WHO HAS KNOWN HEIGHTS

Who Has Known Heights

Heights

The
Mystique Memoirs of a
Melancholic
Mind

A Novel

Wheston Chancellor Grove

True Blue Press

Collected poems of Helen 'Gedny' Cray:
If; I wish you all were here; Where have you been: The revolving door; The way home; attributed to L.A.E.

Library of Congress Catalogue-in-Publication Data
Grove, Wheston Chancellor
Who Has Known Heights: The Mystique Memoirs of a Melancholic Mind: a novel / Wheston Chancellor Grove.

ISBN 978-0-9837007-5-3
LCCN 2016907215

1. Literary—Fiction 2. Romance/Suspense—Fiction 3. Coming of Age—Fiction
4. Contemporary Women / Affairs—Fiction 5. Gender Aspects
6. Sexuality 7. Virginia I. Title

Published by True Blue Press
In cooperation with RJ Communications LLC, New York

Cover design and layout by Wheston Chancellor Grove

Printed in the United States of America

CONTENTS

for

All that was--
all that is--
all that may be—

And the Scatterbird--
who grew old in her tree—

—A Quytman

AUTHOR'S NOTE

T HE circumspect reader may notice a passage that appears more than once. Bravo, but it is no oversight. I do something I like to call 'glimpsing.' As in life, the mind does not operate in a linear fashion. I make use of single quotation marks for dialogue, as is British custom. The narrative utilizes past and present tense. Time becomes secondary to the emotions that transcend the human concept of "here and now." As Westcott explains, "Everything is for the first *and* last time."

This is a work of fiction.

Name Pronunciation

Regn: Ren or Wren
     Origin: German
     'g' is silent; alternate spelling of Regen
     Meaning: Rain

Birçan: 'c' is pronounced as a 'j' Bier-john

Eva: ā-vah, not ee-vah
     Meaning: Life

Fernus: Fur-noose, not furnace
     Origin: Ethiopian

Aloysius: al-ə-wish-əs
     Origin: German Teutonic
     Meaning: Famous in war

I grew up rather alone—
and during that most critical stage, I formed myself.

I live in strange places, stilled silences; others may glance
upon them but rarely take stock—the vase on the mantel,
shadowbirds at five on a morning long ago, the blue dusk, the
wind in the thicket, distant corners. I want to go out in the
main street spinning up with the falling leaves, or into some
open field and let peace come gently, with your presence to
ease the transformation.

Less is more
--
Wheston Chancellor Grove

*"There are many ways of being a man. Mine is to express what is
deepest in my heart."*

E.M. Forster, A Passage to India

WHO HAS KNOWN HEIGHTS

Who has known heights and depths shall not again
Know peace—not as the calm heart knows
Low, ivied walls; a garden close;
And though he tread the humble ways of men
He shall not speak the common tongue again.
Who has known heights shall bear forever more
An incommunicable thing
That hurts his heart, as if a wing
Beat at the portal, challenging;
And yes-lured by the gleam his vision wore—
Who once has trodden stars seeks peace no more.

—Mary Brent Whiteside (1876-1962)
The Best Loved Poems of the American People. Doubleday. 1936.

"In the autumn of a woman's life…there comes always one mad moment when she longs for romance, for adventure, before it is too late."

—Agatha Christie's Poirot

"Once you eliminate the impossible, whatever remains, no matter how improbable, must be the truth."

—Sherlock Holmes
(by Sir Arthur Conan Doyle 1859-1930)

"When I am working on a problem I never think about beauty. I only think about how to solve the problem. But when I have finished, if the solution is not beautiful, I know it is wrong."

—Buckminster Fuller (1895-1983)

Dear Reader:

Love is love.

Sought in goodness, anything is possible—

Regn:

When, as a writer, you know your words have the power to destroy, it is a terrible burden. The truth is painful in the light of day; with time it becomes exquisite. Remember, I am right here beside you on the page. I spare myself nothing. It isn't about you. Only I can set myself free.

And what is sacred remains eternal.

Westcott

Westcott

When I was little after watching the animated version of *The Jungle Book*, I went into the dining room and climbed under the table. I cried. For two reasons: I wanted to be a panther in the wild; I wanted to be Bagheera. Secondly, I was outraged at Mowgli for leaving the jungle.

*

A social worker once told me, 'You're highly intelligent. What's your IQ? Have you ever been tested?'

Another one, a therapist, held no punches and said, 'You're a genius.' I wanted to tell her, *A lot of good it does.* There are different kinds of genius. If being a genius is realizing we are at the mercy of our own understanding, then I guess I am one. 'But,' she continued, 'you're loyal to a fault.' *Yes. O' yes. And I do pay for it.*

In kindergarten my teacher got mad at me for going ahead. When my mother picked me up from school and asked how class went I told her, 'It was boring. The teacher read too slowly.' In high school I took some advanced courses, but no A.P. classes. This was by choice. My teachers were disappointed. In their regular classes my grade point average exceeded 100. So, why didn't I—

My 11th grade teacher took me aside and gave me *Walden* to read. I examined a few passages before the language grew laborious.

In college I took an abnormal psych course. One day when I stopped by her office, Professor Carpenter asked, 'How are you doing so well? What are your study habits—I'd like to know? I design my tests to be deliberately tricky.'

A psychiatrist once suggested I was borderline autistic. Clearly a misdiagnosis. For years I wouldn't make eye contact. But then I, yes I, took control of my confidence and was never again afraid to meet another's gaze. In fact, now I often have the other person looking away, my focus is so intent.

An acquaintance once told me I reminded her of Little Man Tate.

I want to make one point clear—this isn't me talking great about myself here. I'm just telling you what others have told me. Do with this information what you will. To date it hasn't done me any good—at least not that I know of.

I once took the postal exam and passed it the first time out. My career with the USPS lasted 5 days. I couldn't be a faceless worker bee. If anything, I wanted to be the Queen's right arm.

But the truth still remains—I don't relate to my peers, I don't assimilate socially. Is it because I "am" a genius? Because I was *re*born into the wrong body? In the wrong time? Or is it but a combination of each of these factors and something more?

I've always been prejudiced against youth. For a long time I was prejudiced against myself. I longed to be seen for the way I felt, to be old if necessary. I hated my age. Youth was not wasted on me. I just never had the freedom to indulge, to partake of, and enjoy in it.

I've diagnosed myself with borderline eidetic memory.

The Fish Woman was right about some things.

Fluorescent lights, artificial lights of any kind, hurt my senses. I hate loud noises. I have a weak lower back.

If you asked me to name the one feature about myself I most like I'd have to agree with what a few others have told me—my eyes. They are gray-blue. My sister will tell you they're 'battleship gray.' Sometimes if I stare long enough into a mirror I see the mysticism in them. Some old man, some ancient turtle—a heavy burden. My eyes sometimes frighten me—what lurks behind—the capacity for all manner of thoughts. Darkness too.

My eyelids fold on themselves and my eyes are never *wide* open. They are shaped like bird wings. I dislike "wide-eyed" expressions. I prefer shadow within the eyes, seductiveness, a mist of speculation—introspection.

Now where was I—Oh yes, genius.

Exquisite torment.

I suffered from OCD from age 14-17. I still have some mental idiosyncrasies, but nothing paralyzing. I inherited this from my mother. My mother was a knock-out in her youth. Things weren't always bad between my mother and father, but this was before I was born. Besides, that's another story.

I love washing dishes by hand and doing the laundry.

My favorite color is green or blue.

I don't like white socks. Only navy or black.

The story of the Velveteen Rabbit says more than any Scripture. Where was my Skin Rocking Horse when I needed him?

I have a Galapagos turtle in my living room. Not real, mind you, but a life-like replica statue.

If I'd been able to go to West Point like my grandfather I'd have had a pin-up on my wall of Greer Garson, Maureen O'Hara, Jane Wyatt, Sofia Loren, Juliette Binoche, or Meryl Streep.

In looking back on my life I always see myself standing at a window—different windows—and standing alone. I see myself watching the day. I am waiting. Waiting for what, for whom?

For rest.

I've always been very conscious of time—how tedious the years. There is no adequate substitute for intimate frustrations. I was sexually thwarted, and thwarted is the exact term—for most, *not all*, but most of my early adult life—from the age of 22 to 29. My heart stood in the way of my body. I refused to give myself to just anyone. Without love, sex offered little appeal. Lest a genuine connection be felt, I preferred my own company to that of a stranger.

Sex for the sake of sex *is* an ego-driven, inglorious, primal necessity, easily remedied by means of a healthy regiment, with or without someone. But affection—virtue—is what the body craves—the emotional witness—testament to a body not merely needed, but *wanted*. I've always known a single kiss is more lasting than a shag.

Others are attracted to me—women and men, often enough. But *my* attractions are rare. I'd rather be a decent man than a gratified one. Easier in theory. I've never substituted anything! I hate alcohol. I don't like smoking (I'm not a nerd. My only detriment is my receding hairline caused by the testosterone I take owing to hypogonadism). I don't like smoke, I love a mountain wood fire, but I have no desire to transform myself into a living, breathing smokestack. I may chomp on a pipe for aesthetic benefits, but I'd be hard pressed to smoke one. My only vice is talking to *you*.

I love two women. I've only ever *loved* one woman, truly, at a time. And she—

She loved me.

Anything else I feel you need to know I'll inform you as we go along.

Regn

THE BLUE LINE

Don't stop, don't stop for one minute to think
or surely you will be sad

together, the camaraderie of her generation

champagne in hand, glowing the night away on the dance floor

a ride on the train

the boys gentlemen escorts

the girls respectable, both parties willing

but finding more pleasure in the ride, the sights, the freedom, their age, a night of
their lives.

He was absent from this night, a scene occurring four decades ago. But he was
there. He 'was' there, somewhere inside one of them.

∗

The image of breasts in champagne glasses. A German accent and a girlish laughter
seducing her own sense of woman. He took her into one of the compartments on the train
and he made love to her. She was a virgin. He was a virgin. They made slow love, missing
their stop, riding long into the night. She'd taken off her dress and shoes and lain on the
softback bench. He'd untucked his shirt, folded his jacket on a handrail and hung his tie
from a purse hook. She was trembling with excitement. Together, in the dark, lights from
occasional village dwellings passing their window, they undressed each other. She lifted
her back and he swung his arm round gently unclasping the eyes and hooks. He felt her at
length, kneading her warming skin. He kissed her neck. She stroked his naked back to the
crest of his private ravine. They felt through the darkness of time discovering what moved
each other. He slid the cotton blooms from her legs running his Irish fingers through the
darkened spirals of triangular landscape. He came from the side and ever so slowly slid over
her length, as one sliding piece fits within another, only one true fit born, the perfect design.
    He felt himself in a way he did not know, in a way he never had. What organ was this
that stood on its own? He took it in his hand and though she could not see, the wetness
came from his eyes. He suddenly felt a hand on him; it was not his own. She was holding
him there and he could *feel* it. He came down slowly, her legs wings unfolding. He didn't
want to hurt her. He pushed with reserve, withdrawing, thrusting, withdrawing, thrusting a
little farther than just before. It would still hurt she now realized until the rooted innocence
ripped open the beginning of the end of her youth. It burned, she wanted him to stop,
but instead pulled him closer, held him harder, needing to know she was not alone in this.

A cry, a gasp escaped her throat, and he stroked her forehead, brushing her bangs aside, tracing the side of her face down to her chin. Still firm, he had stopped for a moment to give her time. How could he wait—didn't the men always come quickly? So she'd been told. He raised himself, withdrawing slightly and then with a power she'd yet to experience, he entered deepest. She cried in silence and he felt her cry. A warm shower within, a misting of unspoken communion, she had received him.

He lay inside her for a long while and she let him. Something told her, though she could not say, perhaps it was the thundering of the train's mechanical gears and the hush of the compartment, it would be a long, long time before such a night came again.

When the ticket master tapped on their door, the pale hand reached for his billfold, apologizing to the attendant. He explained politely they'd been so engaged in conversation they missed their point of disembarkment and needed to pay for a return 4 stops back the way they'd come.

The ticket master looked at the couple; not a word did he speak nor was one offered by the girl. He opened his mouth and then as though thinking better of it, replied cordially, 'Very well,' and received the payment with a white gloved hand.

There was something old about them, and he knew the girl was safer here than anywhere else. They were—what was the word, respectable? The young man, though his justification could easily be countered, was by all determinations honest in his presentation. A certain polite discretion on behalf of himself and the girl who sat quietly, confident in letting him answer the necessary interrogations so benign in nature.

'Clear night out the window if you keep the lights off,' the ticket master said, sliding the door shut.

'When we get there I—'
'Don't say anything—'
'I have to stay—' his voice drifted.
'Why?'
'I hate to leave you like this. But when we get back it should be light enough out to see you home safely. I wish I could take you home—'
'Where are you going? I thought you were one of Haumer's friends—don't you live in town? You always come with the others, or I thought you did.'
'Yes, but this time—let us sleep for a while.' He took her soft face in his hands. 'Wait for me?'
'But why, I don't understand.'
'You will.' He kissed her then, softly on her mouth, opening his lips to her penetrating tongue. He kissed her forehead. '*Ich liebe dich*, Lass.' He met her gaze and lay beside her, taking her small body in his arms. 'Try and sleep.' He stroked her forehead again, feeling the warmth of her face. She grew still and after a while ceased to intermittently open her eyes. 'Don't forget,' he whispered.

The girl awoke to a rap at the door. Startled she jerked to an immediate sitting position. Hastily tidying herself, a second rap followed.
'Yes?'
The door slid open. The ticket master from the night before gave the station call.
'Oh yes,' she replied hearing the name. 'This is my stop.' And then she became aware again of her surroundings.

The ticket master was already heading down the side panel to continue his announcement. He hadn't closed the door.

'Sir, excuse me!' She got up and stepped out into the hall. 'Sir, there was a young man here late last night, or early this morning, he paid you our ways. Have you by chance seen him? I mean did you see if he got off anywhere?'

'Miss, it is only you in this compartment. I stamped your ticket nigh past 3 this morning. It was only you in the room then. Sorry, miss.' He continued down the aisle.

'Wait!'

He half-turned, mildly irritated. She looked at him hard, verifying her misgivings. She opened her mouth and shut it. No, it was definitely the same ticket master.

She walked back into the compartment and shut the door, standing in bewilderment. In a moment of hope she shot a glance at the hook. No tie. There was no evidence of anyone but herself having been here. Had she really drunk that much? No, but where had her friends gone, and why had they left her? And why was the sun peeking on the horizon? She had no reason to ride the train all night by herself! She sat down not knowing what else she could do. She felt something only she could know. The stealth of intimacy, a private fluid crawling from between her legs. The reservoir gave way and she began to cry. *Why, why give me something and take it away? Wait, he said, but how long?*

The train pulled into the station. She took out a small square handkerchief with green embroidery along the fringe. 'Why did I fall asleep?' She wiped her eyes. Getting hold of herself, she pulled a tiny mirror from her handbag. Looking at her reflection she remembered his eyes at the dance and later on the train before they'd dimmed the light. Blue gray.

'Leeeetzter aufruf!' *Laaaast call!*

She stood up, ran her hands down the front of her dress, looked around once more, and inhaled long.

She stepped onto the platform.

A small group of American pilots idled nearby. 'Hey, Davie,' one comrade called to another. 'You gotta light?'

As the train pulled out from the station it released a stream of exhaust around the wheels. The girl listened to the hiss. Was it her mind playing tricks or did she not hear someone's voice, perhaps those soldiers over there, saying, 'Don't forget.'

$$* \quad * \quad * \quad * \quad * \quad * \quad *$$

He awoke. He went through his body, mentally feeling himself. All the way down he could identify himself. He reached below the abdomen and stopped. Something was missing. He just lay there, not needing his hand to confirm what he already knew. A deep sleep had overtaken him the night before. He'd had two gulps of Chardonnay to take in the holiday at the Christmas party. He felt like he'd been asleep for ages, not just some few hours. He seldom dreamt and when he did the details quickly flew as he rose. But this, this was not the case. He could not get up. Instead he lay still. A sentence came to him. He heard it being said. 'I hate to leave you like this.' He had said it to her that morning. No, this morning! But it wasn't his voice he heard saying those words. It was hers and her voice had a lilt of perfected tone, polished into its accented lightness like wine that enriches and becomes more alive with age.

They'd made love again.

✳ ✳ ✳ ✳ ✳ ✳

He'd gone that night on the train, gone without his knowing, gone on ahead. Ripped from an era he loved, thrust into a generation he could not understand. And she had stayed. Not trusting herself enough she'd succumbed to the resolution, the pressures of social convention that it had been a dream. It *had* to be a dream. The life she had been brought up to fulfill extended its hand and asked for hers in acceptance. And she slid her hand into another's.

Though buried deep down, she kept it to herself—the truth. The knowledge that it had happened and the hope that he would return. They'd made love across the ages. Four decades ago on a train and again last night in his room. His stature was oddly slighter than it had been, but the face, skin, and wan complexion were hauntingly untouched with the exception of a quiet sorrow beneath his brow. He had held the girl he still loved, now a woman, to his chest. He didn't want anything else, just to lie beside one another. He'd moved his head to her breast, listening to the even one-two of her life's drum. Feeling her escalating intimacies his hand stroked her inner thigh and slowly came from above her abdomen, again slipping through the less darkened, closely trimmed spirals, and searching. He watched her face, her eyes closed in coveted ecstasy. She came in silence. Two lives had ushered forth from that small cavern which he now floated in and out of—a graceful ghost carried on the winds of long ago. He missed seeing her give birth, being able to come to her side, hold her hand, wipe her forehead and reassure as she shamelessly revealed herself in performing the woman's right to give life. She slipped her hand beneath his band and moved her finger in circular motions. He felt deadened, the warmth filling him only from the waist up. He was about to say, 'You don't have to—it's all right.' There was wetness in his eyes. He pulled her close and with her free hand he interlocked his own, pressing her cheek to his. He closed his eyes just wanting to sleep. Knowing he would not come he let her stay and moved his legs apart. He felt her reach the foyer and come within. Lying still he held her, silently telling her it wasn't *that* he wanted. Her hands alone, just feeling her touch was enough. And then his words repeated back to him. 'I hate to leave you like this,' she said.

Wait for me. He read the private book behind her eyes.

How long? He did not ask her. He did not ask himself. *Just long enough.*

I'll return her tenderness promised.

Return for good someday? The gentle intensity of his touch *kneaded* to know.

He'd kissed her on the forehead. His way of telling her *I will.*

He fell asleep that night, his head the only indentation on his pillow.

Unlike the girl she'd been on the train, after getting home and sliding into a familiar bed, she did not let sleep take her.

Into the night she lay restless. Someone else in the room was breathing. She listened to the hiss. The indentation beside her. The wind whined now and again and the branches on a tree outside the window scraped the pane. Was it her mind playing tricks or were the four rhythmic scrapes not screaming inside her, like a crazed bow screeching across its cello, again and again—Ich. Lie-be. Dich.

Just as their compartment door on the train was shut for privacy, her breast heaved in its protected confinement. *I didn't forget.*

———

REMEMBRANCES

THERE are times when I am still that I can feel them move inside me. The years. The scent of all the places I worked and my feelings for her wherever I was. Even then I knew it would never be the same. Even in the present moment I loved her as though looking back. I try to remember who she was before I knew her. Just a woman. The woman I worked beside among so many others, but who, for some reason, I enjoyed a little more.

She watered the potted trees in the rotunda, she joked in spite of her age, silly things were funny. The way she stood at the half window that December so long ago. She'd purchased a decorative Santa Claus from the gift shop with her employee discount. She always loved the jolly peppermint robed bearer of gifts. The way Santa was depicted back in the day—his classic tin can likeness and glass bottle Coca-Cola advertisements. I saw her eyes looking over her find while she showed it to us, myself and another colleague in the office; such a simple fleeting expression of delight as she pinched a piece of fabric here, tweaked a limb there. It made her happy. And seeing her happy made me feel alive.

• • •

She gave me The Beatles and paper boats.

I often imagine my life, how it would sound, were it set to a soundtrack. It opens with the theme songs from *Dances with Wolves* and *Out of Africa*. The wide, arcing, timeless score of instrumentals. The orchestra is sweeping, a tremulation of strings merging with the golden horns. Not *Gone with the Wind* melodramatic. No. Patient, expansive, an old steam engine cresting the horizon, coming into the valley after a long, long time away. You'll know when you hear it. It is what you should listen to in reading the entry that follows.

Journal Entry:

from the Book of West

Friday 27 April Twenty Hundred and—

I prefer to write out the year in its original form. To say 'Two Thousand and'—sounds futuristic, metallic, cold. Whereas 'Twenty Hundred and'—exudes warmth. I feel I can fold myself up in the annals of time. Each year a distinguished member of the century. 'Thousand' purports nothing antiquated. It's like a rocket bursting, hard on the ears, stretching endlessly into infinity. I am glad to have been born in the 1900s, to have known life before the millennia, to have experienced the world when human beings controlled the machinery and not the other way around. When the only cells were those discussed in biology class, not a reference to mobile devices. When men and women engaged one another. Before the Me Generation and the loss of self-accountability.

Perhaps I should leave this book as it was and not "taint" it with recollections of the past two years. Too much was said and retracted; too much pain; sometimes sorry isn't enough, and sometimes it's too late. This evening, shortly after six o'clock, I drove down the Parkway with my bike in the bed liner. A sign was sticking out of the ground leading to the Island and a patrol vehicle with lights flashing had stationed itself just beside the entrance gates. I considered turning to see what it was all about, asking the officer—but, eh, it didn't matter. I continued onto the Parkway.

I pulled off at the place—the place where my life forever changed nigh five years ago— five years this fall—September—to be precise. The beginning of the end. I envisioned returning had I truly been gone these five years. But I stayed, stuck around too long. Had I left *then*, what of these memories? Would our love be strong yet and unharmed?

I parked my truck and biked to the next pull-off. It was colder by the river than at home. I did not continue to the large cropping of trees just across the sun-soaked bridge. Too many haunting remembrances lay on the other side. Here I was in my olive green converse tennis shoes and there I was four years ago in my keds sitting with Regn in her Volkswagen Bug one cool early spring morning. I was off for the day; she had to go in to work. We'd talked for some odd minutes. Nothing important in content, but wonderful because of our sharing it. She wore her beige skirt suit. I remember feeling her tongue as her lips softly touched mine and its silent telling. Having never gone there, instinctively I spread them to receive the penetrating bliss. Something inside *rilled* with desire for more. There were other times, later, and maybe even that morning, when I remember seeing Regn's expression as we disengaged for a moment. She bore abandonment and a helplessness in herself, which even then I regarded with mild speculation and dislike. I overlooked it, but that helpless expression annoyed me somehow. I feel that's how Regn sees me now, and yet it isn't so. I am frustrated, but I never exhibit that sheer look of surrender. She'd spoken. 'In a minute'—or maybe it was 'in a second—I'm going to want your hand between my legs.' 'I don't mind,' I said quietly, not moving. She took my hand, reassuring it was safe, I had permission, and slipped it under her skirt. I felt my way up until both sides of her thighs warmed my hand. I reached the cloth barrier and that was all for the time being. She would go to work wet she explained, or something to that effect. I rode off on my bicycle, filled with the high of longing.

————

This evening I turned my bike around before the slight bridge and headed back. A car was parked beside my truck. Blue. License plate Mac78. I walked down the incline observing the loblolly pines. I was about to reach round one to ascertain its girth when I heard branches snapping, coming from a path to my left. A solitary black man clad in t-shirt, shorts, and white socks pulled up to his calves, appeared. I said hello as he approached. And then closer I nodded, made a throaty noise—a second hi, to put him at ease. He took me in, smiled maybe. Not so much friendly as withholding. He stepped into the blue vehicle. Maybe he was just as interested by my being there, curious what I was up to, as I casually surveyed the landscape and counted the trees. Fortunately the presence of a dog provided reasonable excuse. The retractable leash, made in Germany (for once), snapped in my hand. I did not feel concerned or threatened. Had he disposed of something down the path? Did he gratify himself in his solitude with only nature to see him? Or maybe, much like myself, he was remembering someone. Someone who was gone from his life. I'd almost forgotten how beautiful the Parkway is as I rode my Schwinn; it felt good to be out there in the gloaming.

While standing still, regarding my surroundings, I decided I *had to* investigate the path where this mysterious black man had come down. I didn't care if he was watching me. I wasn't going to let him disconcert me. I didn't have my distance glasses, naturally. I say naturally because I seldom keep them on me. They were in the truck, so I couldn't tell where he might be looking.

I followed the path, amazed I'd never ventured along it, even in the days of Regn. Why, we could have found privacy, seclusion for a stolen and much needed embrace. The scene was picturesque. I tell you I could have been standing beside a great river in Africa. The clouds were perfect and a slight haze hung over the marsh reeds and outstretching vista of the James. I imagined the man advancing—coming to kill or rape me. My body was cold, vulnerable, despite the heat of the late afternoon. I needed the pain to be dislodged. A suitable repercussion for having loved so deeply is to be annihilated. Sometimes my mind needed the possibility of *something*. It didn't frighten me. If that was going to happen so be it. Let him come. So many places to conceal a body. I briefly recalled the unsolved Parkway Murders; they occurred before we even lived here, but the thought was eerily present in such stillness of my surroundings.

Some 'kid' with his bike and dog—a nature lover—maybe that's what the man thought. And then he'd look at the facial hair—correcting his judgment of 'kid.'

Perhaps *I* disturbed or frightened him. My demeanor was casual, entirely unconcerned except for taking in the trees. Maybe I was plotting the ideal burial site or intent on hiding something. The trees formed a frame around the scene—a layer of gray-lavender streaked the horizon—it was "heaven." I hadn't wanted to take more pictures so I left my camera at home, purposely. Too many pictures—and isn't it enough just to have been there? Did I really need another snapshot to catalogue the sublime yet painful stealth of underbrush, trees, skies, and the river structure (a roosting fort)? Across the way a vibrant green sign stood in the water. From my distance I couldn't see what it revealed. The place was peaceful, though suggestive in its remote isolation.

Anything could happen here and who would know? It was a "new" place to me, but timeless in its own right. Regn had never stood *here*. All these years since and we'd been so close to 'this' obscurity. Its hidden proximity is what disquieted. But I wasn't afraid. Had I been killed my family and even Regn might have driven to this place and questioned, 'What was he doing out here, all alone?' The wandering or missing dog, depending on the killer's preference, would afford explanation—just out for a stroll. The view was like a window onto another world, another time, another past (and even future) self. I imagined returning, but it would never be the same. This grand keyhole would slip away. It was only now, just for this brief moment.

When I pulled myself away and opened my truck, I heard his door open. Maybe he'd been running and needed the cool down. Or perhaps it had been more sinister out there. I made the pretense of checking the soft red fur of my travel companion for ticks. Robbie enjoyed my thorough check of his armpits and undercarriage. His fur was warm. It was past seven when I put the gearshift into 'R' and backed to my right—face hidden by shadows. I drove right in the continuing pull-out loop before making a left and with my glasses now on, looked back at the clean navy blue car—where once, long ago, another story unfolded some quiet eve.

The place is the same. The trees are the same.
I know. She knows. Does "Time" stand still even when we cannot?
I wish to go *home*.

———

I later discovered my oversight. The camera was where I'd left it—under my seat, for instances just like this evening. *Always keep it with you*, I told myself. You never know when the opportunity will present itself. I was upset at having a rare still shot slip away, but then I understood—Everything is for the first and last time. I didn't want another picture to tuck away in some drawer. It would be a safety net. If it was important enough to recall, well then, I'd view it in mind. How many pictures have I perused in the course of my life? And at that moment, a singular subject, image, could restore. I'd leaf through a photography book or meander through a gallery. I began to grow tired—there are too many pictures, too many lives, too many stories, too many—and for *this one* not to see the light of day I wouldn't allow it. I carry it with me now—that tinge of watercolor regret and dampened longing—running together—the color of melancholy. I leave it here for safekeeping.

———

I intertwine 1st and 3rd person. Throughout my life, up to a certain point, I have lived someone else's life. I was present in form but more often than not, I was far away in mind. Watching. Remembering. Waiting.

. . .

After Regn many scenarios played in my mind. All the various outcomes my life could pursue. This is one of them, the one that often crossed my mind in those years when Regn was gone and I still loved her. It goes like this:

It is hard for me to imagine a world so aligned. I went out this morning, having watched a movie with my wife. So quiet at 1:10 in the morning. All the houses neatly quartered, the cars in their allotted spaces, the energy of motion at rest. Meanwhile atrocities rage in places I can only read about, imagine. As I slip back into the warmth of my humdrum life with nice things to pass the time, I realize how mad we are.

Had a switch been thrown just the other way I might very well have been an assassin or, God forbid, a serial killer. To the average person this would be a startling confession, but I mention it only from a philosophical standpoint. Dualities are often too close for comfort. My life, up to a certain point, afforded ideal opportunities for self-corruption. At any instant I could have turned a darker road and there'd be no coming back. There is no greater possession on earth than trust and I am grateful to have known myself well enough never to violate the unspoken bond, even when many a door invited me in and I would silently say to myself, 'My but we are rather trusting of one another, frightfully so.' Or is it the faith in one's own judgment which is strongest, even when influenced by the presentation and demeanor of the individual standing before you requesting your trust? I was cognizant of detaching myself and looking at these people. *This is a voice, this is just a body, what are you really underneath*—wondering if similar disturbing thoughts crossed their minds. I ventured the specifics of murdering a stranger or someone I casually knew, only as a hypothetical scenario. In the end I couldn't confront myself, in that instance I would have to transform and see the disbelief on the other's face. That singular mechanism, absent in the sociopath, which enables him to kill without regard, steps forward. Though I could maintain contempt for the pleading victim, at the same time I would recognize the power of mercy. I firmly believe what you do to another you also do to yourself. I could never get personal with a target; perhaps as an assassin I would flourish.

I understand what I have just said may be disturbing, but it is such introspection that leads one to debate and question his very nature. One must confront the uncomfortable and realize some things are just thoughts. Virtues must be challenged; how else can they be upheld?

———

I find domestic chores quite calming, which, no surprise, delights my dear wife Q (name unknown, sometimes I inserted a name, like Birçan). And yet, while in the lavatory, I stood looking out into the dining room and at the silver tea tray that needed polishing. It meant nothing. All the vacuuming, dusting, managing of 'things.' As I languidly emptied my bladder I felt compelled to run back outside and wake the neighbors. I washed my hands in the warm water and hurried upstairs. Wife Q was already in bed, her back to me, but the lamplight was still on.

'Cold out?'

'Too cold.'

I hurried to brush my teeth then slipped into bed. I touched her shoulder, she turned. I looked at her for a long time.

'What is it?' she asked.

I leaned down, pulling her close. 'I know it's crazy, but—I'm just so glad you're here.'

She started to smile. I kissed her forehead, but she turned over and slid her upper body over me. Her hand brushed my hair aside. I'd always kept it a shy longer than a close crop and secretly for this very reason.

I imagined she kissed my eyes. A gesture reserved only for rare occasions, something carried over from our days of early courtship. But it wasn't Birçan who did this. Birçan would kiss my cheeks. It was *Regn* who loved to kiss my closed eyes. It was in these moments that I most often thought about *him*. The person I'd been; the Westcott I'd known. An instant and he'd be there to remind me. Should I have felt guilty? But Birçan. If it wasn't for her, would Westcott be telling *my* story instead? Would I have been the one to kill myself? I slipped under the blankets and scooched closer to Birçan's warmth. I reached over and turned the light until it clicked off. Birçan was facing me—as my eyes adjusted to the dark I saw hers were still open.

I looked at her that way waiting for the words. Her silence spoke and I gently pressed my lips to hers, parting them, a familiar exchange but always so tentative, evoking the sensation of exploring. We kissed and I touched her face. Nothing more. That's how it was best. Always so intimate. Always so relieving. After all our early romps and bouts of stolen passion, now we had time. Time. It was something Westcott understood well. Too well in fact.

For a moment I was glad he was dead. Finally. The other part of me, the incorrigible, despairing, tenacious, self-annihilating individual I'd been for so long. But, he gave his life for me—my youth sacrificed. He wasn't going to go quietly though. And he knew I would be restless to finish, to lay to rest old memories, to tie up all loose ends into a nice, handy bundle. *Oh my dear Birçan, if you but knew how close opposites really are.* And yet, you do know. You did know. You discovered. It has been a relief. A relief! I tried to imagine who you might be, long before we ever met. But no image came to mind.

This is a dream I sometimes had. An outcome dreamt while still awake. Prior to, and after Birçan, "Wife Q" resumed being the supposition of life after Regn. I could never have happily deceived Birçan—or lied to myself. After Regn and Birçan I no longer opened up. Never in the same way. My story was off the table. But now I find it critical to get it down, get it out. I'm leaving you see, in a few months' time, and I want a clear conscience. I want the truth to reveal how beautiful the pain was, how good the love, how decent, even when circumstances stood in the way. In death I refuse to hide.

———

I wrote this story many times in my head. But always it changed. I tried when I was young to get it all down. Somehow it's all there, all here, inside. If it wasn't for those years and earlier pages I would not have arrived to this point. This is it. I would often, and up until a month ago, I still *did* drift among the leaves. I'd drive out to the forest, pull a prop table from the bed of my truck, snap its legs into place and take out a complimenting folding chair. I'd sit at my table chewing the cud of hours past. A few uninvited guests. A cyclist that threatened to remind, a laboring squirrel who knew not what to ask, and the chirping chatter—backdrop for one long silent conversation.

I'd drift the aisles. Searching. The library. Leaves upon leaves, a refuge. An asylum. Too many books. Too many stories. The more I picked up, the urgency returned. The sense that I was betraying a necessary duty. There is but one story I must immerse myself in. Diversion of another is no remedy. And to the forest, not far from civilization and the week of work ahead—work to pay my way—I would return. I was in my late twenties by this point.

• • •

The summer sprawls ahead, just as it did then. May it leave me in peace *here*. May the soft gentle winds be a companion rather than an affront to this isolation. May the birds listen so I can take rest from myself. I have nothing left to hide.

—

It was a quietness of presence. A desire to put others at ease. Decency. That's how Westcott lived. Following through no matter how small or large the item of agreement. He learned at Jamestown Settlement, learned at a young age, that people say things because they sound nice at the time or fill a space, but very rarely do they follow through on those throw-away lines. If Westcott said he'd bring in a book for someone to read, he did it the next day or the same week. If in his life someone ever loaned him a dollar or two he paid them back immediately, as soon as they saw one another. He never waited for the other person to ask. He always settled up, however minor the transaction. It was not proper to owe someone.

Mornings, should he need to make a phone call, it became a necessity of habit that he must first brush his teeth, remove the slick film from a night's sleep. His mouth felt clean again, as though his refreshed breath could somehow be detected through the receiver, his very words taking on the minty cleanliness, becoming light to the ears.

At night, when he removed his pants, he always made sure the fly was zipped. It was provocative to leave them open and crumpled on the floor. He called the bathroom the 'privy' or 'restroom.' The expression he preferred was, 'I need to use the facilities.' He had a wry sense of humour and enjoyed wit, there being a time and place for certain language. But he did not care for vulgarity, crudeness, profanity as a second language. Oh he cussed, certain moments required it and it felt good, the emphasis. He liked the words 'damn,' 'shit,' but harsh language—'fuck'—was the exception not the rule. When someone failed to meet the rules of etiquette and offended him, he liked the expression, "Go piss up a rope." Mentally this is what he told that person to do. He had no tolerance for excuses and disdained passivity. He well-knew that being 'shy' was not the same as being 'passive.' He'd been painfully timid throughout his adolescence and empathized with those who were quiet, pensive. But passivity was another matter altogether—a trait akin to cowardice. Passivity was avoidance, passing the buck, placating as opposed to executing. Westcott knew what people wanted *and* needed to hear, but he did not offer false reassurance. Instead, he had a way of softening the blow, listening without speaking; his presence offered a source of level-headed inquiry. The amazing part was he didn't claim to know anything. He just knew it was useless to doubt. Every question ever asked had already been answered. The key lay in remembering.

He could engage in pedestrian conversation out of politeness, nonetheless it bored him. He liked to get to the meat of the subject, into the swing of deep exchange. Garrulousness put him in an irritated mood. His mind clamoring to escape, all the while diplomatically trying to disengage. His thoughts were active and he grew impatient, but he tempered it. For this reason he found most training classes and office meetings useless. He made word lists, drew pictures—anything, anything to keep the creative juices flowing. He could look through the handbook and know the necessary information. Listening to someone speak about it so that the audience could sign a form indicating they'd received all "necessary" materials was a mindless, inefficient way to spend a morning or afternoon. So much waste. His mother felt the same way. She loathed having to go every year to her own company's training updates.

Decency was about purpose. Not motive or intent. Actions made with deliberate preci-sion, a grace that was effortless, without airs, natural as the course of one's fingers running through his dampened hair. In short, it was about consistency of character. A person could never outwardly announce that he was decent, for such traits come to the surface silently. It was not about raising your hand and saying look what I did, give me credit for my generous good will. No. Decency was a hand in the dark pulling a blanket over a shoulder, dropping

5 dollars in an outstretched can and walking on. Giving without the need for spoken gratitude. Surprising others because it pleased you. It was the same as accepting a handshake for
a person's word. The unspoken, communicated code of human integrity.

He judged people who did not push in their chairs. It said something about their character. Westcott always left things as he'd found them or, if they were in disarray, he'd leave
them better off for their wear. Tidy up so-to-speak. He took initiative in that realm of his
life. No one had instructed him, he just knew. It was in his blood.

$\bullet\bullet\bullet$

He'd seen therapists since he was ten years old. First his mother brought him and his
sister to see one because of the divorce. In high school it was to find out what was bothering Westcott and to procure the necessary *letters*. And later it was to discover that none of
them had succeeded in catching him before it was too late. None of them helped him—how
could they? He was seeking 'why' when all they wanted to do was ask 'what?' Or 'how?' His
desire for a guarantee—a certainty, was beyond them, beyond any facts of a psychological
nature. He aimed for the bedrock, the heart of existence. It wasn't his angle, nor did he go
into the sessions with this purpose in mind, but *he* was teaching *them*; he was helping them
to see.

His ingrained nostalgia was often mistaken for depression. He did not need his head
analyzed. All he ever needed was an ear to listen. Someone to bounce ideas back and forth
with—about human nature. His lifelong sorrow came from the fact that he knew much too
soon; he accepted as a youth of 24 that nothing was permanent. Even in those moments of
happiness, a feeling would taint the edges. The smiling face or laugh would vanish, one day
death would have its say, or a cruel sickness. It wasn't fair. What he wanted them to know,
to see, was that loving something too dearly kills it. Life was endlessly painful because his
species realized its own mortality. In everything, he *felt* life to the fullest.

His mother once told him, 'If you were half as determined and passionate about
money as you are about love, you'd be a millionaire.'

Right she was.

But what is wealth without someone to enjoy and share it with? Money can't buy happiness, experience, or knowledge. Money merely buys a level of freedom and opportunity.
Money can never buy real Truth. It can try. Love is something hard earned.

He possessed an unyielding determination, both dangerous and powerful. Dangerous
insofar as his personal well-being was concerned. Powerful in his ability to see something to
the end. He did not like unfinished business, endless speculation, whatever happened to—

His determination was spurred on, kept alive, by certainty. And then he met his match.
The Achilles heel he never knew he possessed. A vulnerability that prodded the very will of
his being. Love. The giving and receiving of a woman's affection required absolute vulnerability and once exposed and subsequently wounded, one is never so solid again. Like a statue
that is dropped and a limb broken, in being reattached it is never as strong or secure as the
original bond. The fracture remains. Even when invisible to the eye, the heart remembers.

$\bullet\bullet\bullet$

Westcott had no guilt for the love. There could be no guilt for something so earnestly and honestly sought. Instead, he was guilty of something he had no control over. Something he could never forgive himself for—of being young. He would not lose Regn to her marriage. In the end, he knew, he'd lose her to age. Yes, maybe, down the road, many years to come, Westcott would find himself in a marriage—a loving, amicable, affectionate exchange. But the passions of his true desires would always remain with Regn. Even after she was gone. It was characteristic of him—a deep-rooted melancholic nostalgia—to miss those whom he loved even in the present, when they were standing right before him or in the same room. An anticipatory loss. For this very reason he wanted to die young. He did not want to witness losing everyone he loved.

—

'I can't be bothered to work.'

    -You mean you don't want to work?

'It would sound that way wouldn't it? No. It's not the case at all. I want to give—.'
He stops. Looks up, expecting a cynical expression from the stranger across from
him. 'Very well then—since I feel compelled to explain—*I am* working, as a matter
of fact, I'm working right this minute. Ironic, wouldn't you say, I'm "diagnosing"
you.'

    -Analyzing?

'Yes. Recording. I must get it right, accuracy is critical. When I'm gone it must—'

    -Is this helping—

'I'm not here for answers that can be found in a textbook. I'm here to talk—for
you to listen. Help? My god. You're human just as me. I'd rather stand on the street
corner, denounce myself and what I am, than exist in the Novocain of suburban
survival—complacency. I've never worked so hard in my life. Melodramatic?'

    -No, I don't think—

'If I stop now the mechanism will steamroll me—iron me flat—bleached and fitted.'

    -Mechanism—by that do you mean industry?

'Society.'

    -Is society so—

'What is society? I am society's foil, mainstream, smallstream, majority, minority—I
mistrust the times. What I know is not what "they" tell us. What I know is what I feel.
And what I feel is what I want to know. There's a freedom in that—'

    -In knowing yourself?

'In trusting yourself. It's impossible not to stand for something. Nothing is still something. Is the Universe a vast nothing?'

    -Do you believe that?

'If I believed so I'd take my life within the hour.'

Twenty hundred and—

This could be anywhere—Tel Aviv, Jefferson City, Denmark, anywhere—but it is here, a small town quickly expanding. A place that ten years ago offered promise of a new beginning. Now it is stagnant.

Why do we read? Entertainment, escape, enlightenment, the comfort of knowing we share similar lives in all too separate ways—and as so what motivates one to write? Each has his or her reason, but here, in this context, I find myself writing for my life. A bit dramatic you may contend. At this point of my life I am not ill that I know of, nor am I on the cusp of my declining years as we so eloquently define senior advent these days.

It's not about age. It's not about time. How does one define life?

I want to go into a cabin in the woods and write. To rest if such is humanly possible for me. To write. And not come out until I am done. How Thoreauian. To slumber with the leaves for a while and remember from whence I came. Be it cold, be it warm, a cot, a fire. If I liked it I'd stay and if I hated the loneliness, which I know I would, I'd remember the outside place and why I'd left.

I cry for the beautiful banality—the often mundane and sheer outrage of comings and goings in this world—cycles, seasons, years—tickita--tickita--tickita--tickita--tickita, and then—it all must go.

It pulses and thrives upon my very being—as though pressing your face to a doorjamb were love enough in itself; feeling what it does not feel, but loving and hating it for it is there to catch you and the expression of your language.

I feel I was left here, lingering, and I'm waiting to go home.

I never attempted to kill myself. I knew I would succeed.

The train often speaks to me. Late at night. Gently calling.

Distant lives.

I feel in being given sight I was denied the joy of a lightness in being.

Summer 20—

Westcott lies on his side on the two-cushioned sofa. Through the window he knows it is summer. Knows by the stillness, the foliage that is a little less than its former lushness. It is July. He will be twenty-five in three months. One hand is sandwiched between his knees for comfort. His head rests on a flat blue accent pillow. His body fits nicely within the beige couch. A black and white wirehaired terrier naps on his side in an adjacent chair beside the window. Westcott is completely still, a feigned pose of death. His eyes are open, fixed. Mr. O' Grady, the terrier, is not asleep.

On screen it would seem a most comical arrangement as the camera slowly pans from one body to the other, while outside a man drives backwards on a lawn tractor cutting the common ground. It is the only active action beyond the sound of a wall clock ticking. Above Mr. O' Grady a smooth green surface is backdrop to a painting. There is movement in the painting and then there is actual movement as the clothesline becomes alive. An everyday chore—laundry hanging on the sea's edge. Westcott is entranced; the sheets billowing in the wind; the unknown woman who stands in skirt and knitted sweater fastening each with clip to the line. He tastes the sea in the air, inhales the sweet salt smell of seaweed, gull, and sand shells. He feels the sun on his hands, the dusting of grains blown against his bare ankles, jeans rolled to the cuff. He wants to ask the woman in her salmon sweater and ocean blue skirt how she does it. Her duties are endless and yet he suspects she is content. Her posture is accustomed, a result of endless routine. The majority of sheets and linens are white, becoming gray with the deep blue breaking just beyond. There are but a few splashes of color. One a foam green, another starfish orange, and one more of butter. He can hear their hands flap against the wind and the sounds of a distant harbor. He does not imagine what's beyond the borders of the vignette; the imperfections and unspoken griefs therein would lie. There is a water basin and a pointed shadow on the foreground—perhaps the roof of a home. Westcott does not want to analyze it too closely. He touches the wind through his open fingers. It cannot change. He wants to let it stay beautiful.

April 1972

Helen Cray "Gedny," my mother,

wrote the following:

If

You're small as you can be, yet
you carry more weight than any
of them; you mean more than all
of them, and you determine the
        outcome of everything.
How is it possible that you mean
so much, yet you are so small—
The size is of no consequence
we know that, but it's puzzling.

How many times throughout
our lives we talk about you;
you're mentioned in every passing
day many times over—
You're plain and you are simple,
but so powerful and significant.
Our directions and destinations
in life are based upon you.

You represent conditions, possibilities,
surprises, irritation, worry, anxiety,
        happiness and sorrow.

There are twenty-six of you, but
        only two really count.

United States Air Force Base, Germany just east of Luxembourg; October 1970

She is eighteen. Everyone is happy. Regn supposes she is happy too. And why shouldn't she be? Jay performs flight simulations. He's a good man. He will help her with the new language.

'Forsaking all others. 'Til death do you part?'

'I do,' comes softly from Regn's smooth mouth. The words are expected; she has no reason to question them. They are going to make a life together. It is what we do.

14 October 20—

It is a Thursday. At 9:07 a nurse comes in, tells him to get the gown, the doctor is waiting. She says to take off everything including underwear and to empty his bladder. Going into the bathroom with these instructions Westcott begins to collapse. He doesn't see why the briefs need to come off unless it is for bacterial safeguarding; even so they won't be working anywhere near that region—it seems unnecessary. 'Please hurry,' the nurse instructs, partially opening the door. He is about to ask if he can keep his drawers on. Not wanting to be difficult, accepting she'll just say no, he pulls the remaining cover from his skin and slips out of them into the gown. His eyes are about to spill over. He clenches the back closed, apathetically trailing behind the nurse. She stops at the receptionist's desk. Westcott presses up behind a beam, trying to hide himself. 'Come on,' she gesticulates kindly. Following her into the instantly ajar elevator, he feels the levy about to give. 'Are you all right?' she asks. 'Yeah. Fine.' The rims of his eyes wet, vision clouding over. Once the elevator opens they walk left into a room lined with gurneys. She motions for him to board one.

Somewhere in the background classical music is audible. Placing a sockless foot on the black rubber step stool, still holding the back of the gown shut, the only thing mattering at that moment, Westcott turns and sits down on the narrow bedding. He lifts his legs from the stool, ever so carefully, not wanting to reveal anything. Keeping his knees together, he scooches on as the nurse draws a green surgical sheet over his white, pathetically hairy shins, up to his abdomen. Westcott remains sitting, propped by his elbows, a position he is not accustomed to and finds straining. He doesn't want to lie down. Placing a hair cap atop his head, the nurse tells him to lie back. 'Are you sure you're all right?' He replies hoarsely, 'I'm just a very private person.' It is the only thing he can think to say. Staring at the ceiling frantically, the doctor comes in, instructing him to sit up. He has a slight shadow on his upper lip and chin from an unclean shave, very debonair. There exists a touch of George Clooney in his physiognomy. The female patients at the Residence fawn over him.

Cautiously Westcott shifts his legs, the knees firmly pressed together beneath the sheet. Dropping them from the gurney, he pulls his torso forward, maneuvering his body to the right so he faces the doctor directly. The doctor wears his surgical cap. He removes the already slipping gown from the slender shoulders. Using his bare hands with a straightedge, he makes measurements. Though they are soft and kind hands, the sensation is *foreign* to Westcott. Innocent and professional in manner, Westcott has never experienced a man's touch, excluding the more definitively nerve-racking but brief palpation the afternoon prior. He stands so close to Westcott, this man. This bona fide man. Gazing out the windows behind him Westcott detects the surgeon's eyes looking into his own and the detached stricken face they occupy. He feels ridiculous in the hair cap—ashamed of being examined—and searches for a mental escape in the grayness outside—the fall leaves of Montreal yellow and orange in their hue, fluttering crisply in the breeze. His albino-like arms lie limply at his sides as the surgeon moves him to sit up straight, adjusting Westcott's wrists and neck for accurate measurements. Another nurse comes in; a side-glance flash of horror escapes Westcott.

'Don't worry,' the doctor assures in his French accent, 'no one will see you.' Aligning the flexi ruler across Westcott's chest, he continues marking in sharpie. 'You can cover yourself now, I have to get the camera. We take the pictures digitally.' Westcott draws the gown up as the surgeon goes behind him into another room. Taking the pictures he explains, 'Your head is not in the photos. Nobody will know it is you,' he reassures. 'Great,' Westcott responds dryly before lying down. The surgeon rests the gown back over his chest, pulling the green sheet up to his neck. A soothing warm, white towel is placed atop the length of his body. Shrouded in protection once more, his heart and nerves receive a moment's repose before the final act.

'Any last words?' the surgeon asks. A tall foreboding anesthesiologist stands at his side.

Reaching the Rubicon, hesitating, Westcott answers. The surgeon laughs in a tone that speaks of his good will. *Don't worry, of course*, it seems to say. Then he is gone. They wheel him into the surgical room; he can hear the classical music more clearly. His eyes move rapidly about the ceiling like a battered dog, defenseless, but one who still expounds trust. He looks out through the skylights at the lifeless dome and then at the bright lamps anchored above the operating table. He is told to slide off the gurney and onto the surgical bed. The nurse at the foot gives him a most disconcerting sinister stare, probably in response to his youthful appearance. Does she know he is twenty years and a day old...he means young? Perhaps it states so on the chart.

Immediately, the anaesthesiologist takes his left arm, straps it down, an execution, and begins flicking veins for the best I.V. location. A white clock hangs on the wall. It reads sometime after 9:00 a.m.

'They had trouble finding one when they did the blood test,' Westcott volunteers. 'They took it from the right.'

'It's easier for operating purposes if we do it on the left.'

He feels that maybe he shouldn't have spoken. After all, they know what they are doing. He turns his head away, expecting the discomforting prick as the vein on top of his hand is rolled and punctured. His eyes penetrate the window in an effort to disappear.

'You'll start to feel a bit drowsy,' the white-haired man informs, injecting the sleep-inducing drug.

Westcott stares at the lights, his head instantaneously heavy. *Stay awake, resist it*. Out.

Germany, 1968

The doctor whom she has been working for agrees to examine Regn in his office. It is her first examination.

At 5' 2" she wears a skirt and medium pumps. She steps behind the screen, softly slides out of her shoes and begins unclasping the many buttons down her blouse. She draws the zipper and slips off her skirt. She hangs her bra from a hook on the back of the enclosure; a tiny tab shows the size at 34 B. She is not afraid and dutifully steps out of her underwear before taking the gown hanging over the screen and bringing it around her *klein[1]* body. If anything she is relieved for the familiar face.

The doctor comes back in the room. There is no protocol for the presence of a female assistant, nurse or otherwise. It is just the two of them. She moves to the table and lies down comfortably, resting her head back. In school they studied gymnastics. Her joints are lithe, relaxed though naturally tense, not in fear or embarrassment, but in anticipation of not knowing what to expect. She positions herself near the edge of the table, her dark brown hair loose around her head. She bends her knees and spreads her legs apart.

The doctor examines her sex, making light conversation throughout the process. He is checking to see if it is safe for her to take the pill. With gloved finger he probes inside then withdraws and pushes the two folds outward while using his other hand to slowly insert a metal instrument. Her body accepts the foreign object without resistance. She feels the pressure of its head raising inside her and opening to stretch its bill. It does not hurt. He spins the knob, fixing the individual calibration in place. He sees no reason to the contrary. He will prescribe the pills. 'Klein aber oho!' [1]

He leaves to get the pills while Regn dresses.

She does not imagine that forty years later she will be telling a young man how right everything seemed that day. How right and good.

---

1 *Klein aber oho.*

Small but whoa.

14 October 20—

Shivering, he wakes himself—his head lolling side-to-side. An oxygen mask has been placed over his mouth and nose but begins to slip. Feeling as though his arms are leaded, Westcott can't move to fix it. The first thing he sees is another white clock, different in its location. It is mounted on the right wall and reads five past 1:00. The surgery itself was supposed to last 2 1/2 hours at most. He's been in the recovery room for quite some time. *They must have slid me onto another gurney while I was still out, covered I pray.* Two other patients are beside him. He shakes, chilled beneath the gown, sheet and towel, going in and out for another twenty minutes.

A nurse inquires if he is in pain. He struggles to nod after rasping, 'Yes,' still unable to fully speak or move his limbs. They feel so heavy. His throat is sore, dry from the respiration tube. A sensation of pressure dispels in his hand as something injects into the I.V. Soon after, the oxygen mask is removed. They wheel him downstairs to his bed. There he will lie, flat on his back, for the next 24 hours.

U.S. Hospital Base, West Germany, Spring 1979

She is shaking uncontrollably. The lights hurt her eyes; she cannot focus; their voices come in and out, they are so far away. It's so cold. Her forehead is damp with sweat. Someone wipes it with a cloth. Something's not right. It wasn't like this when Dee came. She feels helpless amidst the commotion of those standing round.

'She's hemorrhaging.....your son is fine, don't worry.'

Regn hears the words but they do not register. Her hands are cold, clammy, her legs are trembling and the place between them weeps. She has been torn apart, her strength slipping. The gaping wound of strain leaves her too exhausted to protest. She closes her eyes and waits for the shaking to stop.

California, December 1979

The small creature looks into Gedny's green gray eyes. *Is something wrong?* The newborn is quiet. No, she's perfect they inform. It's her first. Ellis. Westcott's sister.

Madrid, Spain 1975; Regn

All the words, where do they go? All the love, where does it go? A young woman opens her eyes. The room has become home to her in the past few months. She throws the heavier cover aside and lies interwoven with the sheet. Her husband of five years has already left for the day on assignments. It is silent in the room. Too silent. A fear finds its way into her breast. A terrifying sense of being trapped. She is alone in this place; she does not speak the language. She lies on her back, her head propped on the pillows, and she waits for the wave to pass. She closes her eyes. When they open a translucent form perched in mid-air looks back from across the room at the foot of the bed. She, he, has no gender. Its presence is ethereal. *She*, for all practical terms, is the embodiment of the olive leaf. Her expression is calm, unmenacing. The young woman waits, experiencing what she can give no other name to but a sublime entity. Angel is too angelic and suspect for mockery, but such is the only apt term. The host-less spirit, revealed in its true form, unclothed to the seeking woman, speaks in presentation solely. A sense of absolute surrender, a peace so vast overtakes the young woman. Her honey brown eyes impart a mutual respect. As gentle as a breeze wisping through the balcony and lifting the curtain inward and upward, the apparition flows from itself into obscurity.

Virginia, Summer 20— After High School

Time is a funny thing. You tell yourself you won't forget the present and then, slowly, subtly, steadily, it slips away, displaced by the future tide you 'hoped' and thought would never come in. The present is safe. It is what you know. Yesterday is a haunting photograph, next year an unexposed obscurity.

Bitburg 1960

'Minchin?'

No answer.

'Minchin! Was machen Sie? Come now, you be late. Vaht are you doing child? You must be on your way. Your bruder is waiting.'

Regn is in her room. She straightens her bed, aligns the few books on the shelf she just dusted. She smooths out the hem of her dress and grabs her leather pack by the door, then steps once more to her side table and readjusts the brush to its customary location. She surveys her work before hurrying to her mother. Everything is in its proper place.

Sudschule, Bitburg 1967

They stand in procession. The girls in two lines, the boys forming a complementing set. Each wears her best; a modest flower pinned on the breast of a few. Regn has left her mousy brown hair down, her bangs fall across the side of her forehead and brow, tucked behind one ear. She is fifteen. Her father died in her brother, Wolfgang's, arms three years ago. The line advances. It is a small ceremony and by the end each student is given a child's hand-sized cross, inscribed and artistically engraved with design. On the back the year. The inscription reads *Ich Bin Bei Euch Alle Tage.*[2] In private Regn traces the circular lines with the tip of her thumb. She takes it to her breast before putting it away for safekeeping.

Some weeks later she finds herself in her cousin Gaby's room, staring out the window. Regn's older sister Ursula has come with her.

'What is it, doll?' Gaby approaches the window looking to see what Regn is so intent upon.

'I was just wondering what we'll be like—twenty years from now.' Regn turns and brushes her eyes across Gaby who just smiles quietly and shakes her head to say *I don't know.* 'Ever the dreamer. My sister,' Ursula sweetly scoffs, studying herself in the portrait mirror hanging, for that sole purpose, on the wall.

---

[2] *Ich Bin Bei Euch Alle Tage:*
I am with you every day

Church of St. Peter and Paul, Miami Florida
11 February 1967

Helen Cray, Miss Gedny as her grandfather affectionately calls her—a name she's kept—stands in the small white church beside Anthony "Tony." She will be 22 in little more than a month. She is happy, so completely happy. How can she know the pain that awaits? How can she know the father of her children is not to be this man beside her, but a stranger 10 years in coming? And still a stranger after 22 years of marriage. 22. She will have traveled the continent by then. Born in Port Chester, ripped to Miami, a place she can never love. Fleeing to California, and then escaping to Virginia and then—then—what of the years inside?

Virginia 20—

He does not tell anyone his dreams. Does he have any dreams for himself beyond just the one? There is no talk of girlfriends and boyfriends. He endures the distress of physical change twice and both times alone. The girls grow into their breasts and learn to accept the power of womanhood in exchange for its monthly hardship.

August 20—

Westcott slips his hand into the briefcase. The lights from a neighbor's house and the lamp at the end of the cul-de-sac illuminate through the window. He feels blindly in the dark compartment of the leather bag. He moves aside some papers and at the bottom grasps a bronze object. It is cool to the touch.

The cross fits securely in the entire of his palm. With thumb he traces the circular lines where the two pieces merge into solidity. He knows the words and strokes the raised letters. The same lines Regn's hands once touched.

It is not the symbol, but the knowledge that this item belonged to Regn which he holds so dear. In grasping the object, he feels he is holding a part of Regn.

They'd been together in Group Arrivals all day. Two springs ago she'd held out her hand with the offering and he'd received it. He knows the embossed date on the back. 1967. The year Regn graduated from high school. His talisman, he presses it firmly and kisses it on this particularly wearisome evening. *Do not ask for anything but strength.* 'Is anyone there?' he cries in silence. 'Come to me—something.' He knows—no—he feels no other forms of prayer. He is not a praying man. Prayer is a crutch. He is asking himself for strength.

~

He sits on the sofa, slouches for comfort, putting his head back, breathing lightly, shallow as to rest. The skies darken. One cat looks out the window. The larger grey male huddles on the throw rug in front of the coffee table. Westcott watches the birds. They dip their heads into the suspended feeder. A squirrel scavenges the deck for morsels. *How I'd like to be you, bird.*

The fish tank on its stand to the right lulls his restive state; the pump filters the water in auditory tranquility.

I wish I could stay right in this moment, just here, now. He feels himself slipping into midday requiem.

Outside, just through the sliding glass door, a white wicker chair and matching ottoman. The woman who owns this house is a widow. Nancy. She's gone for the weekend. He is watching her four legged companions. There are closets, rooms, spaces, privacies within. They do not interest. He does not venture to violate, has no reason to—they will remain things. And so it is, he thinks. He sees a woman in that vacant chair, an old woman—any woman, sitting in her chair, pontificating. It is time to reflect on her life, construct her memoirs. He knows her age, feels it in his own tiredness for want of sleep at that moment, and yet somewhere between half awake and half asleep it registers that such intimate history takes a lifetime to shape. It could not be adequately put down in this time and place where he is concerned, but only from a distant pulpit from which to peer at the congregation of experiences and examine each in relation to the other. A long line of communion offered to each.

The woman outside has nothing left to fear, all is decided, and now she can put it to paper, lay it to rest. From his distance upon the sofa, he wants and feels her internal calm, the peace of knowing the only question that remains is when. *When* will she go? Will it be easy, painless? The gentle waterfall, the little birds beating wings, an empty chair. Sleep.

In waking within he finds himself on the expanse of a green hill. The skies are alive with thunderheads, a gray white cavalry of storm clouds shadowing the valley. He sits atop a deep wooded horse. Mane and tail wisping in the breeze. The wind breaks across his brow, his shirt billows. The tall grass ripples in the current. He rides bareback with just the reins held fixedly across his palms. His inner thighs ache; the muscles and tendons are not accustomed to straddling, but the power between them diverts his thoughts of discomfort. The horse ascends the crest and reaching, stepping from the rocky crags onto the plateau, lets loose in a fury. He gallops hard; the skies hug horse and rider. He gallops without command. The rider's bones crack until the smoothness of stride graft him. Without warning the horse halts, an impossible feat. The inertia of body in the blink of an eye just stopped. The rider vaults over the mane, skyward. Flying, falling through the imperceptible divide. He feels the rain on his brow and lets the cool grass and wind's hands course round him, as though his love runs out from his limbs in silver tracers of magnetic field. The grass a storm of windlust, an ecstasy as pure as an untouched stone deep in the river. The sky becomes one giant canopy of a mushroom, the air scented in earthy redolence. He is somehow unclothed and unafraid. And the wind, the wind he sees in the way it swirls the grasses, slips inside and withdraws from him, again and again. He gasps quietly.

———

What remains more or less is a box. And within the cardboard enclosure a canvas handbag with a name neatly monogrammed in script. *Regn.* Another box, long and rectangular, ideal for storage of neckties, shows its contents to be minute cassettes. Tapes upon tapes, some with dates, a word or two of notes, others blank. These he will never listen to, he hasn't the strength or will. He doesn't need them. They are simply proof. Even in their making, somehow he knew, he understood the weight of the present moment. He knew one day the tiny cassettes would be all that remained, all that he had to remember his youth, his life—the jewel of his existence.

———

There are places I go, so far down and the strength to recover, climb back out again, requires exhausted resolve.

I need those extremes, for a moment will come, a moment so brief, so absolutely fleeting, but beautiful. My depression is not of the new age brand and will not offer its hide as a rat for ever forthcoming experimental drugs put out by the government. Ah there is much discontent. I can go to some dark room and raise my serotonin in a passing interval of lonely shame. I'm in a trance, in a chair; our house across the street, seeing it through the eyes of our neighbors. This is how I live now, in this hour, in this day, this month, this minute, this second. For October the crickets are still beating strong. Everything in its proper place. Will it ever be put down? There's a great thick novel on the table leaving me empty. *The Tale of Edgar Sawtelle*. He is mute. I am not. But I am silent. I carry something I never speak of. I can tell no one about Regn. About myself. Is it my time?

Go back to your work, fade into the day, these leaves will remain. You there, the engineer, I know you for we share the human condition. The mathematician—there is no formula for the finite solution of: borne X; unknown Y; and the remainder of years equals: we are all destined to die.

There is a picture of the parking lot at Kaiser Hospital on the day I was born. It is either dawn or dusk. I came in the morning. I believe the photograph is of the sun setting the evening of the day I arrived in protest. The nurses were there as was my mother, to confirm my rebellious cry, never ceasing the first night through—the entire nursery disrupted in its slumber. I was 10 pounds two ounces. A week after arriving I looked a month old. A bundle of boyish joy strangers assumed. People in grocery and department stores asked my mother all the time if they could hold me. They said I was adorable. It's true. Even my sister would remark with levity, looking back, 'Yeah, you were such a cute little shit!' I was photogenic and always smiling. And constantly on the move. I loved to get into things, investigate. Ellis was four years and ten months old when she lost our mother's sole attention. She never got over being displaced. I didn't ask to be born. Ellis is more like my father. I take after my mother. Ellis and I were never close as siblings, emotionally.

—

White horses always frightened—no, they bothered him. Maybe it is the pureness of coat so startlingly contrasted with the darkness of their eyes that disturbed him so. Something other-worldly. A dark mystery.

'Do you believe in unicorns,' he'd asked her.

'Yes.'

He loves the firm jawline. To stroke the side cheek. The powerful vessels and veins running as traces like tree roots rippling the turf. He holds out his hand, palm up with a slice of apple. The dark wooded mare gobbles it down. He inhales deeply.

I love the smell of horseshit.

So do I.

An oaty redolence, a meadow of soft moss, damp soil, the power of this being. Ears twitching, hooves stomping. He cannot tell her, 'I didn't bring the treat for you.' He is standing on the second log. She is getting impatient, sensing the feeding is up. *Don't go. Don't go—I just.* In a flash he is up the railing and throws himself over, saddling her bare back. Alarmed, she thromps in confusion, backsteps, shakes her neck, whinnies to the other shadows in the distance. Huhphhhh. He tightens his fingers round her coarse mane, hugs her sides as tightly as his muscles will go. They begin to spasm. Huffing she turns and begins to canter, trying to loose this strange object. Feeling his legs slip, he lowers his chest where the horn should be.

She wears the earth. He takes a long drag of her scent.

She eases up, slows, and settles.

'Whoa there, lass. Where to? Lead the way.' His voice is inaudible.

He pats her shoulder. It was just a vision.

Westcott sits on the fence post, one leg on each side. The mare is grazing far off in the field. His hand is mildly sticky from her muzzle and the fruit juices. He holds his hand to his nose, as though to hold his chin, a pensive stance. He inhales.

Had I not been so young I'd never have had the courage to love her.

The evening is deep in the soft shade of blue. A gentle breeze plays with the wisp of hair falling across his forehead.

—

As a child I broke out of the wooden crib. I remember crawling across the floor, maybe four feet distance, through the open doorjamb and grabbing my sister's hair. She was on the trundle bed. I was seven or eight, maybe younger—I can't remember—when I occasionally stole into my parents' room and crawled into bed. I didn't think of the room as theirs. It was Mother's. I wasn't a little boy then, which you'll understand in a moment, so it was all right. There was nothing weird or Norman Batesy about it. Like all little kids I felt protected by my mother and wanted to know she was near. Some distant mornings Father would scoop me up and carry me downstairs on his back whistling a happy tune. 'Zippity do da, zippidy eh, my oh my what a wonderful day.' A blue robe. My father always wore his blue robe. He was quite young then, that I know for sure, but I can't say when Father stopped sleeping in Mother's bed. It was a high bed. A deep wood frame reaching to the ceiling. Two steps led up to a slight rise in the bedroom, then a trunk, my grandfather's trunk, of thick, dark, solid, rich wood. Always cool to the touch. Pillars to grasp and many drawers on the sides. A little rectangular door opened on each side. Sometimes I'd contort my limbs in an effort to squeeze into the cubby space. I didn't call my parents 'Mother' and 'Father' at that time, but as I grew up and when I entered my twenties, it seemed the proper thing to do; it was gentlemanly. It suited the Victorian surroundings of my childhood. More often than not I called my mother, Ma or Mom, and my father, Dad, though he always wanted us kids to call him Papa, something we never did. A name has to be said with meaning and I didn't know my father well enough at that young age to call him something without real feeling and sentiment behind it.

The house was built in 1888. An occasional spider sometimes wandered across the silk black sheets. The headboard was made of glass. I sometimes pressed my nose against the mirror, or more often studied the room in reverse, looking at its reflection. An overhead reading lamp was attached on each side. Lying in bed, on the left was a window. Summer nights we'd sleep with the window half-open and just a cover sheet, the scent of Mother's oils and moisturizers giving life to my young history. She has psoriasis. Sometimes when I couldn't sleep we'd play the whispering game. I'd say something very softly in my mother's ear and wait to see if she could decipher it. I'd trace words or pictures through the night-gown on her back—pictionary, though the game had no name, and she'd have to guess what the object was or what my index had spelled. Mornings I had to go to school it made getting up nice. Mother was right there—I'd hear the alarm. She always set it a little ahead. 'You have about twenty minutes; we don't have to get up yet.'

My sister sometimes slept in the bed. I would be sandwiched between two sets of limbs, my head at the foot of the bed, while Mother and Ellis slept properly.

On the nights after my birthday I'd often cry myself to sleep, stifling a congested nose. It was always so much fun. All the activities, the cake, the classmates, and bags of candy, erasers, small toys I gave to everyone. Mother gave the best birthday parties. I usually had two. A planned party with friends on the weekend and then a quiet family celebration the *actual day of* my birthday.

Sometimes when Ellis and Mother stayed up late watching a show downstairs I'd lie awake in the dark and see an ominous face staring down at me. There were two large panels of heavy glass directly above the bed. Mother said she'd told my father she thought it was dangerous, especially with the tendency for earthquakes where we lived. At my age I had no notion of what those mirrors meant. At 12 I remained young, blithely innocent. To me sex referred only to one's gender, not a comingling of body parts and passionate energy. My innocence afforded an unconscious haven. On the right of the bed the sliding closet doors were made of lighter more practical mirrors.

I would stretch my limbs beneath the cool silk sheets on hot still nights. Being an authentic vintage home there was no air conditioning. Sometimes a floor fan would be plugged in to circulate the still night hours. Sometimes mother played an audio cassette of thunderstorms. The rain would be pouring down, thunder crashing as the ribbon on the tape player unspooled itself. Meanwhile the night just outside the window blew the lace curtain softly.

I would read. I'd look up or just before turning off the lights, glance at the turret in the left corner of the room.

It was a large spacious master bedroom. Two sinks and a small cylindrical alcove—the turret—on the left. I was eleven the first time a book moved me to cry. I was alone. Old Dan had died from a terrible wound inflicted by a mountain lion. His partner, Little Ann, succumbed a few days later—her will to live gone. Billy Coleman knelt between the mounds of his redbone coonhounds staring at the red fern that had mysteriously sprouted between the bodies. I wasn't just so sad that they had died. I was sad because of what their death meant. Billy was leaving the Ozarks. His family was moving away. His boyhood had ended.

• • •

The room, my Mother and Father's room, was blue and yellow as a child. It felt warm and safe. A few years later, when it became Mother's room, the yellow carpet was changed to green with a crisscross pattern, bowed, like giant candies. The *room* became green and purple, lavender—the color my mother loves. It was elegant, but I missed the color of the sun. The purple and green felt cooler.

On weekends we'd play Jaws. When Ellis was younger Mom had played it with her. I would just be stirring and the hunt would begin.

'Dun-dun, dun-dun, dun-dunt.' My mother's voice a light whisper. 'He's coming in the sunroom. Now he's in the kitchen. Dun-dunt, dun-dunt. Now he's at the foot of the stairs. Don't move. Dun-dunt.' I was frozen, the coverlet hiding my face and head. I could feel the warmth of my trapped breath under the blanket. I felt the closeness of the Great White, his stealth approaching. 'He's coming up the landing, he's going left.' Left meant a momentary reprieve. Through the guest room into Ellis' room then my own and Trillia—Trillia was the name of a make-believe land where Ellis' stuffed mouse named Bunny came from; Mother had invented the fantasy. Of course the elongated work area called "Trillia," just off my bedroom, did exist. Ellis' desk was to the far left with a window overlooking the driveway. You could actually climb out the window and into the office above the garage. My side was directly to the right with a window opening to the walnut tree. The whole length behind was windows above the sunroom—and then—'He's in Ellis' room. He doesn't see her. She's asleep. He's looking in your room, he's coming to the closet, hold on.' The large closet was Mother's and cut through between the master bedroom and my own. The two-foot wide, very tall door was nothing more than wallpapered cork board. Very light to open and shut, and always a slight muffled ripping noise where the wallpaper sealed the hinges. I felt my heart pounding. 'Don't move he's right by your side of the bed. He's stopping. He's going on.' A relief. 'He's back in the hall. He's going down the stairs. He's going out the front door. It's safe. He's gone.'

• • •

When I was 8 and my sister 13, the family took a vacation to Hawaii. In one of the hotels we stayed at on Waikiki, we were riding the elevator. I looked up and saw my father kissing my mother. Well, *kiss* my mother. I didn't know what it was exactly; I just knew I'd never seen that sort of display between my mother and father.

At home Father lived in the cottage, the annex out back, a large addition built by my parents. My father wanted it. Mother had protested; it didn't flow aesthetically with the main Victorian. I don't remember when my father first started living out there. I do recall the long arguments. Mother telling us to stay inside. It was boring. One time we went onto the back deck to listen—the window in the upstairs of the addition was open. 'You bellowing cow!'

Ellis was very upset. I took her cue. Mother wasn't heavy. She came out—was it from the garage door or the cottage room below the addition—? It doesn't matter—it seemed like forever, but she was agitated, her voice high, crying. Other times we could hear mother yelling, 'Son of a bitch.'

Summer nights we'd go for a bike ride. When I was real little I'd sit in the hammocked seat behind my mother. I remember our walks and the Witches' Lot. About six houses down from us was an open space, overgrown with weeds, dry grass, and old trees. Why it had been left free I do not know. Mother made up stories about Brunhilda, the good witch, and her cackle of *broom*mates brewing away.

Sometimes after our late night walk or no walk out at all, we'd sit on the front porch in the wooden slatted bench with the white wrought iron siding. Mother and us. The moon would be shining through the hanging wisteria. No need for the porch light to be on. And then just before going in, we'd have our moon kiss. Mother would kiss us both and make a wish on the moon. I felt safe.

• • •

Ellis and I liked to play Businessman or Shop Clerk in Father's office upstairs. Ellis was always the accountant or store clerk since she was the oldest. She used the adding machine. I would go around pulling out all sorts of things and bringing them to the large desk. Ellis sat in the rich burgundy leather wingback. It had wheels. I'd bring the pet carrier, sometimes Piccolo—our neurotic Russian Blue who was purebred to the point of being inbred—if I could capture him, and paint swatches—the long rectangular metal ones that were such fun to fan out. A level, the corner plant, the shells in the glass case—a sea horse skeleton and snail shell were in that collection which always intrigued me. A radio, wallpaper books, the three-sided triangular ruler. Each side had a different colored line going down the middle. It was only a foot, maybe 18 inches long, but what a fun shape for a ruler. Mother had a rolltop desk on the far side of the office. Ellis got locked in it once with the key in the drawer with her! I liked to hide behind the enormous desk. It was angled between two walls. Perfect for climbing.

• • •

My father was an abstraction. In his emotional and physical absence my mother overcompensated. She did not want us to feel alone and vulnerable, as her brother and she had been as kids. She made it her purpose to be at every event, every function no matter how big or small. Something she'd never known as a child. Naturally she assumed we always wanted her there, to suggest otherwise would be taken as a personal assault and we in turn, as her children, would feel guilty. How can you criticize your parent for being too involved? All of this was unspoken or more often in early years, unconsciously absorbed. My father showed up late to soccer games, or not at all. But it seems to me it's always been my mother and I. That sounds too oedipal. Strike that. What I mean is, emotionally we were psychically connected. She'd suffered as a child. And in my own suffering that came later, she wanted to spare me. Of course she couldn't. Having been hurt so much in her own life, and hiding her skin as a child because of the psoriasis, she had no capacity for tough love. Years later she justified by saying, 'From the day you were born you had an iron will. Nothing I did worked as a punishment, whether I took this or that away—it made no difference. But neither you nor Ellis ever got into serious trouble. Teachers and friends always complimented me on how well-mannered you were. I did what I thought was right. I never meant to hurt you.'

On some level I attribute my private nature and discretion to the prolonged feeling of never having my own life. For a while it had been tied to my mother by circumstance rather than choice. As a child I confided everything to her; *I wanted to*. No one else was there and she never told me, 'Be strong in yourself.' When I grew older, I would tell her nothing. I realized it did no good. My privacy was deemed by her as secretive, cloak and dagger she liked to say. I turned on her, turned further inside. At times I felt guilty, more often it seemed right. Though I was no longer a teenager, naturally I sought the autonomy of self I never had. I experienced no social adolescence. I went from 12 to 20. Because we still shared the same living space only my emotions remained a bittersweet haven. I needed something all to my own. I don't know which has been more of an influence, perhaps a detriment—having a father who left little impression other than regret until I was in my twenties and we tried to make up for lost time, or having a mother who was too sensitive. She believed love was enough—that giving and being there would sustain—she wanted us to fill a void that she could never fill herself: Confidence. With age vulnerability sets in. She expected and in a quiet way demanded our love and attention be returned, else we were taking her for granted. This had nothing to do with our father who I knew was often irresponsible. Seldom punctual. My mother needed an emotional anchor, a husband who understood her. I wish for her sake things had been different. Aside from their both being highly creative and inventive, my parents were not well suited for each other, much like my sister and I. I do not hold my mother or my father accountable, singularly. Neither was right for one another. She divorced my father at 50 years of age, exercising the courage her own mother never used.

Like many men, my father remarried after several years. My mother's heart was tired, not only from my father but a lifetime worth of hurt. She no longer trusted or had faith in anyone but her children and brother. She couldn't help it—her need for emotional reassurance increased with the years resulting from the neglect of her childhood. In spite of her unconditional love for me and Ellis, the situation in my own life found me completely alone. I wish my mother would have thought more about herself instead of worrying about her children. She tried so hard, too hard. In the end it slapped her in the face.

But I can't complain, not fairly. Both my mother and father have always accepted and supported me in sentiment. Though each has a very different way of expressing it, they love their children and want the best for us. Underneath all the emotional hardships, if it came right down to it, I always knew they'd give their lives for me and Ellis. So why is love not enough?

Of the three of us—Mother, Ellis, and myself—I was the boldest in a back-door sort of way. But isn't being bold storming in through the front door and making a brouhaha entrance? No, not always. There are dramatic arrivals and exits; sometimes the most dignified ones resound with a stellar poignancy. I was always quiet in my comings and goings. Not like Ellis who moved around and did something on the fly like running a marathon with no physical preparation. The real trauma, the tragic theatrics in my life, came in privacy when no one could witness the distress and the need for comfort. Being the boldest, I realized to my discontent, necessitates being the strongest. You cannot rely on others or falter when others may need or turn to you for reassurance. After Regn I tried to manifest an ironclad strength independent of *all* external sources, becoming reliant only on myself. I failed. And what I discovered was this: even the strongest oldest tree in the forest takes sustenance from the same water source. I felt parched in being alone. An arctic desert.

—

I remember once, on a rare occasion, Regn came to my house—the second one, after we had moved. She was on her lunch break. We'd gone up to my room with the yellow walls. She sat on the edge of my bed. A wooden chair was positioned sideways near the bed. She'd slipped her shoes off. The fabric on the seat of the chair being quite formal. *She'd slipped her shoes off* and rested her stockinged feet on my chair. This singular gesture. The consideration and respect in it, the silent process—obviously made an impact in its sheer simplicity. I wonder what the chair felt like to her feet through her stockings. What did it feel like to be this woman? To be in her small body? To be so loved and not just by me?

———

My Name is Westcott A. Rowan. When I was 20 years old I underwent GRS to become male at the hands of plastic surgeon, Pierre Brassard. If you are unacquainted with the acronym G.R.S., that's fine by me. I'll say it this way so you can feel the statement rather than digest the definition. It's absurd even to me. So if you don't understand, I don't blame you. I was born female and lived as such for 17 years, well, really only 4. Childhood is a period of unisex freedom and I was very unconscious of the approaching divergence that comes with the onset and development of secondary sexual characteristics. I was fortunate to remain in that blissful limbo of carefree existence until 16.

There is nothing wrong with being a woman. In fact, they are the stronger sex—it's scientifically proven. Women endure child labor, their life expectancy exceeds men's, they are better equipped to adapt. But *I* remembered who I'd been, I longed for the return. I became a man so I could be free. So I could love a woman more easily and traditionally. I did not want to endure the burden of monthly courses. I did not want the added weight up top. I wanted to be free from physical encumbrance. The irony of such a statement.

When I was 23 I had a love affair with a woman. When I was 24 I knew life would never be the same. I knew love was the only consequence in life. It is the only meaning to be had. When I was 26 I tried to die. I would sprint from a standstill to full speed in an attempt to rupture my heart—induce cardiac arrest. It was passive and as close to the real thing—suicide—as I'd go. When I was 28 I determined the world, or rather, society in general, needed a wake-up call and to be reminded of what is at stake, what matters in the end. When I was 29 I had a second affair that would last until my death.

And then—air. I shut the door. Carried one suitcase, the old kind, made to last, with silk lining. I closed the door, tipped my hat at the sun, and walked *through*.

I put it away. Began to live for the first and last time. I put it away. Until now.

Dear Reader:

I ask you to take a few minutes before coming with me, to acquaint yourself with the significance of auditory sensibility. Listen to the pieces and if there is a sound for what I feel and have felt, which there is, then I leave it here for safekeeping.

Dvorak: Humoresque
Master and Commander soundtrack: (Corelli's
        Christmas Concerto *Third Movement* "Adagio"
        of Grosso Op. 6 No. 8 in G minor)
Empire of the Sun version: Suo Gan
Coldplay: In My Place
Sarah McLachlan: I Love You
Ennio Morricone: Once Upon a Time in the West
The Last of the Mohicans Soundtrack: Cora
James Blunt: I Really Want You
Loreena McKennitt: The Highway Man
London String Orchestra: Let It Be
Hugh Laurie: Changes
Credence Clearwater Revival: Have You Ever Seen the Rain
Rihanna: Stay
Ennio Morricone interpreted by Yo-Yo Ma: Guiseppe Tornatore Suite
        "Playing Love"
Dvorak: Humoresque*

*Even in its tragedy, life has an ironic sense of humour.
I list it twice, for emphasis.

No, don't turn the page. Go listen to this music. Listen and remember.

———

The heart is broken in by degrees. Once love is lost the imagination is blunted. In my case I could never write about anything else. I'd sit down with one thing in mind and it would always lead back to the same place—love's departure. An urgency to write this story has pursued me over the years. I always felt I was existing elsewhere. I had my day-to-day life, yet I circled as if on the wing too long, needing to rest, but knowing that in standing still, coming upon the one place I wanted to be, I feared getting stuck again. For sure as the sun rises, to invest in the past is certain damnation. Stagnation. In going back, I knew I might not want to return. I had a plan. Somewhat Gatsbian in its conception. I knew it was possible and when I'd start to envision the process the fervency would kick in. Patience was hard. I knew I could never allow the pedestrian activities of life to become routine else complacency would seep in and life would be manageable, typical. The dream postponed or worse, discarded. I had to ensure it remained my priority. Happiness in the larger extent depended on it. My plan was to publish a story, this story.

I knew it was only a matter of time and a spit-lick of luck, the right place, right contact. But it had to be gone about in the right light and purest way. One does not achieve success if his motivation is money, notoriety. A solid financial return on the sale of such a book would generate freedom. It was the gateway to potential realized and years upon years of preparation. With the money generated from novels I would be in the position to make things happen. First I would return to the house on Shackleton Lane. I see myself anxiously strolling up the driveway, the driveway I'd parked in so many times, bordered by the neatly trim lawn I'd once cut in a plaid jacket and loose jeans. I'd be wearing my shirt and tie. Knock on the front door that was no longer patriot blue. I'd introduce myself, explain how I used to live here, that I was the original owner, or my mother was, and how relinquishing it had taken something from her. In short I'd make them an offer they couldn't resist. I'd pay to have them relocate, have the movers come and pack all their things. Give them time to find a new place they liked. I needed this house back. For my mother.

I'd discreetly have furniture transferred, get the home prepared and spruced up, not completely as it was, but similar. It would be purchased outright. No more mortgage headaches. And then one day I'd tell my mother I had a surprise. I'd hand her a small box sized to fit a pair of earrings. She'd open it. Inside a single key would be waiting. She'd look at me, then I'd take her home without saying a word. Not tell her where we were going. Just wait for proof when we pulled up in front.

I wanted my mother to be happy. I couldn't leave with a light conscience unless I knew she was all right.

The house was still beautiful.

Once my mother was taken care of I'd approach a more delicate matter. It had to be done right. Regn could not be forewarned. I knew she'd be much too afraid and panic if I told her my intentions. It wasn't simply a matter of financial independence that had kept Regn with Jay. She had a duty to fulfill, not only to him, but her children's memory of her. I would lay everything on the line. No secrets. Only the truth. Jay would hear all from the horse's mouth, for once. I didn't want to give him a heart attack.

I wouldn't be whisking Regn away forever. I would just be buying us some time. A decent proposal. If I could accept him in Regn's life why couldn't he accept me? I'd make sure their house was paid off. It wasn't bribery, but a trade-off. And then Regn and I would travel for a while. Do all the things we'd never had time or freedom to enjoy. Everything would be out in the open. Jay would always share a history with Regn. She belonged to neither of us. To envision such things was not daydreaming. I accepted that the past was gone and only the future remained unknown. I wanted to create the future and make it wonderful. All I wanted was contentment. Peace.

Money. I hated money. But a person needed it. Freedom can be bought so long as the money is used as a means and not viewed as the grand reward. My lifelong motivation was affection. Perfection.

• • •

Loneliness is an emaciation of the spirit. It is a pain like no other. Before Regn I was alone, but not lonely. After Regn I became conscious of it and the loneliness was unbearable.

With her it wasn't just a desire. With her it was a need. In losing her I never loved again without hating the need for love itself.

At the end of the day, at the final curtain call, will it stand you well to know that throughout your life you were wise in always purchasing—oh say, the generic brand of mouthwash—Equate, instead of Listerine? That you saw through the masquerade? Same components, different brand. Same spirit, different containing vessel? In the end the only answer is: let go.

—

My mother was born breech. Throughout her life she was always doing things back-wards. In filling a take home box she'd put the leftovers in the top of the container instead of the bottom. She often went in the exits of driveways and doorways. She'd open boxes on the wrong side. I mark this last example down to impatience. If she couldn't open a plastic sealed snack, she'd take scissors and cut it open so that a clip would be necessary to keep the meat, or whatever item it might be, fresh. My mother's justification was always the same: "What do you expect. I was born feet first. It's no wonder I'm always going the opposite direction." For a woman born ready to land, I would have expected my mother to be extremely confident and ready to take on the world. Perhaps she might have been had she received encouragement while growing up, had her mother—my grandmother—been a different type of person. The emotional and psychological trauma she experienced at such a young age influenced the way she raised me and Ellis. A single choice, generations before, bears endless speculation. For instance, I am alive today because my great-great-great grand-mother survived the potato famine. I am also alive because a neighbor saved my mother from a potential kidnapping.

Helen was five years old and playing outside on the front lawn. Across the street a young man and his girlfriend sat in the open doorway of their van. They waved Helen over. They seemed nice and welcoming. As my mother tells it, they began showing her pictures of naked women and men.

'Helen, come here. Helen!' A neighbor called. My mother looked both ways before crossing the street and coming up to her neighbor. 'Now, you know better than to talk to strangers. I'm sure your mother has told you before not to go wandering off.' Her voice is gentle, concerned. 'You'd be better off playing inside today,' she looks across the street at the couple and shakes her head. 'Where's Charlie?' At seven, Charlie is on the back porch fixing his pigeon coop. There's a major tear in the screen. He's worried about a rat he's seen lurking around. 'Keep your brother with you if your mother sends you to the store today. All right, honey?'

That evening Charlie is upset. 'Let me stay home, I don't want to go with you! The pigeons need me.'

'They'll be fine. You fixed everything just right. Tonight we're going to dinner and we're going as a family. I want no arguments. I won't hear any more about it. Now, put your good clothes on. Hurry now.'

Arriving home that night, Charlie hurries to the back porch. Before he even steps outside to the coop, he knows something is wrong. The Florida night is quiet. Too quiet. Not a sound, not one coo or feather ruffling. He turns the light on.

All of them are dead. Their necks bitten. They lie on their sides. Charlie circles the coop looking for the hole. Then he sees it. Fresh gnaw marks. Maybe he should have left an opening near the top so they might have been able to escape. Fly up and out. Fly away. Pigeons on the run.

———

Groundwork. Pay attention. This is really where it all starts. Where it all went wrong. In the fall of 1949, Margaret Ann Cray left my grandfather. She took my mother, Helen, and my uncle, Charles, to Florida, leaving her home and well-to-do family in Rye, New York. She told my grandfather, Thomas Bamford, she was taking a trip for the week, to visit friends, enjoy the warmer weather. My grandmother filed for a divorce soon after. The man she'd followed to Florida with the intent of marrying stood her up in the worst way and shortly after, as fate would have it—and fate it could only be, she met Mel. A handsome boy, charming on the surface, dark brown hair and brown eyes, a regular playboy in every sense of the word. At 19 he was 13 years her junior.

•••

On a cool afternoon in September Helen and Charles are loaded into the back of my great-grandfather's Studebaker. He'd succumbed to his daughter's insistence that she drive to the train station with the children and no one else. She does not want to inconvenience Tom. He can send the chauffeur for it. The day before Aunt Ida stops by—Thomas' sister. "Now you children be good and have fun. Listen to your mother. And Miss Gedny"— grandpa's pet name for Helen which Aunt Ida has also adopted—"here's a little surprise for you and Charlie. You two share them and make sure to save some for the trip tomorrow! They're from your grandfather and I." She places a bag filled with individually wrapped marzipan candies, tied off with a lavender string, into my mother's small, trusting hand. Aunt Ida kisses Charlie and Gedny; embraces Margaret. The following day my grandfather pats them on the head, slides some comic books through the half window—*Little Lulu*— and kisses Margaret goodbye until next week. Margaret scans the yard over his shoulder, taking in her home, the scene. She pulls back a little, to see Thomas' blue eyes. "I'll call when we arrive. Don't worry about us." With forced deliberation she gets in the car, adjusts the rearview mirror though it needs no adjusting—catching a glimpse of herself. Her eyes are deep brown. For a second she checks herself. For a split second my mother and uncle might be spared. For a split second she thinks of opening her door, telling Thomas she's decided she doesn't want to go after all. Somehow she'll make it work. Somehow.

She looks once more in the rearview mirror. This time checking her appearance. Such soft, flawless skin, beautiful dark brown hair, a contemplative gaze. *I'm too young to stay and be unhappy. I have every right.* Something in her chest won't stand to be ignored. She turns the key in the ignition. Her mind is made up.

As the car starts along Pine Lane, Gedny is too low in the back seat to look out at her father without sitting on her knees. Charlie has already flipped open one of the comics. Thomas is walking up the path into the house. Margaret looks only at the road ahead.

It is the last time my mother sees my grandfather until she is 28.

•••

Discovering too late that his wife has no intention of returning, Thomas organizes the kidnapping of his own children. He manages to nab my uncle at his new school in Miami. My mother is not old enough to go to school; he cannot get to her. For years she believes her father wanted only Charlie.

Bewildered, uncertain, Charlie is brought back to Miami. Their father is no longer a part of their lives. They do not ask why. By the time she is old enough to seek the truth, the pain has been suffered. Gedny's father tried. Desperately. To get them both.

At four years old my mother's happiness ends.

•••

Life with Mel is a gradual unfolding. Rationed toilet paper. A light bulb unscrewed and removed from a room. A hand slipping by the shower curtain turning off the water when Gedny and Charlie are still soaped up. And for no reason other than he can. On one occasion he forces Gedny to drink a bottle of ketchup. The summer before third grade she breaks out in psoriasis and just about has a nervous breakdown. She is afraid to go to school. She wants to hide her skin. Mel holds himself accountable, but he does not know how to voice his guilt. His behavior is sporadic. In all likelihood he suffers from manic depression. Undiagnosed, he is left to his own devices. His dark periods release a toxicity that destroys anything in his path with one word, one look. Margaret is at his mercy.

When Gedny is 14 an argument ensues—something incidental—the reason forgotten with time. For two years Mel forbids Margaret to speak to her daughter. In his absence, when he goes to work, they talk. When he returns a mood settles over the house; a terrible gloom killing Margaret, thus poisoning the woman my mother will become. Mel is a miserable man, a womanizer. And yet he adores Margaret, loves her dearly. He serves on the police force. To the outside world he is charming, the perfect husband. No one suspects. At 16 Charles is bigger than Mel. He pulls a knife, lunges across the kitchen table. The desire to kill is palpable. Charles looks at his Mother, then his sister. Stays his arm, sets the knife down. Mel isn't worth it. Charles walks out the same night, joins the Navy. Does not ask if Gedny wishes to come. After boot camp his friend kills himself. Charles goes AWOL. Gedny has been left again. She is alone. Her mother says nothing to reassure. She does not know where, or if, her brother is.

• • •

Summers are a dream. Gedny visits her Great Uncle Charlie, for whom her brother was named. Uncle Charlie is Margaret's father's brother—my great-great uncle. He has a cabin on Lake George. The water is so clean, a shock to the skin; the cold a pleasant pain. Uncle Charlie is president of a bank in New York. He is a gentleman. Always dressed in full suit and pocket watch. A genteel man. A silent sorrow kept at bay by the precision and details of his life. He never marries. The woman he loved wouldn't wait—Uncle Charlie was enlisting for WWI.

That was a long time ago. No one asks or talks about it anymore. Many years later Gedny wishes she had.

August ends. Back in Miami she meets Tony. A wonderful boy. Four years older. They go steady for six years. He is a good man. A hard worker, a true Italian cook. They will marry.

• • •

I never met my grandmother. Even my paternal grandmother died just as I was born. At 45 Margaret suffers a partial mastectomy—that is, one breast is completely removed in a time when reconstructive surgery is not an option. 13 years later she is gutted from sternum to abdomen—an exploratory procedure. Whether she had the cancer or not is never conclusive and highly doubtful. At 60 she finds her escape from Mel-anoma. She stops fighting and dies. By this time my mother is already living in California and my sister, Ellis, has been born. My mother speaks to her mother for the last time on the telephone. The reason she left my grandfather, Thomas, is so long ago it goes unasked. Remains unanswered.

Mel did not recover from Margaret's death. Though he remarried, he kept a shrine in his house full of pictures honoring his first wife. Atonement assumes many forms.

I know my grandmother only from pictures and words. Ellis has her legs, her pose. Growing up my mother imparted to us the words her mother loved to make up. 'Hopssah-hopssah-soukess-boose' means the bus. And when playing the game, Clue, the 'luh-wall-awa' refers to the revolver. I miss my grandmother. Such an attractive woman with moments of hilarity. Why did she punish herself for so long?

Why didn't she have one more bout of courage—that same stroke of ardency which ushered her from Pine Lane? Why didn't she protect her children?

• • •

Senior year, Gedny is Captain of the Majorettes. Two years after graduation from Miami High, my mother marries her high school sweetheart—he is in the Navy when she is still in junior college. They love each other completely. Her friends compare her to Suzanne Pleshette. She could be the actresses' double, hands down. Even her voice is the same. Not high, but an alluring suppleness. By my regards my mother does not have a deep voice. Even so, she has often been mistaken for a man on the telephone or at a drive through window. I've seen Alfred Hitchcock's *The Birds* and watched *Rome Adventure*. My mother's likeness to Pleshette *was* uncanny. I know from the pictures in photo albums. Six years later, after her marriage to Tony, working for Accurate Insurance Co., my mother is in her prime. Stockings with the seams aligned, running up the back of the leg. Nice skirts. A beautiful body. Men in the office look at her. She is respectable, charming. Desirable. Gedny does not feel confident. Everyone calls her Mrs. Cray or Helen Cray. Gedny being reserved only for those on the most familiar terms. One day she brings a file into Bob Schneider's office. They've known each other for some time. Casual pleasantries.

Nothing dangerous. On this mid-afternoon his look frightens her. She is not afraid of *its* intentions. She does not consider what it will mean. She doesn't invite it and yet she doesn't dismiss it either.

She is afraid—not of Bob. She is afraid of her own desires.

———

Regn is feisty. She has a certain spunk that sets her apart. Despite her age, she often makes jokes like a kid—silly things. You could say she is young in spirit. Her company is warmth itself. She emits an energy—an aura. She is 5'2", klein, the German word for small. Her voice languid, smoothly seductive without intention. Sometimes her cheeks look slightly packed—a squirrel storing a snack—the folds of her jawline formed long ago so that her accent and pronunciation usher forth from these sweet, ever so subtle pockets of stores. One would not notice this feature at first, but in careful observation her muscles form the words differently, beautifully.

You know without hearing her that she is from another place—somewhere 'over there.' There is something in the skin of Europeans—the term European being used in the broadest of terms—be it Mediterranean, Turkish, Italian, or the heart of Europe, German and French—that enriches the skin, making it well-preserved. In women a certain glow of vitality exudes—even in those who have lived in the United States for over 20 years. Their skin retains moisture—it does not become dry and old. Even in senior advent the muscles of the neck show firm—their bodies are reasonably fit and lithe. Walking is a frequent pastime, this and bicycling. It seems inherited, a cultural norm like language—learned early on so that a foreigner, even if she's lived in America longer than her native land, always retains her heritage.

In skin tone, hair and eye color, she resembles Susan Sarandon. If the latter could affect a German accent, she'd exhibit a strong likeness to Regn. In trying to imagine her young, I think of the up and rising Juliette Binoche as Tereza in Kaufman and Zaentz's 1988 film, *The Unbearable Lightness of Being*. Regn was mousier, shy as an expatriate who barely spoke English. But her form, her sexuality, the very spark she possessed, exuded from her eyes—this is what she and the young Juliette had in common. The eyes and the smile never changed. In actress and Regn alike, I can see their earlier selves in the slightest expression borne of affection. Character-wise, Regn was modest, domestic, unsure of herself. Binoche's Tereza could, and did, stand on her own.

Regn's naturally brown sometimes redwood hair, depending on the brand of dye, compliments the honey brown of her eyes. She calls them piggy eyes. They are not vibrant or lush colored, but ordinary in color. It is the shape of her eyes that attracts effortlessly. Isosceles. That's what they are. Two wedges opposing each other—the longest side of each slanting seductively to the corner socket, giving the appearance of eyes that hide themselves. At a distance her eyes seem shrouded. Up close, that pair of isosceles. Flags turned on their sides. You have to look hard to penetrate. She has a long nose, sharp in its own right—a half triangle to compliment her gaze. Her face, however, is not angular but soft, offsetting such pronounced physiognomy. And her eyebrows, faint with gray—one does not notice them without consciously telling himself to. Her front teeth are straight, though ever so naturally, marginally, protruding. As a toddler she sucked her thumb too long. Her breasts are perfect. Just the size Westcott prefers. Nothing cumbersome. A respectable B cup. Delicate in appearance, but still full to the touch, one imagines.

She is always so clean and fresh, smelling of, of what? Soap and oils, coffee, and Caleche perfume. She does not wear the scent. She exudes it. It is not body spray like the young spritz themselves with in harried movements. It is light, subtle, quiet. Pleasure and refinement linger as qualities of the application.

This is how I remember Regn. Some things have changed.

• • •

I wanted the years without putting in the time.

There is a picture of Regn and her sister when they are knee-high children. Regn sent it to me a long time ago. Regn is the littlest, the newest addition to the family. Her older sister, age two-and-a-half, wears a plaid petticoat and holds hands with Regn as though holding her up, helping her to stand on the broken cobbles. In the background an old cart with the odor of manure. A village street. Neither poor nor rich in location. Ursula smiles—a warm, angelic innocence. Regn, at 10 months or thereabouts—seems to be testing her tiny legs. Both stare into the camera with amazing intensity. A snug white woolen cap fits over Regn's soft, still malleable skull. You know it is Regn and it can be no other. The same isosceles eyes. Ursula has them as well, but her smile lightens her face. Wedges, suggesting a sorrow yet to be determined, show from Regn. They are not sad eyes, but inquisitive, quiet, and yes, uncertain. I look at her forehead, the trust she unwittingly displays as her shoes stand on an uneven broken part of the stones. To see Regn before she changed, to see her as a vulnerable tot, and knowing what the little child in that picture cannot possibly know—makes me search her face with longing sadness. Her body is pure. The Regn I know is eons away from the image staring back at me. I want to step back, scoop her up like she was my little sister, smother her affectionately, watch her learn and take in the world. I want to tell her, "You can't understand now, but when you're a young woman, barely 18, and a nice young man of 22 takes you aside and says, 'Hey, kid, you want to get married?'—tell him kindly you'll think about it. Don't rush, Regn. Don't say yes before you've considered what it means for you. Don't deny your own potential!" I want to bend down, scoop her up as I've never done with any child, hold her close against me. Hum to her. Not as a mother. Not as a father. But as a distant guardian. I want to protect in her what was shattered in me. Is this sentimentality? I misgive that it's a mistake to think this way. For the truth remains, Regn never needed anyone but herself. I study the pronounced frontal lobe of her head, a furrow just above the eyes. Already she seems alone, in spite of her sister's hold, in spite of the love behind the camera. And I realize what the image of her says. We are all alone, from the day we are born. Her dimpled knuckles, her small nose—who would imagine it becoming so long—her perfectly drawn lips becoming irresistibly kissable in time. Her eyes will remain the same. A quiet enduring. Behind them, even now, lies some truth which she has yet to fully discern. It has always been there.

———

For some unknown reason I find airport terminals in the early morning hours and at dusk—just as the sun is cresting the horizon—terribly melancholy. It is the transience—the to-ing and fro-ing of so many passing lives. And the uncertainty. There is also a degree of finality. Traveling brings reunions, happiness. It also signifies absolute departure. A firm goodbye. It brings to mind looking inside a box—a tidy compartment, where everything seems ordered—times, destination, tickets, luggage. Looking at the edges in a geometrical way, all seems stable, bearing the weight of custom, the movement of the times. An airport or a train station is its own entity. Like a box—a parcel of contained changeability. Now peel back the lid, just a corner and look inside. The chaos is overwhelming. Why doesn't the structure just unhinge—with so many variables it seems inevitable something will go wrong. If you believe at all in the odds of statistics then you surely must reason that nothing can be controlled absolutely. Peering into the box, movement is what catches the eye—the ceaseless flow of figures. Most with cell phones; few to none look up or at one another as they pass. Passengers who've forgotten the friendliness of the voyage and think only of the task at hand. As for myself? I study the utilitarian luggage—the coldness of it. The sloppy clothes—jeans, t-shirts, sweatshirts with hoods, and most grotesque of all, flip-flops. Not cute little sandals or low-heeled shoes the ladies don on the weekends with a dress or skirt— no, I mean a thin little slab of rubber offering no pedestrian support, and revealing one of the least attractive features of our species' anatomy. I spend all my time saying goodbye to the present moment. Some of the specimens are well-manicured, but it is the location of such flaunting that appalls an individual, such as myself, who believes in discretion, decorum—there being a proper time and place for certain dress.

To get to the point, I am watching the demise of social etiquette, the practicality of standards, not to mention self-respect. It is my job to observe; I'm a journeyman studying to become the Old Man on the mountain. No, not Moses. Religion is a crutch and divides the masses. I do however, believe faith—whether it is in the moon or the rising sun, or even in yourself, is essential. For life without faith is a type of spiritual myopia. Neither am I so detached that I find it essential to mimic John Muir in his peregrinated search. I do believe he was right though, as I somehow always knew but one day forgot—as often happens as we move further and further away from our origin—the day we are again born: the true source of inquiry and answer lies in nature—the trees, the mountains, dirt roads, untainted lakes (how few remain). The animals have it right, but man has gotten it into his head that because he can reason he is, therefore, superior, and immortal in legacy. Animals are not arrogant and I dare say the vast majority of human beings are not pompous, but they assume an emotional state of stability as a means of survival—not truth. (Yes 'they'—I've just dissoci- ated myself from the human race. Forgive me). And after a while, this non-reality begins to blur and is accepted as true—everything can be ordered, controlled, life is manageable from this viewpoint. But some things are not so neat or concise. And when events occur— whether global, national, or personal—and they cannot be efficiently trimmed of their raw edges, rationalized with a satisfactory explanation of why—then a person is bound to lose his head. He has conditioned himself or perhaps been born into an infrastructure that suggests control is a personal choice rather than a silver lining cast over the mind—leaving him vulnerable and underprepared for the shattering of glass. These illusions, dreams, and beliefs are a joy if never tested, but if something is never tested, never questioned, how then can one know its true worth?

When I was a young man, I wanted the years without putting in the time. I was old before my age, having cut myself off much too early from those explorations that form, establish, and influence the personality. I observed, but I did not observe myself or take into account my role and when, finally I did, the price had been paid. At such an early age, the price was too great.

———

In the years to come I would often consider an old reoccurring question: why Regn? Why not? There was something protective in her nature which I wanted and needed. I began to feel safe in her presence. I sometimes imagined just hunkering down in the back seat of her car or sleeping soundly beneath a warm blanket on her sofa. I couldn't say why these thoughts came to me. I just liked them. Her voice, her smile, her upbeat energy was a comfort and sometimes even, an overlooked presence. I might not have taken account of it right away, but when it was gone it was noticeable—at least that's how it was in the very beginning—long before our dancing at the Christmas dinner. We didn't even dance. I wanted to. My heart knew how, my emotions imagined exactly the right steps, the old ways, but my body was awkward, rigid, self-conscious. I lacked the confidence to actualize my desires.

In truth, even I didn't realize my own desires, their full extent. Not then. Not yet.

Regn always carried herself confidently. Her gait was sturdy but lithe. Her straight shoulders and perfect posture were something I longed for in myself. Much later I became angry when I'd look in the mirror and see my rounded shoulders and curved posture. I was not standing up tall, proud, or open. I had been hiding something for so long and not all traces could be erased. I hated that my lower back was weak. I can't stand hours on end, lest I pace. Earlier jobs that required prolonged standing took conditioning. My legs would ache and my back felt like someone had squarely thrust his fist into it. None of this was detectable to the untrained eye and my self-consciousness made it noticeable only in my mind. My shoulders were slightly rounded, nothing more. But I knew why. The years of contorting, trying desperately to conceal what a woman naturally takes pride in—her body. But I wasn't a woman. Nor was I a man. Regn took for granted the poise with which she walked around, her sure-footed gait. She liked to attract silent attention. I could not know until it was too late, but her self-assuredness was a façade.

Inside she doubted herself. It was an insecurity formed early on, in childhood. Growing up in a small town in Western Germany, boys liked her, she had many opportunities but she always held herself in check. When she married and followed her husband to the U.S. in a way he became her lifeline. She did not speak English fluently. She had no close friends anymore. Her family and husband became her axis, her sense of purpose. She went along with things, let the flow carry her. Her only control was maintaining those things around her: cleaning, ordering, fastidiousness. She read a great deal—not realizing she was actually escaping the malaise of discarded hopes, desires, ambition. Her ardent desire to stand firmly on her own, independently. For her life to mean something because of what she accomplished as opposed to the meaning bestowed on it through walking into a role—a place to be: wife, mother. I once asked Regn what she had most wanted to be in life. When she told me I started to smile. 'Don't laugh, or I wouldn't have told you.' I realized she was being serious. A ballerina. Yes she was petite, lithe, sensual. But it seemed so stereotypical. Didn't all little girls dream of growing up and becoming ballerinas and all little boys want to be cowboys chasing Indians or superheroes? Of course not, but in the era of baby boomers wasn't that the ambition instilled from an early age? What Regn meant was that she'd wanted to be a true artist. Like the child's ballerina encased within its glass globe, Regn watched the years merry-go-round, forever anchored to her pedestal—her role. Very early in life she reconciled herself to making the best of things. She had a good life, not always exciting, but it was stable, productive. She was neither an involved nor uninvolved mother. She loved her children, but she was young, restless, too soon a mother in that era of gender role expectations. Somehow she had expected more out of life. She would never admit it, but at times she felt so disappointed. Was it life? Was this what others went through? She did not know for sure; if Jay felt this way he would never talk to her about it. They were intimate, friendly, attached to each other, but they were not close in the emotional sense. She did not tell him the things that she wanted or needed. She let him do what he liked and let him believe it was enough and satisfying. It was, at times, satisfying. But it lacked fulfillment. She was still young and seeking answers. Eventually it dawned on her—the sun she did not want to gaze long into: the truth she always knew but denied. She was disappointed in herself.

In matters of philosophy and the afterlife Regn always spoke with an air of certainty. Spiritual but not religious, she spoke of reincarnation as a fact not a possibility. We chose our lives so something new could be learned by the soul. I did not disagree, but whereas she found the idea a comfort, I found it troublesome. I did not want to be reborn again. I longed for the last return. I was weary of carrying the muted memory of other places, other times. It made one old much too soon. I'd been born old. Regn did not like to be challenged or to consider another's viewpoint on the matter. She'd listen, but all the while her mind remained beyond penetrating. If she'd made up her mind about something, then she was right, and it was done. This could be frustrating and irritating at times. But I overlooked it; I appreciated her finer qualities too much to allow her stubbornness to get in the way. Eventually I would learn that she hated to have her decisions, opinions, or beliefs questioned because she clung to them. They made life orderly, allowed her to cope. Intensely self-critical, a counter-viewpoint or challenge to her line of thought was always taken as a personal affront. She could not detach herself from the item being questioned and consider its possible flaws apart from herself. To question its validity or absoluteness would send Regn into defensive sulkiness or cool detachment. I often wondered, much, much later, how someone so close-minded in most realms, could be so accepting and receptive to an individual of my dichotomies.

Though exteriorly reserved for the most part, I have always gone my own way. I do not like crowds or following the masses. It would be easier. But it is boring. And one day you wake up and realize your life is gone, you are old, and what was it all for? I've always stood on the outside, watching. It was in Regn's veins to conform and to a certain extent, conforming is practical, a means of necessary survival. Sometimes it is better to be content *without* happiness. Those who walk their own path, the solitary ones, have to be careful of not being accused of jealous cynicism in judging the masses. I have asked myself this question many times: do I scoff at the ways of society because I cannot fully partake in the fruits and luxuries of such, or do I not disdain its policies, regulations, imposing demands, because it undermines the instincts of humankind and discards the importance of the natural environment? At times I am lonely, angry for being cut off from the mainstream, but undeniably I know that it is the latter explanation which is the true source of discontent—in my case anyhow. What I am driving at is this: I have always followed a separate drum—distant and aged. I was different before I met Regn. But was it those differences by themselves or was it pure desire that led Regn and me to want each other? I know with certainty it was a combination.

I died in WWII. Scoff if you wish or don't believe, but why is it so impossible? It's true. I do not know who I was—my name, nationality, political affiliation—that is, was I persecutor or victim, but what I do know is Regn embodied a time and place I missed. Seeing her, listening to her, was like an old familiar song, long forgotten until it is heard again. When at last our bodies had contact, being held in her arms, or holding her close to my chest, cupping the back of her head, it was the same as coming home. Stepping into the foyer after a long time away. Age was irrelevant.

It was an awakening and an unearthing. To love in such a way is not unguarded youth. To love completely is to remember a time and place before; the knowledge of losing it only strengthens it. I wanted to know what entity inhabited this *klein* woman with the languid voice. Who was she at the core, before life changed her? Sometimes I saw Regn, in her full stride—the character of her being apart from Regn the body—her shoes, clothes, hairstyle. She would look at me, and I could look back, unafraid, trusting whatever she was thinking—it was never harsh or unaffectionate where I was concerned. The same, however, could not be said of me. Throughout my life I've had the discomforting propensity to think terrible things about a person. Even if it is someone I've known all my life and love or whom I consider a friend, I sit across from them and the thought comes to attention. I imagine him or her being shot. A head severed. I hear his or her voice distantly as though listening for both of us—wondering if the other person is conscious of his or her own voice. I wonder, with mild discomfort, if others ever look at me and imagine the same. Let's just pop this guy's head.

If I'm sitting close to someone and that person is speaking, lost in his or her own thought or looking at the day, then it makes me uneasy to study the face, the details. I feel guilty scrutinizing and yet this is the only way I know a person best. Stealing glimpses when he or she isn't paying any attention. Regn once said she wondered what it felt like to stab someone. Not that she would. She just wondered.

The mind is mysterious terrain and those who analyze it for a living must take into account the role of correlation. Is what we do governed by intuition—emotions, or intellect and logic. In any given situation which is the first element of charge that snaps? In life, it would seem once again, a combination. However, I argue that unless you're a sociopath devoid of all emotion, even that of narcissism, then 99% of what one does is mandated by desire. And any desire, after all, is the progeny of emotion.

I am curious also, whether my mother having me so late—she was 39—influenced my tendency towards the mature woman—an influx of hormones say, impossible to know, though the body is said to go through cycles every 7 years. Maybe hers did. Maybe not. After Ellis, in trying for a second child, she had experienced several miscarriages. But then, I really do not wish or care to give the logic of Freud a free ticket into the mysteries of the heart. Besides, the personalities of Regn and Birçan were nothing like my mother's.

I do not like the times, the loss of standards, the bastardized attire. No wonder I bask in watching reruns of *Father Knows Best* and the very idea of how things 'could be.' Perhaps my attractions are owing entirely to having died too young in places and times before—a sense of unfinished life and a desire to go back. Whatever the case may be, Regn was that doorway I'd been looking for all along. I just didn't know it. In walking through, even in that moment, I knew it was essential. There was no going back. Not in this life or the last.

———

I have been bored often, if not most of my life. The earth feels like a holding pen. I yearn to go home. I never had the chance to get bored with Regn nor do I believe I ever would have been. The rare individuals I loved provided a harrowing challenge for which I was starved. I never take anything at face value. I have an inferiority and superiority complex. If, say, I'm in a room where a lecture, performance, or speech is being performed, I like to be positioned where I can view the crowd. Not necessarily on the perimeter, but not right smack in the middle, and never in the front, lest I need to pick my nose.

I like to look at the eager listeners and watchers. It seems funny what we do when we pull ourselves back and see what we're doing by watching others do the same thing. I look for others like me. This is the only way to hone in on my kind. I look for others whose attention is not on the performance, but the sea of people. Those individuals who never allow themselves to ever be fully swept away or taken in, taken up. To step back from events doesn't equate to boredom or lack of enthusiasm. Sometimes it does in young children or sleeping grandparents who've earned the right to snooze. But to really step back is to be aware, conscious at all times, independent from the faceless mass around and before us. I am glad to look away when others watch. I don't have to see to be listening. But I always question. And that is the point. My sense of superiority finds contention with those people—you know the kind—those micromanager handbook teetotalers who follow every-thing because it's policy, abstaining from common sense. We've all worked with them—they feel the need to condescend or nitpick, to use whatever little power they wield to make matters of common sense complicated. They will never look the other way, let efficiency slide if it doesn't follow outlined procedures. They are the squelchers of free will, imagina-tion, and self-reliance. To add insult, they often address you with grammatically incorrect or cursory, droll language. I don't mean country talk, or slang. I mean words that barely serve to communicate, they hurt the ears. There is no consideration of the topic, no understanding of the value of words. These individuals merely throw them around, like used Kleenex. Their lack of effort, or even desire to speak meaningfully more than correctly, purports to a laziness of mind. They are content to go along, be pushed along with the crowd. More often than not, they are either a. blissfully content in what they choose not to know, or b. painfully aware of some sort of deficiency, and when they encounter someone who challenges their sense of well-being they feel the need to attack.

———

Anytime I see a Volkswagen, it doesn't matter the year, the make, or the color, I look at it hard. I smile for a moment knowing how important Regn's car was to her, but then her fanaticism seeps in and the memory quickly fades. Her fanaticism over the littlest thing. A minute scratch. The time a small rock chipped her windshield and the very same day she, or rather Jay, called the repairmen to come to the employee parking lot to fix it. The crisis couldn't wait. The whole day she was in a mood because of it.

I have very few collections. Toy replica cars are not one of them. However, on occasion I'll find a miniature Volkswagen, replete with all the detailed features.

I have one such tiny model; it fits in your palm. It is styled after the early Volkswagen bugs—not the newer model like Regn's—but those that seemed to shine with their chrome and had engines in the trunk. This one is of that line—cream with two navy blue stripes rolling over its back. I study it sometimes. Look up as though expecting to see a miniature hand waving. The incredible shrinking woman emerging from the shadowed interior with deep redwood hair peering out the rolled down window. I know it's ridiculous, but that's how it is.

———

In having an affair, if you're unfortunately lucky enough to be *in* love, the stakes are never so high. You never feel more alive. Love is not something you go looking for. It finds you.

I often anticipated, in confiding to someone 'This wasn't a typical affair,' the response it would produce.

'And just what *is* a typical affair?'

We never had dinner together. We did not go away on any particular weekend. There were no performances we saw; our physical interludes were anything but ample and consistent. We did not take long walks or even *sleep* together. That is, we never shared a bed and awoke side by side. This is the truth. Our affection for one another was so stifled, compromised, upon already being compromised given the physical ramifications of my situation. Not one second could be taken for granted. It was stealing time, a minute here, a half second there. There seldom was a window of prolonged relief or even ecstasy and when on the rarest occasions there was, the need to remember every moment, every detail, weighed so heavily that its gravity rendered me exhausted. By the time these things occurred I was too limp in heart to partake of their rapture—we'd either waited so long or enjoyed but a taunting taste. There was never true freedom, always the shadow of a door or a window waiting nearby. Waiting for an exit, a goodbye, a temporary parting. There was not, for a single moment, the freedom of heart.

———

I have only ever treated one person rottenly. On occasion. That is my mother. I could not help it. She never understood me. She understood the pain, but she never understood her own son. She took everything to heart. Sentimentality has no place in an indifferent world. She believed I turned cold. But what she couldn't know was that I wasn't cold by preference. It was a necessity. Regn taught me this well. Regn taught me what it is to show no remorse, but to carry it inside. No one knows the sorrow, guilt, and pain that goes on inside. Nobody. That is why I leave it here.

I will be sad when I die. In spite of the pain I've had a richness unparalleled. Though my high intellect and insatiable appetite for seeking resulted in endless grief, it enabled me to see life at its extremes and to contemplate it at a depth few experience. I do not wish to come back as another. I will miss myself in relation to others. The rareness. The exceptional differences. I will miss the gift that comes with hardship and paying the price. I will miss the tragedy of my own life. As I once spoke to Regn emphatically, but I now repeat here, quietly—the pain, the pain is what made it so God damn beautiful. I endured. You can wait a lifetime for thirty seconds, 5 minutes, or for an hour to come into your life—a brief interval that makes all the suffering purposeful. In such moments of splendor and rapture— even if the rapture be stilled, the private hours and years of reckoning are unloaded, a burden lifted and the spirit feels as it did on the happiest day of its life when it was young and untormented. Or rather, unconscious of the torment waiting to be ignited inside.

———

Some die too young,
Some die too old;
The precept sounds strange,
But die at the right age.

    —Friedrich Nietzsche

Regn (left) with her older sister (right). Germany; circa 1953.

Westcott

Helen Cray "Gedny"

Circa 1972

I've gone back to visit Jamestown Settlement a few times over the years. The last time was seven years after that first summer. The quadricentennial. Two summers. That's all we had. I was with a male friend that last time I walked along the corridors of my mind, running fingers along the banisters of concrete memories.

The museum possessed the same distinct smell it had always had. Warm, fresh, verdant. Redolence of wood shavings. The same audio sounds, same videos still played in the massive indoor exhibits and the grand copper chandeliers still appeared buffed to a natural sheen. Not polished, but still clean. We went on the ships, my friend and I. The costumed interpreters were different. Young. Strangers to me. I only saw one or two familiar faces. Rose Marie had been at the front desk in the visitor center lobby when we walked in. She was slightly thinner in the face, older.

Walking through the site everything was the same. Why wouldn't it be? It made me feel alone, and I knew. We change. I knew those years before were gone, could not be gotten back for anything. They existed only because I existed. No one knew or remembered. Only I did. And Regn. In our separate ways. And what did Regn remember?

I also knew what I'd known to be true in the hours of youth. No love would ever again be so strong. Regn and I had been halved. Sometimes when I'd see a ton of tourists or huge crowds I'd think, how can every life have the same importance. There are just too many of us, the entire world over. And then I'd find relief in the sheer odds of it all, the wonderment. I'd look at the situation inside-out. How amazing that two individuals should find each other in the masses of millions.

And this is how I knew. I knew it was intended. The love. The pain. The truth.

As I left my friend to take in and peruse the 30,000 square foot indoor museum I'd once strolled through with Regn, I wandered around, taking more interest in the material. Reading the facts in a way I had absentmindedly done in those years while employed with the Settlement. My mind was not filled with passion. The history of Jamestown had never enlivened me—it was gone. Dead. Irretrievable. I did not know those people from before. And yet, I felt it was now time to let the history of the land inside. Who would remember me, or even Regn, in 400 years? I might leave the details of our stories behind, but of equal significance was the audience. Those who would come after and preserve the telling, remember the words, and find affection for other places, other lives, other times. I realized that day—my memory, Regn's, and everyone I had known and influenced, and those who had changed me forever—all of us required the future. Someone, if only a single individual, to pick up the story of these lives, my life, and relive, reawaken passions of the past. I would die. As would Regn. But the passion we held, the feelings we shared, would remain intact, contained herein, so long as I told it as it really happened.

I felt older, removed. Nothing about Jamestown revealed the unrequited love that had throbbed between us. The walls showed nothing. The breezeway was filled with a new energy, albeit, a foreign one. People I did not know and never would. I was merely visiting this time. For me the Settlement would always remain inextricably tied to my youth and those two summers, long ago, when anything *was* possible.

PART I

JAMESTOWN: THE BEGINNING

THE PURSUIT

We buried a bird.
And to the cemetery went.
You left flowers on a nine-year old boy's grave, not finding the friend you'd
come to bid farewell.
It was spring. I'd gone to the half window.
'Regn, there's a dead bird out here.'
She came with a paper towel, scooped her from the patio.
She looked around.
I watched.
Over here will do. We walked to the little boxwood hedge on the outskirts of the grassy
mall. With bare hand she scooped the dirt and made a hollow. Her long bony fingers,
shortly trimmed nails, churning the ruddy soil. She knelt, I stood half bent. Patting the
soil she bid her soul go peacefully. It was late spring and the sun beat down upon my fair
skin. My tie dangled; a noose to pull as I leaned forward. In the close heat of the afternoon, voices of students and groups buzzed from afar. Being there, but watching her,
I never felt a more intimate purity of affection.

The little bird's remains are still there—

© Wheston Grove

What's inside—bears no age.

© Wheston Grove

Regn
"Woman in Distress"
Jamestowne Island

Regn did not come to me all at once. After the night at the dance my pursuit in earnest-ness began. It would be nine months before anything came to pass. It was a tedious advance. I lied to myself constantly, but I was not conscious of it. I believed friendship was enough, anything would have to be enough. But with every small gain, any new intimate detail revealed, my determination hastened. On the surface I sought familiarity, a friendly exchange. But deep down, something else had ignited. There was an insatiable desire. That night we stood on the wooden dance floor and Regn held me more than I dared to have held her, a switch was thrown. I wanted to know this woman, anything and everything about her. What made her so melancholy? Why did she feel comfortable around me while I was so nervous? From that moment it was as though a reel had been inserted into my frontal lobe. A taut line, transparent. Pulling. Here we'd been working together, side-by-side for a year-and-a-half, and nothing like this burning, an emptiness that rendered one without appetite. And to think, one of us almost didn't go to the Christmas social that night.

• • •

"The way of love is not
a subtle argument.

The door there
is devastation."

—Rumi (1207-1273)

CHAPTER 1

BEING

HE'D BEEN bolstering what little confidence he still possessed all morning—maintain eye contact, quick gait, firm handshake, *maintain eye contact*. He steps through the double set of glass doors and approaches the main desk. A woman directs him to the only interior benches, 15 paces away, on the opposite side of the lobby, and asks him to wait. The current Visitor Services staff, without a doubt, studies the young man before them with skepticism. In an atmosphere of mostly older women, he will never fit in with their ranks. He is only playing at professionalism. Tucked shirt and belt aside, underneath he is just another transitory college boy who likes his fun and needs the money.

It doesn't matter what they think at that moment.

I just need to get through this interview.

Another lady strolls out from the corridor leading to the café. Westcott stands. 'Are you Mrs. Bellefont?'

'No. She's with someone else right now. It'll be a minute.' Her Ethiopian accent is thick but languid.

He sits back down, wiping damp palms on his thighs.

A tall, slim black woman advances. She could be 47 or 65. Westcott shakes hands sincerely with forced bravado. He follows her halfway down the hall before turning right into a lighted alcove housing a variety of brochures. They proceed through the first solid oak door then make an immediate right where Mrs. Bellefont enters her number code into a secondary keypad. They are in the office, behind the scenes.

'I'm sorry you had to wait.' The interview goes cordially. On her desk Eva Bellefont holds three copies of his application.

'I guess you really want this job.'

Westcott smiles. 'I wanted to make sure you received it. I emailed and faxed the application but never had confirmation of its arrival, so I also mailed one.'

They discuss proper dress code and grooming. Westcott fits the bill in his slacks and corduroy coat.

Probing his character, she says, 'We're always on camera here.'

'Yes, I see that.' Westcott lifts his eyes upward to the small black globe protruding like a bullet from the ceiling.

'You're very insightful.'

It was the wrong adjective in this context. You mean 'observant' he wants to tell her, but knows he won't.

She walks him out to the lobby. They shake hands in parting. A final test.

Strong. Maintain eye contact.

'A firm hand shake. That's what I like,' she says.

The interview over, head swimming, Westcott lets himself come down slowly. Tired, but relieved, he walks into the late morning. He steps through the first set of glass doors into the narrow vestibule then pushes out the second door. He feels the bricks under his shoes, the cold sweat under his arms. So light and gentle is the hour. He is not so old as he thinks he feels. It is as though—but standing in the midst of the very moment itself he cannot see—the Great Scribes themselves are merely dusting some minor erasures from the breadth of the day.

He does not know it in that hour, cannot know, but already events are in motion. His life will change. Not for a while yet—another 19 months. April transpires to May.

A few weeks later the phone rings. Eva Bellefont's voice comes over the line. She does not tell him this: in the interview she saw a young boy. A decent boy who deserved a chance.

'I'd like to offer you a position with The Jamestown-Yorktown Foundation— if you're still interested?'

His heart thumps. He *needs* this job. He wants it. He can't think at that moment about being let go from his most recent position and the bitterness—

'Yes. Of course.' His mind continues to race. He doesn't hear the rest.

'See you this week then,' Eva Bellefont closes.

'Thank you a lot.' He sets the phone down. It is a landline.

Thank you 'a lot?' What a jerk, he shakes his head. *Can't contain your nerves long enough to eloquently respond? You're an English student for God's sake and that's the best you can come up with!— nerves. Damn nerves. Why can't I speak like I write? As I think? There'll be time to set the record straight.*

———

He starts working from two to five. He is taking his bio-lab as a summer course at the university forty minutes south. It runs from ten to one. It demands some breaking-in to be at the register for three hours, stuffing maps between customers, but the season is *just* starting. The summer will be long and the work often grueling in repetition. He is given one white and one navy polo shirt with the company's monogram. It is hand stitched of durable, fine quality. Made in Mauritania. He wears only the navy with matching slacks, never khaki. That is one of the reasons he'd been fired from his last job at Target, not the main reason, but the excuse he was given. He'd always worn a belt with his white shirt tucked in and a clean, nice fitting red short-sleeve overshirt, which he wore open. Some guy's pants were falling off; others never had their sloppy shirts tucked in. Westcott looked professional. They told him he had to tuck it. He protested. 'What about—he never has *his* tucked in and besides?!'— Then one day they call him into the office. The male manager sits in as his female supervisor explains they're letting him go. He hasn't been asking customers if they have a bonus card or if they'd like to sign up for one. And his shirt—. Westcott looks at the young man opposite. Buzzed hair. The only reason for his presence, he knows, is in case Westcott gets visibly outraged and turns physical. It disgusts him—the insult. *The very idea—you know nothing of my character. I don't need this petty shit job, I—.* He is grateful to go; on the other hand angry. He knows why he never tucks his shirt in—he hates khaki pants on him—they are not flattering to his posterior, they accentuate his hips. He hates his hips. Narrow shoulders, lean torso, giving way to moderately flared hips. A nice hourglass figure. Bah, the humor of it all. He doesn't want or need an hourglass figure. He is not at all heavy, but he feels exposed in lighter colors. His rear end is not masculine. His first day working in Visitor Services a small woman with gray hair—cut in a mannish, practical style—shows him around the upstairs gallery. Jill Conway. Westcott impresses her by providing the name 'Oxford' as she mentally searches for the actual location of the real Powhatan mantel displayed as a replica in the museum. She is in her early seventies. Her kind green eyes peer at him through spectacles. In years to come she will prove a most loyal and reliable friend. An employee ID badge is made for him, which to this day he has tucked away in a box. The picture is hardly flattering. His face is heavier.

He looks thirteen though he is twenty. He exhibits no facial hair or even a shadow and not because he's recently shaved. He's never had to shave. His features are soft; his hair full and shiny. He wears a silk navy blue dress shirt and stands against the brick column. He weighs 155 lbs. maybe 162. His head tilts to the left in self-consciousness. He doesn't like the woman who takes his picture. She's in her thirties. Frail-boned, condescending. He hopes he won't have to work with her often, but he is polite and wants to get off on the right foot. The picture is captured. It is printed on the backside of a 3 ½ x 2 inch placard. Thankfully the picture won't have to be seen and can remain hidden on the flip side. Both logos for Jamestown Settlement and Yorktown Victory Center, three ships and a cannon, are on the front with his name printed below. He wears the badge with pleasure and pride.

—

A TASTE OF FREEDOM

It is the 27th of May 20—. Westcott boards a plane. He flies on a thirteen row commuter to Fort Lauderdale. Thirteen—a lucky number for him. His sister Ellis will be coming in from New York. The airport in Florida is so large you need a tram to get from one unit of terminals to the next. They unite without a hitch and take a bus down to the port where they wait for customs to check them through. They make it aboard the cruise liner shortly after three. Inside the massive ship you hardly know you're out to sea. The nights are hot, salty. Together they play many a good round of ping pong. Ordinarily Westcott would never consider a cruise as rip-roaring fun. But he's never been on one. Besides, this isn't any week-long excursion—it's just through the weekend, three days, ample time. Ellis found a good deal. He doesn't like long vacations that involve lounging around, soaking up sun. He prefers to be active—doing something—hiking, reading, absorbing information, contemplating. Vegetating is unacceptable. He prefers the mountains to the ocean. However, they are on a moving island of sorts. They stroll the decks in search of rare picture opportunities. On the topmost deck, accessible to the public, they stand in the pitch black night staring off into the lightless ocean. During the day it is open to topless sunbathers. Westcott imagines falling over the rail, sliding down the ship into the shark-infested abyss. He thinks of the original *Poseidon Adventure* film. What if a rogue wave capsizes the ship? He is not a fast swimmer. He can hold his breath for a minute, but only if he keeps his body still. He has always feared drowning. It cannot be peaceful. It is violent, the retching of the lungs, the bursting, and then the intake, the flooding of water. Maybe he will sleep out on the deck— that way if the ship is turned over, he'll be flung into the ocean—he'll find a piece of debris and hope a nearby vessel comes in time to rescue the survivors before the gray fins start cutting the dawn blue waters. Standing in the night, Ellis nearby, he hears the wind whip through his clothes. There is something exciting and adventurous in this trip. He's never vacationed from home as brother and sister. He likes the freedom.

Saturday they sign up for an on-shore excursion to a private lagoon. Westcott leaves his t-shirt on to go swimming. On the island he buys a $15 authentic and fully functional conch shell. It reminds him of Ralph in one of his favorite stories: *Lord of the Flies*. The freedom of boyhood, the dangers of human nature. He'd first read the book when he was 14. He ached for the sparseness of clothes the boys on the page displayed. The camaraderie of a shared age and gender. To swim without clothes, the awareness of his sex *and* no shame. He remained innocent for as long as he could, ached for the boyhood he could not have, until the red sea jarred him to attention. It was not a crashing wave, but a crawling breaker. He was 16.

Another souvenir comes in the form of a watch. The Bijoux Turner is rectangular and silver, its band perfectly coordinated to the color dress code of his new job—blue, tan, and maroon. Even more astonishing is the fact that it has a notch to fit his slender wrist. It is meant to be. Such a find esteems itself at only $10—duty-free—in one of the many gift shops aboard the ship. He admires the rectangular face. It is rich, just right in shape for his spindly arms and slight wrists. It bears a quality of masculinity. He prefers square edges to round. Even in the shoe department he searches out those with squared fronts, curving gently around the foot. He doesn't like snub-nosed shoes, athletic styles, or loafers. He likes a distinguished dark brown leather—not real leather, but not a plastic cheap imitation either. He doesn't want a glossy appearance, but the natural tone and texture of the material. A good tread, not heavy or bulky, a gentleman's shoe—both practical and stylish. Functional and pleasing to his senses. Concerning pants, he can't stand buttons on seat pockets. They remind him of eyes, smiling, from rounded buttocks. He knows it is false, but he believes men who let their posterior buttons show are nerds. Westcott snips the buttons off, should there be any. Besides, he always carries his wallet in his front pocket.

He parts with Ellis at the Fort Lauderdale Airport. Returning home he feels deflated. Three days. His mother cries seeing him exit the terminal. She is happy to see him. He wishes she wouldn't cry. It's only been three days. What about all the young men through the centuries departing and returning home from war? He'd like to have been a soldier. Not because of any sense of duty. Battle, men blowing one another up, and now women— the whole affair is a waste. A waste of life. Destruction. He wants to be a soldier for the uniform, the pleasure of precision, routine of hygiene, and honor. But the Armed Forces have changed. It is no longer the pin-up of integrity. Men and women join as a means of escape. There is free education. It is not arrogance nor snobbery, but a sense of refinement and breeding which finds Westcott pondering what it would have been like to go to West Point Academy like his grandfather. A tiredness descends. He holds it in the whole drive back from Norfolk International Airport, an hour-and-a-half spent waiting.

Home, he goes upstairs, shuts the door quietly. Breaks down in the privation of his room. Now who's crying? It isn't that he misses his sister. He misses what she represents. So full of life. Independence. The freedom to move around. The freedom of youth. Something inside tightens. In that moment he has nowhere to go *and* no reason to go.

—

THE RUSSIANS

Westcott adopts a little red dog. It's July. He names her Miss McGillicutty. Lucy Ricardo's maiden name in the *I Love Lucy* television series. She is a Dachsund-Corgie mix, her fur not so much red as crimson. That same summer the Russian exchange students come to live with Westcott, his mother, and their elderly tenant, Lucy. There are four Russian students who occupy the guest room, not at the same time. They are slobs, an imposition to Westcott's routine, causing more problems than their rent is worth. He wants to ask them why they never close the bag on their loaf of bread—don't they know it will go stale left for hours unwrapped? Lucy doesn't like sharing her bathroom—the middle one, with the young ladies. Lucy is a sweet woman, tidy, a jewel of a tenant. In years to follow Westcott regrets the timing. Had they come later when he didn't look so young. Foreign girls. Attractive, sexual, a whole summer in close quarters with three young women! Westcott had no notions of desire. They were latent, arrested, deferred. The opportunities were right under his nose and he felt nothing.

Two days after bringing Miss Gilly home they break her ceramic bowl without mention and leave the door to the garage open as they pull their bicycles out (their only mode of transportation to and from work, unless either Westcott or his mother are around to give them a lift). Some nights Westcott drives across town to the restaurant where one of the girls, Elena, serves tables. He struggles to lift her bike into the bed of his truck. She gets in the truck's cab. The other servers look at the young guy driving her home. Westcott does not look at her as a man should.

He feels no attraction. Elena talks to dispel her silent questions. Unlike Alexandra, Elena speaks English fairly fluently.

It happens one evening. It is abrupt. Elena and Alexandra are flipping through the photo albums stored in the twin bookcase of the living room. Westcott walks in, sets his keys on the counter. The shelves are home to a collection of leather-bound, gold leafed classic books as well as the family albums. Elena and Alexandra look up. They are sitting on folded knees. They say nothing, quickly shove whatever they've been looking at—book or album—back into the shelf. His mother and he foolishly assumed the dust of disuse would silently deter examination of contents. The next day the albums disappear into storage under Westcott's bed. It is his silent admission of guilt, but the Russians aren't going to come forward with what they unearthed. Westcott isn't about to explain. He could joke about it. Tell them his twin sister died. But *if* he had a twin, then why were they never photographed together as brother and sister?

—

The new tenants, Alex and Daria, were equally sociable. Alex was curious about American culture and in all fairness, Westcott and his mother were not the ideal host family. For one thing, Westcott was too self-conscious to warm up to a young man and become pals. As for his mother, Gedny was set in her ways and her commentary could be derogatory as opposed to neutral. For instance, Alex was looking through the videotapes and dvd collection one evening. He asked what might be a good choice. He'd watched *Men of Honor*, which Westcott also enjoyed, as well as *Master and Commander* starring Russell Crowe. Gedny suggested they watch *The Birdcage*, the American version, with Robin Williams as "Armand" playing a gay lead, partner to the flamboyant Nathan Lane as "Albert."

Why not expose the Russians to a little culture? But cross-dressing? Westcott found the movie hilarious, especially the houseboy, Agadore. As Alex watched he made a comment that revealed his cultural upbringing and the narrow-mindedness of certain beliefs. He said in reference to Val, the son of Armand and Nathan, 'Wouldn't it make him gay being raised by them?' Mother was quick to dispel this line of thinking. 'You can't *make* someone gay,' she half laughed trying to disguise her shocked dismay that anyone in this day and age could maintain such beliefs. Alex did not stay to watch the rest of the movie as he had an escape in the form of Daria who he was going to meet within the hour when she got off of work. Or so he claimed. Had he stayed, Alex would have discovered that in the movie Val is engaged to a fine young woman, the daughter of a conservative senator, and that the entire movie is about a ruse to convince the fiancée's parents that Val has a regular family. Westcott didn't pay Alex's opinion much attention. He merely sided with his mother and thought nothing more about it. Looking back, it annoyed him that they hadn't been a more 'typical' American family. Mother, father with two 'normal' children. He did not blame Alex for his misguided reaction; it was the way he was brought up, the social milieu. Perhaps it was in poor taste to choose a film so extreme as to prompt awkward conversation. Why hadn't he or his mother been more diplomatic? At that time, in that age, Westcott did not like to ruffle anyone's feathers. He was a traditionalist; albeit a self-professed contradiction because of his condition; nonetheless, his value system was founded on discretion and conducting one's self as either a lady or a gentleman.

· · ·

On two rare occasions during those summer months, after Elena and Alexandra made haste to find vacancy elsewhere, Westcott was walking down the hall to his room. Someone or something was pushing against the guestroom door. Alex and his girl, Daria. Alex was nineteen turning twenty, fit and trim with the stamina of a young wolf. His dirty blonde hair fell straight and loose. His skin was evenly tanned, a lean body of solid muscle with blue eyes that often flashed arrogance. He was undeniably handsome. He looked older than Westcott who easily still passed for twelve or fourteen. Though Westcott was one year his senior, he had full cheeks, soft features. By no means overweight at 168 lbs, he had gained twenty in the past six months. That was to be expected with the injections of testosterone. He couldn't help noticing one day while unloading the clean laundry and putting in the wet, how matronly his own briefs were compared to Alex's speedo-sized skivvies. Daria had told Westcott and his mother her reason for finding another room to rent. The paternal figure in the house where she'd been staying had taken her, or followed her, into the forest behind his property. Alex was at work. She'd felt uncomfortable alone with this older man. After the incident she sought new living arrangements. Daria was beautiful. Westcott took little notice. She had brown hair and brown eyes; she was thin and like Elena and Alexandra, she smoked daily. She always made sure to smoke outside on the deck.

In passing outside their room at night, he heard Daria's high terse moans while the door banged in rhythm with their acts of loveless sex. They took it for granted. And because it was readily available to them, because it was a physical release, the presence of love was not the motivating factor. Sex was. Their bodies were young. They knew each other, may have felt love, but that love was not being tested. It came too easily and what their bodies and throats expelled in the night as sounds of passion, was really the appetite of youth. A rite of passage, a healthy outlet, the progression of age. At first Westcott was appalled—the audacity—to be so blatant in a room that belonged to a house they were merely boarding. There was something else, a sense that quickly displaced his feeling of disdain. Here they were, thousands of miles away from home. He lingered a moment further down the hall, staring out the window on the landing at the end of his cul-de-sac. Mother was downstairs. Lucy had gone to stay with her daughter and grandson for the weekend. Those sounds coming from her throat, a few feet away. He knew what they were doing. He knew what it meant, but he'd never been so close to it. And yet, at the same time, so completely removed. He dismissed it, went to his room and keeping the light off, slipped into bed.

✳ ✳ ✳

I DO NOT REMEMBER the exact days upon which I met each of the various staff. There were 13 solid, core crewmembers at Jamestown Settlement: Eva Bellefont, The Visitor Services Supervisor; Jill Conway; Sharon McCrady; Fernus Ferome Tillie; Ida and Rawlings (married and in their 70s); Regn; Hugh; Bryan; Deborah; Magda; and myself. The mean age was 55. Eva, Fernus, and Tillie were the only Classified employees who received State benefits and who were required to work full-time. I remember my first introduction with Eva, Jill, and those few words I exchanged with Fernus while waiting to be interviewed. After hearing someone call 'Fernus,' I thought what an attractive name. It suited her characteristic languor. I did not meet Regn immediately. I'd seen her name on the daily schedule in the office, mistaking its pronunciation. I soon came to know that 'Regn' in German translates to 'rain.' Regn had dropped the 'e' when she first came to America in an attempt to minimize phonetic blunders. She disliked the hard 'g' in the English language that made her name sound like 'Reagen.' That particular name conjured memories of "The Exorcist" with the possessed 'Regan' on screen spewing split pea soup. She'd been 21 when it first came out. Like most cinemagoers, she was pleasantly entertained and terrorized for two hours. She liked a good thriller. It wasn't the movie that had upset her, but what came later.

That night, after the movie, she'd had an argument with Jay. Almost three years they'd been married. She longed for the days of freedom when she went out with her friends. She missed the excitement of harmless flirtation and the presence of her female cohorts. She missed her native tongue. In short, she was lonely now that it was just the two of them—herself and Jay. She'd erupted over nothing while Jay remained solicitous, even going so far as to sleep on the sofa for the night. Regn imagined another life. She didn't want to hurt Jay—he was a good man—but he didn't arouse her, spiritually. Just as morning was making its advance, she'd finally succumb to sleep. When she awoke, Jay surprised her with breakfast in bed. She'd been prepared to tell him how she felt—to lay herself bare. Seeing his eagerness to please, his loyal affection, she softly smiled. Another man might have recognized the sorrow behind that smile. Not Jay. He only saw what he wanted to see. He might sense the truth, but he would never be the one to call it out of hiding. It was his nature to let sleeping dogs lie.

Weary of telling others how to say 'Rey-hen,' she dropped a syllable instead of another letter. The 'g' she would not part with—it reminded her of Germany and Germany represented her youth, her dreams for the future. She never told anyone this, but it was the only thing she had left of the person she'd once been. If anyone asked, she was 'Wren'—like the bird. As with Fernus, I found it equally pleasing to the ear.

At the sister museum, Yorktown Victory Center, the Supervisor was Rose Marie Ryzon. Displeasingly, the location no longer bears the moniker 'Victory Center.' In years since it has been renovated and now bears the droll, simplistic name: The American Revolution Museum at Yorktown. All those years, then some marketing board comes along, decides the obvious needs to be pointed out. The name "Victory Center" had pizzazz. And Yorktown was the site of the last battle—the so-called patriot victory of 1781. All the signs along the Colonial Parkway were amended as well. The "slaves" were replaced with the term "African Americans," which falsifies history. "Americans" did not exist in the 17th century. The country was comprised of colonists, also known as settlers, and Indians. The unfortunate laborers imported from Africa were known only as slaves and indentured servants. For accuracy the informational markers should read "African slaves." In these minor adjustments I question the efficacy of historic preservation if the very memory of past events is being rewritten, softened so as not to offend. It is an injustice.

Slavery and slaves still exist throughout the world in just about every culture. To suggest otherwise is naïve at best, not to mention idealistically foolish. Semantics cannot erase the truth or tone down its ugliness with a prettier word. Calling a spade by any other name than what it is denigrates truth. *And what am I?*

A much smaller museum, farther from the hubbub of Williamsburg, Yorktown's staff proved significantly less with only four employees, all of which were full-time, "Classified." A few young college girls filled in here and there, but it was a summer job for them and nothing more. It was mandatory that periodically we each put in due time at the other museum. Those at Jamestown did not enjoy trekking to Yorktown—a distance of 22 miles one way. The drive was beautiful but the destination made for a long day. The small Visitor's Center was austerely quiet, a time warp. The building, which no longer exists, exuded a dank musty odor. There were only three ticket counters with two primarily in use. Working there one had the distinct feeling of always being watched. Security stayed on the premises 24 hours a day. I wondered what they did at night. How lonely, creepy, and boring. The place was downright austere in the day; I didn't know how anybody could endure watching the clock after the sun went down lest his home life was so unpleasant or nagging that work became an escape. A person can only read so much. Now, if there were two guards on duty that was different. They'd have each other. Conversation would take them through the longest hours, 2-5 a.m., then the sun would be up, and come morning security guards would arrive to relieve the graveyard.

Manning "The Hub" was simply depressing. In the summer I welcomed the activity of tour groups and students walking through—it was always so dim in The Hub—black corners, lonely alcoves—the feeling of time standing still. No wonder I began to find diversion elsewhere.

The permanent crew at Yorktown possessed a particularity about them. This stringent adherence to policy, I surmised, lent itself to there being too much time on their hands. Duty and routine were all they had to keep busy. Any deviation threw them off or elicited a mild correction. The entire space felt and *was* cramped; the silence deafening. Just through the glass doors a long narrow path along a timeline led tourists down to the indoor museum and Hub. Branching to the right an outdoor exhibit displayed a 17th century farm village. The museum was always cold because it was so dark. A perfect escape during summer humidity. Sitting at the attendant's station in the Hub, a small circular desk with a little lamp underneath, I would read and listen to the piped in audio of ocean water flanking the immersed sunken ship on display. The chair sat quite low. One had the distinct feeling he was a bird craning his neck, popping up, to scan the dark peripheral of his nest. But it was only summer. My first summer with the Foundation. I'd yet to experience the tedious hours of winter solitude, alone for hours in the Hub. For the time being I was content to go to Yorktown once, tops twice a month. The amusing part, no one enjoyed swapping museums. Even those at Yorktown preferred to forego the long drive and stay at their home base. Frequently staff switched shifts in an effort to get out of going.

———

There doesn't seem time to think; the summer season brings hordes of tourists. I can't stand to work more than three days in a row. Taciturn by nature, I find that the muscles of my jaw are sore from endless repetition.

'Hi.'
- How much is it?
The ticket sign stands right in front of them.
'$11.75 for adults.'
- What's the combination?
- Does the Golden Age Pass get us in here?
'No. That's honored by the National Park, which is a mile down the road— also called the Island. We're run by the State.'
- Do we take the Ferry over to the Island?
'No, the Ferry takes you over to Surry. It has no relation to Jamestowne Island. The Island is not really an 'island,' just a peninsula. You drive through the gates. You don't have to have a ticket for the driving portion or 5-mile scenic loop, but if you want to tour the museum they have their own Visitor's Center.'
How did you get here? Did you read anything in the brochures?
- What's there to see over in Surry?
'It's more rural. They have the historic town of Smithfield—about an hour from here—Bacon's Castle, and there's the Nuclear Power Plant.' My voice trails off in a mild laugh, hoping to sell them the ticket, be done with it. Maybe 'nuclear' will deter them from further inquiries. 'Did you watch the 3-minute orientation film?'
- No. Where's that?
'Just down the hall. There.' I point. 'If you go see it and then come right back—'
- No. That's all right. We'll go in now. How much again?
Finally. Why do I waste my breath!
I take their money. Politely. 'What's your zip code?' I say this phrase in my sleep:

'Now, go out the first set of glass doors and down the hall to the left. The movie plays every twenty minutes.'
- What's the movie about?

Hmm, let's see. Jamestown: The Beginning. I wonder. Patience. 'It's an introductory film about the first 13 years—what the settlers went through when they landed.'

Sitting at my station in the lobby entrance of the Settlement I stare up and out the windows on the mezzanine. Looking at the tops of the trees I am in Africa, inside some U.S. Embassy or consulate. Outside, beyond the framed vista, I know without seeing, stretches the Serengeti. The green foliage and blue skies are anywhere. I can be anywhere and the great wooden support beams of the lobby structure fan out in a –W–. *W for Westcott.* Already stagnancy is setting in.

The humidity comes and stays. It's hard to imagine a day so hot you feel the air envelop and hang on your shoulders. Stepping out from your car the atmosphere hits you; so thick it is a wall. It is too hot to exert the energy to complain. The sweat as you walk from the employee parking lot to the building's interior rolls down your back in rivulets. The base of my spine, my belt-line, is always damp, especially anytime it is my turn to go down to the ships and collect the donations from the barrel.

• • •

August. Two-and-a-half months on the job. My cat, Annie "Strum," is euthanized. Strike that. She *was* killed. A tumor pressed against her heart. A tumor which was the direct result of the 3-year FVRCP inoculation.

She is yowling, panicked to catch her breath when the doctor removes her from the oxygen tank, brings her into the examination room. One injection to disorient, the second to bring violent peace. The veterinarian gives us no time for goodbye. Mother is at my elbow. Strum is on the cold metal exam table. She *isn't* unconscious when the doctor administers the serum to stop her heart. His manner is too efficient, routine. My hand rests on the counter. *Why is it wet?* Then it registers. Incontinence. Side-effect of the lethal injection. I've never known death so intimately. Suddenly. I am angry at the vet; the procedure is just that—a procedure. *I* could have done better. Taken her home. Let her fall asleep in my truck with carbon monoxide. Let her calm down instead of being pulled from the oxygen pumped incubator, screaming in protest, fear, pain. It was wrong. The whole process. I wonder what Strum thought, beyond instinctive defense. The confusion of being manhandled by strangers, brought into a bright room, laid on a cold metal table, a quick familiar stimulation of the ear—voices she recognized—mine and mother's, and then, still gasping for breath, the shock of having her heart stopped while her senses were still awake. Humane? She deserved a better ending. I was angry for not saying, 'Wait, give us time.'

I went to the Jamestown Gift Shop and with my employee discount purchased a knee-high birdbath to set beside Strum's grave.

I buried her with a poem I'd written and my blue rabbit's foot. Her body had stiffened in the short span of two hours. Ten years earlier she'd given birth to five kittens. We'd rescued her from "death row." The SPCA wanted to take her unborn kittens and then if she wasn't adopted, put her down as well. The litter was due any day. One died. I still remember their warm, milky scent. They'd fit in my palm, mewed in blind confusion, calling—searching by sound and scent for their mother. Their innocent bodies pliable, emerging as over-sized kidney beans. I remember my horror and rolling stomach in witnessing Strum eat the after-birth. But oh, the warmth of their scent. It was a soft, welcoming sensation.

Her death had a profound effect on me. We'd had another cat, an Abyssinian, who died when I was ten. Her ears were like gramophones. She growled the same as a dog. She loved french fries. She'd been hit by a car. I didn't see it. I only saw her body. It, too, had been rigid, a patch of blood the only visible injury on her lower jaw. But seeing something killed, being present, giving the consent—is different. It's a decision. The day before Strum's euthanizing, the vet had called to say she was doing much better. The sudden turn in events was jarring.

• • •

That same August, a week-and-a-half after classes resumed, the start of the term, I withdrew from CNU for the fall semester. After Strum it seemed ridiculous. It *was* more than that, of course. Tess had asked me, 'Why are you leaving? You can't go just because your cat died.' It seemed absurd. 'I know, it's not *only* that,' I'd answered. 'I know,' she said. But she *didn't know* and she never would. I was in need of something and I couldn't recognize what that something was. Strum's death had been an impetus. I was restless. Tired of pacing my mind. Fulfilling what was expected. By whom? My family? No. Society? Maybe. Me? Yes. I did not have the words or the distance, but I knew the routine of college meant nothing in the shadow of loss. Strum was a cat, not the best cat, Helmsley far exceeded, and yet I'd had affection for her. I hurt but I did not suffer. With Regn the suffering never went away.

• • •

Tess liked me. We'd met a year before in our Reading Literature class. Professor Glass was impressed with me and my work. Sometimes she'd talk about her husband who'd died. He was a firefighter. She had three sons, her youngest was still in high school. In the beginning, after the loss, she'd cry in the shower so her children wouldn't know. With Kleenex in hand she'd wipe her eyes and resume teaching. She was a good professor. I liked the class and the material was easy. I memorized authors' names—Bharati Mukherji, Charlotte Perkins Gilman—their spelling, aced the exams, loved the short stories and discussion. Years later it occurred to me why Professor Glass felt the need to talk openly to us about her loss. Maybe it helped. Maybe it made her feel less alone in the grief. Maybe it kept the memory of her beloved alive. For some reason Tess didn't like Professor Glass very much.

Tess had blonde hair and blue eyes. We dined together in the campus restaurants. I never ate. I didn't have a dining card since I did not live on campus. But that wasn't the real reason I didn't eat. I was still self-conscious. I commuted from Williamsburg 45 minutes north. One time Tess invited me back to her dorm room. We watched a clip of Johnny Cash—a memorial tribute. Afterwards Tess put a piece of pizza on a red plate for each of us. I sat on the edge of her bed listening to Johnny Cash, trying to understand why she was showing it to me. I ate cautiously. I didn't think of myself as a 19 year-old boy, clearly a virgin in Tess' eyes.

19 was just a number. Sex did not exist in my mind. Tess was not a friend or an object of desire; for me she was an acquaintance. I couldn't recall what it was to make friends, to have friends. I don't remember how long I stayed, I just know it wasn't very long nor was it very short, but she'd walked with me to the door or maybe it was the elevator. I stepped

on. There were four or five guys going down. One of them joked, 'We could have quite a party—five guys in here.' Reaching the first floor the doors opened. I felt relieved to be out of the elevator. I felt nothing else.

* * *

OCTOBER. Mother and I will be driving up to New York in a few days. Ellis and Rodger live in an apartment in Manhattan, a few blocks from where the World Trade Center used to stand. Ellis works for L'Oréal. Rodge is an analyst in some financial district, Credit Swiss Banking and later, JP Morgan. They met in college. William & Mary. Ellis moved away from home to New York a year-and-a-half before.

Where else does one spend his 21st birthday than the Big Apple? I don't care about being 21. It's not really a question of *if* we'll go to New York; it's assumed. I have no desire to go anywhere else. Besides, Mother wants to see Ellis. It's been a few months.

Gedny misses Ellis' old apartment in Queens. It might have meant a long commute, but the apartment had space and a lovely tree outside. They'd been on the third floor of a brick building. Westcott misses it, too. There was a kitchen, a living room, a small dining nook on an elevated step, the hallway which could be closed off—its own entity—and then the bathroom and bedroom. It really was spacious. The new apartment, Rodge's choice—is ridiculous in price because of its Manhattan location and it is your railroad apartment. You walk in—fall into the bed just to your right. About three paces further the bathroom. Two more paces a small inset—the kitchen which is open to the living area. And that's it. There is no privacy, no room for guests. No doors to section off relatives. Rodge and Ellis will share the Queen bed, naturally. Mother will have the sofa and a twin air mattress will be inflated for Westcott. The loveseat is too uncomfortable for him to fold himself up in—he needs to stretch his long legs. Sometimes after Rodge leaves quite early in the morning, Gedny moves into the bed with Ellis.

We have dinner at Del Monico's, right around the corner from the apartment. I have the 5 lb lobster for $100.00 and a Bacardi which I force myself to drink. Rodge drinks most of it, thankfully. I hate alcohol. The lobster is delicious. We take most of it home. I lay in bed watching the small clock on Ellis' side table, wait for the hour to rollover past midnight. Feeling the weight of those last five minutes before "20" is lost forever. A silent tiredness descends. I listen to Mother, Ellis, and Rodge, just a few feet away—it's a railroad apartment—one narrow hallway—so tiny—I listen to them laugh and talk watching something on television. I'm not interested in the show. Before going out to dinner I'd sat on the bathroom floor, unzipped my fly, quietly coaxed myself from arousal to plateau. Not quite a year, the hormones keep my sex drive elevated. My body is still adjusting. I received some wonderful gifts, nice presents—a picture of Gregory Peck on the set of *To Kill a Mockingbird* and the airdate. Dinner was expensive and enjoyable. I don't ask myself why I'm depressed. What's missing? I'm 21.

———

Thanksgiving is the busiest day I've worked. The line is relentless. Non-stop repetition. As the day progresses my spiel gets shorter and shorter; I devise new ways of saying the same things, anything to keep the creative faculties in check. I make over five thousand dollars. A moderate day brings in 1,500 to 3,000. 5,000 and your mind's numb, you've worked a hard shift. Each register opens with $150.00 in its till. Tickets are $11.75. At least that's what a general admission adult ticket cost back then. We sell a combination to both Jamestown and Yorktown for $17.00. You do the math.

By the time I get home for a delicious, satiating Thanksgiving meal my face is tired—the movement of my jaw. I don't want to talk, I just want to savor the dinner. Mother is a superb cook. Ellis is visiting—she has been helping mother with the last minute trimmings. I leave on my shirt and tie. We sit down to dinner and offer a thanks more than a prayer. It is a beautiful dining room. Four panels of glass on one wall. The model only had three, but the sales representative had taken a fondness to my Mother and even Ellis. He made sure the little extras requested by Mother and those not requested were taken care of. The room has crown molding on the ceiling and at its midriff. The wallpaper is anything but passé, nor is it too Victorian. It is elegant. Gold and blue-green stripes with a solid gold pattern above the wainscoting. A small border at the top. The front windows look out onto the porch and the white wicker furniture. The lawn has a steep hill. How can we know we only have two more Thanksgivings left in this beautiful home? The dining room table is pure mahogany; its clawed feet are an ornament of bygone eras. The house is warm. The evening light glows on the mirrors and casts shadows on the floor.

• • •

On one or two occasions, but no more, Regn and I are both scheduled for Yorktown. We give each other breaks in The Hub. Before going back up to the front we speak for a few minutes. In coming to relieve Regn, I find she's not at the station. She never seems bored; she never allows herself to appear idle. Regn won't sit at the little desk even though it's perfectly expected and there for that purpose. She walks around, maybe straightens an item of clothing in the children's costume room. As much as I have perused the museum I have no interest in reading all the facts and fine print—I won't remember it; it's taken for granted. It's the same as living in a historical town or maybe even New York. When the information's right there, surrounding you, the interest goes out the window. You don't investigate what's in your own backyard—you seek much further.

And so it is with the history in discussion at Yorktown and Jamestown. I know all too well the main points of the American Revolution, the final battle and the date of the surrender in 1781 at Yorktown, but it feels so distant, removed. I'm not interested anymore in reading about history. I want to make history.

I enjoy talking with Regn. She is easy to speak to; I don't feel I have to be on guard or act a certain way—besides, I'm glad for the conversation to break the monotony. They are stepping on each other up front at the ticket counter with too many scheduled for the day and nothing to do. Regn is always immaculate and well-dressed, but then most of the ladies at Jamestown are attractive. Even Ida, though up in years, exhibits an air of charm. And Rawlings, one can tell, was a handsome Southern Gent in his day. The women display subtle ornamentations. Each has her own distinct style. It is a remarkably diverse crew.

Regn says something light—'don't fall asleep down here' or something funny—then I'm alone. I walk through the gallery—there are two narrow passages—one leads to a room of vignettes. It is like looking at a dollhouse or diorama. When you push a button a certain square, hovering above, lights up and the display of statues, all in white, start to speak. There are four separate narratives—one a soldier, another a wife—two others that escape me—each giving his or her account of life taken from actual journals during the American Revolution.

The other hall leads down and down to the replicated shipwreck. The light seems green in the darkness, though it isn't. There is also the theatre which shows its 19-minute film. I dread having to make an announcement on the loud speaker. More often than not I stare down the microphone, then get up, walk through the gallery to personally tell anyone who is present that the show will begin shortly and there's a cannon demonstration at 3:00, just out back of the museum. I've yet to master my own voice. Customers tell me I have a wonderful delivery and ask, 'Have you ever thought about being an announcer?' Narrating books on tape would be nice.

There are more things to check and turn on/off in the gallery at Yorktown. Everything at Jamestown is automatic, on a power timer. Yorktown has yet to undergo its massive renovations. The focus is Jamestown with the 400th Anniversary right around the corner. Sometimes I go into the children's costume and hands-on learning room. I straighten the drawing sheets and crayon boxes, make sure the items of 18th century clothing are hung up, then I look out the floor-to-ceiling windows, studying the forest and winter light, waiting for the boom of cannon fire. I feel the hollowness resonate in my chest.

I am alone.

EARLY FEBRUARY

Regn comes into work despondent. I initiate a greeting as we walk through the tiny black gate; it is evident she doesn't want to talk. We stroll down to the ships that afternoon to collect donations from the barrel located aboard the Susan Constant, the largest of the three replica ships. The sky is securely overcast. It isn't as cold with the company. Regn had asked me to join her. We stand on the pier, lingering. She does not say but I know something is wrong.

The next day Regn tells me one of her three cats, Dieter, was put to sleep. That night I rummage through mother's roll-top desk, find a card with a country cottage. A cat looks out the window. I leave it in the office the following morning for Regn to find.

IN THE WINTER of his first year at Jamestown Settlement, he's been with the Foundation eight months. Rose Marie is lead supervisor at Jamestown for the day. Westcott sits at the front desk—the main desk perpendicular to the other stations. This is where registers 10 and 11 are located, along with the telephones and electronic pass machine. Rose Marie sits beside him. She is a large woman and knows it, dressing accordingly. The blue velvet jumper and white shawl fit her respectably. Despite being in her 50s, Rose Marie takes pride in her long golden hair. It is shiny. She often wears it up, jelly-rolled in the back with a clip. Her glasses rest comfortably on a prominent nose, another feature that mimics her ample proportions. She has blue eyes and the minute she opens her mouth there is no mistaking her New York accent. 'Hey, sugar,' she sometimes says. A coffee mug always rests within her grasp.

This particular morning she looks at Westcott, the lobby quiet. 'Are you familiar with the movie *Harold and Maude*?' Westcott replies quietly, deliberately. 'No.' 'You remind me of the young man who plays in it—your personality and character. You should see it, I think you'd like it.'

'I'll look into it.'

Westcott goes to the local library. Sure enough the cult classic is on the shelf. The library offers a wonderful collection of old and new films. The best part, they are absolutely free and available for a week's time.

Surprised by its dark humour, Westcott understands why Rose Marie would draw a parallel between himself and the actor playing Harold, Budd Cort. The youthful face, devoid of any facial hair, soft cheeks, dark brown full hair, and blue often fierce eyes. Harold even dresses like Westcott—formal. And his preoccupation with death. Westcott isn't into pulling elaborate pranks of mock suicide, but the idea of death *is* a preoccupation. He laughs when Maude rescues the tree and puts it in her car. He even has a stringed instrument, much like the one Harold strums—no tune in particular—at the end of the film right after he sends his sports car, remodeled into a hearse, over the cliff. Maude has killed herself and off Harold goes sending his empty car to its own demise, symbolic of his leaving death and all thoughts thereof, behind. Harold will live. Westcott likes the Cat Steven's song at the end. "If you want to be free, be free."

There is one thing about Westcott and the character of Harold that is not the same—something Rose Marie will never find out. Rose Marie claims she has healing powers. She is a hypochondriac—symptoms, perhaps, of being deserted by her husband who ran off with a younger woman. Whatever the case may be, unless she also has the power of clairvoyance, Rose Marie will never know Westcott has not always been as he now appears.

He wishes he could tell someone. Would she understand? It's none of her business.

NEXT SEPTEMBER

Westcott carries in the cardboard box with handles, sets it down in the living room. Opening it a very long-legged cat jumps out. They've just brought him home from the Humane Society. They estimate he is 7 months old. His former owners were in the military and surrendered him along with his dreadful name: Dipstick. Westcott has been going over a list of names all week. Bagheera would be good. He still thinks of Mowgli and his panther-friend. He decides on the aristocratic sound of Helmsley and calls him 'Bloke' for short. He's the Tennessee Walker of felines. So tall, Mr. Stilts. Masculine face; yet he's lithe, delicate in his steps, and very affectionate. A year has passed since Strum died.

OCTOBER

I sit in one of the two striped chairs behind the information desk in the Rotunda. It is cold. A small portable heater is plugged into the outlet and sits on the floor warming my navy blue slacks. I pull my heavy dark brown suede overcoat close to me, one hand tucked in the pocket. I squeeze my crotch, anticipating the high I will enjoy in a couple of hours when I am home, alone in my room. In two years the testosterone hasn't leveled off. At 22 my body is experiencing the libido of a 16-year-old. I have no one to practice sex with. My other hand turns a page. It's leather-bound, gold-leafed, one of the classics from mother's personal collection. I am reading about Hester Prynn. For no reason at all other than I was never required to read the story, I feel it is now my duty to literature to do so. In time it resonates a certain irony. Of all the books I could have picked from the shelf at home—*Ulysses, The Ambassadors, Return of the Native, The Mill on the Floss, Tom Jones, Goirot,* I decided on this one—by Hawthorne, about a woman who has an affair. My mind is in a fog.

I close the book, stand to stretch my legs, move around to get warm. Stepping through the tiny swinging door behind the desk into the foyer between the Rotunda and the Great Hall, I can't wait to leave. The entranceways to the indoor museum are walled off—construction is underway on the new 30,000 square foot museum due to open sometime next year. It is quiet, overcast out, immensely solitary. I feel a pulse between my legs, a throbbing that quickens when I focus on it. Pace to ignore it.

I consider more words. I put together word scrambles and bring them into work for everyone to do. It reads: "More Antics for Your Amusement; in the Spirit of Fall Doldrums." The volunteers love them. So does the crew.

I provide definitions as clues; these are no ordinary words. *Lorgnette; dieffenbachia, tintinnabulation; calliope; harbinger; vestibule; troubadour; armistice; meringue; parsimonious; antimacassar; pusillanimous; maudlin; basenji; matriculate.* It is a game I sometimes play at dinner. Mother and I, if we're at a restaurant. I love looking at the letters and knowing the answer lies in them. Visualizing, rearranging, and the satisfaction of a quick solve. Sometimes the obvious ones take longer if you try too hard. When you're calm the answer just presents itself. David is a volunteer. We often talk. Before he retired he was a psychologist. White hair, blue eyes. We seem to understand each other without actually saying so. All the volunteers have taken a liking to me. Karen, pronounced with the Danish dialect, Car-en, is attractive and always pleasant. The volunteers come to pass the time, contribute something or fill their own lives. I'm a young man to them, the world stretched out in front of me, prime for the picking and experiences. In their eyes.

I wait to see security at the end of the long hallway—they've cleared the outdoors—all visitors have gone. I do a quick run through of the upstairs gallery. I shut the doors and walk down the double staircase. Grabbing the radio, daily schedule, and tiny counter (a mechanism for clicking how many visitors come through), I head for the front. Leaving the Rotunda, my shoes step from carpet onto the brick corridor, passed the café and to an alcove on the right with a small keypad. I enter my four-digit code, then hit star and I'm in the staff stairwell where the wheelchairs and strollers are stowed. Another door leads into a small holding area. There is an elevator, the security room, a solid door leading into the Visitor Service's office and a one-person private restroom. I enter my code into a second keypad—this one is attached to the door handle, and leads into the office. How routine it's all become. The lights off—a pair of purses rest in the small window that opens onto the lobby. It's a half door window—the ladies put their belongings on the shelf just before heading out so they don't have to walk back into the office. I return the radio to its charger, carry my book, and walk back through the door and out another leading into the alcove (on the public side) and dimly lit hallway connecting the orientation theatre room, the café, and main lobby. It would be fun to crawl through the little half-window. I never do. Everything's locked up, we're free to go. The ladies open the half window, get their purses. Sharon locks it and shuts the small wooden door. We walk out together into the fall evening. The ladies and I.

I enjoy leaving together. The trees are black, silhouetted against the warm sunset coming off the James River. Sometimes the beating of wings, a steady swoosh catches my ear as a black V flies overhead, Canadian geese coming home.

It's my birthday in a few days. Mother and I will be driving up to New York.

THE MUSEUM IS CLOSED. It's six o'clock. Thursday, the twelfth of October. The Settlement shuts its doors to the public at 5:00 p.m. Westcott didn't have to work that day. He took his mother's car, he doesn't know why—maybe she dropped him off—he doesn't remember.

He and his colleagues were asked to come or stay late (if they'd been scheduled to work, whatever the case may be) and take a preview tour of the new 30,000 square foot indoor museum. For months the Great Hall has just been a thoroughfare, the panels on the left sealed off as construction continued, but now the museum is preparing to open to the public. In the Rotunda the small upstairs museum has been sustaining patrons, along with the short documentary film. Of course the main exhibits are always the outdoor replicas: The Powhatan Indian Village, The Ships and Pier connected to The Riverfront Discovery Area, and The James Fort where they fire the muskets.

Westcott wears his blue carpenter jeans and a heavy navy blue button-down shirt with a plaid inlay that doesn't show since it is buttoned.

The whole crew is there—they start at the far end of the museum by one of the three gift shops.

It is quite impressive. Westcott remembers nothing informative pertaining to the tour. What he does remember is Regn and how in the dimly lit ambience and quietude of the museum she lightheartedly, casually, slipped her arm through his and said, 'Here, Westcott will escort me through the gallery, won't you!'

'Oh leave him alone,' Sharon half-mocked, understanding his reserved nature. Sharon is two or three years older than Regn. Her British accent endears itself to Westcott. She has blue eyes and short, but full blonde hair. She is slightly heavyset and carries it well. Her skin is always tan—she has a pool and loves to soak up the sun. Her exterior can be hard at times, but Sharon never means anything harsh—in fact Westcott sometimes views her in a similar—not the same, but a similar light as Regn. After all, they are both foreigners.

Westcott let Regn hook her arm through his. He smiled a little self-consciously, but he didn't mind. Regn had come to him. He would never have gone over and said, 'Can I escort you?' or 'Here, let me,' even playfully. And to be perfectly honest, though he sometimes liked to watch Regn's reaction to the tour guide or see her face looking at the exhibits, he felt no inclination to touch her. Regn had come to him. He hadn't felt anything other than politeness on his part. He and mother would be driving up to New York the next day to spend his 22nd birthday with Ellis and Rodge. Other things were on his mind.

They finished making their way through the expansive museum ending where the tour would typically begin—with the Powhatan Indian exhibits. They walked through an English country street—horses' hooves clopped on cobblestones, a door to a tavern squeaked, a cat meowed—the piped in audio. Reaching the Indians an enormous fabricated tree sprawled overhead and birds chirped—behind plated glass a boy mannequin extended his arm with a fish. His expression was buffoonish. It annoyed Westcott. The Indians were intelligent. But here this one boy stood, arm extended, with a droll blank stare. Where was the medicine man? The bronze statue of Opechancanough (opie-can-canoe) had been impressive, so why this placid, savageless boy? And then it was out into the Great Hall. The tour concluded.

In leaving that quiet evening they all said goodbye, a couple—perhaps Sharon or Magda and Regn wished him a happy birthday. Westcott said goodbye in return, eager to get home and pack. He felt no need to linger. He made no note of what Regn was wearing. He got in the car and the evening was complete, locked away, unalterable. In months to come he would remember: she came to me. Even then a certain familiarity had existed between them, some sort of ease that made her feel or want to step over and say, 'Westcott will escort me.'

—

"The Great Hall"

"Coming"
Breezeway Leading to the Rotunda
(Photographs by Wheston Chancellor Grove)

Westcott is driving. The Jersey Turnpike is a breeze, but coming into New York City through the Lincoln Tunnel is like gunning it through the two walls of the parted Red Sea. All the lanes converge. A bottleneck is the norm. Once through the tunnel you are prey for all New York drivers who see your out-of-state license plates. You may be parked at a red light but just for the hell of it, for no other reason than they can, horns blast in a wry attempt to raise your non city-slicker dander. Westcott loves it and honks back. He won't give them the satisfaction. In Virginia you can turn right on red, he checks himself in anticipation, wanting to turn, but knowing in New York you'll get a nice ticket if you don't wait for the green.

The chaos of the city is amazing. It never stops. It is not exciting. It is exhausting.

It is dusk. Parking is impossible. Ellis and Rodge live two blocks from Wall Street and a stone's throw from the gaping crater of Ground Zero. The safest place to be if you think about it (no one's going to strike the same place twice). Mother's legs have deteriorated. Her pain threshold is very high. She's brought a wheelchair from work to use in the city. The cartilage is gone in her knees. The doctor says it's "bone on bone." The legs, from the knees down, splay out. She pushes the car seat back as far as it will go. If her foot catches on the lip of the floor only then will she cry out in pain. She's been sitting too long after the drive—she is more stiff than usual.

They double park, then Westcott circles the block with Ellis' suggestions of places to check for an empty space. It's madness in the city. He's glad they're only staying a few days.

The idea of New York is romantic; in reality it's not always the case. His mother loves Old New York, as does Westcott and even Ellis. It still exists in places like Woolworth's, Union Staion, The Empire State Building, and the architecture of the Waldorf Astoria. One just has to know where to look and be able to tune out the bombardment of sensory stimulation. The notion of applying for a job or an internship in New York is not overwhelmingly enticing to Westcott. New York has changed. Once it was the place to be for a young writer, artist, or engineer. Any decade prior to the dawn of computers and he'd have thrived in the city. The atmosphere has become saturated. Now he finds life in a city equally, if not more lonely, than a quiet town. One can easily become swallowed, faceless, lost in the masses. The mind needs space and silence. Balance.

The next evening Westcott finds himself exceedingly bored. The close quarters have gotten to him. He sits in the hallway in mother's wheelchair reading the rest of *The Scarlet Letter*. Rodge is upset. He hears him turn to Ellis. 'Please tell your brother not to sit in the wheelchair in the hall. What if someone sees him?!'

'And what if they do—what's wrong with sitting in the hall—he's just reading!' She is not so much defending her brother as she is indifferent to Rodge's paranoid concern. She doesn't care one way or the other what Westcott does.

And so he's 22 and he sits in the wheelchair his mother must use because her knees are so bad—bone on bone, the cartilage all worn away. And he reads to pass the time, not interested or disinterested, merely discontent. Nothing has changed in a year.

• • •

October 29th, 20—

(Sitting in the Student Building of the University)

There is a wildness about me; an untamability. Its origins as old as the instinct of primordial beast. Sometimes I imagine myself on an island. I know such a place sensory-wise, though I've never been there before. Lying on my chest, my chin a few inches from the earth, I lick the smooth untouched, gritty sand. The dry sod-like grains are held in my mouth before reluctantly being spit out. *Lord of the Flies.* I long for the boyhood I never had. I relate to Simon—the part where he's shrouded within the foliage, hidden, safe from the world, but watching and listening to the others all the same. In the end Simon finds himself persecuted and murdered.

Loneliness is—

The scent of exhaust as a bus full of nameless passengers pulls away—going some-where, anywhere—and I am left behind to ingest the heavy, comforting fumes that always envelope the one who stays.

NOVEMBER

He sits in his professor's office in the English Department.

'How's it coming?' Professor Pardeaux asks. He teaches Fiction Writing and Poetry.

His freshman year Professor Combes nominated Westcott for Sigma Tau Delta. Professor Combes was in his sixties and had a three-year old son. His younger wife worked in the English department. Professor Combes admired Westcott's work. When he realized his boyish features were not age-related pure youthfulness, Professor Combes no longer exhibited friendliness towards his favored student. Westcott said nothing. Years later he felt the hurt.

'It's going well,' Westcott answers. 'Your notes—'

Professor Pardeaux extrapolates on the comments. He is a fit man, tall, looks like Ed Harris and Mr. Clean rolled in one, but more wiry.

Westcott listens, trying to look attentive.

He moves his hand that's resting on his three-ring folder. An imprint of his palm, the moisture of his nerves, reveals itself on the blue notebook.

Professor Pardeaux says nothing.

Westcott knows he sees the residue. He doesn't want to be here anymore.

Nothing's changed—socially. In graduating from high school he merely picked up right where he left off in his solitary routine. He's made no friends. The other students like him. They're friendly. He's closed off.

It doesn't make sense. It doesn't mean anything! The classes, the assignments, the lectures. He gets A's, an occasional B+. It's just passing time, something to do.

He's tired of the same things.

IT IS 1969. The band of airmen, comrades in cheer, carry Regn across the field. She'd given up resisting and mildly plays along. It's a German tradition for the bride-to-be. They will stash her away and the groom must find her. *How romantic, being traipsed across a muddy field!* Such fills her mind as she waits. Jay does not come. He is an American in the U.S. Air Force. These aren't his traditions. It is all foolish nonsense to him.

That same day, walking near his base, she does not tell him how disappointed she'd felt that he didn't come. The tradition was foolishly silly, but she'd have liked for him to have come after her. He does not ask. She does not volunteer. *I'm fine. Everything will be fine.*

DISSATISFIED WITH COLLEGE, dissatisfied with his job, Westcott determined to leave both in the New Year. In early December the Jamestown-Yorktown Foundation had its annual Christmas party. Westcott remembered the nice event, having attended the previous year, and decided it was worth going again. The music, hors d'oeuvres, and good cheer were pleasant enough. He didn't drink. He didn't dance. He didn't have a date per se, but what did that matter? Had he not gone that night would he have stayed on at the Settlement for another two years? It was on this night, late in fall, that he fell in love with Regn.

OTHERS USED TO TELL Westcott that when he ate something it was as though he were tasting it for the first and last time. Even Westcott agreed with their claim. He savored the moment before plunging his fork or spoon into a perfect edible display. Not greedily, but deliberately. The mental anticipation. Sometimes a spoonful was all he needed. He'd always been a delicate eater. Regn said he ate like a bird. He was a grazer. He couldn't help it—his stomach became quite uncomfortable when he over-stuffed himself. He didn't like the feeling of gorging. Certain dishes were ecstasy to his palate. His tongue humorously mocked the divinity in such a splendid moment of gustatory routine. He loved to take his time. What was the rush? Eating to fill the stomach he hated. It defeated the purpose of eating. What he ate never had to be gourmet to satisfy. Sure he'd tasted the elegant, sampled escargot, dined in some fine restaurants, but his favorite dishes were fairly typical. Cheesecake, artichoke soup, mushrooms with pizza. Warm bread. He was particular in many ways, but his appreciation for refinement of simplistic pleasures made him easy to please in the kitchen. It didn't take a lot—it was knowing what small details moved him.

• • •

Whenever he heard a siren, an ambulance or fire engine en route to some disaster or human emergency, Westcott had the urge to laugh. It wasn't the destination that amused him. But the process. It seemed so comical. The hurry, the critical rush to *get there in time.* Lives might be in the balance, every second counted, but was it not an illusion? Humans do the best they can. Life and death matters are never indelicate. But to see and hear a whirring siren suggested absurdity. 'Quickly now, move aside, we "must" get through.' Yes, of course, but you can't win them all. Look at us, so trained to just move into the other lane, look up maybe in a startled moment of surprise. Do we consider that one day the siren may be coming for us? For an instant we become excited, the urgency in the sounding alarm. Quick. Quick. We look up and around if we are not annoyed by the inconvenience of having moved over. We realize we are part of the endless motion. It reminded Westcott of Hugh Laurie's fun rendition of *Changes.* Life often seemed a veritable circus. The whistles, the parade, the fanfare. How foolish it seemed and yet in queer moments, how equally heartbreaking. He was always conscious of his own impending leaving. He never laughed or felt amused by the shadows and sunlight in a private glade or in watching the foliage gather shadows. Such overlooked locales silently resounded with a passion so quiet its representation of life hurt to even ponder at length. Westcott lived in those shadows—in the most perilous zone between waking and night—the shadowlands of watching and waiting, questioning and listening. He lived in the glade of remembrance.

———

OF HUMAN BONDAGE

8 DECEMBER.

There's a picture of me. A photograph taken that night, just before the dance. Our Foundation's annual Christmas party in the Westminster Ballroom of the Hospitality House across from the College of William & Mary. (The ballroom no longer exists. The hotel has been transformed into *more* dormitories. The college campus is no longer intimate). I am standing in front of the Christmas tree in our living room, wearing my navy blue velvet coat and jeans. My bangs are damp, falling in a gentle strand to the side. The hair on my crown is full, shiny, healthy. I am young. I am handsome. Mother depresses the button on my digital camera. The picture is taken. She is dressed for the occasion. A green and black embroidered jacket, black blouse, Swarovski Christmas tree pinned on left breast. Getting into the car, the garage is cold. Waiting for mother to get in, I casually wonder will I maybe dance. The thought quickly leaves me as we head out. I look at the Christmas lights I recently put up—ours is the most festive on the block. A set of deer—mother and fawn—fixedly stand in soft light atop the frosted lawn. I particularly like the netted green-blue-green pattern I arranged on the front flowerbed boxwoods.

———

Mother accidently cuts off one of my colleagues in the small parking garage. I internalize a head shake. Mother raises her hand at the other car as if to say 'look out.' It's Sharon. I dare not look. Sharon will hold her own. Inside I introduce mother to the ladies. She shakes hands with my supervisor, Eva, one of the shipmates, and with Regn who wears a silver dress. We all sit together at an eight topper. I am between Regn and Eva Bellefont. 'A thorn between two roses,' Mother makes light conversation. 'A diamond in the rough,' Eva counters. Mother turns to Regn. 'Why don't you dance with him?' At the kind suggestion between two women, Regn leads me to the wooden square. She takes my hands, places them on her waist.

One could argue the self-consciousness of youth had me feeling the eyes of everyone in the room, but make no mistake, they were watching intently and some of the men, though I did not yet know the privilege my innocence afforded, envied my position greatly. Regn had always been desired and she knew it. In their eyes I was but a boy, harmless. It would not look proper for them to ask her to dance.

We danced twice. The second time the band played "Unchained Melody."

I trembled. I was glad my hands had something to hold onto. Regn asked, 'Is this your first time dancing?'

'Second.'

She smiled. After all we'd shared one song just minutes before.

'You'll probably want to wash your hands. Mine are sweating.'

Regn held us together. I barely moved. I wanted to study her, to look at her evening attire, the features of her face. Rose Marie, Tillie, Eva—all the foundation staid my confidence. I bit my lower lip, looked down, away, my face blushed. I wanted to stay in that space with her but I also wanted to flee from the attention of everyone sitting. When the song finally ended I pulled away, leaving Regn to trail from the dance floor. Running out of the limelight, I fled from myself. God knows not from Regn. Such a perfect gentleman! Had we been on the floor with the surrounding room empty it may have been different. I wanted to stay there—frozen in time—to feel the friendship. She held onto me. Kept me close. Contact. It is rare that I brush against another body. I could feel her presence—it taunted and assuaged.

Back at the table I watched with discretion. Regn discreetly handkerchiefed the corner of her eyes. When we danced she'd been remembering. I felt in her hold and that faraway look someone—something inside her still believed in the expectations of long ago hopes. I read it in her gaze—it was her first time also. No one had ever quite found her stride. In that moment something inside, something that had always been there, latent but waiting for a signal, came to life. In that moment I loved her. Inside I became bound. An electric current stirred in both of us, but in separate ways. In all the years since and with everything that's come to pass—all the hurt—the affection is still there. I was a man, or trying to be—learning to be, and before me stood the other half. Until that moment I did not know definitively what had been missing. Now I was sure. I was alive. As with any experience, it came at a price.

———

It was a wonderful night, and yet, the sadness came sweeping back as we left—that same desolate sense of regret I'd felt someplace before. I couldn't even look at the short, sweet, little woman before me. I was reluctant to leave, but equally awkward to stay. Mother and I did not remain until the end. I felt ill-mannered not saying goodbye to Regn and Sharon who were on the dance floor when we left. For an instant we had been beyond the realms of work and mere acquaintanceship. We were new to each other—this lady *wanted* me to be there with her on the dance floor. An innocent companionship so yearned for, dare not initiated by my hand.

Why did her husband never take her? Even Regn had said she usually never attended the Christmas social. Why? She liked to dance. It was a perfectly proper and delightful event. Did she stay home in the past because Jay wouldn't go? Did she feel awkward going alone? Why did she deprive herself of these small pleasures? Did she believe she was content in her own secluded world?

'You held her like a china doll,' Mother said.

You're never quite cognizant of how important contact is unless it's absent. Like the old man that gets all dressed up to go out to the movies or down to the corner drugstore to buy a newspaper, the night was my social event for the year. I was making up for lost time. I had the strangest feeling of déjà vu as we danced a measure the second time around. "Unchained Melody" brought back recollections of another night. My prom. I hadn't danced but one song—I was with my sister. Here it was, years later. The same *music.* And still I trembled.

It is 28 degrees out tonight. Clear. Very still. Bright moon. Funny thing, I feel *more* sad than I did at last year's party when I spoke to none of my colleagues and sat in a corner eating hors d' oeuvres. Something's gotta give.

———

A few days later

Westcott is sitting in the cafe at lunch with his colleague, Ann, casually passing the time. The sickness has taken a firm hold. He has little appetite. The minute he sees Regn his heart pounds—his body feels alive, every nerve, every synapse. The nervous sweats begin. A girl who works in the gift shop passes their booth en route to her own table. She is taking her break. He merely glances over to see who it is and if he knows her. He turns his eyes away, benignly.

'Go ahead an' look, don't mind me,' Ann speculates.

'I'm not like that.'

'You're a man.'

'I'm not like that—I'm—discreet.' *You mean decent, a gentleman.*

He doesn't want her making excuses for men's stereotypical behavior. He wants to tell her some men lead with their hearts and not their—. It is too honest. She—any woman, would scoff at such a statement. *And what makes you so different?* I tell you not all men are males in the same way. There is a gentler breed that sees the woman as strong in reserve. He is silent. *And to think this is how you wanted it?*

You're a man. The words suspend, fall—

Shump.

Shump.

Shump.

Like weights.

AN INTERESTING MOVIE is on television. Seeing the name John Malkovich in the credits, Westcott stays on the channel. The time frame is World War II. Anytime he watches a period film something is emotionally aroused. A nameless longing, a recognition. An arresting cold sensation moves inside him—he feels a presence enter his skin, take hold. He wants to cry—the pain, the loss. He isn't watching characters portray life from that era—he is remembering. For him it is going home. He appreciates the attire—the colors are muted, they blend in with the environment. Even the automobiles assimilate themselves—the black Ford sedan, or navy blue, or a deep hunter green. The metal suggesting durability—machinery built to last. Westcott despises plastic. Some sixty years later and everything made is throw-away. Things are increasingly sterile, artificial, removed from the natural world. Westcott watches the boy on screen. The brown leather shoes that bear no brand name. The gray coat. A very young actor, Christian Bale.

He finds it suspicious that in three years the boy's voice never cracks.

A new song in the soundtrack is playing. Suo Gan from the movie Empire of the Sun. The pure exultation of the young choir boys. The Welsh lullaby needs no translation. Its beauty is mesmerizing to Westcott.

• • •

So what are you going to do? He'd taken the long way home from the park. Instead of going straight to his street, he veers right onto Cherry Walk and circles his neighborhood. "Cora" on *The Last of the Mohicans* motion picture soundtrack is playing. He doesn't want the music to end. His stomach is hollow, on edge—that same sensation he used to feel when having to stand up and give a speech.

He is conscious of being distracted. He is thinking of Regn.

They'd been working together, side-by-side for over a year and a half. They'd always enjoyed each other's company. How could he have failed to see that which was in front of him for so long? Two months ago he was hating his job—exhausted with the mundane spiel doled out to every customer. Repetition. Patience. He enjoyed his coworkers from the first day he started at the Settlement. But they weren't enough to make him want to stay. He'd resolved to leave in January. But now—

——

One of my earliest memories is being on my back in the TV room of our home on Magnolia Avenue. It is early morning by the way the light enters the curtains. My mother is at the bureau to the right. Ellis is changing my diaper, or rather, assisting mother by getting it ready. Ellis is four years and ten months older. Too old not to be jealous when a new sibling arrives.

It is a story they have often recounted but I remember breaking out from my crib. Loosening the wooden bar. 'Couldn't keep you in' mother would say. 'We heard this thump, thump, thump. Why, you used to stack your toys in the playpen and climb out head first. Ellis was content to just look up at the trees.' I like that I was so fearless. 'And cry—cry, cry, cry—that first year you had colic.'

How we played, hours on end—always something to do. On a rare occasion I'd be so engaged in the moment I didn't dare waste a minute going all the way into the house to use the restroom. I went outside in the lava rocks. A magnolia leaf for my hands. In those days, in that time, I simply *was*.

• • •

When I was 13 my family drove across country to Virginia. I'd grown up in the Bay area, San Jose to be precise. It wasn't until high school and thereafter that I realized how well-educated my sister, Ellis, and I had been. After preschool we entered a program named Challenger before attending the Catholic elementary school. St. Martin of Tours, at the time, consisted of no more than 380 students K-8. There was a waiting list; space was limited. Mother worked in the rectory on occasion and Ellis and I had been baptized in the church. To this day I remember Father Tim and Father George. I remember them only in terms of appearance. They had no influence or effect on me. Father Tim always gave a kind and wet kiss on the cheek. He was tall, slender, Irish, of advanced age, not ancient, but old enough to be someone's grandfather. I liked to look around the church and study the way the sunlight cast an ethereal glow through the stained glass. I don't remember being bored nor do I remember being particularly interested. We never drank the wine. All those people sharing the same cup wasn't sanitary. I'd keep the thin brittle wafer in my mouth. As children we'd turn and shake hands, all of us, offering a 'Peace be with you.' We didn't take it seriously. It was what we were supposed to do.

My kindergarten teacher yelled at me for going ahead in the workbook. I'd covered the page with my arms. When she asked me if I'd gone ahead I lied. *Circle the item in the row that doesn't belong,* it read. What was wrong with going ahead—the assignment was easy, boring. I'd done it, I wasn't disrupting the lesson? My second grade teacher loved football. She was an elderly woman, Mrs. D'Angelo. Blue eyes, a trim small figure, short reddish blonde hair. We often counted kidney beans in mathematics. I liked her and she liked me. My third grade teacher, Mrs. Bates—yes, that was her real name—didn't like me. Her appearance was ghostly, faint. My name was forever being chalked on the blackboard with three check marks for talking too much. Imagine that! Me talking too much. One time she called Mother in for a conference. 'You'll never guess what [he] was doing during prayer and reading time!' 'What?' My Mother asked, eagerly expectant by the tone of Mrs. Bates' astonishment. '[He] was picking the threads of his socks!' Though I was not present, years later my Mother would tell me how she had to do everything she could to stop herself from bursting out laughing. My god, to think, if that's the worst crime I ever committed! Another time I walked up to Mrs. Bates and asked, 'Do I frustrate you?' She studied me for a moment. 'Where did you hear such a word?'

My fourth grade teacher, Mrs. McAvery, didn't care for me either. It wasn't until 5th, 6th, and 7th grade that I grew to enjoy my teachers. Jackie Moss was my favorite teacher, who later became my friend many years after I'd moved away. Having been a nun, she came to the school to teach. She loved the Iditarod and owned a Siberian Husky named Molly. She shared a home with two other women. She was in her late 50s early 60s. An attractive woman, gray, peppered hair, cut very short but stylish, spectacles and warm blue eyes. We were each given a name which we pulled from a hat. A musher in the Iditarod which we would follow. We had a journal to track them. Our school also had pet day. Everyone would bring their dog, cat, bird, reptile, rabbit to school one afternoon and the priest would come out and bless them all. There's a picture of me with Ms. Moss (we were still on a formal name basis at that time). My Golden Retriever is sitting at my knees. Her Siberian Husky by her leg. I wish I'd gotten to know her better before it was too late. Even over the years and through written letters there was something never discussed. It would be a long time before I could confront myself and when I did, Jackie would have passed away. An aggressive cancer of the lymphocytes. An active woman, so good. A nun no less. Why her?

My art teacher was completely deaf. We had to scroll notes on little pieces of paper if we had a question. She had white hair like cotton candy. No one knew it nor would they have ever guessed, but once upon a time she was the recipient of a state beauty pageant. As students we never called her our 'deaf teacher.' I never thought of her much, in fact. She was a good teacher; she even played music on the piano. The fact that she was deaf had no bearing on my opinion of her. It was all normal to me.

In 7th grade we had a male teacher. Mr. Hegarty. He was 24. Only 24, but somehow to us, at 12 and 13, he seemed well-established in his years. He always seemed to wear corduroy pants. Slightly heavy or husky, he was a nice man. He introduced us to more wonderful books. We read *Of Mice and Men*, *The Wave*, *Shane*, Ray Bradbury novels. Our curriculum included textbooks that I would later see in 9th and 11th grade in the public school system back east. One day, we were either at lunch or on recess, I was having a snack, leaning against the pole under one of the basketball hoops where we usually loved to play Lightning. I noticed Mr. Hegarty standing at the closed door leading into our classroom. He was inside, just looking out, casually observing. He was watching me and his look suggested what I could not articulate, or rather, was unaware of at that time. He saw something about me that would be years in emerging. It was the look of speculation.

St. Martin of Tours was, and still is, comprised of two one-story buildings cream-colored with brown trim. The terra cotta tiles overlap like halved cylinders, reminiscent of a mission. In my day, and I suspect it has not changed, K through grade 5 attended one wing. The faculty offices connected the lower school to the upper school, 6-8. They had lunch with the nice green field bordered by the convent. A large gym was built. I can still smell the smooth lacquer of that enormous space, the worked in grubbiness of sweating youth and rubber athletic equipment—basketballs, volleyballs.

There was a wooden stage at the front of the gym and to the right an enormous stencil of our school mascot, The Bengal Tiger. Our principal, Mr. Eagleson, had a son in college who sometimes filled in as the P.E. instructor. He'd painted the mural. Mr. Eagleson's wife had been my first grade teacher. I'll never forget bringing a penknife to school. It was faint blue with a Hawaiian dancer in a hula skirt. I loved the colors, some token of my father's from when he was a boy living on one of the military bases in Hawaii and climbing Banyan trees. His father had gone to West Point and was henceforth stationed in many places. I did not pull out any of the blades. I merely lifted it from my shirt pocket to show a classmate. The next thing you know Mrs. Eagleson was trying, to no avail, to put the fear of God in me. She took my face in her hands, making the matter seem all so serious and grave. I don't believe my mother ever said anything to me about the matter. It was all so harmless, inno-cent she knew. A little lady on a handsome penknife.

Mr. Eagleson had gray hair, wore a suit and tie, and would always jovially swat a kid on the head with his papers as they passed in the hallway. I smile at this because nowadays a teacher can't even hug a student or use red ink. How controlled and regulated we have become.

I can say every one of my classmates' names—first and last. There were 35 of us, 36 at one point, together from kindergarten on up. Sure we had some who moved away or a handful of transfer students—but even their faces and names I recall with clarity. My best friend, Ashley, transferred into our school in fourth grade. Ashley was black. There were only 2 or 3 black students in the whole of the student population.

...

When I was very little I suffered from countless earaches. Doctors suggested inserting tubes in my ears to relieve pressure and for drainage. Mother didn't want to put me under with the anesthesia. I am grateful to her for seeing that we attended private school when the public school system in San Jose left much to be desired. I am equally grateful for her choice to let the earaches run their course and let my eardrums develop. To this day I still can't dive to any depth beyond four feet in a pool without feeling pressure; nor can I do a somersault under water without my ears clogging with water. But I can hear a pin drop. Loud noises anger me. Especially those entirely avoidable. For example, a slamming door. I always shut a door gently. The rancor and deliberate carelessness of a slamming door reflects a character temperament that is impatient, too hurried, and lacking in etiquette.

I am grateful to my mother for her singing voice and the hours on her lap that go unmarked when she read to Ellis and I. My mother gave us—her children, everything she *never* had, everything we could possibly need in love. Everything in herself. What she could not know was that love wasn't enough. What she made up for in love she left out in guidance. Ellis and I found our own ways. We instinctively knew to study, do our homework, turn in assignments. We never had to be told. It was silently expected. We expected it of ourselves. Mother read to us, quizzed us for tests, looked at our assignments, but inside we possessed the desire to learn, to excel. Father never asked. Occasionally he helped with our math homework; that was all. We needed Mother, but what we couldn't realize then was that she needed us as well. The love of her children.

A scribe of the skies once told me I'd been a general in the Civil War. Perhaps another reason we moved all the way from California to Virginia—I had strong ties to the east coast and even stronger connections across the sea. I was returning to former origins. As General, my decisions had to be swift and accurate in the midst of relentless carnage. I had to remain calm; I could not lose my head, literally and logically speaking. This might explain my habit of automatically looking away anytime scenes of brutality or gore occur on screen. Something inside me shies away—not fear, but horrid fascination. The only way to *avoid* becoming immune to violence (immunity being a survival mechanism for anyone long in the trenches), is to look away so that when a glimpse of cruelty meets the eye the depravity registers, lingering in the conscience. The minute anesthesia sets in a person becomes capable of anything. One must guard himself against complete numbness. Having held a position of high-ranking command reflects my current adherence to self-discipline and the desire for mastery as well. The scribe also told me that my mother and I were psychically connected. It *is* true.

Often we'd be watching a movie or television show and comment in the same words about a detail no one else would likely mention. 'You know, I didn't expect her voice to sound like that,' one of us would say. Odd things and we'd announce them almost in unison so that we knew we'd been thinking the same thing. It was uncanny. Certain visual patterns disturbed us in the same way. I'd been internalizing the emotions of those closest to me from an early age and abiding sensations from other lifetimes. I was carrying luggage before

I'd packed my own suitcase. If only for the inviting illusions of childhood—to return to that unconscious state of observing without analyzing. Living without the gravity of questioning.

—

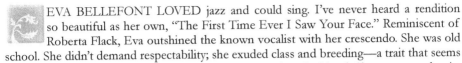 EVA BELLEFONT LOVED jazz and could sing. I've never heard a rendition so beautiful as her own, "The First Time Ever I Saw Your Face." Reminiscent of Roberta Flack, Eva outshined the known vocalist with her crescendo. She was old school. She didn't demand respectability; she exuded class and breeding—a trait that seems to have vanished in the 90s and early 21st century. She'd worked hard. She was a vocal artist who'd found a way to make a living and still cultivate her passions.

Eva always dressed stylishly, with a scarf or neck wrap for adornment. She was direct, but she was also one of the crew. There was never the feeling of division or any pretense, no hierarchy. We were all equal, that's how it always felt. Our time cards were hand-written and left in a long rectangular tiered rack on the wall. Everything was founded on trust and respectability. We'd speak as one person to another—all of us. There was no crusade or need to establish authority. The line of respect was mutual, genuine, and a wonderful testament to businesses still running on the basis of a firm handshake. She was one of the baby boomers and she instinctively knew what management required. And it was not handbooks, quotas, and micromanaging. She kept efficiency flowing and we got the job done. She was competent, productive, and my first real supervisor and ally. I didn't realize how much she made Visitor Services comfortable until three new supervisors were brought in to undermine her seniority and dismantle the morale of our department.

It was my first taste of real disdain for management and the waste of funds. The new-age fresh blood, with all their lectures and slideshows stored in their heads, and a white binder of policies invisibly tucked in their back pocket or purse, infiltrated our tight-knit crew. They were hired for the sole purpose of helping out with the approaching 400th Anniversary celebration scheduled for May. Their positions were supposed to be seasonal. Not one, not two, but *three* extra bodies, three more salaries. Not one of them was familiar with the ins and outs of the Foundation. They weren't inter-office transfers, but complete outsiders. Eva was being ramrodded.

Years later, in confidence with Jill, I would hear how tough Eva played. She wasn't about to be ousted with her retirement just around the corner. She fought and she won. The details of such a transaction one will never know for sure, but the contempt she felt must have been palpable. Little by little the screws tightened. All the old school charm quietly disappeared. First a kiosk was installed in the main lobby. Which no one ever used. Wasted money yet again. The worst assault came in the form of a tiny square box placed on the shelf in the office. It was a time clock. Gone were the days of trust and handwritten 'punches.' Now our honesty was being questioned under the guise of efficiency. We could no longer perform returns. Only Classified Personnel could perform a return—a password was necessary. Shirts were ordered for the spring and summer. The women took one look at the button-down work shirts and tossed them back. Thankfully our attire was left to our own discretion from then on. I always wore my dress shirts and I decided to start putting on a tie regularly since my collection was expanding. The ladies continued to wear their navy blue blazers and white, maroon, or blue blouses. We were an attractive crew and in came the 3 interlopers—Jared, Celia, and Nim—with their workman shirts one would expect the manager of a construction crew to don. More money wasted. All the while Eva kept her cool and persisted in her role. Her title after more than 10 years had been superseded. She was no longer in charge of our schedules; nor was she the individual to come to with complaints or transgressions. Even so, I always approached her first. I avoided "the others" by displaying moderate indifference.

IN DECEMBER WE HIRED some new blood. Three younger men. Parson is a year older than I. Tall, broad-shouldered, blue-eyed with reddish brown hair. He's from Texas. A nice looking guy. His fiancée is finishing up her law degree at William & Mary. Stephen and Thomas are high school seniors. We also took on some part-timers who will be working from 10 to 2. There's Pauline, a retired principal, Jean—who will be quick to make enemies, and Christine—a stay-at-home mother who is homeschooling her children. She makes delicious apple pies. I am polite but impervious to the changes taking place around me. My mind is in a swoon. I make light jokes. I am friendly. My attention is elsewhere.

• • •

One morning I approached the front desk. Regn was at 11, Sharon on 10. 'Ever seen what a real jackass looks like?'

They stared at me, uncertain. I pointed to the entrance doors. As they both looked away, I placed a small, quarter-sized figurine of a burro on the counter. I waited for them to notice.

'Ohhh Westcott!'

'I tell you, this guy, what are we to do with him!' Regn answered, thoroughly amused.

• • •

In the afternoon, after a killer day of $4500 in sales, himself alone, Westcott steals down to the Rotunda. Walking through the galleries he finds her, at the very end. She wears a red sweater tucked in a khaki skirt with a slit up the leg and black boots. Shoulders back, her short torso, immaculate posture. *You look like a statue just standing there,'* he surprises her. Her back was to him. He delighted in watching her. They talk quietly on their way through the dimly lit museum, stopping in the Race and Class exhibit—host of the King James Bible display. They listen to the chorus piped in, "O' Magnum Mysterium." It is soothing to Westcott after the incessant noise of the lobby. With heels she comes just to his chin.

• • •

Regn would be off for two months, having recently obtained the position of a 10-month classified employee; the same position Mother applied for as I planned on leaving the Settlement quite soon. She was interviewed and received great remarks from the panel. However, Eva didn't know my intentions and wisely indicated that an applicant from inside would be better-suited for the position. Had I announced my departure maybe my mother would have received an offer. But the future was unknown and I still didn't have any direction or concrete prospects. And yet, things *were* aligning.

With the new position Regn received state benefits, but she was limited to only ten months per year. In time these details took on great importance. Classified status offered security, at least that's what everyone believed. It was a meager raise in pay, but a steady income with decent health coverage. She would be on leave from January until March. Westcott eagerly awaited the time when he'd see her again. Somehow he mustered the nerve to call her once. He'd worked himself up all day, rehearsing what to say, especially should her husband answer the phone. He just wanted to say hi, see if Regn would like to take a walk.

Regn stopped by the Settlement maybe two times on her leave. Once for a mandatory training class and another time to bring her granddaughter through the museum. Regn never reciprocated the offer to take a walk. She never checked her email either. It was not deliberate. She was simply remiss.

Westcott was assigned to go to the training classes, but on different days. Useless lectures. But he was getting paid. Afterward, off the clock so-to-speak, he'd stroll up to the mezzanine, a book in hand. A sandwich he'd brought with him. He didn't want to go home. The silence and loneliness waited in every corner. Mother would be home, but there was nothing new to say. Even just sitting on the mezzanine listening to an occasional voice below offered possibility. Interaction. Stimulation. He had nowhere else to go. No one to see. So he'd sit and wait and then the restlessness would return, the ridiculousness of passing time. *Where to go, what to do, where to go.*

When Regn returned in March things picked up where they'd left off. Her presence quickened something inside him. The winter that had lulled him thawed overnight. Something inside burned. He awaited each new day of work both with dread and longing. It was a tedious advance and for the longest time one-sided. Regn was fond enough of Westcott; she even declared so to him. She said he could write to her anytime he needed. She would listen. The spring passed with everyone discussing the big event. The 400th Anniversary celebration. The quadricentennial of Jamestown as the first permanent English Settlement in America.

Westcott was wistful and excited at the same time. To be a part of history. His colleagues couldn't wait for the event to be over and done with—they were sick of hearing about it. Their lack of interest made no sense to Westcott. Was it such an inconvenience? Maybe Regn, Sharon, and Fernus had no interest in the history because it wasn't theirs—they had each immigrated to the U.S. Somehow Westcott never truly bothered to interview them on that matter. His energies were elsewhere, analyzing what seemed more important pressing matters. His pursuit of Regn. But even he, a natural citizen, didn't feel cultural ties to the historic event.

He merely felt the importance of sharing in a landmark occasion, a once in a lifetime opportunity—the feeling of being a part of something—together with individuals he considered his friends. But sometimes being thrown together inclines others to a degree of friendliness. Lasting relations reveal themselves only when separation occurs and both parties maintain interest and correspondence. Of those he worked beside for four years only one remained his friend. Only one. Jill Conway. No one else. All the rest spoke empty words. It bothered him. Hurt him. But then what did he expect? They had nothing in common beyond their job. He was a young man. It seemed natural that he should disappear into the world and not be heard from again. Or was it something else?

In May, Queen Elizabeth II returned to Williamsburg. She'd made another visit in 1957 during the 350th anniversary. A picture of the young Elizabeth hung in the Jamestown rotunda and perhaps does to this day. Westcott looked at it on many an occasion.

The summer passed, but the fever never broke. It grew stronger. More fervent. Regn said back in April they'd take a walk. It hadn't happened yet. Months upon months. Could she never find a good time? Or was it—was he—just not that important to her? Yes she was married and had things to do. Even he had "things" to do, but when you care, when you are fond of someone—you "make" the time. Was she afraid? Afraid she'd like it? He sensed she was.

He remembered the attention he gave to any new detail she revealed about herself, however casual. He studied her clothing, her jewelry, the movement of her body in completing a transaction. Her movements were languid but deliberate. Everything about her was womanly. She was completely comfortable in her sexuality. Privately, she found flaws and was exceedingly self-critical, but to the outside world she was the model of sensuality. She did not flirt with men. Her alluring demeanor was unconscious, a feature as natural as the nose on her face, or the texture of her hair. It was part of her and nothing she had or wanted to work at. It simply was. She was what Westcott called a woman's woman.

Above all her voice moved him. He had not known that an accent seduced his emotions. But he'd always been drawn to those with an accent. Be it woman or man. It sounded nicer. A lavender husk. More proper, elegant. American English was clumsy, clipped, flat. No lilt, nothing guttural, boring, unpleasant. Not always, mind you, but in general. He had no exotic fetishes. His attuned ear seemed to be remembering voices from another life, another time. He could never escape the sense that he'd lost a life dear to him and that life was lived in another language.

JANUARY

Magda is quite an attractive woman. One would never suspect her of being in her late 60s. She has thick gray-white hair and no sign of thinning. She wears it modestly and easy to keep at a short, bobbed length. Her eyes are a crisp blue, Maine blue. Maybe Maine comes to mind because she was raised in New England. The coldness of such winter regions seems to have imparted itself into her blood and slowed, if not arrested, the aging process in freezing the nerve cells of her body. Her face and neck are tight and naturally so. There has not been any work done. It, too, appears as though the cold has numbed it, glassed over, frozen it implacable to frown lines or crow's feet. She talks a little too much at times, sporadically, but she is nice, attractive, and part of the 'good' crew. She does not work often, seldom in fact. She does not need the money; it is something to do. She is retired, well enough off one can surmise from her car, yearly excursions, and attractive attire. She has a black Labrador Retriever, the English breed, which is broader, bulkier, solid. The Lab's name is Lady Godiva.

I was standing or maybe it was sitting—it doesn't much matter—at the main desk one afternoon. Magda confided that many of the ladies respect and truly care about me. 'You're *real*,' she said. Such irony. I doubt the Russian exchange students saw it that way. But then, what did *their* opinion matter? 'Thank you for letting me know that,' I replied. Something inside twinged, but I wasn't lying.

My *character's* real. Her words sank down, momentarily soothing the walls of my stomach, filling the bottomless well.

• • •

Deborah asked if I had a girlfriend. She wouldn't disclose who she was messenger for; I have my suspicions of possible candidates. Shortly thereafter a young intern by the name of Sarah, on two separate occasions, found reason to stop at my station and feign asking questions pertinent to the Settlement. I was polite. It hardly seemed opportune to ask her out even had I *wanted* to—she was young, attractive, but we were miles apart. Besides, I've never cared for the name Sarah. I think it goes back to *The Land Before Time*. I love the "long necks" and Little Foot. Sarah—the triceratops, was proud, a bully, and unlikable. It's also too faint a name. Sarah. Its cadence soft, without fierceness. I prefer the pronunciation Sera—Sir-Rah! Doris Days' clear as a bell pure singing voice. Qué sera, sera—what will be will be.

• • •

It is a dry ache. Loneliness. Staring down the Great Hall as the sun dips behind the James River. The great chandelier hanging motionless from the cylindrical radius of the

Rotunda ceiling. Still snapshot moments—the steadiness of silence, watching the sign for the ferry flash its motorist information. *How much can you stand?* It seems to ask. The tedium wears you down; one becomes much too tired to show true emotion—you become numb, complacent, accepting—conditioned to the state. Then again, you have no choice; you're still breathing. You tell yourself you're going mad; you feel morose disposition of your mind as boredom unleashes its wrath. Worst of all there is no one to tell, no one to listen. All this anguish must be dealt with independently within the private domain. The self-conversations, the noise within one's head, "deserts of chit-chat" without—*someone said that, who was it, ah yes the woman at the library*—the sound of silent discussions transpires to a deafening drone. The need so much, the want unsatisfied—to give love in return. I heard it said last night watching *The Letter* (a classic black and white film) 'It is like a disease I wish not to get well from—even in my agony there is a [perverse] joy.' In my case rendered by isolation. You hate it with contempt, but are loyal to Her because she is yours and of you.

• • •

He imagines they're together—some of the ladies, enjoying a friendly lunch engagement planned a week before. They talk of their day-to-day hassles, their lives, and of work. Work. Yes, where he is. They speak of him as one lady to another. He wishes he could be there obscurely and know without their knowing, what they say about him. Someone or something will divert the one's attention and just like that he'll be swept aside. A book set down on a coffee-table.

GERMANY, 1974

'Ah, let me look at you.' She hugs her before pushing the girl out at arm's length for affectionate surveying. 'And how's Jay?'

'Fine. Good. Everything's fine. He's being transferred again.'

'I remember you saying something about that. It will all smooth itself out. You never guess who stopped by the other day.' Her English is broken, she leaves out the contraction.

'Who?'

'Remember Hans Schmirgen—?'

Regn looks up as though her mother's voice is just now coming into range.

'Hans Schmirgen?'

'Well, he asked about you.'

'Oh.'

'I told him you'd gone and been married—almost four years isn't it? My youngest off and married—'

Something registers in her daughter's eyes.

'I could see he was hurt when I told him. He always did like you. A mother knows. Well, tell me what's new!'

Regn does not mention they've been trying for a child. She can't seem to get pregnant.

Walking down the few steps outside, she builds a composite image of Hans from some distant memory. It's not just who Hans Schmirgen is, she later realizes, but what Hans Schmirgen means. What would her life have been like had she married him or—*Josef—I don't even remember his last name*. The American. He'd danced with her that night, some night—and as he left, the dance concluded, he lowered his neck and gently kissed her forehead. 'I want to make passionate love to you,' he whispered in her ear. She'd liked him and not because he wanted to take her to bed. She hadn't slept with him. *Where had he gone? Back to the States?* A faraway dissatisfaction, a familiar stranger, wavers through.

Soon after, she is late. The pregnancy is strong. This one will make it.

FEBRUARY

Lying in bed, it is 8:30, he thinks about rising. How would he manage it? Another day. What smattering of distant hope would he light upon *this* time, perusing the dusty shelves of his mind—home to the most private of anthologies. He had never wanted so little so immediately. Once he had wanted a great deal immediately, but *that* at long last was remedied. The tedious wait had left his will vulnerable and delicate. Now what seemed so simple, even laughable, lay attainable. He needed the silence broken; another moment and he'd lose his mind.

He decided, 'I'll go for a walk.' He didn't want to go for a walk. It was 5:10. The sun was quickly going. He hated the cold, but loved it for wearing him out to the point sleep would not be an effort. He hated sleep. He took Miss Gilly along. He was not walking to get anywhere. He walked for the sake of walking. Beyond such fronts as something to do to pass the time, he walked in the dismal hope of their seeing him. A colleague on her way home from work might drive by the park and detect such a young man with his crimson dog. They might ask him the next time at work, 'Was that you, Westcott, I saw at the park the other day, walking your dog?' They'd be moved by his placid expression, his silent plea to initiate further. *Don't put it all on me.* He'd never volunteer information. He wanted them to ask more than ever. But they never did. They respected him too much and he was too timid to pursue the hanging sentence.

• • •

Yorktown Hub

Magda loaned me *The Devil in the White City*. I've been reading uninterrupted. It's so quiet here. Sometimes I close my eyes, walk about—see how many paces I can go around the railing, not touching it, before bumping into something. Anything to test the senses, keep the faculties alert. The storeroom closet is open. Housekeeping keeps the shelves stocked with supplies to use in the restroom. I grab a handful of 5-inch long, marker-sized, "tubular products" on reserve for the women's restroom. I will use these later. In the absence of a sexual partner, a natural outlet, I must find other means of penetration.

• • •

In January and February Westcott goes to Jamestowne Island. He is listening to Corelli's Grosso Op. 6 No. 8 in G minor, the beautiful "third movement adagio" included in the film *Master and Commander: The Far Side of the World*. He goes under the premise of needing *and* wanting something to do. As he gets out there and begins to walk he knows he has really come to be closer to Regn. He wants to discover what she loves about this place, what draws her to it.

Westcott takes Miss Gilly. He does the 3-mile loop first.

In February, feeling daring, he takes the 5-mile tour. He spends three hours walking and stopping, taking picture after picture. A latent passion, something always within him, dormant, requiring only an activator, suddenly comes to life. He doesn't know it but an ember has been ignited. The flame will grow over the next year-and-a-half until it is a soaring inferno. As he snaps picture after picture he loses himself and all sense of time—for once he escapes Time. He is *enjoying* himself.

There's no one out there—it's timeless with the exception of the sandy-colored paved road and infrequent passerby—no doubt a tourist, as license plate dictates, scoping out the natural landscape. The narrow, one lane path snakes peaceably and accordingly. Vegetation is quite dense for February. He catches the brackish scent off the James—mildly salt-laden. Quiet, still. He rests on the wooden railing atop the longer of the two exposed bridges suspended over the cat-tailed marsh. Last February Regn had wanted to spread the ashes of Dieter at the Island. He can see why—it's such an untouched place; pagan-like; temperate and embracing.

He reviews the pictures—they are beautiful. Even in the photography class he'd taken in high school with traditional film, he never felt such surge of intent and control. He knows the angle, the lighting, the perfect picture. In creating he is alive. He's freezing time. This is no hobby or newfound pastime. Photography will become one of his mainstays throughout life. It is a means of preserving Time. That he had been born an artist—in all ways—a paragon of romantic torment out of the likes of some Brontë novel—has yet to make itself known to him. He watches himself unfold.

• • •

Journal Entry:
from the Book of West
Tuesday, February 20ᵗʰ Twenty Hundred and—

Weather- [Sunny; generally pleasing w/ occasional wind gusts likened to an early spring day—still brisk]

How small I can make my world when reducing it to simplest of means—things become stagnant assuming the illusion of 'never ending'—changeless, 'safe.' If you try to remember everything you'll go crazy. I'll be driving, stopped at a traffic light and look to the dome, scanning the arced horizon in all directions—assessing the sheer magnitude of the world. What in the hell are we doing—fenced in by man-made superficialities. It's too much, too big. So much left unsaid.

Depression—Hopeless Resolve—Second Wind

|

Desperation

———

It's a little known fact even to natives of the town, or those who have lived in Williamsburg long enough to forget they aren't natives, that Route 199 and Humelsine Parkway are one and the same road. The locals, 99.9% of the time, will give directions using the name 199. If you are coming from the south on Interstate 95 and get off onto I-64, it will lead you to 199. Driving from say Virginia Beach up to Williamsburg, you will take a left off 199 onto Route 31, more commonly referred to as Jamestown Road. It is 4 miles long if taken to the left, a straight line from a quiet 7-Eleven (with a green and white sign only—the primary colors are not permitted by city ordinance because of the historical location) all the way to Jamestown Settlement and the Scotland Ferry which takes you over to Surry. If you turn right onto Jamestown Road at the Junction of 199, you will go 2.5 miles passing Walsingham Academy, Lake Matoaka, and The College of William & Mary. Ending at the historical main street of Colonial Williamsburg, Duke of Gloucester. Locals shorten the stalwart name to DOG Street.

Now, as I was saying, in turning left onto Jamestown, you will see it is shrouded by trees on both sides of the road and inset neighborhoods. The most serene image occurs 1 mile down, after The Lightkeeper and Rapunzel's Salon, just before coming to the open bridge. The branches form an arch, a hollow tunnel as though you are putting your eye to a telescope, it is perfectly cropped in the spring and fall—the leaves restore one's sense of pleasure in being alive. 2.25 miles beyond this point you will see two roads, one on the right and one on the left, access roads. Olde Oak Stables (though you would little suspect horses being there, you never see one) sits on the left, and a field with trees, beautiful trees, grows natural, untouched.

In the summer the open field surrounding the trees vibrates optically. A green luminescence. An abundance of tiny lanterns, levitated. Fireflies floating in 'J' formations—the males signaling for a mate to approach. They come late at night, when the world is asleep and no one but the horses in their stalls, peering out the cracked walls, watch.

The narrow road continues parallel to Jamestown Road then Greensprings Road, running into Jamestown Settlement. The narrow lane is lined with daffodils and historic markers that shine in the spring evoking a somber nostalgia in the fall. I call it the Avenue of Trees. Standing at one end it would appear you are permitted to step through into another Time. You are away from the hubbub and development of shopping centers only four miles away. It's taken for granted you can have such beauty, solitude, and still be within a stone's throw to contemporary civilization. It is sad also. How long before *they* buy up this remaining land? Much of it is privately owned. Pray the current landowners never cave, pray they never decide to up and move. It is hard to conceive that once, men and women in buckskin were treading these same grounds. This, right here, is where settler met Indian. This is where the white man forever negated the Native American. This is where America finally took root. It is not Plymouth Rock. If you're looking for The Mayflower, you're about

400 miles off in your estimate. We have replicas of the three ships that sailed. They are The Susan Constant, Godspeed, and Discovery. Looking at them it's amazing a single soul survived the 3 ½ month voyage.

A large building stands on the right across from the Settlement, what used to be the campground headquarters before the county purchased it years ago. The letters are still anchored to the tin roof: Jamestown Beach Campsite. With the National Park being just 1.5 miles away, it is a shame the campground was ever closed. The land sits, waiting.

Directly across from the Campground spreads a wide asphalt parking lot, bordered by shrubbery and manicured hedges. There is a loop for charter and tour buses and then the main lot. 50 tall flagpoles, 25 on each side, delineate a grassy rectangle. Each state flag whips in the wind or hangs motionless in the summer humidity. Coming up the walk a circular fountain spurts as ol' faithful round a copper ship with billowed masts. Beautiful, enormous, *original* trees cast lace on the walkway. Not recently planted twigs, but the trees that witnessed the 350th anniversary in 1957 of Jamestown's founding. The Fort-like structure is just that—thick, rustic beams and a moss gray siding. A vaulted, tin roof dormer. A panel of windows and doors to let all the light enter. The walkway is red brick and continues into the vestibule—a little horizontal hallway, a vacuum of space in which to wait on a bench, peruse a brochure, or just look out at the day, basking in the leisurely pursuit of vacation. Standing out front looking at the building, one can raise his eyes to the windows on the second floor of the brick edifice. It is the mezzanine and not accessible to the public. Just inside those windows on that second floor—the windows to the left—a woman sits, or used to sit, with a book or without. She peels a tangelo, has a green bottle filled with mint tea, gazes out at the day. Gazes at the one sitting across from her.

Outside the branches wave. The fresh but humble sign in its wooden letters—green, gray blue, blending with the environment—hangs from the roof. Jamestown Settlement. Cheerful noise filters through—tourists luncheoning on the patio of the café, the burgundy awnings draping the scene in color.

Just through the second set of glass doors the vestibule opens onto the wide, spacious lobby. Four support beams, all wooden—how high is the ceiling—it goes up and up so that 'ceiling' cannot be applied to this remarkable structure. No, it extends up to the 'rafters,' where, on occasion, a bird will chance to light and a certain woman will fret, calling in her accent, propping the glass doors open until she sees it fly free. Across the lobby, just beyond the wooden stations with their registers for ticket sales, lies another panel of glass windows and doors. Another hallway—but this one continues down—and the last set of doors leads to the grassy mall and 100-ft brick tower, its significance dubious to prompt the question 'What is *that* structure used for?' It is rectangular, solid brick, 100 maybe 150 feet high, and appears very much like an enormous 3-dimensional number 1. It is a commemorative symbol of the first permanent English settlement in America erected during the 1957 celebration. It has no functional purpose outside of stimulating the general inquiry of curiosity.

The present Visitor Services, café, gift shop and educational building is new—only four years old when Westcott receives his position. It exudes warmth with its multitude of windows, the red earth tone of its brickwork, the smoothness of wood. In its own rustic way, it is quite charming, timeless, inviting.

—

If you curve past Jamestown Settlement and do not turn into the parking lot with the flagpoles, you will see a sign for the small marina and winding your way further you will arrive at an impasse. Your first indication of this impasse will be the muffled reverberation of tires as the terrain changes from the smooth snaking asphalt to the sandy-stone rubble of the Colonial Parkway. Standing inside the Settlement one can often hear the approach and change-over of the tires without any need of looking up. In the summer motorcycling groups rev their engines, the mufflers become a singular cloud of noise. It is the very epitome of carefree, lazy summer days. In those engines, thankfully muffled by the glass panes, a young man's attention is beckoned, and the sensation of restlessness wavers through. The sound suggests escape, adventure, the very idea of going, going, going somewhere, anywhere. A group on holiday, just taking in the sights. Nothing of the Hell's Angels sort, just your typical bandana-swathed bikers, with that air of easy-go lucky—whatever happens, happens. We're riding and that's all there is now.

Reaching the junction the uninformed tourist must be observant to the signage. If you take a left you will be entering onto the 22-mile parkway which leads to Colonial Williamsburg and then Jamestown's sister museum, The Yorktown Victory Center and the National Park's Battlefields. It is the width of three lanes with slabs of glazed over stones. From the sky the road looks bathed in sand—a natural path winding through trees and marsh reeds and thickets. The brackish, dusty-colored James River is viewable from the road.

If you turn right you will be heading for the APVA's Historic Jamestowne, more easily called "The National Park." The extra 'e' on Jamestowne is a good indicator of your location. There is yet another sign for the glasshouse of 1607 where, to this day, tradesmen are firing and blowing glass beside a 2000 degree kiln. The National Park is the original site of the English settlement. It is run by the Federal government. Jamestown Settlement is run by the State. It is a recreated site, a living history museum with interpreters and "The Ships." Everyone comes to see the replica ships. *The Island*, as those more familiar with The National Park call it, is more appropriate for the historian or true scenic traveler. There is a small museum, the archeological digs, the archaearium (displaying all the recovered and excavated artifacts) and the quaint church. Beyond the museum civilization ceases, one enters the past. A 5-mile walking or driving loop through the forests and marshlands embodying an atmosphere of time standing still. Here lies the real history. It is amongst this forest floor that the Powhatans moved like deer. It is here that the Englishman first staked his claim. Only 400 years ago. Leave this Island in Time and you will discover what civilization can do to the land. Stay for a short while and it seems something you always knew but had tucked away is brought to recollection. Something in the reeds and the river, the watchful trees, suggests not much 'has' changed—not really in all these years. Mankind is still seeking, but not gaining. He seeks and seeks, and seeks. It's never enough. But here— here in this quietude, all one could ask is answered in the flicker of wind with the reeds. As quickly as you glimpse it, She—the answer—vanishes.

• • •

"Winter Reeds"

"Jamestowne Island"

"Stay"

"Her Resting Place"

"Convergence"

View from Parkway Bridge
"Summer of Love"

"Windlust"

"Waiting for You"

"Jamestown Beach"

"Somber Passage"
(Photographs by Wheston Chancellor Grove)

Ode to Miss McCrady

1

Of Great Britain, born and bred
Little more than this be said

Sharon, Sharon—Miss McCrady
Ever a woman was the lady
Features likened to Doris Day,
Tan complexion, crisp blue eyes—
        hair of golden ray

She's of class, she's of style
Ever a woman could make me smile
Proper, smooth, accented UK verse
holds its own—unyielding,
        what steepled church

2

Though we met nigh two years past
So many questions still burn un-asked

3

Chocolate on chocolate theory apply—
Your confidence and directness I can't deny
dissembles with countenance brisk and firm—
beneath it all, at the core, lies something warm?

4

Your coat of arms doth humbly show
The tusks of ivory crossed—

You that loves the gray Majestics,[3]
whose memory is not lost

5

I cannot explain if you wish not hear—
But listen, beg listen closely now—
Time 'is' our greatest fear!

6

Young and old—Age aside
Experience alone is Life's divide!

In the absence of Regn I paid more attention to Sharon. Perhaps in some ways I reminded her of her own son. She was lonely, too, even though she didn't speak about it.

---

3 Sharon had a fondness for elephants "gray Majestics"

I knew she missed her family—her many grandchildren in the UK. She had a sister nearby in Virginia Beach, and her husband, but it wasn't enough. She needed to come to work. To stay on track, get out, put a little money aside for her trips home to England. She commuted 40 minutes to work—one way! She liked the drive. Sharon was flattered and impressed by the whimsy of my Ode. I knew it was hardly my best work, poetically speaking, but for Sharon, it captured the essence of who she was. I have never favored writing poems *about* close acquaintances. It feels contrived. I can only compose something if I *feel* it. With Regn, the words flowed. I did not have to think, I just knew. Later that spring Sharon asked me to help her write an article about the Queen's visit. It was submitted to The Virginia Gazette.

• • •

I was at Yorktown Victory Center feeling morose in the stillness of hearing the inner office clock tick. To pass the time I devised a questionnaire and asked Rose Marie if she'd answer it. She was quite receptive. I told her I'd pass the survey around to everyone and gather the results.

Rose Marie tells me about her life. After her husband left her for another woman she said she was a mess, took any job she could find.

'How did you recover?'

'Drugs. Lots and lots of drugs.'

I mistake her meaning, thinking of narcotics. Then realize—oh yes all the modern drugs—like a trendy fashion craze. What drug are you on? Depressed, take this. Overweight, swallow this one. Can't sleep, down this. I just listen. I don't cast judgment.

• • •

Personality Questionnaire

Name_____

1. If the world could be seen in only one color of different shades/hues what would you pick?
2. Favorite flower?
3. What if the entire ocean were only 2 ½ ft. deep?
4. As goes wallet, purse, belt, shoes, etc. which color leather do you prefer—black or brown?
5. Fishing, hunting, walking, or gardening?
6. Train or plane?
7. Plastic or glass?
8. Black or blue ink?
9. You go to the Zoo. What's the one animal you must see?
10. Which one of the Golden Girls are you? (Men—which most resembles your wife)?
11. Which war do you most identify yourself with?
12. Would you rather have one week left to live or live forever?
13. Car, bike, or horse?
14. Favorite time of day?
15. Who do you think is stronger—men or women?
16. Cigarettes, cigar, pipe, or chewing tobacco?
17. Island or mainland?
18. Favorite day of the week?
19. Do you believe other life exists in the universe?
20. Favorite instrument?
21. Black or red licorice?
22. Row boat or motor?
23. Ice or no ice in your drink?
24. At the movies where do you sit? (Give location in theater as well as proximity to other viewers).
25. Pavement, cobblestone, or dirt road?
26. Crooked or straight?
27. Wristwatch, pocket watch, or the sun?
28. Young or Old?
29. Would you rather be attacked by a bear or shark?
30. Cremated or buried?

MARCH

Mornings I sometimes lie in bed thinking how wonderful it would be to have oneself. Regn and Sharon experienced life—married once or in Sharon's case, twice, divorced, married again, had children, and grandchildren—so straightforward. That normalcy of human behavior is not known by me. To find a woman and not be able to freely act upon your emotions is agony; the burden of detached impotence merciless. Were circumstances otherwise, on *both* our accounts, physically I long to be with Regn.

• • •

I'd been quite nervous about starting in Group Arrivals. I'd gone over to shadow a couple of times. When the tour guide comes in or the teacher, there is no time for questions on procedure and often groups arrive simultaneously. You can't interrupt your colleague and there is no one else—just the two of you.

I can still remember the scent of those days—the excitement mixed with nerves, and not just the newness of the task at hand, but of Regn. It was the smell of the gift shop employee exit which also ran into the breezeway where the groups passed through. The scent of sun, newspaper, and tiles. Check-In was located just off the breezeway through a set of doors. This adjoining building was known as the Education Wing—the ground floor being comprised of classrooms and lecture/training rooms. A small desk to the side, under an alcove, was the Group Arrivals Check-In. One could stand looking at Group Check-In and gaze upstairs—it was an open atrium. Upstairs lay the development and marketing offices, the President's quarters. The carpet was blue-gray and sunlight always shone into the open area. Scuffing shoes and chattering kids could be heard through the glass doors, muffled and obscured by the Group Check-In desk being set back a little. In spite of the human traffic, the building still retained its scent of freshness, cleanliness, openness with all its windows and natural light.

I enjoyed picking out a new shirt and tie from my closet every morning, especially if Regn and I were working the same schedule. I alternated between two separate colognes. I'd never worn cologne until Ellis bought me some. To this day when I inhale a light scent of Wrangler—its sweet sharpness—or the stronger, darker scent of Musk, I return to those hours and it ceases to be just cologne that I take in but the very scent of age, of youth at its most beautiful peak. It bears the memory of possibility, of unknown forests, unchartered territories, and a heart light and skipping, hell-bent as the captain of any of the three ships, determined at all costs to prevail to the new world. Turning back was no option. Whatever the gales, whatever the emaciation, whatever the casualty to self, onward I kept my course. My heart felt the magnetism of its own compass guiding me on—its direction constant and sure. There was no other way through. I feel it again as once it had been, before it was broken-in; its strength and resolute ardency. The years of solitude were nothing compared to what lay ahead. In sailing for the horizon that part of my life had been sealed up, a gentle eddy, a trough of gentle waves diminishing further, receding away. Whatever loneliness and pain went with the years between the ages of 14 and 20, was closed, irretrievable—I was already cast in form and direction in a certain course.

When I open the little bottle of eau de toilette five hundred different days unfold within me, conversations so strained, breaking slowly, so painstakingly, to a comfortable place.

A place so warm and inviting after the years of silence and introspect, of hiding. A place in the sun that would burn me alive before I let it cast a shadow on me. Until that time I had not known, I had not been conscious of my loneliness. Yes, I had been taciturn in school, alone, I had set myself apart when others tried to engage. But though I was alone, I had not felt the pangs of loneliness. It had not burdened or tormented as such when I first felt the clear tang of its opposite in the form of another's company. Of Regn's company. We came, each in our own way, in our own need—listening, wanting, tentatively, as though we came upon each other from the side in spite of having seen each other head on for two years. It was a gradual advance, much again like a vessel waiting for its sails to catch wind, grasping hold of the ropes and learning much too quickly, all at once, how to move in a certain direction. There was no practicing. It was everything and all—for the first and last time. Everything had to be right, whether it was or not. The waters were beautiful, the work harder than anything in my life, but the very glimpse of any tempest of defeat was never in my line of vision. I'd never failed at anything. And though this may sound quite an exaggeration, I tell you earnestly, it is true. Everything to this point I'd ever set my mind to, I'd achieved. But this wasn't about conquering some land, nor had any of my other desires ever been about proving something. It just had to be—I could not break, could not turn or retract once I'd committed myself to my course. You cannot force a clock to run backwards when it is made to persevere always, and ever, forward. Had I not been so young I'd never have had the courage to love her.

I feel the tightness of some mornings when, tired, the want of sleep would pull at the corners of my eyes as I walked into work at 8:30. The morning still breezy before the heat might set in. I feel the neatness of my clothes. The solemn pride of donning a shirt and tie and cologne and being welcomed. Of dressing, not only for my own satisfaction, but also the pleasure of another's.

One particular morning, when for the first time I would be in Groups all day with Regn, I chose my white shirt and a beautiful silk tie with slanted bars of navy and green. I fastened my watch, the one with the maroon, tan and navy band and rectangular face. My, how some customers did compliment me on it.

I wanted to make a good, strong impression in Groups. It was a break from the noise of the lobby on busy days and the gift shop with its doors flung open to the brick foyer of Visitor Services. I don't believe, except when my company afforded, that Regn appreciated Groups as much as I did. Even at lunch, on particularly crowded days, she'd sit on the mezzanine upstairs with her book and lunch, letting all the noise from the lobby below rise up as she looked out the corner window at the brick walkway and trees leading into the Settlement. It was blessedly quiet in Groups except for the 5-minute rush when guides would come in—it is from these details that I gathered Regn did not like, or rather, could not endure silence.

I, on the other hand, relished stepping away from the lobby and letting the quiet descend upon my eardrums after incessant noise. I admit, on more than one occasion, I sacrificed this respite for the pleasure of dining with Regn on the mezzanine should our lunch breaks mercifully coordinate with each other.

In Groups we handled large sums of money. I'd had tills in excess of 10K at Busch Gardens, so the amount did not concern me and the sum would mostly be in checks. I was more worried about efficiency. It was actually quite easy and in time I would think nothing of the privilege of being in Groups alone, which I eventually was. There were some colleagues who wanted nothing to do with Groups—Jill, Magda, Ida and Rawlings, for some like Ida and Rawlings it was age. They didn't want the headache or pressure of it (though there was no pressure). Even Parson never came over but once or twice to see how things were handled. He ended up doing other things like being a Museum Program Assistant and giving small tours in the outdoor areas. Group Check-In was mostly verifying numbers. For every ten in a group one adult or chaperone was free. I liked stamping the checks and seeing that everything balanced. If there was a discrepancy I'd go into the system and add or subtract from the total count. Seldom did we utilize cash when working in Groups lest there be a large amount of people who did not show or had not yet paid. When we went to lunch one of us always had the keys to our separate cash drawers. There was never a notion of pilfering. We were a family of sorts and even had one wanted to pocket a 10 or 20, which was evidently possible, it would not do. We, well most of us, respected each other and the level of trust between Regn and I was unbreachable.

I still have those exact bottles of cologne. Not new bottles of the same brand, but those same *exact* two bottles from that time so long ago. They are still mostly full. For some reason I never quite felt the want or desire to spray a dab again. On a rare occasion, I might perchance, but it is rare indeed. Afterward, in leaving the Settlement, somehow the scent had to stay with it so that now when I pick up one of the little bottles it all comes flowing back to me without being tainted or transposed by other places, times, memories.

• • •

In April I went to Staples and bought a tape recorder. The kind that still used microcassettes. It was small enough to fit in my pocket. It seemed the right thing to do. I still have it. Still use it.

I remember the first time I brought it to work. Regn and I were on the main desk—it was busy. I couldn't decide where to keep the recorder to pick up the best sound. I was afraid that in my pocket it would be muffled. The keyboards on the main desk were pull-outs on a sliding drawer. I tucked the recorder at the top, never pulling the drawer completely out, but just enough so it could pick up a clear voice. I covered it with a napkin. Colleagues came and went. Sometimes I'd have to get up from my chair—it was risky leaving it there. I decided to keep it in my pocket for good. Later I discovered it picked up everything just fine through the thin cotton of my slacks. I had no intentions for my recordings. I seldom listened to them unless an argument had ensued or some sentiment had been spoken that I wished to preserve. It wasn't unusual—in fact it seemed quite practical. I was making notes. For what I didn't know. But somehow I knew even in that moment, one day those tapes would be all that remained of our—what? What did we have? At that point we were still crossing the waters. I also wanted the recorder so I could practice my speaking voice. I read some of my work aloud and recorded it for Regn to listen to. I played the piano and composed a piece with Regn in mind. I let her borrow the recorder to listen to it. Much later I even gave Regn a short story: *The Blue Line*. After it won in the contest. I gave it to her with my newer digital recorder in a yellow envelope. I asked her to read it and record it in her voice. I wanted to hear it in her accent, to have it spoken that way. She kept the envelope for a month or two. Then forgot she even had it! She said she didn't have the time, what was she to do, pull over somewhere and sit in a parking lot doing it? Her unwillingness and helplessness annoyed me. I was also hurt. 15 minutes. She couldn't find *just* 15 minutes to set aside and read a few pages out loud. She made excuses. 'I feel funny sitting there with myself talking to a machine.' There were so many instances when she could have done it. What this told me was she didn't "want" to do it.

The recorder was a back-up. I couldn't be sure I'd remember every word or detail—so I would have it as a reference. I also missed talking to Regn—just hearing her voice. I anticipated that maybe years from now I would want to be reminded of how her voice comforted and excited me.

I never have listened to those tapes.

· · ·

I wrote my first letter to Regn in June of that same year. The fever had to break. There were two things I wanted to tell her. For months I agonized which would be better to come first. I wanted her to know my affections and I longed to reveal my story—the truth about my gender.

I still have that letter among hundreds more. Did I write a thousand? It's possible. And I don't mean little short missives or foolish sentiments. Everything I wrote was with an earnestness unparalleled. Sometimes in looking back, I know my writing brought Regn to me in a way my actions would never have let me—not at first, anyway.

I kept copies of my letters, and not just to Regn. Be it business correspondence, a casual thank you, or even a friendly how-do, throughout my life I always put aside a duplicate. My own personal archives.

In the beginning I never explicitly told Regn 'I love you.' It always seemed so trite, cliché. My letter spoke of many things. I concluded it with: *You move me in a way no person ever has.*

'I had to walk through the upstairs gallery with tears rolling down my face. It was so cold up there, I thought they'd freeze.' Regn said she read my letter in the restroom before going back into the gallery. Did the location matter as long as the message was heard?

Regn would have to discover who I was another way. This part of me would have to wait. The thing I concealed for so long and whom no one knew a thing about—this I suffered in silence another year. I had to find out if Regn was the one to tell. I could no longer carry it alone. At the time my desire seemed to be the impetus driving me on—both physical and emotional desire. I had no plan. There was no notion of such. Rather, I had a mission. I wanted Regn to know me and above all, I wanted to know Regn in every aspect. However long it took, I would wait.

· · ·

Regn was not a writer. Even in her native tongue she seldom composed anything of length. It was always just a few words. She could write. She didn't like to. Only once or twice did she ever draft something of five or more lines. Regn was afraid of writing. Yes afraid. I once bought a beautiful green leather notebook with gold-leafed pages. It was a journal. I gave it to Regn. She didn't want to take it. 'What am I supposed to do with this?—I don't know if I can—'

'Just write about anything. Write about us.'

Regn never put a single word on those unmarred pages—not to my knowledge. I did insert a small picture of me. I suspect it's still there, waiting to be discovered. By Jay? Her children? Her grandchildren? In it I wear my olive green Fedora, a heavy dark brown suede jacket. My neck is turned, I am looking to the side, standing at Jamestown Island, the trees and national monument behind me. It is the one and only picture Regn *took* of me with my camera.

Regn did not like to deviate from her comfort zone. I learned this by degrees. She had her way of doing things and that was the only "right" way. I found this character trait irritating and narrow-minded. I told her, 'You miss so much.' She always had a rebuttal.

APRIL

He makes the most sales ever in the department, totaling $8,001. He photocopies his end of the day report. It is a record. 'You're the man,' they all start. Jill makes a note of it on the board. Eva whispers something to Regn in the back office. 'He's a golden child.'

'And 8,000 yesterday—that kid,' Regn rejoins.

'I can hear you,' Westcott tells them as he stands in the outer office.

Regn shuffles through the drawer, picking out a rubber pig the size of an almond. He's pink. 'Here, a reward,' for his performance. They sell them in the gift shop. This one had been found, perhaps left by some tourist and picked up by an employee, then deposited in the drawer with miscellaneous paperclips and pens. It's not the object so much as the source from whom the token is offered. Westcott cherishes the little pig because Regn's hands had picked him out. In looking at it, he was really thinking of Regn.

Westcott wears a new white shirt with his blue and vibrant green-striped tie. The weather is sublime—the epitome of spring—warm 70s. Earlier he'd joined Regn for the end of her lunch break. She was upstairs with her legs propped on a chair and her shoes removed. He'd glanced at her bare feet, the tabletop hiding their tips. *So private, how does she do it?* An executive director walked by coming towards Regn from behind Westcott. He had a perfect view of the soles of Regn's exposed feet. She was comfortable with them out. It disturbed Westcott. Disconcerting as it was, he wanted to see Regn's feet. Somehow viewing the soles was more intimate than mild cleavage.

The foot should be concealed, *especially* the underneath displaying the hideous five—he hated the name given to the phalanges and never said it. Fingers were fine, but their basement counterparts were ugly, even on the most attractive foot—they were ridiculous. For this reason he always wore black socks or slippers, even in the company of his mother. He wanted no imprint to show. He had beautiful arches, slender white fronds for walking and running, but even so, it was a matter of decorum, discretion. One just didn't go around flaunting such unappealing wares. For the moment he pardoned Regn.

He quickly noticed she was flat-footed.

His extreme aversion to feet was something he acquired from his mother. The ball and heel didn't bother him. If going without shoes at the beach, he made sure to walk in such a way as to only have the heel and ball make contact with the sand. He couldn't stand the image of footprints, let alone the word itself. Idiosyncratic perhaps, but then he was reminded of aviator Howard Hughes' fixation when it came to having all the items on his dinner plate separated. If one should touch another he became mortified. This didn't bother Westcott, but it proved he wasn't alone in his particularities. He also did not like to look at faces with rounded nostrils. It made the person look ape-like and worse, it appeared as though he or she was always smelling shit, or something unpleasant as his mother liked to say. It wasn't a judgment, but an observation. He knew they couldn't help it. Genes determined the structure of a person's columella. Westcott was grateful for the cartilageic contours of his own nasal passages. If he tilted his head back they looked like angels' wings. Regn's air passageways were elongated, kidney beans. He liked that they were paramecium or colpidium as opposed to tetrahymena-shaped, if one ventures to compare the nares to that of a protozoan.

• • •

At home he sits in the quiet of his room listening only to the ceiling fan's rhythmic whir, the evening birds, and trilling insects. *What an utterly brutal day at work!*

He studies the pig she gave him and her handwriting scrolled on the receipt paper— *glucksweinchen*. It is a "good luck" token. He asks her for a good German name the next day. Westcott keeps Friedrich in his breast pocket.

CALIFORNIA 1996

Milk in paper cartons—little square houses with roofs to open, pinch and turn on end. A light blue windmill printed on the side—a Midwest farm. So cold and quenching. Tiny wheels and a thin layer of peanut butter—too thinly spread across—two wheels pressed into one. He counter revolves, pries them apart. Discards one wheel in the trash. Filling-to-cracker ratio equalized. Strangely enough the cool liquid does not disturb his particular stomach. Semi-lactose intolerant, it tastes good, not too much and the taste of the paper and milk—the taste of the late afternoon air—a taste still pure. After school snack.

He colors to pass the time. Looks out over the field beside the convent. Watches and listens to the others play. A rubber ball smashes the fence. It rings in vibration. He will wait to do his homework. Wait 'til he's alone and doesn't feel watched. He prefers to do it by himself.

WHEN WE DIE IS that the precise moment we're born? Slight belly extending over belt, otherwise fit. A Schlitz tumor. Heart surgery not too long past. Rawlings wears his burgundy knit pullover vest. 'We have to talk about *that*—' he fingers his own top lip, indicating Westcott's faint mustache. 'My god, boy, you're thin as a zipper. But you're a good boy, a company man, I love ya!' In leaving he adds, 'It looks debonair, sexy.' He sweetly mocks. Westcott laughs; his eyes flash over the southern gentleman standing before him. When Rawlings gets going Westcott can't pick out but a word or two of sense; a briny voice, a good-will drawl. The muscles in Westcott's face quiver, muscles he's not used to exercising. *I've never had to shave my mustache. Never.* A "bear" hand of friendliness rests on his slight shoulder. A current of sensation as Rawlings touches him. Westcott feels guilty. All the times Rawlings tries to get him to banter. He had four sons. He can tell Rawlings was a good looking chap in his day, and Ida, a looker in her own right. Rawlings will say: 'So tell me, young fella, you going out girlin' tonight? I can just hear them calling around town—here comes Westcott!' He means no harm. There is nothing crude. It is familiarity he wants, camaraderie between the sexes. There aren't many men in the department and in a way Rawlings wants to relive some of his fine memories—his youthful nights of charm and dandy by hearing Westcott's stories.

Westcott has no experiences to share. When it comes to the male species he doesn't know how to talk light smack, or doesn't want to. He wishes he could paint a vivid yarn for Rawlings, more than smiling politely. Sometimes the ladies are in earshot. Tillie might say, 'Look, Rawlings, you're making him blush.' He wonders if they assume he is a virgin. And later if he is homosexual—his extreme gauntness, his friendliness with the ladies, his attention to detail, his sensitive disposition, his fine dress. He wants to tell them but he can't. It isn't the kind of thing that you just bring up and lay out on the table—'Oh by the way—'. Besides, why should they know? It isn't their business. No one has to know lest they are his partner. And yet it bothers Westcott. Somehow he is still pretending. He wants to be male, wants to be perceived as such, but inside none of the male qualities dominate. In finding out, he doesn't know if their friendliness and inclination toward him would change. If they knew the truth would they still like him? Who would remain his friend and who would reveal a prejudice? He considers these feelings especially when it becomes obvious to the others that his relationship with Regn is something more.

'Well, I need to shake the dew off this lily. Hold down the front for us!' Rawlings scoots down the corridor. Westcott smiles. He's never heard someone put it that way before.

A LETTER IN THE MAIL. Jackie Moss passed away. His sixth grade teacher. A nun for many years. She'd owned a husky, followed the Iditarod each year—went sledding herself. They read *Woodsong*. Gary Paulsen was a favorite author of Ms. Moss'. The summer reading had included *Hatchet*. The summer before 6th grade Mother had been seeing a lot of her own therapist, Sue. It was about the divorce. Westcott waited in the reception area, listening to white noise blowing from the cream-colored domed hive beside the door his mother entered and came out of. She had been crying. Westcott liked reading while he waited. It was worth it. After mother's appointment they'd get cheeseburgers or chicken sandwiches for dinner and then go to the park—a wonderful, huge park with iron jungle gyms. He was 11.

In *Woodsong* Westcott wrote about the musher's longing to stay out in the wilderness—his reluctance to cross the finish line. He wanted the moment to remain. To stay out there, savor the distance.

Information on the service, a brief note. Rare cancer of the lymphocytes—he'd known she was terminal. He sent her a card a couple weeks before—not knowing those would be the last words of his she'd ever read. He included a scenic picture—timeless in its sepia tone—the one of the tree trunks—the one he titled 'Stay.' *She was a better friend to me than I was to her—depression breeds selfishness, I am always concerned with my anguish. She was 3,000 miles away—a different suffering; my pain is here, immediate. That is no excuse.* It hasn't sunk in—she was his one link to the past—someone who knew him before and after. She passed on Good Friday. Sitting in his truck, not wanting to leave work that afternoon, he did not know her fate. He drives around town after taking Miss Gilly to the park, listening to Regn's cd.

Jackie. A void. No one to write letters to anymore. It's queer; he doesn't know how to feel. He doesn't cry. But a definite void. He'd always liked her name. It struck him as being unisex. He'd seen her two years ago. She'd visited with a friend who owned a timeshare in Williamsburg. Jackie, he, and his mother had gone out to dinner at The Whaling Company. It was the first time she'd seen her former student in 7 years. Oh, they'd sent pictures back and forth of pets and occasionally he was in one of them, but Jackie had not seen Westcott since his surgery and starting hormones. Besides, he'd only been on them for 3 months. In spite of their correspondence over the years, he still thought of her as his teacher. He was still just a kid when they saw each other, even though he was 20. None of them could know that in two years Jackie would be gone. For his 21st birthday she sent him a black ink drawing from a local artist in Alaska where she vacationed. It showed an Eskimo crouching, arm extended vertically, an eagle cresting the top of his hand. The illustration was called, "Renewing His Strength."

CALIFORNIA, *Magnolia Avenue*
He is eight years old and goodness finds him waiting to talk to spirits.

• • •

Westcott never knew any of his grandparents. Scratch that—two days after he was born, his paternal Grandmother, who Ellis called Lala, had seen him, held him *in spirit*. She passed away while vacationing in Spain. He saw his maternal grandfather once when he was 7. Nothing else. Through a program in his elementary school there were grandparents who could be adopted. He had surrogate grandparents. He loved his grandmother as if she'd been his biological one, but a longing revealed itself as he grew older. A longing for his history—traits—their lives. He felt estranged from his past—cut off. All he had were the pictures of relatives in heavy frames.

• • •

He's written a letter—two letters. One to his 'real' grandmother—his mother's mother. The other to an elderly woman whose backyard was transformed into a magical, immaculate garden—for an absurdly high price—completed by his father. She is a family friend.
The one with the tiny greenhouse that makes him feel safe. Green plastic siding, aesthetically blending, quaint. Tilled earth and shadow. He likes the earthy redolence inside, the stacked flowerpots. For the first time he sees the shadow of foliage, the warm glow silhouetted through the green corrugated structure. It is a feeling. And the feeling speaks to him. The little old woman who looks out her window. The woman with the strong name. Ruth. She has a pull chain to flush the chamber—the toilet in her house. A fascinating line of buttons on a rare television, one of the first models. It is quiet inside. Time has stood still. An auto repair and mechanic next door. Roses stenciled all along the whitewashed wall of modern cinder block to paint out the encroaching unpleasantries next door. These roses will remain. She has a lava lamp on an entrance table. How strange; even at his age it seems mesmerizing, out of place to Westcott for her to have a lava lamp. It was a gift to Ruth. From his father. He watches it. The little woman who lives here has many stories.

He once cracked walnuts with a hammer in her carport. The trick was tapping it just enough to split the outer shell and dislodge a whole nugget.

His mother had a tea in that garden—Ruth's garden. Invited many of her friends. He grass-stained his knees. He liked to climb on the small shed just beneath the back railing, stand at his post before the garden, and joyfully fling himself to the ground. Heights didn't scare him.

Ruth dies when he is 8. His first funeral. He remembers little of it. He hadn't been present when she died. His father had come upstairs and sat on the small daybed in Trillia and told him. His father's tears had fallen on the shoulder of Westcott's t-shirt. His father had cried. They went to Ruth's house that evening or the next. And then Westcott cried. He held the little stuffed brown rabbit Ruth had given him. He held it in his hands behind him. He cried because his family was sad about Ruth's passing. He did not know if he would have been sad on his own. Later he took everything Ruth had ever given him, even a woodpecker tree ornament from her garden, and put them all in a small green box. He wanted her memory contained. No one suggested he do this. He often kept small boxes of important items.

• • •

He goes outside, down the deck and follows the long slab of pebbled path up the side of his house to the wrought iron gate that opens onto the front yard. It has an archway. He sticks his foot, crookedly to fit, between the iron. He stands *in*, not on the clasped gate. Tapes the envelopes to the arch. Says a word to bid them fly, farewell—a prayer? He doesn't recall the words. Later he comes back. The envelopes are gone. For a moment he feels blessed. It worked. He moves closer to be sure. On the ground to the right smudged with dirt are the letters. They'd fallen. No one had come. No one had answered.

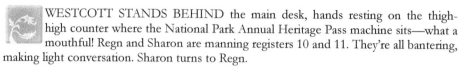 WESTCOTT STANDS BEHIND the main desk, hands resting on the thigh-high counter where the National Park Annual Heritage Pass machine sits—what a mouthful! Regn and Sharon are manning registers 10 and 11. They're all bantering, making light conversation. Sharon turns to Regn.

'He needs a girlfriend—someone vibrant instead of *us* old women. What do you say, Westcott?' She swivels round in her chair.

Westcott smiles.

'You have excellent taste. But you'll have to run any girlfriends by me to make sure they meet approval and deserve you.'

Listening to Sharon, Westcott stares at both ladies, wanting to concentrate full attention on Regn. He needs to see her expression. Sharon is looking right at him; he does not want to betray his affections for Regn.

• • •

Wednesday the 25th

Regn is at Yorktown. Eva calls Westcott into her office. She's found the post-it notes with Westcott's scrolling on the side binding.

Bloody hell long day.
I'm in need of a sabbatical now.
My head aches!

'And how are *you* doing?' She shows him the notepads.

'Oh, I was just speaking in jest.'

'All right. But I don't want anyone else finding these. You know who I mean.'

'Yes.' The Sups. The three who ousted Eva from her own position. It's an unspoken allegiance. Eva's on his side.

'If there's anything you need, my door is open. Anytime.'

'All right.'

'We don't want anything to happen to you.'

'I wouldn't go postal—I love my co-workers.'

• • •

Saturday 28 April 20—

I gave her my truck keys to cut open a box of maps, watching her hands touching the keys I touched every day. Usually Group Arrivals wasn't open on the weekends; they checked in at the lobby. We spent all morning and the better part of the early afternoon in the company of each other, talking for hours. Groups were sparse. The day had been a gift.

Regn showed me pictures of her life and family, even her house. When she spoke of her mother she wiped her eyes. It was strange to see pictures of Regn. By looking at them she was becoming real. The mystery about her dissolving. She pushed her hair back, relaxed and reclined in the chair. I saw her age for the first time. It startled me, but I saw the attractiveness, too. She asked if I had a girlfriend. 'No. I do not,' I answered with simple precision.

Regn said in so many words, 'I guess I'm passed my prime.' 'Not necessarily,' I strained to confess. We ate lunch together in Group Arrivals. Her father died when she was thirteen. She had two older brothers. The second, Dieter, died as an infant. Her sister was the middle child and Regn the youngest. After Dieter, the pregnancy with Regn had not been planned nor initially wanted. As a kid Regn owned a parakeet named Hensien. She lived in Madrid while pregnant with her first child. She also lived in the Midwest.

'You reach a stage in your life where you don't want to be alone.'

I wanted to tell her, 'I'm already afraid of being alone, it has nothing to do with age. It's human.' I remained quiet. Listening.

'Sometimes I feel trapped. I could never afford to live on my own.'

I let her go on.

'And then I think I'm a terrible person or that others think I am for wanting to be on my own. But they don't understand.'

'Why is that?'

'Oh you wouldn't want to hear.'

'I don't mind.'

'If I were on my own I could do things, go out with friends, and have fun—I don't want you to get the idea my husband's bad, he's a good man, but I just don't want to be dependent.'

The conversation meandered comfortably with Regn doing most of the talking.

'There was this guy one time, at another place I worked—my manager's husband—' Regn is thinking back. Westcott waits. 'Well he—he rubbed up against my back in the storeroom while I was getting something—it was horrible. I left after that. I also worked in a dentist's office. And the doctor was all the time giving me these looks. When we were young kids, the neighborhood boys caught me and my sister sunbathing in our backyard, nude.' Regn started laughing nostalgically, reviewing the intimacies of her life, long unspoken.

I wished to study the photographs, but I was nervous. She showed me her children, husband, friends, father, brother and sister. One was of her as a nurse back in Germany— she was very young. I recognized her by her eyes—a sorrow and warmth in them.

'If you had to choose, what would you say was the happiest time in your life?'

'The happiest time'—she is quiet for a long moment.

I feel the air conditioning, the tightness of early morning dissolves from the corners of my vision. The time is going so quickly. I am relaxed. Regn is relaxed. It is good. We have found the perfect stride, the simple fluidity of two people completely engaged in the moment. For the next two years that feeling will only grow stronger. Never had I been so focused, so alive, so present in *the present*, as I was with Regn.

'—I'd have to say when I was 16 or 17 working as a nurse in Germany. Sometimes I checked blood sugar. This one old guy would always jump when I pricked his finger. I also had some men bring their urine samples to me in beer bottles—' she laughed remembering those good times. Those years when anything was possible. Her whole life waiting ahead.

The overcast morning transformed into a gorgeous day, rich in color with gray skies off in the distance. I wished I'd brought my camera.

Fernus called. 'Oh please, can't we just be left to talk.' For the first time Regn didn't want to be bothered—our interaction was taking precedence over work—she obviously had things she needed to say and Fernus had interrupted at a crucial point. Having answered the phone cordially and putting the phone back, we continued to talk. It was relief for both of us.

I spent a good 45-minutes alone for the remainder of Groups. Regn had already closed up and returned to the main lobby. I paced in deep thought. So much had she given me to think about.

I told her just before she left, 'This is my best day of work yet.'

'Me too.'

I went to the ships after closing up Groups. *Elizabeth* (a substitute when the *Godspeed* or other ships are out sailing) was the only one in port. Just as I arrived onto the Riverfront the cannon exploded at the end of the pier. I watched the blaze of fire as the gun reported over the James.

• • •

Sunday 29 April 20—

Two days in a row!

Regn and I were on the front desk. I held a book she'd brought in from her small hometown in Germany. An amazing little historical keepsake—hardbound and full of wonderful photographs. Slipped in were newspaper clippings and pictures of her family.

'I should have been born a boy—I was always a rebel,' she laughed. I know she didn't really mean she *wanted* to be a boy—there's a big difference between should and want, but she could not know how her statement hit me. She did not know. Not yet.

Flipping the pages she comes to one and stops. 'This boy, Josef, was a friend—very sweet. He died ten years ago from AIDS. He was a homosexual.'

Her words meant more to me than she could know. I looked at the two lines of students. Tucked in the back row, peeking out, was Regn. She was maybe 11 or 12 years old. The same secretive smile, mysterious eyes.

I looked at my light blue shirt and my yellow silk tie with the civil war cannons evenly dispersed. I always liked it when a customer complimented me in the presence of Regn. I wanted our private conversations to stretch on forever. We were still getting to know one another—the details of our lives. It would be a long time before I let her find out. Another year. A year filled with quiet aching and a joy that quickened the heart every time we saw each other walk through the door.

MAY

My eyes stung. It was still dark when my copper double-belled alarm clock went off on May the 4th. I was the second shift. I had to be at the Settlement by 7 a.m. Those who volunteered for the early shift would already be there, having arrived at 6 a.m.

We—the staff—parked in the vermilion meadow across from the employee lot. The morning dew was damp, a chill in the air. For two hours we stood around in the lobby, the Great Hall, the mall just outside the glass doors, and did nothing. Why was it imperative we arrive early?

Parson and I headed to the end of the Great Hall. Celia had dismissed everyone and said we should just go back up front and stay in the lobby or rotunda. Parson waited with me by the metal detector scantrons. We held our ground. I wore my maroon dress shirt, it looked like silk, and a beautiful silk tie depicting Washington in conference amongst delegates. If tilted, a feathered, quill-like pattern behind the scene attracted the eye. The gold, silver, lavender, and maroon of the tie complimented my shirt perfectly. I'd left my coat in the office. I didn't dare leave to get it, lest Celia waylay me. All other departmental staff had given up and headed back to the lobby. Most stood outside on the mall waiting to watch the screen prompt. Secret Service and security repeatedly instructed that no one else would be permitted access. All check-ins were complete. We waited. The cold made me jittery. The trees were in bloom, lush in their green foliage. We waited over an hour in the cool spring morning. I wished for my coat.

Then something miraculous. Security says, 'Step over here, we'll let you through.' I don't believe it.

Parson goes first. He empties his pockets. The wand scans each side of his body. He waits for me.

I fumble taking the batteries from my camera—they examine *everything*. I feel at any moment they'll get a message in their earpiece telling them not to let us pass. It's too late. I make casual conversation, I don't want my quietness to be suspicious, I'm overcompensating. As Parson and I walk together up to the Fort, we are the only ones left. He is taller than I, modestly built, a nice full smile, a decent young man. His presence undoubtedly masculine.

'I wasn't going to go unless they let you through.'

He meant it. What a guy I thought, the kind of guy I would only hope to be by my side were we in battle. A true comrade.

Stepping inside the wooden gate at the Fort everyone looks at us—two guys just strolling in, crossing in front of news crews, big commercial cameras. Throughout the procession I stood behind a pressman. I saw a rectangular placard clipped to his black bag.

USA Today. We waited another hour. My legs wanted to give out. The dampness setting in. Not even Sharon got into the Fort. She was on the walkway leading up from the ships. She would not hear the speakers. She would merely see *her* Queen in passing. I photographed the festivities. A swarm of shutters, clicking, zooming. The Queen walked solemnly, elegantly. I never heard a single word in the program I was too busy shooting. Events unfurled before me, individuals stood, walked to the podium, spoke, I never heard them. I was still in awe that we'd gotten through, *we* were the last to enter. We'd stuck it out, and it had paid off, our patience proved worthwhile.

I took pictures until I was tired and then it was time to exit. I wondered, standing there—had security been so generous because they saw the youth of history before them? They'd thought to themselves, these guys will very well make it to the 450th why not let's pass them through—what's the harm in a couple more—let them have something and live to tell about it?

By the time the Fort cleared, most staff had returned to their posts. Walking back through the Great Hall, glad to be in from the cold, Regn, one of our new supervisors and a few others—namely Magda and the volunteers, stood by the desk. 'We saw you on the screen.'

'You did?' I wondered what I was doing. Did I look like some gaping tourist taking a gazillion pictures? Some months later Parson showed me the news clip—he'd saved it for me on his television. All you can see is the back of my head and my body turning as a delicate lady, adorned in turquoise with matching hat, walks by in front.

The supervisors were displeased that we had disobeyed their instructions. But they wouldn't reprimand. They were more upset at themselves, the fact that we'd waited and they'd given up.

Regn, dressed for the occasion in her light beige skirt and matching blazer, turns to me. 'So you got to see the Queen. I'm happy for you.'

———

It was the kind of event grandparents tell their grandchildren. 'When grandpa was a young man, oh in his early twenties, he saw the Queen of England. Not many people do, not in person mind you.' Westcott wanted something to pass on. He knew he wouldn't have any children, and that was perfectly fine. But perhaps a niece or nephew, if Ellis had children of her own, would someday visit, someday ask, 'Uncle Westcott, what exciting things happened to you when you were young?' He'd restrain himself. A flash and Regn's name would fill his mind.

He would not mention her, though he'd like to. Instead, he'd say, 'Well, did you know about the time I saw the Queen?' Young children loved those kinds of stories. When they grew to be older, much older, maybe Regn would surface in his stories.

Looking at Regn in that day, in that hour, this is what he imagines.

BITBURG, *Monday September 1959*
Wolfgang pushes out his rear to mimic his little sister. He puts a hand up to each strap of his lederhosen and parades in an air of brotherly jest. 'Look how your bum sticks out with your pack on!' He breaks wind for emphasis.

Regn is seven. She walks tall despite her 'klein' size. Her posture is perfect, sprightly and poised.

'You still believe the Queen of jolly ol' England doesn't use a *throne*, then?'

'Of course not, she's *the Queen*! She doesn't have to go to the bathroom.' Regn is emphatic. She doesn't quite believe her own words.

Wolfgang smiles and laughs. He'll be seventeen soon. 'What did I do to deserve not one, but two lil' sisters? And you the whippersnapper!' Playfully he swings an arm around her.

FRIDAY 11 MAY
Anniversary Weekend, Day 1

Mild tiredness finds my face tight. I turn onto the bumpety gravel of Drummond's Field and pull into the grass. 7:35 a.m. Wearing my sky blue long-sleeved shirt, brand name Crazy Horse, and silk tie with the locomotive billowing red white and blue as steam, I walk through the dewy grass across an isolated, peaceful access road and into the campground. The little road to my right, had I kept on, leads to the 4-H club. Ahead, overgrown now, lies the old campground. I'd gone camping there some distant summer, years before, collected oysters in the river. Cut my foot on a rock, laid out in a field. Played catch with my father who was visiting. The air is cool, anticipation hangs on the shoulders of such a day. I halt, lift one foot, tying my damp shoelace on a rotting picnic bench. I like that my shirt's brand name is obscure. Crazy Horse. It reminds me of an Indian name. It suits me. I walk down the shady path.

Green corduroy overalls. Blue t-shirt, two wolves baying at the moon covered by the bib. There's a tent. And inside the tent someone in overalls; I can't believe it—she unclasps the hooks, removes her clothes, and pulls on a one-piece bathing suit. She does not see me watching. Looking down, the flesh of young breasts puckers side-by-side. 'How old are you,' I ask? She looks away, but not from my presence. She can't see me, though I can see her. She is looking away from herself. '15,' her tenor voice answers. Ratty hair left to its own, falling free. Fair skinned. Quiet eyes, fiercely pondersome. I remember that day. I'd been changing out of my wet bathing suit and made the mistake of looking down. A young boy, about 11 had been camping with his mother and their dog. I'd looked at him in his shorts. He wore an unbuttoned overshirt and nothing else. His skin was bare, his chest free to the day. I'd envied his flat chest, his freedom. *Now* I wear a tie. My torso is flat as a pancake. I'm still hiding.

I come into the open sun-washed field of Anniversary Park. The state police have no idea where the shuttle is located.

I traipse across the main pavilion, cut behind tents, reach the main road. I stroll past security. What a joke. Their presence is merely for effect.

I run into Regn while making a trip into the main entrance. She wears her large sunglasses. I'd taken mine off. Regn is assigned to the Group bus loop way the hell out in No Man's Land—the Boonies. Eva comes to my station, asks me to go to the lobby and bring some maps so we can all stuff them. Fine mess of a day this is going to be, I think. How utterly disappointing. Business is not the expected numbers—we, or I should say everyone else is, or appears to be sitting in fold-up chairs staring into space. The frustration is present. That we should be so idle, but I cannot be with Regn in her section. I want to be with her, to spend the day talking. At last Eva affords an excuse! At the expense of sweating profusely in the heightening sun, I take the dolly, pull it all the way out to Regn's tent. I make sure to have my sunglasses on—not simply to keep the brightness out of my eyes. They protect me from meeting another's gaze and I want Regn to see me in them. The others say I look like a movie star. I like to hear this, who wouldn't, but it also hurts me. It hurts because I don't know how to use these looks to my advantage, or rather, I feel that I am fooling them. Strip away the clothes and sunglasses and I am defenseless in my shame. I am the only one wearing a tie. I make two more trips to no avail—she isn't there. I know at one point, after lunch, she'd switched with Sharon who was in the lobby. Maybe they traded back again.

Later, at lunch, Regn tells me she'd come outside a couple of times to the Surry post, in my absence, asking where I was. It comforts, knowing she was looking for me.

After lunch four of us have our picture taken. Regn, myself, Fernus, and Sharon. I grip my brown lunch bag in hand, Fernus holds her soda can, Regn makes a funny expression. But what strikes me about this photograph is the shadow. We are standing in Group Reservations, the sun streaming in from above, through the skylight, and directly behind my head a giant starred reflection is cast on the wall. It is cast there as a pointed halo of sorts. I am next to Regn, she wears her sunglasses though we are still indoors. My face looks so young, my eyes do not betray any weariness. The pain is gradual. The pain is two years and more ahead. Is the star the crest of my youth? Does it suggest what I've always known— that something more, something far greater was in store for me? Looking back and all that's come to pass, I can tell you yes. With a full and tired heart, I can tell you *yes*. I am not inclined to whimsy or overly-superstitious; however, there are signs and sometimes they must be noticed or you are a fool to dismiss them. I knew from an early age I was different. I saw the world from a distance. I was born to suffer and endure, but in so doing, if I succeeded, I was born for distinction. It was not conceit, but the knowing of Self and sometimes the frustration, the tedious ache of patience, rendered me doubtful.

'Will you hold this, Westcott?' Sharon hands me her purse, stepping to the restroom. I feel like the lady's personal valet and am pleased. We walk out front and across the street to Anniversary Park—I slip my sunglasses on again, raise my hand to my brow. It is oddly, sadly quiet for opening day. A staccato painting, daffodils bloom the length of Jamestown Road. The air is close. Still. And thick.

'Why don't you take that off?' Many a colleague suggests, acknowledging my tie. I stuff maps along with them, never loosening my Windsor knot. I stare into space. Staff in vibrant yellow t-shirts—staff brought in—volunteers. My colleagues in fold-up chairs, a long stretch from one end of lots down to the Ferry. Plastic flags lining the avenue, feathered white flags. Tents, a stage. Grander yet in 1907 when *entire* buildings were erected; *this is the best they could do and twenty years worth of planning?* Grand now only for the lives that are beside me. May. Twenty Hundred and Seven.

A man sits with legs apart. Bill, my colleague. Heavy, a beach ball from stomach to groin, a smooth arc. Navy blue pants, hiked at the ankles. I glance between them, at his crotch. A form, a wad—the only apt term for it, is gnashed to the left, naturally uncouth, unavoidably so. I can see the shape of Bill's penis through his sweat-clinged pants. I suspect, without derision, he doesn't much use it anymore. He's crowding eighty and doesn't look a day past sixty. Bill's all the time admiring my ties. 'Hey, handsome,' he says laying a hand on my shoulder. Most of the ladies find his tactile liberties just that—too free. He comes right up on them, easily slides a hand along the shoulder, hovers. It doesn't bother me; it arouses my curiosity. I would never be so forward with the ladies or even Bill. Fancy me sidling up to him, a hand on the shoulder. 'Hey, Bill, how's it hangin'?' I shake my head half-laughing at the notion. And Regn—I wish I could politely touch her person.

Sharon and I take the shuttle back together. She gives me a ride across the field in her white van. Her car's in the shop. She had to drive her husband's for the day. We wobble and bump along the unlevel terrain to my truck. 'Hey this is fun, sure is something isn't it?' Sharon laughs in her British way. I wonder what it's like in Regn's car.

The evening is gorgeous. At home I mow the lawn, thinking about the day's events. I'm annoyed at washing my work clothes the day before, only to have them saturated with onion-odor sweat. Everyone said I should take my tie off, roll up my cuffs. I didn't want to fling it to the wind. Besides, my arms are long, wiry, like a lad's. I have not filled out, probably never will. I never hike up my sleeves in the company of others.

SATURDAY 12 MAY
Anniversary Weekend, Day 2

I ride the shuttle without anyone from the Visitor Services department. After an hour of mindless pacing in the rotunda where I've been posted, I bolt for the lobby. The confinement is too much. We're over-staffed. In the lobby I wade through congestion and find relief in the sight of Regn. I take a piece of lint off Regn's back. 'Wait, hold on, you have something'— I announce my intentions lest she be startled. For a second I consider saving it.

Just as we are about to get off work, at a quarter to six, it starts to rain. We planned to head over to Anniversary Park to hear Bruce Hornsby and Chaka Khan. Regn isn't going to come. She's in a mood. I go back into the lobby for an umbrella. I arrive with Sharon, Fernus and another Sharon—Sharon 2 from the Executive Department, at the currency exchange tent. We wait in line. Suddenly, from behind, Regn appears. I conceal it from the others, but inside my irritation subsides and I am beaming. We convert our cash to commemorative script money before buying some much wanted dinner. I continue to hold one of the umbrellas over Regn and myself. The rain soaks my sleeve into a dark blue. Sharon has a poncho. I am shaking mildly and not just from the damp. We forge on in spite of the foreboding weather. Soon the drizzling rain lets up, ceases altogether. It is an evening I know will haunt me in time. I know because in that moment history is being made. Not just in commemorating four hundred years. Right here, right now, my own private story is being laid out as we pass the evening together.

The ladies devour their ribs, while I pick away at my BBQ chicken and square hunk of cornbread. The cornbread is dry. Regn enjoys the only vegetarian item she could find— steamed vegetable stew over a tortilla. After sitting down to dinner the ladies want a drink. Sharon opts for wine. 'Cheers!' Regn holds her dark lager up, enjoying herself. I wonder if she remembers that just half an hour ago she wasn't going to come. How sour her mood had been. I weigh this visible change in attitude. Sharon has already polished off her cup. I sip my Sierra Mist wishing they'd had Ginger Ale—a true gentleman's beverage, smooth. The Sierra Mist is too sweet. After taking a quaff of beer, Regn offers me a taste from her glass. 'Are you sure?' I drink from her cup, my lips meeting on the same circumference where hers had rested a few seconds ago.

After dinner we wander to the field. I find some fold up chairs for all of us, arranging them for better viewing. I sit restively. Regn still stands. I carefully situate myself behind her for the night. She knows I am watching. But she is relaxed. Sharon gets up. With Regn she sways to the music. 'Come on Westcott, get up and dance with us,' Regn half turns. 'I'm quite content, sitting right here.' My voice smiles. From the side I see the breeze brush Regn's forehead; her hair wisps gently. Her shoulders teeter like a seesaw in opposition to the side her knee bends.

"That's Just the Way it is" and Chaka Khan's, "Tell me something Good—Tell me that you love me," fills the cool night air. I take out a small chocolate donut from my brown bag which I'd asked if Regn would put in her purse while I'd carried the umbrella and my camera. Regn had feigned annoyance, but I could tell she didn't mind stowing the lunch bag. As soon as the umbrella was no longer needed, I requested my brown bag back. In the dusky light I ask her, 'Would you like one?' She laughs. 'It looks like an asshole.' And that's Regn. Her accent has the effect of making it sound less crude. To look at her you wouldn't think such levity would come from her mouth. She kids sometimes like a young girl; I appreciate her willingness to be lighthearted and funny. 'Well,' I say, 'you're not going to deter me from enjoying them. The chocolate is de—ee—licious!'

It is dark when we leave. Riding in the shuttle we all start to weave like some gravitational pull holds us. Regn thinks it is the alcohol going to her head, but when those passengers who hadn't enjoyed a drink notice we know it is a faulty alignment in the vehicle.

'What are we going to do now, girls?' Sharon thinks aloud. 'We've made it, now it's retirement—'

I am quiet. Tired they think. They are secure in being together, having their age as one. They will leave me someday. *I am sitting next to Regn, our bodies in contact, her thigh against mine, so close.* I wonder what it would be like to hug this woman beside me, to just lie down and rest my head on her lap, sleep for awhile.

I pull out of the field beneath the floodlights before Regn and Sharon. Sharon turns left. Regn and I continue into the night. With her in my trail, I ease up on the accelerator. Reaching the intersection I move into the left turning lane for home. The light is yellow. I should run it. I could. I wait for Regn. She pulls up beside me, in the lane to go straight. Just then her light turns green. She waves. I wave. I am left to wait out the light.

SUNDAY 13 MAY
Anniversary Weekend, Day 3

The morning begins overcast, dank, drizzling. I arrive at 9:45, thirty minutes after boarding the shuttle. Security is the Gestapo. Employees are instructed to throw out their lunch.

I stuff the dried apricots I brought in a small plastic bag into my pants. Regn is forced to relinquish her apple, yogurt, and Flax seeds. Where's the sense in it! Her mood is edgy as a result, her disposition sulky for the entire day. I tell her later she should have stowed the snacks somewhere on herself or deep in her purse. For three hours staff mill about, chatting. We step outside by the mall to view President George W. Bush, on screen. He'll be speaking in the Fort shortly. Except for the heightened security, there's less to-do about his visiting than there was for the Queen.

Regn and I exchange words while we wait.

'I always wanted to fly a fighter plane, to be one of the Blue Angels.' Her voice is distinct while her thoughts wander in figure eights. 'I don't have a bad life, but—'

There is a mockingbird nearby; invisible. Regn knows her ornithology; identifying it by chirp alone. I hear a scrub jay. It sounds like newspaper ripping; muffled.

'If I was gone, you'd miss me.'

I feel it is a statement more than a question. I answer her anyway. 'Yes.' *And something more.*

~

We head for the festivities shortly after 7:00 p.m.

'Wait. Let me get your picture!' I take out my camera. The ladies scoot next to each other—Deborah, Sharon, Fernus, Tillie. Four sit on the cement highway divider. Regn humors me, stands on the far left side, a forced smile, protected behind her large sunglasses. The strap of her purse bag over the right shoulder. She wears a white cotton long-sleeved shirt and the navy slacks I think look good on her but am still too shy to compliment her about. *My Ladies of Jamestown.* I snap the picture. I wanted to be in the photograph with them. Somehow it seems befitting that I am behind the scenes—the one capturing the moment instead of being in it. The banner sits right behind them. Deborah with her pageboy haircut. Fernus' smooth brown skin melting with the glint of the sun. Tillie's hair, always a dither; she is the only one not looking into the camera, just like her. Sharon smiles full-heartedly. Regn's expression bears traces of impatience around the corners of her mouth. I put my camera away. Everyone's set to go.

'I'm not coming...' Regn stops.

'What?! Come on,' Fernus, Sharon, Deborah answer in unison.

'I'm tired; besides, there's nothing *there* I can eat.'

We all try to persuade her. The word that comes to mind is sulking. Not to mention starving. Everyone asks why she hadn't gotten her dinner earlier—during our designated break times. She's making excuses. Her attitude perturbs me.

As we stroll across the road Deborah says amongst her cohorts, 'She does everything to the extreme, she's dropped so much weight.'

'She gave me some of her clothes that don't fit her anymore,' adds Sharon.

'She told me she'd eaten too much today and felt fat,' I throw in—feeling the camaraderie. After all, Regn is being unreasonable. She's the one who's missing out.

I find it bizarre that she doesn't want to stay, see the finale. A once in a lifetime event. Her husband has attended none of the activities. Three nights and not a one. Regn is stubborn. I'd had dinner with Mother earlier in one of the classrooms in the Education Wing. Afterward, I'd stepped into the single person restroom for some quiet. The Group Arrival restrooms would be filthy with all the thoroughfare. I was conscious of the moment. Of time. Many thoughts crossed my mind. Regn had kept to herself all day. I'd found her at one point in the upstairs gallery. I tried to engage a light conversation. It was obvious other things were on her mind. I tried not to take it personally. I felt bad, guilty about Mother. Over dinner I'd been distracted by analyzing Regn. It had been that way for some months now. I'd become increasingly private, resentful of my mother. Underneath I resented circumstances; I resented myself.

Of course, all this did not formulate in my mind in that moment as I washed my hands in the restroom and flushed the latrine. It would be a gradual breaking-in, and a painful breaking away. I had yet to realize how much my mother depended on me emotionally and how I'd gone along, too wrapped up in the denial of my gender, to realize the future had arrived. Illusions must shatter one day, but when they shatter all at once and you have no one to fall back on, the ramification is death in many forms. I did not see that my youth was soon to end.

After dinner mother and I parted. She must have sensed I wanted to be with my colleagues. We shared too much together as it was, I needed something to myself.

After Regn up and left, the rest of us strolled across the road into the field with the stage. We watched the fireworks together.

~

The ladies buy a beer each. A shame Regn missed this, I think. They seal the time capsule. I don't pay much attention to what's going inside it. At the finale's end, wading through the crowd, Sharon holds onto the back of my shirt so she won't get separated in the mob. It is cold out. I shivered the two hours we spent on the field watching the screen.

Walking, I think again of my mother who is somewhere out there in the midst—I'd gone to look for her once the ladies were situated before the show. I couldn't find her. Maybe I hadn't wanted to—I'd made the pretense of looking only to alleviate any sense of guilt rather than with the intent of a successful result.

We ride the shuttle back together—the ladies and I. Thus the 400th Anniversary draws to a close. It seems I am the only one disheartened to see it end. Everyone else is saying how glad they are they won't have to answer any more questions about the 400th. The fear returns. What, in years to come, I will term "the generational squeeze." The fear that I will be left one day with just the memory of tonight; more importantly, the memory of them. I do not belong to my own age. And the age I love will die away.

———

"May Day." Awaiting the Queen as she walks up the pathway, having visited the three replica ships. Staff members at the Jamestown Settlement look on through chinks in the bulwarks of the Fort.

Hats and fanfare for the Queen.
(Photographs by Wheston Chancellor Grove)

Left to Right: President of the Jamestown-Yorktown Foundation (JYF), Philip Emerson; Queen Elizabeth II; Vice President of the United States, Dick Cheney. All entering the James Fort, Williamsburg, VA.

Queen Elizabeth II listening to one of the speakers. Sandra Day O'Connor, former Supreme Court Justice (back left), Dick Cheney, VP (front right). (Photographs by Wheston Chancellor Grove)

JYF President, Philip Emerson, escorts Queen Elizabeth II through camera crews.
(Photograph by Wheston Chancellor Grove)

Standing in the James Fort, a senator's wife looks on.

"Picnic on the Lawn." Main entrance. Tourists visiting Jamestown Settlement
in honor of Anniversary Weekend. May 9th-11th, 2007.
(Photographs by Wheston Chancellor Grove)

The dubious tower that tourists always ask about. Many claim it signifies the No. 1
for the first permanent English settlement in America.

Posterior view of Jamestown Settlement.
(Photographs by Wheston Chancellor Grove)

*The mezzanine as seen from inside, looking up from the lobby
atrium of Visitor Services.*

*Sunlight through the mezzanine windows; morning as seen
from the lobby of Visitor Services, Jamestown Settlement.
(Photographs by Wheston Chancellor Grove)*

The meadow where staff parked on May Day, the 4th.

Sunset as seen from The Colonial Parkway.
(Photographs by Wheston Chancellor Grove)

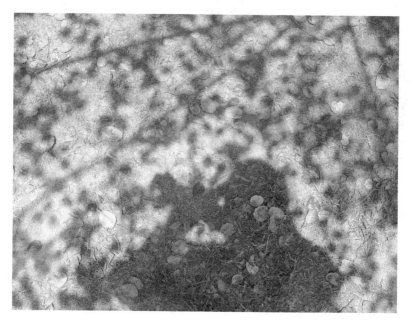

The grounds of Jamestown Settlement.

Westcott's childhood home in California.
(Photographs by Wheston Chancellor Grove)

JUNE

I fly out to California to visit my father. It is the first time in ten years since I've been back to the house where I grew up. My father has always visited us on the East Coast.

I meet my father's new wife—she exudes the genuine sweetness that comes from a patient heart.

My father says, 'Why, hello, mutton chops,' when we stop to get petrol. My sideburns are coming in—it will be a while before they connect into a beard. And when they do my sister tells me I look Amish. If anything I look Colonial which, living in a historical town relevant to the 18th century, makes such appearances ideal.

I take no offense to my father's statement. My father's had sideburns with a beard and mustache for as long as I can remember. I look at his leathered face—so tan from working out in the sun. His blue eyes, light ocean blue, not like mine, and his skin tone remind me of Kevin Costner. I don't see him that often so when I do I notice these things. They're always new to me.

• • •

The Victorian structure itself seems smaller; many things are in disrepair much as they had been when we left. More on this in a moment. The wisteria is gone from the front porch. A piece of wood is missing from the steps. The patches of green on either side of the hedges are now synthetic grass. It doesn't look like an impostor—not like that hideous cheap AstroTurf they use in mini golf. No, this grass looks and even *feels* real; this grass doesn't yellow if you are lazy enough or not vigilant in monitoring where your dog goes. But somehow, knowing that it isn't real, dissatisfies me.

The front door is the same. It's beautiful solid wood, not that styrofoam plastic synthetic material. And it has the stained-glass oval inlay with the family name's last initial: R.

• • •

In the foyer a familiar scent hits me—it is cool. Antiquated. Still. The small table where mother always laid holiday decorations now displays the same tiny lamp with its peach Victorian shade and tassels—it is turned on—warming a collection of seashells. The shells are nice but do not lend to the furnishings or adornments typical of a traditional Victorian. My father says he's left the lamp on ever since we left—similar to the JFK memorial and the burning torch. He always keeps it lit. I don't know what to make of this.

The same banister and dark green carpet grace the stairs. The pocket doors on the right—closed—lead into the living room. A beautiful ceiling covered in real green and gold leaves then lacquered over by my mother and father when they first purchased the Victorian and began restoring it. Wooden floors. 10-ft ceilings. The alcove in the corner, attached to the second story turret where the Christmas tree stood, where Ellis and I played Chinese checkers. Where I studied the squares of the chessboard, wanting to learn the mysteries of the game.

Moving through the foyer an 11x14 panel catches my eye.

'Hey, I remember that—the alarm keypad's hidden behind it.'

'What is there?' Kim asks.

My father never told his new wife that the home's alarm system, which no longer works, is hidden behind the panel. A beautiful copper plate depicting a Victorian home etched in black, mounted on black velvet and framed in a wooden white square, betrays no evidence of concealing push buttons behind it. I look up.

Not many hallways have peach ceilings and wooden lattice work. These are remnants of how the Victorian was. In a moment it will be a jolt to the system when my father opens the white wooden door leading into the TV room. By itself the TV room is stylish, a nice den motif—yellow walls sponged with marigold, black leather furniture and a fake palm tree! The décor itself is nice but in this context I must hide my disbelief. It is anything but appropriate for the style of house. I want to remember it as it was. The bathroom door across the room has no doorknob and hasn't apparently for several years. Kim doesn't seem to mind though, or if she does, she's given up mentioning it. We walk into the bathroom, all of us—the memories flooding me. My father asks, 'Now, I bet you don't remember where the light switch is in here?' But I do. It's in the wooden cabinet that used to house all of mother's ointments for her skin and her curler pins. I want to step closer, see if the familiar scent is still there. Instead, I flip open the dark wooden door—it is very narrow—maybe 10 inches. Out of sight, tucked in the corner, without a cover plate is the light switch. I flip it on. My father smiles at Kim as if to say, *Well, I'll be damned!*

I look at the backside or rather the inside of the bathroom door. The pewter emblem I always liked to look at, a silhouette of a person—obviously a woman with her hair rolled up, a slight rise on her breast and a singular leg protruding upward from a tub in preparation for scrubbing—is no longer there. It was something from the 1920s or even before, so why would he take that off? I ask, 'What happened to the lady in the tub, pointing?'

Back in the TV room I see the armoire that used to sit in the corner—where I climbed in to hide—is no longer there. Father says he moved it upstairs. I remember the top of it fell and hit me on the head when I was young. I was afraid to tell Mother. Anytime we were hurt she got upset. I didn't know she was just scared and not angry.

We step into the dining room through the open, doorless jamb. It is one of the few rooms relatively untouched. The glass panel over the non-functional blue tiled fireplace. The silver wallpaper, its ornate design. The two twin arched alcoves now house modern picture frames of family. The table is the same, so is the carpet. It all looks doll-like—especially the table. The chairs used to be so heavy to move, they seemed so sturdy. Now they appear rickety, worn, frail. The table has faded from the sunlight streaming in; its center is a solid rectangle of glass, divided with iron tracers into small rectangular patterns. To the right another set of pocket doors leading into the living room is also closed. The chandelier is the same. And it is dusty.

Just off the dining room lays the kitchen. My own mother filled this kitchen. All the aromas of her cooking—sautéed mushrooms, her famous chicken, broccoli, and cheese casserole. All the holiday and large family get-togethers. All gone. The linoleum has been replaced. But the small square tiles all around the sink and countertop still remain. The old windows throughout the house are from my time, my childhood—they seem real—like true glass—not the new age safety windows that are impossible to break and feel almost dulled like plastic. The small wooden garbage bin that swung open like a wedge from the side—when I was very small I used to climb behind it and hide—is still there.

The old corkboard pantry, wallpapered blue, is gone. But the gas stove remains and above it the little ceramic clock with the pig in spectacles and chef's cap and a wooden spoon. It has been hanging there for at least 23 years. The old stove is an original still going strong. They don't make anything to last anymore. I look at the tin-foiled burners. The smell of silver polish comes back and a tinge of cigarette smoke. Arlene. Arlene was an Indian—a true Native American. She'd been our housekeeper when we were little. I remember coming home from school and seeing, or rather smelling the newly vacuumed stairs—we had one of the blue Kirby's—another machine built to last. Solid to lug around. Arlene used to wrap aluminum foil around the dirty burner plates every once in a while when smoke, grease, and general use found them needing a change. I remember her blue glass ashtray, left here and there for her cigarettes. I wonder now what she thought of us—me and Ellis. Did she think we were spoiled? Did she think my mother was nice? Did she like us? I liked her.

The neighborhood kids, those next door and directly across the street, were not allowed in our house. We could play in the driveway or in the tree-house in the backyard father had built. Sometimes they'd ask if they could come in. I don't know the reason Ellis and I gave, but there was a clear division. The neighborhood was hit and miss—one of, if not *the*, longest streets in the city. Our house was built in 1888, originally surrounded by farmland. Other homes had cropped up around it. It was a jewel in the midst of the unsavory. When the little old lady who always wore a plaid shirt and wool pants—Emily—when she passed away next door and her relatives took over the place, the yard was left to rot. Her son was a talented graphic artist, but he also had the misfortune of being a drug addict. On the other side squatted the tiny blue house—one story. They had two young husky boys—one with a serious heart condition who always breathed asthmatically. They were Spanish. Across the street was a Mexican family. They had a sofa on the front porch and it always seemed lots of people were coming and going. We played many fun games. But we never went into their house and they never came inside ours. There were other vintage homes on the block, with all sorts of interesting inhabitants. Sometimes I imagined who lived in them.

Our home had a white wrought iron fence and hip-high gate. I balanced atop the entire inch-wide fence from one side to the other, even along the gate portion that wobbled hysterically. We were contained. We were the kids who lived in the mansion. We were the kids who wore uniforms and went to private schools. As children we did not ask for many "things." We were not spoiled so much as we were unprepared. We'd been raised in a fairytale of illusions—literally. A miniature castle. Arguments seeped in, tension was in the air. We always turned to Mother instead of Father. I trusted my mother, believing unconsciously that she was planning for the future instead of doing the best she could. She was always holding on. I didn't know my father, not really. It was always us against him. It shouldn't have been. But *he* wasn't present. I had no male figureheads in my life. Had I been closer to my father would I have realized the truth sooner? At 10 years old or even 12, you don't think about how you're going to feel at 25. If you're anything like me, you might have thought about what you were going to do on the weekend, what would be for dinner that night, could you maybe invite a friend over? I missed not seeing any love between my mother and father. It had been there once, but it takes two for a marriage to sink. The captain at the wheel and the deckhand on the bow just feeling the wind, watching but not communicating. One searched the horizon; the other clung to the wheel.

• • •

The back deck is no longer—it has been torn up and replaced with Tuscan terra cotta steps. By themselves they are nice but the style clashes with the Victorian aspect. I sleep in the downstairs room of the cottage. When I was five this room had been turned into a public daycare which my mother ran. Later it became a rec room where Ellis and I played Atari or watched Mario and Luigi risk their lives. Innocent, fun games.

I awake to a gray damp morning. The air is damp despite there being no rain. It is quite early—about seven—I am still on Eastern time—it feels like 10 o'clock. I am careful to be quiet. I want this time alone. I look at the backyard, the garden. The enclosed spa that no longer works. The pagoda enclosure mildewing. And in the corner, surrounded by the ivy lined fence—our fig tree. I remember this tree from earliest age. An amazing specimen to climb. All the knots and gnarls. A handlebar to swing from, a seat to perch upon comes right over the little sidewalk bordering the garden. I always liked looking at the air balloon shaped figs. The way the light plays through the transparent leaves. The white sticky glue—the sap of the figs. Beneath this tree my father laid to rest most of the family pets. I never thought of it as a cemetery—to me it appears as a clue or symbol. I imagine that stepping beyond this tree—climbing through it to the fence beyond, there will be a passageway through the ivy.

I do not envision any 'secret garden' on the other side, but a porthole to another plane, another state *of being*. And the fig tree—this fig tree—long steeped in ancient lore and tradition, has been my playmate from earliest of years. The swing that hung from its branches and a wooden bar coming down to hold me in—the things we left in the pooled armpits—cavities in the tree where rainwater had accumulated and snail tracks remained amidst cobwebs. The grayness of its bark, its stout, squat presence and climbability. You can step into it and then pull yourself up. How it danced during the Great Earthquake of '89. The doughboy pool slammed its contents against the cottage where I'd been playing. And the tree swung across the yard.

Mother had come onto the deck, through the *glass* sunroom, a spatula in hand—in the middle of fixing dinner, trying to get to me. She was pregnant at the time. She miscarried.

I often wonder how things would have been had I been the middle child instead of the second?

• • •

I walk around the house taking pictures—it's no time before I have a hundred. So much has changed and yet—the past is all there. Some improvements have been made, but like I said, they stick out—there is no uniformity. A giant red British telephone booth—iron—the real deal—stands between the doors to the cottage and garage. Where once the sunflowers grew. One was photographed and put in the *San Jose Mercury*. It grew to 15 feet! It doesn't feel like home—my home anyway. My mother had made it our home.

• • •

While in California we go to Costco. I find a book on the sale pile. *Evening* by Susan Minot. I will read it on my flight back.

Though it's been many years since I viewed those pages, I remember Harris Arden and the scene where the woman—funny, I don't recall her name—I'd have to look it up—is standing by the table with the checkered picnic cloth, digging her nails in—knowing life will never again be the same. The parting of lives.

Harris Arden's "root" had been hard and unfolded. My root will never be hard. I will never feel what it is to lie inside Regn completely and be still. My sole erection is of the heart.

 SHE TOLD ME HER GRANDDAUGHTER, Rebecca, who was seven at the time, had left for Florida where she'd be living for the next two years.

• • •

'It's really going to be hard on her *and* me,' Regn says.

Here is a big void that needs filling. If I could have but known or seen how vulnerable we each were, yet how pure and decent our intentions, our needs—

Late in the afternoon with a moment to spare Regn says, 'I got your letter. I told you.'

I'd given her another letter.

I feel sick, *not those words, please.* A customer interrupts. The lady approaches the counter. I seek her out.

'Yes, can I help you?'

'I want to speak to *her*,' she says, indicating Regn.

She needs *a product.* Regn comes over to the drawer beside me. The till is in the top drawer, office staple supplies in the middle, the third one houses specific items and unmentionables.

Regn retrieves a tampon tucked in the back. She waves the lady around the corner, discreetly stuffs it in her purse.

Housecleaning prefers we hand out such necessary items upon request. I don't see the logic in this. I tell Regn about the time I'd been looking under the counter with our hunched over volunteer in the Rotunda. He's hunched over because he's ancient. He breaks wind all the time, silently, and falls asleep in the chair. The customer said, 'Are those them?' I was a young man in her eyes. There was a box of candles that happened to resemble the size and height of a Tampax box. As I recount this experience I know my face is red. I feel the blood. Regn laughs.

'So you can light your flame! There should be a sign in the restroom on the machine that says: *Please see attendant.* I'll have to check if it's still there. I'm not sure if you've seen it—' Regn laughs again realizing what she has said.

'And how many times do *I* go in the lady's restroom?'

'Yes, I know. I just feel natural talking to you. It happens.'

I like that she can joke with me about these things. *But*, she still doesn't know.

The conversation takes a turn. 'You're stubborn for not believing me, Westcott! Don't take it the wrong way. You're special because I consider you one of the true artists.'

'Thanks.'

'About your letter—'

The issue I *most* wanted to discuss. My stomach clenches.

I remembered the afternoon a few weeks earlier—I'd been counting out my drawer telling myself, *Say it, say it. Now.* The more I wanted to, the longer I hesitated. I knew the opportunity would pass. Someone would come up to the desk.

'Can I ask you something?'

'Yes. You don't have to ask.'

'Would you ever join me in going to a movie or something? I mean friend-to-friend.' I'd looked away, fumbled with the coins in my drawer.

'Oh, *V*hestcott. You're a nice young man. I'm just old fashioned. There are things you can do as a group, but just you and I, it's different. Count your drawer,' she'd said kindly.

I'd dropped a quarter on the floor. It had taken the strength out of me to ask.

~

We're at that point again.

Old fashioned. Maybe that is why I'm drawn to you. I do not tell her this.

'I'm a very busy woman.'

'Don't you trust me—' It is intended as a statement, rhetorical.

'Oh, *V*hestcott.' Her beautiful language transforms my name. I love to hear the effects of her accent. 'I'll find the time for us to take a walk sometime.'

'That's *all* I'm asking.'

It would be many months before we took that walk. For the moment receiving a 'yes' was enough. *I've got the golden ticket*—my heart was lighter. Like Charlie Bucket who finds the silver piece under the grate and goes into the shop. A gift, a splendid treat. He does not go in with the hopes of winning the ticket, but merely to enjoy the pleasure of tasting and savoring the chocolate—what others take for granted.

I'd waited for those last ten minutes all day—a moment of privacy stolen. Alone with Regn.

Even the air conditioning unit sounds brighter, somehow more cheerful when I pull into my driveway. I hear the sound of summer in it, not the drone of despair. I look forward to our walk.

• • •

Westcott finds a "planted" twenty dollar bill under his mouse pad. He tells Regn, asks if anyone had been short on that register the previous night.

He's exceedingly thirsty, has a headache.

'You need to take care of yourself, Westcott.'

'I do.'

'Here.' She hands him the orange juice she bought from the café with a straw. 'I got it for you.'

'Perfect. How did you know? I always get a straw. I try to drink juice with a straw to minimize the acid on my teeth. Thank you. I'll buy us a cookie next time.'

'Don't worry about it.'

He reports the twenty dollars to Eva and turns it in. It has been a set-up, he's sure, by the Sups. Eva agrees. Westcott is insulted. An employee was let go last Christmas. He'd been doing what Westcott always knew was possible. He was a law student just working summers and winter break. *Apparently* ringing up false returns and pocketing the cash. What a shame to make the stereotype true. No such thing as an honest lawyer! But, was it true? Westcott believed it was. Eva had tested him once when he first came on board. He'd gone to the window for change with a 100 dollar bill. Eva pretended like she didn't know she left the bill inside the pouch with the 10s and 20s she gave him. Westcott came right back. It had been different with Eva. More direct. Not some random 20 left waiting at his assigned station. With Eva, Westcott knew. The Sups were passive.

That evening Westcott watches *The Village* starring Adrien Brodie. Regn recommended it a while back. He is struck by a certain line in the movie:
'He has feelings for you.'
– How do you know?
'He never touches you.'

I can never initiate contact with Regn. She is free to do so—as a lady she has the control. It would not be proper for me to put a hand on her—though I long to tap her on the shoulder.

• • •

In reciprocation of the two films Regn loaned me, *The Quiet Man* and *Madame Butterfly*, I had given her *A Tree Grows In Brooklyn*, which I find endearing. Regn had this to say about it:
'I didn't like it. The ending. And their father was always poor and a mess, then just died leaving them problems. Why did the mother need a man to be all right—it was like she couldn't go on and survive without one. She should have been able to stand on her own. But when the man comes in at the end—as though he's their savior—it wasn't my thing. I'm sorry, Westcott. I know you like it.'
'We're equal then because you know I don't like how the woman in *Madame Butterfly* kills herself over that louse. I find the opera exhausting. How can you enjoy it? The idea is the same—she can't live without him and he's taken her child. So she kills herself? That doesn't bother you, but *A Tree Grows in Brooklyn* does?'
I would later find Regn's reaction to the film to be another clear example of her self-resentment.

• • •

Friday, 29ᵗʰ of June 20

Regn is floater for the day, in charge and on the late shift. Walking by, she slips a Dove chocolate into my right shirt pocket.
I am sprinting down the Great Hall. Shaking the morning dew from my bones. Relieving the frustration that will leave me wanting to explode if I don't act out somehow, some way, physically. After the *inane* morning meeting down in the maintenance building—where I bring the Group list for the day—I open the Rotunda. It's the only time I can run through the museum without causing a stir from onlookers or security. I used to love running in younger days and playing soccer.
I pass the morning hours drawing sketches of my colleagues beside their names on

the daily schedule. I make a list from memory of all the state capitals in the U.S. I love maps and geography. At home I look at the globe, examining names of mountains, seas, the parts of each continent. At work I have a folding map. I take in the flags and location of obscure countries. I scroll German phrases and practice writing the date, my name, and short sentences with my left hand. *Heute ist Mittwoch.* Today is Wednesday. As a child I started writing with both hands so that now I am a bit ambidextrous. I open all bottles and mail with my non-dominant hand. It's good for the mind to use both sides of the brain. My colleagues enjoy the sketches, but wonder why I always draw myself so seriously. The renderings bear strong likeness to everyone. Regn is always smiling; the focal point being her eyes. I always wear a tie. Sharon is depicted with her glasses.

During the last fifteen minutes of my lunch Regn comes in from the breezeway to find me on the stairwell, sitting with a book on my knees.

Later I am asked to get change. Regn is on her lunch in the office. I stagger a moment. I hadn't slept well the night before because of my stomach.

'You should go to the doctor.'

'They might find my unborn twin, or—!' The organs that never dropped I want to say.

'Maybe there's something they can give you for it.'

'I don't need to pay *them* to tell me I have a nervous stomach—I know that—I'm always nervous.'

'There's no reason to be. Why are you always so nervous?'

I smile. She understands.

'What am I going to do with you, Westcott?'

'Shoot me.'

'What would I do without you? I need you.'

Her words cheer me.

Regn wears an African grass necklace purchased in the gift shop. It is red and marigold. She has on a white blouse with elbow length sleeves and loose burgundy pants that cut off at the bare ankle. Her shoes are black, heel-less slip-ons. Closing register 8, I join her on the desk at the end of the day. *Regn's Sumptuous Delirium.* We are joking that her necklace is made of grass—marijuana—and that she is high from it being around her neck.

She gives me a yellow boat or a tricorn hat—whichever way you prefer to look at it— she'd folded from paper. Her only testament to origami. It's one of several things she taught me that I've never forgotten. She places her hands on my shoulders as I sit in the chair. I feel her hand, then her fingers, squeezing my shoulder. 'Oh *V*hestcott.' Her voice is quiet.

Those two words are enough.

I WAS GOING for the excellent dinner, the socializing of colleagues. I'd told Regn I was going to go. She never went to any company events. She'd worked four, five years longer than I, and never had the desire to attend. Her children were grown; what else did she have to do? Why not try it at least once? It was Thursday. My favorite day of the week. Since high school I'd never cared for weekends. Most of the week was over; just one day left. It always felt like a place of safe holding. Thursday.

It was June the 21st. Parson was supposed to pick me up. He was running late. I wanted to arrive a few minutes early. I'd planned to save a seat for Regn. If she and I didn't sit next to each other the evening would be for naught. I called Parson to let him know I was getting another ride. Mother drove me. I am stringent when it comes to being punctual. Regn always zoomed in at the last minute, I would learn. It drove me crazy. Why I didn't just drive my truck that evening I do not remember. It was a good thing I hadn't. A great thing.

~

The ceremony rolls by, dinner is delicious—salmon, potatoes, asparagus. And dessert. Regn has the vegetarian dish. It's only within the last year that she's turned vegetarian. It annoys me, in time. She is fanatical. She won't eat anything if it's had contact with meat or been cooked in chicken stock. I could understand it if she'd been a vegetarian her whole life, but all of a sudden, and then to the extreme? Long after we'd become close I posed a hypothetical question, in good humor. A ridiculous scenario. 'If someone said they'd give you a million dollars to eat a cheeseburger, would you?' Regn was annoyed, wouldn't answer. I thought it absurd. Why couldn't she answer the question? Her children would benefit from the money. And I knew she could use it as well. She didn't like being cornered. But I wasn't cornering her. It was just a simple question. When Regn made up her mind about something, that was it. There was no penetrating. It wasn't determination. It was sheer stubbornness. Her stubbornness would do great harm.

That night I was not looking for her flaws.

~

Tillie received an award for 7 years of service, maybe 10. I looked at Regn, casually. I wanted to catch every detail.

This window of time is a gift. No interruptions from customers. I am free to simply enjoy her presence. She is seated to my right and behind me when we all turn from the round table to face the speaker. I'm glad when the ceremony is over. Jill has her camera. She takes pictures of the staff. Tillie with her award. Parson and myself. The first picture of Regn and me. To a stranger flipping through an album we look like mother and son, where age is concerned. When *I* study the same picture from so long ago I see only the woman I loved and who, in that moment, was becoming *more* fond of me.

I asked Parson—Regn happened to be in earshot—if he'd give me a ride home.

Walking into the lobby, Parson has to use the restroom. I'm grateful. I wait, silently hoping Regn will walk out, see me and we can share a few words. How long will Parson be—long enough—just a moment more—that's all I want. And there she is. She comes towards me.

'I'm waiting for Parson. He said he'd drive me home.'

'I'd take you.' She uses the past present tense.

Parson returns. 'You don't mind,' I say, 'Regn'll take me.' And off I go.

It's all I wanted of the evening—time with her—and here we would be alone. I'd secretly hoped for such an opportunity; I didn't want to give it up. Parson and I could get together any old time. If I felt guilty for standing him up twice that evening I didn't let it spoil the brief time I was going to share with Regn. I could make it up to Parson. I would.

~

I was too nervous—on a high—to look at her, study her clothes. We walked into the cool night air along the sidewalk. The presentation hall had been sweltering with body heat and no air conditioning.

'I have to stay five more years in order to collect my retirement. When I get up for my award I'll walk like an old woman with a cane.'

I want to tell her, *I'll walk you.*

Regn forgot where she'd parked. Then I saw the silver bug, gleaming beneath a street-light. I open the door gently. Conscious of stepping into her car. The interior is cloaked in her scent; light, warm, mild, and clean. I've never been inside a Volkswagen. I've never been inside *Regn's* Volkswagen. I've always liked them—especially the originals with their chrome—the newer models are slightly larger even in width. I am amazed at how wide the black dashboard is—I'd never seen a dashboard stretch out so far in front of the steering wheel. I can't get used to it. When she turns the ignition over the James Blunt cd I'd given her is playing. It makes me happy to know she's been listening to it. "You're beautiful," comes on. Neither of us seems self-conscious—the music is turned low. Out of the parking lot we find our way.

'I have to go across, right?'

'Yes, unless you want to go into oncoming traffic.'

'Maybe you shouldn't have gone with me. Rebecca always tells me, "Oma, now you do this." '

A couple months ago Regn had loaned me her McKennitt cd in reciprocation of my offering music to her. I'd watched as she leaned into her car. I could have opened the passenger door, leaned in and simply received it from her hand. I was hesitant to overstep, to lay even a hand on her car, to be so forward as to open the door. So I waited for her to step back out and walk over to me. Sliding the disc into my console that afternoon I was conscious of having an extension of Regn come inside my own private world.

~

We catch many red lights. I am beaming. We speak lightheartedly. Regn wants to keep the conversation going. As do I. For separate reasons. She tells me about a book a nurse read to her when she was sick in the hospital as a kid. She had the mumps when she was twelve "with big cheeks"—she adds for emphasis, bloating them like a puffer fish. Since that story she's always wanted to own a Volkswagen.

'Twelve. God am I old. That was so long ago.'

The story was about a family who drove all over Europe in a Volkswagen beetle. We mention the awards—casual exchange of words, staving off awkwardness. I am more talk-ative than usual. Here she is. My hands are cold. I try not to look at her too much, or turn my head, for fear she might detect my gaze studying her. The headlights in the rearview mirror make her a white-masked raccoon. She says she doesn't always see well at night.

'Third one. On the left.'

'This is your house?'

'Uh-hm. I'm glad we live on a cul-de-sac.'

'It's nice.'

'Thank you.'

The slightest of hesitations. Does she want me to hug her politely? Shaking her hand would be ridiculous. Too formal. I do not know, cannot know at that moment, but if I just reached across and hugged her, she'd think nothing of it. I don't know how.

My pants squeak sharply along the black leather when I go to get out of her car. Unbuckling the belt I inadvertently let it go—it snaps back, hitting the side panel. I apologize, shyly, knowing how particular Regn is about the maintenance of her beloved bug—that's the reason she parks so far away from everyone else in the lot—she doesn't want a ding, scratch, or dent on it. I thank her, bid her good night, at least I think I did. I know for sure I thanked her—I was in a state of euphoria.

Regn lightly hits my arm with the back of her hand. Contact.

'See you *to-mah-row.*'

I'M COUNTING MY DRAWER when Regn comes into the office. I hear her before she enters. I listen for her. The sound of the keypad, the sound of three doors. I saw her pull up on my way in. The anticipation is what I love. The details. The security of knowing she's arrived and will be here for the day. Even if we don't have the leisure of time, we have *time*. It is the unspoken acknowledgments to self. The constant checking and watching for expressions, inflections in the voice, mannerisms. It is a gradual advance. The more we are restrained, the stronger it grows. It is innocence and age that allows the affection to mature, naturally, as it should. Something inside stirs, the heart itself is attracted, much before the body responds. Knowing Regn looks forward to seeing me as much as I do her makes me happy.

'Good morning,' she says, touching her hand to my left lower hip. I don't mind. 'I missed you Monday.'

Our break went fast. Before leaving, without my ever asking or hinting—'We'll make time to take a walk.' The reiteration of her previous statement secures my hope.

'What's the book you have?'

I'd been strolling the aisles at the library not coming upon anything intriguing when there it was—just like that, waiting. If it had jumped off the shelf or mysteriously fallen, I'd have been no less surprised. It was hardbound, gray, a thick novel.

I hand it to her across our wooden slatted hexagonal table. *Green Darkness* by Anya Seton.

'It's intriguing. About these characters who are reincarnated and meet in another life in different roles. I like the time frame and setting.'

'There's a reason we met. Maybe I'm meant to draw something out of you—' she pauses. 'Something good.'

Regn listens to my tape recorder and the piece on the piano I'd written. I watch the wind swaying through the trees outside our window on the balcony.

'So, you're a composer as well, Westcott.'

'I don't know about that.'

The other night I had a dream about Regn. Something was distressing her and so I instinctively put my hand on her shoulder to comfort. We immediately became alerted by my first and *only* move to touch her. In the dream Regn recoiled, not so much physically, but in her expression. I moved to explain. Even in the dream feeling my hand on her shoulder and the strap beneath the shirt and blazer, I loved the feeling that we were close to each other, the feeling of safety it generated, and the want to stay close to her.

Late in the afternoon, I drive to the Island, go into the Visitor's Center. With the protection of my sunglasses I walk to the church, sit a while. It is so still.

The heat is close, humid, but the church is inviting, rustic in its redolence. I stay a bit, inhaling the scent of cold bricks, well-worn benches. I wonder what I'll feel 30 years from now. Will I remember this day? This summer? The memory of passion at its finest? I wish Regn would sit beside me. Before venturing outside to the river's edge I deposit a quarter into the donations box.

Benches have been placed for scenic viewing beneath the foliage. I choose one on the far left. The wind off the James is loud and cooling. I watch two ferries pass each other coming and going. The light flickers through the giant trees, a dusty haze streaming the clouds over the river. I'd brought the large grey hardbound volume with me. I pick up a toothpick-sized twig, tracing Regn's and my name in the dusty earth. I think, years from now, if I am still around, I will come to this place and think of *you*. How young. How foolish. How innocent. How true. Much as I hate to admit, and cannot at that moment, I *am* young. Forgive me.

• • •

I was the last to leave of the early crew. Regn was alone at the desk. I lingered before we said our customary farewells. She waved with that sad look. She had the crazy topper on her pen—the one with the purple spiked hair and the beak—the bird that almost looks like the road-runner. Its expression and nose reminded me of Regn. *Scatterbird.* I had a matching one with blue hair. I'd brought them back with me from California—funny trinkets I'd won at dinner one night. The other afternoon she'd left the pen at her station. When she returned it was gone. I saw her dismayed and worried as she actively looked for something—the some-thing I of course knew. I was disheartened to consider that maybe a customer had walked off with it. She said nothing as she shifted papers, distressed lest it be gone forever. I looked on the counter. The beak of the purple haired creature hooked the main desk sign. 'Regn, it's right there.' It was the first I'd spoken in her moment of fluster. 'Where?!'

I pointed. I wanted her to know I knew what she was thinking. I was glad she should care so much for a token of fondness, that she troubled herself never to misplace it, some-thing as small as a pen topper. Even then I knew it wasn't the object. It was that I had given it to her.

JULY

I hadn't expected it. An entire day of waiting. Regn studied my bumper sticker. 'Treehugging Dirt Worshiper,' she read aloud. 'I've had that since I've worked here—you never noticed? Gosh—your observations!' It's the only time I'll permit the use of the term 'worship.' I hate that word in the traditional context. Honor, hold reverence, kneel down, pay homage to—such expressions are perfectly acceptable, honorable. But worship?—It sounds so groveling, supplicating, prostrate. I *worship* nothing.

My truck was pulled in the opposite direction; the driver's side faced the main road opposite cameras mounted high on the brick edifice. 'Let me give you a hug,' she said advancing, putting her arms around me. My right hand was encumbered with book and lunch bag, my left touched her back. I wanted to press us together. It was abrupt on my part, I wanted to hug her, linger, her chin hit my shoulder. We wished each other a good time—she with her granddaughter and I with Ellis who is visiting. So often have I longed to embrace her again, and yet out of the blue—I was taken off guard. Always I restrain myself. To love and long in quiet is a heavy throb that does not cease. This morning after I'd pulled in, I saw Regn arrive. I'd gotten out of my truck and headed toward the gate so Regn wouldn't think I'd been waiting for her. I knew she followed. I heard her call my name softly. '*V*essst-cott!' I turned and did not move.

• • •

Fernus said to Eva, 'He looks like a professor.'

Regn told me several times how much she liked my haircut. 'It's very nice, your sister did a good job.' I brought in a gift bag full of L'Oréal sample products Ellis received at one of the plants she toured. The ladies quickly devoured them. Interspersed were a few men's hair rinses and creams. Regn took the white sunglasses and Ellis' long navy blue blazer.

I was strolling out from the office to the lobby with my new shoes and matching briefcase. I'd found both when Ellis and I went shopping. A haircut, shoes, and briefcase—it was a rare splurge. I love my shoes! The shiny leather is rich, the front squared and the heel elevated giving me an inch and a half more height. For some reason they remind me of a den designed in African motif. There is a slight marbleizing swirl of black dusting over the rich mahogany hue. They are Bass and were on sale for 55.00. I didn't have a pair of dress shoes.

And my satchel—what a find. A clasp was missing and it was placed in a clearance bin for only 45.00. Brand new they usually run $180.00 and up. Besides, this one has character in being slightly worn. Parson loves it. I didn't want something pristine. I like the natural give already showing in the dark brown leather.

189

~

I still have the satchel even to this day. I've been considering to whom I should leave it.

• • •

I wish I could go back to that afternoon in February when *we* walked together down to the pier and collected the ship's money. I liked her then, but this is something more.

I can't imagine a time when she didn't fill my mind. A time when I didn't make a copy of the master schedule to see when she'd be in. A time when I just came to work when I was supposed to, not earlier—five, ten minutes, it didn't matter who was in, I just showed up. A time when I ate lunch alone. How did I make it all those months—there she was.

I imagine kissing her and venture to fantasize over the bedroom. I'd be content *just* to lay with her, feel her next to me, lie on her, but not do anything. To put my hands on her chest. Her makeup case was on the counter the other day. She and Sharon always leave their cases in the cubby or by their drawers. Her white handkerchief with the green lace around the border peeked out. Sometimes it has pink fringe, on a rare occasion lavender or peach. I appreciate that she still uses handkerchiefs. I stared at the little blue case. Admiring it, loving it because it is hers. I wonder if she ever thinks of me in a romantic manner, though she dare not entertain the thought long.

• • •

Regn gave me her log-in password/access code to do returns. We used to be able to do them on our own without a classified's pass code. It is a nuisance when we're busy and need to do a return and the Sups aren't around or the classifieds are tied up with customers of their own. We never had a problem before. Since they came—the 3 Sups— new "counterproductive" procedures have been installed—returns being one of them. *It's being circumvented. I can do returns anytime now.* The insult of it all—it is a safety feature—obviously they don't trust the individual staff. Before it was possible to ring up a sale, not fulfill (apply) it in the system and simply pocket the money, reprint a previous ticket and void the sale on the screen without ever performing a return.

• • •

Sent: Sunday, July 1 3:51 PM
To: <regn.tompkins@jyf.virginia.gov>
Subject: Regarding Friedrich!!!!

Regn,

You know the chocolate I keep in my shirt pocket—I go to eat it and what do I discover, an ailing squeal coming from Friedrich.

Turns out he took the liberty of indulging on a chocolate high! You can't blame the fella for feeling sick—the delectable confections are bigger than he is, so I mean where can he put it? I guess that's why he's a PIG.

He's keeled over and I'm out my pick-me-up! You must talk to him. He speaks bilingually, but he only listens if it's in German!

It's such a paradox. You always hear of the older generation longing to be young again. But O' to be young and wish to be old. When your life seems like a sentence you envision a release. I guess we can never look too closely at life, else everything will crack and you will find yourself saying, 'What's the point in anything?'

I've often said to myself I wish I were ending up here rather than just starting out (in terms of age). I know that must be unbelievably hard to accept, but how long can a person linger? I try to live for the present, but the present always becomes the future.

Would you believe Friedrich is taking on a brownish hue--the amount of chocolate he consumed is seeping through his skin. You've heard of someone's face turning orange from eating a few too many carrots--well, Friedrich has *not* been carousing in the mud!

Later Mate,

Mr. Westcott

I find this piece quite poignant.

"I walked a mile with Pleasure
She chatted all the way—
But left me none the wiser
For all she had to say.

I walked a mile with Sorrow;
And ne'er a word said she—
But, oh! The things I learned from her,
When Sorrow walked with me."

— Robert Browning Hamilton (1812-1889)

• • •

I haven't mentioned Molly before. She came after Parson, was it in late winter, early spring that she joined our crew? Well, anyway, Molly's here just for the summer. She brought her family to tour the site. We—Regn, myself, and Molly were standing around the main desk.

'My mother thought you were cute as pie yesterday. She said I should seek you out more,' Molly is honest.

'Oh, well—'

'That was nice of her.' Regn filled in the space.

After Molly slipped away from the desk Regn turned to me. 'Maybe you *should* ask her out? She seems to like you.'

'She has a boyfriend.' It is true. But from what Molly indicated in casual chatter, he isn't ideal.

'She's cute. She has a Victorian voluptuousness about her,' Regn observed.

'She's nice. But not my type.'

'And what *is* your type, Westcott?'

I thought about her for a moment. Molly. *Mop? Jackie Moss' Siberian Husky. Sounds like Mall. I don't like malls.* Even her name did nothing for me. I brought her image to mind. I could never feel thronging desire for her or any 'Molly.' She was nice, yes, she had brown hair and brown eyes, but her skin, her form was so young. That elusive quality was not present. No sorrows lay behind her gaze. Her skin did not beckon me—I looked to Regn briefly. Inside every fiber of me yearned.

I studied the veins in her tanned hands and looked at her toned arms. She had on a double string of pearls. Her breastbone revealed a farmer's tan as her square cut blouse framed it. Regn possessed a quality that intimated a bygone era. In style she was a woman in every sense of the word. I'd been ripped away from my previous life. She was a link to that era of womanly grace and silenced grit—post WWII. And that is where I belonged.

I walked out alone.

• • •

Entering the office she hugs me from behind, pressing her cheek to my shoulder. 'How was your weekend?' she inquires.

She is in charge—the Lead classified for the day. We are both on the late shift (9-6).

'The postman came—you have mail.' I hand her my letter. She shows me a dress in a magazine she is thinking of buying; she plans on going to the store this evening.

'They're open 'til nine. Do you like it, what do you think?'

I am glad she values and wants my opinion.

Regn stays in the back all afternoon. She makes the schedule for tomorrow, putting herself on # 4 and me at # 10. 'Why do that to yourself?' I ask. Secretly I know. She'd gone out of her way to ensure we'd have lunch together the next day, sparing me the crowds of # 4 by placing herself at that center location.

• • •

'Gosh, Westcott! You're so thin,' Magda declares. 'You've lost so much weight since I've been here. You were never heavy, but now you've lost even more weight.'

• • •

'How do I take your essence? It would be a bad thing if I did. I don't want to do that.'

'There's a couple of truths. I don't know *which* would be easier to say,' I pondered.

'Don't I make you smile?'

'Yes.' Long pause. 'You cause me much grief.'

'I do, why? You'll have to explain yourself.'

'I don't say that to hurt you.'

'But it does. Can't I help you?'

'I don't know.'

Regn was about to cry. 'Don't I make you happy?'

'Yes—but it's bittersweet.'

'I know age doesn't matter to you. In ten years I'll be wrinkly and sagging.'

'It doesn't matter.'

'You're how old—? When's your birthday?'

'October.'

'I've lived half my life.'

'I feel for every year it's twice that for me.'

Regn spoke of her 'almost' affair and how she'd lived past it. Another man she knew a few years ago. He'd wanted to take her on a vacation. He was married with three children. Nothing happened. Jay found out, somehow. 'We never did anything. He just always liked to come into the store where I worked. But there would have been too much hurt. I went to the Island a lot after that. By myself. I'm all right.'

'Are you?'

'Don't be shy, Westcott, or embarrassed to tell me anything. Don't be so awkward. Are you afraid of what I'll say—my reaction? I wouldn't be mean or—'

'Yes—that's just it.'

'I—don't know if I can feel the way you do. I like you.'

'That's good.'

I put the top back on my salad. 'I didn't like it.'

'Was it because of me?'

'No—it just wasn't good.'

She waited while I fumbled to pack my things up. We took a quiet walk down the stairwell back to our posts.

'I'll have to make up some excuse why I'm late,' I said.

'Just don't say anything.'

• • •

Regn said, 'Hold out your hand.' She placed a dried insect in my palm that she'd found down in the Rotunda. It was disintegrating. She threw it in the trash. She'd wanted to share it with me. The conscious decision to pick it up, carry it with her, find me, and place it in my palm.

When she stepped out, I fished through the can and retrieved it. Sometimes I think I'm trying to get over her in small increments. And yet I still hope. There is harm in fantasizing and yet that's my only solace, as goes physical love.

• • •

I can never have her—even were it possible, I wonder, would she want me? An impossible question. Why torture myself relentlessly?

Rawlings is bantering again. Hugging me in one arm like a chum. 'I love this boy, he knows it!' He and Ida wave as they drive off in their Mercedes.

I trip on the stairs going up to the gallery while carrying a box of maps for Ann to stuff.

I'm growing weary of the Settlement. What Regn and I have will never be enough. So what do I do, where am I to go from here? She is what I want, but—

Eva and I have the same days off. She'd turned to Magda in the office and glanced at me. '*We* have plans,' she joked.

Magda had said, 'Hello Mrs. Robinson.'

I smiled at her joke. Irony resounded within my private thoughts. But Regn is no Mrs. Robinson. She would never come up to me and solicit.

• • •

When I looked at the daily schedule it was a delight—I would be on # 11—next to Regn.

'Aren't you lucky, you're beside me today.'

'Don't state the obvious,' I reply.

Late in the morning Regn confesses, 'Eva knows you and I are friends so she put us together. You know what she told me. 'You'd better watch out, you're a married woman.' I told Eva we're just buddies. I heard you called in sick Saturday. Were you really sick?'

'I needed the break.'

'I worry about you, Westcott.'

'You and everyone else.'

'No, they all worry about you in their way. I worry about you *more*.'

• • •

'I'm always *yelling* at you.'

'Why, because I'm honest?'

'No, because I like you too much. I think you and I could argue for a day,' Regn laughed.

I'd been trying to explain to her that I'm a realist and not a pessimist as she believes.

Before leaving, Regn flipped to a line I'd delineated in the book I loaned her, Virginia Woolf's *To the Lighthouse*. 'This is you.'

The sentence read: "How could a man that was so brave in thought be so timid in life?"

It was the same sentence I'd underlined.

AUGUST

It's been a long time since I *heard* the birds. It was so still and quiet as I walked out of work with Thomas, who will be leaving soon. He has a shaved head, smooth almond skin, and handsome blue eyes. He's a couple years younger, college student; a nice guy from the little interaction we share. Summer is making its turn. A sense of fall's advance presented itself in the evening air. The stillness was arrestingly poignant. The sightless birds chirped from their bowered nooks, but there was an austere vacancy. I've heard that sound before in other places. It's a comfort and yet, simultaneously, it brings everything into scope. Where have you been?—it seems to ask. I've been here all along, but you were far away.

• • •

I'm forever battling society's unpublished standards of 'success.' Standards defined solely by mankind. A college degree does *not* equate to happiness and success. Take Faulkner. Never even finished high school and later dropped out of the University. Have you ever been in a room at dusk when the lights are off and watched how everything assumes a blue tinge? This is more important than any class lecture. I'm not discounting the value of college *entirely*, but I maintain too much stock is placed on it—it is now a racketeering business. Prerequisites, technology fees, textbooks. I believe it should be based on merit not procedures. If you are prepared then you should be permitted a waiver from certain requirements. Of course, these waivers *do* exist. But they don't want you to know about them. You must research all the exemptions on your own. And even then there is a line—you can't test out of all the courses and there is a fee to obtain the waiver.

I long for the days of yore. When education was about knowledge, not procedure—the next move—society's determining factor of qualification. Such a lie. It takes more, a key ingredient no classroom can instill. A fire inside, an ambition unyielding. Tenacity. Facts are just that—facts—anyone can acquire facts, memorize and apply them, but to create something new, to invent, to strike a new road takes relentless self-reliance and confidence. There is but one person only you can ever fully trust and that is one's self.

Enough with such enigmatic talk.

• • •

She gives me part of her orange. She has one piece of gum left and tears it in half. 'You don't mind that I touched it, do you?' 'Just as long as you weren't picking your nose before.' She tells me about her doctor's appointment the next day—a physical exam—followed by the dentist. I can't suppress the fact that such reference to woman's routine maintenance arouses in me a frustrated desire, erotic, mixed with curiosity and shameful dread.

'Do you think some of the others are jealous? I didn't expect to be employee of the month.'

Regn was proud of her achievement. She'd been selected as employee of the month not from the Visitor Services Department, but out of the entire Foundation. I wondered how the nominations were made.

'I'm not jealous. I'm happy for you.'

'I'm glad. You know the picture they printed, Rebecca took that of me at the Island. She has an eye, even at her age. Jay helped with the bio.'

This last part hurts. *You could have asked me to look it over.* As though knowing my sentiments, Regn cheers me. Standing to go back downstairs she says, 'I love you, Westcott.' I know she speaks more for my sake than her own. It is friendly, but hearing it soothes me. I want to answer. Somehow, in spite of all the months, I'm not prepared. Like many desired dreams, when at last they come to pass, it is without ceremony. Her words offer affection, but they are offered in casual transience, not lingering passion. Not yet.

It is 5:15 when Regn exits with Deborah from the office. She comes right over to my register. I'm closing out. She is concerned about my hours for next month. I told her they'd shorted me. 'You have seniority over the 10 to 2s. You need to tell them,' Regn places her hand on mine—she needs something. Reassurance. Deborah is watching. She walks halfway out the door, hesitates. I sense she is feeling insecure and worried about her appointments the next morning. Was it more than that though? She truly would miss me—earlier when I'd been standing with my back against the wall by the main desk, feigning not to look over at her, she walked by on her way to the office and rubbed my shoulder with her hand. She has the freedom to touch me—*Quod me nutruit me destruit*—"That which nourishes me, destroys me."

Ain't it the truth, boy. O' Regn how I long—

· · ·

There are certain things you can't say when she asks, 'How was your weekend? What did you do?' I can't tell her I hurt when she's right in front of me, and when the evening comes and one of us is left to stay. I can't tell her I thrust my fist against my chest in utter frustration at moments. I can't tell her no matter what we're alone. Everyone. I feel there is no one to talk to—my mother—to tell all would be an ultimate betrayal of myself. I couldn't face her thereafter; she would think she knew what I was pondering anytime she glanced at me and I looked far away. I can't speak of certain things to Regn when the very matters involve *her.* I'm better off on days that we don't work together. When she is there I am in earnest to make use of the time, distraught in the hopes of her 'hearing me.' I never change do I? When she's not there, there's no need, no urgency, no one 'might' be watching. Is it all an act on my part then? No. I want to make something of it when she's present, we have so little time together. I want to say what I've thought in private. I want to tell her the things that seem safe to say in the dark of the night, but come day sound foolish, rehearsed. To look at her, listen to her voice, and hear the silent reply 'you can't have me' takes strength to endure. To be so close to each other, but unreachable—is a cruel twist of fate. Isn't it hard enough already? She seems to justify everything with her spiritual beliefs—but there is no comfort in that for me. She said today, 'Who knows, in the next life we might be married, eccentric, and shoot each other.' What good is thinking of some life that is not now, an unknown? I'm alive, she's alive, this is the time we have—right now.

I was sitting in my truck when I heard Regn tearing down the parking lot in her bug. I looked out the passenger window to see her zip by. We walked in together. She gave me her Beatles cd. I'd never listened to the Beatles. I like engaging in new tastes. Some of the songs are great, others you can keep.

At lunch we speak of music. 'There's a song, from back in the 70s, "If you can't be with the one you love, love the one you're with." It's not by The Beatles, but I sometimes think of it.'

'What if you're not with anyone?'

I'd momentarily stumped her.

'You have to make the best of it.'

'And what if the best isn't good enough?'

Whenever she seems completely at ease I notice she puts her head back. She reminds me of a bird—one that comes out of the cuckoo clock now and again. When I meet her gaze it can be so still. Other times far away.

A customer comes up to the counter, asks *the most* annoying question we get. 'What will I see here?' After giving the *long* dissertation, Regn turns to me. 'I hate when a guy pulls at his willy to fix it. Did you see him over there do that?'

I can't believe she said the word 'willy.' It's not the term I would use. And yes, my sentiments precisely. There's no reason to adjust yourself in public. If anything slip your hand in your pocket, discreetly rearrange yourself. I've had to often enough. If anyone has to readjust himself it's me.

'When I was a kid I just couldn't imagine the Queen sitting on the pot! Can you believe that?'

I smile at Regn's openness. I feel bad for switching lunches and not going with Ann. I see Ann back at her station watching us talk.

Closing my drawer for the day I walk into the office. Regn has her beige blazer hung over the back of a chair. She's wearing a navy blue tank-top. Her black brassiere straps show, modestly. There is something else. I see for the first time her incredibly short stature. Her shoes are off; she is walking around barefoot. The top of her head comes to my neck. I steal glances at her feet. How flat they are—no arch. I see her age at that moment and think of her confidence to kick off her shoes. Was there a part of her that did it for me? Her feet might have been hurting and it is warm in the office, but could she not have felt reassured by my fondness?

Back in the lobby one of the outdoor interpreters comes to the desk. She needs a volunteer badge. She is always nice to me. 'Hey dude,' she says in her husky voice. Sharon is beside me and asks how she's doing. Kai mentions something about them giving her a hard time. 'Some crazy stuff,' she tells us. She now *volunteers* at the Settlement. I'd seen her working down on the ships, easily mistaken for a guy.

I know they'd given her the razz when guests confused her for a man and used the wrong pronouns. She takes a nice picture. I silently sympathize; her androgynous appearance is no reason to ostracize. Putting the clip on the photo placard, I offer for camaraderie, 'See you around.'

• • •

I'd bought a pack of lighters to burn some pages, give them an antiquated appearance. I asked Regn if she could get the damn things to work, or was it a lemon pack. Handing over the lighters, in one quick snap she ignited the flame. In that instant she assumed the role of an older woman—again I saw her age—she made me feel so young. That twinge returned. She is such a woman. The way she just flicked it. And voila! She's lived, I thought—been around. She did smoke as a teenager, but who doesn't? Well, I never did. I'd hit the wheel before coming down on the lever, but the damn thing wouldn't light. I'd never used one. 'It's a good way to build up a callous,' I told her while I fiddled with the thing until the flame stayed lit. Regn talked about how she and her friends had this place above the movie theater where they'd go and hang out when they were young—listen to music, smoke, drink a little. It was fun, she reminisced. I couldn't tell her how such memories had the effect of making me very sad, envious. They had their music—The Beatles, Rolling Stones—I envisioned her younger, cigarette in hand, the way she must have acted as all teenagers tend to do at some time or another. Somehow I could see her back then and here she was decades later. I don't like to think of her as so much older. It forces me to realize I've yet to live enough. Some experiences you just don't want. I enjoy hearing Regn's story. I showed her my license. I wish I hadn't. She remarked how I looked so young in it, that I'd matured quite a bit. She sees me as a boy, I know. I confessed to her, at long last, that there's a reason I look so young. I didn't tell her what that reason was. I asked her to guess how many times I've had to shave my mustache. 'Never,' I answered. I told her it would be easier to tell her if I didn't feel the way I did about her.

Just before heading to lunch, I called to her '*Viel spaß*.' Have fun. And '*danke*,' I meant for the cookie she shared with me from the café and for showing me how to use the lighter. Without a beat she replied, '*Bitte schon*.' You're welcome.

My head started to hurt the last forty-five minutes 'til my lunch at 1:00. The afternoon went slowly, we spoke with a relaxed ease about things that normally, for me, would be incredibly awkward. Somehow she makes things easy. Nothing bothers her. I regrettably told her I'd had a dream Sharon was kissing me. Sharon is sixty. But her hands are smooth and her joints limber. 'Maybe unconsciously you have something for her.' And so began our conversation about who is attractive at the Settlement. I told Regn the dream had been the right place but the wrong person. After divulging who I found attractive I expected the same of Regn. It hurt me when she said, 'If I were single I'd probably be dating Guy from the Gift Shop. Deborah has it made. She's on her own, plenty of money, and still she's miserable. You should smile more often, Westcott. You have a nice smile. It lights up your face and eyes.' Coming from anyone else this would have sounded bromidic, but the way she said it was matter-of-fact. She spoke of Tillie and how she was a sex maniac. 'Sweet, innocent, Tillie?' I replied. 'I'm a visual person and imagine certain things. I can't help it. All that huffing and puffing—Tillie and her husband,' she laughs lightly. 'Maybe that's why she's so happy,' I said, smiling. Regn spoke candidly and openly about sex lives—mentioning her own, though not in detail. 'I once told Tillie there's better things in life than sex. Like standing on a mountain. There are more important things than what goes on under the sheets. I don't have to have that.' I couldn't help wondering if she'd given up long ago. *How many lovers have you had*, I wanted to ask but knew I couldn't. Not that day. If you've only been with your spouse you have no measure of comparison. I told her it meant more when there was true love involved.

I was almost mad at Regn for no other reason than she is decent. Even if she did run off with another man I would not be the one, which is all the more devastating. She loves me yes, but she sees me as a boy. Could she *ever* love me the way I do her? I noticed the thin layer of clothes she was wearing. It hit me. I imagined being intimate with this lady and how close physical contact really is in such moments. I knew even if she'd have me I couldn't get away with it. I couldn't hide myself and the truth. That's what makes it all the more cruel. Up to this moment I've never admitted in a straight-shooting manner, what is so apparent, what I've said in every way but the clearest. I long for a love affair with Regn. This is not purely a physical attraction. My love runs deep—the more I can't have her—the stronger it becomes. 'Sex isn't everything,' she says. 'I've known bliss and it's not that important.' I can't help but think she gave up. The frustration is without pacifying—

'I don't know, I think you and I would always be fighting—at each other's throats—we're both so eccentric. A love-hate relationship. I can be a very difficult person,' she admitted. I told her she reminded me of a bird. I could see her strutting on her branch back and forth.

'You have so much energy—like a hummingbird. You're exhaustive.'

'Why? You just look at me and you're exhausted?'

I couldn't help laughing—for it is true. Though the exhaustion be for other reasons.

'Can I ask you something?'—I'd wanted to for a long time. 'Why'—my voice became shy again. 'How come you don't wear a ring?'

'Oh.' She looks at her hand. 'It was stolen and it also bothers my arthritis. I remember when we came home that night—the cats were acting really strange—someone had been there—'

I didn't ask if this was many, many years ago or more recent.

'I didn't want another one. I don't believe in those things. Is that wrong?'

'No. I don't really go in for those tokens either.'

'I guess that makes me bad, but in the winter the cold hurts my hands.' She touched the joint of her finger.

A storm moved in late in the afternoon. Regn was watching her beloved "Weather in Motion" camera on the computer. She always got a kick out of watching it. She said, 'I should do the weather,' meaning herself.

'If that was the case, Regn, no one would be watching the weather.'

'Oh thanks.'

'It was a compliment!'

She realized what I'd meant and we both laughed.

When we got to the parking lot, Regn moved to hug me—someone from the gift shop was coming out behind us—I worried she'd see or that Nim and Eva would be coming, too. Regn grabbed my arm, pulled me close, squeezed it. I wanted to hug back, but what if they saw? Sometimes I care, sometimes I just don't give a damn what they think. I get tired of being on guard. Driving away I listened to the tail-end of "Yellow Submarine." As the rain fell harder, "In My Life," played. The melancholy of the song made something hurt. It is nostalgic and the lyrics prophetic.

My favorite part is the solo instrumental played on the piano amplified in speed to make it sound like a harpsichord. After reading the biography *John* by Cynthia Lennon, I discovered that this segment of the song which sounds just like Tetris, or I should say, Tetris sounds just like it, was played by George Martin, manager for The Beatles, "Les Beat" at that time. The power of music, much like writing, is that it evokes universal emotions—in this case sorrow—while being intensely personal. I felt what The Beatles felt when they penned the song, but though the feelings were the same, they were prompted by entirely different events. "In My Life" had not been about the love of a specific person, but infinite affection for a time and a place—Liverpool—the cradle of youth for The Beatles.

• • •

She'd loaned me a German and English copy of Das Weiss Rose: *The White Rose*. The story of an anti-fascist brother and sister in Germany who were executed for what at the time were deemed treasonous acts against their German country. I passed the morning reading *it*. The part recounting Sophie Scholl's last hours sent a chill up my back—literally. That same old presence stirred—a cold sensation entering my chest cavity. Anytime I read or watch something pertaining to the late 1930s through the 1940s the hair on my arms and neck stands on end; a stiffened chill wavers through and for a fleeting moment I feel— something passes over me or through me. I know I was of that era and a longing sweeps in, but also a profound awareness. I remember things from that time—not individuals or places, but *things*—manners, language, dress, scents. Was I a remorseful Nazi and now, this time around, I am serving my retribution? Did I die an innocent soldier yearning for his lady? Regn's accent reminds me of *home*, I feel I know her without saying anything. I am afraid of a pain I feel I experienced before and its potency still remains with me, though years have passed, shells slipped away, and here I am.

• • •

Someone turned in a red bird to Lost and Found. He chirps when you squeeze him.

I went into the office with the plush toy behind my back and made him tweet. Regn looked at me, laughing, trying to see behind my back. I moved so she couldn't, then revealed the lil' guy. I named him Portly Pete.

'Just watch it with the supervisors. You know how I feel about *you*. I don't want you to get into trouble.' Regn sounded concerned.

The Sups are getting on my nerves with their asinine policies.

Retrieving my bag I discovered a paper inside. Regn stood beside me. 'I left that for you.' It was her schedule of days off for October. 'So you can put in for the same days as me.'

I didn't tell her I'd been doing that all along. Pulling her sheet out of the folder posted to the bulletin board to see the days she'd requested off.

• • •

For lunch I cooked a meal in the microwave, which I rarely do at work. The attention standing in front of the microwave brings bothers me. I don't want anyone to see when I eat. I carried the dinner upstairs. The three Sups sat opposite at another table across the mezzanine. 'I wonder what they say about us,' Regn commented. 'I'll just tell them you're my toy-boy,' she laughed.

'Did I annoy you today?' Regn asked.

'No, I thought it was the other way.'

'You are one person who could never annoy me.'

My how those words resonate after all these years.

Regn proceeded to write her signature on the daily schedule after I told her I could sign her name.

'Here, now you can really practice forging it.'

I kept the sheet with her handwriting. And not for the purpose of forging.

We were told by the Sups to clock out at 5. I lingered an extra fifteen minutes off the clock. Finally I told Regn my being there was too conspicuous. I headed out, alone. The weather was mild. A sure sign of summer surrendering to fall temperatures.

SEPTEMBER

It's Monday. The third. I'm sitting at our table—the one Regn prefers. If you are standing outside facing the Settlement the window is on the left. I put my sunglasses on; my stomach is tense with anticipation. I look at the giant trees gently blowing. It's been a fairly quiet day. I glance at my watch. Hopefully she'll be up soon so we have the full 45 minutes. Through the mesh railing I can see Ann downstairs at her register—number 7. She can't see me. My hands are cold, I take a sip from the raspberry spritzer I brought with me. Just then Regn comes through the doors onto the mezzanine.

She has her purse and a cardboard plate with french fries.

'I wanted something greasy today. I brought my lunch, but I just felt like something else,' she justifies.

'And soda?'

'Yes, why? Can't I? It's diet anyways.'

'Diet's worse—it has aspartame in it which is very bad for you.'

'I don't drink it often.'

I'd switched lunches with Pauline so I could go with Regn. Pauline was more than willing. I deliberately did not run the swap by Eva for fear she'd say no. There wasn't any problem in the switch—neither of us had Rotunda duty so what would be the harm?

'You're wearing your sunglasses.'

'Yes, they're a great defense mechanism—protection—but if it makes you nervous—' I slip them off, set them on the table.

'What are you drinking?'

'It's a raspberry soda. Natural sugar and raspberry. I love them. They're hard to find. This one is Swedish.' I turn the glass bottle so she can read the name. Kristall.

'Do you want to taste it?' I pour some into an empty cup—I'd let her drink from the bottle, but I don't want her to think I'm going to start something with us sharing drinks all the time—not that I'd mind. 'Well?'

'It's good, but a little too sweet for me.'

'It's not that sweet. I love the combination, the soda aspect of it. I made a copy of the James Blunt cd you wanted.'

'You're too good to me.'

I know, I want to say but don't.

And then the moment I'd been waiting for all day, maybe even all week. With the cd wrapped in paper I hand over the card and gift. Tomorrow is her birthday. I won't get to see her. I'm scheduled for Yorktown. She will be 55. I don't think of her in terms of numbers. Her energy is younger.

'Can I open it, now?'

Her hair is darker I notice. She's colored it again—

'I'm not ready to go gray,' she tells me.

I love the rich reddish-brown color on her.

'It's beautiful. You did this?' She holds a photograph taken on the Island with her image from a snapshot I'd taken during Anniversary weekend superimposed in color against the black and white background. On the reverse side a piece of prose I wrote titled, *The Fountain Bird*.

'I'm touched.' She studies it. 'Let me give you a hug.' She gets up. I want to let myself go, hug freely, naturally. There's the camera and people down below, and most of all there's Regn watching and myself watching me.

'Thank you, Westcott. And thank you for the card and cd.'

'I'm glad you like it.'

Regn sits back down, has set the picture safely to the side of her lunch. I'd deliberately put it in a plastic sleeve for safekeeping. I glance at my watch. It's five to one—just enough time to get back downstairs and to my post. Right on time. The time flew. Just then movement catches my eye. Eva is barreling down the mezzanine with purpose. She comes right up to the table, as close as she can get.

'What time did you go to lunch?'

She's looking at me. Something inside sinks.

'12:15. Pauline and I switched.'

'You can't just switch lunches and not tell anyone.'

Inside I'm cringing, her tone has me feeling terrible. I don't want to look at Regn. I know her gift is on the table in plain view. Eva's too busy interrogating me; she doesn't seem to notice.

I've been chastised. I am embarrassed, hurt that Regn should be there to witness such scolding. It's not as though we were very busy and Pauline is back at her station—I can hear her voice rising from the lobby—she is loquacious—everything had been covered. Mortified and crushed, I manage to look at Eva. 'I'm sorry.' My voice is quiet, sincere.

'All right. Just don't do it again.'

The incident leaves me dejected.

Alone again, Regn tries to assuage. 'She's yelled at me before—she has a lot on her mind with her health and the Supervisors, but it wasn't right of her to do that in front of me. I'm going back down.'

'Leave your trash with mine, I'll be down in a minute.'

Packing up my gift in her purse, she hugs me from the side—putting her hands on my shoulders and her head close to mine. I watch her walk away. She looks to the side just before entering the office wing. I neither smile nor frown. I look back out the window. I want to break down. The mood had been ruined and the rest of the afternoon dampened. To be scolded in front of her and the knowledge that Regn knows I did it on behalf of spending time with her makes me feel all the more chagrined. All the way back to my station I tightened inside. Earlier this morning one of the Supervisors jumped on me for my briefcase. 'The ladies can't bring their purses out here, so would you mind keeping your briefcase in the office.' How many times have I kept it by my chair on the floor without incident or comment? The only thing about today—I'd set it *on* the chair beside me. They're just putting the screws to us.

As a cover I do a walk-through of the galleries. I need a pretense to escape to the restroom. I'd put off bladder/bowel relief. How many times have I done this—countless.

I'd rather be physically discomforted than sacrifice a few minutes of Regn's company. After relieving myself, I enter the gallery.

Late in the day Eva steps to my station.

'I was on a crusade. They'—she points upstairs indicating the new Supervisors, 'were on me. I shouldn't have done that in front of Regn. In the future, any changes in the schedule—you must run by one of us. All right?'

I nod. 'Yes. I will.'

Though appreciated, the apology is too late. The harm has been done—the moment upstairs spoiled. In time her apology will mean much more to me. Where Regn was concerned Eva was just looking out for me. Where the Supervisors were concerned, Eva was only doing her job, and at that she was biding her time.

WHAT DOES THAT say to you? All the times she's passively turned me down. She's told me in casual conversation discussing others that she doesn't like to hurt anyone. Sure she's remiss and has admitted to such—but how long can I use that as the sole justification? She may not have wanted to hurt me by refusing friendship, but by opening up to me she gave hope and in so doing the harm she's caused is far greater than had she just come out with it from the beginning. In a way she led me on—although I credit myself with running away on fantasies. *In a way couldn't you say she's used you?* Yes—it is true—I am someone she can talk to freely—I told her so myself—'If there's anything you want to talk about, I'm here.' The ladies don't want to hear about it—they don't understand how she could ever consider walking out on *him*—her husband, which she had entertained in the past *long* before me. He *is* a good man. But she married when she was 18—just a kid.

Anytime she doesn't like something or want to hear it she ignores the matter by saying nothing—she deals with it that way—how many times has she not responded to my letters? Remiss only goes so far—

Had she ever been interested in me, back in January when I first invited her to walk with me at the Island, she'd have jumped at the suggestion. Can I really be so blind? It just goes to show you can't reason with the heart. Why tell me though that we're such 'close friends—that we have a special bond'—but never let me near when she knows from my confessions I'm no threat to her physically? Though I may reiterate certain points they must be stated here. Our friendship has been so rationed and that is entirely her own doing. Maybe she is afraid of allowing herself to like me—but then, why not say so? I am a foolish fuck, a foolish boy, tenacious and stubborn just like someone else—*she* should know—after all she's the Queen of wrought-iron stiffness—she will not bend if it doesn't suit her convenience and needs.

O' listen dear boy, dear reader, listen to what you already know but must find out.

One of my fondest memories is of last October. Almost a year now. The VS staff had all come after hours to tour the new 30,000 square foot gallery. At that time I gave little weight to the event—I was nostalgic for it as I am with most things now. I was heading for NY the next morning—my birthday. That evening Regn interlocked her arm in mine. *She'd* come to me—in that one moment—the only time before my fondness overpowered. The other ladies had looked at her speculatively—'Oh, leave him alone.' I'd liked it, but my heart was not yet hers then.

'Isn't there anything I can do for you?' she's asked.

Yes, of course—you have to know—. If she really cared we'd have taken that walk long ago—why string me along—is she so blind to her own actions? 'When the weather's cooler, nicer,' she assures me.

How long will she use that excuse? I'm afraid it's time for goodbye—*that* word dredges it all up again. I always knew it was going to be hard. She has the years to protect her— I may have to survive much longer with it—to live with the memory. 'Think of it as a learning lesson,' she once said. *Yeah, sure,* I tell myself. *Don't ever get too close.* I feel abandoned by her in my pain, but then she was never mine to lose. I must be strong, but for what? She took my love, though I volunteered it. Always remember, no one really cares, unless they're pathetically sentimental like myself.

I should cut her loose before she does me—just one more avoidable hurt. I don't want to sound sullen and I don't want to think of her in anger—this lady I love—but the pain, the torment. She can't fire me from this friendship if I've already resigned myself from it—but my heart's not yet in it to walk away.

I try to think of a time before the Settlement—

Am I insufferable or am I real like Magda said?

. . .

Saturday 8 September

I saw an infant nearby. 'Hide it,' I joked. 'Take it away.'

I don't like infants. They're conniving, manipulative. I like them when they're "human," around three or four and you can actually talk to them and they're not spitting up and messing themselves. I think of animals and how they fend for themselves—tend to their own bodily needs the minute they drop into the world. Human beings are so needy, helpless. Love is a separate matter.

'Remember, I was twice a mother. I nearly bled to death with my first.'

'It's strange to think of you that way.'

I don't see Regn as a mother. The other day at Yorktown in the kid's kaleidoscope room it hit me as it does from time to time—I understood how she could stay with this job—she's lived, done so many things and is for better or worse, happy or not, settled. I saw her there, envisioning the way she does her job and how she'd pass the time in the Hub—probably walking about reading the material—always so attentive to her duties. She wouldn't be caught sitting behind the desk reading.

I vaguely remember one time long ago when we were out at Yorktown together. It's hard to recall the way we interacted then—so much has come to pass and the same question follows—'What good has it done for either of us?' The years ahead stretch out before me. Again I hate to admit she's lived her life and is content to stay in this *place*. I can't wait for her; she does not wait for me. She'll get along I tell myself. I don't want to get over her. I sat in one of the scooters this evening gazing out the glassed vestibule of the Settlement. I told myself again, *You're the one that must go.* Why must she have already lived her life—it's too hard. How can I go on when I want to stay but know I can't—it's a dead-end. The emptiness descended once more. Sharon I'm sure saw me—but what does anyone really care?

It's all up to you, I tell myself. I clocked out quickly and walked with Regn. Ann was coming up from the Rotunda—we waved to her from the hall. Strolling to the staff lot Regn's keys clanked her water bottle. It sounds like a cow's bell. 'The cows are coming home,' she laughed.

That they are—a hollow tone. Regn had parked right beside my truck. No longer so far away where no one can tap her car.

No one was around. She made no attempt to hug me; she's withheld all physical contact from me today.

'Well, another day,' she said heading to the *passenger* side of her bug.

'Don' tell me! I know what you're doing—checking to see if anyone hit you.'

'Yeah, why?!'

'You're crazy.' I shook my head. I'd allowed the moment to get lighthearted when I'd wanted more. To be earnest. Serious. Take charge of the situation. Reluctantly, I climbed in my truck, rolled my window up—I always keep it cracked to spare the interior the warm temperatures. Regn never does and I'm perplexed that she never puts a sun visor in her windshield. With a black leather interior things heat up quickly. She who loves her car so much doesn't want it scratched and yet she lets it bake in the sun!

OTHERS BELIEVED, or at the very least thought and often told me, I possessed a delicate disposition. It wasn't so. Isn't so. I am quite sensitive physiologically and in an emotional sense, but it is not "fragility" that courses through my blood. Not much phases me in respect to society at large. What I've always possessed, however, is a *genteel* quality. I believe in discretion, a certain time and place for expression. Decency. Proper, respectable dress. Punctuality. I'm acutely light sensitive and loud noises not only bother my ears, they anger me. Particularly loud noises that are entirely avoidable. For example, someone who just lets a heavy door slam shut or a shopping cart collector who slams the carts together, pushes them across the asphalt, clattering and roaring, as if demanding attention. I hate when customers pull a cart from the line. Instead of grabbing the metal wire panel and stopping it from clanging, they just let it bang shut. Worst, bussers at restaurants who confuse efficiency for going hand-in-hand with being louder—dishes piled into tubs, utensils pinging, glasses clanking. I prefer the quietness of an Indian, to silently appear rather than announce myself. Too much noise, obnoxious noise, self-made noise, drowns out the details of the day. I need to hear the wind, the tick of the clock, the sound of my throat as I swallow. Others saw a rail of a young man, who presumably would topple over at the least bit of thunderous wind howling through; what they could not see, what they could not know was that I was anchored. A rod ran the length of me, a staff of relentless, tenacious willpower. I might double over, and I did, but like a tent pole that can be pulled apart and folded into a bundle, then opened back up and inserted one into the other to form a sturdy pole, the core inside never snapped completely. My being was tested, pulled taut, battered in a relentless downpour of grief. I could not come in from the rain. I would still hear it coming down on the roof, I would know it was just outside. I could not pretend. Pretending was just a polite euphemism for lying to one's self. For a long time I remained staked, resolute, firm, unyielding. The greater the obstacle the more I dug in—nothing was impossible, I knew, except if you were dead. Even so I grew weary at times.

I knew pain was useless, it came just the same. I knew being sad solved nothing, sometimes the sadness wanted to stay. I would get to thinking: who wants to marry a man who is content to die tomorrow? Not morbidly so; I didn't drag myself around, but if I were "to go" the next day, I'd have been all right to say adios. Since the likelihood of this was relatively unlikely, I realized I could never fully be myself with anyone. I would always have to hide the private torment, the sensitivity, the source of pain. This emotional loneliness is what bothered me—had always concerned me. I could be in a room full of people, it didn't assuage the sense of isolation. The detachment was inside. The mingling bodies had an ionic effect on my physical body, the energy was good for it, I suppose, but it also magnified the internalized emptiness, the realization that in this room—whatever crowd happened to be occupying it—I did not belong. I did not want to belong to these people. To groups, to crowds. I just needed one, yes, a single individual whom I recognized emotionally, with whom I could engage and fall in love, and who would love me in turn unconditionally. It seemed so simple, almost cliché, trite, but there was nothing easy about it.

People no longer look at each other. All the empty smiles, conversations with angles—I felt the room narrowing, being stretched and pulled taut—to a point. And on the farthest apex—the point—was myself. Like a slingshot I wanted the point to be released and for me to be belted through the passageway girded by faceless, countless individuals. I wanted to be shot out the other side where my own kind could be found. And let me be very clear when I say "my own kind." I am referring to those Robert Kinkaids, John Muirs, peregrines of heart who understand what it is to be displaced, born in the wrong time, an insatiable yet quiet aching for yesterday's twilight. Others who know what it is to travel down the centuries and to desire nothing greater than the return to one's origin. People talk about their jobs, the clothes they buy, their bank accounts, salary, sex-life. I wanted no part in it. I wanted a private conversation with just one woman and I wanted that conversation to never end, but to last me, to walk with me, to the end of my life.

I had that with Regn. Without it I would be as good as dead. My life would be defined in terms of absence, what was missing rather than in fullness and brimming satisfaction.

CHAPTER 2

THE ANGELS ARE BAKING

SHE STEPS AWAY FOR a minute to the restroom. A family comes to the counter. Their son sits astride in his wheelchair. A helmet on his head. He has no arms. His mother, in charge of the leash, directs the service dog—a cute little pup.

'I'd let you in, but we close in fifteen minutes. You'll essentially walk out the door and security'll tell you to turn around,' Westcott explains.

Regn returns.

'Everything come out all right?' he asks.

They watch the family head for the gift shop. 'How terrible, the strength of the parents to care for him,' Regn offers.

Westcott knows this must be a big outing for them—had the hour been earlier he'd have let them in free of charge—*What kind of a life is that?*

'Sometimes I think maybe it would be better to just be out of it. Your spirit's closer when you're like that, to a higher place.' As she says this, Regn looks far away.

AN ABSOLUTELY MAGNIFICENT DAY, weather-wise! I wasn't even scheduled. I'd switched with Parson so he wouldn't have to go to Yorktown the Wednesday before. It is actually cool outside despite it only being September. In Virginia summer seems to hang on. I knew the day would be bleak and boring. No one was in—well, none of my preferred ladies. I wondered what Regn was doing, probably sunbathing with a book in her lap.

~

Coming back from lunch, having dined with Mother in her car, the cannon reports. Startled, caught off guard, I am angered by the loud pitch, or rather its lack of warning. My legs buckle. I lose a breath. The ground reverberates. I feel the hollow boom resonate within my chest; it has traveled the length of the ground, up through my rubber soles and penetrated me. I see smoke from the report wafting skyward. It is a true fall day despite it not being fall officially for another two weeks. The morning opened overcast and wet from last night's rain. The early hours have given way to sunshine and blue skies. A person could have fall fever—why is spring fever only ever mentioned? Customers are steady and the fact that we're short staffed doesn't help. I wish I could leave early—another two hours on the register. Days like this make working at the Settlement 'just' a job.

I type on the computer to pass time. This is what I write:

Someone was chasing me—
With a knife
I couldn't make out the face
What do you do before you go to bed?
I said—
It was the past you know
And the blade? I awoke before it could take me.
The blade—
Regret

In the afternoon the armless boy returns. His mother is in her motorized scooter with the Jack Russell terrier. The father pushes his son. The boy appears to be of sound mind and only physically maimed. They are across from me at register 4, being waited on by Rawlings. The boy had been sitting upright, but now maneuvers to sit sidelong. He looks to me. I smile and nod my head. He hesitates, on the verge of offering a head nod. He looks away to the little dog. I'm sure he is used to this sort of reaction. But I'm not *staring* at him. It's something else I wish to offer. His eyes look so dark with the black helmet and hair beneath. Sentences run through my mind. *So you're back, you were here yesterday,* anything to acknowledge, let him know *I still think you're human.* But they leave out the door. *Now here's someone who will never know sex. The kid isn't even able to take care of his own bodily functions with appendages missing. And yet here he is, out braving the world. What choice has he?*

I go out front at twenty to five. Letting the day fall from me. Stand there—watching time. I look up to our window—the one Regn peers out of at lunch. I study the knots on the trees, comparing them to human anatomy, thinking how Regn would see it the same way, smiling wistfully in thought alone. I listen to the water in the fountain tumble down more heavily every time the wind blows through—a dusting of spray marks the pavement.

'How far to the National Park?'

A last minute tourist straggling in, too late.

I don't mind answering—it is gorgeous out, I am too tired to resist, and it is almost time to close.

'Just a mile to the right, down the road, but they close the gates at 4:30.'

I watch the sun coming through the trees and tell myself, 'this is fall.' I tell myself to take it in. Enjoy this brief moment. I look to the place where I'd taken Regn's picture during Anniversary weekend. She'll be going up to the mountains at the end of the month. They go every year.

I wish I were going to the mountains.

I clock out earlier than usual. Tillie is alone at the main desk shutting up the closet. 'Bye Tillie.' I am making up for all the times I may have overlooked her presence.

'Take care,' she tells me.

EIGHT-AND-A-HALF MONTHS. I'd waited 8 ½ months for this day. My expectations were too high. I spent those 2 ½ hours somewhere else—I wasn't there with Regn. I was too caught up trying to think of what to say next I didn't hear her. I'd been anticipating it the entire day. Eight months to prepare; I failed to relax. I let myself down.

• • •

I arrived to the Island at 2:50. The agreed time was 3 o'clock.

We saw a fawn in a thicket—standing alone. Regn moved a caterpillar off the road. I like caterpillars. They have legs. It's worms I'm afraid of and snakes. Legless devils. Okay, so worms are harmless. I still can't stand the way their bodies telescope in on themselves as they move. No fur, no hair. Now where was I—oh yes—Regn and I.

'I regret not being a better mother.'

'Give me an example.'

'Many things. When my daughter had her first exam—you know a woman's thing—'

'The gynecological exam—'

'Yes. I wasn't sure if these things bothered you to talk about.'

'No, it's fine.'

'You see, you're easy to talk to. I'm glad I can say these things. Well, her first exam I didn't go with her. Something happened—it can be intense not knowing what to expect and she came home crying. I should have—just things like that.'

My legs were quite sore and my lower back was beginning to ache from the long walk.

'Do you think you can ever truly know someone?'

'Yes, I think so.' I looked at her.

'I don't think you can ever really know someone—'

She was right.

'Well, no, there are certain things—' I wasn't thinking about myself, my physical secret. I knew Regn was speaking of emotions.

'There's a part of every person that's very private that you should keep for yourself.'

'Of course,' I agreed.

In the distant years ahead and the span of them behind, I would often consider her words and our causal exchange of commentary. We were getting to know each other more and yet we were talking round the issues. *Yes, Regn, a person has so many sides, I wish you hadn't shown me all—*

On the latter half, the back-side of the 5 mile loop before it rejoins with the 3.2 mile path, Regn stopped. Pointed. 'See that group of trees?'

Seven, all converging, sprouting from the same roots. I was amazed and mildly disgruntled at myself for not noticing them before. I'd never thought to look to the left—the other direction—in all my bicycling on the Island. She'd mentioned them at lunch one time. I'd tried to locate them when I'd gone for a ride some weekend. I took it as an unspoken symbol. An analogy. I'd never looked on that side of the path. Love is blind. And then Regn answered what I'd been thinking.

'You never know, you might meet someone else.'

'I don't want to.'

'Mary from Yorktown is nice.'

'She talks too much and she's always saying 'like' this or 'like' that in *every* sentence.'

'You could just be friends I meant—'

'I'm not interested. She's not my type.'

We continued onto the last and longest trestle bridge over the marsh. Regn wiped tears from her nose that came from behind the protection of her sunglasses. She used the word 'fucking' to describe her frustration. Her desire to do things. She spoke candidly to me about sex and her opinion of it again. 'It's important, but for me it's not everything.' We sat on the long bridge. My legs grateful. I'd like to have stayed on the bridge for a while longer. I looked at the sky.

'Sex changes things, ya know,' Regn says as we start to walk again.

'I can't say that I do.'

Regn saw a friend at the end of our walk. I walked ahead.

Regn caught up to me. 'You could have stayed. Why did you walk away? She probably thinks you're my toy-boy.'

'I didn't mean to—I just—'

'It's fine. I don't care. I was jealous of her at one time—she'd taken the step to be on her own and have lovers—her husband was a real asshole. Don't think mine is bad though—he'd go out in the middle of a storm if I asked him to—I don't have a bad life.'

'No, of course not.' I was disappointed. I didn't want her to be hurt, but if Jay wasn't a nice man it would make things easier.

~

Regn was thirsty. I offered her the bottle of water in my truck.

I brought out my album. I'd been working on it with intense concentration and energy the past few weeks. It was a scrapbook of the 400th Anniversary at Jamestown along with my photographs of the Parkway, some of the ladies and the ones I'd taken of Regn during the celebration.

'Oh, Westcott—this is wonderful. What are you going to do with it?'

We sat on the curb. The parking lot had cleared a great deal. My hips still hurt. Regn flipped through the book. I was disappointed she couldn't take more time with it. I'd let her keep it for a few days if she wanted. She said something about one of the pictures—I didn't hear her. I was too busy thinking what to say next, anything to stall, give us a few more minutes. I detected her crying again.

'Who are you going to give this to?'

'Who should I give it to? You're the only one who's seen it.'

'Well, you know if you bring it to work—'

'What do you take me for, geez.'

She hugged me. I always let her initiate. Feeling it was safe, I pressed her back with my hand.

~

I was probably the only one who had been looking forward to the staff meeting scheduled for that evening—it was an event to go to—*something* to do, and Regn would be there—it was another 2 ½ hours to take her in. I drank from the bottle of water where she'd placed her lips. When we arrived to the Central Support Complex there weren't any cars. We looked at each other, raised our hands in question.

Another staff member, one of the 10 to 2's, approached my truck. The sign on the door said: *Visitor Services Meeting Cancelled.* Cinda had come back early from a trip, all the way in North Carolina and was perturbed. The three of us chatted on the sidewalk. I studied Regn's face—her hair tucked behind her ears—she never wears it like that at work, I thought. I looked at her graying eyebrows, affectionately.

We'd left the Island for no reason. Then I saw the opportunity in it. We could go to dinner; she'd be able to look through the album at leisure—or we might stay there and share a few more minutes. It seemed perfect.

'Let's just call it a day.'

A day. We'd only spent 2 ½ hours together. 'We could go to the park by my house, or the one I take Gilly to by the college.'

'I don't know what I want. It's already 6. I'd better go. There's probably a message on my machine.'

'Your husband will wonder where you are.' I climbed in my truck. She said something; I rolled the window down to hear her better.

'I didn't hurt you, did I?'

'Yes.'

'You're hard-headed.'

'I'm not the one that's hard-headed, you are.'

Cinda was listening. Where she'd gotten to neither of us paid much attention. She must have been in her car.

Regn waved. I drove out ahead of her.

FALL. JUNIOR YEAR OF HIGH SCHOOL

He sits at his desk copying the notes—it is merely dictation, not application they are teaching; who is he to protest? He listens to one of the teachers lecture and extrapolate. If she asks a question he knows the answer to, inquires if anyone has been to the places they are studying, he makes no attempt to respond. His fingers give way to shaking; his eyes dart around the room. One day his teacher asks if the boys sitting nearby are bothering him. *Not in the way you think*, he wants to tell her.

He never raises his hand to ask a question. He relies on himself. Trusts himself to come to the right conclusion.

On the rare occasions he does seek a necessary answer, he must first devise a plan on how to approach the teacher. He goes over in his mind what he will say, there is a process to follow; he has to work himself up to asking the question. And then there is that aspect— that freedom—of undisturbed observation.

~

It is a Monday afternoon the last week of September. The 2:40 bell sounds its tone four times, vacating all classrooms. Westcott remains behind, listening to a roar of voices fill the halls. Outside he hears the bus engines running; a slight high-pitched toot of exhaust, a shift in gears like indigestion, and a rev on the accelerator, then they are off. Gray clouds are beginning to accumulate in preparation for a thunderstorm. Above the door a digital clock reads 2:45. *They sure don't wait long, glad I don't have to ride the bus often.* Mrs. T enters the room, having gone to her office. Pulling up a chair from one of the twin desks she says, 'Have a seat.'

'No thanks,' he replies shakily. 'I've been sittin' all day.' A reasonable excuse. He feels less intimidated standing.

'So, um, this place you wrote about in your paper, is it real or just something in your head?'

'Just a place in my head.'

'I loved the imagery, I know what you mean. I grew up in a rural farm-like setting myself. You could go outside in the open air and yell, not be heard for miles...You moved from the west coast, right?'

'Yeah.'

'That must have been quite a difference. You like it better here?'

'Yes, it's far more quiet, no cement jungles...' he drifts off.

'Well, why don't I walk you over.'

Westcott grabs his backpack and heads across the corridor to the last door on the left corner of the school's exterior wall of classrooms (the high school has been constructed in such a way as to have two squares stacked atop each other with a hollow core serving as a scenic courtyard). A lady steps out.

'Ms. Garlow, this is the student I was telling you about.' Mrs. T motions towards Westcott. She had not used the term 'the student' to identify him, but rather his name.

Ms. Garlow holds out her hand, receiving a sweaty palm to shake. It is his first time meeting her, but for the life of him he does not recall what she was wearing. Of course, he can always describe with accuracy his own wardrobe. He has on a cornflower blue and white plaid shirt, a navy under-shirt, close fitting jeans, and coordinating converse tennis shoes. Over time he comes to formulate an opinion based more on abstract than concrete characteristics. There is a certain freeness about her, an airy-fairy naturalism. She displays a relaxed, laid back demeanor, a borderline Bohemian style that he doesn't quite warm to, they are qualities not of his type. Albeit, since Ms. Garlow is a good friend of Mrs. T's, he takes to her all the same. She can best be described as someone thought to frequent coffee houses and art galleries, but this is only an assumption. Her skin is incredibly pale, a *casperian* hue partially accentuated by the naturally dark brown color of her hair.

~

Throughout the Fall and stagnant winter months Westcott intermittently attends weekly literary discussions headed by Ms. Garlow, coming and going without so much as clearing his throat. On days he stays after he waits for Ellis or his mother to pick him up, and if by chance a meeting has been cancelled, he has a two-hour stint of idleness to pass in quiet observation. Taking the 4:30 activities' bus would be too conspicuous to even consider. If he is lucky the single bench situated perpendicular to the school's main entrance and beneath the metal letters anchored to the brick wall reading D-R-U-M-M-O-N-D-S F-I-E-L-D, might be unoccupied. If not he stands with his back up against the building and his legs extended slightly at an angle for support. He will not pace. No *physical* movement. His presence, though casually dismissed, seeks distinction in his gaze. He watches students engaged in extracurricular activities. Athletes and the sort make their way out the double doors toward the fields, returning after a hard day's practice short of breath and profusely sweating. Studying a track runner wearing shorts and a t-shirt with aptly toned muscles, he begins to envy him. Patiently he waits. He listens to the wind whip the flag chain against its pole in the little island of trees forming the car loop. He refrains from doing any homework or paging through his textbook lest he appear the geekish bookworm, which he is not. He dissembles his academic dedication, feigning a nonchalant, easy-go-lucky nature. After daylight saving's the skies grow dark by four casting a cold, strangely refreshing blue shadow across the surrounding forests, baseball diamond, school, and figure. On occasion, he'll see Mrs. McCormick or Mrs. T leave the premises. He offers a hinged 'Bye,' in exchange for a pleasant 'See you tomorrow.'

Westcott watches the sky closely, its transformation from fall to winter to spring. Steady. Subtle. Movement.

'MARIA CALLAS…Puccini…I'm going to see Tosca on Sunday.' He sits across from her, listening, eating animal crackers, hiding the box shaped like a circus freight car in his brown lunch bag. A pink 6 oz. Juicy Juice juicebox he sets aside for later. He tries to remember himself, knowing how his skin felt when he was 14, 15, 17.

Regn didn't like musicals, although she loved operas. Westcott always enjoyed *The Sound of Music*—the time frame, Captain Von Trapp's uniform, the harmony of their voices. And the young Liesl. A beautiful actress. The young woman who plays her, Charmian Carr, never appeared in any other movie. There is a scene in *The Sound of Music* when Fraulein Maria (Julie Andrews) slips away to the garden and sits on a bench. The screen color shows green and blue suggesting it is twilight though the hour is much later. It is the feeling of this scene in terms of color which makes it stand out in memory. Yes, the Captain (Christopher Plummer) is coming to find Maria, and they will confide their mutual sentiments of affection to one another. But it is the ethereal calm and nostalgia of the hues that makes the emotion timeless. Take away the characters on screen, the love still remains. It is the very atmosphere itself. It is how I envision the summerlands to be. Cool in color, warm in sensation. An enveloping feeling of eternal peace. Twilight after a *long day's* work. A lifetime of private battles.

He knows the woman across from him in more ways than one. Knows her body though he's never seen it unclothed. He knows to a degree what her body can feel because he shares a woman's knowledge. There are things about Westcott Regn cannot fathom. He wants her to see his hair wet and shiny having just been combed after his shower. The scent of his light safari deodorant permeating a crisp fitting white t-shirt. He takes a bite of his grilled chicken and cheese sandwich when she's not looking. He still doesn't feel comfortable eating in her presence.

He's peeled away the top layer of the bun—only a soft thin layer of white caps his sandwich.

Her long fingers. *She wears no ring. It had been stolen. She doesn't believe in such tokens. Besides, it only agitates her arthritis.* All the details she's told him.

A pile of napkins and discarded crust. He never *buys* a drink in the café. It's always his glass bottle of Swedish import, Raspberry sparkling soda. That or an 8 oz. styrofoam cup is all he needs. A complimentary cup. He fills it with ice and a little orange soda from the café.

'You eat like a bird.'

'I've always been that way. My stomach. I eat throughout the day, small amounts. I have to or I get a headache and feel faint. I'm probably hypoglycemic.'

'You remind me of Jimmy Stewart.'

'Because I'm so skinny?'

'Well that, but I mean the way you sound sometimes, your voice. You sort of talk like he did—serious but with humor, too. And his mannerisms.'

'I'd classify his tone as being earnest. So yes, I relate.' Funny Regn should notice this quality. Westcott sometimes did an impression of Stewart saying "Zuzu's petals" or "I'll lasso the moon for ya." He only did this in private when he could be sure no one was listening. 'He is one of my favorite actors. I may be thin, but he was quite tall. I wouldn't mind being an inch or two taller.'

'Then I'd really be short! You're the perfect height.'

'A guy likes to be tall. Don't you know by now, Regn, I love things in small packages.'

'Finish your lunch.'

'Yes, mother.'

'I'm going to smack you!'

'Please do.' Westcott smiles impishly in a way Regn finds irresistible.

 THE LEVY BROKE on a Friday. It would break again. Many times more. I was scheduled to be behind Regn on register 6, she was on 4. Fernus called in sick. Eva asked me to move to the front desk beside Tillie.

I didn't mind, but the frustration of seeing my lady, unable to speak to her from my register—. I was tired and hungry—not hungry in the sense of needing to eat—when Tillie said she'd switch lunches. I didn't want to unless it was all right by her. I didn't want Tillie swapping lunches on my account. I was worried what Eva would say.

Eva looked at the schedule. 'I see. You're in cahoots.' Register 4 always went to lunch at 12:15. Not too early and not too late. 'I'm trying to help you. Be careful. Watch it. Oh, I know—'

'We're just friends.' I tried to pass it off, harmless.

'Anyone with a briefcase like that *isn't* harmless, Professor.' Eva's tone was light but meaningful. I did look rather serious walking into work with my soft leather satchel, my tie and vest. Lawyerly. I shut the half window, returned to the main desk.

'Well?' Tillie asked.

'It wasn't definitive.'

I went back to the window. 'Tillie wasn't sure if that was a yes or no?'

'Will you go to lunch with me—' it wasn't a question. 'Since you're on the main desk then it's fine.'

I now knew our being kept apart, Regn and I, was deliberate.

We dined together—I couldn't help feeling it might be our last time. I told Regn about Eva.

'She was probably joking.'

'I didn't think so. I'm worried.'

'About Eva?'

'No. Not her.'

'Do you think I'm cold?'

I answered strongly, firmly. Without hesitation. 'Yes.'

From her purse bag she pulled out the miniseries she'd mentioned she'd loan me, *Mulberry Days*, starring Geraldine McEwan and Karl Howman. It's a British series she likes. I was eager to watch it.

After lunch I saw Regn crying at her register. I felt it best to keep a distance with the others looking on.

A man brought in an inch-long viewer from 1907! It was minute, smaller than a dog whistle, incredibly crafted for its day. It was a telescope shaped gadget, so small, so easily discarded. I liked the idea of holding something from 1907. A return—I felt in holding the object, I was closer to something. Something that had been so much a part of me, somewhere, sometime.

I called our curator to the front desk. The man who brought the item let me look into the viewer while we waited. It was amazing something that tiny could hold such perfect pictures.

Eva summoned Regn to the office. I feigned nonchalance. I made excuses to go into the office. I opened the window to see if the inner door was shut. Regn was taking a plant outside which she'd watered. 'Some guy's wondering about a monument being dedicated in Yorktown, do you know anything about that?' I had to say something on the fly.

Eva was in the back office. Receiving the expected negative on the monument, I quietly shut the half-window and returned to my station.

When Regn *still* wasn't back on her register I went into the office. The *inner* door was closed.

A colleague was counting down her cash drawer. What's going on? I mouthed the words.

'Regn's in there,' she whispered back.

In the meantime Tillie received serious news—her daughter's friend's child had fallen down a flight of stairs and was airlifted to Norfolk. I tried to comfort her by listening attentively. I listened closely to Tillie's situation, not in sympathy but to take my mind off whatever was happening in the inner office.

When Regn returned, at last, I was aching for a moment to steal. She came strolling down the hall from the café with Ann. She'd been crying again. I didn't hesitate when she sat down at her register. I didn't care who was watching. They already knew.

'Did Eva confront you about me?'

'Yes. Six people had gone to her with statements about us. Such dirty minds. Even the other day, when we were at the Central Complex—'

'You mean Cinda—'

'Yes. She said she saw us standing by our cars talking when we found out the meeting was cancelled. Like it's a crime to talk or something.'

Interruptions were rampant, customers straggling in—we weren't steady, but plenty of tourists were milling around. The afternoon dragged on. I couldn't get another second alone with her.

Tillie had come back from break crying. I told her I could manage the desk.

'I'm all right,' she assured.

'A lot of people just say that.'

She wanted me to keep talking to her—I joked, hoping to ease her mind, my mind.

Everyone left early or promptly. I told Regn I knew it bothered her that co-workers were saying things, even though she says she doesn't care. It's the suspicion.

'And to think how nice Cinda has been to me and then to say something—'

'It really grates on me—someone who is rarely at the Settlement—and to put her nose in our business, make accusations,' I conferred.

We both wondered who else had said something.

I turned off the videos, went to lock up the front. Regn brought her key for the door that doesn't work with the Allen wrench.

'I'm sorry,' I told her standing in the breezeway. She was outside turning the lock with the regular key.

~

'I don't want you to be awkward around me. Now you'll distance yourself, I know you.'

'I'm more worried about you than myself,' Regn assures.

'I don't care what they think.' Westcott is firm, inserting the Allen wrench in the door, locking up—going down the line releasing each push bar efficiently, systematically, with slightly more purpose than usual.

The task is good, it takes his mind off the situation for a split second.

Westcott grasps the cane he brought from the closet behind the main desk—the cane they use to reach the switch on the handicap accessible doors. All he needs now is a top hat. He loves a man's walking stick. He hits the black switch high up in the doorjamb; the bumper on the cane's foot switches it off.

They walk out together. Eva Bellefont behind them. Regn and Eva discuss tomorrow's morning meeting. Regn's in charge Wednesday.

In the parking lot Westcott's step stalls. Eva is going on about some movie—*Midnight in the Garden of Good and Evil*—she walks in the direction of her car. Was she stalling, trying to give him time to get in his truck, drive away?

Regn and Westcott head left.

'I feel terrible.'

'Eva is a friend. Don't be mad at her. It's the others. You want to go somewhere for a couple minutes, talk about it? Eva takes that route. Wait 'til she leaves.' Regn looks in the direction of Eva.

'You lead the way.'

She pulls off at the first inlet on the Colonial Parkway. A truck is parked there with dog carriers in the bed. The top on Regn's car is down. She is exposed. Westcott wants privacy. He looks over his shoulder to see who's in the other truck.

'Can I borrow your phone—my mother will wonder where I am if I'm late.' He is embarrassed to admit it, but he'd been a few minutes late before and just as he was pulling in his mother had been backing out the drive to go look for him. He let her have it that day. 'I'm twenty-something years old! It's ridiculous. What the hell could happen to me? Maybe I just got hung up at work.' She'd justified, 'Well, I know you don't usually go anywhere, and I just worry, maybe more because of your situation.' 'Oh please!' It had angered him. He was tired of her worrying. It did no good. These thoughts pass in a matter of seconds. It is an old phone. Regn's phone. He wanders down the bank, out of earshot. He doesn't remember what his excuse is, but he must keep this to himself. He wants to. He slides his hand into his left pocket, depressing the play back button by feel instead of hitting record. Noise breaks the tranquil silence. Regn looks at him for a moment. By the grace of God a faint radio turns on in the truck beside his. 'There's someone in there,' he says. They both look.

He steps closer, peering from the front of his hood. Sure enough a man is reclined in his front seat. The radio justifies the noise.

Westcott doesn't tape the conversation.

~

She keeps her sunglasses off. Westcott had removed his when he got out of his truck. He'd placed them in his breast pocket. Now is not the time to conceal anything.

'I wish there was something I could do for you. I wish I could tell you it'd be all right. We'll always be special friends, you know that.'

'Would it be better if I left?' Westcott suggests.

'No.'

'I mean the Settlement—'

'We'll take walks, but I can't always be there when you want...You're a beautiful, nice young man....I'm strong, I've had times where I just didn't want to go on.' Regn is sitting in the passenger seat of her car. The door is open. She faces him. Westcott stands, arms akimbo. His back to his truck. The colors are so sharp. Everything defined. His tie—striped, blue, cream. His shirt blue. His nice shoes with the heel giving him an extra half inch—the leather shoes he loves because of the color. They remind him of the '40s. She shifts her naked legs, straightening the hem of her navy skirt in a manner not to reveal anything.

'You have to be a friend to yourself—I guess we're the talk of Visitor Services now. Don't give them the satisfaction. How people can be so mean—it's horrible. They blame me—these mature women.'

'It's my fault. I'll tell them if you don't want to. Go ahead, tell them. Put the blame on me, I don't mind.'

'I wouldn't do that. I worry about you.'

'I've told myself over and over—I don't want my life. I look at it as a sentence. I think years from now when I'm gone they'll say, 'He was just some guy crazy about her.' It's not accurate. It's not like that....You don't think I'm a crazy fool do you?'

'I understand, that's why it's so hard for me.'

'I wish I could just stay *here*—' Westcott steps forward. 'I think if it had been different I might have met someone, just been able to go with them—What? Don't look at me. I hate the way I look. I *hate* what I am!'

He steps back, closer to his truck. 'What? I'm pathetic.'

'No.'

'When I said if you were me what would you do, I wasn't asking you to tell me what to do, but just asking what you would do.'

'I always try to see the positive......A friend is someone who's always there for you.'

'That's just it—'

At last the man in his vehicle drives away. Maybe he'd had enough.

'Can you do me a favor—I'm so scared to ask, I don't think I can.'

'Write it if you have to.'

'It's just—I mean no harm. I know you're a married woman. You must know what I'm going to say.'

'Just say it.'

'Don't look scared. It sounds so bad or lame to say it out loud. Would you...I mean some time, would you do me the honors of—' He's afraid to hear himself say it.

The leaves are falling from the trees down the hill. Cars pass on the main road—tourists. A nut drops on Regn's hood. Another minute executed. He must.

'—being my first—'

The evening remembers those words.

'—kiss—'

His nose starts to run. Reaching into his breast pocket, he puts on his sunglasses.

'You don't have to....Don't cry.' It is so quick. She moves to hug him. He puts his arm around her, tentatively delicate. She kisses the right side of his face.

I meant—and then in the same singular motion, as if knowing, she moves her mouth to his. It is polite, over before the sensation can be processed. Later he thinks her lips felt like a balloon.

Turning to her bug, a small distance between, Westcott says the only thing he is sure of. 'I'm glad it was you.'

Regn smiles.

'So am I.'

It is almost 6:30 when they part. She pulls out first, checking in the side view mirror to see if he is coming.

He waits, palm to eye, before following in her trail. It is the first day of fall, the sacred autumnal equinox.

He is 22 years old.

OCTOBER
Monday the 1st.

Why was he here?

'Why am I here?' he asked himself. So often he just needed to get out, to get away. It never worked. Momentarily it served to tame the restless ache of loneliness, but *She* always returned to him. Always.

Where was he today? Oh yes. The train station. He loved the train depot even if he didn't have a ticket to board. The prospect of others going somewhere was exciting, then again, he considered 'If I went somewhere I'd just be thinking about the time when I could return.' Coming. Going. Neither satisfied him. It wasn't the physical state of transience he desired, but the movement within that wrought his patience so. It was that constant, constant troll of tempered desire.

He looked around him at the passengers. 'Are any of you happy? Really? How do you do it?' No, that wasn't what he meant for he knew a state of prolonged happiness did not exist. Contentment, convenience maybe, but not happiness. *It's the familiar,* he thought. *My gloom is familiar and so I do not leave it.*

He didn't want to be anyone in the room. He was tired of himself, but seclusion offered perspective. He remembered the feel of her kiss and what it meant to him—to live "there" forever.

The bottomless pull in his gut returned. He envisioned her uncovered skin, lying beside her with no expectations of carnal union, but just to have her near, feel her closeness. To hold her in his arms. Ageless. Timeless. To know and rest easily in the knowledge that she knew he would never hurt her. She was his heart's station. The luggage he carried was his past. He might lie forever on top of her, but he would not board—that was the conductor's right, her right. An embrace before she'd depart yet again, and then the loneliness of wanting to go with her.

The indelible pain.

• • •

'I'm going in here, shutting the door and not coming out. I'm going to yell,' I told Regn and Tillie. I slammed the door for effect then opened it with exaggerated composure, a bundle of visitor maps in my hand.

'I thought you were going to yell,' Regn laughed.

'I'm scared to hear myself yell even when I'm alone.'

• • •

WHAT HE REALLY CAN'T STAND about "the customer" are the ones who silently crack one off, that is, break wind. He knows Regn would laugh at this. When the Boca machines get jammed they make an er-er-er constipated sound. Regn calls it a farting noise. Westcott will never use that term. Whenever someone else says it he feels embarrassed for them. He hates the word more than the bodily expulsion. It is a stupid word and stinks to high heaven. He prefers the expression 'breaking wind'—it's genteel, maybe even literary. As a last resort he'll tolerate flatulism. Belching is permissible; he can resound from the soles of his feet. But emissions from the posterior are vulgar, improper, impolite—such indiscretions are simply that—indiscretions. He's gagged, holding his breath, bowing out as quickly as possible from his register making any excuse to get up—more maps, receipt paper, anything—just to escape the foulness and let it dissipate before returning to his post. How rude the customer can be! God forbid a co-worker come near and think such expulsions were from him. He'd let them know for sure it was the guest's doing.

Another thing that really irritates him is anytime he has to print a Heritage Pass and ask the customer for his or her name. They spell their name B-e-t-t-y H-u-g-h-e-s or J-o-h-n H-a-r-t-m-a-n. *No shit! God damn it, give me credit. I'm an English major for crying out loud! Throw me a real zinger like Shumacher or Pflueger and I'll put you in your place.* It's funny. The man will be paying, doing all the talking, while the lady might rummage through her purse appearing completely occupied. The minute Westcott asks for their zip code the man is struck silent and she, out of nowhere, responds. Voila! *I love it. The things you see;* sometimes it's a fight between the spouses as to who can get the zip code out the fastest. Most times he no longer asks, making up postal codes or typing in Canada/UK.

The repetition is wearing. Who keeps track of all the data? It's futile, manmade, contrived, substance-less. He prefers the foreigners. They are almost always polite, informed, and genuinely interested in the contents of the museum more than the gift shop and café.

• • •

Some say they touch the skies
some say they see the wind
a whisper of spring is near
can you hear it say—
these are mulberry days

Some say they'll understand
some hold an open hand
a shimmer of moonlit haze
can you hear it say—
these are Mulberry Days.

WESTCOTT IS SAD THE LAST EPISODE of *Mulberry Days* has concluded. He and his mother have been enjoying the series immensely. There are only two seasons. For some reason, maybe ratings, the show was dropped. There is no conclusion. Something in Mulberry's character comforts Westcott, as the screenwriter purposely wanted. But it is more. He feels a kinship, an understanding. In the opening ensemble and credits, for the last time Westcott watches Mulberry rest on the brick rise taking brief stock of the melancholy pond. How is it Death can be cloaked in such colorful "vested" companionship? Mulberry wears vests in every episode. He is also "vested" with insight. He is the embodiment of Death come to take Miss Farnaby. Miss Farnaby has lived a quiet life. Never married. No children. Why is the opening tune with the credits so familiar in its yearning lyrics?

Will anyone ever be able to hear the music to these days? Westcott wonders. He does not tell his mother Regn loaned him the series. He says he checked it out from the library.

SATURDAY 20th OF OCTOBER. I often receive compliments from the customers on my name. A gentleman asked, 'Is there a story to go with that name?' Preoccupied, I offered a terse but pleasant 'No.' I wanted to reply, 'You wouldn't believe me if I told you.'

Lunch began casual. It was obvious *I* was going to have to direct the conversation to get anything out of her. I asked if she'd listened to the cd. She said she'd flipped around. I had to draw it from her. 'What did you think?'

'You have to be in the mood. I like Sarah McLachlan, Jewel, and McKennitt.' Her response deflated me.

'I ju—' I kept pushing my napkin through the flip top I'd snapped off my can of ginger ale. I worked the paper through the small opening. My hands wanted to be busy. 'I just wish you could let me love you. I just want to lie beside you and study you.'

'That can *never* be. You're hopeless.'

'That hurt.'

'What am I going to do with you, Westcott?'

The door was open for the brunt of this conversation—what we both had been waiting for. While she wound her way into it, I avoided the very thing I wanted to address. It was just my way. To come right up to the point and shy away. I was still learning.

I went into the vacant restroom in the executive wing. Switched the light on. Let it come, the tears. I didn't care if they wondered why I was late getting back from lunch.

'You're a fool,' I told myself. 'Gave too much, you knew, you just didn't want to believe it.'

Into the afternoon I was sweating profusely. While customers continued to come, I lied—telling them I had a cold. Parson noticed. 'Man your allergies must be bothering you.' He doesn't know I don't have allergies.

I asked Tillie if I could go to the ships for her—said I wasn't feeling well. The seat of my pants revealed a conspicuous sweat stain in a most embarrassing location. I told Parson who was sitting behind me on register 9 that I'd sat in water—some residual from the rain, in case he should notice.

The day was beautiful. It hurt. It mocked. The leaves were turning, smoke in the air from the Indian Village made me want to take Regn in my arms, hold her long and hard. I entered the family restroom down by the dock. My bowels felt loose. Using the facilities I detected my hipbones jutting out. The last self weigh-in read 132 lbs. My drawers were uncomfortably damp. I retched. A dry heave. I continued to heave. Nothing came. My sides ached. Looking in the mirror, I considered how this day would seem to me years from now. *What are you going to do?* Taking the boardwalk back, through the trees, all the colors ran together. I half-listened for the firing announcement, readying myself to put my hands over my ears should they report the cannon. I was gone 45 minutes. I didn't care if I went back. The only thing waiting was pain.

I was in the office counting the ship's money. Everything inside wanted to come out, but there was nothing left. It was a cold sweat. I wanted to turn to someone. There was no one.

'Are you feeling any better? What made you sick?'

'I'm just under an enormous amount of pressure.'

In that moment I wouldn't have minded hugging Tillie. If Regn wouldn't come, I needed someone and Tillie's so good and sweet.

'Is there anything I can do?' Tillie asked.

'No.' I paused wondering if I could shoulder the emptiness alone. 'But thank you.'

Regn's make-up case was open on the counter. I peered inside it—the black slit her hand slips in and out of throughout the day. Her lipstick was upright with the identifying color label. "Raisin Rapture." *Rapture, it fits her.*

Tillie was at the main desk talking about dinner, what she was going to buy at the grocery store, how her husband liked the gumbo. Hearing the word 'husband' struck the nerve of isolation in me. They have their lives, their history with a partner, and in Tillie's case, love. She is, I believe, the only *genuinely* happy person in the mix of us. With the others it's convenience, familiarity, security, a buffer against loneliness, and last but most of all, accepted peace at the expense of complacent resignation.

Eva wanted everyone to clock out. I went in the back. Regn was trapped—I couldn't get to her. I grabbed a yellow post-it and scribbled in script: *I still need to speak to you.* I stuck it to the inside lip of her purse.

Heading out of the office Regn was putting the change bags in the safe. She heard me punch my card in the time clock. She kissed her hand to me and waved behind Eva whose back was to us as she sat at the counter doing paperwork. It wasn't enough. I found a daily schedule lying around for scrap paper, and raced to get the urgency across to her. I wrote the first thing that came to mind. *Please understand. I know what time does. Westcott.*

'Bye Tillie. Bye Fernus.'

The pain makes me more social. Always, in the past, speaking someone's name seemed too intrusive, too personal. In that moment I spoke confidently, naturally. The pain made me less afraid of such mild idiosyncrasies. A larger fear dislodged the smaller ones. Everything else seemed easy. By comparison.

• • •

He pushes his way into the open hall. Outside he finds an upturned Japanese beetle on the bricks. He squats down, in no particular hurry, happy for a reason to delay. He picks him up, equally pleased to know 'she' would do the same and returns it safely to the wild flower bed. It is so quiet out. A perfect evening.

He looks over his shoulder. The breezeway is empty.

In the parking lot he sits in his truck a few minutes with the door open, listening to a squall of evening birds chirping away in a nearby tree. In one spattered black swallow, the birds take off, leaving the lot soundless. He starts his engine. Turning out of his space, Parson is exiting the gate. Westcott waves.

• • •

I had to take Mother to work. The battery in her car died last night. She was worried about driving herself, getting off work and discovering it wouldn't start up again. No one was in the office when I first called The Settlement. I didn't leave a message. I was on Jamestown Road. It was 8:40. I knew Regn would wonder where I was. I'm never late.

I called once more to let them know I was coming. Regn picked up. I could hear it in her voice—the relief.

When I stepped into the office I saw that same relief in Regn's eyes mixed with recent fear. She'd really been worried. I went back into the office for something and nearly hit her with the door while she was getting the Group sheets. 'Sorry,' I said almost bumping her. She lightly tapped me with her hand. Touching me reassured her I was there. I saw how hurt and worried she'd been.

I would remember this in years to come when that same voice of concern walled itself away. How a person can change without regard—how every sweet word, every affectionate sentiment, becomes lost—

Another incident occurred that morning. The security guards in the gallery insulted a customer who came back to the lobby requesting a refund for her complaint of grievance. Ann waited on the couple. I could only hear bits and pieces. Studying the woman—her mannerisms and voice—I knew what it was about. The guards had made a remark loud enough so other guests would look. Her husband was in the military—she stood bigger than him, broader, but comfortably so. I listened intently to the commentary, especially my co-workers. Tillie was oblivious to the whole thing, so we thought. Later she asked Regn and I if we'd recognized that the woman *was a man*.

Regn went to lunch from 12:15 to 1:00. I was washing my hands in the restroom with the lights off when she came out of the office. 'I left a little surprise for you in your bag.'

I bought my lunch. Sitting on the stairwell I held the envelope, studied her handwriting. I always savored the feeling of 'the moment before.' The card depicted a mountain scene with the river cutting through the hillside—in watercolor. I smiled at her misspelling. I love her misspelling of an English word.

I held the little Glücksschweinchen, "lucky piglet," in my palm. She wore a white bow carefully tied in string around the neck. '*Her name's Frederika,*' the card read. I placed her in my pocket with Friedrich.

I wanted to hug her again.

I bought my lunch. Sharon was in the café getting a cookie. 'You're not having dessert?!' Sharon remarked. 'You're a man—you have to have it.'

If you say so. I would have a cookie later. How conscious her statement made me feel. What would she *think* if she knew? It would be hard at first—a shock—but I think she'd come around.

In the afternoon a woman turned in a lavender floral scarf she'd found. I wrapped it around my neck and waited on a couple of customers before Regn said, 'Take *that* off! You look like a frew—'

'I'm flaming?'

Sharon observed, 'You look like a puff.'

Had I really become so comfortable with the ladies as to joke about being gay and putting on airs?

I went over to Sharon having removed the ridiculous accessory. 'I have a foreign hair on me from the scarf.'

'It might turn you into a woman, Westcott! What would you make of that?'

She didn't know. She couldn't know.

~

I thanked Regn for the card and Friedrich's girlfriend.

'The artists do it with their mouth and feet—the paintings.'

'I loved the scene.'

'I tied the string on Frederika.'

'You did?'

'Yes—'

'That was a delicate procedure. It took patience, I'm sure.'

JUNIOR YEAR. NOVEMBER

Often the Drummond's FHS marching band can be heard on the field running through its half-time repertoire. Westcott listens to the hollow knock of wooden block setting the rhythm for the other instruments to follow. Emptiness in its tone. He is seventeen. A gust of wind sends autumn leaves fluttering to the ground before him, while the "maestro" fills his ears from behind. He likens the sound of its beat to the Kalahari bushman's language—the clicking made by rolling the tongue off the roof of the mouth and down upon your bottom teeth. Weekends he practices driving in a nearby church parking lot and along the Colonial Parkway—a very scenic and historical highway spanning the width of three lanes running parallel to the river; ideal for beginner drivers with its little to no traffic. During the week at eleven o'clock at night he'll go out with his mother and circle the neighborhood. He enjoys these late hour excursions—the air's crisp with the scent of fall, the sky clear and still, the moon distant, chilled with a bronze penumbra.

···

5 YEARS LATER. NOVEMBER

At the end of my break I entered the office. She'd purchased soup from the café. She looked around to assure privacy. I glanced to the camera. 'I don't think they have it bugged.'

'Sometimes you scare me, Westcott. Really.'

'How so?'

'It's hard to explain.'

'Maybe scared's not the right word. Overwhelmed—' I supplied.

'I'm not used to this. It's new to me. Maybe I'm scared of the way *I* feel.' The attraction was unfamiliar, but the feeling wasn't. She hadn't felt this way since—

She was alive again. Desire had taken hold. And she recognized the truth in herself. What she had denied or side-stepped all the years. Every woman wants her chance at passion. Even just once in her life.

Someone came to the window wanting change. When they shut the door, the moment had been shattered.

'I guess we're a hopeless case,' she said at last.

'It's a good feeling though.'

'Yes.'

'I love you a lot,' she added.

'Write it down.'

'I just told you.'
And I shut the door.

I left early that evening. I scrolled a note on a yellow post-it. Regn was in the inner-office. 'I put it in your bag.' I smoothed the sticky side onto a green folder in her purse.

Never forget—overwhelmed can be a rare privilege. It's no easy feat.
Always, Westcott.

• • •

I didn't worry *as* much what others thought. If I had any concerns about being conspicuous that morning, I don't remember them. With my large wheeled-in suitcase I walked into work. The wheels rattled along the grooved bricks in the breezeway. When I arrived my friends and colleagues looked at me with an air of speculation. Reading their unspoken questions I said, 'My mother kicked me out. So which one of you is going to take me in?'

'I will, Westcott,' Magda volunteered.

We all laughed. 'Where're you going?'

I'd brought my work—my paintings and photographs. Folded in towels, carefully packed to safeguard from jostling and scratching the frames. No one had asked me to bring them. I just went ahead and did it. There were moments when even my boldness amazed me. Regn had brought something out of me. Whatever that 'something' was, it was not guaranteed. Other times it eluded me; I'd revert to my old timid self. The only person standing in my way was me.

~

At lunch Eva suggests I prop the photographs on the counter. I was in Groups with Sharon. Though we'd been working the same days, it seemed Regn and I had had little chance to talk lately. The phone rings.

'Hey, kiddo, your work—I'm impressed, everyone is—you have such wasted talent. It's amazing, but I always knew *it is* in you.'

Parson drops by while I'm with Sharon. 'You're a talented young man.' Everyone keeps complimenting me. 'I'll be your manager,' Sharon offers. 'You need a promoter. Did you take art classes in college?'

'No.'

'You mean you've never had any formal instruction?'

I shake my head. 'It's just in me.'

'My God, Westcott. Why is it some people get all the talent!'

I ask Magda to walk to the ships with me. Magda keeps a steady pace. She is always immaculate in dress, even if it's casual. When she gardens I imagine she always wears an attractive straw hat. She asks me what my plans are for the future. 'You don't want to stay here at Jamestown do you? You have more important things to do.'

'Yes. *This* is hardly a career.' I look around indicating the Settlement.

She laughs.

'If you like, maybe you can come by my house next Monday. That way you can meet Lady Godiva. You don't mind watching her in March? She can get to know you beforehand.'

The last hour of the day I spend in the Rotunda with Sharon after Group Arrivals is closed.

'I'm exhausted.' I'm not used to all this talking. I'd been socializing all day and the compliments, though wonderful, found me weary.

I enter the office. Eva is talking to Regn and showing her the tenderness in her neck. Regn wants to talk to me—her expression says so. I come back in a few minutes. It's no use, Magda is getting her stuff to head out for the evening.

Will we get a chance?

Regn strolls to the lobby where I have been waiting for her.

'There is one picture you haven't seen.' We go into the office. I should have gestured for us to step to the stairwell. I reach into my satchel, pull the frame out of the protective pillowcase I wrapped it in. Knowing we can be heard I read Regn's words as she moves her voiceless mouth. 'It's beautiful.' The nameplate reads: *Waiting for you.*

In our silence Eva reads something, too.

Eva is *still* in the office when Regn and I walk out together. The lobby is warm and inviting. Outside night has descended.

'Can I carry anything?' she asks.

I have the suitcase, my briefcase, and the bag with my album from Anniversary Weekend. I'd inserted blank pages where Regn's pictures were included so no one else would see them when browsing the book. She takes the album. We stroll to the employee lot in the darkened evening, cool and refreshing. She mentions my work again and the private showing of the one item.

'It was conceived with you in mind.'

'I know how you feel.' Those words made it sound one-sided again. I wanted to respond to her, *And you?* She stood by my door before I opened it. She'll be off for four days—her granddaughter is visiting. I missed her even then. She looks around without actually moving her neck. Feeling it's safe, we hug. I want to tell her how nice she looks, that I'll miss her. I want to hold her a moment longer. I wish she'd kiss me again. I must love her; even if it seems hopeless I must find a way. I want to rest in her arms and for her to feel the warm protection of mine around her.

• • •

He'd gone to the privy. Regn stands in the lobby by his register. Through the many windows the trees loom darkly against the orange, lavender, and pink skies.

'Here, something for you.' She slips a yellow folded note into his hand and walks away. He savors it before reading its contents. There is time. Feeling its corners and all the possibility it contains. Finally, he unfolds the paper.

When she comes back he looks her in the eye. 'I don't need a translation.'

Stepping into the breezeway he feels achingly happy. Happy because his feelings are shared by Regn. Sad because he still can't touch her.

He'd been planning what he was going to say since the previous evening, rehearsing it in mind as he closed up the main gallery.

~

He tucks the note into his breast pocket. Thinking of the words. Only the essential had been written.

Ich liebe dich.
Fur Immer.
Regn.

They walk into the cool night. 'Look at the sky,' Regn's voice is wistful. 'You should take a picture.' It is purple melting into orange interfused with streaks, heavenly. '*I* have many like it,' he replies. They approach the gate. 'You know what my mother used to say when the sky was like this around Christmas?' Regn's voice is close in the dwindling light, nostalgic. Westcott looks to her, the sky illuminated behind stark trees. 'She'd always say, "The Angels are baking." ' He smiles softly. Sadly. Wholeheartedly. The window is shutting; he feels his nerve about to fail. Sharon, already in her car, comes plowing toward them in comic relief and honks her horn. 'Did you hear what she called me?' Regn laughs. Westcott is far away. 'Didn't you think it was funny?' 'Yes,' he answers politely, mechanically—for the pressing moment is soon to be lost if he doesn't speak. He's waited several days, several months not to be afraid of his own voice. His own desires.

'You want to know something,' he rattles under his breath.

'What?'

The evening is cool, refreshing like before. His voice sounds different then how he'd heard it in his mind. So quiet, gentle, sharp in the winter air. She was squeezing his arm before he'd spoken, protected in the dim light.

'I'd give my life to be with you.'

'I know.'

She hurries away, her heels echoing on the asphalt. A need to escape, to hide—not from him but herself—in the way her steps check themselves in pained flight.

DECEMBER

I drew a cardinal and set it as the desktop for Regn's register. Most of the day I spent hanging at the main desk. I told her my new sign-in password. It used to be Atticus7finch. Every few months the system requires you to change it. I chose Alwaysstay1.

'Westcott, you are *unverbesserlich*.' Incorrigible.

She bought me a cup of tea. Regn had on the pin I love of a Russian castle nestled in the countryside. It is oblong, shaped like a zeppelin and just needs a basket on the bottom to be a true blimp. I love the artistry in it.

Sitting alone in the office after closing my drawer, I considered again with betrayal that Eva may have been right in her attempts to keep us apart. In her own words, 'I'm just looking out for you.' She wasn't wrong. I hated her intervening because I didn't want to face the truth. I didn't want to believe it. I couldn't. I wouldn't.

I think of my colleagues. Rawlings, a teddy bear of an old man, Tillie with her lists for inventory and personal things to do, Sharon always dusting and sanitizing the work stations, all of them with a spouse to come home to, living each day with what they've come to expect from it, reasonably pleased, or if not, damned great at concealing it, Sharon especially. I envy that they have a partner, even if they're not completely happy. Then there's myself and Regn.

• • •

Wednesday was ours. A rare joy in such a long time. I was going to talk to the national park gift shop about selling my pictures in their store. I stopped at Flemings Engravers to have the nameplate mounted on Regn's picture.

Regn called again. It was going to rain. We'd better meet earlier. I waited for Regn. The drizzling rain gave way to sun. I took her picture in the hunter green cloak I said she should wear. The cloak her husband had bought her for her birthday.

'If we lived together would you be happy?'

'Yes,' I replied.

We spent four hours together. In the end she didn't want to leave.

~

She keeps talking; he hears "Steal Away" faintly playing in his truck. It is his ringtone on his emergency mobile. So faint, Regn cannot hear it. With his acute ears, Westcott listens. He knows who it is. No one else has his number. No one else would have reason to call. It is his mother. No one knows where he is—where they are. It is just Regn and him, a vacuum of sanctity.

'How did you get your name? Westcott—Wes.'

He wants to tell her. He notices the shortening of his name. He likes it.

'Some things are a mystery.'

I TREATED IT LIKE A DATE. 'Hey Wes.' Her voice seemed pleased to say it. She'd used a sick day and spent the afternoon at home. I'd cleaned out the cab of my truck. It wasn't dirty. It needed a freshening up. I wanted it immaculate for Regn. Her Volkswagen had no pet fur, no streaks on the window. Gilly's presence was known. I took Ol' Reliable over to the Buggy Bathe to have the exterior washed. There's something calming about a car wash. Watching the machine ejaculate its soap and the mop swinging back and forth, I felt excited. Tonight Regn would be riding with me. I wanted everything to be just right.

She arrived at 4:44 p.m. I did not pick her up from her house. She'd told her husband she was going with me to Magda's. It had been unwise of her, 1: not to let me pick her up from her house and, 2: if she told her husband who she was going with, then why hide me from him? Groundwork for suspicion had been laid. I didn't worry about it. We were going to have a nice time. There was nothing wrong with two colleagues sharing a ride to a social gathering. Nothing had happened. Words had been offered, but we were still in control.

'With the suitcases in the bed it looks like we're eloping,' she laughed. I wanted to say if she told her husband the guy driving her was the man who wanted to whisk her off her feet and make sweet love to her, he'd never have believed her. I said nothing except, 'You want to hear a great song? The lyrics are priceless.' It was the Kingston Trio singing, "The M.T.A." (Metropolitan Transit Authority). I played it only to make her laugh. I also like "Where Have All the Flowers Gone."

Regn had on a silk red blouse and black slacks with a dainty silver necklace and matching earrings. I wore my navy blue velvet coat and a tie. Sitting beside her she seemed, for once, a much older woman. I felt conscious of the age gap, which I preferred to ignore. Sometimes I couldn't. She was beautiful. The lasagna she baked rested on the floor by her feet in a glass dish covered with foil. If she noticed the truck was newly cleaned, to my quiet disappointment, she made no mention of it.

We were the first and last to leave Magda's house along with Parson who arrived fashionably late. She'd hosted a holiday dinner. I had unwrapped all my pictures. It was a private showing of sorts. Magda told me to bring them. Her husband was on the board for a local art gallery. I carefully wrapped each back in their towels and made haste to pack them up, trying to arrange them as systematically as when I first put them in the suitcases. Deborah had been the first and only person to say she'd buy one. I was shocked by her enthusiasm. She'd made no deliberation. She saw the one she liked and that was it. I sold it for $55.00. My favorite piece, titled "Stay." It was a sepia photograph of a tree stump on the island. What made it striking was the shadows, the composition of contrast in texture and lighting. In the background tall grass, marsh reeds border the river. Regn would buy the same picture as a gift for her daughter. I'd made a set amount of copies. Regn would be taking hers later. She was my best customer that Christmas.

I wonder what happened to those photographs? Who is looking at them now? What will her daughter, her son, her grandchildren think if they ever read this? What I want them to know is simple to say, not so

easy to believe. But it's the truth and the only thing remaining of the past. What Regn and I shared was
decent. We didn't set out to hurt anyone or ourselves. The affection was rare, rooted. It came from inside.

Arriving to the dark parking lot, hers was a lone car. Though she said otherwise, I
hopped out of my truck to assist in putting the pictures—Christmas presents she'd
bought—into her bug. We hugged tightly. 'I have something for you.' In my hand I held a
wishbone leftover from Thanksgiving. 'You know what it is, right?'

'You want me to break it?'

'Make a wish.'

She closed her eyes. It snapped on my side. 'I guess your wish will come true then,'
I told her. In my other hand I fished out of my right pocket a tiny folded piece of yellow
paper. I handed it over creased between my fingers.

'Don't be upset if I don't come tomorrow to the Foundation dinner.'

If she came, tomorrow would be the seventh day in a row we'd seen each other.

Regn unfolds the paper.
You're the woman I love.

SCANNING THE LOT for parking he sees a silver bug. It must be her. When he
sees the antlers and KRAUT 2 his heart leaps. He hurries to find a space. There
isn't one. He circles the lot, goes out, drives down the street. He can't believe she
decided to come.

Standing in line to get drinks from the bar, he compliments Regn on her dress, the new
one she'd been talking about getting. 'You're the only one who's said anything.'

He turns to Sharon who seems most flattered when he tells her the lavender eye shadow
she is wearing matches her blouse. She gives a Bugs Bunny look. She blinks and opens them
with the effect of a silent movie picture. *Boy-ing!* He reads her thoughts. What heterosexual
young man would notice such things?

Westcott gets a ginger ale and a Heineken. He doesn't want the latter. He has to make
the pretense. Sitting beside Regn the front of her black dress opens enough. It is respectable
and nothing more. He does not like a woman who flaunts her cleavage. Regn is not one of
those women. Westcott cautiously looks to see the elusive hummingbird etched above her
right breast. He finds himself inhaling deeply, with complete imperceptibility to anyone who
might be watching—though no one is—to catch the scent of her perfume. Sharon drags
him onto the dance floor. Her husband doesn't mind. After all it *is* innocent. They meander
across the floor to Regn who is shaking out a rhythm by herself like so many of the dancers.
None of the men ask Regn to dance. Everyone more or less has a date or spouse. Regn and
Sharon each take one of Westcott's hands. The three move together. Or rather they move
his limbs. He wants to step lightly, freely, to sweep across the floor. He knows he could if
it was just he and Regn and no one was watching. But no, that won't do either. He wants
to dance as a gentleman—to lead *and* direct this woman with precision, the precision and
deliberateness with which he's pursued her, unwittingly. He wants the world to look upon
them and see what he hides. He wants to be applauded and yes, even envied a bit, for his
grace and certainty of step. More than anything he wants Regn to move with him. Had he
the confidence, the experience, were he a true man, it could never have happened. It is the

slow advance that makes her love him. In many ways he is just a boy. She wants to protect him, but sometimes that look, that expression, is so old, determined. He knows what she wants. She can't deny the way the feeling of being loved makes her feel. It's been so long.

Parson and his fiancée arrive an hour later, about 9, and jump into the fun as young couples so easily do. He is loose, easy going. Unafraid. His Texas spirit coming out—a free range of command.

Two of the Sups have come. Celia and Jared. Westcott lets the holiday cheer smooth the veneer of animosity. As he had the year before, he enjoys the lovely atmosphere, the dim lighting, and *hors d'oeuvres*.

Halfway through the band takes a break. There is a raffle with door prizes. Everyone attending has automatically been entered. The third drawing catches Westcott's attention. 'Regn Tompkins!' Regn is surprised, strolls up to the podium and receives her gift. Sitting back down, she unwraps a commemorative 400th anniversary Christmas ornament.

The band starts up again. While the ladies congregate on the floor, Parson turns to Westcott. 'Have you ever met Regn's husband?'

It is an innocent question. How can he know such a question strokes Westcott's sorrow like an exposed nerve.

'No,' Westcott answers politely.

Why does he never come? Westcott is curious, but thankful her husband shows no interest.

They all stay to the end.

'Will you drive me to my truck?' he asks Regn. He wishes he hadn't. When she turns the ignition on the James Blunt cd is playing again. 5 months later. At the corner he tells her, 'Turn right here left.'

'Don't irritate me.'

He quickly apologizes detecting strong agitation in her voice. He'd been making a joke. Lucille Ball says the same thing to Desi Arnez in *The Long Long Trailer*.

'Just think, if you hadn't come, you wouldn't have received the ornament.'

'You're right.' Her mood is lighter.

She takes him to the church lot where he parked.

'Thank you.'

'I have a headache—from the drinks,' she says perhaps to soften the effect her irritation may have had.

Westcott opens his door, assuring her he's going to get out. The lights come on in her car.

'Can I see your hand?' he asks.

'Why, what's wrong with it?'

It is clumsy. His intentions falter. He hadn't meant *to ask*. He'd planned on gently taking her hand, kissing it—a perfect gentleman.

'I was going to kiss it.' He lets her hand go. 'I'm such a fool.'

'See you tomorrow, kiddo.'

That one word and she made him feel his age. He is devastated. He doesn't feel like a man driving beside a woman tonight. In that one statement an invisible line forms. She sounded more like a concerned mother. It is the same name she called her granddaughter when the two of them stood in the rotunda talking to him. She's used the term in the past when addressing him, but it was lighthearted, fun-loving. Never before has it sounded so impossible in its meaning. The feeling of that word is one-sided. Regn meant nothing by it.

At home he escapes upstairs feigning the pretense of being tired, having to work the next day. In bed, he finds himself crushing his body into the mattress, tossing and turning. The streaks of frustration stream down his face. He rolls onto his stomach burying his head beneath the pillow. He holds the pillow over his face considering how horrible it would be to die by suffocation—too close to drowning. He wants to melt into the mattress—the longing for another body comes over him in waves of chills that fill his chest in the visible form, which he feels without seeing in the dark—goosebumps on his arms. He wants her next to him, pulling the covers closer. He will not let age deter him.

Why, he wonders. *Why had he danced with her a year ago this night?* He feels worse than he did that night so long ago. Then he'd had a mission, a mission wrought with undying hope he would never abandon. Tonight he'd been consumed with absolute hopelessness, hearing her determination in the one word which she had undoubtedly offered affectionately, unaware of the effect it carried in its shadows.

REGN AND I WERE PRIVILEGED not to be interrupted during lunch. I opened the gift she'd left in my bag. A silk Santa and reindeer tie. Also tucked in the box was an air freshener in the shape of a cat's hind quarters. It said 'Cat Butt Air Freshener.' We laughed. She took my hand at the end of her break, squeezing it. She'd caught me fumbling with something under the table. I said I was putting money back in my wallet. My tape had run out; I was putting in a new cassette. Whether she believed me or not, she didn't say. 'You're so funny. You make me laugh and make me sad,' she offered. She loved the Elton John cd I left in her purse Tuesday. 'It was a wonderful surprise. I put it on immediately.'

I wish I'd gotten out of my chair and hugged her after opening my gift. I let her come to me when I want to go to her. I always wait for her to come to me.

In the late afternoon I tried on my prescription glasses for Regn to see. She thought they were most becoming and added to an intellectual appearance. 'Your voice is very calming,' she observed. We talked the day away. I had a headache from not eating enough. She rubbed the back of my neck with her hand, knowing my head was hurting. 'You look like you're in pain.' The sky was a distinct blue as we walked out together. She hooked her arm through mine. I put strength in my grip as I pressed her close. She'd parked next to me again.

• • •

From: Ryzon, Rose Marie
Sent: Friday, December 21, 20— 10:39 AM
To: Rowan, Westcott
Cc: Tompkins, Regn
Subject: What a JOY!!!!!!

Dear Westcott,

I am writing to you and copying to my precious friend, Regn.
Regn gave me such a beautiful Christmas gift today. This gift was given to me

by Regn with so much love that I wept instantaneously. The gift is one of your beautiful photographs, "Elsewhere". It touched my heart because it struck a chord very close to home for me and because it is so evocative that my soul felt full.

Thank you for bringing such beauty and creativity into my life with your special talent and gift.

Love and Blessings Always,
Rose Marie

THE DRIVE IS PLEASANTLY SOMBER. The Sunday road wet and gray. I could barely discern the sleeping trees. Headlights were in order. Still and quiet. "Dante's Prayer" fills the interior of my truck. One could not drum up a more appropriate song for the haunting atmosphere. The view through the windshield is cooling soup, an ocean of possibility. I don't *cast my eyes* to the horizon; I enjoy what is immediately in front of me. I do cast my *soul to the sea* according to McKennitt's lyrics. I arrive first and a little ahead to the location I'd suggested. I listen to an occasional acorn drop and the soft patter of tapering rain; I sit with shivering anticipation in this inlet along the Parkway. The mist and fog are dense, enveloping the trees, masking any evidence of the river, eliciting a melancholy atmosphere at that hushed, solemn hour. I look at my watch. 7:27 a.m. It's the Eve of Christmas Eve.

Elton John plays softly when Regn pulls in beside me. We hug with the scent of earthy dampness surrounding us. I carry my present over, which I'd put in a brown grocery bag to be inconspicuous. I didn't want my neighbors seeing me with a Christmas gift on my way to work! Not that they'd care. I didn't want the attention. We sit in her car.

I acquired Mother's knack and love for gift-wrapping. The other evening preparing my gifts for family, I relished the last gift to wrap. A square box. I placed the bronze item I'd purchased inside a soft striped piece of blanket adorned with wild horses. I got the blanket at the fabric store. I cut a small piece and kept the larger portion for myself then placed the bundle in a box. Square boxes are very difficult for achieving perfect seams without excess paper on the sides. I smoothed them taut and added a ribbon and bow. Last I placed four Santa stickers on each cross of ribbon and a label. I inspected my handiwork with satisfaction. My, but it did look perfect. I took a picture.

Regn does not seem to notice the Santa stickers or the way the blanket is carefully folded so the horse is evenly displayed. It is very dark in the wee hours of the wintry morning. She enjoyed opening the package though. That I did see. And she loves its contents. A bronze carving of a woman leaning against an ornate box with lightly painted flowers near the base of her silver blue gown. I'd ordered it through The Victorian Trading Company. I thought Regn could keep something in it, an item of jewelry. I also bought a delicate silver dragonfly necklace. Regn loves dragonflies. I included a letter folded in a special origami style and set a few imitation flowers inside the box—nothing large or tacky. Just some delicate lavender flowers for accent. I didn't consider whether a man would go to all this trouble. It wasn't trouble. I took delight in getting it ready. I was excited to give her the gift. It was my pleasure.

A woman once,
a woman always—
Your heart's your own
even now in the fall of your days—

My letter concluded.

She rubs my scruffage—my downy sideburns, holds my hand as we sit in her bug. I'd given her my gift. I couldn't forgive myself for not knowing *how* to be a man and, after all this time, for still being afraid. She held my head close. Was she going to kiss my mouth? It's just what I wanted. But I turn my head away. She kisses me on the cheek. 'Don't be so shy, Westcott.' She rubs the smudge of lipstick from my face. I long to kiss her. I am cold, tired, shivering more from nerves than dampness. I want to stay with her there—. The leaves are falling on the windshield. The James River remains a sheet of gray. Her scent rubs off on my skin, stays all through the day. When I get home I take a sock and rub it against my skin to gather the scent in the hopes of preserving it. I put the sock in my shoebox of belongings. I want the courage to take the initiative. It's complicated on her front and on mine.

~

I wanted to live in that hour indefinitely. The day gave way to rain. I thought of her as it came down.

In the afternoon Ellis and I went biking along Greensprings and onto the Island. I wasn't with her, my mind was far away. I felt guilt. I should have been enjoying the ride with my sister; my thoughts were of that morning. I didn't share this place—The Island—with anyone but my Lady. My Lady—it was a term of affection not possession. We rode out to Black Point, got off our bikes to stretch our legs at the river's edge. Though it bothered me, I couldn't help turning my back in silence on my family. There was nothing they could do and to be alone was, ironically, what I preferred. It wasn't fair to my sister; I was taking her for granted.

• • •

New Year's Eve

I listened to "My Guitar Gently Weeps" on my way to work. For a moment, walking in, I thought I might be all right if I never came back. There's a reminder of Regn around every corner. I'm beginning to see the impossibility of it. I'm working against years and years of mindset. *And yet* she has more freedom *now* than if we'd met when she was younger. Her kids are grown, living lives of their own—I am the reason—I hate myself for something I have no control over—my "chronological" age. I've been changing right before her eyes. I envy her age. The situation prompts me to love and despise life all at once. She's watched from her perch of experience.

I KNOW THE SCENT of my love for her, the scent of it in the spring and how it was. The senses return late at night when I lie awaiting the escape of slumber. She comes to me and the memory of love's beginning—the scent of its fever. After all these years.

• • •

To be punished for not feeling the way I look. "I guess that's why they call it the blues," Elton sings. It was cold, damn cold when he left work. They agreed to rendezvous in Colonial Williamsburg. The main street. He wore his thick, heavy, dark brown suede coat. In leaving work he quickly made a b-line for the large wooden wastebasket by the restrooms. He heaved. His stomach retched. A dry heave. Nothing. The eager anticipation. The reserve. He couldn't keep anything down. He drove to the historic area and stepped inside his favorite store smelling of mothballs.

The Scottish Store Unlimited: Tweed caps, bagpipe music, an enormous 7-foot bear in a kilt. He waited just inside, keeping warm. She hurried by on the cobblestone. Thomas Jefferson held his bronze pose on a nearby bench.

'Regn.'

She turns to the side. Sees him in the lighted frame of the store. They walk in the coldness. To the world, a few passersby, he is handsome stepping from the doorway in his white shirt, gray diamond tie, the silver tie-bar in the shape of a ship, navy blues, and his distinguished overcoat hanging round his gaunt frame. She is graceful in her hunter green cloak, shrouding her elegantly. Sound of heels on sidewalk. Regn takes out her handkerchief, wipes her nose. The streets are relatively quiet. It is warm to look upon. They are from another time—the streets—as are the two walking them.

Reading his reserve—he does not move—cannot move—she takes his palm, clutching it to her. He trembles. He can hardly look at her. She holds his hand in her lap. He squeezes it. 'I never get to hold anyone's hand.' He struggles to maintain composure. 'Well you can hold mine now,' almost desperately she adds, taking his palm. Her skin smooth. His entire body is trembling. She moves his arm to her gut. Knowing it will never be like this again, afraid she'll never let it, something inside gives way, a physical release within the walled breast, a surge of coldness infusing with warm. *I* hug her with all the years. Let go of the restraint inside, *release myself.* 'You're shaking,' she says. I feel myself shaking, hold tighter.

A wall has come down. Silently we let it fall. Moisture finds its way onto her shoulder as I study the quiet night through her window. Soundlessly I cry.

I hug her for my life, sensing the memory might very well have to sustain me. She gives me her handkerchief. I want to tell her the cold from our walk has my nose running.

I clutch the delicate material in my fisted palm.

'You keeping it?'

'Do you mind? Yes.'

I give her a handwritten letter. She holds it to her nose to take in its scent from my pocket.

I slide from her leather seat into the cold night air.

JANUARY

I'm in the rotunda watching the sun over the James ripple in squared shadows on the wood paneling. It's cold—the room is so large. I hear the piped-in audio of birds from the main gallery, the violin in the 2 ½ minute film upstairs, the hum of electricity, and yet the light on the walls is loudest. I want to insert a tampon and relish the sensation of something entering me—the boredom yearns for it. *Insert.* The word arouses me.

In the beginning you don't give much regard to new surroundings and persons simply because they've yet to establish themselves in degree of meaning. Do I remember what it was like first touring the museum—taking it all in? Little did I know how familiar the place would become. A new job with tasks made interesting by the simple fact that they were different—something I hadn't done before—not that they were exciting in themselves—it was the varnish coating of *new* that was inviting.

In the cabinet, below the desk, I know they are kept. A sign in the ladies restroom, on the silver casing, where they are expected to be says, *Please see attendant.* No quarter needed or was it fifty cents now? Standing, the camera has me in view—the black boo globe fixed to the ceiling across the room. Another down the hall, and another still behind the stairwell near the restroom and theatre exit. I squat, open the cupboard, remove a bottle of cleaner and set it on the countertop. From my pocket I take the paper towel I'd brought from the men's room. I lift my head. A bird in a nest. No customers coming. The Great Hall is quiet. The film is running. I reach into the box amidst the miscellaneous items—flashlight, Windex, a volunteer's jacket—and remove three rods protected in cardboard, a sealed wrapper peeking from each end. There are plenty left. Not enough to miss. I fold the paper towel round them. Extra fingers. I hurriedly stuff them in my front left pocket, push them down, keeping my hand over them.

'My sister called and said...I told her we had...A guest needed one...I brought some from the front to restock down here and just forgot to take them out...'

I imagine my response were I happened upon, or security to somehow see me on film suspiciously slipping something into my pocket. Should one, say, just fall out of my pocket while I sit at my post, what *would* they think? Just curious? Weird? Disturbing? Shady? The seat of my pants is damp. Nerves, anticipation, restlessness. I relish the prolonged expectation and consider going into the restroom now. Coming inside, the gentle push. No, it's too early, shouldn't keep one in that long. This evening. Tonight if I'm not tired. Best before dinner, on an empty stomach. Alone in my room. I feel my body preparing.

'When's the film?'

'Every twenty minutes. Next one will be at 4:15.'

They head upstairs to see the smaller gallery.

In the quiet of my room, winter cold outside. Better in the spring, when the light lasts well 'til half-past eight. Natural light. Dimming twilight. Warmth without the electric heat. I go through the processes, mentally, unwrapping the delicate apparatus. I look out the windows of the rotunda, the sun is setting. The pull is never so strong as that moment just before dark.

Standing, I feel a shudder between my legs, a jolting shiver twitches my shoulder to attention. I press my groin to the wooden corner near the small swinging gate.

Discretion triumphs. No movement. My obscure bulge from "packing" remains decently checked. A crease on the face of my navy trousers that never stiffens. I press the corner into me, feel nothing. I swiftly step from behind the desk, leaving myself, opening the gate with my thigh as I push out, pace the dulled tile and royal carpet, picking faces from the thread. Monkeys. They look like monkeys—the flowers and swirls. The monkeys have flowers for eyes. I take in the giant chandelier anchored above. The twin elevators. The corridors leading to the breezeway, lobby, and down the Great Hall. All empty.

HAVING STRETCHED his back he puts the comb in his mouth. It has become a ritual. There is little pain to warrant biting down on something, but just in case— He stretches his arms and spreads his feet apart, the left a bit in front of his right. Unbuttoning his jeans and lowering the waistline just enough, his torso turns toward the mirror. A hard angle to manage, his straining muscles remind. He searches for the right point, anticipation building. Countless times but the idea of sticking himself with a 24 gauge needle still isn't appealing. Sometimes he enters too high or too low. The thigh is too muscular—it hurts more than the gluteus maximus.

It's only twice a month, but what if I went away to a foreign country, what if I were marooned on an island and couldn't order the supplies—it makes me dependent. If I just stopped—it makes him tired just thinking about it. He stands tall, his shoulders thrust back, his chest open.

The 1.5 inch needle goes in almost flush to the skin before he depresses the plunger. He is sparing, always injecting the least amount, not even a ½ cc. His prerogative. Discarding the used syringe his flank stings as the foreign liquid begins to migrate through the muscle.

He feels certain he is shortening his life.

———

Regn walks the Island, alone. Distant expectation. A fresh dusting of snow sharpens the bare trees and crystallized silence. She sits on the railing of the bridge, slips a hand inside her pocket and pulls out an envelope. Inside she finds a solid acorn, dipped in a golden coating, heavy, the size of a kernel. A note and something else.

THE COLOR OF THE MOUNTAINS

For Regn

It's cold out tonight.
The wind was a sad reminder, yester eve,
of the silence between. How I want you to know—
Your blazer on the chair—
reading glasses, make-up case, Raisin Rapture on the counter—
Your suit that compliments your hair
The sound of your shoes in your sure-footed gait
Your conjugative charm of consonants into beautiful accent—
The T's become D's and W's V's
When you look at me and I feel it cannot wait
Your multitude of smiles—
distanced melancholy,
silly sweetness with a
slight droop of the mouth to the left—dissembling sorrow
Your eyes—Ah yes, so hard to see
A somber, resolute complacency in their
mild tilt of silenced battles
For being a woman—I saw the tears come
from behind your sunglasses one day,
stolidly down the crease of your nose—they seemed
to seep up through your skin—
Your hand without the ring
I love you the color of the mountains—
deep, soft, long shadows—
Would my lady receive me—it *is* my greatest dream

Wednesday 30 January

The wind whistles—breath through teeth, as rain falls on the eaves of Westcott's house. He awakens suddenly. His feline companion, Helmsley, lies stretched beside. Feeling Westcott move he, too, stirs from his slumber and steps to the foot of the wooden bed, peering out at the wet, stormy pre-dawn. Westcott reaches to the floor on his right, lightly picking up his brass, double-belled alarm clock. 5:19. He sets the clock down, lies there, no longer welcoming sleep. The words come in the dimness of his unlit room. Things he wants to say.

Outside, the slick black damp streets trace a zip-line path from Westcott's home to Regn's, three miles away.

Regn is up, already out of bed. She sits finishing some cereal, leans over the boiling pot contorting her face in the steam—ooh, eeh, ahh—the muscles around her mouth and neck contracting, firming, strengthening. Her cat strolls in—she lets her lick the remaining milk from the bowl. She enters her garage. The silver car backs out. Jay's truck is still in the driveway.

Regn is on the rowing machine and then swimming. She wears a black swimsuit. An elderly gentleman is soaking in the whirlpool. They exchange polite greetings as she walks by. In the main pool Regn's form is smooth; like a frog she swims.

Having bathed in her tub to wash the chlorine from her skin, she studies her naked body in the mirror at home.

'Genuinely becoming,' she scoffs in her accent, mere reiteration of what Westcott had told her. She lifts her breasts, brushes her abdomen, turns to examine her hinterlands. It is a ritual she performs every morning as denoted by her sigh. She knows she is aging. Her breasts are no longer firm, perky. And if she isn't vigilant the supple pouch just beneath her abdomen, the woman's nemesis in older years, will gain weight. But all is not lost. She still has her looks. She still has something—. She sighs in disbelief. That her body could be so desired in spite of what she sees as flaws. She knows Westcott *isn't* smitten. He's serious. Hard-boned, young skinned, iron flat stomach. He wants her. On some level she knows this. The way he looks at her makes her feel alive again. He notices everything.

It is a little past eight. Westcott gets out of bed, pulls his jeans on over his pajamas. In the bathroom he steps on the scale having just flushed the latrine. 130 lbs minus any water. He brushes his teeth, washes his face at the vanity sink in his mother's room. He looks at his reflection in the mirror. Dark brown hair. Pallored face. Gray blue eyes. Skinny fellow. His Irish heritage discernible. His white shirt does not ripple or bulge with muscles. He is slight and gaunt. The house is quiet. He takes Miss Gilly out the back door, down the tall deck, into the yard. He quickly returns to find Lucy in the kitchen. She is the best tenant they've had. Beginning in high school they started renting a room out, just for a little monthly supplement. There'd been the Grad students. A wonderful gentleman from Romania and then a classmate of Ellis' at William & Mary, Everett. Then Lucy and the Russians. Lucy was more like a family member, an adopted grandmother. A sweet woman with beautiful white hair. She asks if he can open the clasp on a pair of nail clippers. Her pure white hair and glasses twinkle. She's in her late 70s. She wears her solid wedgwood blue sweatshirt. Her favorite color. When she showers she turns the sprayer off to conserve water. Habit. She is not Polish, but Westcott and his Mother joke warmly by calling it a Polish bath. There is no need to be sparing, but it is habit instilled from hard times. Lucy has always been thrifty, conscientious, conservative, but happy. In fact, Lucy has never been anywhere but Virginia, her birth state. She's had a hard life, left school after fourth grade 'to help her Mama at home,' she says. Her husband died. Now she looks after her daughter who still lives nearby and her grandson. She remains good, bitterless, in spite of all. With some effort Westcott releases the hook, hands the clippers back.

'Why I thank you, Westcott. I'll be sure to dance at your wedding.'

I'd like that. A wedding? Or for her to dance at it? Both.

Westcott smiles opening the kitchen blinds, a flash of quiet sorrow in his expression. He goes upstairs to his mother's room. She's in bed. Her day off. He opens the front window blinds, pulling on the beaded cord. He touches her arm.

'I'm going.'

'You're off at 3:30.'

'I should be.'

'Love ya.' She turns onto her side.

'Yes.'

He closes the door. In his room he puts a handheld recorder in his pants pocket and picks up a dark copper-colored bottle. Wrangler cologne. Squirts a dab on his neck and grasps the handle of his brown briefcase. His blue truck pulls out of the drive. The storm has lifted. The sun is shining.

"Hey Jude, don't make it bad, take a sad song and make it better...you were made to go out and get her..." The engine creaks as it silences. In front of him a fitness center. 'Curves for Men.' He watches the far right corner of the lot, scanning the cars turning in—he glances at his watch. It's just now 9:30. His face brightens. He gets his keys, lifts his dark gray tweed cap from the seat—the one Lucy gave him the Christmas before, though her budget is tight—and gets out as Regn pulls up. The sound of passing traffic on the nearby interstate filters through his alert senses at such a fresh hour. Celtic music, "The Book of Secrets," performed by Loreena McKennitt, fills the interior of Regn's Volkswagen.

'You okay?' Regn asks.

'Yes, why?'

'You look tired.'

'Do I? Something woke me up at five o'clock this morning.'

'At 5 o'clock?'

'Yes and that never happens.' He wants to tell her it was the anticipation of today. It is too early for serious conversation. They have the whole day to talk.

A dinging sound goes off in the car. Westcott reluctantly pulls the seat belt around to fasten it. He hates this feature in newer vehicles. He never wears his belt. Where's the risk, the freedom, if you're always buckled in?

She is wearing jeans, a maroonish-purple high neck cotton shirt. Westcott looks at her slightly less than shoulder length redwood hair. It covers her ears, the bangs fall over her forehead to the left in a natural wave.

'I made you a cd—it's a mix. I titled it B-E-E-M.'

Beatles, Elton, Eagles, and Mix she reads.

'That French song is on here.'

'We have a long drive; we can listen to this for a bit and then put it on,' she says.

He fiddles with his cap. Unbuttons, snaps it.

'Stop that. Why do you—you don't have to be nervous.'

Westcott lays the cap on his knee. He wears his heavy suede, dark brown coat. It is stiff to move. It hangs on him, 'fits' him. It wears him and not the other way around. He should take it off. He doesn't want to cause a fuss. He leaves it on.

"The Highway Man came riding, riding—the highway man came riding up to the old inn-door." Westcott loves the prelude of McKennitt's rendition—a solo violin and the hailing wind, no lyrics. It is masterful.

In the tunnel to Norfolk he tells Regn, 'Better hold your breath.'

She smiles. 'That's something a kid does.'

Westcott wishes he hadn't mentioned it. He doesn't want her to think of him as a kid. He's not. Silently he holds his breath.

'Well,' Regn asks when they've hit the sunlight again.

Westcott had been quiet. It's a long tunnel. He needed to conserve every last breath.

'I made it. It's good for the lungs.'

'I don't know if I could hold my breath that long.'

At the Volkswagen manufacturer they sit and wait while Regn's car is serviced. They drove all the way to Virginia Beach and now sit at a small counter. Regn has brought pictures. He looks at them, at her in them, and then looks back at Regn. One in particular strikes him as 'glimpsing.' He reads it in Regn's eyes. Regret.

It is a photograph of her with friends, a housewarming, a wedding shower. On her lap sits a dish and utensil drying rack, the kind you put in the sink. He looks at it and at the girl's expression—the girl in the dress holding the unwrapped present. It seems to him and even Regn, she is holding fate in her hands. An emblem of domesticity and all the years to follow. She is so young sitting in that chair and not simply young because of the woman now sitting beside him, but because she *is* young, just a kid looking into the camera. It does not occur to her—the girl in the photograph—to ask, 'Let me, I wish to take the picture.' Looking at herself through time's eyes, she now asks the girl in the picture, *Why did you just sit there? You wanted to be on the other side. You know you did.* She demands. Questions. Regrets. Awakes.

~

Regn is scanning side streets for the restaurant she's been to with Rose Marie. She can't remember what street it's on. She sails through a red light.

'You just went through the light.'

'I did? Shit!'

'It's fine, no cars were in the intersection. No one saw.'

'I never do that.'

'You're fine. It's all right.'

The streets are quiet, strangely sparse. Westcott hasn't been to Virginia Beach since, since—he remembers it was the tourist season, years ago, hustle and bustle.

Beach front. Strange in the winter. So still.

Regn is about to give up. On the second time down the street she turns left. She sees it. The Heritage Café.

It's a bohemian environment, spiritual, inviting peace to all walks of life. The servers and clerks are adorned in Celtic attire. There's a sign that says 'Palm Reading.' It is a nice restaurant attached to a natural, organic grocery store. They have books on meditation, yoga, the Dalai Lama, Nietzsche. It is the type of store that would furnish the motto—*healing comes from within*, if it had a motto—*Love your body, replenish the soul*. Westcott is glad it *doesn't* advertise such things. He doesn't like that sort of gushing lovechild atmosphere. Come to think of it, that's just how Rose Marie talks. Her Christmas thank you, though meaningful, was an effusion of adjectives. Westcott prefers direct brevity. Letting the object itself reflect the sentiment rather than adding ridiculous fluff and ornamentation. Sometimes saying too much has the effect of killing the genuineness behind the sentiment. Regn and Westcott stand at the deli counter.

Westcott pulls out his wallet.

'I'm buying.' Regn counters his intentions.

'Oh no, I don't feel right about that.'

'Hey, times have changed. Besides, I asked you along.'

Westcott orders a turkey on rye and a lemonade. Regn gets the vegetarian dish—something with beans and potato salad. Westcott runs to the restroom. Regn pays and gets a seat. She picks a two-top beside the window. The sun is coming through. It is warm. Westcott removes his heavy coat, hangs it on the back of the wooden chair. Feels better.

'Tompkins,' the attendant calls. Regn doesn't notice.

'I'll get it.' Westcott is up before Regn. He brings the plates and drinks one at a time. Setting his drink down, he tells her, 'Thank you for lunch.'

He takes small bites, intermittently tastes a delicious chip, covers his mouth with hand, sips thoughtfully.

'Don't be shy, Westcott. Everyone eats.'

'I don't think I have a right.'

'Why not!'

'There was this girl in college. We'd sometimes get together for lunch and I'd never eat.'

'Did she?'

'Yes, well—she was a finicky eater. I'm pretty sure she was bulimic.'

'What was her name?'

'It was Therese, but she went by Tess.'

'Did she like you?'

'Yes. She sought me out.'

'And?'

'I hadn't experienced that before. I think she knew too much—about me.'

'What do you mean?'

Westcott turns his head, looks out the window, feeling Regn studying his gaze.

'What happened?'

'She was taller than me, which I don't like. She was also blonde, blue-eyed. I prefer brown hair, brown eyes, but I left college briefly and well—'

A man behind Westcott looks at them over his newspaper and spectacles. It is clear to him that they are not mother and son.

Westcott folds his remaining sandwich in a paper napkin. For later. He takes his lemonade with him. Standing to walk around the store his eyes reciprocate a silent question for the man with the newspaper.

Spell books, health books, spiritual healing, candles, greeting cards, jewelry. They take their time. Regn purchases a cd. Enigma. The two step over to the grocery portion of the store. They peruse the aisles. Westcott picks up a book on nutritious remedies for every ailment. It's alphabetized. 'Impotence,' he reads aloud. Regn mildly laughs. *That's what she probably thinks. O' Regn.* He told her he couldn't have children. She still doesn't know why. He puts the book back. Regn finds the lip balm she hoped was there since the last time she'd been in the store.

They park in a vacant lot near the beachfront and boardwalk. The two step onto the sand. Regn in her low-heeled black boots; Westcott in his brown leathers.

'Did you notice that lady in the store checking us out? You see, they look at you and think you're my son.'

'It makes it interesting. At least we were in the right place. The atmosphere in there seemed pretty open.'

'Should I start calling you son?'

'No. I could be your manservant or valet. I'll call you Miss Tompkins or Miss Baron—' (Bear-rohn) her maiden name pronounced with the German inflection.

'We're an odd couple,' she offers.

The wind is blowing out to sea. Regn's hair parts on the right of her scalp. The gray roots show, belying the dye. Westcott smiles internally. The intimacy of such a casual, endearing detail. Her face is free to the sun.

'If you could afford it, would you like to live here in one of these places on the beach?' Regn asks.

'I don't know, I'm not much for the beach—but if someone gave it to me I'd take it then sell it. I'd love a cabin in the mountains.'

'I prefer the mountains.'

'I know.'

'If I won the lottery,' she begins, 'I'd buy an old car for you—the 1930s Ford you like.'

A few seagulls. No one on the beach. No one. Early afternoon. The great tourist hotels looming sadly. Sleepily.

'You know I made a list of the things I want to do.'

'And, what are they?'

He hesitates in prelude.

'Well?'

'Gallop away on a horse. Publish a book. Jump off a small cliff or bank into a lake with just my shorts on, look down at a valley in Ireland or somewhere amazing, and...' *make love to a woman. Make love to you, Regn.*

'And—'

'The last one I think I'll keep for myself.'

'I think I know.' She stoops to pick up a small butterfly shell.

Does he hear the waves? Does he see the winter birds scurrying on the sand as though they're on stilts and being blown hither? He watches her boots cut smoothly into the sand.

They turn. Head back the way they've come.

A quarter, grain-grazed. Regn points with her shoe. Westcott picks it up. Something to remember the day by.

They sit in her car. Regn applies the lip balm. It's peach.

'Want some?' she mocks.

Westcott shakes his head, is quiet. Watches Regn apply the chap.

'Have you been to the Edgar Cayce Museum?'

'No, I've wanted to though.'

'We have time,' she says and they make their way.

It is warm inside the building. Regn goes to the restroom again—her third time, first at the service station, then the restaurant, and now here. Regn says it comes with age. Westcott moves toward the lavatory. The doorway is so skinny. He will always remember that, how narrow the entrance. So odd those doors. Inside he steps into a stall, pulls out his dated phone. His mother picks up. 'I'll be a little late from *work*.'

'Are you meeting Regn?'

'Yes, for a little bit.'

'All right.'

The toilet next door in the ladies' room flushes. 'I have to go.'

'All right. See you when you get home.'

'Yes.'

His back itches. A mild hot flash from the testosterone. They look in the gift shop first. A soothing rhythm, a Tibetan chant. One of the cds the store sells is playing. A meditation chant. Statues of the Bhadshavitah. Little Buddhas, small trickling water fountains. The music pulses softly. Hah, hah, hah, hah—and then lower—a cadence. He is sad again. His stomach needs privacy.

'I'm going to step to the privy. Take as long as you want.' This time he really uses the facility. He feels pressured knowing she waits, but somehow Regn understands. *We all do it.*

He takes off his white under thermal, puts back on his white t-shirt, blue overshirt, and coat. His back itches again. Hormones. The heat triggers it. In the winter his ears alternately become bright red, blood warm. He strains to hurry, go so as to be comfortable for the long trek back.

Coming out, Regn is right there.

'Okay?'

'Yes, just a bit warm.' He gestures to the shirt balled in the crook of his arm.

They walk up the stairs, into the Resource Library.

Westcott scans the bindings. 'Look,' he points to the section on Theosophy and Regn's favored author, Madame Blavatsky. Regn pulls one from the shelf. After a while he says, 'I think we create our own afterlives.'

Westcott goes round to the other aisle. Regn takes a pair of books and sits comfortably in a corner chair. A rustle of paper. He finishes his lunch discreetly. He pulls out his Olympus recorder. The screen shows it is still running. He comes down the aisle, looks upon a row of books running along the wall. Helen Keller. He picks it up, comes to Regn. He watches her read.

'I have a pen, you want to write the names of those books down.'

She takes it, finds a piece of paper, scrolls the titles.

Westcott shows Regn the opening sentence in Keller's novel, *Midstream.*

"When people are old enough to write their memoirs, it is time for them to die, it seems to me. It would save themselves and others a great deal of trouble if they did. But since I have the indiscretion to be still alive, I shall add to their burden by…setting down the burden of my life…"

It's getting late. They head to the top of the stairs. An exhibit on psoriasis—

'Hold on,' he steps to the side. 'My mother has this—'

The cold air is refreshing.

Outside, before getting in the car, Regn glimpses Westcott's expression.

'You look sad.'

'Do I?' He hadn't thought to look that way—

Regn hugs him. Westcott *lets* her.

They hit rush hour traffic on the way back entering the tunnel. Westcott feels his stomach compressing, laden, inert. He is silent. There are many things to say. Regn asked him to come. He doesn't want to scare her away. His mouth is dry. His head aches. He hasn't eaten or drunk enough. *That lemonade from lunch would be nice.*

'Mind if I eat something?'

'Don't get any crumbs in my car, you know how picky I am.' She means it, too.

Westcott eats some cheese nips he'd stowed in his pocket.

The evening light bothers his eyes.

'Mind if I put this down?'

'You can.'

He flips the visor. The road turns, they are no longer driving west, but perpendicular. It glows on the side of his face. He feels the discomfort in his stomach. The closer they get to their destination. Time is running out. What is it he wants to say?

Regn takes the long way home, through the historic area.

It is 6:30. They sit in the shopping center. *How fast the day went.*

'Well, it was fun. A nice time.' Empty summation. Westcott wants to respond, he wants to reach for, and hold her close again like that night not long ago. Where is his boldness?

'Yes,' he answers. He looks to Regn. Feels the seconds slipping, dropping like heads. *Mayakovsky. Aren't you a cloud in trousers, my boy.* He hesitates, searching for a silent cue. Would she hug him again? He doesn't know, should he say—

'Don't forget to listen to those songs on there,' indicating his cd. He fails himself. 'Thank you again for lunch.'

'Have a good evening.'

'I had a good time.'

'So did I.'

'Take care.'

Westcott steps into his truck, waves to Regn. In that moment he knows he will pay for being reserved. Inside he is freezing.

Regn pulls into her driveway and garage. Jay waits inside.

• • •

The next morning on her way to work Regn puts on *Westcott's* cd. His voice has an Irish accent—he is singing "When Irish Eyes are Smiling." Her face wears amusement. And then she is sad. He plays the piano—"Für Elise" and the song he wrote for her titled "Always," a brief solo, only instrumental. Words are not necessary.

Westcott sits in his room. At his desk, working, he rests his hand on a solid white handkerchief, trimmed in green—her handkerchief. The evening of that handkerchief revisits him. She'd pulled him close, moved his arm around her, and something inside gave way. A physical release inside his walled breast. *He'd* hugged her with all the years stored up in him. The hardness in his chest hurts. He needs it to come, he needs the warm embrace of affection to ease his heart.

~

He steps into his closet. Under the hanging clothes, on top of the chest, he reaches back. He bends, retrieving what cannot be seen from the height of standing. He pulls out a box of Q-tips stored inside a plastic bag, sets it on the small bookshelf, starts to unzip his pants, stops. The Q-tips provide an easy, slender means of masturbation when he's not in the mood for a long self-interlude. Something sleek, clean to slip inside the emptiness between his legs where no hand but his own has ever felt. He drops to his knees, clenching his fists. Leaves the Q-tips as they were. He doesn't want that particular 'high' at the moment. The closeness of the closet envelops him. Suffocates, but cannot hold his body. He wants to feel her arms around him. To be loved before carnal intimacy.

FEBRUARY

Westcott stands on the pavement looking out at the marshland along the James River. Regn's bug pulls in next to his truck. He casually turns, ambling toward her.

'You want to go this way,' she gestures.

'I thought we could sit in the church a bit.'

'You want to take this and cut around—'

He would prefer to sit. He speaks less when walking. But he lets her lead the way. They head off on the trail.

'You like my belt? There's a story behind it.'

It is a navy cloth belt with a light stripe of blue between—a brass buckle engraved with a tree is clasped in the middle.

'I had to sew this to make the buckle work. It was my father's. He had it twenty-five years.'

'It'll be an antique soon.'

'It already is. So, what are you going to put for the one fact about yourself?'

'Fact?'

'Yes. At work there's a sheet for the meeting.'

'I was there yesterday, just checking-in and didn't see one. Eva didn't say anything to me about it.' Regn is curious.

'The envelope is right by the time cards. It's an anonymous fact about yourself.'

'What about you? What did you put?'

'I was thinking—it's the god's honest truth—I didn't like my given name so when I was 18 I legally changed it.'

'At 18 you changed your name to Westcott?'

'Yes.'

'Why? Was it common, you just didn't like it? What *was* it?'

'Boswell Incubus.'

'Really. You have me wondering.'

'I can't say.'

'You won't even tell *me*. Now that hurts.'

'There are things you've said you never tell anyone and this is one of them.'

'I have to know. It's going to drive me crazy. Bartholomew, Charles, Ryan?'

'I'm going to have to smack you—' Westcott smiles playfully.

They take a service road to the right that gives way to a clearing. They head across a field. Canadian geese mill around. Regn steps to a nearby dogwood. Wraps her arms around its girth. Presses her face lightly. Pats its trunk.

'I love trees. Do you think it's strange, hugging a tree?'

'No. It's not strange.'

'I'm enjoying the time off. It's nice to be a Classified and receive two months paid leave. How have you been doing, Westcott?'

They sit on a bench overlooking the river. A tree stands sentry directly to the right. It truly is a scene one expects to find contrived by filmmakers. This is genuine. The bright sun shining off the water. Both Westcott and Regn wear their sunglasses. Regn puts her feet up on the bench and her back against the armrest. Westcott sits forward. It is not a large bench. He looks at her neck, focusing for a moment on the silver dragonfly necklace he'd given her for Christmas. He smiles ever so slightly. He does not say anything.

~

'That sandwich was scrumptious the other day.'

'What sandwich?'

'Last week. At The Heritage Café. It was very decent.'

Regn does not find his description odd. That a sandwich is decent or scrumptious makes no difference to her. She's grown used to Westcott's eloquent language.

'Can I ask you something completely off subject?' He's been preparing for this since that afternoon he left her car without so much as reaching for her. He's tried all morning to come out with it.

'Yes.'

'My saying it doesn't flow naturally or anything, probably sounds completely inopportune and foolish, not to mention absolutely downright ridiculous. Don't look at me like that.'

'I'm waiting for you to say it, Westcott. You can look at other people when they say something. You don't want me to look at you?'

'I'm not used to these conversations.'

'Well then say it.'

'It's so simple it seems rather ridiculous.'

'Say it.'

'I mean something so—'

'Say it.'

She'd let him that night they went for a walk, but *she'd* been the one to take his hand. Would she let him do it again, if he came to her?

'Would you mind if—I—felt your face?'

He is relieved before she even responds. Relieved to have gotten it out. A weight has been lifted. The expectation of his own words set down.

'No, you can feel my face. I don't mind. You *can* feel my face.'

Westcott doesn't move.

'I—don't know how.' His voice is soft. Quiet.

Regn takes his hand in her hand, presses it to her face.

Silence.

'There. Is it soft enough?'

'Yes. Very.' *And so warm.*

'Is that what you want to do? Hmm?'

'Yes.' He answers quietly, almost—ashamed. 'It's the simple things I tell you.'

'You have cold fingers.'

'I know.'

'You can feel my face. You can feel my eeeaaaars.' She laughs. 'You can feel my neck if you want to.' She moves his hand over the right side of her face and down to her neck. Still he does not command the direction of his touch. He allows Regn to guide him, though he yearns to brush her bangs and direct his hand. 'You can even feel my leg. It's *just* a leg.'

'I tell you there is nothing natural in what I do. It is so—stilted.'

Westcott is shivering, not just from the wind.

'I told you about those characters in the Golden Compass. You ever read it?'

'No.'

'The two characters at the end can't be together. They're from two different worlds. If one goes to that other world they will eventually die. So they each have to go back to their own world. It's sad. You want to go to the church?' She means the small Island church. All stone with beautiful windows letting the light in, no feeling of religion, only timelessness. Vastness.

~

It had been quiet, peaceful on the Island, inside the little church. At Regn's suggestion, she drives them to Waller Mill Park, 20 minutes away. She has no desire to go home.

'You said something the other day that made me sad. It probably sounds odd to you, it's something someone says in casual passing and you wouldn't think much of it. You were saying if you won the lottery what you would do. You'd put a large sum away for your granddaughter—for college, a car. And you said in a few years the guys will be chasing her—. Well, I just thought it's so fair. Here's someone who has her whole life ahead of her—it's exciting, it's absolutely right—and that's how it should be.'

'You didn't have that?'

'Yes and no.'

"A Life Uncommon" faintly plays on Regn's stereo. They've circled back in conversation.

'A one-line fact about myself that nobody knows—' Regn thinks aloud.

'Your hair's wind-blown.'

'So?'

'Nothing. It's natural. I like it.'

'There's one thing I do that I don't think I should tell you.'

'Go ahead, I'm not going to tell anyone.'

'I—I don't think you would. But it's very private.'

'You have to tell me. My imagination is going to run away with me and that could be worse.'

'It has something to do with the human body.'

'All right—'

'And more. The—the private part of the body.' Regn laughs, hoping to brush over it.

'Shaving or what?'

'Well, I shave my underarms and legs, but I also—'

'Yes. For fun? Or all the time?'

'No. See I do it regularly because—'

'Hygienically?'

'That, too.'

'Is it a European thing?'

'No, I'm different. It's a "Regn thing." Some women do it when they wear bathing suits.'

'Right, but they don't completely—I mean they'll shave the swimwear line.'

'I don't completely shave it.'

'That's how you made it sound. What you're telling me is you wax your crotch.'

Regn laughs. 'Nooooah. I trrrrrim it! So it doesn't become really bushy and—. See, I'm telling you something now Westcott that isn't good. I saw one time growing up—when we always went to the pool—there was this woman and she had this bikini on and everything there was sticking out.'

'You should do it with scissors and not a razor.'

'I do it with one of those—that you use for sideburns, one of those things that has the safety thing on top.'

'If you do it with a razor—'

'I don't.'

'Well no, but when it comes back you'll itch like wild fire.'

'Hey, when you give birth that's what they used to do. They'd shave you and then it itched like hell. I don't do that. I TRIM it. A light little haircut.' Her voice raises an octave for emphasis. 'I mean this woman was ridiculous. There was hair coming out everywhere. I thought, *Oh, Christ, never.* I like to take care of myself and for me that is part of it. Maybe I should put that as my fact.'

An ambulance is in the *oncoming* lane. Regn slows and moves to the shoulder.

'You don't have to pull over,' Westcott tells her. He can't stand when people stop. It feels sheepish. There isn't a fire engine barreling in hot pursuit of the ambulance. There are no cars for the ambulance to pull around. It's going to *stay* in the oncoming lane. Hesitation is what causes accidents. Westcott is wired for efficiency. Regn's mistaken sense of security registers in the back of his mind.

'Don't criticize me while I'm driving.'

Westcott is surprised, mildly offended. He was only stating a fact.

'I can't believe I told you this.'

'Lots of women do it. You are a contradiction though. You're very open in some ways and in others incredibly not.'

'What do you mean? I am very open with you.'

'Yes. I just said that. But in other ways—'

'Well, some things—there's a limit. There's a line where you stop.'

'I think you just crossed that one.'

'I know. I feel stup—'

'Don't feel foolish. What you told me isn't unusual. I wasn't shocked.'

'You weren't?'

'No. It doesn't offend.'

'Good. I'm glad. That's how much I trust you. That's what I think of you. I can tell you things. I might say I always eat the whole apple. Everyone knows that about me. I make a big thing about it. I think it's a waste to throw the core out. It's the best part.'

They detour to the restrooms before hitting the trail. Regn stands outside the men's entrance waiting for Westcott.

'Not fair. You shouldn't finish before me. I told you I suffer from paruresis.'

'I'm just fast,' Regn explains.

'Expeditious urinator! That's what you can put as your fact.'

'I'm going with Magda Thursday to lunch and then for a walk. The two perfect women.'

'There you go. You can say, "I'm one of two perfect women." '

'Yes, we always say that. Oh my god, we can't stand ourselves we're so perfect!'

~

'I tell myself I don't have to stay here, but at the moment there's nowhere else I want to be.'

'You want to stay at the Settlement forever?' Regn asks.

'No. Of course not. I'd go out of my mind.'

They let conversation wander with the path, heading to a square wooden box up a small flight of stairs. It is a lookout. The lake is calm. On the ledge, written in permanent marker, inside the shape of a heart, is an inscription. Regn starts to read it.

You believed in me when others doubted me. No one compares with you. I never loved like this before and it's killing me inside. You are my everything. I love you so, so, so, so much. If this isn't true love I don't know what is. Keep your head up and do the right thing no matter what happens. If we ever break up I'll always carry you, you know that.

'That's beautiful. Someone put down what they thought. Don't you think it's nice?'

Westcott is quiet. He knows someone young wrote it. Young lovers. He doesn't tell her it sounds maudlin. It says too much. Romance is words. Love is unspoken. And romantic passion is movement, knowing without asking.

'It's cute,' he says.

~

They find a picnic bench.

'Here, you can feel my scars,' Westcott allows.

Regn takes her hand, rubs the front of Westcott's shirt.

'You're right. I can feel them. Why do you have these scars; did you do it to yourself?'

'No. I'm not into self-mutilation.'

'Were they inflicted by someone else?'

'In a way.'

'You don't want to tell me?'

'Oh Regn, it's not that I *don't* want to—I worry you'll have some latent prejudice. I often wondered if you were some test.'

'Believe me, Westcott—'

'You want to hear something odd. You made it possible for me to love a woman's body.'

'My body's hardly the best looking. Why didn't you like the woman's body?'

Regn pulls Westcott close again holding his head to her breast—she pulls his arm around her waist. Brushes the side of his head with her hand. He listens to her heart beating and the sound of her breath.

'Don't worry, I'm not looking down—'

'I'm not worried.'

Westcott sees the gray wing of the hummingbird above her breast. He wants to look down her shirt. He pulls his eyes away.

Regn takes Westcott's hand. Runs it up and down the top of her thigh.

'Here, a new experience. How silly it is.'

They laugh.

'It's sad but true.'

'Once, in Germany, there was this guy, I'd gone out with my sister to a dance.'

Westcott listens to Regn's voice reverberate within as his ear presses softly against her breast. 'This pilot in the Air Force whispered in my ear, "I want to make passionate love to you." I wish I'd gone with him. When he said that chills ran through my body. I wish I could have known that once. I don't think we're meant to get married and stay with the same person, but you still owe it to the one you're with to be true. There was one time when my husband was gone for over a month on business. I was pretty sure something happened. When he came back he was acting a little strange.' She trails off. 'Listen. There's this bond. It doesn't matter the distance you're apart, it's inside and no one can take it. We have that. And will again.' Regn looks to Westcott. 'You don't believe me.'

'I don't disagree. It's after death that I worry about.'

'You'll still have the same core person and know each other—'

'But I don't want to see you another way. I like you just as you are.'

'Why?'

'Because I *have known* you before. What if you come back as some backwoods Redneck?' Regn laughs. 'I don't think I'll return as some he-haaaaing hillbilly.'

They stand.

'Look at dat.' Regn gestures to initials carved in a tree.

'I thought you'd mind.'

'Do you?'

'It doesn't kill the tree,' Westcott explains.

'No, but I don't know if the tree can feel it. Can I ask you something?'

Westcott looks over to her.

'I'd better not—'

'You can't just make the statement and not finish it.'

'If you were to love a woman—would it be me?'

Regn walks a little ahead on the narrow path.

'I say this with absolute certainty. It is not youth speaking, this is unflinching truth. Without a doubt. Yes. It's not a fascination I have with you. You have the letters. There aren't words for it. It is—what it is.'

'I just don't want to hurt you anymore than you have been. I don't want you to have expectations, and yet you will anyway. Do you understand?'

'Yes. I don't expect you to leave—' even as he says this, he knows he is lying to himself.

'What am I to do with all the things you give me? I mean what if my kids ever found them—they'd think there was something between us,' her voice whispers. 'I have to keep them hidden. Things like that can hurt.'

'I don't want to put you in jeopardy—'

'Did you ever see that movie—'

'*The Bridges of Madison County*—'

'Yes.'

'You could put them in a safety deposit box and will them back to me.'

'In the movie her kids discover it.'

'You could have it sealed,' Westcott offers.

'The part where she's gripping the handle and you can see how badly she wants to go with him—'

'It was incredible. I have to know. Where'd you put my box?'

'It's in our dining room on a tea tray.'

'You remind me of Meryl Streep's character in the movie. Not just the circumstances but the way you carry yourself. She's one of the true classics.'

'My mother's nose was kinda like Meryl Streep's. You know how hers is long and pointed—'

'Yes. If I had a pin-up she'd be it.'

'Hey, I thought it would be me.'

'After you, of course.'

———

The Path that Leads to Nowhere
—Corinne Roosevelt Robinson (1861-1933)

THERE'S a path that leads to Nowhere
In a meadow that I know,
Where an inland island rises
And the stream is still and slow;
There it wanders under willows,
And beneath the silver green
Of the birches' silent shadows
Where the early violets lean.

Other pathways lead to Somewhere,
But the one I love so well
Has no end and no beginning—
Just the beauty of the dell,
Just the wind-flowers and the lilies
Yellow-striped as adder's tongue,
Seem to satisfy my pathway
As it winds their scents among.

There I go to meet the Springtime,
When the meadow is aglow,
Marigolds amid the marshes—
And the stream is still and slow.
There I find my fair oasis,
And with care-free feet I tread
For the pathway leads to Nowhere,
And the blue is overhead!

All the ways that lead to Somewhere
Echo with the hurrying feet
Of the Struggling and the Striving,
But the way I find so sweet
Bids me dream and bids me linger,
Joy and Beauty are its goal—
On the path that leads to Nowhere
I have sometimes found my soul!

— *The Poems of Corinne Roosevelt Robinson*
New York: Charles Scribner's Sons, 1921.

The rain fell atop the slick in dry translucency. The rivulets of precipitation on the window were psychedelic in their movement. I held the *Victorian Trading Co. Magazine* in my hand, the cover dry, safe within the interior of my truck's cab, except for its reflections. It reminded me of the Loch Ness monster, good Ol' Nessie, cutting through the waters, slicing so gracefully. I'd recently read *The Poet of Loch Ness* and the sea creature's existence was something I'd never doubted. Maybe it was just the play of light and angle, maybe there was nothing on the horizon at all, but the possibility always remained. Looking at the cover and the reflection of the rain from my truck's window, I was transported.

The magazine carried intriguing apparel, jewelry, and decorative vintage furnishings. It was from this very magazine that I ordered my Christmas gift for Regn—a beautiful bronze pedestal box, about 6 inches by 4. A woman leaning against the front with delicately accented flowers of pale blue and light marigold. I'd seen it advertised in periodic issues. I wonder what Regn did with hers? A year or two later, I was drawn to a teardrop necklace with a gray stone cresting the orb. Looking at the magazine spread, I was delighted to find the pleasing piece still in circulation, but something distant sounded. I recalled reflecting upon a pretty little necklace I'd bought for Regn, the only other item I ordered from the magazine. I'd never seen it on her. She'd loved it; hadn't wanted to keep it though, was afraid. "Just keep it for me a while," had been her words, but I knew if I did she'd never ask for it. So I insisted she take it then. It was summer; I was working at Contradite Health Care. She'd come into the late afternoon office. I was always alone as the receptionist. The lights were off to keep the room cool. The air conditioning didn't work. How my body yearned for hers.

I missed seeing her every day. It was quietly astounding seeing the necklace after all these years.

~

As a young kid and even into high school I confess I did not entertain the library as much as one would suspect. Sure I went and pulled out books on the Civil War, perused photographs. Attending a small private elementary school consisting of only 350 students K-8, on the times I did visit the library just off the main corridor housing Lost and Found, I'd hit upon two books. *Little Soup's Hayride* was a favorite. And then there was the special hardbound edition of *Swan Lake*. An inch-wide binding showed royal purple on the shelf. The librarian would roll the hand-held rubber stamp to the correct date and depress the seal to my scrolled name on the small rectangular index card in the back of the book. A tangible card catalog—wooden—stood to the left of the desk. No computers.

In the sunroom at home I'd leaf through the beautiful, full-spread pictures of the swans. I never bothered to read the text, the pictures were too lovely.

———

I've often been fascinated and bothered by most people's quick decision to trust. Beyond the realm of work Magda knew absolutely nothing about me. She gauged my character by how I behaved toward the customers and colleagues alike. How I presented myself, how I spoke and my sentiments within the friendly exchange of daily discourse. Trust is not so much placing your faith in another person. Trust really comes down to relying on one's own judgment, trusting in your own sound assessment of the other. For this reason we are often angry and distressed with ourselves when another betrays us. At first we blame the one who has wronged us, but then we turn on ourselves. At any rate, within the course of a year I would acquire three lasting clients for whom I would pet sit and house sit.

Trust was never a matter to be taken lightly. But I never quite got over how Magda opened her doors to me, literally. She was fortunate I am not the type for self-gain. I'd known refinement and possessed many great furnishings. I never longed for monetary items others possessed. I had no need of them. In fact, having seen both sides of the coin, I appreciated the burden of "things" and how they come to own a person. Magda worked at Jamestown not for the money but for something to do. She bought a BMW. Finances were hardly a concern. In a way I knew she felt she was doing us both a favor by having me pet sit Lady Godiva. I was not only taking care of a member of her family, but in turn she was giving me a place to escape for a few days, with fair and generous payment. It was friendly business at a rate of 20 dollars per day. My own home was beautiful, but sometimes the confinement of not having my own place got to me. I was a young *man*, after all. Magda wanted to help me gain independence. Or at least feel it for a few days until I could strike out on my own.

I always made a point to observe the home before settling in—in fact, I never settled in—I would never allow myself to get too comfortable. If it rained I took my shoes off just as I would at home. I left the pillows on the sofa as I'd found them. I made the bed, fluffed the throw pillows. If a bar of soap had been left for me to use in the guest bathroom, after washing with it I checked to see that no stray hair had been left on the cake or in the sink. I always closed the lid of the commode.

I did not use the telephone, lest it was for a local call, and that would only be to my own house. I took in the mail, causally glanced at the address of senders, but without intent. I did not go in dressers or closets. There was no interest. We all pretty much have the same articles.

The first time I pet sat for Magda was in early March. Regn had just flown with her husband to Germany. Their first big vacation in several years. Regn would be gone two weeks. The back of Magda's house was all glass windows, a beautiful view of the lake. Mornings a swan could be seen gliding along the smooth surface. If it was too ideal to believe, I didn't consider this. After all, I'd grown up with 1888 Victorian architecture. I appreciated the surroundings at Magda's and I was well suited to them, but I did not desire to occupy the place myself. I loved my own home. Circumstances weren't ideal—living with Mother and having to have a renter or two to offset the mortgage, but the home was beautiful and well-groomed. A two-story four-bedroom, well-lit home on a hill, on a cul-de-sac with trees, plenty of trees. Actually, Magda's house was smaller than ours and decorated somewhat in an early American motif. My first day I sat in different chairs, felt the sunlight on my bare arms streaming through the window. It rained late in the afternoon. I listened to a small clock on the side table tick away. Looked at Lady G, flopped over on her side—half on her circular mat, the other half on the wooden floorboards. *You big lug*, I thought—*you're sweet, but stubborn like an ox.* She was difficult to walk. Being of the British line, as a Black Labrador her cranium was broader. She was solid. When she didn't want to move, she dug in. Sometimes I'd lie on the floor, rub her belly, kiss her forehead, grab her big forearms. She had presence. I was glad of that. The silence would get to me. I read quite a bit; I had nothing else to do, nowhere to be. I did look just once into Magda and John's bedroom. How chaste! Two small single beds on opposite sides of the room. It was the 1950s. They were a deep almost black brown wood. Magda was in the latter part of her 60s; some things were probably not desired anymore. Even so, sleeping arrangements of that nature were the exception.

One night I baked a plate of cookies. Magda told me to help myself to anything I wanted. I ate very little, cleaned up all evidence. I put the dishes away—the one or two items I used and reused. I can't stand a person who is too lazy to rinse his own glass or utensil and just grabs for another one.

The room I stayed in was downstairs. The basement had its own sink and oven, which I didn't use. I went down an all wooden paneled stairwell and stepped onto cool square stones. The basement always felt damp. A dehumidifier was turned on. The basement opened directly onto the backyard. So in actuality, the main floor was elevated more than usual. I had a king sized bed all to myself. A white blanket. The white made it look even larger. It hit me. I stood in the doorway, taking it in. All this—and no one to share it with. Magda wouldn't have minded if I'd had a girlfriend over. She knew I didn't have one, but if I had, she'd have expected us to have a nice time. Staring at the empty largeness of the bed the old sorrow, the tiredness came on—I quickly slipped into bed, put the plate of warm cookies on my lap and with deliberate attention, chose which cookie I wanted to enjoy. I tasted it slowly, relishing the feeling, the sensation in my mouth, the subtle, private satisfaction of taste. I took a swig of milk. It was wonderful. A nice bed, plenty of blankets for warmth, Lady G- as sentry on the floor by my side, and a book on the other. Silence.

After 2 ½ cookies I wiped my hands on the paper napkin I'd brought with me then resumed reading the book I'd started that afternoon. Regn wandered through my mind. I knew it was useless to think of her, to miss her—she'd be back soon enough, but somehow I wished she could have been with me to share all this.

The book I had was like reading my own autobiography. The situation paralleled my present dilemma, but what aroused my mind and emotions was the very character of Robert Kincaid himself. The way he's described are the exact words I've used before to describe myself. Obsolete. A dying breed. But Robert Kincaid's story happened in 1965. It was now 43 years later and I still shared his sentiments about life, society. What would he think if he were alive today?

I knew the author had modeled the character after himself. Robert James Waller was still alive—even if I wrote him a casual letter—he'd likely never get it. The letter would be man-handled, waylaid and probably replied to with a stock, typed letter and an electronic signature. I wasn't going to send a fan letter. Those assigned to sort through his mail, if he had such a small crew, would screen it, mark it, and put it in with a pile. What I wanted was to make contact, to know and let the other person on the other end know, there are others like us, who, for some unknown reason, remember the "way it was." We are born nostalgic.

" 'I sometimes have the feeling you've been here a long time, more than one lifetime, and that you've dwelt in private places none of the rest of us has even dreamed about. You frighten me, even though you're gentle with me. If I didn't fight to control myself with you, I feel like I might lose my center and never get back.' He knew in some obscure way what she was talking about...He'd had these drifting kinds of thoughts, a wistful sense of the tragic combined with intense physical and intellectual power...when other kids were singing Row, Row, Row Your Boat, he was learning the melody and English words to a French cabaret song...he liked words and images...words have physical feeling, not just meaning, he remembered thinking when he was young.

"Robert lives in a world of his own making [his mother had said]. "I some-times have the feeling that he came from another place to which he's trying to return."

I looked up from the page. *My God.* It was me to a T. And not because I wanted it to reflect me. It was. I'd always felt I was waiting for my return. That I'd been left here, on this plane, looking up, away, inside, wanting to go home. I felt bound.

"...His body moved with the kind of intensity and power that comes only to men who work hard and take care of themselves...the easy way he moved his body, old ways, disturbing ways, ways that draw you in.

"There was something, something very old, something slightly battered by the years, not in his appearance, but in his eyes.

"We're all getting lashed to the great wheel of uniformity.

"Francesca said nothing...wondering about a man...who seemed like the wind. And moved like it. Came from it, perhaps.

"His grace, his quick eyes...mostly the way he moved...the men she knew seemed cumbrous compared to him. It wasn't that he hurried. In fact, he didn't hurry at all.

"One of the last cowboys. 'There's a certain breed of man that's obsolete... or very nearly so. The world is getting organized, way too organized for me and some others. Everything in its place, a place for everything...Rules and regulations and law and social conventions. Hierarchies of authority, spans of control, long-range plans, and budgets. Corporate power...a world of wrinkled suits and stick-on nametags....Eventually, computers and robots will run things. Humans will manage those machines, but that doesn't require courage or strength, or any characteristics like those...All you need are sperm banks to keep the species going, and those are coming along now. Most men are rotten lovers, women say, so there's not much loss in replacing sex with science. We're giving up free range, getting organized, feathering our emotions. Efficiency and effectiveness and all those other pieces of intellectual artifice. And with the loss of free range, the cowboy disappears, along with the mountain lion and gray wolf. There's not much left for travelers.'

"[He had] incredible intensity, but controlled, metered, arrow-like intensity that was mixed with warmth and no hint of meanness.

"She [began] to turn in her mind, breathing heavier, letting him take her where he lived, and he lived in strange, haunted places, far back along the stems of Darwin's logic...she could smell rivers and wood smoke, could hear steaming trains chuffing out of winter stations in long ago night times, could see travelers in black robes moving steadily along frozen rivers and through summer meadows, beating their way toward the end of things.

"She began to understand what he meant when he said he was at the terminus of a branch of evolution and that it was a dead end...he saw nothing beyond himself along the branch. His kind was obsolete.

"That old uneasiness...just being in the presence of a woman for whom he felt something. He never knew quite what to say, unless the talk was serious. Even

though his sense of humor was well developed, if a little bizarre, he had a funda-
mentally serious mind and took things seriously.

"The old ways struggling against all that is learned, struggling against the
propriety drummed in by centuries of culture, the hard rules of civilized man. He
tried to think of something else…anything but how she looked right now."

At least Robert Kincaid had had the chance to touch, to hold the woman he loved.
To dance with her, share a quiet dinner. I knew Regn was busy, an itinerary, things
to keep her mind occupied—visiting her brother and his wife, seeing old sights,
enjoying the break. I wasn't so foolish as to believe I'd be on her mind. But might
I cross it? Might she look upon a pleasant sight in her travels and wish I were there
to see it, for her to show me her country?

I listened to the silence, the book open on my blanketed abdomen face
down—it was too soon for the crickets and frogs. The silence was sterilizing, the
more I listened, the more the emptiness expanded. I heard Lady G sigh. Quickly, I
picked the small book up and lost myself in it before loneliness took over.

"Such physical matters were nice, yet, to him, intelligence and passion born
of living, the ability to move and be moved by subtleties of the mind and spirit
were what really counted. That's why he found most young women unattractive,
regardless of their exterior beauty. They had not lived long enough or hard enough
to possess those qualities that interested him."

If one does believe in reincarnation then it is possible I had been Robert Kincaid. Need
a person really have been alive to be reborn as another? Kincaid was quasi-fictional and died
in the early 70s. His spirit had ample resting time—a good decade to evaluate and select a
new life, waiting unconsciously, maybe even contentedly, in the Summerlands. What a film
that would make. The story of a man who doesn't know a book's been written about him.
He is acting out his own life and the ending has already been laid down. Written.

Yes, oh yes. I'm not crazy. It's what I've always believed. Long before I even knew the
text existed. But why, why must Regn be my Francesca Johnson? How will it end? I could
turn away. I should turn away, but somehow, we've always known one another. She's like
coming home whenever I'm in her presence. Love is not a choice. Acting on it is. Finding her
was half the battle. It would be wrong, foolish, to throw the chance away. You can spend an
entire life searching for the glove designed to fit and never find it. With Regn, never having
made love to her, I already knew she'd slide over me perfectly. It was a heightened sense of
knowing. There could be no logical explanation, no hard evidence of the matter, but inside
we recognized each other, and that recognition, that unspoken affection was stronger, more
powerful than anything our bodies could or might give each other. Loving Regn made my
entire being alive. I didn't just *feel* alive. The pain, yearning, patience, and desire, made me
alive. I knew I loved her because I hurt. Soon that pain would be ours to shoulder together.

———

CHAPTER 3

WHEN I AM AN OLD WOMAN

BIRDS ARE CHIRPING all about. One flies so close my hair blows. It is evening on a Monday. Overcast. And for February a burst of warm temperature. I look at my watch. 4:45 p.m. Four weeks before Regn leaves for Germany. A month before I find myself alone reading in the guestroom at Magda's with Lady G- sleeping restively, black chin on forepaws.

I wear my green t-shirt. John Deere arches in yellow letters below an oval that once beheld a tractor. The melted print has completely peeled away. Now just a black silhouette of what once was shows. It looks more authentic this way. I wear my belt with the brass tree buckle and formal leather-brown shoeware. I ride alone, stop only to watch the deer moving stealthily in the twilight forest. I am at Jamestowne Island. A biker pedals by—

'Hey.' She keeps pedaling.

I have time only to nod with my tweed cap. Behind her a fair distance, out of view, a man follows. Coming upon me he offers no recognition. Though we've never met, I know who he is. He passes and then I feel free to remove my hat for a second, let the air breathe through my hair. It's a monotonous bike ride. Coming out into the main parking area I see *his* gray truck is there. I pedal around the bend and down the row of parking spaces behind the truck. AT1DAY, I strain to refocus my eyes and read his license plate.

The driver's door is ajar; a pair of bicycles lie in the open bed. Regn and her husband are cooling down. Regn watches me discreetly in her side and rearview mirrors. Her facial expressions reveal nothing of the pull she feels. The years have forced much inside.

I am parked farther down, outside the park gates, still a mile to go in biking.

I arrive to my truck on the little hill called Powhatan Creek. There isn't a creek. Only the river and marsh, and forest. I hear the hum of utility boxes coming from Jamestown Settlement. A huge gathering of trees, vines, and ground brush provide seclusion. It is a little shoulder, an arch of history. I load my bike and waste no time. I'm bored. I don't want to cool down like Regn. Even at rest, the heat is always present. Turning right from the pull out area, headlights appear behind me in the waning dusk. I think, *In a movie the director would want the audience to see this from Regn's perspective.* She looks at my license plate, QUYTMAN.

The man beside her is in no rush. My truck pulls ahead. She trails me, though Jay is driving. She does not speak to the one who sits beside her. She is thinking of the one who waits ahead.

• • •

A few days later we're still riding circles round one another. I like evening bike rides. The Island is quiet, away from major traffic. I do not want to bike alone, to be confined with my own thoughts. I go to the Island with the slight expectancy, the chance that Regn might be out there and a few words pass between us. Miss Gilly accompanies me; she needs her run.

I see the gray truck and know Regn is somewhere on the trail. We run into each other three times. Stealing seconds when he is so close. Regn crouches to pet Gilly. I take in her purple sweatshirt, dark gray-blue pants and her orange sneakers. She wears a cap. When I was on the longest of the four trestles having let Gilly run free, she said, 'Better watch it.' 'Oh yeah, some biker might run her over.' 'Uh-huh, one with a weasely cap,' she laughed kindly. I'd looked at *him* as he passed before; he was wearing gray sweatpants that hung loose in the seat, a green sweatshirt and what they call nowadays a beanie cap. Regn pedaled away, in case he appeared at the other end of the bridge. When he came by, *this time* he smiled seeing Gilly. 'Hi,' I said to dispel awkward suspicion. Here he was. There she'd gone. And here I sat. A triangle with only two informed. The proximity of all of us made it seem dangerous. It wasn't. I was heading to the parking lot when I heard Regn's bike coming—she went to the lot but soon returned discovering her husband wasn't there—she went to look for him. I decided then to make another loop. He passed first and then she followed— deliberately in the rear. 'I found him,' she laughed. By the time I reached the lot again they'd already loaded their truck and were pulling away. I was the last to leave. It was comforting to have seen and exchanged words and yet how could one not be jealous as the one he desired drove home beside her other.

• • •

I am loading Gilly into the truck after a jaunt on the Island when Regn comes and taps on my window. I put my fedora on to meet him. Regn introduces her husband to me. I shake his hand, noticing he has a gavel nose—each nostril its own entity, a bolt on either side of the stem. What he lacks in profile his full white hair satisfies. Lucky him! He will never go bald. He seems so tall. Or is it that Regn is so short? He makes a comment about the cool weather. I politely, casually reply, 'Yes—it's rejuvenating.' I mean invigorating.

The next time I speak to him will be 4 years and 9 months later.

• • •

I'm at the rec. center. I pad from the locker room to the edge of the pool. The lifeguard idly watches. I hang my legs, perch on the edge. It is much too cold. Always too cold. Not for any geriatric or therapeutic leisure. Some local high-schoolers are doing laps, the lanes sectioned. I lower myself with my arms. The water chills the unwet cotton t-shirt. I want to dive under, plunge beneath the surface, just get it over with. It hurts. Without a sound I duck down to my neck, gasping without so much as a breath. My mind shivers. I begin to tread water. I eye the lifeguard. *Go away. Can't I swim in peace.* I'm not swimming, I'm flailing. I want to take long strides; it feels like a brick pushing down on the lower lumbar of my back. I hold myself in check, though I wish to splash and surge, uninhibited, free of clothes, free of study. It is hard stepping into the locker room dripping wet. The blast of air opening the door, cold against the wet. I rinse in the communal shower. A man soaps up, his buttocks pale, but masculine in structure. Another turns, rinses white foam from his scalp. A purplish part. The extension jiggles. I stand under the shower head, enjoying the penetrating heat. I let it soak into my skin, further still, thawing my bones. I pull the neck of my shirt out so water can spill down and wash away the chlorine. The sleeves have been ripped off, I wear a skin-colored tank top. But the cotton material is thick, naturally heavy when soaked. I glance at the men glance at me. I want to peer closer, examine longer. They would misunderstand. It is too dangerous. I sneak a look when I can. I hoped my aisle would be empty, at least 'til my wet shirt was off and my dry one back on—I pull the wet shroud—hunch, concaving my chest, hastily throw a towel round my back and dry myself. Wet shorts, I sit on the bench before pulling on my white t-shirt. I move the towel down and fashion it round my waist, holding it in case. I tug at my shorts, slide the gripping material from each hip and let them fall to the floor. I sit down again. Lockers bang. A man just down the aisle, somewhere in his twenties, turns, bends, quickly slips on a pair of boxer briefs. I pat my thighs and shins with the towel, terry, hoping to be alone for privacy's sake. The man pulls on his pants. His socks. I get out my briefs slip in a foot then the other, pull them up, towel firmly grasped round waist. Don't pull them all the way up. Get out jeans. Slip them on; stand close to locker, let towel drop and in a swift move pull drawers and pants into place. Quickly zip the fly.

• • •

He's at work again. Bill sees him pacing. 'You look just like a lion, raging hungry.'

It's quiet in the lobby, inside he is on fire. He runs through the parking lot. A man in shirt and tie racing the length of asphalt through the bus loop. A co-worker is watching. He hears their thoughts, though they do not ask. *What are you doing, Westcott? What are you doing?*

Running for my life. He does not say.

Westcott walks Miss Gilly, sits in the chair in his room reading. The perfect sized, green wing-back chair he'd purchased for twenty bucks. He moves to the keyboard in his mother's room. Limply plays tunes and then a fury overtakes. His fingers are too fast, he crosses his arms, plays the right hand's part with his left and the left's with his right. *"I'm comin', I'm comin' for my head is hangin' low, I hear their gentle voices callin'*—" When not on the piano he blows into his M. Hohner German-made Harmonica. "Red River Valley," "Shenandoah," "*Tammy.*" He plays beautifully when no one is there to listen.

He looks through photograph albums, does his laundry. Watches Helmsley bask in the warm light, content. He sits at the kitchen table eating the lunch he made—macaroni and cheese with a diced hot dog thrown in—looking out at the day. He is riding his bike with both arms outstretched like a tightrope walker. He is pedaling without his hands on the handlebars. The wind is blowing through him. He wears his sunglasses. He parks his bike, sits on the wooden railing of the bridge, takes his glasses off, studies the reflection of the forest and marsh in the lenses. He is suppressing all natural tendencies.

• • •

I meet Regn at Waller Mill Park. Wet and cold. Last night her husband started making speculations that she was having an *affair*. What those speculations were she did not say. 'I'll call you next week,' she tells me.

• • •

The phone rings. I know. Who else calls my number? I don't answer in time and have to call her back. We speak of nothing important, easing into the conversation, whatever the true reason for her calling is—it's not to tell me 'have a good day.' Then she says it—'I've made a decision. I think I'm going to stick it out.' Happy Valentine's Day indeed. Not that it matters. Valentine's Day is for suckers. *Stick it out.* Interesting choice of words.

• • •

Sixteen days. Regn leaves for Germany in an hour from Dulles Airport in D.C. I picture her sitting in the terminal reading a large book, waiting for the flight. Here I am, three or more hours away. Do I wish to be going somewhere—yes. It wouldn't matter if I was going to the corner as long as she was beside me and we were going off together. It's not that I don't have avenues to seek company, but it has to be a company you enjoy *and* desire. These days are interminable. She'll have the pleasant diversion of following an itinerary, while I find it a relief just to get through another day. It doesn't matter where or how far, the pain is within. Fill the time as I may, complacently ravaged, I hunger. Due to recent domestic uprisings, her husband suspecting she's having an affair to the point of questioning Regn, I fear Jay will want to rekindle something on this trip. The very thought of her appeasing marital duties—however false in heart it may be for her—to imagine him atop of her, loving her— is too much. And yet I know with certainty at that very moment, her mind would consider me. Two men fighting over her for separate reasons. Her plane leaves in fifteen minutes. The excitement of it, how I wish to be going. I'm fairly certain she'll discuss me with her cousin, or at least mention my name. Already I miss her, so wonderful to fly.

• • •

I am at work, at the Settlement.

The shadows are on the floor.

From the corridor I wait—if no one comes I will pounce on myself. If I sprint down the plaza I may outrun the silence—dislodge the tedium held up within this ribbed cage. Run. Yell, God damn it, yell. Can you hear me? I'm afraid of my own voice! Let me split my shadows—the sun will sleep and the silhouettes draw like a curtain. To run with pen or knee—there is no liberation of soul. Fly I say—Lie down and die. Let me soar. Let me live.

In Regn's absence I seek Sharon out—relying on her company. I haven't heard Regn's voice in ten days. So much is coming all at once. This weekend our tenant of three years, Lucy, is moving out. The following week Ellis will be coming down from New York. She's resigned from her job at L'Oréal. I should enjoy the added company; I feel it as an interruption.

MARCH

Friday the 7th. It's been raining most of the day; he takes a nap. When he awakes the rain has let up. It is again coming down. From his vantage point he overlooks the reservoir through Magda's sunroom. The trees are stark; one would think it's the midriff of winter—cold, dank, and gray. But spring is just a few weeks on its tail.

He can smell the hops in the air carried from the Anheuser Busch brewery on the shoulders of the wind. The night before he'd taken Lady G- for a long walk around 9:00 p.m. The rain momentarily ceased, it was warm out, a mild breeze. Having read until sleep came, he awoke at twenty to seven. He lay in bed for another forty minutes. *What is the rush?* He took Lady G- out, collected the newspapers. From the back window a swan now glides across the surface. He's finished the slender story of Robert Kincaid. The rain is still coming down. A few minutes ago the phone rang. He didn't answer. It's not his place to do so. The sound of the ringing startles him. Thunder makes him wistful. He's writing on a glass table made out of a wooden-spoked wheel setting atop a barrel about four feet in diameter. The bare silhouettes of the naked trees reflect in the glass. The lighting is gray, white, and early morning cold. Though the temperature is warm, the light shows 'cold.' Wakes and drafts of water rush along the reservoir—rippling torrents, currents that roll. Here he sits listening to the rain.

~

A music box. Westcott turns the slivered wedge. No cute music box, the sort given to your niece or daughter on her ninth birthday. An intricate carving. He closes his eyes. Lady G- watches, reposed on her throw cushion. The rain has let up again. Arms raised in pose, hands grasping air, he shifts his shoes. A subtle sway. Gentle. Slow-dancing. With Himself. Lady G's eyebrows bob in their seesaw musing. The music stops. Westcott stops. Someone is watching? He looks at Lady G-. His only audience besides his own reflection in the evening window as he dances alone.

• • •

I try hard not to think about it. I'm tired of thinking. Today is Rebecca's 8th birthday, Regn said. She hugged me this evening walking to the parking lot. Fernus and Magda were right there with us. To cover Regn exclaimed, 'He's my buddy,' and then 'So are you,' as she hugged Magda. I'd rather the feeling have gone unspoken between us—I don't want to be her 'buddy.' Magda asked if I'd mind house-sitting and taking care of Lady Godiva again. I hate it because of the loneliness. But she pays generously and it gives me freedom from home. I accepted.

•••

Regn and I buried a bird. A sparrow out back of the Settlement. She scooped it up in a paper towel, and with her bare hand dug a hollow in the mulch beneath one of the boxwoods. She was right in the middle of her lunch when I asked if she wanted to be a part of a burial service. We did it together. And I watched this woman, her hands, and her goodness to bury a fallen bird.

•••

Ellis is arriving tomorrow. The only thing I can think is to ask when she heads back. It's terrible, you'd think I'd relish the company. I feel like such a shit. I can't help it though— I can see and talk to Ellis *any time*. With Regn we have to make time.

•••

I went riding my bike one evening along the Avenue of Trees. The nice little access road running parallel to Jamestown Road on your way to the Settlement. There was no reason to be there, except one. It was 5:50 when I heard a honk. There she was in her bug on her way home from work. She made a right U-turn onto the side road. She'd been asked to work the next day. We were both disappointed I hadn't picked up the shift. There was another sadness in her eyes, she saw me riding alone. She extended her hand out the window; I squeezed it, held on a second. 'I'll miss you,' she said. We agreed to race. Me on my Schwinn bicycle. Her in her Volkswagen.
    'Who do you think will win?' She called out.
    'We'll see.'

———

Regn sometimes referred to Jay as her husband. Other times she addressed him by his name. In the beginning when we were still getting to know each other I wasn't sure which reference I preferred. 'Husband' was general, removed. As time passed Regn began to only use his name. It gave him a title. Using the name Jay made him more real. He was no longer a nebulous entity. A 'husband' could be anyone. But Jay was someone specific, someone who she knew and I did not. Her familiarity with the name and her use of it in my presence connected the three of us.
    Sometimes I didn't want to be reminded she was married and the name Jay was better than hearing 'my husband.' And then there were days when I wanted so much to know and study Jay, more than our chance meeting while bicycling. I wanted to look at him, talk to him, know what he was about. Who was this other half of Regn from which I was entirely removed? Jay was to me what I would become to him—a stranger known only by proxy through Regn. We may have shared many things in common, but greatest of all was Regn, the one we loved equally, though very differently. Regn and I did have certain pet names for one another, but nothing proverbial. I always disliked the degrading use of babe, baby. We never said sweetie or honey. And I never said "my Lady" or "Lass" to Regn. I could write it in a letter, but if I addressed her in person it always was in German, *meine Dame.* Regn would say, 'My Irishman.' Sometimes I signed my letters, Kinkaid. To me Regn would always be my Scatterbird. These terms were more or less concepts than actual functional

names. They were private and used only in those moments of honeymoon heights, when everything seemed beautiful because the pain was always nearby meaning the joy, the happiness, was fleeting and could never last even in the most ideal circumstances. Happiness is always temporary.

For St. Patrick's Day I wore my navy blue velvet blazer and a green shamrock bow tie. I was at Jamestown. Regn was at Yorktown.

Regn called in the morning, then again late in the afternoon. 'Where do you want to meet?'

It would be our first time getting together, outside of work, since her trip to Germany. 'Well, we can start driving towards each other until we collide.'

I left immediately at five and took the parkway. I pulled off at the ancient Oak. The setting wasn't right, there was no cover, it felt exposed. I continued on to Williamsburg before calling Regn to let her know where I'd parked. I chose a discreet corner of the Colonial Williamsburg visitor's lot, buffered by cars behind and a forest in front. I was surprised to see she found me immediately. I looked up and there was her bug with the rabbit ears and pink nose for Easter. We stayed late into the evening—seven about.

She spoke of her long trip. 'What if I told you I couldn't see you anymore—like this?' Regn asked.

'Then you'd hurt me in a way that wouldn't repair itself.'

Several years ago I wanted a gold wedding band. Ellis bought me a beautiful one, for Christmas, when mother and I were visiting her in the city. 14 karat, it has slanted notches. A beautiful wave-like design. I never had cause to wear it. I just wanted one.

I gave it to be given.

Regn slipped the ring on my hand. We held each other. She breathed heavily, like a restless lover, squeezing the skin on my back through my blue Crazy Horse shirt. My head rested beneath her tilted chin. She exhaled. I inhaled her warm breath. I felt her back, her body in my arms. For the first time ever passion gave way between us. All the thoughts and emotions became palpable. From that time on there was no going back.

I led the way home. My window rolled down; the air cold. We drove through the historical area onto Jamestown road and turned right on 199. She followed. At the intersection she moved into the left turning lane. I raised my hand with the ring. Waved as I drove through the green light.

• • •

Easter Sunday. Thinking I was upset with her, Regn went into the gift store. Passing my register—as I was helping a customer—she slipped her hand into my velvet coat pocket. I reached in the right side, felt something hard. I waited for the customers to take leave of my station. I pulled the object out to find a purple, heart-shaped stone etched with designs. That morning Regn and one of the Sups had jumped on me for not being at my register. I was busy opening the front doors and a group was crowding the lobby. They couldn't see me in the midst of the mob. I told Regn with derision that she'd insulted my good nature by assuming I was shirking my duties. Hurt to think I was upset with her, she wanted to make it up to me. After finding the stone in my pocket I walked over to the main desk. I put my hand on her shoulder, making my way to the privy. Conscious of the change—the ease with which I felt allowed to touch *her.*

I asked Regn if I could have her keys at lunch. I went out to the parking lot and from my truck got the trio of potted tulips I'd bought the night before and walked them over to her Volkswagen. The pot was on a silver pie pan for leakage and soil. I set it on the floor of the passenger's side with a note. *One for You. One for I. And one for Us.* One of the tulips had opened since that morning.

Late in the afternoon Regn was absent. I was going into the office when she came in from the stairwell, her mobile phone in hand. She'd been trying to call her children. I knew she kept the phone in her car, so she'd seen the flowers. She said nothing. Closing out my drawer in the office the phone rang. It was Fernus at the front desk. Regn answered it and stood beside me, receiver to her ear, stroking the ring on my hand as I balanced my drawer.

The next day one of our security officers stopped me on my way into work. 'You're so pale. Are you sick?'

I was tired, hadn't slept—stomach cramps. But, I was gaunt. Regn's bug zoomed into the lot; I lingered as she strode up the walk so we could go in together.

In the office, before we opened, she lays it on me.

'Something happened. I need to talk you at some point.'

'What, did Sharon say something?'

'No. My husband found something.'

With those words lingering in mind the day stretched out interminably.

Sharon had brought lunch for myself and her. I tried to enjoy it. Distraught, I hid on the stairwell in the Education Wing for privacy. Who should appear then but our supervisor, Jared. Why the hell was he even over in this wing—I just wanted to be left alone. Turkey rolls and strawberry shortcake was lunch. My stomach in knots, it still tasted good. I thanked Sharon. We went down to the ships together. She asked me to come. Her friend had unexpectedly died a few days before. Linda Haydn had worked as an interpreter on the ships. Sharon didn't want to face the Ships alone. Of course she would never say so. I listened as we walked—she mentioned everything *but* her friend, Linda. She went to the end of the pier. I let her take her time. *Is this how goodbye is done?*

Late in the afternoon, with loose bowels, damp drawers from nervous sweating, and a cold sweat, I ate the rest of my lunch. I was beyond tired. The anticipation. Why lay something like that on me to endure for the whole day?

5:15. 'We'll talk later,' Regn says. A whole day of waiting and now she isn't going to explain!

'You at least have to tell me *what* was discovered.'

We stood alone in the office, everyone having left for the day. She'd asked her husband to change her password for her email. He'd read a message I'd sent. None other than, *Subject: Silent words*, with the link to the highly incriminating song, "I Really Want You to Really Want Me" by James Blunt.

We headed to the parking lot; she said she had to go, but *not* to worry. I felt violated. She seemed surprised I was upset with her. How could she be so remiss, naïve, as to let her husband work on her email account without caution! She invited him right in. It could have been avoided. She'd been careless. We were all hurt, including Jay. I was foolish to send anything in an email. I'd trusted Regn.

I allowed the initial suspicions to churn inside me, granting some pardon. But it was her negligence this time that caused much grief. As it says in *Love in the Time of Cholera*—age *should* protect us. Her husband does not know the certainty. And Regn did not betray. That

her husband mistakes the love for youthful infatuation is best. Regn and I know it is otherwise; this is of utmost importance.

March

Westcott likes where he is situated in Mrs. Talmedge's and Mrs. McCormick's classroom. In contrast to first semester, his desk is in the very back, positioned directly in front of one of four square windows lining the interior square wall. Initially the seating chart had him placed next to Maradine, an eccentric girl who, because of her "in your face" personality, had no real friends. Westcott remembered her standing up in Algebra II and singing "Tomorrow." Another time he watched her egged on to do push-ups in the cafeteria. Detecting his passive display of incompatibility with poor Maradine, Mrs. T tells him he can sit in the empty desk at the back of the room, for good. He loves walking into fourth block every day, dropping his backpack by his seat, and peering out the double layered glass at the sky. It would be nice to open the windows, let in some real, fresh air. The sort of windows he grew up with. He rests his hands on the white sill, studies the enclosed courtyard below with all its young trees, taking in the spring warmth. It is so calm to him. He's never walked across the courtyard, never sat out in the yard. He never will. Too many people could see him from any window. He doesn't want to attract attention and yet his silence demands to be heard. He wants—

His teachers come in wheeling their skinny carts, laying worksheets on the corner counter. Sometimes he'll be sitting quietly taking notes or listening to a lesson and a gust of wind will whip against the window, roll across the roof. Rain pelting sheet metal, a jostling freight train. The noise lasts only a second or two, leaving as silently as it came. When the lights are off and all the room is dark, except for the bright glow of the overhead, the day will shine in through the panes, and if the blinds are drawn up the world outside falls upon him. When Mrs. Talmedge isn't teaching she's at her desk located to Westcott's left. He's glad she is on the same side; had she been on the other a folding partition running along a track in the center of the classroom to divide it in two would prevent him from seeing her entirely. He curiously looks over to see what she is doing then returns his attention to the transparencies Mrs. McCormick is extrapolating on with sharpie in hand. He watches the latter's features outlined from the light as she bends over the overhead. He glances at the various posters and sayings stapled on the two bulletin boards taped against the white cinder blocks. A huge 8 x 6 ft. American flag lays strewn across the left wall.

One day while Mrs. McCormick is busy instructing the class, Mrs. T sits at her desk discreetly eating some chips, a diet coke resting within grasp. Hearing the crunch a blond-haired student turns around.

'Mrs. T, are you eating?'

Caught with her hand in the cookie jar, plainly—mildly annoyed, she answers the girl. 'No.'

An innocent white lie, Westcott *knows* Mrs. T knows he knows. Sensing her secret is safe with him she goes ahead with the lie anyway and winks. He is a silent trustee, a fact she uses in her defense. In spite of her efforts, Mrs. T's accuser later sees the incriminating evidence, a Pringles potato chip bag. She had forgotten through the course of the afternoon; it is rolled up and placed conspicuously on her desk.

There exists only one drawback to being in the very back of the room. For about three months Westcott manages to strain his eyes enough to read the notes, but after a while the astigmatism cannot be conquered. He wears his glasses that had been bought some seven months earlier.

~

As three-leaf clover cut-outs make their way into hallmark windows and manufactures, at the discretion of marketing strategists, change the color of their cookie fillings to mint green, Westcott and his fellow classmates learn they are to be guinea pigs in a pilot project for American Studies. They just finished reading the short story, "Maggie, A Girl of the Streets," about the 1920s, and are moving into the latter part of the decade. As devised by the hands-on assignment, students will impersonate famous figures from the Charleston, pre-Black Tuesday era. A list of individuals, some notorious, others not so well-known, circulates the room until everyone has a paper. Mrs. T instructs the class to select three names from the columns, numbering them in order of preference. Westcott notices the males have a greater variety of roles from which to choose. Scanning over the list of names, some he has never heard of, Jesse, a boy with an uncanny resemblance to Denzel Washington asks, 'What if a girl wants to play a guy or...' his voice trails off with a hint of laughter. 'Well,' Mrs. T interjects smiling, sensing where the question is going, 'if anyone wants to they can.'

The entire class, including Westcott, finds his remark amusing, but now he concentrates on deciding who he wants to play. After a moment he pens a circle around Ernest Hemingway. He likes the idea of portraying a writer. Next he chooses Dashiell Hammett, unaware that he, too, is an author. Lastly, for no particular reason except that the name sounds intriguing, he picks Blind Lemon Jefferson. He chicken-scratches numbers alongside in accordance with predilection. When Mrs. T comes around to collect papers he hesitates. He resolves not to care and hands in the loose leaf.

For the next two weeks they research character biographies, compiling a first person account of *their* lives. Westcott is more than pleased to be playing Ernest Hemingway when it comes time to revive the Harlem Renaissance. As part of a short three-minute presentation, each student is required to dress in attire representative of his or her person. Westcott has been wrestling with the idea of cutting his hair, not merely for the sake of creating a more realistic Hemingway.

~

April

Reluctantly, Westcott zips up his book bag and meanders towards the right exit. He waits in the front of the room facing the desks-the same position his teachers always occupy. He is complacent, incapable of displaying the least bit of joy that it is a wonderfully warm and sunny Friday afternoon. Studying the room and its static decor he reads over a familiar quote written on red poster board pasted high above the left countertop.

"On the impulse of winter
   Midnight,
   Streetlight,
     Small town rain." - Allen Ginseng

He ponders its poetic words, creating a mental picture of icy precipitation melting away beneath the yellow warmth of an old fashioned street lamp. So many adjectives, so few lines. Often, in months prior, he has studied the phrase while waiting for the bell to ring, ingraining the words to memory; a form of unintentional elaboration brought on by short intervals of idleness. He returns his gaze to the floor.

'Yeah, I'm going to the game and then out to dinner with some friends,' Westcott overhears a classmate.

Mrs. Talmedge has just finished talking to some students about the school baseball game scheduled for that night when his expression catches her attention. He glances up—for a split second makes eye contact. She looks at him, pauses.

'Have a great weekend.' Her words, though few and simple, brighten his spirits, comfort. They seem genuinely just for him so that he replies in his quiet way, 'You as well.'

APRIL

Something gave way, shattered. *I* shattered. I was at Yorktown. On my break I tore off to the fields and edge looking over the river. I left work early (it was so quiet they said I could go) and collapsed. The anger consumed me, I couldn't be still. I wanted to grind myself into the floor. I punched it, squirming around on the carpet in the recently vacated room. Our tenant, Lucy, moved out of what used to be Ellis' room. The rage came in great waves; I wanted to scream, to crush myself into the wall, melt into the floor. I was tired of *just* looking at Regn day-in, day-out. I needed to feel her. Completely.

Through gritted teeth I betrayed my frustration. I'd desired Regn for a year and four months.

'I want to fuck someone mean and hard.' The tears of restraint disappeared in the carpet.

Ellis put a hand on my back. 'Why don't you come this week, get away.'

In the absence of a hardened penis my heart wanted to explode. God it hurt. It never stopped.

• • •

My Lady and I met before work. She was the late person and didn't have to be in 'til 9:30. I told her I was going away—to the Riviera Maya for a week with my father, sister, and some friends of his. She gave me a handkerchief dusted with her perfume. I spoke of the day before.

'It was like my heart was trying to unhinge the floor.'

Despite the risks she'd come that morning. To be with me, if only for a few minutes. Nothing more had been said by her husband. He did not like to discuss the matter.

Regn assured me everything would work itself out.

I WADED INTO THE WARM SEA, farther and farther. A safe distance from shore, still touching ground, I struggled to remove my damp white t-shirt. I replaced my baseball cap and sunglasses in the hopes of shielding my fair skin in spite of mild sunscreen. Anything could have happened. I gave no thought to the obscurity of the waters or what may or may not be lurking nearby. Free to move my arms, free to feel the salty water break against my bare chest, I bobbed in the waves, not wanting to turn and face shore or meet anyone's gaze who might be watching. In spite of moderate use of sunscreen, my face swelled from the heat and lotion, itching with a rash.

Ellis and I had fun taking pictures of each other in the tropical environment. If not for the frustration I was trying to kill at every corner, it would have been *the* perfect trip.

We went to a small town one day, and another the next. I was amazed at all the old Volkswagen bugs we saw—such exotic colors. I took pictures of as many as I could. Regn would be pleased.

One night a group of small children put on a show. I thought of Sharon, how much she would have adored the activity—her vacation is often spent going to the beach with her sister. She flies to the UK every chance she gets to visit her grandchildren. We played cards while torches burned on the beach and board games I'd stowed away in my suitcase from home. Ellis and I shared a queen bed. There is a picture of me in shorts and an ocean blue t-shirt. I hold an authentic guitar, feigning to strum it. Mac, dad's father- in-law, bought one. At 80-something years old he decided to learn the guitar. What sustains a body? In that picture I know what I want. I want to make love. Lots and lots of love. I do not want just sex. The desire must be there first. Always. The desire has been building for months with Regn. My hair is thick and full. My limbs wiry. I look 16. The youth I never had.

Toward the end of the week, the main swimming pool was completely empty. I pulled my shirt off, slipped into the pool. Even with the lights I was protected by the water. It was wonderful to be open with myself. I wished Regn could see me free. No one has. I looked at the night sky. Black, a mild breeze. Somewhere far away someone loved me, desired me, as much as I did her. Despite the longing, I did not know it, but I was happy.

There were beds out on the beach with canopies. I couldn't help wondering in the wee hours just before dawn who might sneak out there, or nearby, and relish the opportunity. Sex on the beach.

I'd never eaten such a spread of delectable dishes and it was all included. I was glad I'd come at the last minute. A part of me still remained far away, selfishly.

The nights hung close and black as I ran along the shoreline, listening to the Mexican gulf. The waves reminding me of the body I wanted. Regn's body. The freedom I longed for.

———

Journal Entry:
from the Book of West
Wednesday 23 April 20—

To get so close only to have it all taken away. How can I write about it, when all the clichés seem to come into play and yet it is anything but. Last Saturday after having lunch together on the mezzanine, in the darkness of the office wing upstairs, Regn and I hugged each other. No one is in the office during the weekends. I told her, 'I love my tie.' She'd bought me a surprise that morning in the gift shop. It was a beautiful silk tie of Ireland. Very expensive.

I closed up the Rotunda in the evening. 'I can only stay a minute,' she'd said, 'but if you want to meet me at the creek for a hug—.' I left before her, as she waited in the lobby with the others. We had more than a minute. It was drizzling much like our love that wanted to come down, pour, but remained interred. 'If we could have each other once and then I think I'd have to leave, for both of us—' I told her.

'You don't have your condoms with you,' she joked. 'Besides I don't need to worry about *that*—'

No, Regn, you don't.

'I have to go.'

I open the passenger door, one foot out. Straighten my navy vest. Smooth my tie. She kisses the edge of my fingers, takes them to her breast. I bring her hand that holds mine, to my chest, press it to the smooth plain of my shirt where the heart would be.

'That's the closest thing to an erection you'll get from me.' I press her palm for emphasis. She laughs sweetly, though tears are close. I know she still doesn't understand.

We left utterly high, on top of the world. We were fools in love. Too passionate to check ourselves; too excited to heed fair caution. She sent an email that would, in less than 24 hours, destroy us both. It was a note that had restored my faith. I was believing with enough determination anything is possible, and then one evening later I couldn't believe there was a god, not a kind one if one at all—for the cruelty of getting so close—only to be annihilated. But aren't I the one to blame? This isn't any matter of gods or supernatural powers—we'd sabotaged ourselves. It could have been ours. The hurt was needless. We could have had each other and I left quietly, on my terms, without threats; why was I so stupid to have trusted my soul to technology? But try to understand Reader, I also trusted Regn to protect us.

The passion is blinding. Yesterday morning was wonderful. Regn sent two respectable pictures of herself in a bathing suit haphazardly shot. I worked on my photographs, framing them—the ones of Jamestowne Island. I took a nap in Ellis' empty room, mentally practicing for when the time came to make love.

I was out with Mother when the phone went off. I should have known something was wrong—Regn calling after five o'clock. Initially I was sorry I'd missed the call; Mother had answered while I was in The Frame Shop. The caller hung up. We were three minutes from home when it rang again. The minute I heard her sobbing voice, and *sobbing* is the only word for it, I knew. I was angry at her shaken composure—she sounded so—young and helpless.

'Something's happened, Westcott. I *need* to talk to you.'

'Can I call you right back?'

'No, I need to talk to you *right* now.'

'I'm not at home.'

'Pull over somewhere.'

'I'm not alone. Give me two minutes and I'll be home. I'll call you back.' Sad as it would have been, I hoped without hoping she would tell me her cat had died, or even—

I went upstairs to Mother's room, the furthest part of the house, my stomach in a knot of fire. Regn answered immediately.

'He knows everything. He read the emails, he's seen the pictures. He said he'll send guys after you if you don't leave. He'll publish everything at Jamestown!'

I confess here and now, the photographs I took of myself were artistic, tactful, and nothing I was ashamed of, except that *he* didn't need to know. In my own way I was proud of the pictures, not in some male egotistical aspect. Nothing indecent was exposed. I would never—. Less is more and having discretion is key. Did a part of me want him to publish them? At least then we wouldn't have to hide. There I sit holding a handkerchief in my hand and in the second photograph a plant, Kincaid—my bonsai, sits nearby in the empty room. Black and white. Classic. I lie on my stomach and naked groin, only the lines of torso revealed. Eroticism lies in suggestive absence, not vulgarity. The shadows and contours of shoulders and nethers are decent, muscular, striking—perfected composition and nothing more. I look like a young sexually potent male. The injury lies with our intimacy being discovered. *And*, I didn't want to hurt him.

'Get in contact with Rose Marie to let me know you're all right.' Regn hung up.

Was she pacing in her backyard? Was Jay watching from the window? Waiting? All I could do was pace. As long as I kept pacing, *just stay pacing*, what was I going to do?

I was supposed to meet Parson that evening for chess and a drink at a local coffee shop. I canceled.

The stupidity of my judgment—*I knew* it wasn't safe—he'd already seen her emails once, and yet I was a god damn fool and trusted it—her. She reassured me even when I said there are ways and your husband works with computers. I trusted her, I trusted our love. You think you know yourself.

• • •

26 April 20—

It is time I ask you, Regn. What do you want?

It is your company that calms and not some counselor of mainstream society who chalks it up to mid-life crisis versus some young man's sexual exploration. I was too good, always too good to recover. You know where the coldness comes from. There's little if anything left to hurt and I'm supposed to live, to be strong, carry on—we all are—. I came too far, and too close only to be shot in the back by my own hand, with you 'right' there. Wait, I'm not being fair—'We' came so close. Your husband may hate me, I do not care; I am not scared—I am very angry, and the rage will come in swells of frustration, but unlike Jay, you are not here in those instances to talk it through. Letters don't give answers like face-to-face dialogue. Right now he still has a bed and a wife in "physical" form. Does it make me the stronger man? You know to tell anyone it will not subside, because an ear is not what you need anymore. It's all been said—you've been too ravaged to let anyone else in—and you tell yourself keep quiet.

I may not be an old man, but I 'live' as one. No, even were I a ready-made man, sleeping around doesn't satisfy. I've made it impossible for myself— there's no other way to put it. Just how does a personage sustain himself when all reason tells him he is mad, one day you may resent her for the pain, you can't, you just can't wait with your life on hold and you can't wish it away.

Is it pig-headed bullshit, a disillusion that fills me? The day I no longer believe and trust in my own senses is the day I am lost. It's true, by God, and I've said it so many times, what matters in a life?—It's so god damn hard, that doesn't even cover it—but why SETTLE for the common, why turn the other way just because it's easier? You can maybe find physical relief that way but—why, why—I say this simply—rather I pass away with this love intact than live my life trying to recapture—. It is suicide. It means something more. At what expense? I cherish our rarity, but at times when I'm out and I see that man and woman together, I tell myself you could have that, you can find a woman who can be yours now. I don't have time to tell it again—I don't, and sex without love, well, it doesn't move, but rather strands us! I want it and I mean it with all goodness; you shouldn't have to work at it this hard. It sounds so black and white, all or nothing; will I go out fighting? How much will we sacrifice? I try to tell myself in those hours of isolated reckoning and bitterness, some go their entire lives without, or complacently settle.

He is in my mind and I wish never to think of him as he does of me. Our disdain for one another is mutual—though my anger for him lies in the <u>*waste. You were right fucking there, always right there, and what was*</u> <u>*done about it?*</u> *I feel I handed him over the key to your mystery and yet I'd like to think it is an allusive lock that must be searched out. Perhaps you are like one of your mystery novels, filled with panels and doors that open different directions when slid opposite ways. To look at you, Regn, devastates because I want to hold you hard, shake you in tears of anger for loving you. Why did your love have to be so good? I fear the window closing in on us. I can't spend my life wondering, forever left standing in this place. This is no fool's game. No debauchery of lives—let us keep what was already said and have this pact. I will be quiet for you. This is not an undermining. You say you feel helpless—it's not so. You have choices. If we wait for your freedom, I fear a draft will shut the window I look out, and there you'll sit, perched on my sill, with no one to answer. One day we must bid the ultimate farewell in parting from this plane.*

But not now, not while we're here sharing this time and place. I will think always of that day we were in the library. You had a book in your hands, the winter sun was warm among the shelves—and we were safe from the world.

For you, Regn.
Now burn this when you know it by heart, as I'm sure you will.

It is raining and I could go down with it.
I need you now, but the silence comes
 when you are there;
I am the one who waits, the one who always waits—
the one who can always be;
the anger billows and then I'll grieve
 for my remaining share—
and such is expending oneself, without relief,
 it is not fair to me—
The days rise and the eves fall, the heart breaks
and the axis keeps its time—
Not tomorrow, not another minute, Right Now,
 while the Pain resounds!

MAY. JUNIOR YEAR

Mrs. McCormick has brought the students all the way up to the 1930s and the Great Depression. Westcott savors his time in American Studies; he enjoys doing his homework and reading through the textbook. To highlight the era Mrs. Talmedge has the class read the literary classic *Of Mice and Men*. Westcott is familiar with the novel having read it in elementary school. He doesn't mind and is more than happy to read it again. He takes an unusual interest in the Great Depression—a certain attraction he cannot place his hand on. The characteristics of that time—Americans mentally and physically uprooted from the life they knew, their perspectives forever altered. *Did the Depression take such a toll on the people because of their inability to accept the inevitable truth?* A human flaw he cannot escape.

~

Westcott looks down at his Coleman watch wrapped tightly around his right wrist. It annoys Ellis that he does not wear it on his left since he is mostly right handed. He studies the little lantern embroidered on a square tab stitched to the band. A thin frame of rich green borders the face of the clock. It is 2:31 in the afternoon on Friday, April 19th. Westcott sits at his desk quietly. Mrs. Talmedge has finished reading and discussing Steinbeck's tale. The class is getting to the crux of the story when she calls it a day, tells them they'll pick up with it on Monday. Everyone shoves their books and binders into their backpacks, slowly drifts to each side entrance knowing full well the teacher's disdain to have them all crowd up at the door. Some students still stand by their seats exchanging information about plans for that weekend. Westcott remains sitting. It has nothing to do with obedience.

On Saturdays his mother is off from work so usually they do something. Sundays he has himself to himself, unless Ellis is off from her job as a colonial server. He loves when she brings home Tavern biscuits and sweet potato muffins after her shift. It doesn't matter if it is lame, no one will know, no one will ask, and so he watches one of his favorite childhood movies, *Shiloh* or *Where the Red Fern Grows* starring James Whitmore. Memorizing the lines. It isn't the idyllic dogs, the content, or storyline that enthralls him so. He wants the seemingly impossible—to be a Marty Preston and Billy Colman. He thinks about JP's character in *The Orphan Train*—a movie he hasn't watched in years. It occurs to him why he always felt so disappointed and betrayed when JP, living on the streets as a newspaper boy, reveals *herself*. In watching *To Kill a Mockingbird* he feels a camaraderie with Scout, as though he knows her through appearance and behavior. It seems to him she is on his side. He finds himself dressing in anachronistic attire. He loves the gray tweed-style caps reminiscent of the 1930s donned by George in *Of Mice and Men*, JP, and Joseph Donnelly of *Far and Away*. His uncle wears those hats. It makes him nostalgic, passively victorious in opposing the obnoxious trends indicative of his generation. He plum wears out the knees of his green, Jordache corduroy overalls. Time and time again he sews them up and when the buttons pop off, he improvises. Yellow twisty-ties and paperclips contort into makeshift clasps to attach the bib to the suspenders. A spokesman for the Salvation Army, Ellis mocks. His mother forces that particular pair into retirement.

Weekends he buries himself in homework.

• • •

'I don't think you're listening to a damn thing I'm saying!' Mrs. T hollers.

The class has been acting up, chattering incessantly when a student flips a bottle cap and nearly hits her. Already fed up with their behavior that day, she snaps when the perpetrator laughs at his error.

'I don't find it funny.' Everyone is serious, slapped to attention by her stern tone, everyone except Westcott. He is already staid. Mrs. T looks at him.

'Now you're going to start reading the first chapter of this book,' she storms out.

Mrs. McCormick says nothing as she grades papers at her desk. Seeing her partner leave, she rises and steps out herself. Never before or after has Mrs. T become this upset and frustrated. It is obvious something external to school is bothering her. He doesn't know why, but it is startling to witness a teacher lose control. In some way it relates back to his "Leave It to Beaver" perception of them as untouchables and his eagerness to believe they are perfect, above such common emotional outbursts. He knows such wishful idealism is a farce. He is glad to see she has a backbone, commanding the students in an authoritative manner; it demonstrates strong character and competence, which is more than he can say for some male teachers. Westcott falls to reading his book. A page later a composed Mrs. T returns, reasserting her job as narrator. Her temporary punishment, a pleasant repercussion to Westcott, is short-lived.

~

Westcott follows along in the book, listening to Mrs. T's changes in voice inflection as she switches back and forth between characters, aptly giving each character his own personality. After the climactic death of Curly's wife, Westcott is eager to read the book again. Even though he finished it the afternoon before, alone in his room—the still warmth of spring outside his window—the conclusion never ceases to grip.

Putting his blue three-ring binder away and placing his glasses inside their case, he zips his backpack, leans it against the table leg. Patiently, he watches the other students stand about, slowly gravitating toward the door. Westcott makes it a point not to rise before a certain time on the clock. The lights remain off in the room even though the overhead projector has finished its prescribed purpose for the day and class officially ended five minutes earlier. Mrs. T is at her desk, the blinds closed behind her. In contrast, a stream of bright light shines through Westcott's window reminding him of the warm weather outside.

Sensing she is watching him, he looks at Mrs. T.

'It's a hot one out today!'

He nods, smiling a little, anticipating the hanging interrogation. He feels his checkered Cherokee coat begin to suffocate and the navy button-down undershirt cry out. Weighing the silence.

'Are you just a cold-natured child?'

He wishes she could know. Innocence of supposition—an erroneous attempt to disrobe his peculiar behavior and unorthodox wardrobe.

'I guess so.'

MAY

Jay wanted to talk to me. Regn discouraged it. I agreed with her. It was something I would always regret. I was not ready to confront Jay. What if I had? What if we'd spoken in no uncertain terms, calmly, decisively. What if I had told him, 'I'm not her boy-toy. It's not cheap. This isn't about me. It's not a young man she's after. This is about Regn. Long before me she wanted out.' But we didn't speak. Things quieted on the home front and Regn and I ached, with slightly more caution.

Regn was at the main desk, bouncing in the chair like a kid. 'Look, I'll fall like Fernus once did, you'll catch me, won't you, Westcott?'

'Yes, I'll save you the disgrace since you're wearing a skirt.'

'Wouldn't that be funny. My legs in the air. Security could zoom right in, see straight up to heaven.'

While closing, Regn stepped into the closet, I got the cane and key for the doors. Having a moment together I picked up the conversation.

'I'd like to see that.'

'What?'

'Up to heaven.'

And I walked away to shut up the lobby, amazed how far we'd come. A few months ago I'd never dare to be so explicit.

Standing by the desk Regn turned, resuming where I'd left off. 'So you'd like to see up to heaven. It might not be heaven to you.'

'I know you couldn't disappoint me.'

• • •

I didn't have to work; Regn was late, scheduled for 9:30. I stood on my bike when she drove up at 8:45. She got out of her bug and came over to my truck. I love to hold her as we stand; I love to press my groin to her in the absence of movement—firmness in my heart. To stand taller and hold this woman to my chest. We walked over to the embankment. The fog hung in a sheet atop the James. A man intending to fish said hello. Inside her car a beige blazer lay on the passenger's seat, so small and sweet. I picked it up carefully and handed it to her while she laid it on the seat behind. I looked at my olive green Ked tennis shoes. Somehow we kissed and her tongue invited me to accept. Never having gone so far, instinctively, I knew.

This was the morning I first touched her down there, the first time she took my hand, letting me know it was all right, and slipped it under her skirt. She said softly, 'You know a woman gets wet, right?' I'd looked into her eyes and then quickly away, afraid of my secret.

'Yes, Regn. *I know.*' I wish I had been older. I wish I had taken charge sooner. When at last I felt ready, it was too late.

•••

I got her sunglasses from her purse and handed them to her. She grabbed the ship's bag. We walked outside. It was quiet, cool, with a nice breeze. No one was about. We headed to the Indian Village taking the longer scenic route on the bridge. 'I'm so glad I got to know you, Westcott. When I am an old woman I will look back on these days and the moment before I die I will say, *I will be with Westcott in the next life. We will spend our whole lives together.* You must believe it and say it, too. We must make the best of what we have. Hold on. I never regret meeting you.'

'I find you in places no other person could see,' I said.

'When I'm alone at night you're with me. I have to use my hands though and I wish it was your hands—that's bad to say. I would never tell anyone that.'

'No it's not,' I answered.

'And that's all I'm going to tell you.'

Words either sounded crude or foolish to say out loud.

'Sometimes you're so much on my mind I have to be careful not to say your name out loud, Westcott.'

'I wouldn't give up having met you,' I said. On the ship I discovered I'd forgotten the key. 'I've never done that,' I smiled.

'Your mind is elsewhere,' Regn defended.

I took out my truck keys from my pocket. It worked—the lock has been turned so often any key will do.

'Fernus once did the same thing. You're clever, she went back to get the keys.' We took the same route we'd come. Thunder was rolling in overhead. The weather gray, a foreboding storm, windy. 'Wouldn't it be wonderful to be on the Island now? I wish I could just give a date of *when.*'

'I wish it could be spontaneous,' I replied.

'I know. I have this passion and desire in me. And I want to use it, you've done something to me.'

'No, maybe I just awakened something in you, something that was always there.'

'You might be right,' she said. 'You're not alone.'

A bang went off in the fort. A musket fired.

'I want it so much,' I said.

'If we could just slip under the bridge here. I often thought it would be nice in the outdoors—to make love—where there was no one.'

'Yes.'

We stopped and looked at the forest. Tourists could not see us, but we could hear them milling about the Yehakins, speaking to the costumed interpreter. Their voices were indiscernible chatter. Wood smoke drifted in the air. To me the scent of wood smoke would always evoke the memory of affection at its finest.

Regn linked her arm through mine.

'Look at the sky,' I said, 'the clouds.'

'It's nature at its fiercest, sometimes you need the destruction. These things I say, I could never even read in books.'

'You know something, it's incredible how we can be so close and not be able to move.'

We entered at the Rotunda. In the hall between the office and the door to the public breezeway, with security a few feet away—a door the only thing protecting us from view, my Lady and I stole an embrace. Someone could come from one of four doors at any moment. We risked it. The skies opened up minutes after our return, a momentary downpour. To cleanse our sorrows or water them with sustenance?

• • •

And here we are again, just you and I. I haven't been feeling well. I'm 100 lbs. plus two days less than the number of days in a month. My lower left side often burns, an ulcer perhaps. Sometimes nausea—the feel of how paper tastes, will overtake my stomach. I get shooting pains in my head. I think it important I put down what follows, should I for some reason mysteriously encounter life's finality.

I like water from a hose, just wiping it on my face, even tasting it. I enjoy standing in the dark, without clothes, having taken a shower and letting the ceiling fan blow its air on my exposed skin.

What does any of it mean? Anything we do? I must define success. Does a career make a person happy; are they a good individual because of it? Going to college, earning that degree—how does it make the world or yourself content? What really matters? Is it enough just to be good? Bottom line—everyone's passing time, whether conscious or unconscious of the minutes. Some are content not to question, but I must. What am I anymore? What has my life meant? Had I not undergone physical transformation what of my state of mind? What is man or woman in me? How did I get to such a point of bleached existence? Everything presents itself as a reason to question. Sometimes I truly think I've gone moderately mad, becoming lost in the search for the answer to the ultimate dilemma of human conscience: how did I come to be and what the hell are we doing? I know "why" I'm driven with such conviction, but in the end it will be my own destruction.

These are things customers have said to me:

You're a wise man
You're a good man
You're an honest man
You have a nice smile

Sharon told me in her no-nonsense British way, 'You're strange.'

'I'm glad you recognize it.'

Eva Bellefont says I'm from another world, an old shoe, an old soul.

What of who I was remains? How much have the hormones altered my thoughts? I feel I've been so many places without actually having gone there—

• • •

He stands with his back against the locked door. He's removed all his clothes. A silicone phallus slides out from between his thighs. He thrusts the organ inwards, holding it firmly at the base. He stops; his heart lurches, the momentary pleasure intruded upon. A voice is calling. 'What?!' he yells downstairs in a nonchalant tone to mask his agitation. He sees his mother in the chair, opened mail on her lap. Sees her in his mind, through the floor between them. Quiet again but now more frustrated by the violation of already compromised privacy. He pushes the shaft hard into himself, to the furthest *depths*, in an attempt to force the tears.

He lays there, limp from the fleeting high, ashamed because he hadn't wanted to do it, hadn't needed it; he needed to clear his head. The coldness still fills him. He listens to the silence. The anger of his own confinement rages beneath the otherwise complacent surface. He wasn't loving himself. He knows. He was killing himself.

• • •

She was printing out poems of Goethe. When I'd finished selling the ticket she whispered what I've spoken on the silence of these pages. 'It's torture being next to you.' 'Should I leave?' I asked. 'No, I don't want you to.' Sometimes it's devastating, but then it's beautiful and I hold onto that.

'You know when you're pregnant they tell you to strengthen your muscles, in the birth canal—that's what I'm doing—' and then she used the word she'd never spoken before— 'they call them vagina exercises—I shouldn't say these things. I would never talk like this to anyone. I don't know why I can to you. You make me a loose woman.'

I knew what she meant, it came naturally. She wasn't being crude, just honest. But that one word aroused and filled me with shame. Not shame regarding Regn. Shame about my own body.

'You mean kegels?'

'Those are for the bladder, aren't they?'

'Sometimes,' I said. Then we got around to me again. 'I still don't think you understand. I can't— Yes, may I help you?'

'We'd like two of your tickets, just for here.'

'Are you interested in the film? It starts in 10 minutes.'

'No, maybe later.'

'All right. You'll go through the doors and take the hall down to the left. Here is your map. I'd start with the outdoor exhibits. The Indian Village.'

'Thank you.'

'Have a good day.' I turn back to Regn.

'Love is love, Westcott.'

'Yes, but I can't penetrate as—'

'You mean you can't get an erection?'

'I can, I just—how should I put this—it would require—'

She looked puzzled.

'You don't understand.'

She shook her head. 'That doesn't matter, Westcott, I told you. There are many ways to make love. You can use your hands.'

'I know. Sometimes I think you underestimate me. I *understand* a woman.'

Our conversation lasted throughout the day amidst interruptions from colleagues and guests. 'If I went to the doctors I'd probably die of absolute shame.'

'Why?'

'Sometimes I think of going as a punishment. It's the closest to having someone lay their hands on me.'

'What, a doctor? You don't have to go to the doctors.' What she meant was you can come to me if you want to have someone's hands on your body. My foot rested on the partially open bottom drawer of the desk. One pant leg was modestly hiked up, enough so that my right shin and calf were exposed. The darkness of hair contrasted my fair skin. Regn looked down at the innocent specimen of masculinity and whispered, 'I want to touch it.' Delighted by her candor, I merely smiled. Knowingly. Quietly.

Late in the afternoon Regn pinched my rear end as I stepped by her. Just then Ann walked up. 'I think there's more going on here.'

JUNE

'How many partners have you ever been with?'

One foot is on the half-open drawer, my other on the floor. My hands fiddle with each other to avoid staring at Regn intensely.

We are alone in Groups. I'm wearing my new olive green Converse tennis shoes. I was walking back from break when I passed Fernus in the breezeway. She'd noticed my shoes.

'You're bold,' she said in her calm lackadaisical accent.

I knew tennis shoes were not permitted dressware so when Eva asked me what I had on my feet that morning I simply explained, 'My other shoes got wet and didn't have a chance to completely dry. Don't worry it's just for today.'

'All right, I hope so.'

I realized my getting closer to Regn was fostering a newfound confidence in other forms. Fernus' statement had not been an admonishment, but more a statement of awe.

Regn was mentally scanning her archives, counting. I was glad her first time had been fairly typical. Even her age when it occurred was typical. It all seemed natural. So she had been with a boy before her husband. Nothing wrong with that. It was the late 60s early 70s. And one boy was necessary to release the first time jitters. Why save that for marriage, I thought to myself. But Regn didn't make it sound like she'd been nervous. It was just something that happened. A boy she'd met on vacation.

I envied her freedom of gender. The fact that her first time had been so normal and shared *with* someone. I listened to her tell about it—and then two other times. The number of partners was astonishingly respectable. One clearly upset her—it should not have happened. The other she spoke casually about. She'd married young, I knew, as had Jay. They'd both had minor indiscretions and it was pardonable. She did not explain this. I justified it in my own mind. These instances went way back to her early years of marriage and were more or less a one-time encounter. The danger of an affair is not sex, but love. I'd experienced neither. I ached for her more knowing she'd kept herself all these years. A beautiful woman who many men throughout her life had wanted, but she let slip by.

~

The word was harsh, blunt, unforgiving. I wondered if it was the definition or the word itself that made it unspeakable, lewd. I used other terms, euphemisms in place of masturbate and masturbation. The word sounded criminal. 'Have you—with yourself?' I probed. 'You mean—yes. There's nothing to be ashamed of. One time I accidentally walked into my son's room and caught him in the middle of it. He yelled, "Maahhm!" He was so embarrassed.' Regn shook her head smiling. The details of family life. 'We all do it,

Westcott. There's nothing wrong, it's perfectly normal.' 'I wasn't thinking that there was.' But somehow in my deepest thoughts the act felt indecent. The manner in which one went about it made all the difference. Regn's openness and ease in speaking of such private acts made everything feel all right. I had never spoken these things to anyone. Once more I felt camaraderie and a level of trust like no other.

• • •

The heat index was 104 degrees. We met at the Creek. No one was about, thankfully. No tourists. We could be ourselves. The air was so still and oppressive outside. Regn's McLachlan cd was playing my favorite song, "Good Enough." 'I don't know if this makes it worse,' she said. 'I worry about what it does to you, I don't want to make you more crazy.' I answered, 'It's too late for that.' We held each other for what seemed a long time before moving. She unbuttoned her shirt, I felt her breasts, and kissed them. My hand slipped along her skin, we were both sweating. She unzipped her pants, took my hand and slid it into her underwear, knowing I wouldn't without permission. I felt the nap of her hair and the firmness of her woman's shape—the pubic bone. My fingers began massaging the slit, and slid inside. I stayed there a moment longer and felt her hand on my wrist and withdrew before she could come. She felt me *through* my clothes. Grabbed me there—feeling the bulge between my legs. 'I can't feel it,' I told her and she held me even harder. I knew she was squeezing something. My mind felt it, but the bulge had no sensation. She did not know. She searched further; I took her hand—I didn't want her feeling too close. We looked at each other for a long time. 'You want to say something, don't you,' she said. 'It's all right you can tell me. It's fine.' 'It's fine if you're not me and living it. I wish I could really feel you,' I said.

'You can,' and then she understood. 'Why, because you don't have a penis that can—? It doesn't matter. Maybe I love you even more because you're so gentle.' We unbuttoned my shirt; she lifted the undershirt, felt my hair, kissed my skin. She ran her fingers slowly over my mustache.

We studied each other. I kissed her hand and straightened my vest. I waited a couple minutes after her bug had driven away then followed the winding road, lest anyone we knew should still be at the Settlement and see us leaving together. My windows were down, my air-conditioning in need of Freon. I could feel the heat heavy and close through my vest, long-sleeved shirt and undershirt. I loosened my tie. Her scent clung to me. I inhaled the hand that had penetrated her body and softly bit the nail, a trifle lick, in want of her taste.

THAT SPRING, ONE YEAR after the quadricentennial, Eva had taken me aside, outback by the grassy mall, onto the benches built into the wooden support beams. Our shoes rested atop red bricks. It was warm. And I was 23 years old. Desperately waiting for a time. For Regn to give us the time. To say when. When. I had been aroused for months, one could reasonably say, years. I had been patient. Regn said we would. And now it was just a matter of 'when.' It was hard watching her at work, being so close. Taunting. The desire was an energy in itself, and one that no amount of hiding, even had I been more experienced, could have concealed. It was palpable. Earnest. And wanted. We both wanted it so much.

'I don't want anything to happen to you. Or to hear you've driven your truck into the river. Is there anything I can help you with? I know people, I can give you their contact information if you need to talk. I'm just telling you, you need to watch out. They're looking for a reason—any reason.' They. She meant the supervisors who never left after the 400th celebration. I'd been written up for something petty. Of all things, reading at my station! In Eva's day, when it had been just her in charge, so long as we were attentive to the guest, got the job done, were friendly, it did not matter what we did under the desk. Read, draw, write.

Jared requested we speak after I'd been admonished in the write-up I had to sign.

'Now, get some water, and just go in there, be calm. And collect yourself,' Eva assured.

Jared was a chump. Uncouth. In my navy vest buttoned over my tie I almost always outdressed him. My decorum put him to shame. Not personally, but outwardly. Others didn't take him seriously. Maybe he thought I was gay. I didn't care. I had nothing to prove to him.

'You always look preoccupied, as though you're somewhere else and don't want to be here,' he said in our meeting.

How true. How true. How true. Yes. I was climbing up the walls of my skin, my mind. The frustration beyond tempering. I felt the box getting smaller and smaller. The confinement of my life. At home. With Regn. My physical being. I often envisioned a summer downpour. Running out the double set of glass doors to the front fountain. Pulling at my tie, loosening it, feeling the slick strand free itself. Unbuttoning my white shirt. Removing it in one full-swoop, whisking it to the ground. Letting the rain pour down. And yes, taking the bottom of my white undershirt, pulling it up over my head and dropping it to the ground. To turn and face them. To let the rain pelt me, saturate. My hair become string, naturally mussed. Jumping into the fountain, kicking the water out with my shoes, tromping around. A madman, alive in agony. The moment of waiting. The desire to silence them. Shock them. Come clean. For my bare torso to speak what I could not. This is why I love Regn. This is why I am quiet. This is why I don't fit in. This is why I gravitate towards the company of women, as friends before love. This is why. This is why. I wanted them to know.

Instead. I waited to make love to Regn. To be relieved. I could not yet know it, but one time was not enough. Not for her or for me. Nor would it ever be.

• • •

We continued to meet at the Powhatan Creek overlook, to ease the desire. For three months it went on like this, April to July. And still no true sex. No unveiling.

What of my domestic life during this time? I generally make little, if no reference to it at all. Ellis had been down in Virginia with us for over a month and was getting ready to bike across country, Liam in tow. She's always been so spur of the moment. She planned the bike tour all in a week and up and left. No long distance training. I was excited for her—if that's what made her happy. Did I envy her going all these places while I remained trapped—yes, at times; although, I preferred short trips. I didn't see a way out. In those hours Regn and I lived, breathed, and died for a moment's freedom. We were each preoccupied. Floating along. The only difference was, I didn't have to answer to anyone and she did. My father's suggestion was always to come out to California, work and live with him. I knew that was not an option, nor a healthy environment for any prolonged period of time. I'd reached the point where I could only take my parents in doses. I'd been researching rentals, but mother and I were financially co-dependent for the moment. My job wouldn't support me and mother would need an additional tenant. I needed and had to live on my own. I knew it wouldn't change the void. I'd done odd jobs here and there for colleagues—framing pictures. The money went straight for bills. I couldn't put enough away into savings. I was tired of hearing about the bills. 'How much can you give this paycheck, come down here, where are you going?' I was weary. I didn't want to have to explain myself to anyone. I didn't expect to live at home for free. I contributed. But I wanted control, my own beginning.

My mother did not force me to stay at home. At the same time she never encouraged me to explore. Her desire to protect me backfired. She never said, 'I think it would be better for you to go away to college rather than stay here and attend one. You'll be fine. You can and will make friends. You need to find yourself.' She never said, 'Maybe you should go abroad, study for a year, get away. You don't need to worry. Besides, your surgery is done, what's holding you back? You need to get out of yourself.' She constantly worried. I discovered quickly that worrying was pointless. She told me she just wanted me to be happy, but she offered no concrete solutions. I realized to my great frustration that it was up to me to change things. In those days it was limbo. I walked right into her lifestyle. And that was *my own* doing. It would be easier to blame my mother, but she was doing what she could, trying to keep life going in a job that was waning in pleasure year by year. Her worrying about me did no good. I'd been distracted, distressed by my own body. These things—livelihood, marriage, a life of one's making—one's own, had been postponed. They were secondary to the paralysis of dealing with being in the wrong body. I had been waiting, floating, drifting and then. Pangaea! Everything came at once, all pieces breaking, leaving the familiar continent. Fracture points. But before that moment arrived I wouldn't leap until I knew where I was going to land. And then it was too late. I was out of time. Events decided for me.

With Regn it was different. I leapt with everything in me. To a certain point I kept my relationship with Regn very private for this reason: I wanted liberation so greatly. I had no one to turn to, emotionally or financially. Mother would listen, but telling her made things worse. Much as she wanted to, she couldn't help. It was entirely up to me. I had become frustrated in every way. On all fronts I felt boxed in—the patience it would require was excruciating. I couldn't tell Regn about these things. Regn needed me to be strong, for her. But sometimes I wasn't. Sometimes I needed her.

I couldn't wait that evening. And for what? A twenty minute indulgence, a tease that would leave me hungrier than when I came? It would be torture. No. For once I had to make her come. She wants to leave it all up to chance—you have to take it by the brunt and make time.

I went out to my truck, scribbled a note. I can't sit around always waiting for her because she won't always call and she can't always come—not without some sacrifices. My heart can't take it—the up and down—to come so close. *Splendor in the Grass*! When I hold her I want it to be our time to have each other. Controlling the passion is exhausting—I can't allow myself to want it. I want to kiss her, all of her, not just a morsel of holding each other only to part with the energy still not released. We want to throw each other down in hysteria of frustration.

In answer to my note we met the next day. Somehow she made time.

*

She drove to me and I got in her car. I directed her to a secluded space with trees in front. She left her car running. I thought of the petrol she was wasting. It *was* hot out, but what of the expense? Her cd played all the way through five times. I held her tight; she began to cry, not the sort associated with climax, but a release of sorrow for all the years. Not an erotic cry. One of heartache. She came in my arms. Three times she came. She wanted to touch me. She scrunched down in the driver's seat, put her legs over the console, her head resting on the door. I maneuvered to lay on top of her, my legs trying to find room under the dash. I caressed her abdomen, felt her breasts. Laid my head on her chest as she ran her fingers though my brown hair. We passed the morning like this. For three hours we felt without completely seeing. Our hands told us what we already knew.

'You want to say something, don't you? Say it.'

I hesitated. 'I love you.'

'That's not what you wanted to say. Come on, say it.'

'I don't want it to hurt you.'

'Say it.'

'I wish you'd take a stand. You're not helpless. Be a Shirley Valentine.'

'You mean leave. I don't know.'

'I wish you could be on your own. I know we couldn't *be* together, but—sometimes I think you punish yourself.'

'I know you don't like to hear it, but my husband's good to me. There's nothing he wouldn't do. He gives me my space.'

'I won't leave you. I think you worry that when you get older I'll run away.'

'It's not that.'

'I don't know if I can stand to have you just once? Can you?'

'I don't know.'

'But I must or it will destroy me.'

'Hold onto this.'

'I never want to think it's the last time.'

'It's not. Sometimes I pray to the gods for us.'

'You can't rely on praying, Regn. You have to do your part. Take action. Make it happen. There was a time when I was more scared if I didn't do anything. I had to change or it would kill me.'

She studied me closely.

'You know, look at my fingers, they have arthritis, even in my feet. In the winter they start to hurt,' her voice began to cry. I took her fingers and held them. 'One day my skin's going to hang, and it's not far off.'

'You have many years left.'

She sat up and hit the horn with her knee. We both laughed.

'How would you love me?'

'I want to, if you'd let me, love you as a man would.'

'But it doesn't matter. You just gave me love, you don't have to—'

'It matters to me.'

'I would let you.'

'I like to feel you shudder.'

'Shudder? What do you mean—I've never heard that said.'

'Shudder.'

'Shake?' she asked.

'It's shudder.'

'You can't say you never gave a woman an orgasm. Now you can brag about it.'

'Even if I wanted to, Regn, I wouldn't. And who would I tell?' The back window was fogged from our heat.

'I'm yours, body and soul. You are my true love, Westcott. If you have more feminine characteristics it's even better. It's so easy with you.'

'Why? Because I don't ask for anything in return—physically.'

'No. We've known each other before.'

I watched the branches blow in the hot wind outside Regn's window.

Tentatively her hand came—I let it slip down, searching.

She discovered what was and *wasn't* me.

'You don't regret knowing?'

'No. To me you will always be a beautiful young man.'

 I PARKED MY BIKE beside Regn's Seven Sisters on the Island. I saw a path through the brush. I knew my lady had made it. She always hugs them. I took my picture in front of the seven trunks, my hand resting on one of them.

The sun was still warm. I was sweating. When I returned to the parking lot I sat in my truck. I tried to imagine thirty years from now—this place, me. Regn would be 85 and I would be her age. It scared me, I didn't want to live to see such a day. And yet, in that moment, thirty years didn't seem that long. Time seemed immeasurable. It didn't exist. I watched a deer on the outskirts of the fence grazing, twitching her tail. I would like to have been that deer.

• • •

We were at our table on the mezzanine. 'I'm glad I met you, even if it was late in life. You give me a peace and I have that to thank you for. I wish you'd talk more—you're so philosophical. You have a beautiful mind. I'm—' she broke off chewing her cheese and crackers. 'Let me look at your eyes. You can see so much emotion in them—sorrow, melancholy, maybe a peace.'

'Anger.'

'No, I don't see that.'

'Sometimes I wonder, you look at everyone and you know they have the career—that's great if it works for them, I'm not knocking it, but I don't—sometimes when you're always on the outside watching you see much more. I question everything.'

'You should. I'm like that myself.'

'It's not so easy though, always going against. You know what I've wanted to do with you,' I said abruptly.

'What?'

'Put your lipstick on—you. Does that sound funny?'

'No.' She told me about a boy named Joseph who'd applied lipstick to her for a school play.

'This isn't any play.'

•••

Regn never liked Pauline because she was a very large woman. She referred to her as the Puffer Fish. She breathed heavily given her rotundity. I liked Pauline. Yes, she could be loquacious and exhausting, but she often had very interesting commentary. For some inexplicable reason she reminded me of the Hamburger Meister. She'd been with the Foundation about a year. She was a retired elementary school principal and quite personable. Though she was of German descent, she had been born in the United States.

'Westcott, are you familiar with the book, *The Reader*? I think you'd find it fascinating.' We were alone at the front desk, everyone else was on their lunch break.

'It's about post-World War II and a love story.' Pauline continued. 'I think you'd like it.'

'I'll check it out.'

'Also, you may not want to mention it to Regn. Read it for yourself and see.'

•••

'You are a splendid man, Westcott!'

If he knew about my gender, if he knew about Regn and me, I wanted to ask Rawlings if he'd still believe I was a splendid *man*.

'I think there's something very sensual in you. When you touch me, I can feel it enter me. And in your eyes, you have bedroom eyes—I have to ground myself—to get away from you—' Regn sat across from me. Her words thrilled and tormented.

'Get away from me—that doesn't make me feel good.'

'I don't mean it in a bad way, or I'll go crazy.'

'Sometimes I think I should be the better man and just give you peace.'

'I don't want you to go away. Not yet. Let's be crazy a little longer.'

'And what do you think that does to me? I'll want to be crazy forever, and I don't know if it's possible, Regn.'

'I don't want you to go.'

Standing in the lobby she told me as I walked by, 'I have the scent of your Wrangler on me.' She remembered the name of my cologne—it's not like her to do that. I was impressed.

'I'd like to pull you down on top of me.'

'So would I,' she answered.

In the afternoon a woman approached me.

'Is Regn here?'

Though we'd never met, there was something familiar in the woman standing before me. I saw my Lady in the bone structure of this woman, particularly in the nose. She had her father's eyes, blue.

It was Dee, Regn's daughter. She was 34. Regn far outshined her in appearance. Her son got the looks. Dee took after her father—firstborns often do—not only in physical traits, but personality as well. Jay wasn't unbecoming, but such features in a woman are not captivating. She was attractive in that she shared Regn's blood. She was not my type. Pale skin, brown hair to the shoulders, and her father's eyes—the looks in the women skipped a generation because both Regn and her granddaughter are distinct.

Regn introduced us. I was about to give my hand. A psychoanalyst might say the thought that my hand had been between her mother's legs just two days ago staid my extension of a handshake. I know it was because I'd been taken off guard. It seemed surreal. It was the one and only time I ever met either of Regn's children.

Regn left at 5:30. We were standing in the alcove by the brochures. She hesitated. No one was around. We kissed in the open—a quick, stolen, love.

• • •

'What did you think yesterday, meeting my daughter?'

I felt safe. I wasn't going to tell Regn our age protected us—her daughter would never suspect, I was secure. 'Side-by-side, I have to say, and don't misinterpret this—you have the looks, Regn.'

'You know, when we first moved here, I was outside with Dee and some young neighborhood guys were walking by. They called out to Dee and said, "Your sister is hot!" Can you believe that? They thought I was her older sister. Sometimes now, when I get coffee, I ask for the senior discount. The cashier doesn't believe me.'

The perks of being a young mother, Westcott thinks but does not say. 'You will age gracefully, Regn. I'm sure of it. You already have.'

The conversation waned in its light-heartedness with moments of weighed silence. Regn looked out her window on the mezzanine. And then—

'Who traps you more, your husband or me?'

'Oh Westcott. My husband more, you don't trap me. He wants everything a certain way and that's all he sees. Sometimes he hugs me and then I think he goes and cries. I don't have the answers. Sometimes I think I know what's right, but then I—'

'You're telling me right there. I should just give you peace; I don't want to but—' I felt the reservoir.

'I don't want you to go,' she said.

'I just want to be good to you.'

'Wish to the gods to let it happen.'

'You can't wish. You have to *make it* happen.'

She took my hand and held it across the table. 'Can't we just live for today?'

'It gets too hard.'

'I don't know what to say. Sometimes it's in both our heads and there aren't any words. I have no one to talk to about this, sometimes I feel so alone.'

'You're speaking my own words. There's no one I can talk to about it. You've sacrificed your entire life, and I'm not saying it was wrong.'

'Maybe I have to keep sacrificing.'

'Don't be a martyr, Regn.'

We had to get back. The offices upstairs were dark. I went around the desk to throw our trash in the can.

'Couldn't we just crawl under there—' she laughed. It was no laughing matter. We both felt the heaviness. On the elevator I set my bag down. 'Don't want to fall over.' Yesterday I'd lost my balance while we hugged.

I pressed my mouth to her forehead. Her neck went back slightly. I pressed my mouth to her lips. She held her eyes closed.

'I'm sorry. I wish it could be easier.'

'Don't say you're sorry,' letting her know sorry wasn't good enough; sorry changes nothing.

She'd been in such a good mood this morning—should I have let her enjoy it? Or was it prolonging things?

• • •

Journal Entry:
from the Book of West
Saturday 28 June 20—

Even in *this* I often hide behind my words, never saying what I want to—sometimes I imagine in dying I find myself wandering through a magnificent stone edifice—the Great Hall of the Settlement. But it's been abandoned, overrun by nature. Vines and foliage fill the hallway and the roof has caved in—water runs from a fountain, it's almost a paradise, and I know without knowing that I'm searching this place for something—someone. It's haunting and yet I feel welcomed. Safety awaits in this sanctuary.

JULY

I arrived to work to find Deborah had opened the office. I was on register 4 and keeping quiet. I wore my new lapel pin I'd bought Sunday. I'd gone to Busch Gardens by myself. In the German town I found a cuckoo clock lapel pin. Black and gold. I was conscious of my mood. Regn mentioned my reserve. I didn't want to be lighthearted, we had such little time as it was. Things needed to be said. Decisions made. She stroked my chin with her hand, just once. I had to point out my lapel pin for her to even notice. 'Your powers of observation, I worry about you,' I added with derision. Throughout the morning I opened up and we joked. My petulant frustration drizzled.

'I wonder how somebody like that—the big guy you see over there—' she gestured 'and the little woman he's with do it. She must be on top. It would be like riding a horse.'

'We're the same weight,' I commented. Despite being 7 inches taller, I was so gaunt our weight made us complementary.

I left for break at 12:11. Not putting my lunch in the microwave, I was too nervous with anticipation, I immediately walked upstairs. Regn was still on lunch with her bare feet propped on a chair, which both disturbed and intrigued me.

'What time is it?'

'It's 12:15, you're supposed to be back.'

She wasn't in any rush.

'Are you just going to move your mouth or are you going to say something, Westcott?'

'Don't ever take me for granted.'

'You think I take you for granted?'

I hesitated on the next question—

'Say it—'

'When's the last time—you had sex?'

'Why do you want to know?'

'There's your answer.'

'It will only hurt you.' She paused. 'Last night.'

No wonder sex had been on her mind in our conversation earlier. I'd been planning the question all night and this morning. I'd prepared myself for her answer to go either way. Something in me wanted to believe she'd say, 'Oh, we haven't done *that* for a long time.' Her response stabbed me. Last night! Just last week she was saying how much she was hurting to be with me. And yesterday we spoke on the phone, 'Irishman, take care, see you tomorrow.' And what does she do? Goes home and is satisfied. Last night. And there she was trying to joke with me this morning, brushing my face, all the while having had him in her arms last night! Just the other evening, Sunday, I'd been defending her *to myself*. Mother was worried about me. Yet *I* had to test the seed of doubt.

The pain of what her statement told me. I'd been looking forward to tomorrow—that we might spend time together since we're both off. But here she's having sex—she doesn't need me touching her a day-and-a-half later. I go weeks, months—years. A stroke on the face, a hug in the elevator, a second-long kiss. That's supposed to last me? The thought of putting my hand where her husband's prick has just been—is too much. How could she lie on her back and let him love her, knowing my longing agony of having gone without? A part of me wanted to say you disgust me, another part still wanted to be good to her, not say something harsh out of pain unknown.

Cold-faced, monotone, I replied. 'That says so much.'

'You're hurt I can see it.'

'Have you ever heard it said that the truth of what one says lies in what one does?'

'What am I supposed to do? I have to keep on living.'

I couldn't believe my ears. Everything inside me backed up. I was stunned. 'That is a very poor excuse. I feel completely used.'

'Do you want to end our *friendship*?'

The word jumped out at me. Friendship—what happened to her walking through the rotunda and whispering in my ear, 'I love you?'

'You don't trust me anymore?' she asked.

'I don't believe what you say. I have to eat my lunch.' I rose from the table and walked away. I didn't look back at her as I turned into the doorjamb. I just walked away. I hesitated by the elevator still in shock, waiting for her to come. She was *already* late from her lunch. For once I was in the right. She didn't come. I turned around. We met by the doorway.

'I realize something.' I looked her in the eye as I spoke. 'I'm stronger than you and I would never use you,' I started to walk down the mezzanine. She motioned for me to follow her. I wanted to take the stairs; she looked at me to ride the elevator with her. I kept my distance.

'Your actions say so much.'

We didn't speak throughout the afternoon. She busied herself with the dolly and loading magazines—I didn't volunteer to assist. Clearly she was fine doing it herself. The others noticed. After all, this morning Ann had caught us laughing hysterically and now there was dead silence. A fierce storm rolled in. I went out front, felt the wind, watched the lightning. I was supposed to go to the ships; the outdoors had been closed. I thought to myself, *Their marriage can't be in that bad of shape if she's back having sex with him.*

I closed my register at 3:45. Neither of us spoke. Returning to the lobby to enter my amounts in the system, I stopped at Regn's register. 'Are you going to say something?'

'What should I say?'

Our body language dictated we were at odds. Deborah and Jill were at the main desk. Fernus was close by.

'Why did you have to ask?'

'It says so much. I don't want to say this out here—' but I did—'if you loved me at all sex would have been impossible—with him.'

'Then you don't know me. You're a man and I'm a woman. A woman can do many things. I meant what I said to you.'

'I don't understand how—' My mind tried to wrap itself around this.

'I'm just going to become so hard, be done with this,' she spoke under her breath, 'and take what I can get.'

'Incredible,' I said in disgust and awe. Staring at her, 'You didn't need me for anything.'

'That's not true. I need things. I've given a lot to others and sometimes I need things.'

'At the expense of others—'

She didn't answer.

'It would have been different if we'd had each other and then time passed and you went back—you're not putting this on me.' I moved around to the side of her register so my back was to Deborah and Jill.

'I told you I was getting back with my husband.'

'*No you didn't*. You did not say that.'

'I remember my words.'

What excuses was she coming up with! 'You did not. You said you didn't have the answers, that you didn't know what you were going to do.'

She looked at me, confirming I was *not* crazy, that what I was telling her was in fact what she'd said.

She was sitting. I was standing.

'I have to tell you I find it weak and selfish and completely deceptive.'

'You know you're hurting me. Ann's watching,' she nodded with her head.

I looked over to register 7.

'Watch it.'

'I'm not the one hurting you. You're doing it to me and I feel absolutely used.' I walked to my register, closed out the computer. I knew she was hurting. She was being cold as a defense, I knew her well, but I couldn't let her off that easy. Not this time.

I was in the office signing my papers when Fernus came to the window needing change. She was casually singing in a slurred voice, 'I think it's love.' How nonchalant. I caught her message—she was singing to me. I got her 8 five dollar bills from the drawer in exchange for two twenties. Regn came in behind me. I could see the hurt in her eyes. Eva was in the back office.

'I meant everything I said. I still do.' She was referring to that day in her car when she'd told me, 'You are my true love.'

I hushed my voice knowing Eva was listening. 'Actions speak louder than words.'

I disappeared to the restroom with note paper and pen. I made a copy at the Xerox. Regn's make-up case and thermos were on the counter. Seeing them hurt me more. A part of her. I didn't want to hate her, lose her. I waited and waited, she didn't come. I used the privy, took off my Ireland tie, unbuttoned my shirt and headed upstairs thinking she might be hiding out on the mezzanine. I saw her bent, practically slumped over the copy machine, her head in her hands.

'What are you doing?' I'd startled her.

'Making copies.'

I watched the reconciliation forms for balancing our drawers shooting out of the machine.

'Here,' I said *dropping* the folded yellow post-it note on the tray. She made no effort to pick it up. 'I wouldn't leave it there. I'm heading out.'

Did she think I'd taken off my tie because it was the one she'd given me? No—it wasn't that. I just hadn't wanted to tuck my shirt in after the restroom. Besides it was raining and would wet the silk.

She picked up the printed copies, followed me out. I was going to take the stairs.
'Come,' she said hitting the button for the elevator.

Tom, our curator, appeared from the offices. I stalled, holding the door open for him to take the stairs, betraying no sign of my emotional distress.

I stepped on the elevator with Regn.

'I meant what I said.' She moved to touch my face. I stepped back; her hand fell to my shoulder.

'Don't—'

'I won't,' she said. I knew I'd crushed her, because if she had been the one to step back from my hand, I'd have been destroyed.

All I could say was, 'Your actions say so much.'

I got my briefcase. Clocked out. 'Bye Eva.'

'All right, have a good evening.'

Regn looked at me, expectantly. I forced a nod. Left without her.

Even in my anger and hurt as I watched her that afternoon in her white sandals I still loved her. A part of me longed to say, 'Let's meet tomorrow.' I needed her, but what dignity would be in that? The skies were gray and cloudy—it was drizzling, cool.

• • •

The next morning my voice is terse, final. 'I'm going for a walk on the Island. You can meet me or not.'

I get into her bug at 9:30. We drive the five-mile loop and pull over by one of the informational markers.

'You hurt me so much yesterday.'

Regn is helpless to make a plan. 'I just want it to be the right time. I didn't mean to hurt you. I just wish we had a bed.'

She cried, then I cried. We stayed on the Island until 1:00, talking.

I am starving when we drive back to the Visitor's Center. Regn had to use the restroom. We'd just gotten back in her bug and I'd started to eat my cheese and crackers. 'So where do you want to go?' Regn asked. 'It's raining now.' We were going to make love. I told her in no uncertain terms, we do this now, we make it happen or not at all.

'We'll go to my house,' I said.

'That's his truck!'

I see it driving down the lot. I get out fast, fumble with my keys, pretend to be opening the driver's door of the car I'm next to. Regn's tires skid. I see his truck coming back on the U-turn. After he passes the second time not seeing me, I go back to my truck. Should I go inside the Visitors Center, stay where I am, or drive and hide my vehicle? I wait.

He doesn't come. Maybe he only saw Regn's car. He'd have returned to the lot and confronted me if he'd known I was still there—wouldn't he? Were they both pulled over and having a conversation farther up the road by the entrance? Why had he been there? I knew he sometimes went to the Dale House café. Was it mere coincidence? I didn't dare move. I'd wait, give them time to argue.

Fifteen minutes went by—no call from Regn to alert me he was coming—that was good, but no call to say all was well, he suspected nothing. *In that moment* I understood her actions and why she'd slept with him. It became clear. I wasn't buying into her excuse, it was true. She'd done it to secure him so that when he was to go away at the end of the month, his misgivings would be put to ease. She would create the facade of peace in order to protect us. This is what I told myself. I wanted to believe it even when I knew Regn was not that calculating. I transformed her selfish transgression into heroism. In reality, she'd entered the act quite simply—putting her needs first—to soothe frustrations, while I held myself for her. There reaches a time when it is betrayal for a woman to sleep with her husband. But I'd come too far, waited too hard, not to have our love actualized. If it killed me we would have our chance.

Now this? What if Jay did see me, what would she tell him? It's like she says—we're doomed. Never a quiet moment, or place of safety. I was so angry and hurt by her this morning and now that this happened I realize her sacrifice. *What was I doing there?* Another man's wife. *You should be at home on such a miserable dank day. You're creating danger for her and yourself.* It's pouring now, where is she, what's being said? Is she trying to calm him down or does he think she'd just gone out to walk alone? Thank god we hadn't started to pull out of the parking space. That I wasn't in Regn's car and he didn't pull up parallel behind us is a saving grace. Or is it? Sometimes I want him to know so it can become easier. But I don't want to hurt him. It happened so quickly—no time to think.

She called and left a message. She was driving home from the dealership. Jay had traded his truck in for a new one—same brand, style, and size as mine—only much newer and a boring color. The color he'd wanted was out of stock. He settled for white. Everything was all right. He *hadn't* seen us and was just out for an afternoon walk and snack. Or had he and he just didn't want to say anything?

Again. Love would have to wait.

There was a moment, a moment when we were driving through the Island in the grayness. We were heading back to the Visitors Center. Regn had her left hand on the steering wheel. "Serenissima" played. Her right hand rested in my lap on my hand. We were driving back so I could get a snack from my truck. I was *starving.* We should have stayed out there in the forest and made love. It was the very warmth of her skin, her hand on mine that stilled me so—a deep calm. Not the throes of clutching, kissing, or climaxing, but just her hand with mine in the early afternoon of a drizzling Wednesday.

• • •

14 July 20—

My love is not meant to hurt you, Regn. You say you fought for many years.

We fight differently then. You fight passively to maintain what is manageable.

My dear Lady, you misread that story. I am not criticizing. Just hear me out. I agree the character in The Reader did resent Hannah. I think he resented her for punishing herself, standing there and not doing anything but slipping to resignation, allowing her person to be imprisoned in order to hide the Truth. He was haunted by her. I do contend that he was wrong not to go to her before the sentencing. Had it been me, fear of the wartimes aside, I'd have gone and spoken with her—asked her why and if she wanted me to confess her secret to spare her sentence. He loved her, Regn, and if you didn't see that and the hurt he carried—his entire life he, too, was 'locked' up. She never left him. He had immense guilt surrounding her. He tried to hide in his work, he could speak to no one of her. It wasn't that he felt nothing; he could not allow himself to revive the emotions, how else could he make a way? To think he ever stopped loving her is to miss the crux of the story.

Regn, not all answers are quick and easy. If you work at it, though it may be long in getting to, there is a solution, even if it has multiple answers.

Of course there is no 'resolution,' not until one of the 'three' of us passes. And I don't say that to sound macabre. I'm not quite sure the peace we seek will ever be had. We may busy ourselves to distraction, 'managing' our emotions, but peace must come in the ultimate end.

My anger is <u>for</u> you—that long before me you did not help yourself, and I venture to say you share that same sense of anger within.

I'm more of an extremist in the search for truth than you, Regn. I search the horizon, living there, while so many cast their gaze on the immediate performance. I'm not proclaiming one is better than the other, but something tells me it's right—that the meaning lives on the mirage of an endless line encircling the world and wraps 'round the mind confounding us so.

I respect you for this, I am grateful to have found you—someone who loves me without question or why of my state. You are rare, and never forget that. And I love that I can let you put your hands on me—without fear. Never doubt the <u>respect</u> in such love.

HE IS 23 YEARS OLD. He has never slept with a woman. Somehow he knows without asking she is accustomed to sex in the dark—not in earlier days, but now perhaps out of compassion for his self-consciousness and to mask her own through his—at her suggestion, she turns the lights out and the waiting subsides.

~

He keeps that first time, that first night for himself. He remembers speaking with her in the evening. Summer stillness fading on the horizon. She said she had some things to do—water the plants, clean the litter box, and then she'd come. Then she *would* come. How ridiculous these things. Idle chores that could be tended to later, earlier. But now? At the time he pretended to understand. But how hard it was for her, how hard, came to him much later. She was just going through normal everyday routine, as though nothing out of the ordinary waited this particular July evening. It was her way of keeping calm.

Jay was in the mountains. Would be gone for just one night with a friend. He never went away. What was this friend telling him? 'Just let her get it out of her system, Jay. You'll see, these things never last.' Regn invited Westcott to her home. But he preferred a neutral place. Jay was too close. What if he decided to turn around and come home?

Westcott woke up early. Before sleep was satisfied. Breakfasted at the only old-fashioned diner left in town—Five Forks Café, where they still took orders by hand and put the tickets on a wheel for the cook stationed behind the counter. The stovetop in view. He was hungry and yet he wasn't. He was glad to be done with breakfast. There were still hours before evening. His sister was visiting. He sat next to her and across from his mother, never letting on, happily sick with anticipation of the night to come.

To this day, I believe, the motel is still there.

11. That was the room number. Across town, an out-of-the-way lodging. There are white silhouettes of horse-drawn carriages mounted on the shutters of the windows. He'd been set on the place for a while. Quaint. Off the beaten path of tourists.

Around two he headed to Magda's and checked on Lady G-. Pet-sitting. His absence from home for the night would be justified. It was warm and humid. Cumulus clouds abounded in the skies. He tried to read. The novel was intriguing, but the Irish brogue hard to get into. He couldn't concentrate. He set the copy of Jamie O'Neill's, *At Swim Two Boys*, on the table and looked out the window. Tomorrow at this exact time, it would all be over. He'd have made love by then. He doesn't want to think about tomorrow or yesterday. In just a few hours it is really going to happen.

Telephone poles stretch into the distance. The room is nicely furnished, a little musty, but in an inviting way. The White Lion has charm—a remnant from decades past—the 1950s early '60s. Nothing contemporary.

He *is* going back to a time that comforts. He imagines it is a different year.

——

He waits into the evening wearing his white shirt and silk tie of Ireland—the one Regn surprised him with. He wore it because of the occasion and secondly because he relished the thought of Regn loosening his necktie, undressing him. Regn is late. She'd been waiting in the wrong parking lot. She wears a loose pair of gray capris sweatpants with pink stripes on

the side leg and white sandals with a white shirt—very casual. He picks her up in the Visitor
Parking lot. He turns his stereo down low. He'd been listening to "And I Love Her" by The
Beatles on his way to get her. Somehow it would seem too perfect, too much, a prelude to
the obvious, if Regn were to hear it. She'd say nothing, but Westcott knew, somehow, that's
what she'd be thinking. Quiet seemed best. Regn seemed distracted. 'You okay? You want to
come, right?' 'Yes, of course. *Yes.*'

He'd left a table lamp on after checking-in that afternoon—a soft warm light, and
smoothed the blanket he'd brought, placing it on the interior bed (the one farthest from the
door) of the air conditioned room. The blanket is salmon with rivers of color—green, blue,
black and New Mexico horses. Beautifully depicted. The blanket he will fold up in time,
keep tucked away. The blanket of summer. The night his youth has been leading up to—the
torment of deprivation.

Opening the door, Regn enters the room. He steps inside. Closes the door quietly, with
intent. It is inviting with the corner lamp. Does Regn recognize the blanket? It is the same
material he used to wrap her Christmas present in.

'How much was it?' She means the room.
'It doesn't matter.' It was $66.00 with AAA.

~

Hungry, in the dark he finds a nectarine he brought. He eats it. Regn takes a bite. He
rubs the juice into her skin.

He is in a daze, starved to numbness.

He isn't there—he's thought of this moment for so long. That night he doesn't feel
desire—his energy of anticipation has all but worn him cold. Months upon months of
waiting. They'd undressed in the dark. There was mild light through the blinds. Westcott
was shocked by the sparseness of hair between Regn's legs. He knew she trimmed it, but it
almost looked child-like. The bone was firm and the current between flowed effortlessly. He
kissed the inlet pond where femur extends to socket in the pelvis. Searching, the thong of
words pressed inward finding the feel of a moistened wound. He pushed tentatively—two
O's linked by his own subtle thrip of salmoned horseshoe. Regn had said, 'With you I'd do
everything.' This wasn't entirely true. Later, in times to come, as he felt free to assert his
desires, there were things he wanted to try and Regn plainly would not. He'd experimented
with himself and knew how to be gentle and what worked and what didn't. His physical
dichotomy offered the advantage since he knew firsthand what moved and excited a woman.
But Regn, for all her bodily rapture and sensuality, was a woman in the most traditional
sense when it came to the bedroom. Partially because she'd never had a lover who wanted
to take her there, to these untapped experiences—nothing crazy—but just on the fringes
of erotic pleasure as opposed to simple pleasure. On this night something inside her raced.

This was a new intimacy for both of them. Westcott didn't know if he liked it or not.
Once he started, he felt he should continue. Her entire body was always fresh and warm.

~

'I wish I'd seen you.'
'Why?'

'I want to look at the person I'm making love to——. It's a privilege,' he says. 'You give me my greatest story. A story I can't write because it has no ending and to write it would be to relive it and I don't have the strength.'

'My sweet, sweet West. You fulfill me in every way. If you *were* a woman I'd still love you. Never be ashamed. We're so lucky. Some never find this. There are a lot of sad, sad people in the world.'

A person can wait his entire life for those words. I was 23 years old. My heart had peaked in its prowess as a lover. Maude would tell Harold to go on loving. But Regn was *not* Maude. She was much younger. I'd felt all the stages of Regn alive in my hands. The girl she'd been and the woman she was. She had no age. Nor I. And the love we shared, the love I'd known, would never be so imperfectly perfect again.

~

Half past eleven the moon is bright. His hand rests in hers. She holds it. The visitor parking lot is completely empty of cars. Regn's silver car glints in the moonlight. He shifts the gear into park. Shuts the engine off and grasps under the dash on the rise separating the floor. He hands her an animal cracker cookie box—the cardboard rectangular ones with a white string to carry it. He knows its contents, as does the man in the moon, and Regn who opens it. No one else at that moment. That's how it should be. He'd bought it at the Spring Art Festival a few months before. The man who made the fine pieces said, handing him the small brown bag with the firm bracelet wrapped in tissue paper, 'I hope she likes it.'

She loves it. At work the ladies compliment her on it.

They stand in the empty night. For a little while he came in from the fevered cold. He can never stay—the earmark of his life—always on the outside looking in. The moon has no emotion—only that which he grants it. On this night it shines for them. The happiness is short-lived. A desolate fear displaces calm.

He doesn't want to go back to the empty room. He feels the opposite of how he should. The sense of vacancy is terrifying as though she's made peace and carried it away with her.

~

He sleeps in his clothes for two hours. Or tries to sleep. It seems a shame to waste the room. He wishes Regn would have spent the night, but in case Jay called she wanted to be home.

He makes a recording, a dissertation to his mother in the event of his death, which he will never give her. He wishes he had the courage to end his life.

He considers going for a walk. Instead he studies the framed picture of this night. The little horse and carriage emblem on the shutters of each room. A hanging flower plant. It really is quaint; the trees still bloom and in the early hours the blossoms wash the pavement.

He returns the key into the drop box at 4:30 a.m., drives home, quietly creeps up to his own bed—closer to Regn—literally, in terms of distance, miles. Skin.

No one in his house stirs. Mother and Ellis are sound asleep.

It doesn't seem like he's only been gone most of the day.
Somehow. It was. Much longer.

*

PART II

THE COLOR OF THE MOUNTAINS

23 July 1975
6:10 p.m.

Helen Cray "Gedny"

I'm passing a cemetery and
I wish you all were here. Perhaps
you are; I'll know in time.

I truly hope you care as
happy as I am at this moment.

How great is the feeling of complete
alienation to pattern. No rhyme,
no reason, such contentment.

Total freedom to drift your
own way.

To glide and be so aimless.
No inhibitions, no self-denial.

Just letting me be,
because
I am.

CHAPTER 4

THE PATH THAT LEADS TO NOWHERE

AUGUST. THE ONE TIME REGN is punctual, ahead of time to be precise. I'd said to try and be there at 7:30. She'd said 8. I look to the grandfather clock. The Roman numerals show 7:20. Just as she pulls into the driveway and parks, Mother is backing out from the garage. I step to the front porch, lean over the wooden railing. 'Hi, Regn.'

Mother opens her car door. 'How are you, Regn—wait one second and I'll back out.'

Regn moves her car to the side then pulls into the garage. I stand at the door leading from the garage into our kitchen, motioning Regn to go to the front. I want everything just right. I press the automatic door lift so it will close. She can't see the house for the first time so informally as coming in from the garage! I walk back through the house.

Opening the door to her she laughs. How long we have waited.

'It's okay. She doesn't mind.' I mean my mother.

Regn steps across the threshold. The grandfather clock is ticking. Dining room off to the left, formal living room on the right, the stairwell, then the TV room that gives way to the kitchen and back deck. She looks around. I show her different pieces. 'You can look at them if you like,' indicating two lady statues—Ertes in the front window backed by lace curtains.

'You're so funny,' she says.

I'm being awkward, I know. I sit on the living room sofa—she has on gray sweats, a light blue cotton shirt and her white sandals. We hold each other. Politely. Gently.

~

She is the first woman, the first guest—outside of family—to ever enter his bedroom. She lies in repose on his bed with the green and beige checkered comforter, as if resting, fully clothed. He sits beside her. Miss Gilly pushes open the door, comes running in, jumps up and sits down like a brigadier right between them. Pronouncing her jealousy or decreeing a sanction? It's a small bed. Hardly big enough for one person, let alone two-and-a-half. They laugh ridiculously. 'What can I say, she's a very jealous stogie-dogie' (stow-gee doe-gee).

He sends Miss Gilly out the door, lets Helmsley stay in the chair with the green and yellow rabbit. They are the only witnesses. Regn lies back. The search begins.

~

It is near nine o'clock when they leave. The summer skies are dark. The soft lamplight of his room quaint. Gedny promised to let them have the evening. She went to the movies. They walk out the front door. My but it's so easy. Simple. No worries of being seen. On their way, stopped at a light, he muses. 'I used to read—you sometimes see after a story the short biography. An entire life summed up in a concise paragraph. It'll say so-and-so did this for five or ten years. It's so brief when read in a mere passage, but "ten years"—saying it doesn't capture the length! I often think of someone reading my—. Sad to think it's all laid down to a few lines.'

'It's what you make of it. I don't know—I don't think like you.' Regn turns the corner.

Three miles. Just three miles. The distance between his house and hers.

There is a light on inside. Outside the porch is dark, shrouded with trees in the shadows. But he knows the house is wedgwood blue.

Pulling into her garage, Westcott looks around. Waits for Regn to turn the ignition off, step out. Regn and Jay's old time bicycles hang on the wall. A pair of boots stand propped, with deliberate precision, beside the steps leading in. The way they are set there—carefully, habitually—Westcott knows they are *his*. Just as he sees the reading glasses on the counter in the kitchen beside a bowl of fruit.

Regn *filled* the house—everything is the way she likes it. She shows him the laundry room where she stenciled the walls with suns.

'Are you all right?'

His face is quiet, taking account of everything.

Regn always said her home was 'cozy.' She is right. He follows her into the living room. They sit on the couch. Tentatively he leans back. She pours them each a drink of chardonnay.

'Very little, I don't want to waste it.'

Enjoying wheat thins and cheese. She holds up her glass. 'Cheers.' She looks at him from her customary seat on the sofa. 'It's strange having you here.'

Yes. He knows she means it in a good way. Finishing his cheese and crackers she leaves him in the kitchen. Without a word, silently, he knows he is to follow. To the right of the stairwell, if one comes in the front door, is Jay's office. Westcott looks at the room, the empty chair laden with anticipation of a return. But it is not Jay he imagines, it is the absence that registers unconsciously. He is simply taking in the lay of the land. On the stairwell there is a line of pictures going up the left wall. He looks at each with every advancing step. He wants to remember each of them. Such care in the alignment of their mounting. At the top he turns right. Regn is in her meditation room. There is a sofa-bed which she has unfolded. This is where she sleeps with her granddaughter when she comes to visit. He does not remember but somehow they get under the covers.

~

His phone rings. At half past one in the morning his mother is calling him. 'Are you all right?' Westcott sits on the edge of Regn's pull-out bed. His annoyance is lessened by the presence of Regn and the chimera of emotions within. She knew he was going with Regn. Why is she calling? He's 23 years old, damn it. Why must she intrude on this night? Can't she ever stop worrying! He answered because he knew it would be worse if he didn't. She'd start to panic. Call again. Leave a message asking him to just call home, let her know when he'd be back. Nothing is his own. Not Regn. Not his body. Of course he's all right, he's with Regn. 'I'm fine,' he answers. 'Will you be very late?' 'Yes.' 'All right. Have a good time.'

She honestly didn't know. Maybe she didn't want to believe it.

'Everything okay?' Regn says from behind him. 'Yes.' He turns over his shoulder. Back to the moment, the night. Back to her.

~

Tangelos and green tea. She'd thrown on her shirt and stands barefoot in her underwear. He has on his faded orange and blue boxers—only one of two pairs he owns, his black socks, a white t-shirt and his overshirt, buttoned to conceal the unnecessary vent of his drawers. They stand in the full light of the kitchen, a quarter past two in the morning, exposed to each other in the intensity of the fluorescents. Their stomachs were growling; a snack is in order. 3 A.M. Regn draws a bath, pours in her Badedas. Steps in the tub. He turns off the light, removes his shirt and drawers. He will not let her see him. He does not open his legs for her to sit between.

'My skin's very sensitive—' Does she understand? He means the place between—

They sit, somewhat uncomfortably in the quiet night. 'What are you doing?' Her voice is soft.

The exhaustion of the hour finds his eyes searching in the dark. He doesn't realize he's inhaling audibly, deeply, as he binds this memory to his senses. The scent of lemons and warmth. They dry each other in complete darkness. She wipes his skin after hers, drifts into her room for a moment. With towel about waist, 'You can turn the light on now,' he calls to her pulling his drawers up.

She rests on top of him. He is still. His boxers still in place. The room is dim, gentle on the eyes, perfect for seeing without blinding. He prefers to make love in the light. To study Regn's body. Every detail. Every flaw. He's waited so long.

She is crushing him, straddling his slender body, his hips wide though bony. It is uncomfortable. He cannot come—not like this. She holds him close. He did not expect it of himself, tears come down his face. The light is soft, yet his eyes strain from exhaustion to stay awake. Beyond tired—too tired to sleep. 'What, what, what'—he keeps saying. A switchboard on the fritz, a power surge, leaving him speechless. On her side, he holds her into him—her hinterlands against his groin, his hands wrapped round her, protecting. He enjoys this best. He cries, he thinks, in relief and pain of waiting—but it is more, much more. Already he is missing her.

She sleeps for a moment. He listens to her snore. She stirs. He rests his head on her chest and begins to doze. He takes her hand in his and for the longest time strokes the fingers, staring at the ceiling, knowing she is watching his face. Regn sees him cry. Wordlessly. He feels each joint, the arthritis in the protruding bones. Her fingers are quite long for such klein stature. She'd have made a great cellist. He likes that she keeps the nails short, colorless. She gardens and works in the soil, she likes to get her hands in the earth. 'We made wonderful love.' Her voice is a whisper.

She drives him home. It is five in the morning. 'I've never made love all night,' she says. Her right hand rests in his on his lap. She drives with her left. They pass the cornbread meadow—a field covered with yellow poppies and black and white cows motionless in the blue mist. Sleeping. A small spread of land in the middle of civilization. He hopes the owners never sell. It is almost dawn. The streets are peaceful. The world does not hurt at such an hour. There is time.

•••

Saturday. He calls to say he'll be into work late. Regn arrives as scheduled, at 8:15, having slept only an hour. At lunch he steps out front, reclines on the bench, fully visible from the lobby registers. He is a peacock basking in the afterglow. He does not care if the others think his behavior out of character, or rather, he is too spent to muster the energy to care. They can't touch him—they can't take away last night. The day hurts. *It is beautiful.* He stares up through the tree at the bright sun, half in a daze of sleep deprivation. Behind sunglasses, light moisture runs from the corner of his eyes. He lies there, head against the iron bench, seeing himself from far away. Someone, something is watching. Not just his colleagues—but the trees and day itself. It is a bold presentation. How far he has come!

Evening. Pay phones are hard to come by he now realizes scanning the shopping center for one. He walks into the grocery store, uses the phone at guest services so the number won't be suspicious on her caller ID. She never has her mobile on.

'A little bird says you should take a sick day tomorrow.'

'I don't know if I can—if I *should*. I'll see.'

Sunday. 3ʳᵈ of August. About noon his phone rings. She'd gone to work. She is going to leave early. They gave her permission, it is slow enough, Fernus said so. *Fernus. Thank you.* Fernus had often displayed sympathy or was it a private envy—in any case, she was always good to Westcott. Does she know why Regn is leaving early? Surely one woman senses another's *passion*. They agree on two o'clock. She calls *again.*

'Would it be all right if I came a little earlier?'

A red letter day—she never—

'I was at work,' she says when she arrives, 'and I knew then how hard it's going to be. I just wanted to be with you—'

'What do you want to do?'

'What do you mean?'

'You know what I mean—'

'I don't know—you give me my soul, I can say things to you I could never tell anyone— the way I can talk to you.'

He knows she is not being cliché. If he read such a statement in an American novel he'd chuck it against the wall. She is speaking plainly, without censorship or theatrics.

'I lost my heart's virginity to you.'

'So did I—I saved it somehow—all these years.'

~

'Will you cut me?'

'What do you mean, cut you?'

'So we'll be bound by blood.' He gets his razor. Lifts his neck, lies back.

'I don't want to hurt you.'

'It's fine. Here, I'll do it.' With several strokes he nicks the back of his thumb instead of his neck. He slices it more than he intended. The blood rolls down. Regn takes his hand, softly stops the blood from dripping, wiping it clean with her tongue. It continues to bleed. 'Let me get some alcohol.' He gets up, goes down the hall.

He keeps the Kleenex firmly pressed. He is part of Regn now. He wants to taste the copper of her marrow, but he doesn't want to hurt her. The exchange remains incomplete. Already his hand feels tight, stinging. They smile.

She leaves his room for the bathroom.

It is so quiet in the house.

Returning, her tone has changed. She's mustered strength again.

'I need to go home, check on the cats. Call my kids. Then I'll come back—about 6?'

Westcott is in his chair wearing *her* sandals. 'They fit!' He slides them off trying to laugh at the moment knowing the alternative. Nothing has been resolved.

'We're the same size, only you're taller.'

~

He hears movement in the hall. No one is downstairs. When he comes back up Regn is still sitting on his bed, looking out the window. She notices the calendar hanging on his wall. 'It's not July.'

'You want to switch it for me.'

She goes to the corner, flips the page to August, tacking it up. He watches her hands. They do so many things. But this—this she will only do once.

~

His mother, home from work, has changed into her comfortable clothes and is downstairs.

'Why was the alcohol out on my counter?'

He lies. 'Helmsley scratched me while I held him for Regn to pet. We're going to Busch.'

'Now?'

'No. About six.'

'Is Regn—'

'She's gone, she's coming back. Then we'll go. This isn't easy, you know.'

'What? Just enjoy the time you *do* have. Call me if you're going to be very late. I don't want to worry.'

'Uh-huh.' Inside he sighs. A sigh he no longer recognizes. The irony.

He silently heads upstairs, into the empty room, Ellis' old room. An air mattress and the hall tree are the only items. He lies down on the soft makeshift bed. The fatigue overtakes him. *She doesn't want to worry.* His mother never discouraged him from Regn. She was concerned, but she never asked for details. On some level he knows why. She'd wanted him to have this, and hadn't she remembered all those years ago—herself, how alive she'd been, and the pain? Leaving her first husband, Tony, for the man she met in the office, Bob. The

German, Bob Schneider, who left his wife and four children for her. Gedny didn't want him to—told him *not to leave his wife*—in the end he did anyway. Westcott knew the story, only as his mother told it. Times were different. Margaret, Westcott's grandmother said, 'Now you *must* marry him.' Westcott had his mother's journal from those days—after the break, after she left Tony and later when Bob abandoned her. Reading his mother's view of the world when she was the same age as he is now, finds him in the company of a stranger. The woman on those pages, her poems—she was more alive. Not just in being young, but the passion made her vibrant. He thinks of the woman downstairs in the recliner. His mother has regrets. He knows this. 'Right or wrong,' she told him, 'it was one of the most exciting experiences of my life.' Westcott understands too well. The mere thought of Regn electrifies him. The memory of her touch, her scent, her voice—

Tony was Gedny's first; she didn't want to hurt him. She still loved him—always would love him. Bob was—what was Bob? If only he'd listened and stayed with his wife and children, if only. Gedny had been pressured to marry him, both by her own mother and Bob. One day, two years into the marriage, Bob would say he was going fishing for the weekend. They spoke that afternoon on the telephone. Bob pretending everything was just as it should be. Gedny coming home to a note. The next day divorce papers were served. No prelude, no warning. No explicit reason. Gedny hadn't asked for this. She hadn't asked for any of it. Bob had said they'd have their own family. He changed his mind. He didn't want more children after the four with his first wife. Gedny wanted children. She was counting on his word. Three years later she met Westcott's father, the last. Might Westcott have been Italian or German, otherwise? During the interim, before her final marriage, she'd had a few persistent suitors. Romantics, men crazy about her. All that remains is a letter or two with earnest intentions and a name. Lives slipping through fingers. Gedny didn't have the confidence. After everything that had happened, she felt insecure. Westcott would have been 39 years old if Gedny had had him when she was young. Might Regn have been more easily persuaded to come with him were the span in age less startling?

From his father Westcott received the blood of Norway and from his mother Ireland and England. Was a tradition being passed down? Had not his grandmother taken her two small children—Gedny four, his uncle six, and left his grandfather because of an affair—a scandal in its day? She paid heavily for it, as did Westcott's mother and her brother. Gedny always felt abandoned. First by her father, then her mother, later her brother when he escaped into the Navy. And then the whole debacle with Bob. Why must one inherit heartache?

But what did his mother think or imagine they were doing upstairs? Just talking, being close? Westcott was private, revealed nothing. She knew they were close. Regn was a confidante for her son. But how close, he never mentioned. His mother, to her credit, knew Westcott would do as he wanted. Saying 'no' was not an option. He'd have done the same; passion must take its prescribed course. He trusted himself. Relied solely on his own sound judgment. In this he felt alone. He was glad of the privacy, but he missed the effort of guidance being passed on—neither he nor Ellis were ever guided. They chose their own direction. Gedny looked to her past for a sense of purpose and explanation. Their mother had given them every opportunity, exposed them at an early age to fine things—cross country train trips, vacations to Canada, Mexico, and Disney World, dining in the Twin Towers' "Windows on the World" restaurant, affluent performances—they saw "Cats" on Broadway, visited the Peabody Hotel in Memphis and watched the ducks waddle from the elevator—higher education, instruments, athletics. And still they wandered. As children they took it for granted, assumed their Mother had all the answers. And the right ones. She never said, 'Go off on your own, find your way. I'll be fine. You are strong. One day I know you'll come back when you've found what you are looking for.' But Westcott knew it wasn't his mother standing in his way. It was himself. It had always been himself and what he was that prevented him from leaping, just grabbing a suitcase and heading out. He was bold, relentless, but underneath his confidence as a man was flawed. In the absence of 5 inches of flesh he felt exposed, vulnerable, and disingenuous. His character had evolved around what was missing instead of what he possessed. It weakened him emotionally; it also gave him the cruel advantage of insight. He walked the borderlands. He looked male in every way, but it wasn't true, physically, and for this he could not forgive himself.

Lying in bed Westcott's mind does not formulate all this at once. He is imagining the night that awaits. Wondering what he will remember of this afternoon twenty years from now. He doesn't want a long life.

~

It is seven and still plenty light out when he steps from his porch. He has a small blue bag in tow, it looks like a paramedic's with the Swiss emblem.
'Does it bother you?' He reads her face as he opens the passenger door.
'No.'
He knows *she* knows its contents.
She's changed out of her white button-up blouse into a white cotton shirt, sweatpants, and brown heeled shoes. 'Can you walk all right in them?'
They pull out of the driveway. Follow the roads they know so well. How easy to take these roads. In the full daylight they pull to the intersection by Westcott's bank, turn left and continue past Regn's neighborhood. It is a feeling—something this simple—a casual drive on a summer evening. She wants to put the top down. It is broken, needs to be looked at. Probably best not to—he likes the private atmosphere.
'Can I?'
'Yes. You don't have to ask.'
Her softback cd pouch is concise, sufficient, orderly. The discs are not scratched or haphazardly stowed like his mother's. He picks out one of the copies he made for her.
He looks at the time on her console. Twenty past seven. They drive through the check-in at Busch Gardens. The man with the orange reflector vest directs them to the designated parking. Westcott's *To Kill a Mockingbird* soundtrack fills the interior with its enchanted instrumentals. If ever there was a gentleman archetype it was Gregory Peck as Atticus.
Westcott looks at the digital clock beside the built-in thermostat.
He tries Regn's cap on, peers at himself in the rearview mirror.
'It looks good,' she says.
He puts his salt and pepper tweed back on.
He wants to freeze-frame the hour.
Their mouths converging, a do-si-do of gum, she exchanges her chewing gum for his, like so many times. Fastidious by nature, this simple act with anyone else would have made him squeamish. He could never have imagined it possible to mingle his own intimate fluids with another. But Regn—her blood, her saliva, her sweat, even her private spring—felt, tasted, and exuded a quality so clean and desirously pure, that he considered them his own. There wasn't a single thing in or without Regn's person that could ever repel his senses.

The park closes at nine. Pulling into the parking space he is euphorically happy, intensely sad all at once. He laughs at something she says. In laughing he feels something inside about to give. The water in his eyes wets the rims beneath his sunglasses—he can hear Time being sliced—a chopping block of minutes.

'So many times I wanted to come here with you,' she comments.

'As did I.'

The beautifully landscaped park is parceled into countries with cultural shows and cuisine. They walk through Italy, decide to keep going to the farthest reaches, Germany. In Das Fest Haus Regn orders a Michelob ultra. Westcott has a lemonade. He hates beer. He tastes hers anyways. It is smoother than most. They get a small pizza as opposed to the expensive bratwurst, cabbage and potatoes.

'I'm paying,' Regn tells him.

'I don't expect that.'

'Hey, you paid for the room at the motel.'

Yes, he had. It was unnecessary, but that first time he wanted it to be safe. Jay had only been going up to the mountains a few hours north and somehow a neutral setting seemed best. They would be on equal ground that first time.

They look at each other amidst the crowded room. A radiance in the dim ambiance. He listens to her reminisce about going out in younger days, having champagne—how both her sister and brother divorced. Feeling the shadow of confinement. He does not think of tomorrow, next week, next month. What is, is now.

They take the Skyride to France. Alone in their blue cable car, high above the eyes of scrutiny, they kiss, just once. Decently. It is not bromidic. They are not free to partake as young lovers do. They are sharing a hard-earned pain, a moment preserved, suspended in the current of their lives.

They sail with the knowledge of landing, the hope of flying. Blue. The cable car is blue. Everything is perfect tonight. They are gliding through the treetops.

The one rollercoaster they want to share, *Griffin*, has already closed. They hurry for Italy. There is no line. They step into the seats of *Apollo's Chariot*. It is no pumpkin transformed into a coach, but this will surely do. 290 feet up, the night spangled, he touches her hand before they plummet, becoming weightless.

For the first and only time, they hold hands in the darkening crowd of tourists who don't see. Instead of taking the tram, they walk, stepping close and into one another. Moving through the crowd Regn runs her forehead into a tree branch. She laughs in pain. Scatterbird.

Out of the blue Westcott asks, 'Did you like being pregnant?'

The second evening begins.

~

She points out a brass cricket by the fireplace.

'They say it's good luck—you should always have one by your fireplace.'

'Yes. Dickens.' He goes to it, picks the brass critter up, examining it closer. Delicately, he sets it down on the brick with intent of his touch. The opera music she turned on delicately transports him in Time.

Regn goes to the restroom. Leaves the door open. Continues to talk. He stands just outside, along the wall between the kitchen and small bathroom. 'It's all right, you don't have to hide there.'

He wants to look. He hears her water. He comes around the doorjamb just as she is pulling up her underclothes. How does she do it? So open. So free to be herself.

~

'They say if you have a limb amputated you can still have sensations of it—you know what I mean?' They sit a long while on the sofa, longer than the previous night. Relishing the prelude.

He loves kissing her. Slowly, tentatively, then penetrating. He is telling her to wait. He feels her losing herself; he pulls away, wanting it to build. Coming closer, closer, withdrawing. A wonderful stirring.

'You know, I never liked kissing before. Until you'—

Before she can say another word, he presses her thin mouth gently, once more, then kisses her forehead, which he loves doing most of all.

They go upstairs.

He sees his picture—the one she'd purchased at Christmas—on her wall.

The nameplate. *Somber Passage.* A picture of the Colonial Parkway in fall.

How far they've come.

'Would you rather—in my bed?'

He carries his small navy bag with the Swiss emblem into the other room.

She does not ask, but waits on the bed.

'Don't look,' he mumbles.

The sound of unzipping. Wrapped in a green hand towel he takes out his stand. Though he will not feel it, he wants to penetrate her as a man. She spreads her legs nimbly. He wishes he could lie inside her—feel the warmth wrap round him, hold him. To know her in that way—completely. He is amazed how easily and naturally her body accepts the artificial extension. Post-menopause aside. Regn's body is used to sex. Is it exercise that keeps her so moist or the fact that she still has carnal exchange with Jay? Maybe it is both. Carnal longevity effects the pH levels *down there*, making the skin glow. It's little wonder why Regn exudes irrefutable vitality. Sex keeps the body flowing—the inertia a preventative against rigidity and infirmities. He remembers the story of the doctor she told him about—the one Regn went to when she was so young. '*Klein aber oho!*' *Small but whoa!* What was the 'whoa' in reference to?

She grips the sides of his head with both hands, her fingers running along his ears, lifts her legs, helping him to move inside. Fully within he kisses her or tries to as her body shudders. A graceful cry. It is his turn. Still hard he slips out of her. The object goes back inside his navy bag. Regn will not push inside him. He does not ask and really he doesn't want it just then. He envies Regn. The knowledge her body has received in all the years of penetration. Shameless. No lifeless prosthetics. No questions to answer, a safe union. She slips her hand beneath the shield of his drawers. He still won't let her see him. She feels the empty nest, kisses his scarred chest. His hand stings from the razor cuts. He wishes he hadn't gashed it so many times in letting her taste him.

'Is this your side of the bed?'

Her scent fills the light pink-beige pillowcase.
'Yes.'

~

'Do you want me take you home?'
'Yes and no.'
'I know,' she says. He wants to spend the night. How would the neighbors know?
She wears her mint green silk pajamas—the matching set of pants and long-sleeved blouse with a faint green stripe—light, cool. I love them on her. We step into her bathroom. She pulls the ring on my shoelace necklace so the clasp is in the back. The gold band rests in the dark spirals of testosterone-generated follicles. My scars do not bother me this night. I wear no shirt. I comb her hair with her brush.
We *stood*—she in front of me in her green sleepwear, I behind her with my hands on the side of her shoulders. And there we *are*—standing, forever.
She shows me her old passport, and her mother's lighter she keeps in her bedside table. I look at the items in her bathroom. A stack of books on the sink by the commode. I smile.
'A doctor in Germany said it helps.' To read she means. Yes, fodder for the duration of bodily processes. It is so intimate. Jay uses this commode. These are the things Regn sees every day.

~

'Will you *daunce* with me?' His voice falls into a Gaelic tone without intention.
'There isn't any music.' Regn has a beautiful singing voice. He's asked her before to sing. But she rarely will. She's too self-conscious. She hums. A familiar tune. *La Bohème's*, "Nessun Dorma." By her bed, in front of her full length mirror, they gently move. He lifts her up off the floor, playfully half spins—
'I'm not a young girl, anymore.'
'No. You're not.' His words have a reverse quality. It is complimenting.
They go back into her room where she does her exercises. She turns on her meditation music. He takes a picture—one where she is lying on her side on the sofa beneath a Renoir painting. Her body is relaxed. Face resting in palm of bent arm. Expression—sensual. The other is of her sitting Indian style in a lotus position, palms pressed firmly together.
She changes into her sweatpants and light shirt. He wishes she'd stay in the silk.
At the top of the stairwell he crouches to pet Heinrich, her Siamese.
'You have such big blue eyes.'
Downstairs in the kitchen he has a glass of orange juice. Regn gets some antibiotic cream, squeezes it onto his hand, rubbing the ointment in, putting a band-aid on the wound that stings. They stand, too mentally tired at such an hour, hearing the minutes drop like heads—Mayakovsky. Again the words—*Aren't you a cloud in trousers my boy?* Breathing into each other the silence. Feeling the hair back against her forehead, he looks at the widow's peak and gray roots. He loves her age. She slips her hands into his back pockets, pulling him against her. They stay so. Holding.
He looks around trying to take it all in—knowing, wondering—*Will I, would I ever be back?* She said she'd done it the way she wanted it—the house. He loves what her hands have done. There is affection in its order. Everything in its proper place—so precise, clean, and

kept. It is warm and safe. Yes, she is this house. He wonders what she looks at through the window above the sink. The window with the dustless, fresh white curtains, mildly plumed. He cannot see the yard.

In her bug, in her garage, they wait. He knows she knows that to start the engine there will be no stopping time. It is 2:45 a.m. They drive through the late night wanting to freeze. It is not the same as before. As she pulls from his driveway he stands beside Ol' Reliable, illuminated by the porch light. He raises his arm in a motionless wave.

~

Tuesday. They leave to find the Botanical Gardens in Norfolk.

'You know, sometimes I think I'm too philosophical for my own damn good. I was saying the other day, all I want in life, and I know it sounds lame perhaps, but I just want to be good. Decent.'

'You are.'

'And when you accomplish that, what's left? I guess the test is remaining good.'

'And why wouldn't you?'

'It's hard—always going against the expectations of society.'

Veering onto the interstate and missing the exit, they proceed to get lost for an hour-and-a-half. Regn's mobile rings. Jay's flying in today. They know this of course, but being reminded makes it real. He's coming home from visiting his sister in Oregon. Such a short trip! He must know. Isn't that why he left? In all the years with Regn, Jay never goes out of town. Is he giving them time? Time to get it out of their system? Is he considering his options? Westcott wants to know. Regn doesn't bring it up. He just went west. Neither of them want to spoil the time with hard questions. Not yet. Five days Jay was gone. Two of which Regn and Westcott didn't do anything or go anywhere. They haven't shared near enough.

Regn doesn't pick up the phone.

'Why don't you call him back—it's all right.'

She doesn't.

It is past three by the time they find their way to the gardens. They stroll into the park, find a secluded bench overlooking the canal. The batteries in his recorder run out—that vacuum of time too private to be taken down. Its sanctity to remain within them. A tram of sightseers rides past across the way. A couple walks on the other side.

'What are you thinking?'

'How easy it is for them.' Regn says, 'How free they are—'

He takes her in his arms on the bench. They eat a pair of tangelos she's peeled and ask the hardest questions of each other. He asks her to put her head on his lap. Brushes her hair aside. Softly presses.

She sits up. Cognizant of the dream, the absurdity. 'I'm scared.'

'Does my presence or absence hurt more?'

'Your absence would—'

'Do I or does Jay trap you more?'

'He does—but I don't want to keep you from living your life—'

'It means a little less without you.'

But these are just words now—he knows. What is said cannot be repeated.

'What do you want?'

'I've changed and I've told him that. It's like I was asleep and finally woke up.'

'Can we do this, are we in agreement? If it's a gift then I cannot turn my back on it. Something in me says it means more to keep it. The easy way—not easy, but what so many do, would be to walk away. I think if we're patient, if you want something enough—you have to work for it. As long as either of us is alive I won't be free. Something inside me would always wait. There is always that—hope.'

It is almost five. He takes another drink at the water fountain.

'If I were a bird,' Regn says, 'I'd like to live here.' She takes his left arm—

By the stairs heading into the entrance they stop.

He turns to her—'Promise me, no matter what, you'll call me back.'

'Call you back?'

'Yes. That you'd come to me.'

'I would always. Even if you went away for a while, but left me a note where to find you, I'd come.'

Westcott feels the burden of patience. But he is happy without being complete. Content in the knowledge of a mutual choice, a shared vision, a decided direction.

In that moment not even Regn knows her own fallibility. Does that make her any less accountable?

~

'Listen, would you mind if I gave you all your letters for a while—I'll take them back, but right now I think it's better.' She removes a soft lady's hand purse. Long, rectangular, the color of a gunny sack. On the front is her name, sewn in script. It is inside a yellow bag from the Scotland store. Westcott receives the vintage hand purse reluctantly. Doubtful. 'I'll ask for them back. Just keep them for me.' He nods, tries to smile. Removing his chewing gum he asks for hers. He mashes them together. His knight figurine has toppled over on his dash. He spreads the gum on the bottom of Kincaid and mounts him to his post. The unspoken seal of agreement.

On 143 he pulls ahead of her and turns onto 199. She keeps straight heading for the historic district. In that instant something breaks. She gives a shrugging look and a smile. *Oh well, I thought you were going to go this way.* She is in no hurry and prefers the longer route. He wants her more than anything at that moment and speeds along in an effort to intersect. He makes a right, getting off the highway, taking the road to Colonial Williamsburg. He pulls in the bus inlet and waits—hoping she hasn't already come this way. He needed to see her—to have her in his mirror—to take her all the way. He pulls towards the intersection seeing her silver bug coming from his right. Though he can't discern her expression without his glasses, he knows she is surprised but glad he is there. They drive through the evening parallel to W&M. At the intersection they turn right. He stays in the straight lane; she pulls into the left turning lane. His light is green. He puts a hand out the window. Waves. It has been a long day—not long enough. She watches him drive away.

REGN BROKE DOWN to Sharon in the office. I wasn't there to witness it. Jay's company is closing. He will not have a job or he will be working from home. Her house—just the other night I was admiring its security, everything in its proper place. I would hate for her to have to sell it. I waited with my Lady this evening. We were both on the late shift 'til 6. I stayed with her until the Gift Shop closed its doors and she could go. I walked with her to the parking lot, assuring her whatever it takes I'm here for her.

•••

I've said it so many times and I say it again: How does one make a life in the shadow of such—

All she has to do is keep on doing what she's doing. How can I not resent myself? Sometimes I think I'm pathetic, but other times I feel it is strength to subject oneself to such pain on a regular basis. It takes more to endure and if we're patient it will come to pass. But such patience is faith in the dark and damn hard.

Take for example a beautiful day. It's made all the more beautiful by the sadness of yearning to be close. The absence of the person you want to share it with heightens its splendor. I said I'd be strong for Regn. I feel myself caving. Why must she be the strong one and I with her, while Jay is insecure? Why must I find equal strength when she's had years of breaking in? I cannot resent her for the fact that she came into strength much later and I must have it now. Find it, somehow.

Haiku—

Sit with me today
The leaves collecting minutes
Hold each other hard

Lady Blue cries out
A brass cricket on the hearth
Dissolved into one

A breath imparted
Your mouth inhales my exhale
The scent of your brow

Suspended in time
Silver bug flies through the night
Destination—free

Gashing the pale hand
She tastes the substance of life
Thread of blood to tongue

Strolling side-by-side
A drink from the fountain stone
The garden wind cries

Eating tangelos
The water canal lulls by
How well we do it

A silent tremor
Rest my head in the cool grass
The brush of your face

Coffee and mint tea
The warm scent of flavored breath
We open the gate

Sad gaze to afar
A trembling embrace of strength
We must keep it safe

"Wish it were easy
I hate when I let you go,"
Her words each parting

My shrouded Lady
I would trade my pains for yours
Our sacrifices

Beautiful Dreamer
Let thy sorrows slumber deep
Awake unto me

• • •

I will sit here so quietly, writing to save my life. The tedium—I could go to sleep. I am at work. I know the terms. I said I could accept them, but I'm not sure I believe it. The strength it takes. I want to be by a river. To put my head down in the cool grass. Rest. When I awake would it be to you? Pacing the ramparts of my mind—stilling myself—to be so quiet, don't move, else cry a soundless cry—feel its coolness like the grass, surge as a tremor—a soundless pain, the brush of your face, a quiver of undetectable relief.

THE WHOLE OF THAT SPRING, summer, and fall, I'd come home, mentally wiped. Mother's car would often be parked in the garage. I'd pull into the driveway, walk into the kitchen, my satchel in tow, climb the stairs to my sunlit room and slowly remove my tie.

I missed being able to tell someone how I felt. It was an isolating experience on top of an already isolated life.

'All I can offer you is wait and see.' Her words. That's what I'd been doing. I tried to make a plan. But the only tangible, concrete thought was when would Regn and I see each other next.

I had dinner, I walked Gilly, and then I'd record any critical details of the day. If Regn and I worked I'd write down exactly what had occurred. It wasn't always interesting; like the little cassettes I used for our conversations, on some level I knew it was essential to record the events as they were happening.

Having each other did not cool things down. Our desire escalated. Every day Regn and I were scheduled it was a mental acrobat. Even on the days we were off there was always configuring. How much time, when and where could we see one another? We almost always just sat in her car or went for a walk.

I was stunned to hear that Regn, at 56, didn't even have her own library card. If she wanted a particular book or movie Jay picked it up for her on his card. He also did all the grocery shopping. Her lack of independence went off like a gong. She soon had her own library card. It was a step forward.

I was willing to wait. No matter how long it took. I did not put a time limit on the process. I knew Regn had to sort things out in her own way. The right way.

Emotions were high one day, somber the next. Our energy fraught with hope and despair. In spite of the hardship, I was ensnared in the rapture of being in love. Of loving and having that same feeling returned. Equally.

She would later say she'd been in a dream and woke up. What to her was a dream had been to me reality. The stakes were high, but we were alive. We were still riding the crest of the wave. Love shouldn't be a state of mind. For Regn it was. For me love was a state of being.

Regn was the dreamer. I was the visionary. But I was also pragmatic. One could not merely hope for things, as Regn did. Putting desires into *action*—formulating a plan—was essential.

SEPTEMBER

Regn was in high spirits. Serene. She seemed to be overcompensating in her happiness towards me. Had sex with Jay occurred again last evening and she was trying to conceal it?

In the afternoon I went down to the Rotunda to relieve my Lady. Behind the counter she takes my hand. I squeeze it, keeping my back to her, so I face any customers walking through to the Great Hall. Regn stays the half hour with me. 'The tension, if you were to read this in a book one would think it madness.'

'I think I'm going to go crazy. Come to the theater ramp,' she says.

We walk through the empty room of chairs—the next show doesn't start for 18 minutes—and veer left into the passageway for wheelchair accessibility. I search the ceiling for cameras. We kiss. She takes my face in her hands. I stroke hers in a single brush. We kiss again.

'If we could live together I'd wear a shroud. I'd wear a shroud for you. If someone said that's what I had to do so we could be with each other I'd make the sacrifice. They wear those for their god, but I'd do it for you.'

I look at her curiously. 'Just as long as you don't worship me.'

'Why not?'

'I don't believe in worshipping. Respect is enough.'

· · ·

Some of the shipmates—the men who work aboard the *Susan Constant* and *Discovery*—are admiring Regn's pants. One asks politely if he can feel the material. Regn lets out an uproarious laugh. 'That's what we need in this world,' the man says, 'a good laugh like yours!' How ironic. We are in acute desperation to hold each other; this man cannot know how his innocent teasing taunts. Regn says Jack Holland, head of Security, has come on to her. He resembles Wayne Newton, considerably. She thinks he zooms in with his cameras watching her and others. As we stride out together, he is entering the building. Regn and I look like twins wearing our dark sunglasses, walking arm-to-arm. He acknowledges us brusquely, but cordially. If he has watched us and seen her hands brush me, he must be saying, *Lucky cuss. If I were still his age with his stamina! What a woman. Wouldn't be hard to keep it up looking at that body.* It's superficial, a stroke to the ego, that with all these "men" constantly wanting to get near my Lady, I have the privilege, alone, of her love. I say alone; Jay is an entirely separate matter. For once I feel the primordial pride of a bull, a lion, any stud who has outlasted his male counterparts. For a fleeting spell I bask in the glow of being seen as a true-blooded fully equipped, masculine individual. I also know at the very same moment that had I truly been male Regn and I would not have met. I'd have gone away to college, gone overseas, any number of likely scenarios. It is the lack of a working penis that made love possible.

Another employee shoots me a hard look as we enter the parking lot. Regn doesn't notice. It makes me uneasy. A most skeptical disconcerting recognition. I don't care what they think. Regn assures me she doesn't either—they'll think what they want. On the surface we're friends to them. But it *does* bother Regn, more than she knows at that moment.

• • •

It occurred to me sitting outside on break. The birds scurried while I sipped my soup. I'm going to die. As simple as that. Yes. We're all going to and know it. But I recognized the finality of the fact. I am going to die and whatever pain I'm in will not last.

I tell myself I may have to let her go, not for her sake but mine. I asked her Friday, straight out, as I've done so many times, if she'd rather I left her be—if I was hurting her. She said if I left her alone she'd be more miserable; I wasn't the one hurting her. 'I hurt myself,' she said. *And so do I,* I was thinking but didn't say. She may not like it and it's not what she wants, but what works for her doesn't work for me. She has no answers. We'll have to see what time does. It is easier for her only in that she just has to keep on doing what she's doing. I make it possible for her to have both worlds—the financial security (though that has been shaken by Jay's perilous job situation) of staying where she is and then the moments with me. Even if it's just sex, if her physical needs find her hard up there's someone to turn to in the night. What am I, is the question? No, she isn't using me and I know that; she doesn't want to hurt anyone and, well, I love her more than my happiness so I wouldn't put her in the position to choose. 'At least if we can see each other at work,' she's said in the past. The job itself is killing me slowly—I feel I've become institutionalized by its mundane repetition of tasks. I feel ill—will I think myself to death trying to keep busy just to get through the day and the boredom? Regn may be there, but we want the freedom to be somewhere else and talk freely. I start to resent the work, which isn't right. Sometimes I already feel gone.

• • •

I am disgusted at the state of the world—this country especially and what society has become. The anger. I wonder what will happen if no one rebels against technologies' encroaching demands. We ourselves will become the computers—tied to artificiality. The Truth is all but discarded for a microchip to entertain. We don't have to think, to consider for ourselves the realm of our unknown origins. It's everywhere and infiltrating—I hate it— always being under surveillance, having to apply online, cell phones making up for letters and face-to-face conversations. The state of mankind, at least in this country, is in serious threat of sacrificing its humanity when the dollar is higher-prized than the goodness of an individual. I'm often dissatisfied with the procedures that make us anything but free, the passive requirements guiding society—the false sense of status, and the need to blend in in order to reasonably live, else survive on the fringes, trusting the empirical to the trenches of mainstream that will bury you alive if one slips into its catacomb labyrinth of appearance's sake calling cards. There is so much to say, so much disdains. The more I wish to dissolve into the natural world.

THE WIND WAS BLOWING. It was somber out, cool, drizzling while we sat in her bug and then took a long walk. We bought a sprite from the drink machine and shared a sesame bagel with honey almond spread. We sat on a bench. It was isolated, but two hikers did walk by. I felt the slightest graze of a would-be mustache. She'd tweezed or more likely taken an electric zapper to her upper lip. I didn't mind. The wind soared with us, calming quietly, blustering unto our sensuality. 'I could never look at someone closely like I do you. I always felt awkward,' she said, 'but with you—I don't know what it is.'

'Maybe it's that I trust what you're thinking.'

As I said this she looked at me absolutely.

'I never thought there could be such a complete love.' Her thoughts conveyed themselves naturally. She spoke not in terms; it was of an innate knowledge rooted within. 'I wish I could tell someone, but there aren't words.'

She counted my buttons—seven. I felt her palm—it was calloused—I liked feeling the smoothness of worn skin—it was from using her rowing machine.

'I noticed it too,' she said.

'I know,' I whispered.

'I know you do and that's what I love.'

~

She brought up sex and how some of the ladies at work, Eva, Magda, and Jill will have nothing to do with it, or rather their husbands, in that respect.

'And you?'

'I have needs. I don't always want a penis put in me though.'

Always—it equates to an option. *At least you have 'the' option.* Not always, *but sometimes.* Westcott stops without stopping. Inside his mind crystals tumble down. Her words cause him shame. He's never felt a real human penis. The straightforwardness of such a statement. He cannot tell her how much her words hurt.

The easy force with which she speaks so directly. Is it just Regn being Regn, or the heritage in her veins, the land that formed her, from which she speaks so vibrantly? He cannot tell her it makes the desolate parts of him damp. He cannot tell her what he alone knows and will not speak. He cannot tell her—*And sometimes, I do.*

He struggles to suppress the idea of sexual fulfillment. *What we have is more, yes.*

~

'Then why do you need it?' I asked.

'It's relief.' That's all it is to her.

'I wish you'd resort to self-gratification. It's something you have control over. It would seem you have the best of both worlds; all your bases are covered. I can't help at times, though I try and rationalize, feeling used.'

'Then you don't know me. It's not like that.'

'It hurts because I want to be the one giving it to you.'

'I know and I want it to be you. You give me everything I need. If I was with you I could have it all day. I just told you I don't always want a penis put in me, but if you had one I'd like it.'

'Maybe were I "normal" and had the luxury of just going out for a one-night stand—I might view sex as just that—a physical relief. But for me it must always be in love.'

'I'd do anything to make you happy,' she said freely.

'You just left yourself wide open. Anything? Would you be celibate then?'

She didn't answer.

'I've tried to explain to Jay I care for him. If he found a woman to go out with I wouldn't mind—sometimes I wish he would. Sometimes I think it would be easier if—. But then I'd feel guilty, as though I'd somehow caused it, just by thinking it.'

I've thought the same things and assessed the repercussions. Say Jay died of a heart attack, Regn would feel responsible. I often imagine him in an accident—nothing lingering or maiming, he does not deserve to suffer, but quick and fatal—something for which Regn could not possibly hold herself accountable. Nor I.

'If we lived together I'd like to pamper you,' she said.

I found chiggers all over my ankles again. 'Shit!' I yelled bending down.

'I wish I could wash them and lotion them up for you.'

We were on the paved path—it looked like a tunnel—trees stretching all the way down, almost to a dream.

'You know,' she said, '—maybe I shouldn't say.'

She revealed the first time she sensed something between us. It had been long before I had—a casual gesture. She'd been watching me get into my truck and just like that she realized she already knew me.

'I love you. My West.'

'My *shrouded* Lady.'

MY OBSTINATE PERSONALITY—what good does it do to fight what you can't change? Am I a horse yet to be broken, or a fool with self-*diluting* thoughts? When will I place myself second and be strong enough to do what I have to—what I should, not what I want? What is right though? Is it wrong to want something for oneself? Would my words, in person or epistle, be powerful enough to send Jay in search of another woman's arms? Regn's circumstances afford her the right—she's sacrificed most of her life—her children are successful, grown, and it would seem reasonably happy. Should she not herself be allowed happiness? She must tell her children this. I well understand that if she left Jay it would be on her own and I would only want it that way. I would not and could not ask, nor expect her to leave on my account. I am frustrated that I can't help her financially. I must ask myself, 'Do I want her freedom solely because it will make it "easier" for us, or do I want it for her happiness?' I only want it if she can be happy. I don't blame my Lady for it is I who cause my own suffering. I know Regn has similar conversations with herself.

'No one knows how I feel,' she said. 'I might smile and laugh all day, but inside—.' She desperately wanted someone to confide in—the only person she said she can talk to is me and yet she may seek a third party objective listener. I can understand—some thoughts are too intertwined with Regn. Even I long for someone with whom to discuss things. She wants to be on her own, but financially she is caged. If only I was solvent, in the position to help her—I'd work two jobs, anything.

'I'd have to sit down with my kids. Jay and I and discuss it. Dee would be furious, I know how she can get.'

I didn't think that was fair or right of her daughter. 'You'd have to explain matters. You may be alone, but I know exactly what it is you feel. So you're not alone on that account.'

'Your hair's all in disarray, you know that.'

'I just ran my hand threw it. So?'

'You look like one of those mad artists—you'd fit right in with a scarf—someplace in Europe, from another time—'

'Is that so bad, Regn?'

'No. That's why I love you.'

Stepping out the doors a rush of perfume filled my senses. We discussed her living on her own as we walked down to the ships to collect the donations. We stood on the walkway beside the forest.

'I'm often in your room holding you.' It had been a month since we were free to make love. We spoke as though our memories of such times were all we had and ever would. I was caving inside, but smiled. She remembered my asking her to kiss me—that first time on the Parkway, and how she'd really *wanted* to kiss, but that it had been a sisterly one and how I'd thanked her.

We've come so far.

'I always remember the first time sitting on the bench and brushing your face. The sensation of what it felt like. It's always that way—every time—Regn.'

I had to go down to the Rotunda and close up—forty minutes—it didn't matter, I was deep in thought. I'd gone discreetly into the restroom, entered the stall, slid the lock, and let it come. I'd cried at lunch, but concealed it. And now the pain came harder. I composed myself before heading out to stand by the rotunda desk near the theater. It was raining. I went to the tall floor-to-ceiling windows—lining the Great Hall—the puddles forming, the rain coming down. How appropriate. If ever a moment reflected a person. I was alone in the pain, I didn't want to think anymore and I didn't care to discuss it, with anyone. It was ripping through me. On our return from the ships she'd said, 'All I can offer you is this. Just wait and see.'

'Have a good weekend, Westcott.'

I stalled in my truck not wanting to leave until she'd started her engine. Fernus was waiting—watching to see what I was up to? I put the gear into drive and slowly idled to the main road. I waited for a car coming off the ferry to pass so they'd be in front. Fernus turned left on Greensprings Road, I headed straight on Jamestown, continuing to look in my rearview mirror for the sight of a silver bug. I thought of calling Regn.

I turned into the Farm Fresh parking lot to pick up dinner at Soya. It was dank out, gray, stormy, the sort of evening I long to take her home, have dinner and make love. I was crossing the street when I saw a silver Volkswagen coming towards me.

I stepped up on the curb, out of the rain. She rolled the passenger window a crack, indicating she'd be in the parking lot. I'd considered going back to the Settlement. *She'd come after me.*

I paid for our dinners, which mother had called in, and headed to my truck. Regn was out of her car, going to Rite Aid. I moved my truck closer to the store—allowing her time to enter alone. She'd already picked out two bathroom items when I found her. 'I knew you'd be here when you said you were picking up dinner. I really do need these,' she explained.

'You don't have to make excuses.'

Walking aimlessly through the small aisles—it's a small store, a black camera was hovering. A song was playing—listen to that—"I just want to take you home"—the man was singing. 'I hate that it always has to be like this,' she said.

She tucked her hair behind her ear. The way she did it I could tell how she felt as I stood so close.

'I'll head out before you,' I asserted, grabbing her in an arm hug, trying not to make it look obvious to anyone passing by. I walked through the sliding doors into the drizzling evening. It had been so warm in the store. I slowly backed my truck out to the right, waiting to see her exiting. Another truck was idling to turn down the row. I rolled my window halfway. She came right up in her beige skirt and blue shirt. It was a risk. She slipped her hand through the window, felt the side of my face in a way that could not be mistaken for anything but passionate affection.

'A ghra mo chroi, Regn.'[4]

I gave the man in the green truck a polite gesture. *Pardon, sir, thanks for waiting, didn't mean to hold you up.*

•••

I get tired of writing—isn't it enough to live it? I went for a long bike ride—three hours—starting from home, going all the way down to the Parkway, beyond the farm with the silos and cows in the pasture. The tail end of a hurricane had come through—the wind was surging, empowering. I sat on the bridge. Clouds hung low and layered, giving the earth's ceiling a flat rather than domed appearance. Far across the marshland the ferry, I presumed, was being propelled by the winds. It drifted at a fast pace. It was white—brilliantly so, electrified to the east—where the sun lay hidden within the billows. The tall grass beneath my dangling legs swept in a fury—rolling and waving, possessed by turmoil, a restless brawl within itself. I watched it rage passionately and then calm down. I stood on the stone rail feeling the rejuvenating circulation whip through me. A beat-up car drove by. I heard a young guy call out his window, 'Go on, jump!' *Yeah, sure—like it's even high enough for a suicide mission.* Sometimes the gusts were so strong my legs burned pedaling into its force. It misted on the ride back then the skies cleared and the sun appeared—everything was sharper in color and purpose along the edges. It's a shame Regn wasn't there to see it.

•••

My colleagues read the article I'd submitted to the local paper, *The Virginia Gazette*, about Ellis biking across America with her Jack Russell, Liam.

We stole a touch here and there, but I was telling myself not to feel it, don't let it in—I couldn't. To want her and then have to be there for myself alone—the pain. I've started holding my words—I can't tell her everything—she isn't always there to listen. It's better if I rely on myself. When we see each other it brings more hurt than relief. She's a kept woman—though I dislike that phrase. We discussed our bills. All she has to cover is her car payment and credit cards. Jay takes care of everything else—the mortgage, utilities—she has it made. If she lived on her own she couldn't make it financially. It is comfort and security that always prevail. I don't blame her, everything she says is right. 'If I were younger, just

---

[4] A ghra mo chroi: My heart's beloved; Gaelic. Pronounced: ah-hraw-muh-here.

starting out—but—' Much as she desires to be independent it's as the story goes, it's too hard to start over now. It's all a gamble. Will she survive him? And what of me? I can live in disillusionment, try and tell myself—convince myself—we are fortunate for our gift—and yes we are—but the heartache outweighs the gratitude at times. A few hours in a week isn't enough to tip the scales and keep one sane—not enough to thaw the pain of isolation and hungering loneliness freezing within. Sometimes I feel she's already gone.

They've really shorted us—everyone—and cut the schedules.

In the parking lot she asked if I wanted to meet for a few minutes at Powhatan Creek. I halted.

'You don't want to?'

Could I, was what ran through my mind? *What good is it to torture myself?* I can't allow myself to need these times, these moments.

'Do you think it's safe? Maybe we should go further.' I suggested.

'I just wanted to have a couple minutes. I wish I didn't miss you so much,' she said.

'I'm glad you do. Is that so wrong?'

'No.'

'I'm scared to touch you,' I said. 'I'm scared.'

'Why?'

I was trying so hard to hold it in. I grabbed her, cradling the back of her head in my hand pressing my face to hers. 'Because it hurts so much.'

'I love you, Westcott. Sometimes I just like to say it.'

'Ich Liebe Dich, *Regn*. I never get to say your name enough.'

I let her in—let myself go. I felt her lips, my finger invited into the cavernous ledge of her mouth.

• • •

'Sometimes I hurt for you down there. I want you.' She paused. 'I don't mean that to sound—'

How does one endure such a statement? We had two hours on the Island. It was wet out; we drove in her bug to a quiet pull-out on the three mile loop.

It was in my hands. I didn't want to talk about it anymore. What was left to say? How many times could we hold each other before I became tired of letting her go? She would never be there in the way I wanted or needed. It wasn't just about sex.

I longed for companionship—someone who would be there all the time, as I was. She went home to a husband, perhaps with resentment that he was there, but it was security, convenience.

We kissed long, rubbing our hands skin-to-skin. I squeezed her breast. I withheld giving her relief. I wanted to and yet there was something in me that wanted her to have that frustration—to feel it as I did. I gave her a tin case with a pocket watch engraved. It read: *Beautiful Dreamer Wake Unto Me.*

'Sometimes I feel like I'm longing for someone in a grave,' I said.

'What do you mean? You think I'm dead, or you're scared I'm not dead?'

'Both.'

A little turtle moved across the road. Regn stopped. I got out and picked him up, setting the shelled critter in the cool grass.

IT WAS ONE AFTERNOON among so many. But the image would remain. Another kodachrome square for the archives to slip into the projector in years to come. Even when the film melted away. This image was ingrained. I'd had the day off. At the end of the street Regn put her turn signal on and made a U-turn—I pedaled toward her as I had seven months earlier. So much had come to pass. We were no longer racing.

She was leaving work. She drove alongside—I rode my bicycle without hands. Elton John permeated the air. Her white shirt, the belt holding her securely in—big sunglasses and the breeze through her crimson hair. She looked at my bare ankles. 'Do you still have bites?' I pulled up my pant leg. The welts had not healed. She was weighing the time—I could see—it was almost 5:40. We arrived to the end of the road. I looked at her hard—knowing then in my nostalgic mind, it was just one of the many images of her that would remain with me forever.

I reached my hand to hers. 'It looks nice,' I told her—meaning the scene. Her in her silver Volkswagen bug, the top down. The essence of charm.

• • •

Westcott stands at the small window upstairs looking out at the forest of his backyard. He closes his eyes, opens them, lights the candle, pools his energy.

Death be not afraid.
Isis, Isis, Mother Isis
Please take the name of the one I say—
Suffer not Jay Tompkins,
Though your soul must go today—

The words are his own. Will they wield any power?

• • •

It began to pour. I sailed on through the rain standing atop the pedals of my bicycle. Motorists looked at me like I was crazy. The rain fell in sheets. My shoes sloshed. It is freedom to stand in the rain. I stopped. Let it fall down. Tilted my head back. Let it come.

Journal Entry:
from the Book of West
September 20—

Sometimes I think I live in the dark green shadows of the foliage. My mind will sound like a tape whose ribbon is winding down. It becomes a slow garble of cyclic thoughts, speaking in freeze- frame motion. I occasionally think of Jackie Moss and miss not having her as someone to write to—a neutral party I could turn to—someone. Parson was the only male friend I had—I could really use his company now—a pal to do things with, just have fun, pass the time as two guys and not have to think. I feel confined. I am bitter, resentful, guilt-ridden, *and* frustrated. I have no escape from myself.

WE—REGN AND I—don't talk about it. What's the point? Why ask what we already know the answer to—it only causes pain. The passion in me has died. I have not the strength or energy to give into it. There were times today I could have said something, stolen a brush. I am too tired. Am I not bored with the pain? I've had to learn to console myself; you can't depend on others. I'd rather be the one others depend upon. We had lunch together upstairs. It was light conversation.

We avoided the underlying discussion.

Late in the afternoon I stole over to Groups. Regn was closing. We rode the other elevator up together. We hugged, she kissed me, but my mouth was not there—*I was not there* to feel it. The door opened on the other side. Guy from the Gift Shop, who flirts with Regn on occasion, stepped on. 'What are you two doing in here?' he joked. We laughed in spite of ourselves. If walls could talk.

Regn printed out a dialogue pertaining to the Dalai Lama and lessons. She asked me to explain one of them to her. It read, "Learn rules well so you will know how to break them properly."

I explained you must question the origin of the rules themselves and who made them. Don't take everything at face value. There can be no progress, no advancement, without certain rules being broken. Regn agreed. I was referring to society's rules. Not nature's. Nature may evolve, but some things never change.

• • •

I am fascinated by the state of life. To just enjoy every moment. Well then, I'll say what I remember if I were to die tomorrow. Seagulls calling from behind—an overcast sky, sitting on a lone bench, perhaps on a pier, the salt wafting in the air. A bit breezy so near the water. The warm interior of my truck, stepping in the front door in the still of a winter's evening—not late, hardly six, but dark and close outside, quiet with the cold and empty trees. The warmth of lights within the houses as you drive the roads, welcoming. The list is endless. Here I sit—the lamp beside me; in a fog of boredom and too much sleep. My head congested with thoughts of what does it all mean. How should we, how should *I* live? I read a line in the trial of Socrates today. It says, "It's not enough to value life, you should value a good life." What defines "good?" How do we set the ramifications and who decides? Long or short, fast or crawling, famous or unknown? It matters not—but for that small space we occupy—our sector of those who knew us. Can we go when we want?

I don't want much, only to die in Truth.

WE MET AT THE COLONIAL WILLIAMSBURG Visitor parking lot and drove to York River State Park. Scarcely a soul was about. We lay on the thin slab of the picnic bench seat. I rested on top of her. Compressed her clothed body. The temperature was fair, the day perfect. Since my hours had been reduced, I rarely worked. It was the "recession," and jobs were scarce. I wondered of my existence. The loving exhausted me.

We ran across the field. It was the only time I'd ever seen Regn run. In that instant I saw her as she'd been. Years before. She was a young girl again, her white shoes, a smile on her face. We'd run across the grasslands. We were alone and the afternoon was ours.

She dried my tears against her face. We felt each other under our clothes in the seclusion of the forest. Waist-to-waist, our shirts covering the wanderings of our hands, I slipped mine under the band of her underwear, penetrating her as we stood in firm embrace. She slid her hand to my packed groin. Arousal was dormant in me. Just holding her was my hard-on. I wanted to act upon her as a man, to lie down and thrust inside her. The frustration of not being 'ready-made' was too much. It didn't matter she said. Yes, it is true, but *I wanted* the relief—to feel myself move against and *into* her body. I can only feel through heart and detached sensation.

I wish I could slip into bed now and fall asleep beside her. Not sex, but to have her close.

Sitting back in the parking lot, it felt like we were at an airport—the light, the air. Her bug's top was down. I gazed up at a contrail. The remnant of thrusting engines.

'I don't care, you're perfect just the way you are—I love you no matter what. I love you, *Westcott*.'

• • •

She had on the shirt I love. 'I wore it for you,' she said.

'Would you believe me if I told you I bleached my cuffs for you.'

Jay had officially been working from home since Friday. Regn's brother would be flying in with his wife. He still lived in Germany. They hadn't seen each other in ten years.

'I'm looking forward to it, of course. But another part of me just wants it to be done with,' Regn looked tired.

I was glad to be at work and serving customers. The days off were painstaking—I tried to keep busy.

'I wanted to tell you my thoughts. About you.'

I was looking out the window on the mezzanine listening to her intently.

'If I couldn't see you I don't know what I'd do. Even if you went away, but I knew you would come back, I'd be all right.'

Her words satisfied me in a way sex never would.

I extended my hand, squeezing hers. We didn't have to worry much about anyone strolling along the balcony and seeing us. Sundays the offices upstairs are closed.

We met at Powhatan Creek. Just after work. The passion renewed. I came into my own. I wasn't just reacting or responding to her movements—I was showing her how *I* loved. I kissed her softly and softer, my tongue rolling gently along her lips, slipping in. She started to kiss more desperately. Our time was running out. I pulled my mouth back from hers in silent direction—telling her without words, softly, slower. She never did like to wait, to savor the anticipation. Even with an afternoon chocolate fix she'd eat the small piece all in one bite. I make it last. The anticipation, the prolonging is the best. Coming so close, closer, withdrawing, and then, then—

We breathed in the scent and oils of each other's hair; I kissed the back of her neck.

'Just yesterday,' I said, 'I was right here.'

'I wish I could have been with you. You don't know—when I ride my bike I say to myself, Westcott, can you hear me? When I'm at home I have to be careful not to say your name out loud. You're always in my mind.'

She had her sunglasses off, I kept mine on—I prefer not to have my closed eyes seen while I kiss. Behind my sunglasses, eyes shut, I felt her face, taking in the contours, the texture of her brow, jawline, chin, nose, like a blind man wanting to memorize her features by touch alone. I looked at the clock without her knowing. It was ten to six. Would she be interrogated when she arrived home, despite whatever white lie she'd told to explain her later than usual detainment at work?

'I'm so glad you're in the world, Westcott. Even in the pain. You complete me as a woman. You don't know how hard this is for me.'

OCTOBER

Her hands were cold and mine were warm—it's always been the other way around.

I felt in her all those months of silent desperation I'd endured.

We had less than 45 minutes. Her break for lunch was at 11:30. She'd called me at home and asked if I wanted to meet at the Island. Her Volkswagen displayed bat wings for Halloween.

'Do you think we'd have a—'

'A child—' I filled in the void.

'I know you can't, but in the next life I say we will get married and have a child,' she openly dreamed.

'But *this* is the life I'm living now, this is what we have, I love you the way you are—'

'I know, but it feels good to believe.'

'If I ever adopt a child I'll name her after you.'

'You're the strongest person I ever met.'

'Sometimes I think I'm a coward.'

Regn wiped my face with her hand. A streak of sorrow had fallen from behind my sunglasses.

'You're very strong,' she reiterated.

'It's going to be hard and it's only going to get harder.'

'I love you,' her voice spoke softly.

'Be good for me.'

She was in my arms, my chin on her shoulder. I don't tell anyone. To explain they can't understand. They all look at me and say, you're young how can you possibly know.

• • •

It was late afternoon when my phone rang. I didn't pick up in time. I called back.

'Afternoon, Lass.'

She was crying. Not again, too tired to fear what might come next, prepared for the worst I thought, *What does he know now, what has he discovered?*

'My position's been taken away. I'll be laid off in November. They're making cutbacks on Classified employees.

'It should be Celia or one of the Supervisors. Their jobs are restricted. They were hired on a temporary basis. It's so wrong. They just march in, wreak havoc and then we pay for it. Eva must be livid after what she's put up with—imagine being ousted. I'm sorry, Regn. I'll meet you for a few minutes, if you want.'

We hadn't seen each other in 12 days.

'I feel sick.' She looks out the window. 'Jay's working from home and if he loses his job—I'm scared. And a few weeks ago I'd brought my brother and his wife through the museum, proud of my job, and *they* knew. Celia and all of them—they already knew and waited to tell me. You're my lovely rock.' She turns to me.

I wipe the tears from her face.

'I want your scent to stay with me. Your touch is like heaven to me,' she says.

'I slow-danced with you last night, in my mind.'

'You are very strong, like the trees. Thank you for coming. I wanted to tell you before you found out from anyone else. Now I have to face going home and telling Jay.'

• • •

Regn will either take on the status of wage employee or leave the Settlement now that her ten-month classified position has been eliminated.

What hurt most was when Eva said, 'I'm too old for this and you're too young.' She meant the bullshit business politics and low morale within Visitor Services caused by Celia and Jared. 'So if you have somewhere else to go—' She put her hand to her forehead in a salute, as in adios. 'If I were you I'd get out.'

That's just it. I'd like to *just* go far away, but I can't make a quick escape. I am forced to linger, gone before I've even left—a shadow unto myself.

I waited with Regn this evening. I asked politely if she had on knee-highs or the full-length pantyhose. They went all the way up, she said. They are her second skin. The way she said it was not solicitous or tawdry.

Together we stood in the lobby and together we walked into the warm October evening. How many more evenings would we have? The sun was framed by clouds. The hour quiet. We'd both parked at the far end of the lot. Side-by-side we walked the greatest length of our hearts. We stepped to the passenger side, nearest my truck and hugged. How much more can I withstand? The absolute desire. I could not allow myself to feel its pull. I was ragged.

17 October
Regn–

At times I could suffocate in my own thoughts. I want to go to my summer-land and wait there—for all of you. Wait there. I question too much. I am frustrated because I don't ask the right questions or maybe it's that no answer can possibly be given to the things I seek to know. I've become so distanced from the world and I think I'll just have to laugh madly to live lightly—not let anything truly penetrate if I'm to make a way, but then I ask, and it is a crucial question of being—is there a point in living mechanically? Is it not better to go out blazing in anguish than lost as some ocean bottom-dweller who swims in darkness, knowing not which way is up and which is down? You gave me the passion of life, my Love. To experience the human condition. Maybe it was in me—in both of us to begin with, but we had to unbind it in each other, that which could never be opened alone. I want a ghost, an appari-tion on the wind or in dream to come to me from beyond, that other place we cannot remember, and tell me it will be all right. There are so many, so many of us, so many lives and I wonder that I should not get lost in the loudness of this world.

I live between the worlds—

I am a horse that will not be broken. I sprint in a fury down one side of the corral, halt and gallop back the same length. An anger, a contempt one fears to saddle, lodges within and I aim to take a flying jump at the fence. If I break my legs trying I do not care. I will go down fighting. I am stubborn, defiant, and it blazes in restless pulsing of restraint. I look at the other horses all in their stalls. They've forgotten what they lost. I will suffer for my defiance. The hand with its lasso approaches. I rear in disdain for what he is and what he's not. I see myself vaulting the fence, fleeing the blaze. You trot the length of the fence and a stable door sees you to its return where shelter and oats suffice to comfort. And I could trample the hand that flips the latch binding you to its quarters. Listen hard; in the dwindling light a wild neighing finds its way to the passive chewers bedded down for the night. He rears and rears and rears, thudding the ground with bittered hooves, billows of dust tight 'round his calves and twitching muscles. The lines of his coat shine in their sweat, the mane tangles with the wind. He 'blucks' his anger, the sound of a snorted sigh. No hand will tame nor stand to fix his power. In his freedom he is an outlaw. He is a prisoner unto himself. He will run until the self bursts within, a firecracker in a fisted hand. He rails in stranglement—the farmers claim he's mad. A gun will explode, he tears the well-trod path of his wandering. He's fighting years and years, generations and generations of convention. He will not stay to watch the starved sacrifice of spirit, nor will he run to save his hide. He 'trunders' to and fro—there to remind, there to remind. Let the fence rot to snap, let the stablehand give way. Borne of free will, let the kept mare assume her rightful ways.

~

Here I am, a fall night in October and you are in the mountains. I have no one to turn to with these things and so it is to this page—this blank, white page—a no man's land I give dialogue, but it responds only in representation. That these letters exist is a comfort—a testament.

I said it to you once, Regn, but I think it bears reiterating. Having your love unleashes a loneliness all the more—a hundredfold, because I know what it is we miss together. The clothes I never get to see you wear. Anything of pleasure, a simple joy, and in its splendor I am haunted, haunted by the desire, the want, the need, to experience life with you. Every hour is an hour we surrender. I want to give you it all. In a way I did. There is a truth and in holding such truth we are afforded a glimpse of perhaps the greater Truth which we cannot humanly formulate. Having touched upon it, what is one to seek, except to keep it so safe from the ravages of merciless time? To see you there within my hand's brush, and stay.

For us to move so slow. To dance with you and thereby transpose our life's rhythms.

It is so quiet—that place from which I speak, a quiet flame that burns steadily through the hollow of this host. I rubbed the day's work from my neck and in so doing I felt it as your hand upon my skin.

I am never ashamed of what is laid to rest here, for should these leaflets ever be discovered, the decency of such graced love cannot be denied.

Let it be known, if not now, then someday to someone, the agonizing tension, the subdued, harnessed passion of a moment in bondage. In bondage I mean freedom clamped—the liberation of accessibility—the innate pulse of free will. To live in constant check is a tether upon one's spirit. To orbit by pull alone, the invisible gravity of pure force, spinning—course unknown, propelled in loving, knowing by its life it must collide, else spin the thread away to a limp, unraveled line.

~

It's been many days and I now resume where I left off this letter. Here it is the evening before my birthday. I've tried hard not to think much about anything. While away camping I passed a couple in the bed of their truck, protected by the night, intimate—startled to have been happened upon. At a fair a woman's hair caught my glimpse. Knowing it couldn't possibly be you I still took a second glance for the memory it evoked. And what if one day that is all I have—triggers of remembrances? The more I consider it, the more ridiculous it seems—all the manmade boundaries we erect. I am sad because one day it will all be over, and by that I mean our life. Everything. We'll become like those individuals who page through textbooks, watch a movie, fill our lives, giving little thought to those gone before. An unknown name, just a photograph among so many. How many times have I said it? The world is so large—did we not win the lottery already? I often wonder how much of what is felt by the heart inscribes itself unto the spirit and thus becomes immortal? The mind, I most fear, does shut down with the body and with it all cognitions. It raises a crucial question—is memory borne solely of the mind, or if powerful enough, can it infuse the very heart, the divine spirit of one's changing forms? It is very much speculative, philosophical, and exhausting to analyze. I don't wish to give any more credence to the 'why,' but only confront the how and the when. I want to tell you this and anyone who would ever read these privacies—I trust you with my Life, and by my life, I love you, Regn.

I'm too tired to think. Really. I begin a thought and I can't follow it through— will it bring me to the same places in mind I've been before—so many thoughts—I simply can't stay fixed on one long enough to hold it. It's a tiredness you spoke of when you said you felt 'old,' a weariness in the tried spirit. It's the spirit that ages or preserves us. I look at you and underneath it all I sometimes see the foreigner in you. The insecurity, that is, remnants of leaving all you knew as a German and being in an unknown "country"—a country I speak of on many levels. An innocence of never truly being on one's own and it protects but inhibits you. Sometimes I think "that" part of you always stayed and a certain confidence of the woman you imagined yourself to be was surrendered. We know each other's vulnerabilities and such defines the bindings of trust. How many times do I see myself walking to you and pulling you close—your arms coming inside my winter coat to secure us. I imagine what it would be like to feel you from within—not because you're a woman, but that you're the woman I love. To fill you from the inside out. I can imagine it in all its gentleness—is the phallus really what the man's about? I have nothing to prove, I just wish the heart's passions could be satisfied as they should—the ultimate inherent right of woman and man, lady and gentleman. The stealth of emotion's force—no crude, searing penis, as you would call it, but a pure extension of the soul's goodness to protect the body, singularly possessed but never claimed. For it is hers alone to pull you inside.

...

The thoughts overflow my mind. Can I write myself to freedom, write myself out of my head? I don't want to carry these things with me. I want to set the record straight—the record to anyone who knows me on the surface. I am a contradiction on every level and to live at odds with oneself—this sounds like pity speech, let me rephrase. I want to set down the burden of Truths; but the story I feel I must always write is the story I live. I don't want to be the recorder anymore. Why can't I be the one who just lives? I want to rest, to rest so far down and deep where it's cool. To tell everything, not just about you and me, but capture each tedious detail—the intensity of a moment—the way sunlight elicits sadness when it finds a certain place on the wall—the scent of the Settlement when walking through the doors. I live in memories and senses—it scares me, the weight of emotions—the smallest of details—things I can't even find words for, they become so abstract in their translation from sense to language. Even now my words probably lose you here and there and I, myself, often feel lost to my mind. I know, though, you understand these things, but the difference is you don't try and put them into definitive words, yet you detect them all the same. The details are too vast to list. I'm speaking of appearances and sounds, scents and tastes. The sound of melancholy—a child laughing and I hear sadness. A gentle breeze and I feel nostalgia. It's all painful to me because it cannot be held—it cannot be kept for its explanation is beyond human comprehension.

I both love and hate that I am hidden to the world, and by world I mean those few who inhabit each personal ring of familiarity. No one asks and so why do I feel compelled to explain, to correct, or even instruct? I am emotionless at times having spent myself completely. My heart does not match my body, which no one can see or if they do, they misjudge. I have felt certain things too intimately, too intensely, too soon for this shell. I wish to scream and scream to the world it's not a weak loneliness that finds me here. It's the fear no one wants to admit and many accept complacently—the very fear of life's transitory state—that I, we, are so alone within ourselves. Some of our wants change every other day, while others remain cemented in their course.

I write to escape, but the words are not always quenching. When you row where are you going? Sometimes I stand before you wanting to move, hearing the silence of time slipping, but I don't speak, for there is nothing left to say that we don't already know. When sitting beside each other or when we're together I feel a certain waiting from you, the energy of what you don't say, that I will move a certain way. And I can come to you as I envision if I let myself go—but how do I let myself go knowing we never wish to return from that place?

It's rough times right now, but you'll be all right, I know you. You are well received by many and like that story I once gave you, the world gravitates in your direction. You are distinct but still know how to blend for the sake of fitting in. Just know I would take your fears on top of mine and carry them would it set your heart free.

I want to be delivered from myself. Delivered. To pass away knowing who I was and for what I stood. How does one ever know thine own self without others to illuminate, or shall we say, eclipse.

I don't want words anymore, only our knowledge. The freedom of 'just to'— Just to walk up to you as a man and kiss the woman who hides herself. A woman whose heart is shrouded. To pray, not to a God but to each other. To pray. Patient to a point and if endeavoring towards a common convergence, find safety and comfort in the thought the pain cannot last. We must come yet again full circle and with our own help find we are still there. I made a bargain once with the moon, but I will not express the terms of it here for such is between maker of prayer and keeper of prayer.

You need not be scared, my Lady. The only way to say this without it sounding contrived or melodramatic is to write the words. It's like our blood that turns red when oxygen touches it. To speak it aloud would at best seem rehearsed, and so I tell it now. Were loving a talent, you'd be my masterpiece.

Westcott

I SHOULDN'T, IN FACT I should feel just the opposite, but I feel alone. I realize you might as well stop analyzing and live, it changes nothing—try and find the meaning to all your questions—the day still remains. I don't want to try and make sense of it anymore and god damn it I don't want to write. I am scared, the unknown future—live in the present, well, the present is stagnant. I sometimes feel life's too fucking long and yet in an instant it can be taken—Regn's friend, Bobbie, for instance. Last year this time she was alive. Today we were at the cemetery looking for her gravesite. Regn didn't know where it was; we scoured the grounds. No one was in the office to ask. We picked a flowerless grave that hadn't seen color in a long time. She set the yellow bouquet to rest on the plaque indicating the remains belonged to a nine-year old boy born in 1953.

Now is all we have. What if that's not enough? I'm angry and sad, I'll say it a hundred times if need be, I want to dissolve away. We left the cemetery and drove to Waller Mill. We entered the forest, left the path. We made love in the forest. I laid my coat on the leafed floor. We held each other. I penetrated the only way I could—my hands loving her. We lay there—protected, unseen, yet free to the day and the open skies.

Regn's head rested at the base of a tall tree. She looked up at patches of fall blue sky.

'I just want to die right now,' she said.

I slid off, we switched places. She lay on me. My hand slipped under the band of her loose gray cotton pants. I felt the curved softness of her hinterlands, as pure as the day she was born. I've always thought the rear end was the most private area. I once told Regn and she'd asked why? Maybe it's discretion, decorum.

Regn looked at me as I stroked the softness of that gentle hillock. Places only her hands ever touched.

~

She hates that it must always be on her terms when we meet. She feels she takes everything and is selfish—she wishes it could be easier. *I'd laid my new gray coat on the leafed floor.* It was beautiful deep in the trees.

Now look, I've stopped crying. It's on paper, am I all right? Of course not.

• • •

Met Regn at Island. Exhausted. A vampire—it is Halloween after all—taking my essence. A beautiful vampire. As though the very life of me had been swallowed. Those early afternoons when all is quiet as we sit in her Volkswagen, the only sound late autumn crickets in the brush and a distant jet, stark in its engine reverberations. The taste of her makes my mouth ache. I am completely vacated of strength, faint as it were. Our tongues enter each other, my hand slides between her breasts, under her shirt and up to the warmth of her bathed neck. I hear her exhale, we breathe into each other. I smell her hair, tweak her nose. 'This isn't good, I have to go back to work.' She kisses me several times, desperately, for this is all the time.

OCTOBER. SENIOR YEAR

Westcott's family—his mother, sister, and visiting grandma—celebrate his eighteenth birthday by going up to the Shenandoah Valley and staying in a cabin for the weekend. Upon returning from the Blue Ridge Mountains, he has a substantial amount of reading in *Beowulf* to make up along with a test he missed the Friday before. On Wednesday he and another girl stay after school. Ms. Hutchens told them earlier where to meet her. When he walks in, the room is dispersing, a teacher and a few students straggling in from a recently adjourned track meet.

'Yes, *Sir?*'

Never formerly acquainted, Westcott has seen Mr. Tennyson and knows he teaches English and coaches the track team. He is the only black person in the English department, which conspicuous in itself, is why he can put a name with his face.

'I'm just here to make up a test for Ms. Hutchens' class; this is where I was told to come.' Ms. Hutchens has been tied up; Westcott studies a few minutes until his classmate arrives. They discuss material from their literary text and plans for the evening.

'I have to mow the lawn tonight. *Real* exciting.'

'Yeah not so much,' Elaine agrees.

She is attractive, a young Joanne Woodward, but Westcott feels no affections.

He enjoys the privacy of conversation. He is too concerned with hiding, and in anticipation of the test, he does not consider what Elaine truly thinks of him. She is nice; the exchange of discourse polite. He senses she is a good person.

Ms. Hutchens appears at the end of the hall, her black briefcase-bag in hand. An hour into the test she announces that another appointment prevents her from being further detained at the school.

'I don't want to rush you, but how 'bout I let you take the tests home to finish? You still have a couple minutes left.'

'Did you want our books?' Elaine asks.

'You can turn them in tomorrow, I trust *you.*' The emphasis extends to both parties. Elaine quickly leaves. Not wanting to hold Ms. Hutchens up, Westcott hastens to pack his pen and papers. Opening his backpack, he decides to lighten his load and takes out his small, orange Literature textbook.

'Here you go,' he mumbles, extending his arm to Ms. Hutchens, confirming her statement. You *can* his answer is silent. In retrospect, he sees that such a chance to whip out his badge of honor had little to do with a test of trust. Simply put, Ms. Hutchens didn't want to lug two extra books back to school the next morning. Funny how the young mind sees things as illustrious when in reality the shine is but a dull display of common exchange, in which the elder party sought convenience. He is, in many ways, still naive to his own wishful thinking.

Ms. Hutchens shuts the door behind them.

'See you tomorrow.' Ms. Hutchens heads left down the hall towards the main entrance.

'Yeah, bye.' He turns right. Wearing his green lumberjack coat and blue carpenter jeans, Westcott makes his way out to the vacated parking lot. He is still walking to his pickup when Ms. Hutchens' cranberry car pulls away. A slight breeze is about, the scent of fall stirring. In the distance a utility vehicle backs up, the tone hollow as building contractors in nearby housing developments prepare to lay foundations. The landscape of his physical world is changing. Little by little so is he.

• • •

It was Friday, the first of November, the last day of Spirit Week. Students wore their class colors proudly. Some had red or green spray-colored hair with painted faces. As a senior, Westcott was to dress in red. He wore his navy blue shirt and plaid jacket. Not wanting to be excluded from his class' pride he taped an American flag to the back of his jacket with the year written across it. During the past four days in English Ms. Hutchens had given her class a reprieve from doing schoolwork. She, and many of the teachers, sensed class-time would be a wash. Students were far too preoccupied with the ongoing festivities and crazy get-ups of their instructors and peers to pay attention to learning. By week's end the hall decorations were falling apart and ready to be taken down.

Westcott sat quietly in second block sifting over a packet from anatomy. Half-interested, he colored in a skeletal diagram. He listened to his fellow classmates talk and banter, laughing to himself if one of them made a humorous comment. Once in a while he'd put his pencil down and look up to glance about the room. Pondering a deep sorrow. *How lucky you are, how very lucky.*

There was a knock on the door. Westcott was situated in the corner of the room directly next to the entrance. He'd been delegated the door hop. It was a student council officer carrying balloons with notes tied to the bottom of the strings. She handed two of them to Ms. Hutchens and continued on to other classrooms with deliveries. The mylars read: Happy Birthday. Ms. Hutchens looked at the folded cards, proceeded to give a balloon to a student named Danielle and one to Westcott. He shrunk in his seat. His birthday was three weeks ago. He shoved the gift under his desk and flipped open the card. *Congratulations from the Student Council Officers.*

'I'm *sure* you're glad to be dragging that behind you the rest of the afternoon!'

Westcott smiled at Ms. Hutchens.

A little while later he hears a classmate ask, 'Renee, do you have any colored pencils?' Just then Westcott had been making his way to return the box of pencils to Ms. Hutchens' desk. Seeing Westcott, Renee turns. 'No, but *he* does.' Silence. 'Uh, sorry,' she quickly adds. He feels overwhelmingly obliged. *No apology necessary, please, you're completely right.* Westcott never forgets that about Renee. She is a sweet, petite black girl who always looks immaculate and fashionably prime. She plays the flute in the school band. Westcott helped her once with their World lit. homework during fourth block. She, too, is in Mrs. Medley's Anatomy class. Renee is highlighter crazy with reading assignments—annotation is more an artistic endeavor than analytical. She drives a small white truck.

Halfway through third block the senior class gathers at the back of the school in preparation for the spirit jam and their march into the gym. Westcott leans against the brick wall. Everyone in their clique chatters and goofs around. He sees an old classmate from American Studies standing nearby wearing a letterman jacket with track medals pinned all over it. He had loved to run once, but he would not dare to do so now. His bones and joints are rusting, atrophying.

Twenty-five minutes go by. Just as they are about to get things moving the fire alarm sounds. Students are in disbelief—many refuse to exit the building until security instructs them to head to the field and track. Disgruntled, Westcott meanders toward the designated area. Once outside, he makes himself all ears.

One of the seniors had pulled the alarm as a prank. He is annoyed. He hadn't been thrilled to be going to the spirit jam either; he doesn't care for them anyway, but that is beside the point. He'd rather have been entertained for an hour and a half than forced to uselessly rot on the field. He considers the student responsible for the disturbance a complete jackass, a selfish fool. What did he gain? In compensation Westcott spends the time watching. He sees Mrs. Talmedge with her green and white Dr. Seuss hat, her Viking-striped face. The tall cap reminds him of a caterpillar; he grins. The leaves have started to turn in the surrounding forest. Every now and then a slight breeze stirs and the clouds drift by unnoticed.

That afternoon as the boy made his way out the door, across the parking lot to his truck, he was unaware of the rare magnificence above him. It wasn't until he headed off that he took note of the sky's uncanny qualities. A dusky shadow descended over the front of the high school. Enormous cumulus clouds united and overpowered the sun in a thin sheath. The wind shifted and the wool broke apart. Rays of smoky light transcended the unobstructed pockets of free space etching the folds and ridges of each cloud in a tinge of blue. It looked like a scene on a stained glass window.

As he drove away he felt the complete content of it. The utter despair.

NOVEMBER

It was just Regn, Pauline, myself, and Eva Bellefont. The weather was overcast, the bloom of autumn with a warm breeze and cascading leaves. Eva asked me to assist her in rearranging the storage closet. It was slow because of the weather and being Election Day. Regn and I had the pleasure of lunch together. Perhaps our last.

'So you have a doctor's appointment tomorrow,' I said. 'Yes, I have to spread my legs.' Her voice sent a twinge through the lateral line of my body, to the cold, intangible sphere within the stomach's wall. She could not know nor was it deliberate, how much her words aroused me. I wanted again to study her—inside and out. I imagined the scene—enduring the details by proxy—lying on her back atop that sterile paper, its crinkling sound as she shifts her weight and lies back, raped of discretion, utterly vulnerable, and inserted upon. The room smelling of latex gloves, warm and medical, discomforting to my own fear. A gown open in the front—hangman of personal privacy; the lights dim. In some strange way I wanted the terrible procedure myself—to feel the shame as I lay exposed, have a practitioner's hands on me in a far too intimate manner to be considered routine examination. In some twisted way I wanted the agony of experience—to have that shame as a form of hi-jacked gratification, an imposture's "penance." I desired a human hand other than my own where none ever ventures.

I'd just closed out when Eva came to the window and said she had it from upstairs that Pauline and I were to leave early.

Regn and I agreed I'd come back at five to the Creek.

She arrived quickly at 5:10. I'd been considering relieving myself in the brush. I really had to go. I felt daring. Erotic. It didn't bother me for once. I waited.

The November wind sailed softly around Regn's bug as slowly the windows fogged. We moved in silence. A reservoir gave way and the restless ache disrobed itself.

The rain drizzled, occasionally a car would drive past, we'd hesitate for a moment.

I thrusted her with my heart, coming inside her, feeling her through the shadows of my shut eyes, feeling her with my mind and hand. She cried, gripping the sides of my scalp. She came beautifully, whispering over and over to me, 'I'm sorry, I'm so sorry, I'm sorry.'

I understood.

We rested, my hand motionless on the nap of her pelvis, my thumb stroking the soft skin, content to lay there.

She wanted me to be relieved. I welcomed her hand beneath the elastic band. I held her close pushing down on her wrist—silently saying *you can go further, it's all right.*

Even in the blue shadows of her car, our faces barely discernible to one another, I could see her eyes. She read the question I wouldn't speak. 'What do you want?' she asked. 'What, tell me.' Our voices were hushed. 'Tell me.'

'Put your hand inside me,' I whispered, afraid not of the action itself, but the sound of my own desire.

'Put my hand *on* you.'

'No.' When at last I spoke it was almost inaudible. '*In* me.'

She wet and came so easily. I felt dry but insisted in my silence her presence within. It burned, it hurt. I moaned gently, the pain wonderful. 'Softly,' I said. We tried. She came close. I tried to hold onto the mounting of gathered tension. I couldn't come. 'It's all right,' I said. And it was.

I let her stay in me, feeling her. For the first time I found myself at peace, complete. I could have fallen into eternal slumber. She repeated my name as though it were her very breath exhaling.

'I'm sorry,' she said again.

'Don't say you're sorry.'

And then I said I'm sorry.

'Now we're both saying it.'

'I love you, Regn. I want to say that strong.'

'My West.'

'We had the wind.'

'There aren't words. You gave me ecstasy and you don't need a penis to do it.'

I started my truck's engine and saw her shadows moving through her fogged window. The light from her visor showed she was fixing her hair, composing herself. Her windshield was defrosting. It was 6:10. I waited for her to pull out. She didn't speed off, but seemed to wait and I followed. On Jamestown road I kept a distance. I followed her through the dark evening, the leaves on either side of the road a canopy. The headlights shone on piles of leaves and the pine needles and crisp tan leaves kicked up by cars into tracks along the center of the lanes. I felt content. Her gum in my mouth, my fleece collar alive with the scent of her essence.

• • •

In response to all the cutbacks and layoffs at Jamestown I wrote the following and submitted it to The Last Word which runs bi-weekly in the oldest newspaper still printing in America, *The Virginia Gazette*.

"Jamestown Cuts"

A recent death has occurred, but there will be no mention in the obituaries. It is the death of better days. Since no one has yet to address the drastic measures taken to compensate budget reductions at the Jamestown-Yorkton Foundation, I feel obliged to express my shared disgust. High-ranking, superfluously salaried positions are not only exempt from cutbacks at Colonial Williamsburg, but such is true of the first corner in our Historic Triangle. It is the sales associates and front linesmen who are the backbone of any company, yet they frequently receive the least thanks, while big-wig execs hide behind the comfort of their desks with comfy benefits and job security. I am outraged by the disbandment of Visitor Services.

• • •

I went with some individuals, five girls from telefunding to dinner. I'd signed up for the extra money—The Foundation held a telethon for a month in the fall and spring. They were girls—just that—young. I felt all the more alone, removed from them, watching—bored by their conversation. It seemed so trite.

I just wanted to talk to her, but no words came—I could hear it in her voice, the weariness, the rational, I hate reality but there's nothing I can do. She's worried about me. 'Don't worry, Regn,' I said. 'I'm fine.' I wanted to see her. We both know a moment only hurts us more. She's trapped in a marriage, laid off, Jay's at home most of the time, and she has responsibilities, as do I. It's time I stopped thinking and shut the hell up. I am selfish and must put wants aside to needs.

• • •

Once again I feel the self-anger rising. I have nowhere to run, not that running would solve anything. There is no one to call, no one to speak with who will alleviate this contempt for myself. I want to reiterate I am not angry at Regn. No. Only myself. I fear she is better equipped to be strong for she has a life to fall back on, a buffer of surface successes and diversions. The other day she went out to lunch with Fernus. I envy that freedom between two women. We can never go out to lunch. It's clear and I recognize it, I am my own worst enemy. I think of all the things Regn has experienced that I never will. It's not that I couldn't, but though a part of me longs for the normalcy of it at times, I don't desire it. She has known a certain type of loneliness, but she will never experience the isolation of being detached from the mainstream. She has her gender and sex. Society will consider her a success for having married, had two children who are financially sound, and a husband that does take care of her. To anyone reading this it might seem, and could be argued, she is selfish not to let me go. The truth is I am responsible, I am accountable, and at times I disdain *of* myself for the pain I have unleashed though it is wonderful.

• • •

I can't help but let my mind wander to the other life she's always had and how if her frustrations and anger rage she can turn to him in bed. He can slide onto her body and in the fury of release she can attempt to masquerade the pain from him. Can he not feel it, though, if she's not really there? It's not the sex she may indulge in and unlikely abstain from that hurts me anymore. It's the simple fact that she has the *freedom* of choice. She's had sex many times, countless times—I'd like meaningless sex for the relief.

At times I feel robbed of my youth. My heart has raped itself, a virgin to man, so that when a girl or woman should look at me, whatever masculine qualities I possess, silently crumble like a house of cards. I know what it is that intrigues her—a woman, for I have felt the same—is it not in want of knowledge of the man, that innate, natural awareness of what it means to be male and how it feels to be taken in by one?

I know not a man's physical endowments, having never felt, nor touched, nor studied in close examination. And so that intrigue comes.

One more day is all we have, one more day of working together.

'I WAS THINKING WHAT IF I had the Christmas dinner at my house?'
'Isn't Sharon going to?'
'She hasn't said.'

'I'd rather do something with just you, go somewhere, the mountains. We're going to the Shenandoah this week.'

'You are?'

'I wish it were with you. I shouldn't have told you.'

I was hurt but then I respected her even more, loved her for telling me. I knew the truth of her words.

'Uhhh, I just want this day to be over, to get out of here,' Regn tipped her head back.

~

I saw her walk through the glass doors. I'd just clocked out and hurried to catch up. We exited.

'Where you goin', Lass?' I smiled. We both knew we'd see each other in a couple minutes around the corner at Powhatan Creek.

I removed my suede jacket with the fleece to see what it would look like on Regn.

'Now it has my essence,' she spoke tenderly. 'I've never loved any man the way I do you.'

Even with my slight frame, the jacket was loose on her, too big. *She's so small*, I thought. We held each other again in the dimming blue light, the moon was already present. We made love, my hand slipping down her leg and entering beneath her soft skirt, sliding up between her thighs. My favorite part, the advance. I love entering from below—the idea of coming under and up rather than slipping my hand down from her stomach first. I took my time, running my hand along her inner thigh ever closer. I moved up and under the waistband, finding her. I felt the dampness of her woman's desire, how easily she came. I slipped inside her. I lifted her shirt, uncupping her breasts from their fabric hammock. Though already white against her tanned skin, they shone luminescent in the moonlight. She lay still. She tried to relieve me. I was too tired to even feel. She lay in my arms, I stroked her face and listened. 'You are a great lover. You make the other person feel important. Like there's no one else in the universe.' 'There isn't, Regn. Not in my book. I love for life.' She stepped out of her car, standing to straighten up. Lifting her skirt she pulled her shirt down to re-tuck it. 'How do I look?'

We stood by my truck embracing, feeling the want to pull ourselves into one another. We kissed once more. 'I can't promise anything about Tuesday. I want to come though.'

'Try. I tentatively plan on you being there. You took all my thoughts.' My mind felt vacated from our passionate explorations. I still looked at her, still wanted more, watching her get into her bug. I waited for her to leave, to see her to the corner—see her safely on her way.

THE REALITY is, standing, holding her to him, listening to her voice hum a tune he knew but could not name, it became clear such a single moment was reason, alone, to endure the labors necessary for pursuing freedom.

She noticed he watched as she laced her brown leather boots. 'What?'

'It's the things I never get to see you do.'

'I'm not going to say goodbye,' she said, 'because that's not what it is.'

'I want to thank you.'

She interrupted, but he continued.

'I wanted to thank you for telling me you're going to the mountains.'

Her voice began to give way. He could hear the pain in her throat. 'Everywhere I look, every place—you will be there.'

He was too tired to contest, too tired to feel anything.

He'd lifted her sweater and she'd removed it. Just looking at her bare torso was enough. He needn't touch her, only to look upon her—

But she was willing and he wasn't a monk, he could not deny the desire he knew was in both of them.

'I want to, as a man—'

'All right.'

He left his room and came back, the apparatus secure around his waist. In opening his door, a completely naked woman lay on his bed. It was too much to believe. She lay on his coverlet, exposed, vulnerable, physically at ease.

He stepped up and over her. He pushed inside, positioning the phallus with his hand, guiding the nerveless staff. It hurt not to be able to feel Regn's grace accept him as her body opened, expanded. He tried to kiss her as she ascended closer to the point. His shoulders spasmed, it was uncomfortable holding himself up.

'You know, being on top is over-rated,' he whispered.

Regn laughed. He looked down. He wanted to see the extension of himself inside her. As though seeing it he could feel the contractions gripping it within. It was possible to believe that his body was whole, completely male. Regn became self-conscious and moved to release the object from her body. He wanted to stay inside her, to look upon the organ firmly within after the wave of pleasure had descended on her. Only for a passing moment had he seen the penis lodged gently between her legs. He wanted Regn to hold him. But her high was fleeting. He penetrated with his heart and just as Regn surfaced, breaching the waves of her mind, Westcott's heart felt relieved. The hardness inside his own breast gave way, a deep calm spread through his skin. He wasn't cold. His was an emotional orgasm, not a sexual one. She'd come to him that morning shaking, in need of someone to listen. He knew *that* kind of desperation, how it manifested when you called someone and no one was there to answer. The immediacy of needing to relieve one's burdens. She'd come to him, though a neutral confidant was desired. He understood and yet he knew there was nothing he could say beyond comforting words. He was frustrated, angered by his own helplessness at that moment. At the precise hour he could not reassure with anything concrete other than he was there to 'stay.'

That night after she'd gone he found himself alone in the room where they'd made love—his own room. He had no earthly desire for it and yet, in a rare act of shamelessness, he entered upon himself. There was no inkling of want, no need to release. He was calm, too limp to protest. She wished she could just go off and be a nun. Those had been her words. He wanted the solace of assurance. He, too, had considered that perhaps a monk's life would be an alternative. A little gardening, prayers, and discipline—a dependable lifestyle. He wanted that hour back, to tell her he'd been forced to the point of shaking often and in those minutes of runaway fears with nowhere and no one to turn to, it lay down within him and he realized as he now did, lying unclothed atop his spread, the mind is alone, within itself, to rescue its host.

He'd become bored with sex *for* himself. Access so often denied by circumstance. But he endured it alone, hoping that to inflict mild physical pain might evoke the tears he could no longer shed. He'd made love to her in the way he experienced it now. He'd meant to ask her, did 'it' feel authentic, not as a means of satisfying her, but quelling his wonderment? Did it feel genuine? The reservoir broke and the idea of sex no longer mattered. Even would she enter him as he did himself, *sex was no requiem for his love*. He wanted solutions, the relief of heart. A part of him cried for the emotions his body failed to erupt that afternoon. The emotions he felt within her. That moment when you don't think you can stand it a second longer; the chest feels as though it will burst if left to teeter on the verge of plummeting. That point of explosion when calm invades the frontal lobe as a warm embrace.

Fully within, one's muscular spasms are constricted—a true woman will say to herself 'to come powerfully does not involve complete insertion, only adequate or subtle stimulation.' It will hurt, burn, and then familiarity takes hold as the body adapts and a firm power is stilled. Your breath becomes a draft where cool air has found its place. All is endured for the furthest point of penetration, and though the heart could give out, you do not care. You are empty. Alone such methods cannot achieve ecstasy. He knew how to satisfy himself, to tease and build the fury before spurring the velvet stallion between the legs. She preferred to come quick, whilst he savored the prologue, the climbing, to study and observe. She'd bite it all off in an outpouring of passion. He took small bites in preparation. He wanted her to feel the stealth of arousal. He had forfeited his capacity to reproduce, and she had fulfilled her natural right as a woman—an inherent marvel, her gender's grace. Sex was not essential, but it still had the ability to give life. An energy between whose pulse of blood had transfused each into one. *It was her presence he could not endure without.* Her presence which he longed to enjoy with a freedom that would defy the constraints of time.

He wanted those overlooked instances—a place at the dinner table—to look up and across at her, fork in midair. To see her enter a room, package in hand. To quietly slip behind her as she stood at the sink and fold his arms around her waist. To argue about nothing and everything, to laugh for the pain of life itself, and to dance gently before going up to bed and falling into endless slumber.

He had been a lover to her that day when all he sought to be at that moment, and what she needed most, was a friend. Dancing, holding her in his arms, like a cradled bird, not secure in its abilities to fly independently, he supported her—while the fluttering of her life's fissure anchored him—a tree and a bird.

• • •

This is my form of 'conversation.' Unfortunately it's an echo because the feedback reverberates off the same walls of my mind. You'd think I'd have multiple personalities for the sake of company, but here I am in the one place no one can penetrate. You couldn't put me in prison. I've made a prison of myself for which I take absolute responsibility. I want to reveal the pain and be forgiven for moments when I sought to kill the anger. I want to go down easy, calm and rest in a quiet hold, a pure condition.

...

23 November 20—

What made me believe it is 'a right' to have happiness? Foolish me, how young I was. It's no right, only a gift if you can manage it somehow. There is no greater feeling of frustration or helplessness than to be dependent, potential wasted. I will do what I must to stand on my own. I will not be the picture of hopeless desperation.

Did I ask too much of you and not enough of myself? The only person we can judge is ourselves.

Thank you for the beautiful book, Regn, though a letter from you is the best gift.

It's <u>of</u> you. Thank you, my Lady.

I paged through the mountainous scenery. Regn had bought me a gift from her trip to the Shenandoah. A lovely book of photographs. I read her inscription to me.

DECEMBER

The days of monotony are wearing. He can barely stay awake, the boredom has lulled him into a lethargy. He's been putting in applications, the winter months are approaching. It is not the most lucrative season except for temporary holiday shifts. Unexpectedly Regn called. The number came up 253-5112. The front desk of Visitor Services. It was almost 5:30. The Settlement was closed. He wondered what it could mean.

Regn was at the Gift Shop Christmas sale. They agreed to meet. Westcott is driving with his mother. She says she'll drop him off. Regn can take him home.

It has been twelve days. Regn drives her Volkswagen to a dark corner of the parking lot, takes him in her arms.

'Sometimes, this past week I just wanted to scream,' she said.

'I get angry for loving you so much and for needing you.'

'I need you. I would imagine touching your face.'

Her fingers trace his jawline. He turns his head to nuzzle her, rubbing his face to hers, gripping her forearm, feeling the sweater she wears. He holds her, feeling himself shake, holds her, afraid to let himself go knowing they have to part yet again. He buries his head in her neck; she strokes his fine hair, running fingers through it; he feels her vest. She slips her hand under his shirt and thermal, touching bare skin, but decently. He keeps his hand on her face, tracing her lips. She moves his hand to her breast. He wants to, but the pain. All the anger dissolves. He gently squeezes her supple breast. 'You don't know how that goes through my whole body when you touch me,' she says.

'Maybe I'm just like an old woman who needs to be reassured.'

'An old man,' Regn interjects sweetly. 'You have a right, you have every right.'

In front of his house he reaches his hand up and softly tweaks her nose. Ellis steps out the front door and down the driveway with Liam. She and Regn exchange 'hi's' and then his Lady heads down the road.

The relief. All the hours and just a few minutes to knock them back. The heart felt lighter, easier—a natural release of tension. Angry as he'd been, feeling her he felt he could go another mile.

• • •

The yellow lights in the parking area illuminated our cars. After the Visitor Services dinner party we headed to the William and Mary campus.

I felt myself in her own movements—her ways having become mine. She was taking her time.

'I wish it was simple, that we could just make love right now.'

'Yes, slow love, Regn.'

'Very slowly. I want to be your lover first and then your friend.'

I remembered sitting across from her at lunch and her saying the exact same thing only the points were reversed. Those words—her words just now—were relief enough, the confirmation again.

'That's all I needed to know.'

'Sometimes when I go home—no I shouldn't say.'

'What?'

'You just—make me crazy—I shouldn't tell you these things.'

'Please do, what?'

'Sometimes when I go to the bathroom I'm wet.'

'Thank you.' I hugged her close.

'And I don't mean that in a cheap way. You turn me on. When I get home you'll be beside me, you always are.'

Friday 5 December 20—

This evening was the foundation's Christmas party. No one I spoke to was going from our department!

...

Friday 12 December 20—

We stood on my back deck, gazing at the moon. I stood behind her, came close, a cat draping his paws, my arms around her shoulders, resting my hand atop her heart.

'It's cold, let's get inside.'

'I love to study you in the light.'

'See all my wrinkles. You don't have wrinkles, yet.'

'That's the least of my problems.'

I watched her looking around, warmly. At the Christmas tree and my mother's casserole recipe when I pulled it from the oven. She would never eat it, naturally. It had white chicken smothered with cheese, broccoli and slowly baked in cream, a cream of chicken base with curry…Wild rice, biscuits on the side.

'I can't make head or tails of it anymore.'

'What?'

Silence.

'What?'

'You know what I'm going to say.'

'Say it again.'

Silence.

'Tell me,' she pressed.

'I just know I love you.'

She pulled me closer. I kissed her forehead.

'You are *schön*,' beautiful.

'I love the way you say that,' she laughed.

She had to go before the others arrived.

'I hate this,' she said. 'I wish I could stay—'

'Don't—'

'But I do—'

She wore a green sweater and brown vest with a leopard collar. Over her shoulder I said, 'I don't love you to hurt you.' We squeezed each other. 'God knows that.'

She opened the door to the garage where she'd parked her car. A few minutes later the others pulled up. They would never know. What if one of them had arrived early and she'd still been parked in the garage?

Jill and Sharon arrived first. Jill brought a small Christmas plant for Mother. 'Where is she?' they asked. I told them she'd given me the evening. Standing in the kitchen, everything precise and festive, I felt mildly foolish. It seemed too perfect. The candy dish his mother put out. Anticipation. It was by no means an illusion, but he felt, as a young man, they'd think he was overly hospitable, trying too hard. Rawlings was a little late. Ida wouldn't be coming, she was not feeling well at all. I was disappointed. Only three, but it was still wonderful company.

Rawlings loved the pistachio ambrosia. I gave him the recipe for Ida.

Later, just as we were starting to eat, the main phone rang. I looked at the number. *His* name. She never called from that number. Was it her? I answered, hesitantly, praying everything was all right—he hadn't asked anything when she arrived home. Her voice was relief itself. She wanted to know if they'd showed. 'I wish I could be there. I love you.' The others were a few feet away in the dining room; the pantry door was open to buffer the conversation. The only barrier. I spoke in a hushed voice. Forks clinking, gentle conversation, I faced the wall for privacy.

'I'm glad you called. Thank you. Ich Liebe Dich.' I wanted to say her name.

The others asked why she hadn't come. I made up an innocent excuse. 'You know Regn, the vegetarian.'

· · ·

Tuesday 16 December 20—

She called it Lilac.

Westcott circles the lot once before seeing a car back out. He waits, pulls forward. The space is to his left, parallel to the curb. There is ample room; he makes a go of it. He turns his wheel hard to the left, begins backing up. It is too sharp; his rear tire goes up on the low curb by the tree roots. He shifts gears and moves forward. Back and forth he maneuvers rolling down his window fogged with condensation.

If anyone's watching, he shakes his head smiling. *Well, that will have to do.* Throwing the gearshift into park a car just on the other side of the island backs out of a straight on space. *Honestly. What timing.*

He locks his door manually, heads through the passageway leading to the main street. Williams and Sonoma is on the corner where the old drugstore used to be.

It is cozy inside. The lights a gentle warm, ivory and yellow with the almond exterior. Rich is the word that comes to mind, like smooth dark chocolate. Westcott steps inside, innocently scanning the walkways around holiday displays.

'How are you?' A sales attendant makes her pitch.

'Good,' Westcott responds looking through the clerk just beyond at the woman advancing.

They tuck themselves around to the corner. 'I like your haircut.' Westcott thought Ellis had taken a little too much, but after the initial shock to the shoots it seemed it was rather refreshing. Regn wears a cotton turtleneck the color of lilac and a wool skirt (the ones Westcott had given to her from Ellis' wardrobe; items she no longer wanted), black leather boots rising just short of the knees, and her deep green cape. She glows in the light. Her silver corkscrew earrings slip in and out of sight beneath her redwood hair.

'They're just giftwrapping my things, it should only be a couple of minutes. I spent $186.00!'

They stand by a shelf of copper cookware. Westcott holds her gaze, feeling the lavender come alive, the depths it prompts in her hidden gaze. Naturally seductive without intent. Her energy of goodwill radiates. She moves through the store, a woman knowing just what she wants to buy. The rugged sturdy eloquence of dress. Men at work ogled over her, even in this store the gentleman wrapping her parcels is more than eager to assist. *That I should know and experience her love, how fortunate I am.*

Regn shows him the items she's purchased. Westcott grabs one of the packages and offers to carry the other. They aren't heavy. Each handle has a wooden grip bar for added support. Into the cold evening the couple walks. They head to the rear parking lot. Westcott turns his neck. He'd been wanting to tell her since he first walked in, 'You look so nice, I mean that.' 'Thank you.' Low and behold Regn is parked just by Westcott's truck on the opposite side of the tree and curb. 'I didn't even notice.' He'd been so busy trying to park. A deep puddle floods the passenger side. In her high-heeled boots, Regn steps through the pool, puts her package in the backseat. Westcott extends his arm from the curb; she gently grasps it from him.

They take a walk, her arm hooked through his. The basketed fires along Duke of Gloucester Street burn for warmth.

'I'll have to have a large drink when I get home. I'll have a stiff one since I can't have you,' she says. 'I wish we could just go back and—there are so many things we could do.'

Westcott is thinking about that.

'I don't mean it that way—'

'I know. I wasn't thinking of that.' He'd had an image of them sitting side-by-side in a church or by her fireplace.

Coming up to his truck Regn asks, 'You parallel parked?'

'Why, you can't?'

She shakes her head.

'I have a confession to make,' Westcott smiles. 'I had a helluva time.'

• • •

I hadn't worked in more than a month. I knew something would come through and when it did how quickly the days of idleness, the malaise, would be forgotten. Another job. A job that would fill my time. I missed The Settlement, the camaraderie. Regn resumed working in mid-December. She went upstairs to work for the Development Office as a receptionist. At least she got to be out, earn a paycheck, and interact. I knew it was quiet there, alone at the reception desk, I'd worked it myself the winter before. But it was something to do!

As soon as the holidays were celebrated it would become much harder for us to see each other—her excuses limited to the library and an occasional errand. No more holiday shopping.

We had the evening. 5 ½ hours. The plateau would come soon enough, the sadness. For the moment we enjoyed the minutes, every word, the presence of each other, free for this window of time. It was Sharon's Christmas party. I told Regn I'd drive her bug around to the next neighborhood to show her the amazing lights on one particular house. When I got in I laughed. 'It's cute,' I said. The seat was so far up. 'You have longer legs,' she said. 'Here, you can move it back.' She was uneasy. Her car was very important. She didn't trust me. It hurt. I'd planned on driving us all the way to Sharon's—a half hour away. *She* wanted to drive even though she didn't see as well at night, so we switched seats. We pulled into the park. I gave her the small box I'd purchased with Ellis' gift last week at the silver shop. 'Close your eyes.' I slipped it on her finger. 'I know you don't wear rings much because of your joints, but I thought it was so nice. It was a silver ring with an ornate setting. 'It's beautiful.' I could feel she meant it, especially when later that evening she said again, 'I love it.'

Sharon asked Regn who gave her the lovely ring. 'Was it Jay?'

I wish she had been honest or lied convincingly. Say 'Yes, it was from Jay,' or tell Sharon, 'No, Westcott gave it to me.' Instead she made it obvious and said, 'Someone special.' They knew. They all knew. Didn't they?

Sharon had invited Celia. A few of us, myself, Jill Conway, and Regn thought it was in bad taste. Sharon was placating the Supervisor. Sharon didn't have to invite anyone. It wasn't the departmental Christmas dinner, it was her own private soiree. We were glad when Celia didn't show up.

On our drive home Regn said, 'I hate when people say things like pussy. I don't like when they talk about it so crude. I think when two people love each other it should be kept between them. Sacred.'

'Yes,' I adamantly agreed. 'I hate when they use names—'

'Oh you mean like sweetie and darling?'

'I draw the line at darling, it depends on how it's used. But Honey, Babe, or—' I forced myself to say the unpleasant term, 'baby—it just seems like nonsense.'

'I feel the same way.'

'Yes, you're my Lass. *Meine Dame.*'

We went inside. Mother and Ellis were downstairs. Regn exchanged greetings and pet the animals. We went up to my room. I opened her gift to me. A tweed cap from The Scotland House Limited and a stuffed yak and a card painted by the artist who uses his mouth to hold the brush. I cherished the gift wrapping—Regn had done it at work. The yellow box was covered in tissue paper designed with ornaments and a wired bow ribbon that fit its girth. I was disheartened by the present. I love tweed hats, but even Regn noticed while lying in my room I already had more than one. I knew she liked funny gifts and the yak was cute. She always seemed to buy practical gifts. And her note—rather formal—was addressed to include my family. I'd hoped for something of depth, personal. Having herself received the ring I think she felt dissatisfied with the gift she'd chosen for me and wondered if I liked it. It was a good color choice, not one I had, but it seemed she never quite knew what to buy so she would settle on something. I'd rather she waited until she really found something unique. Though I did love that the hat came from the Scotland store. I felt a pull in my chest. I tried the cap on. It was too small. 'You can exchange it for a larger one.'

Hiding my disappointment I said, 'Would you just rest beside me.'

We lay next to each other on my bed. I didn't want anything else, only to lie beside one another. This was the gift. We kissed, her tongue tracing my lips. I gripped her tongue softly with my teeth and let it be pulled from my mouth. A pulsing throbbed between my legs. In holding her I could feel the movements of her pelvis. I took my time, wanting to fall asleep with her more than anything. I moved to her breast. The door opened. Regn looked up. It was Helmsley. I got up and shut the door. I lay down again, still in my brown tweed vest, buttoned shirt and tie. I removed my wristwatch, set it on the floor, while slipping my shoes off. Feeling her escalating intimacies I moved my hand down her hip sliding her olive green dress up her thigh. She was on her side. She'd worn an ankle-length jumper which did nothing for her in color. It muted her. It was plain, even drab. I pulled down the skin-colored tights with her black underwear. The slightest residue of beautiful dampness marked the cotton lining. Seeing the dab of moisture aroused me. She shifted onto her back to release the other side so the undergarments could be pulled down. She kept her knee-length black leather boots on. We slipped her breasts from her clasped bra. The door suddenly threw open again. Regn startled.

It was Gilly! She came prancing in. Grabbing her by the collar I shooed her out, pulled up on the loosened handle and ensured the door was tightly shut. Returning to bed Regn laughed with her hand atop her face, her arm across her forehead. My hand stroked her inner thigh, slowly came from above her abdomen, slipping through the darkened, evenly trimmed spirals, and searching. Finding its destination the pointer gravitated inside. Helmsley rested at the foot of the bed.

I watched her face, her eyes closed in coveted ecstasy. She came in silence. She slipped her hand beneath my band and moved her finger in circular motions. I felt deadened down there, the warmth filling me only from the waist up. I was about to say, 'You don't have to—it's all right.' There was wetness in my eyes. I pulled her close and with her free hand I interlocked mine with hers, pressing her cheek to mine. I closed my eyes just wanting to sleep. Knowing I would not come I let her stay and moved my legs apart. I felt her reach the foyer and come within. Lying still I held her, silently telling her it wasn't *that* I wanted. I didn't need it. Her hands alone, just feeling her touch was enough.

I used my brush to fix her hair and she ran it through mine. We stepped across the hall into Ellis' old room. Standing before the old hall we looked in its tree mirror. The hall tree was one piece of furniture that had stayed in the family since I was a child on Magnolia Avenue. It reflected the early 1900s. A beautiful piece, light-weight, with ample hooks for hats, coats, a stand for canes and umbrellas. It was a very old piece. Our reflections captured themselves in the looking glass. Regn standing in front of me, my hands around her. The roots of her hair gray. She straightened my tie. 'What will they think we were doing up here?' she said playfully without concern. We stepped out from Ellis' room and there was our tenant, Dan, heading into the middle bathroom. He was a professor at the college. Regn turned quickly and headed halfway down the stairs keeping her back to him.

I didn't care what he thought. I walked my Lady out to her car, but not before she said goodbye. 'Merry Christmas, Regn,' Ellis said. 'Merry Christmas,' she returned.

'Someone's watching from the window,' Regn said. I looked across at Bob and Patsy's lighted shades. 'It doesn't matter. They know about me. They're probably saying, '*Well it's about fuckin' time!*' Bob and Patsy had known me since we moved in, since I was 14—a normal young girl and then an awkward tomboy and then—. They'd always remained friendly. I liked Patsy. She suffered from some illness, it was hard to say what. Manic depression, schizophrenia? Sometimes she'd come right up to your face and speak, sometimes she'd be in the middle of what seemed in-depth conversation and in one breath she'd wrap it up and be out the door as though some tiny voice or bird in her head had, from nowhere, said, 'Let's go.' She wasn't crazy, but she was not normal. Crazy or slightly off individuals possess an uncanny ability to be exacting and speak directly. Patsy was always eloquent in her language, particularly in her phone message etiquette. No hemming and hawing or 'ums.' It flowed; she sounded like the operator.

Because Patsy suffered from something unspoken, there seemed to be a certain kinship. She didn't bore me. I found her eccentricity oddly calming. In short, I liked her.

Regn laughed. 'Yes, they'll think you go for old crows.'

'Hey, you're *not* old. I get to drive next time.'

'I promise,' she said. I waited at the edge of the driveway as her bug went to the end of the cul-de-sac and looped round. She blew me a kiss. I waved.

Standing in the foyer I noticed the bottom of my shirt was slightly rumpled and untucked just above the belt buckle. Mother was studying me. She didn't say anything. I went upstairs and slowly unbuttoned my vest. Two years ago we'd danced. This night a vision inconceivable. I'd sought her in goodness and hadn't faltered.

• • •

The Gift Shop at Jamestown called me regarding working in their warehouse. They asked if I could come by to discuss availability. I knew Regn was working upstairs at the reception desk; it would be a pleasant surprise. A relief for us both. I walked in the main entrance at three o'clock. Someone at the front desk waved. It was Tillie. I didn't want anyone to know I might be picking up work in the warehouse.

I halfheartedly waved.

We, the three gift shop managers and myself, took the elevator to the second floor and sat in one of the cramped offices—Chloe Manestead, Guy (the one who often looks at Regn) and another man in charge of the Gift Shop. They weren't promising any hours and nothing would be needed until March. *What a joke.* It was still December. My days at Jamestown were truly a memory. I was still angry considering what they did—the Visitor Service Supervisors and the head-honchos, all the bastards! They had no right to come in, clean house. Out with the old, in with the new.

After our quick meeting I stepped through the door leading directly to the Development desk. Regn looked up, startled to see me. Her shorter haircut was very becoming. She wore a striped cotton shirt—pink, blue, black, and a pair of slacks. I stood while she continued to stuff brochures behind the desk. We talked for more than an hour. Occasionally, people working in the offices would pass by or the phone would ring, but for the most part we were undisturbed. I gave her one of my stories to read. Before leaving we stole a hug. I waited on the stairwell, watching her take her place behind the desk. She looked up and through the narrow rectangular window. I waved.

It was strange being back there after two months. I missed working. I stepped into the Visitor Services office (my code still worked in the keypad) hoping to say hi to Eva and whomever else was there. Everyone, what few remained of the old crew, were in the lobby. Jared among them. I didn't care to give him the time of day. I took a scan of the office for old time's sake and left as quietly as I'd come. I wanted to work.

SHE SAID IT would take time, she had to do it her way.
'Just tell me to wait.'
She said, 'Wait for me.'
'I can endure if I know we're going towards the same direction.'
'Yes,' she answered. She often imagines being in her own place. 'I will miss you these next days, desperately and'—her words relieved me. 'I hate this part—having to leave—'
'Let's look forward to a time when we don't have to worry about clocks.'
'I just want it to be good and right,' she said, 'and I have to do it my own way so certain people take it easier. I would always come to you. Sometimes I think you're stronger than I am. You're a very strong person even though you don't think so.'
'You're a good woman. You have a good heart. I'm not saying that to cause guilt. And I don't think you're selfish. You're my Lass. I don't want to love each other desperately. I want it to be easier as you do. I love you always as a gentleman, you know that.'
In spite of her joints she wore her ring—the one I'd given her last Thursday.
She blew me a kiss. 'Blow me a kiss,' she called to me as I stood by my truck. I did. It was unnatural for me. I made a gentle salute.

· · ·

Wednesday 31 December 20—

He listens to the wind chimes on the front porch.
He's at the Fleisch's pet sitting, Regn has come by.
'I need you with me in this,' she says.
'I don't think of myself as a man and I don't think of myself as a woman.'
'I don't know what to say to that—to me you are an angel.'
He knew she had never seen the movie: *To Wong Fu, Thanks for Everything! Julie Newmar,* with Patrick Swayze and Wesley Snipes dressed as drag queens. Her words are just that—her own. Original. Spoken in earnest.

Upstairs they lay dressed side-by-side on the very high bed. Still and quiet they face each other. O' Grady whimpers from the stairwell. Westcott moves perpendicular, his legs dangling from the bed, resting his head on her lap. The sun pierces through the crisp air and bright window.

Regn slowly slides from the bed. Westcott sits on the edge, reluctantly rises, holds her to him.

'It's an honor to be loved by you.' Her voice could paper the walls.

Downstairs she gathers her keys, another letter from him. A rich leather chair in the TV room. The woman on the wall in the oil painting Westcott admires so much is still hanging wash. Her back is to them. O' Grady hops into his chair.

'I can't let myself enjoy this. I know in a minute you're going to walk out that door.' The chords in his throat tremble.

She reaches, brings him closer. Westcott feels his own tears coming—too long staid. He turns, walks into the foyer, puts his sunglasses on—she asks something. His voice shakes, revealing what the sunglasses conceal.

'I told Rose Marie how selfless you are and how you yourself said if I get old and decrepit you'd carry me and hold my hand.'

'What did she say?'

'She smiled. Just knowing you're here keeps me alive. You made me a stronger woman so that I can take a stand. You gave me something—'

Her hands press to his back. '—Never forget the gift you gave me.'

• • •

New Year's 20—

At 12:36 his phone rings. He is lying in bed just drifting off. He is a guest in this bed. Grady sleeps at the foot. He looks at the number.

At this hour.

'Hello?'

'Happy New Year, Westcott.'

Regn had to take Jay to the emergency room.

'Why?'

'He has an infection.'

'Of what?'

'The bladder.'

'Oh.' *Prostate you mean, but didn't say.*

She is alone downstairs.

He pictures her, from what images still remain of her cozy home.

'We watched the Three Tenors. Maybe we can watch it one time.'

Yes. Yes. How nice.

'I wanted you to hear me say it. I love you. Please don't think I'd use you.'

He sighs. 'You hurt me.'

'Happy New Year. Say it to me.'

'Happy New Year, Lass.'

It was the first and last time he ever ushered in the New Year with words of love.

JANUARY

How I cherished those evenings, those minutes with the James River a mist in the darkening twilight of winter. And there we were—are, an occasional car coming down the road on the right towards the Island only to make a U-turn seeing the gates closed. We'd look out the window at the headlights, an edge of safety in check—might we be happened upon, would we be seen?

'You want to know something odd,' I said. 'I was never afraid of dying myself, until I met—loved you.'

'You're not afraid of dying?'

'I said I wasn't afraid of dying *before* I loved you. Now I am.'

'You must stay healthy and strong for me.'

Over her shoulder I whispered, 'I'll always be here, you don't have to worry about that. I'll be here for you.'

'Thank you.' She squeezed me tighter. Just the forest around us and the early night closing in—

'Ich liebe dich.'

'Du bist mein licht.' *You are my light.*

I put my hand to my forehead. A slack salute in return to her blowing kiss.

A new routine.

...

Saturday 10 January 20—

It's been two months since I last worked at the Settlement and now that I think back I was getting away with minimum service at times. I pushed the envelope, headed for burnout, but it was more than that. The Supervisors had the effect on me of "not" wanting to please them. Because they demanded and tightened the amicable working conditions a resentment brooded and I, along with many of the others, just did our job—they destroyed the simple good will. It's a damn shame. I miss slipping on my wristwatch, the professionalism of going to work in a shirt and tie, being surrounded by good company—but, it was hopeless. I'm faced with simply making a living now.

The other afternoon I received in the mail a newsletter from my University. One of the articles pertained to a philosophy professor. That's when it hit me. I am a philosopher. It became so clear. It was evident. I should have majored in philosophy, but to what end? You don't need to acquire a degree to philosophize.

I want to study the ramifications of my own mortality. Given due consideration or not, it's inevitable some might argue, so why bother to waste precious life dwelling on the natural course of all living existence? I counter, why not? To understand one (life) you must consider the other realm (death) and not merely on the surface. I am not of this era and yet here I sit. There is a dull sorrow for this acute sense of displacement, though I can remember no previous life, only things that move me in such a way as to have always been there, dormant, still a part of me. And there is the fear of one day never awaking again to this life, not knowing who I once was—if the feeling of memories themselves are subscribed into heart what of the memory in terms of mental recollection? Which way is the correlation? The latter may store the details but the true recorder resides in the breast of intangible striations—the human condition.

• • •

Friday 23 January 20—

I'm losing my mind. I haven't worked in more than two months. I've been putting in fucking applications! And when I do get called in it will be a trial to get through the day after these weeks of laxness. I want the sense of accomplishment after a day's hard work. I wish I had tests, homework assignments, a paper to write, something mentally demanding, logical formulas. My mind is so restless, so desperate to take in more knowledge, however trivial, starved to have its temporarily unused regions stimulated again. My mind drifts, becoming rabid—exhausted—too tired to think a thought all the way through. Sometimes I talk as though I am a robot. Words are issued but I don't know what they are. I hear them, but I don't think of what I'm saying. I don't talk much these days anyway. By talk I mean have a conversation beyond filler dialogue. I take Gilly out, put the laundry in the dryer. My whole clock has been thrown off. I used to wake instinctively at 7 or 7:30. Now, days seem much longer. Can a mind just explode like a light bulb gone dead, the picture tube in a television? My head is flour and dough now—I need it to be smoothed with a roller, pounded, kneaded, cut into shapes.

No doubt I've slipped into a further depression. The sky is white today, your typical winter forecast. I just lay awake in bed for an hour, almost catatonic, but thinking. Are we or are we not going to sell the house? I can't move into an apartment with mother—share even smaller living quarters—I *will* go stark raving mad. I should be writing, working on a novel, but I don't want to be in the quiet of my mind—I need to get out. I want a job—reliable, long-term, steady salary and benefits. My hope, my patience is dwindling.

• • •

Sunday 25 January 20—

I peered in the mirror and was absolutely detached, looking at a complete stranger. We spent the weekend looking at houses—nice ones. How many cycles before the mechanism breaks down for good? I feel myself falling deeper and deeper within myself—a slumber heavy in its fog. I went to the Kimball Theatre this evening, alone, and saw *Jellyfish*, an unusual but interesting foreign film. In one of the scenes a character makes a paper boat. Just like the ones Regn showed us all how to fold, although I believe I am the only one who remembers. My vocabulary is slipping. Redundancies. What day is it? Does it matter? If I don't get an active job soon—. I now understand why an individual who goes to a nursing home quickly declines. I must stay strong. I study the cracked knuckles of my winter-dry skin.

The List

I like the feeling of hot, hot water on the back of my neck to soothe muscles. No wonder I take long showers; I savor the routine

Putting my head down into the pillow

Shucking the cream from a razor after a few strokes, rinsing the blade and resuming— the mild scraping noise of the flesh

Washing my face first with hot then cold water

Drinking water from a hose

Watching a room being painted with a roller brush

Seeing fresh poured cement smoothed out

Holding wet pumpkin seeds in my hand

Lying on my back with one hand, palm down, on the flat surface of my chest, gazing up at the sky

Small bottles, containers, boxes

Opening a jar of peanut butter or butter and studying the unraped smoothness of its pure contents

Lifting the blanket and letting Helmsley come in and hunker down beside my stomach

The taste of salt water in the air

Dusting wood with Olde English furniture polish

Grating cheese

Striking a match and seeing if I can let it burn itself down to the quick without having to blow it out before it reaches my pinch on it

The scent of orange peels

A hard firm banana—just one bite (AND I mean the fruit—stop smiling)!!

Holding a frog

The feel of a flower's petal

The fireflies' light show

The sound of horses chewing their oats

A nap resulting from sheer mental fatigue

To lie down in the grass and project a view through the blades seeing the world from an insect's perspective

Watching the flow of dust particles in suspension amidst a beam of sunlight

The feel of closeness—sanctuary in a hay barn

The smell and feel of worn leather

The feel of a well-worn banister or bench

Watching cars go through the automatic wash and seeing the cycle

The lonely sound of a buoy

Water knocking on the bottom of a drifting paddle boat or canoe

The sound of motorcycles tearing down the road in the distance some lazy summer evening

Making love on a train (have yet to do)

Drawing pictures in a suede or velvet material—say a jacket sleeve

Spinning really fast (works as a natural high); who needs marijuana?!!

Eating pizza with a fork and knife

Very thin drinking straws

Squeezing those little critters and star shapes that contain bath oils

Crayons with paper stripped off

Popping the bulbs on washed up seaweed

Listening to a jet plane pass on a humid June day

Bicycling without hands—my arms outstretched like a tightrope walker

Walking with a stick or cane

• • •

A wonderful two hours. She'd gone walking with Magda on the Island. I'd waited out of sight before picking her up. I drove us in my truck around the five-mile loop. We got out at Black Man's Point, then pulled off at the cemetery.

She told me of her days in Germany working as a lab technician. The pill was made available to her. She spoke frankly about such intimacies. The doctor had said after examining her to see if she could take the day-after-pill, '*Klein-aber-oho.*' Small, but whoa!

As I told her about my past she stroked my hair and hugged me. We talked about us and how persistent I'd been. 'You don't have balls but you *have* balls,' she declared smiling. I drove until the five-mile loop merged with the 3-mile marker, taking us back to her bug. She had to go to the bathroom and decided the woods would work. Into the trees she stepped. I couldn't see her. I called playfully, 'What ya doing, Lass?' A car drove by and stopped to read the historical marker. Regn came out from one of the trees straightening her pants and sweatshirt. 'I went on my shoes,' she said. 'And no toilet paper?' 'I have a wet butt now.' We held each other, shivering, then got into her bug. She continued to shiver, her lips trembling. She looked so young at that moment. 'There was a reason our paths met.' 'And what is that?' I asked. 'I'm not sure. I just know I love you.' I got her shawl and the application for a receptionist position I'd picked up and handed them to her. Her position at Jamestown wasn't permanent and only part-time. While looking for jobs myself I scanned any that Regn might be interested in pursuing.

She would never leave the Settlement.

• • •

It is night. Cold. He walks to the entrance of his neighborhood and back. The noun catches on his lips. He mouths it. Whispers. *Vagina.* The Vagina. Her Vagina. A word he never speaks or even forms upon his lips. It can be said in mind or read in a passage without moving his mouth, but never uttered *aloud.* A word he attaches to her alone. Such a strong, unmentionable term, a shock to the ear because of its intimacy. Penis does not pain him, but the representation of its recipient, the very sound, stirs in him both longing and a repulsive shame.

I have a—

• • •

Items on a towel. The bare shoulder of a masculine body. A naked back with a dark brown shoe-string around the neck. A gold band laced through it. On the towel a silicone penis, erect. Beside it is a condom. We do not see his face. Only his hands and actions. We watch him tear open the prophylactic and roll it onto the artificial phallus. The items have been carefully set on his bed; he is standing over them. We see his unclothed posterior as he slips into bed, lies stark of clothing atop the sheet. Beside him a small radio. He turns on his soundtrack: *The Hours* musical score, *Out of Africa*, *Last of the Mohicans*, *Suo Gan*. We see Westcott's body through his eyes. The angle assumes his viewpoint looking out and down the length of his body instead of in—we see his triangular patch of landscape—we see what is not there.

His knees are bent and his socked feet, the only item of clothing except his necklace, are flat on the mattress. He takes the hygienically prepared penis in his hands and turns the shaft towards himself. The director focuses on his face, his rising and falling chest. We watch as slowly his legs slide out and down. His facial expressions dialogue the action happening just below the frame. He moves with himself in ecstasy. We do not actually witness the penetration, such is not needed. We can see it in his movements, the pelvic ebb and flow of retention. He holds his hands firm against his groin, gasps, and in silence cries. The wetness rolls from the corner of his eyes, subtly, singularly. He is still. Having come, he grieves—not for the momentary high, but its opposite—the heightened sense of aloneness. The emptiness it brings with it. The director is me.

~

The thin lubricant sheath removed and disposed of in a plastic bag behind the door of his closet, Westcott now stands at the vanity sink in his mother's room. He pumps the head of the soap dispenser, rubbing the shaft, rinsing it smooth beneath the warm stream. He looks up, conscious of the dramatic irony. Embarrassed. Freud had an unhealthy preoccupation with phallic association. The tenants use the middle bathroom. He has no choice but to wash at this sink.

IT WAS THE STARVING SEASON. In the winter of 1608 the settlers were quickly dying, their provisions had run out, they had no surplus of crops stored away. Some of the Powhatan Indians left meat or grain for the Englishmen—compassion did exist. But unlike the settlers, I was scrounging, not for shelter or a meal, but purpose. After being laid off in November, officially, I desperately looked for work. Still in disbelief, believing that come spring we'd be called up again—*we* being the individuals laid off—my search for new and permanent employment was halfhearted. I just needed something to tide me over 'til spring when the tourist season picked up. I immediately landed a job as a banquet server. I lasted one evening. The pay was terrible considering all the schlepping around, and my back felt like someone had punched the lumbar. I could hardly stand by evening's end. I bowed out diplomatically. Truthfully, I'd earn more collecting unemployment. I wasn't going to live off the system, but why break your back for less pay when I could take my time and find something more suitable? It was simple logic.

Being without a job unleashes a routine of monotonous apathy. I felt trapped, cutoff, powerless to take action. Depression set in with lack of productivity. I had nowhere to go.

No one to see. Fortunately, I still had Regn. We spoke almost daily on the telephone, met frequently enough. But I was slipping.

Ellis resigned from L'Oréal and moved out of New York City. She was coming home. She needed to get away from Rodger and the hard, tiresome city. It was time to reevaluate. 5 years it had been since she moved up there. 5 years. Tired of the city, she thought about heading west. With savings to tide her over for a little while, she came home. Being in constant close quarters did not help matters. I felt directionless and everywhere I looked, from Ellis to Mother, I saw the same. The frustration multiplied. Meanwhile my body still yearned for Regn, especially with the cold setting in and the withdrawal of activity, social interaction. No diversions.

I was emotionally haggard. My sleeping habits changed. I read to wile away the days, not actively or with intent to analyze, but merely as a pastime—anything to diffuse the boredom. I continued to put in applications. Ellis read as well—we frequented the library. Mother would be laid off just after the New Year—the usual two months of paid leave. Employees of Colonial Williamsburg are typically given two months off and afforded unemployment compensation. We went to the library often and took Gilly and Liam to the park.

I slept late even though I set my alarm to wake at 7 and sometimes 6 a.m. But my body felt the warmth of the blankets, the softness of the pillow. Waking up early meant more hours in the day to kill. And so I slept late—'til 10. I puttered around the house. When I read I'd start to nod off—too much sleep always makes me feel more tired. The lethargy would last for a couple of weeks and then a change in winds would rush through—I'd be able to get up early, my mind felt active again. This lasted a week, maybe, and then back to the excess sleep. I felt I was in a fog, drifting from one room to the next. The only highlight of the day being 15 minutes to 5 o'clock when Regn would call me or I'd call her. She was still working.

In February I received the position of receptionist with a veterinary hospital. The same one where Strum had been brusquely, cruelly euthanized. I needed the job, not just monetarily. My sanity depended upon it. Regn was glad I had the job. When she asked where she became concerned. It was the same vet she took her pets to. 'What if Jay comes in?' Her concern annoyed me. *And what if he does—I have a right to work there.* I wanted to say, *Let him deal with it. Last I checked it's a free country. He doesn't monopolize the town.*

There were three other receptionists—all women. This was the main reason the Doc, as we called him, hired me. He even said after the interview, 'It'd be nice having another male around.' Besides himself and his colleague, the rest of the staff—techs—kennel crew, were all women. Juliette had tattoos below her ears and multiple piercings. She sounded and acted much younger than 38. To listen to her voice you'd assume she was 22.

The shift was palatable. I got to sit down, which my back appreciated. The location was ideal—minimal petrol expense—only 1 mile from home—and the work constant. The first day my head ached from smiling and taking everything in.

I wanted the staff to like me and to assimilate nicely.

I worked from 1-6 and every other Saturday. Evenings I'd sometimes see Regn turning the corner, on her way home. I missed not being able to see her regularly.

Lest questions arise about my orientation and just to make casual, amicable conversation I told the other receptionists I had a girlfriend. And why not? I did have one, didn't I? I asked Regn what she wanted me to tell others, if she thought it all right. She agreed. I liked Juliette, but as a friend. I didn't know how to make friends. It had been a long, long time.

In March the outdoor area supervisor at Jamestown contacted me for interpretative work during Easter weekend. I jumped on the opportunity. No, it wasn't Visitor Services and it was only for a few days, but I was going back—back to the familiar sights—I missed my colleagues. Just being at the Settlement made me feel closer to Regn.

Soon after the Gift Shop Warehouse was hiring a delivery driver to work between the Settlement and Yorktown Victory Center. Technically still an employee since I was only laid off, the Warehouse division interviewed and agreed to hire me. The work as it turned out would be monotonous, dirty from all the products wrapped in newspaper. *And* fruitlessly boring.

Wanting a semblance of old routine, I would be lying if I did not say I took the position to be closer to Regn, with the solace that on occasion I could stop by her desk while making a delivery to Jamestown.

By then Regn had officially received the position I briefly held the winter before. In hindsight I wondered if they'd been testing to see who, amongst the Visitor Service staff, should go and stay—who would best fill the position of receptionist upstairs? Regn still worked weekends in Visitor Services. Perhaps they felt they owed it to her to give her something. She'd been with the company longer than I. The others—the non-classifieds like myself—were expendable. I held a certain resentment. Regn didn't lose her job. It seemed I was the one having to make *all* the big adjustments.

One afternoon while still working for the Vet, a customer brought in a fecal specimen in a plastic bag. He pushed it across the counter. I knew then I was in the wrong place. I didn't want to come into work in a scrubs uniform and see feces being examined under a microscope for parasites! I missed donning a tie, being complimented on my attire, bantering with colleagues, laughing with Regn. Sure the work had been dull, monotonous, mind-numbing, but I felt welcomed. No one liked the Supervisors—so I wasn't alone there—and Eva remained an ally. I remember my last day—my official final day with Visitor Services. So uneventful. I honestly believed I'd be back in a few months. Eva had asked me to take some boxes of magazines and brochures from upstairs and move them to the storage closet just off the hallway in the lobby. I mentally composed a letter. I wanted to say something prophetic about our time together.

It was anticlimactic. Part of me wanted it to be done with—the waiting had become too much. There was no pomp, no ceremony. I said goodbye to the staff. A few were over from Yorktown. None of the regular crew—my crew—were in. I looked at the office, the shelves, the pattern on the carpet. I do not remember the exact words spoken, but Eva understood my meaning. I thanked her. Eva had on a nice blouse, ascot, attractive high-heels and a pin-striped lady's suit with matching blazer.

I felt guilty leaving the Vet after only two months. But I was eager to get back to Jamestown. I would be stationed at the CSC—central support complex—the midway point between The Settlement and Victory Center—where HR held its offices and the Warehouse kept its bulk inventory.

One day, toward the end of my brief stay in the warehouse, I was sitting with much relief after having stood all morning unpacking items and price-tagging them. I was resting at a tiny desk in a quiet room just off the warehouse. Nick, the head clerk, a year or two younger than I, had gone on his lunch break. I was carefully unwrapping marble-sized animal figurines and verifying that the count matched the attached inventory sheet. I wore jeans and a button-down shirt. You definitely wouldn't wear a tie and clean shirt in this position! I constantly washed my hands to clean the newsprint from them. I was remembering a conversation with another warehouse clerk. A tall guy, much older than me—forties maybe, nice, soft-spoken. He was gay. Somehow we'd gotten to talking about artifacts and travel destinations. I mentioned my affinity for Germany and wanting to go abroad, maybe even teach there.

'So *that's* why you liked Regn so much and the two of you were always talking.'

Who hadn't noticed, I began to wonder? What was said in other departments? Regn and I did dine often enough, every opportunity we could on the mezzanine.

I played it off innocently, although a part of me—was it pride, wanted to tell the whole truth. 'Yes,' I answered.

Nick was a nice kid. Hardworking, had his own house in the country and a girlfriend. When checking items he would always say 'these ones.' I hated that, but considered it wrong to judge someone simply based on a grammatical discrepancy. When I decided to leave the warehouse it wasn't him I had to answer to, even so he asked where I was going. To this day I regret my reply. 'I got a *real* job with a law firm, doing some paralegal work.' He wished me the best and I reciprocated the offering. Afterward I realized what I'd said. 'A real job.' And what was Nick doing? Wasn't that real enough? Had he thought I was insulting him? I didn't mean it that way. He was good at his work, he seemed happy enough. He had a home and a girl—what more could a person want? He was responsible, paid his bills. He was more free than I was—independently speaking. I'd never lived on my own. Never had a full-time girlfriend. I resented it in myself.

The wonderful part—perhaps it was intended—the Foundation never asked me for my ID badge or name placard. All employees are supposed to turn these items in upon separation from the company. I put them away and have kept them since.

But that day as I sat at the table remembering my conversation, I looked at the lines of "things" people buy. Little mementos. *What are you doing here?* I knew I couldn't stay. I'd sunk too low. I was so far off course from where I was intended to be.

In May I would land another job. Amazing considering the unemployment rate and competition for jobs. Four in the last six months. I was a tumbleweed ablowin'. I knew why.

I was trying to hold on. To Regn. To a certain place and time.

FEBRUARY

I was at the grocery store in the entrance getting a cart when the attendant started talking to me. Real nice, older gentleman. He asked how I was doing. 'I've been laid off from my job.' He was from the era when a handshake meant a man's word. He was from a time when morale came from within and not the accumulation of comforts. He was authentic. He put his hand on my shoulder. 'Hang in there.'

I met Regn at Powhatan Creek. It had been six days since we last saw one another. It was urgent we speak.

'Sometimes I think the only way I will ever be free is if he—. And then I feel like a horrible person. How can I think such a thing? It will come back to get me.' Her voice began to sob.

I understood her exactly, having thought the same things. And the guilt I felt at times for wanting to be free at home. What she meant was Jay's *natural* death.

She was scared and powerless. There was nothing I could do at the moment but have strength. I took her in my arms for both of us. In that single sentence the depths of her regard for me unequivocally stanchioned itself in Truth. I took her face in my hands.

She could give no answers. 'I have to do this the right way. The other night he cried out in his sleep. I pretended to be asleep. He's just so scared of being alone—'

We both knew the situation placed a long road in front of us. I couldn't be scared. I must, first, do what I could financially to secure myself. I had to be strong for Regn's sake. I would do what I had to, willing the energy of peace into manifestation. I could not, would not, rely on helpless prayers as Regn did. I knew if we were patient and both wanted it, which we did, goodness would be ours, mercifully granted.

'Woman to woman,' I said, 'trust me.'

'I do.'

Time stood still that evening as we laid each other out.

She wore her lilac knit turtleneck, skirt and black calf-high boots. It was still light when we left. I removed my sunglasses and smiled for her standing by my truck before climbing in the cab.

370

MARCH

It had been three months since they last made love. Since he made love *with* someone. The coldness in his chest left him forever cold to the touch. He was at Magda's again. It is cold outside, very dark for lack of streetlamps and the pattering of heavy rain. He hears the train from Busch Gardens; smells the hops from the Brewery. The sheets have been changed as has certain furniture and the bath mat downstairs. He is amused—the things a person does. Magda, mother of three grown, successful sons, grandmother of countless grandchildren, does these small things to keep purpose. These rooms, he imagines, few ever see. New furniture or furniture rearranged as a means of keeping order, a sense of productivity, to keep from going crazy. It's a nice house, very comfortable. On the bedside table sits a sampling taste of chardonnay, which he poured. He forces himself to drink a mild night-cap, hoping it will mellow him for sleep.

An impulse, a need to have sex so badly had overtaken him that afternoon. The withdrawal felt desperate. He found himself looking under the Entertainment section of the yellow pages. Escorts. A gray, rainy day, a large lonely house—quiet, and the night hours. Then he imagined some strange woman *actually* showing up and him opening the door. He'd feel like a kid. Would she be expecting the overflowing hormones of a beer-satiated bench presser hard-up ready for a wild time, or perhaps a narrow, tall, computer geek with whom she'd have to remind herself she was here for the money. But she would arrive to find neither. Maybe the thought was enough. The idea. Besides, he liked to know a woman's history. He couldn't just slap on a condom and have a 'romp' as Regn called it. He liked to feel a woman inside and out. The thought of entering a stranger, someone whose line of work lay in pleasuring just didn't feel clean. Regn was safe in so many ways. She did not share his frustration.

A large bed. He longed to be laid out and made love to—to be loved. In the past he was the one who gave the love, not knowing, or rather, not opening himself up to be loved physically in return. He needed to have love made to him in the manner he loved Regn. To be taken, let himself go, be stripped of protective barriers. He always hid himself. More than any sex, at that moment, he would have settled for being held.

Am I so weak? What of those in prison? They go years without the touch of a woman and they don't go ballistic. I am not a monk—is it my heart more than my body that is starved? Regn can have relief whenever. I can be angry at her for what is and continues to be. He's been entering her for years, more years than I have been alive. She knows a man's body in ways I do not.

He hears her words—'I just don't want you to be so sad.' Oh, Regn, this sadness is my very being and I am accountable for it. Our pains are separate. You have some form of fulfillment and you always had security. To marry and be taken care of. No, you never explored your own capacities, but you had the luxury of not being on your own. By my age now you were married five years and with child. Being alone isn't so great, Regn, in spite of your desire to be on your own. You probably want to say it's not so great always being married. That can be true. I've made a prison of myself. We both want what the other never had. Do I expect too much from you? You have security, a legacy. I am a shot in the dark. I am often scared, though I may say otherwise. I must always take care of myself. Who will be there to look after me in companionship—and with whom to grow old? I can't say it enough, to feel the way I do and be the age I am, is terrifying.

I was *unverbesserlich*, having nothing to lose, not knowing the risk unto myself, I was relentless. I wish I could make it right, so much pain has been shared. Sometimes I think I must go away and leave Regn to 'make the best of it.' I feel I only cause you heartache. You can't be there for me and that's not your fault so why should I continue to torment us both? We were living in a dream, I see it now. Foolish me. My words of anguish only serve to hurt you.

Regn flies with Rebecca down to Florida tomorrow. I have no place here—how fortunate she is to have Rebecca, someone who looks up to her, another form of love—just as she's known her children's love. A body to hold, to play games with and laugh. I make it harder for her and I wish I had the strength to be good about it, to just keep my silence, but I'm not strong in that way—I could be grateful. I take my family for granted. Sometimes I find myself seeing right through them. I'm distanced, somewhere else. I try to hide it—the constant sorrow within.

'I just want you to be at peace,' she said. Peace. I have nothing solid to press my hand on—financially, emotionally.

Much as she may want it, reason will triumph desire—I misbelieve Regn will ever move to be on her own. And I don't blame her. At her stage in life and financially. The hard cold reality has hit and the only one I am angry at is myself. Who am I to disrupt what little peace she can still have? I ask too much. I've become a cynic to my own dreams. And there's no comfort to be had. What Regn cannot see from her perspective is the loneliness. I want her in a separate way. She does not need me as husband. I want her completely; I mean to share this life and that cannot be. If we have each other someday it will be for her an icing, an added sweetness on top of a life dutifully lived.

She does not need me absolutely, though she may love me so. I hurt myself. For a millisecond I start to hope again but then I think my hopes are a form of suicide. I have caused much pain and yes I hold myself accountable. Regn did try to stop me, I remember, but I could not be deterred. 'You overwhelm,' I hear her saying long ago, the November before last. I try to think of the positive, but the pain triumphs the splendor. You've given me so much and still I want more. I don't know how to reconcile the hurt, and though I wish more than anything to turn to you, bury my face in your warm neck, kiss your mouth so softly, I feel it is me who always asks too much. It's me, always god damn me for whom I can't forgive. I'm not strong enough in myself to leave you be without your asking.

Oh, Rebecca, never grow up.

• • •

I drove down to CNU for the spring Writers' Conference. I listened to the keynote speaker, Chris Phillips, on philosophy, thinking he and I could have a damn good conversation. It was only ten in the morning when we adjourned for writing workshops. I wasn't interested in them so I meandered into the new campus library. The building is rather impressive, despite its phallic headdress that pierces the skyline. The center is a rotunda with a campus design etched in marble on the floor and a double staircase that splits on the landing, going to the right and left, just like the one on the S.S. Titanic. Being the weekend, it was relatively quiet. I went into the restroom and was pleased to discover they'd chosen manual flush toilets over those horrible, irritating automatic ones. It was clean, and the building itself inspired a sense of possibility. I imagined it would probably pale in comparison to European universities, but it was still nicely done. I made my way back downstairs and into the wing of library books. The aisles had cranks on the end walls so the entire shelving could be moved—it saved on space. It was so quiet you could literally hear a pin drop, a whisper, the slightest clearing of the throat. I looked at the low ceiling—they'd kept this part of the original library facility. I remembered the days when I'd come and sit in the library, hidden away, studying my readings, or more often, write to pass the long stretch 'til my next class.

I returned to the Ferguson Center, perused the art department and went into the Faulk Exhibit of Dogs. Then it was time for lunch.

A note. This morning when I first walked in the woman at the check-in table asked if I needed to register. I said I already had and she asked for my name. Upon giving it, I detected a sort of recognition. I was quiet and kept to myself throughout the morning. My face was sore from last night's emotional deluge and I was rather tired from having awakened at 7 to get down to the campus by 8:30. I went to a conference after lunch. Those with whom I sat wished me luck, as I did them. Finally the awards ceremony came. We returned to the auditorium we'd been in for the opening address. The moment of suspense. I hoped the day had not been in vain—I know that sounds miserable, but all in all I wish I'd arrived shortly before noon instead of having to spend the entire morning waiting. In hindsight I'm glad I went on time; it would have looked in bad taste had I just come for the awards ceremony. I wore my navy blue work pants, crazy horse blue shirt, a tie and my rain jacket. It was cold, even inside. My pants were annoying—they were new and felt tight, riding up on the hips, snug. I couldn't wait to get back into my loose comfortable jeans. I sat on the side in a single chair—easy to get up and access the aisle and easy to exit the auditorium. A cute elderly woman all dressed in purple sat in the angled chair to my left. The awards were doled out quickly. They began with poetry. I felt my heart quicken. Each time, just before a name was announced, I was sure I'd hear a familiar one. But as the fourth slot (honorable mention) was given, my hopes dwindled. There was still the fiction category. I held my breath. First, then second and third. Was it all for nothing? I felt sure I was going to win something. The truth is, and this was before the awards, I felt certain individuals had taken notice of me. There was a woman at lunch sitting at another table who looked at me, or rather watched. She was the same woman who read the names of the award recipients. I knew her from our poetry readings at the Norge/James City library. She reminded me a bit of the wicked witch, in appearance only. She had all white hair, but her voice was cottony and her hair pointed along with shoulder pads. She looked prim. Amidst all the crowd, and well-over 1600 submissions, I heard my name called. Honorable Mention for Fiction.

Afterward, I went to the table to collect my submissions and purchase a winning entries booklet. I only had a hundred dollar bill. How many times do I carry a hundred dollars in my wallet? They said they would send it if I could mail them a check. 'What's your name again?' The other lady was about to write it down when her table partner said, 'Oh we won't forget *that* name.' I ran to the ATM in the student center and got a five. A couple of individuals congratulated me—those same women whom I'd shared a table with at lunch. When I returned to the entry's table, the two women who'd been there all day received the money. 'So what place did you win?' she asked. 'Recognition,' I said, meaning honorable mention. 'Did you read it?' I inquired. They said yes. 'We were in charge of the proofs—not like that—but putting the proofs together after the judges had decided. When I saw you I—umph—.' The sentence hung in the air. I wanted to answer what she did not say—

I suppose you were expecting someone much older. Both women looked at me and I say this with no flattery to myself, there was a certain intrigue as though they hadn't pictured the author as he stood before them, so young. 'Congratulations,' they added.

Later I read the three printed stories in the booklet. Honorable Mention is listed in the index, but it does not receive publication. Of the placed winners I felt only one deserved its prize. Had my piece been too much to actually be put in print, but nonetheless worthy and demanding a place of recognition? I felt my own piece out-shined both 2nd and 3rd place stories. Second place was boring; it had some good points, but its ending was absolutely impractical, outrageous. As goes the third place winner—well, there was nothing new about the storyline. It had been told before in countless other ways—a castle, a damsel in distress—and there were multiple spelling errors! Initially I was proud of my accomplishment. Having read the other contestants, I felt slighted. I deserved, not necessarily first, but one of the 'ranked' positions. The judge's comment was worth it, but I still wondered if my submission of *The Blue Line* had been considered too passionate for print? I didn't agree with the judges choices. It is all a matter of opinion when you get right down to it.

The sun's coming out, and at least some blue is visible. The white swan just glided in and landed out of view. And here I sit, half past ten—I hear the clock's pendulum, the rain water draining from the gutters, Lady G- breathing, the small wooden clock to my left ticking, the sound of this keyboard, the distant trill of a bird. And, the quiet of waiting.

• • •

Monday 30 March 20—

The other morning Regn called me on her layover in Charlottesville. She was going to visit her granddaughter. Told me how much Rebecca loved Talis and noticed the Converse tennis shoes. I'd given Regn a favorite stuffed cat of mine—small, packed with fine granules. I donned her with a pair of miniature Converse tennis shoes I'd found with cute honeybees stitched in for design. Regn had bought Rebecca a black and white pair of Converse. She said, 'Rebecca tells me, Oma, I'm not one of those girly girls.' She was deeply moved and slept with Talis that night in the hotel.

'Who did you tell her it was from?'

'I said a very good friend of mine. His name is Westcott.'

• • •

When I watch a movie like the one last night, *The Courageous Irena Sendler*, I have no right to stake a claim in suffering. What they went through in the Holocaust, the abandonment, the forced separation—my discontent is but little elbowed by such pains of another era forever framed in history.

I pace sometimes. It's the only tactic that seems to calm me. I'll pace aimlessly from room to room, occasionally picking an object up absentmindedly, looking at something or rather through it. I pace in loneliness for want of diversion. I dare not pass a word of complaint. What right have I and besides it does no good. The sky is heavy with storm, thunder is infrequent but evident.

I am impossible—it's either not enough time to think or the drone of my own voice uninterrupted for hours on end.

The evenings are very hard and the days off very long. I want to go so far away from myself. In the film last night one of the characters says she is reading a book and in the text the author writes, 'Happiness can only come from exercising free will.'

I'm trying damn it!

The work is so fucking boring—'ape work' as Jill Conway would call it. Pricing, unwrapping products—there's too much shit in the world—just too damn much meaningless 'stuff.' It's money. I have no choice. I despise myself for human needs, or should I say, wants.

I sometimes find myself looking through my mother and then the guilt comes because I should be present in conversation, but I give stock answers or placating replies. I am too far away to be bothered, untouchable in my selfish emptiness.

Regn said she'd call tomorrow. I don't think I want to talk. I only hurt more. The rain has come and as I sit here in my reading chair, my eyes a reflection of the day, I am complacently despaired. I am despondent.

It's a downpour now and yet the sun is out.

I am often sick to my stomach. It's a terrible thing to hold yourself in contempt for the things you feel.

It's incredible to have to keep it all within, but no one wants to hear it, not really. The irony is in loving Regn and having her love in return, my loneliness assumes a depth unparalleled. I now list through the days knowing that to rage in frustration, no one will come.

What no one can know—the minutes, the seconds, the hours, divided into days. When you stand in the restroom having washed your hands and look into the mirror while on your lunch break. Alone at the kitchen sink, sitting in your car before you leave for work and right when you get home—the feeling of going for no reason other than what's left to do. I look for distractions and I fear were I to have a child it would just be that—something to do, what we're supposed to do—going through the motions. I am going to destroy myself with these endless thoughts that come back to the same place and one day I really will be alone and unhappy. Let me just have the strength to keep this to myself.

APRIL

I have to be careful, else I'm quick to wear myself out. What if someone or I were to read this in twenty years? Mother's at work. It is a Thursday morning in the full bloom of spring. The leaves erupt into fruition overnight. Even in my overwrought condition I watch the buds and now the forests cannot be penetrated far in mere looking. They've become dense and rich—lush again. It is overcast, a white, blank-less sky and a bit cold. Last Friday I made three deliveries. Yorktown, Jamestown, Yorktown. I took the Parkway to the Settlement. A trooper pulled me over. I was so lost in thought I'd been exceeding the speed limit. He only gave me a warning, driving a State vehicle it could have been a hefty fine. As I labored with the mountain of boxes I knew, *I should have made a clean break from the Settlement. Lingering in these odd jobs only hurts more.* The days of Visitor Services were gone. I knew they would be and yet, even while cherishing every minute of them, I still had not been able to keep them. I saw Fernus. She was working in Group Arrivals. 'I'm not cut out for this—' I was pulling a pallet full of precarious boxes. Her expression indicated I was cut out for better. She'd confirmed my own private thoughts. *What are you still doing here?* A key-shaped handle worked as a lever to crank the pallet up so it could be hauled. Once the boxes were loaded I had to wrap them in cellophane to keep them from toppling. It was grunt labor and grossly underpaid.

Monday I finally spoke to Regn. She'd tried calling Saturday on her lunch break. Said she'd call later, but never did. The silence was too much. Monday I told her, 'You don't have to be so brave.'

'I'm going to be a grandmother again.'

She sounded tired.

Her son and his second wife (each already has a child by their first marriage) were six months pregnant. And just a month before her daughter had surprised them all with the news she was going to have her first child. Dee was 35 and older than Regn's son, but had remained childless despite attempts. Like her mother, she'd had difficulty getting pregnant. Regn had been looking forward to her freedom from all obligations. She loved Rebecca deeply. With her this would make three bloodline grandchildren and one step grandchild!

Very seldom is it that my voice can be clear when describing circumstances at home. I am at odds with myself. Mother is very insecure and I realize she cannot be there for me in the ways I need. She has always been loving. How can one accuse his mother of loving her children too much? She is too afraid.

I look at Regn's children. She may not have been the most involved mother, but both of them are well-adjusted. They don't have fancy jobs, but good practical positions. Nothing exciting, and yet they're successful at what they do according to Regn. I wonder, are her children satisfied, truly? Or is it, too, just a life they walked into—marriage, children, job? They may awake each day and be reasonably content, 'satisfied,' but are they fulfilled? It's frightening to one day look up and realize you were somehow never prepared, left to manifest your own strength. Ellis is like an island. I wish many things. I will say this though. I am grateful for my passions and the drive and discipline to pursue them. I know what I must do to be fulfilled.

It was an afternoon in spring. I'd applied for another job and interviewed for the position. Coming home the panic hit me. Nothing was right. The only thing I was sure of was Regn. I wanted us to be together. But how? Patience, yes. Then what?

I stood in my room. Ellis came in to talk to me. I understood what she already knew. We were alone. I hugged my sister. Shaking. 'I'm so scared,' I said. She pressed my back. She was more alarmed by my needing to hug her than the source of the fear. Had I turned to Mother, she'd have started crying. Ellis wouldn't. I was still hoping, seeking reassurance. I needed a rock. 'You have to buck up, kid, it'll be all right.' What else could she say? I knew Ellis didn't have the answers. She was still trying to find them herself. So was Mother. I was alone.

• • •

I found myself sweeping the warehouse. There I stood, broom in hand, calmed by the constant motion, the need to get the debris cleared, lost in thought. I felt like Ethan Hawley's character in *The Winter of Our Discontent*—the way he talks to the jars on the shelves. *I am so unhappy*, I said to myself, standing there, sweeping. Where was my shirt and tie? What was it all for—the A's, 3.9, the college credits? Where did I go and how did I come to this—this small 2x3 piece of cement floor—gashed from pulleys and boxes? Driving the truck isn't so bad, but it's no livelihood. I am alone. I see myself in flashes always alone. Standing in an aisle at the University library. In the restroom, in my truck. Is it who I really am, or what I've become in over a decade's time? The work is petty, someone has to do it. I felt the walls on all sides, the confinement of life and wanting to break loose from the structure. What does it mean to be successful? I again asked. To be a good person—do we define ourselves by society's definition or defy majority and establish our own standard? I am disgusted by the situation in our country. No doubt Sophie Scholl once confronted the corrupt nature of her own government, their manipulations, propaganda. Our principles have been flushed down the toilet; there is no standard anymore—from proper English to decent apparel. I feel at odds, right down to my very skin. I am androgynous. I say it again. I am androgynous. I am 24 years old in terms of dates. And you can never be completely prepared. *They* can't tell you how to live. '*They*' don't have the answers. In the end you must always decide for yourself. Always.

I sometimes have the image of those old film reels in my mind—the way the soft light would sputter from the projection onto the screen—as though light cutting through the blinds and a fan's arms splicing the ray of bars—a rolodex as the leafs turn—whether fan or pages, the flickering—timp, timp, timp—of quartered self.

MAY

I was scheduled to work. I called the Gift Shop Warehouse to notify them I wouldn't be in. I had an interview for a full-time position. Actually, I had filed a new unemployment claim—not that I wanted to—but the amount was *more* than I was making picking up two days a week doing shit work, loading, unloading, shrink-wrapping and driving around for tuppence—less than what I was making at the Veterinary Hospital! The morning and afternoon were mine. I did chores in the house. In the afternoon Mother arrived home and had a huge argument on the phone with Ellis. Mother tore out of the house claiming she wouldn't be back. I left despondent and headed to the glasshouse.

I sat in the quiet parking space, gazing at the restrooms and surrounding forest through my windshield. The intricate design of the small structure always fascinated me. The bricks crisscrossed like a Linkin' Log house with numerous 8x4 inch rectangular windows—black spaces throughout—giving it a chinked appearance. Why would someone invest such tedious labor in a public restroom? And, one so far off the beaten path? It blended nicely with the environment, rustically nestled into the trees. A miniature Fort Apache. I pretended the blank spaces were my life waiting to be filled in. I didn't want to turn to Regn. It wouldn't be right. What was left to say, what could she do? I called my father instead.

Some 3,000 miles away he was standing in line checking out at Home Depot. The conversation was brief and held no definitive answers. I hung up, if not dissatisfied, disheartened. I sat there and decided to use the facilities. Walking from the hood of my truck I thought I heard the familiar tune—"Steal Away." My phone. The sound of it made me jump inside, a lurch, my heart always skipped a beat. Its very sound was tied to Regn. I continued inside, telling myself wishful thinking, I'd imagined it, I'm hearing things. I often feel I have to go to the bathroom; my bowels are a train wreck. I only had to urinate. False alarm. Returning, I looked at the face of the silver phone. A missed call. I flipped it open. It was Regn. She'd called from work. She left no message.

I don't want to call. I want to call. I hesitate. She came to me—she had called this time. I am merely returning her attempt. I dial the number—it goes to the recording, she must be busy on the other line. I wait a few minutes, try again. Still the answering machine. I try once more. She answers.

'Thank you, Regn,' I say in a quiet voice.

'For what?'

'For calling.'

She goes on and on about work, then describes a movie she watched the night before. I'm listening, clamoring inside to speak, waiting for a window of opportunity to say what I really need to. But I feel it's best to restrain the well inside, not tell her the volatile situation at home. I answer with a heavy heart, thinly disguising the reservoir about to give way—the sense of being absolutely alone, the frustration of no way out. Then she says it.

'I can only offer you friendship now. We had our time. It's for the best.'

On top of everything. I am too tired to counter, to argue. I speak the truth. I speak about the day's events and now the loss of her.

'I can't just be *friends*. I can't be your long lost friend,' I respond. 'I can't make any promises. You might lose me. I don't know if it's in me to forgive you.'

She is hurt, frightened. 'Can I call you sometimes?'

'And what? To say what?'

'Nothing.' She gives up.

Silence.

'Can we meet for a couple of minutes?'

'Yes,' she says without doubt. 'We can talk for a little bit.'

I get my bike out from the bed of my truck, pedal languidly to the creek pull-off.

I park my bike behind the sign, walk down the small incline to the vista and water's edge. It is so gentle out this late afternoon, windy, soft, beautiful. I stand there staring at the day preparing myself. Trying to hull up the pain inside so Regn won't see. I open my shirt a little and tilt my head back letting the breeze caress me. I want to fade into oblivion. I casually glance back every once in a while in expectation. I see her bug. The mere sight of her coming saddens and excites me.

I pretend not to notice. I stand still unsure how I want to face her. Finally I shift my whole body in her direction—I let her come to me. She walks down the incline. I step back in hesitation not wanting her to touch me. She comes closer. All is lost. We grab each other. I hug her with everything in me. The levy gives way against my wishes and need to talk. I feel myself shaking, we continue to embrace. Not in passion. In pain.

The conversation falls to my mother more than it does to the issues I really want to address, Regn and Jay. I feel the minutes slipping.

She holds her sunglasses in her hand.

'I promise I'll be here for you, as much as I can right now. You can trust me. Always.'

A pair of geese honk on the water in front of the reeds. A jet-ski zooms past, sputtering towards the arena. The wind sends a nearby branch brushing into my sunglasses. It whips through our clothes. 'Your pants are falling off,' Regn says and lifts them up at the waistband. 'You need your belt. Have you lost more weight?'

She has a welt on her neck from an insect bite. I notice it first by touch. We hug again, she kisses my mouth. I pull her close. Kiss the temple of her hair and then her forehead. Have I been too easy? I want at times to yell in pain at her, 'Go to hell!'

I don't say all I need to—I relinquish the upper hand in relieving my emotions, showing vulnerability.

She believes I am strong. She is wearing a skirt, a raspberry cotton shirt, a necklace with a large circle at the base with a rock stone. Her scent has been imparted to my skin.

'I love you. Never forget that.' And in a manner only she could pull off without it seeming bromidic or phony, she takes her hand and puts it to my chest.

'I am *here*.'

'There's not a day goes by I don't think of you.' I pick her up.

'I'm too heavy, you'll give yourself a hernia.' I pick her up as though carrying her across a threshold. My hand underneath her bent legs, the other supporting her back. She laughs.

She is a featherweight. We walk back up the path. No one has come. She has my hand in hers and pulls it to her lips. No music plays in her car. She blows me a kiss. I go to the glasshouse.

For a long while I sit on my bike seat. Minutes pass. My hand rests on the black lining of the bed of my truck. One foot on the ground. I stay like that, in a trance.

If I don't move, if I just stay like that nothing will fall apart. I watch the evening sun through the lush foliage. I love it here. 10, 15 minutes pass. I feel no want to go. I need to keep those words alive, somehow, to trust them, to know this moment, preserve it and know its touch, so it will sustain me in the silences and the hours to come. I stay there, watching the sunlight play with the leaves. I stay and it watches me.

• • •

I speak without loftiness. I feel it is my destiny to do something great and then die young. Did you accomplish what you wanted in life, Regn? It is my passion that will not have me rest. I will not, cannot resign myself. Though life seems long, it is short. I wish no harm to my fellow man, but I must not give care to what the crowds 'decree.' It is not my course to go their way. Rather I go as a blaze, a thunderbolt, a brooding storm, than quietly wither away. I live between the lines and were it to mean something in the end, I'd willingly suffer for it—again and again.

• • •

Another day. Regn doesn't want to be touched. We were tired—there'd been too much hurt—so we spent the time laughing.

'I care for Jay, but I think he is more dependent on me.'

'Emotionally,' I said, 'and you are financially dependent on him.'

Finally we hugged. It was so good to hug. I gently put my hand on her tanned breast-bone, played with her beaded necklace, momentarily conscious of myself again, how far I'd come—we'd come. I never overlooked these subtleties of contact.

I tweaked her nose. 'You just got it all, didn't you?' With her widow's peak and the cleft in her nose.

'Oh yeah,' she looked up in sarcasm. 'I just got it all.' A slight sorrow just beneath the surface of our humor. The things we really meant but could not bear to speak anymore.

'You dyed your hair again.' It had an orange tinge. 'Now I can call you carrot top.'

I asked for Regn's purse and took out her wallet. 'May I?' I slipped something inside.

'You can see it later. I put it in front of your Shell petrol card.'

It was a poem. My favorite poem by Mary Brent Whiteside.

'I'm very difficult. I don't deny it. I can be horrible at times,' she said.

'I know it. And I'm not going to deny it. Regn? Will you stand with me, before you go.'

We got out of her car. We'd met in the Colonial Williamsburg Visitors Center Parking lot.

She kissed me then and I knew she was all there. Her petite body within my arms,

I said, 'This is just how I love it—not too much, just like this.' Against her mild protest, I hoisted her into the air.

Some men off in the distance made a ruckus. From my peripheral, one seemed to wave a thumbs up, another gave a slight whistle of approval. I shifted so my back was to them. Regn slid down, her shoes touching asphalt, my teeth gently knocking her forehead. We laughed.

'You're crazy,' she smiled.

I half-turned to look in the direction of the noisy men. 'Is that so bad?'

'I don't know.' She laughed all over again.

• • •

Tuesday 26 May 20—

My first day working at Contradite Health Care. When they offered me the position I was so happy. I could wear a shirt and tie again. No more ink from newsprint on my hands. No more standing on my feet checking barcodes. How have I managed to secure these last three jobs in spite of the market, the enormous candidate pool, *and* considering my constant turmoil? I have a knack for seeming at my best when I've just been at my worst. People have often told me, 'You look so well.' Little do they know the day before I was in the throes of a nervous breakdown. I guess a catharsis has the effect of purifying one's body. Maybe it's like they say about sex. The day after glow. In hurting so much, shedding all the frustration in tears, the pain exits your body—you appear lighter.

I am eager for the steady work. Hours are full-time—everyday. 3:30 p.m. - 8 p.m. M-F and 9-5 Sat and Sun. I am alone, the office is all to myself. All I have to do is answer the phone should it ring.

I told them I have a vacation scheduled in June—I'm flying out to see my father. First I fly up to New York to meet Ellis then we will fly west together. They won't hold the position—will only allow a certain number of days off. I have to change my flight—there's a ridiculous fee—is it worth it?

I need the security of the job. I *need* the job for my sanity and sense of power, control. I assure them I will be back in time.

• • •

The man takes off running along the Parkway. He lightly jogs then slows to a quick-paced gait, whether to give his atrophied muscles a rest or dispel suspicion from the occasional passerby?

His very presence is brazen, his attire denouncing the white envelope he's moved from inside his buttoned shirt to his back pants pocket. His inconspicuous intentions are undone by the navy Puritan slacks and true blue Crazy Horse dress shirt, tucked and pressed with a modest belt. The same one he wore two years earlier. He takes care of his clothes. He is white-collar. A jogger might be out here, a bicyclist, but a man in business clothes? Did his car send him walking astride the James River, a passerby might wonder? There is no gas can in his hand. Just that rectangular white paper peeking from his hip pocket and his clean look, a business man on lunch. But today is Saturday and not yet half-past seven. Not too warm yet. He's been up since twenty after five. Remarkable how light the dawn hours of May. He'd wanted fog, a mist to shroud them.

There were the quiet fishermen already at their posts when he'd turned into the second pull-out, the location agreed upon the day before. Stepping from his truck, he decided to take off down the road. It wouldn't do to be seen here. He felt watched. These gray morning men, speaking the dialect of reels and carp, sitting on upturned buckets with too much room for speculation in the morning stillness.

Westcott stays to the edge of the road, on the left side closest to oncoming vehicles. Canopies of shade guard him from the petulant sun he fears will enlarge any skin or facial marks—a blemish constituting a freckle in his book. Completely exposed, he holds a hand up to the side of his face, feigning to scratch the inside of his ear as an excuse for this peculiar behavior of keeping his hand up.

Over-sized flies harass his hair, zip in and land, flick at his neck. Westcott swats the air, a madman waving his arms. He quickly ignores them, finding they bother him the same regardless of brushing tactics. Phrases are running through him, all night, the anticipation, her reaction. It could go so many ways. His head is tight inside, pressed to the rim with rumination.

'Can I touch you?'

'Where?'

His eyes meet hers. 'Where?' she repeats again.

He comes to her, taking her left globe in his hand. He slips beneath her thin navy blue cotton shirt, releasing her breast from its cradle. In kneading her he feels the sensation in his own body as though touching her is his own hand upon himself. He gently presses as he would want to be pressed upon and feeling the constraint of 'just minutes' he quickly draws his hand beneath her waistline, emerging in the coarse depths, sliding down the soft line, a gentle storm of index pushing inside, her warmth little moistened in such haste, drawing him further.

She tries. She is too tense. He holds her. Traces her eyebrows with the tip of his already dried hand, kisses her softly. His heart, like a diver submerged, begins to drop its weights. He holds her, sighing through the breath exhaled through his nose. He hears his own breath. She lets him do as he pleases. She takes his hand again to her breast, pressing it still. He moves down her shirt, taking the delicate flesh from its hammock, lifting to free it and see the skin he blindly touches, seeing only with his heart. He looks, searching to reveal the nib on the deeper-toned crest. He feels it between thumb and pointer. Moves his head down, kissing the softness of her breast. She enters his mouth, and then releases herself in a moment's slough of kisses, penetrating exchanges. He holds her, strokes her neck, plays with the necklace and its white rectangular pendant with the ivory dragon. His heart spent itself. That place between his own legs untouched. No tangible rod to stir, to grip round, only the invisible staff of being—a mutual understanding of the woman's body, knowing her as he knows himself. And he surfaced, having held his breath to the point of suffocation. He surfaced, a breath of air so light, so cool and imparting.

• • •

Saturday 30 May 20—

I spoke too soon. This is a damn long shift. Utterly alone for 8 ½ hours in an office. I'm alone all the time. These are long days; I'd rather be busy. Regn wouldn't be able to stand it here. I'm about to go out of my mind. Only so much reading and research on the computer to do. I write, bring my books, study German. I can listen to music; it's still lonely as hell. Lady Gaga plays often on the station, and in the evening Delilah has her show. I hear about love—it's gushing, ridiculous. Only occasionally does a caller on the radio sound contentedly peaceful. I dislike the young callers—their passion spews from them. I am not jealous. It makes the idea of love seem stupid from the objective listener. All the emotions. I begin to realize being *in* love is a state of mind. True love, the enduring kind comes softer, quieter, calmer. I hear it in callers who are older, have been together a long time. I like interactive radio, I like hearing other people's stories, but it makes love seem typical. Real love is rare. And it must be worked at to keep it alive, strong.

I spoke to a resident today. Elinor Davis. She's been here 9 years! My god. She keeps herself busy with word puzzles. Another lady came up the hall, screaming. She had one green and one cream-colored sock on. Then Ms. Smith made her round—she sings in an Italian voice though she looks not to have any such heritage. Her *singing* is an absent-minded humming. She asked me to phone her daughter. I went along with it for a few minutes, explaining she couldn't be reached, she wasn't coming today. Ms. Smith typically comes up, sits in the chair, then rolls back with her walker and the yellow stuffed monkey hanging from the handlebar.

It is depressing in its quietness here. Even with music. I hear the clock ticking, the airy sound of power coming from the computer. Better to be busy. No wonder they pay *more* than $9.00. These are 'hard' hours. Alone. Alone. And then the hours I'll have on the plane, in the sitting area, the silence of being within one's mind.

7 YEARS EARLIER. SPRING. SENIOR YEAR

He sinks into his chair, eyes glancing about the walls. He'll stay fixed for a long moment on a particular picture, then surreptitiously discarding the emblazoned image, move on to the next. His head drops down between his arms, resting against his hands. *I'm sorry, I'm*—he cries to his mother who cannot hear him. He stares down at the floor. A clear liquid slides from his nose. He flicks his tongue above his upper lip in a levying attempt. Finally he is forced to use his hand and smears the slub on his tired jeans.

The argument unfolded moments before.

I have an idea of the kind of day I'll die on.

'I'm so damn tired!' he'd yelled, jumping up from the decrepit, floral sofa which he had begun to hate because of its outdated appearance with the foam innards seeping through frayed upholstery. His mother had looked over at him.

He mentally whipped himself; he didn't mean to hurt her. He now looks out the window to his neighbor's yard. The pinwheel glints in the sun. Round and round the wings go. The bird never moves. Forever treading the same winds. Beating its artificial extensions to no avail like the endless thudding of his heart. A flight of no escape.

Neither you nor I am free to go where we want.

A NIGHT TO REMEMBER

MAY. SENIOR YEAR

Westcott sits on the edge of the bed in his mother's room lacing up his shiny black shoes. Ellis is busy at the sink futzing.

He steps into the middle bathroom, studies his reflection in the mirror. He turns every which way. The shoulders. The shoulders are too broad because of the pads. He feels like Frankenstein in the coat. He wishes it fit him better, or rather, he wishes *he* fit *it* better.

'Are you ready yet?' he implores.

'Almost, darling!' She affects a thick N.Y. Jewish accent.

Westcott returns to his post on the edge of their mother's bed; a moment later he hears the stenciled chair in front of the vanity creak. Looking at his sister then, in her black and white gown patterned with a Victorian vintage, she is elegant.

The afternoon had been overcast, lending itself to a drizzling evening. Westcott drives to the restaurant following the mood of the day. The hour is young. There is no particular reason to hurry. They dine at The Olive Garden. After a helping of vegetable soup, a genteel proportion of mushrooms, and a sprite, Westcott is full. He squeezes a few bites of chicken along with Ellis' shrimp scampi and pasta into his bird-sized stomach, then his eyes spin like an old register, stopping on the letters f-u-l-l. It is a vision his mother spawned in his head. She'd kid him whenever he complained of feeling sick and unable to eat another morsel. 'I don't see the full sign on your forehead.' A take-home box is in order.

Brother and sister return with a generous amount of leftovers for their mother. It will be a while before they leave. Fashionably late is best.

~

They are greeted politely by two staff members familiar to Westcott in face alone. Side-by-side, they enter from the drizzling rain treading atop a red carpet. Halfway down the hall, he glances up. His teachers sit at a table, a jury in waiting. He falters in his step.

'Those are *all* my teachers!' *The ones that count anyway.* Westcott informs Ellis in a sickened whisper.

'Don't worry.' A hand presses his shoulder edging him onward. He does not feel it.

He is an insect under a giant magnifying glass awaiting death and scrutiny at the hands of the executioners before him. As they approach the table, nervousness overwhelms; he wants to throw up. Mrs. Talmedge and Ms. Hutchens are present; off to the side sits Ms. Garlow. He couldn't make eye contact if his life depended on it. He feels their gaze. Yet, as he and his sister turn, proceed up the spiral staircase, a sense of relief fills him. He is being seen by everyone. On this one night he is himself. The silence has been broken without his ever speaking a word. In the ballroom Ellis removes her long black overcoat, draping it on one of the many vacant chairs. A moment or perhaps ten minutes drifts by. Scanning the dim room Ms. Hutchens catches his eye. She is walking across the dance floor in his general direction. As she passes he hoarsely says, 'Hi.' Amicably she reciprocates the greeting.

She has on a scarlet red dress with matching lipstick. The color is too bold for her complexion, drowning her eyes away. She needs a pastel to bring out her baby breath irises and dough-blonde hair. The red is fierce, offering little compliment to her features.

Upon the arrival of more guests, Westcott checks out what the other guys are wearing. Maybe he shouldn't have rented the traditional style tux with a bow tie. He begins to wish he'd chosen a darker vest with a full necktie. A tie running down the middle of his shirt would provide an extra barrier. He refuses to take a seat, paranoid that his tucked in shirt will bunch and create the appearance of something being *there, up top,* when in fact it is just a wrinkle in the fabric.

Westcott and his *date* wander over to the sparse side of the dance floor. It is darker, fewer people around. He takes a picture of Ellis next to one of the many wooden cut-out movie stars propped against the walls. They are detailed in black, white, and gray paint. Ellis poses beside her favorite actress, Audrey Hepburn. Westcott walks over to the window, rests one knee on a chair, peers out through the vertical blinds at the liquefied night. In the daytime this room would be like a bird aviary or observatory, with its panes running from ceiling-to-floor it provides a fortress to look out at the world. It is the William and Mary Sadler Building.

Tired of standing around, Westcott and Ellis make their way through the rapidly increasing sea of dancers, under the decorative arch, out into the upstairs lobby. The cool air feels refreshing compared to the body-generated heat inside the ballroom. As the two walk about the mezzanine Mrs. T. steams by, her head bent down.

'Hey, Tugger,' she offers in her sweetly gruff voice. Charging by, he doesn't have a chance to respond.

Mrs. T wears a simple, formal black dress, very conservative and appropriate in style for such an occasion. As chaperone she can't go flaunting about or be too revealing, she still embodies the role of teacher. Waiting for Ellis to return from the restroom, Westcott rests his wrists on the iron rod banister, observing the lobby below. Funny how even if he'd wanted to he couldn't follow his sister into the restroom anymore. Sitting in two parlor chairs are Ms. Garlow and Mrs. Sumner, another English teacher he knows but never actually met; both wear casual attire: pants and a blouse. Watching them converse in the dim lamplight situated beside them, he rotates his class ring back and forth on his middle finger.

He received the ring yesterday. In tenth grade the idea of buying a trinket he would never put on seemed a waste. Such an unnecessary item now serves as a memento. He likes the deep blue color and rectangular cut of the stone. The left side pictures a wildlife scene with his name engraved above in capital gold letters. Opposite, he had chosen the symbol for education, a shield divided into four quadrants displaying a torch.

Inside the band is his signature. He'd wanted to order the male's ring—wishes he had—but mother persuaded him that the sheer size of it on his soft, delicate hand would be overstated. He does not wear the ring after that night. Wearing it had never been the point. It was a memory. A keepsake.

Ms. Garlow looks up. Caught, Westcott withdraws from the railing. He sees Ellis approach. For three-and-a-half hours they move back and forth between ballroom and reception area. Never dancing.

As is customary, a slow song brings the night to a close. Westcott rises from the red clothed chair, having sat for the first time that entire evening. He proceeds with Ellis onto the dance floor. She instructs him to put his hands on her waist. His face blushes; he laughs giddily. Not at dancing, but the fact that he is attempting to dance with his *sister* while Mrs. T and Mrs. Hutchens are there to watch. Westcott hears Aerosmith's words, "I don't want to fall asleep 'cause I'm missin' you—" He doesn't like the song. Feeling his heart pound, half praying the lyrics will end yet wishing he could go back to 8 o'clock again, he is strangely sad. All the couples in the room cling to each other, lost in the blind love of youth. The idea that some will make love on this night never enters his mind. At 18 he possesses no sexual desires. Westcott finds himself somewhat sickened by their hanging on one another—their neediness. In a way he is glad to be with his sister, but the pangs of separateness, difference, are cause to envy such innocent affections. He is always an objective party looking in. He feels old for his age. He looks upon his peers as an elder spectator, shaking his head in disdain at the music they listen to, their falling over each other in the school hallways, and their boisterous inclinations. He is ancient, emotionally miles away. Socially, they have the protection of each other.

All the way home Westcott tries to dissemble the pain tearing through him. He peers out the window at a low sheet of heavy fog rolling in over a ravine, the clouds a solid sheet of white, strangely luminescent beneath the absent moonlight. The ground has transformed into a bottomless haze, an abyss the color of watered down milk. Trees on the hillside appear suspended, levitated in mid-air. *Perhaps Puck is light of foot this night, out gallivanting about the fringes of illusion and reality, mischief within the forest.*

Westcott and his sister enter their mother's room, switching on the light. She has yet to fall asleep, waiting, he knows, to ask them.

'How was it?'

'Good,' he says complacently.

'I even got my bro' to dance. You should have seen those moves.'

'Hardly.'

'Didn't you stop at the theater?'

'We drove by, but he didn't want to see anything.'

'There wasn't anything playing that interested me.'

He starts to turn away; he can't fight it any longer.

'You all right, West?'

'Yes, I'm…fine.' Standing in the doorway, resting his palm on the handle, Ellis saves him.

'Hey, you want to go to IHOP?' She is unaware of the escape she has afforded.

He hesitates for a moment, not knowing what he wants. The thought of going to bed, lying awake in the dark and quiet night with only himself to hear is more than he—

'C'mon Westie-poo,' she coaxes, trying to liven him up.

'I guess so.'

Walking down the hall, his strength gives way. He begins to visibly cry. Very slowly, with a sense of nostalgia and precise care, he takes off his coat, the bow tie, and his shoes. He hangs the rented tux back on its hanger, cherishing the items as a widow would the belongings of her deceased spouse, or a mother who's lost a child, taking in the scent, studying every detail of her child's favorite stuffed toy. He does not want to forget.

After pulling on a loose pair of jeans and his beloved red and white shirt, they leave for yet another dinner, or what one might call an unusually early breakfast. As would be expected at half past one in the morning, the restaurant is catering to only a few customers. Westcott orders a club sandwich. He watches Ellis pick at her ham and cheese omelet. For the first time he feels tired and so the bill is quickly paid, the meals packed up.

Ellis goes upstairs leaving Westcott to himself in the dim kitchen. He places the boxes in the refrigerator, steps to the back door, gazing out at the chilled moon.

Lying in bed, he dreads waking. He thinks about Government class and how maybe if he fails they'd let him stay another year. He knows such a scheme is far-fetched; he can't fail.

Resting on his back, staring at the picture on the wall, he contemplates killing himself. Hanging is out of the question and he doesn't have access to any gun; pills seem the most practical option. Ideally carbon monoxide would be the least painful method. He prefers to end his life away from home, beneath the open sky; a running car in the garage wouldn't do. He'd clog his tailpipe. By the time anyone found him his heart would have stopped.

He sifts over the details, pondering what to say in the suicide letter. He'll leave a list of people he wishes to be at the funeral, a choice few his family might overlook. Before leaving, the Civil War calendar tacked up to the right of his desk will be taken down. Turning the pages ever so slowly, he'll study the pictures and their captions, seeing all that the future months hold. His solitary medium of anticipation still remaining, will be obliterated. The tuppence of hope distilled by his waiting to flip the leaflets and the certain delight anticipated by a scene he has never laid eyes on will be instantly effaced from spirit.

He shifts to his side, resigned. Suicide is not possible. The taking of one's life is never condoned by any religion, lest it be for honour. He possesses a mild approach to religion, reserved in attitude, embracing a myriad of beliefs with the natural world as his chapel.

The muffled pattering of rain atop the roof rouses him from sound sleep. Through the orange slice window to his left, his mood displays itself in the sky and forecast. He is perfectly still, lulled by the crackling echo of rain running down the grooves of the eaves, bypassing the gutter, and splattering onto the driveway. Again he faces the debate which emotional exhaustion—a few hours ago—had left unresolved. A debate which is to become an endless tyrant over him. Westcott throws the covers aside, rises. If nothing else, perhaps disliking something familiar, such as life, is better than confronting the unknown.

~

The following Tuesday Westcott finds himself entertaining his customary pastime of staring out the window. Outside the essence of spring permeates the air; a warm breeze triggers a wave of flapping, synonymous with a dolphin waving its flipper. Throughout the newly bloomed foliage, the leaves whip up and down like a stack of papers flipping rhythmically before a table fan. It occurs to him then that his 2x3 window on the world should be open on such a splendid afternoon. It isn't his room to restructure; he does not bother to assert his desires. The dimness and awkward silence within the trailer stir his unconscious fatigue. There are two others in the makeshift classroom. Together they wait. Westcott assumes his taciturn trance. Reanne speaks. Her comments are idle conversation, rhetorical in nature. Then something brings him back inside, his attention snaps to the board; his eyes abandon their post on the window and forest beyond.

'I can't believe it's already the 20th!' Reanne's voice mumbles, foggy, spit-lisped.

'Humph,' he acknowledges, glancing at Ms. Garlow's hand-painted clock of Stonehenge that has gently rested on the bookshelf for a year, still waiting on end to be hung. Reanne adjusts her glasses. Andrew has long hair, to his shoulders. He sucks his lips in, drawing on air to form a high-pitched squeak; a habit that seems to coincide with the appearance of a mouse some six months earlier, a mouse that took up residence in the musty classroom.

'I don't want the year to end...' Reanne's voice trails off. A door slams heavily from across the back parking lot housing the Driver's Ed and custodial vehicles. All stop to catch themselves instinctively. Westcott has just been impaled by a bolt of realization and is deep in thought. He studies the upper left hand corner of the eraser board. Scrolled in blue marker he reads: May 20th, 200—. He traces the date over and over with his eyes. The numbers curve in such a way as to smile easily at him, almost mocking. Nothing harsh, belligerent, or obtuse in their strokes as sometimes displayed by a 7, 9, or 5. They arch gently and yet he does not share their joyous qualities. Between them he sees a clock ticking away. He glances at Reanne. A comrade in his nostalgia. Ms. Garlow's footsteps are audible on the ramp leading into the trailer. Westcott looks once more at the date. A silent absolution of inevitability. The pit in his stomach bobs up and down once, a gastro-swallowing.

He does not know what the others received; in his hand he holds a copy of *The Last Unicorn. What are you saying?* He silently questions Ms. Garlow. He isn't one for the fanciful— he won't say anything. It is a gift; a kind gesture on behalf of Ms. Garlow. A different book for each of them. Three odd-balls. The Lit Mag's most dedicated attendees. A girl. A boy. And something else. *Does a unicorn choose to be a unicorn?* She is not born with the horn, but the memory of something presses—she is free when the truth of what she possesses penetrates the world.

JUNE

I'm in a payphone booth at the Salt Lake City Airport, Utah. I just finished some chicken tenders from Burger King. As I sat alone, there were two other men—one probably in his fifties another in his forties—each at their own table. The three of us giving attention to the task at hand—eating. None of us had diversion; no newspapers, cell phones. It was comical yet sadly illuminating. Three 'men' all waiting in this *place*, all going about their business—a weigh station. No one talking. A little boy was playing—he traced the engraved letters on the garbage door pushing it open. His older brother—around six, came over—asked him, 'You know what that says?' So strange—the stages of us—human life, each represented in that moment.

I felt forced to eat all my chicken since I'd paid for it. The tenders were stale on the ends. And here I am, the tarmac to my left, the night skies deeply blue, the lights from the runways. Here I am tucked away in my booth.

I see us all marking time, it's especially clear in an airport—the comings and goings—I look around hoping to make contact, establish recognition with another solitary observer. No one's paying attention. They're asleep or looking at a screen. They have music piped into their ears. No one is talking *to* each other. Was it a pointless trip? Not entirely. Damn, this wooden bench is hard on the rear. That and my stomach's bothering me—bowels all cemented, pain in the side. I don't belong any place. *Pretty Woman* just came on and is playing softly through the terminals and bi-ways amid the scrape of chairs, footsteps, luggage rolling, the dull vrrrrb of jets. But others prefer their own private music; they don't wish to share anything with those around them. Music on top of music. Most have earphones to block out the world. I like *Pretty Woman*.

I imagine, I feel I am that deep, soft, steady troll you hear returning to your cabin aboard a large cruise liner. The room is safe, the sound slightly subdued, the lights not harsh on the eyes. The feel of cool sheets after the open sea breeze. And underneath it, as though sleep itself, the bhhhrrr—rhythmic troll of the engines within the deep hull of the vessel. I know the sound and in becoming the sound it is a comfort. I sometimes allow myself to imagine, one day, lying down beside Regn, pulling her backside into my chest, holding her body through a night, feeling her *without* the twinge of pain. It's peace I want with her. That peace has no timeline.

I just looked at the telephone—the going rate is 4 minutes for a dollar. My flight doesn't take off for another three hours. I have no one to call—well, I do, but what's to say? I'm reading a book. *Stealing Athena*. A good read. My eyes need a rest, and to just sit still hours on end is enough to drive anyone mad. I can talk to the characters but they don't respond.

I sometimes consider being pregnant. The prospect of delivery is erotic to me—painful no doubt. I almost want it as a form of self-punishment—to endure.

I'm getting tired—all the artificial ingredients in what I ate. Artificial. Is anything real anymore? I feel detached, and to face the hours this weekend all day at work—. I am not looking forward to the return.

The visit in California was good until the last two days. Tension builds anytime the three of us—Ellis, my father, and I *or* me, mother, and Ellis are together. With Dad, Ellis takes over. She dominates the conversation on all accounts. In the case of mother, I sometimes feel I have to choose sides; Ellis or her. One afternoon in Sunnyvale I was driving with my father in his old truck—the same one he'd bought when he was still married to Mother—the four-door white Ford with the cranberry stripe. He now calls it, "The Beastie," it's so broken in. We were alone talking and he asked if I'd met anyone or had some relationship. I wanted someone to tell, I needed a witness. The things Regn and I had done, experienced, weren't just wonderful. They were ineffable and yet, I wanted validation, that yes, something *had* happened. I blurted out, 'I made love to a woman in the out-of-doors.'

My father was glad to hear it, but I could not give the extra details I so eagerly wished to—I wanted to tell someone how I felt. Why did something so wonderful have to be a secret? I wasn't ashamed. I was frustrated. My mind conjured the feel of Regn's smooth hillock, the feel of her body compressing mine, clothed, but exposed to the world in lying on the forest floor.

• • •

Exhausted having flown all night. Delivered picture to *This Century Art Gallery*. Went into work at 4:30 p.m. A zombie. Mother stopped by and brought dinner—the lady I work with finally left so Mother could bring in the meal for us to eat.

• • •

It's about to storm. Someone is playing the piano down the hall. I dare not think of the 5 1/2 hours of solitude remaining. Why contest what I must endure? I am perturbed though worried about Regn. Having passed each other on the road yesterday, there has been no word from her.

Regn came shortly after five. It was as I'd suspected. She was on register five yesterday, she couldn't access her email until the end of the day. A phone call at lunch or something would have been nice, I thought to myself. 'You could have left a message,' I said. I opened the door for her to come into the office. She sat at the empty desk. My legs started to tremble. We started so rigid, formal. I gave way—it never fails; all the restraint breaks down. There she was stoic and composed, while I struggled to fight the sorrow from overspilling. She eased up a little. We stepped into the back office. She always pushes her tongue inside me, I never have to invite it. As I held her I knew she was still *there*, with me, but so much is happening in her life. She didn't have time to miss me, she said. 'I do love you, even if you don't believe it,' she assured.

I picked her up, scooping her legs under my left arm. She wore brown pants, short at the ankle, sandals, and a white cotton shirt with her ivory dragon pendant. Yesterday she'd gone to Waller Mill Park alone with Tamerlane "Laney"—the little dog she and Jay found abandoned. They took her in, gave her a home. 'We will get another chance,' she said with conviction, 'but my granddaughter is here this week. You have to meet Laney.'

'I want to keep myself pure for you.'

She took me close and replied, 'If something comes along don't pass it by. Be good to yourself.'

'I demand so much, expect too much of myself.'

'No one can take away what we have. We had some wonderful times.'

'I believe we will again.'

'If there's ever a chance—'

'Never stop wanting it.'

'I don't,' she said.

I walked her out of the lobby; told her to have a safe and good trip, stop by the gallery with Rebecca and see my picture. I went back inside and waited for her to get in her bug and pull out.

...

I wore the same shirt as yesterday. I'd chosen it for Regn. She didn't come. The olive green one with a navy blue undershirt. It's a good color combination on me. I waited 'til a little after three seeing if she'd be first to make contact. Nothing. No phone call. I had to know. I sent an email. She was at Yorktown and replied to my note. 'Sorry I can't make it by this evening.' It was terse, perfunctory.

I had plans that evening to meet with a former colleague, Juliette, from the veterinary hospital. It would be good to talk to someone. Regn had Rose Marie to exchange conversation with all day—she still had her friends at work. I had the silence. About 5:20 I went to the restroom. I was in no particular hurry—I had another hour to kill. I used the facilities, straightened my shirt while studying myself in the dimly lit bathroom mirror. I was thinking about the evening. Guilt fisted itself in my gut. I didn't like the idea of spending time with other women. I had the right; Regn didn't expect me to hold myself for her. I expected it of myself, even if the company was purely casual. I was tired and hurt. Sad. Stepping from the restroom I replaced the key on its hook outside the door. An elderly patient walked by mirroring my placid state. There, at the end of the hall, someone was standing. I narrowed my eyes to see better. Was it true? She was in her white Volkswagen cap, sunglasses, blue shirt and khaki pants. I lost all train of thought. I didn't let myself hope she would come, gauging by our conversation the day before. And now here she was.

I led her into the office. 'You're persistent,' she said.

'But you came.'

'I'm a mystery to myself.' She put her hand on my jawline.

'Please don't regret coming.'

'I don't, but I can't see you if it involves a blatant lie.'

'I don't make the terms, Regn. You know if we are ever to see each other that's how it is right now.'

She was under immense stress—she would be going down to Norfolk for her citizen's exam the next day. In all her years as a legalized alien she'd never applied for citizenship. Jay wanted her to, especially should something happen to him. I walked Regn out. No one sat in the rocking chairs under the portico. Her gait was quick as she cut across the parking lot. I felt, I knew, it was not only because of the time and getting home without having to make an excuse. She was running from me—from the way she felt. I was guilty having been in the restroom considering the evening with Juliette and then walking out to see Regn standing there. I wanted it to be her that evening.

~

Juliette and I walked in Colonial Williamsburg. The night was sultry, I still had on my burgundy dress shirt and slacks. We watched the fireflies over a bed of flowers. Juliette put both her hands on my shoulders in an instructive manner, casual, nothing improper, showing me something. 'Look!' We sat on a bench—it was a full moon. We sat in the dark beneath a giant tree, hidden from the world, a little colonial house softly aglow with lamp-light. I kept thinking of Regn. I wished she could see this beautiful night. I wanted to sit beside her in the quiet shadows. I reminded myself to try to be present. Juliette deserved my attention. She was well-read, great with language and spelling, interesting. She only liked old men, like Christopher Plummer, or famous figures who were dead, safe, untouchable. Alexander Hamilton for instance. She said I reminded her of Little Man Tate. Juliette was 38. To hear her speak you'd think she was in her early 20s. Her appearance was a less attractive, hardened Jane Hirschfield. We looked in the window of Williams and Sonoma, the same store I'd stepped into last December, Regn radiant in her attire. 6 months ago. It should have been our evening. I felt I was deceiving my Lady. I realized then what she must feel concerning Jay. How can I expect her to lie, when I can't tolerate doing it myself? Regn doesn't have a choice. She's married. I do. I don't ever want to feel torn. Yet however casual the meeting, between Juliette and me or any other woman, I felt I was cheating. Socializing is always intimate.

There was a message on my telephone. Regn had called on her excursion to Norfolk. I expected being with Jay that morning there was little chance she'd call. I was overjoyed she had of her own will. Where was she and where was he when she did call me? 'It went well, I'm glad it's over, I'll tell you all about it. Have a good day.' I wish I could have gone with her—stopped at the Botanical Gardens, had lunch at the Heritage Café. Her message cheered me.

• • •

'Good night and don't forget to write!' The old woman laughs.

On duty I talk to Ms. Smith. Turns out she is from Bremen, Germany, still humming her little tune. Anytime a guest leaves, whether or not they respond, she bids them, 'Good night and don't forget to write. One day I might just wake up dead,' she says.

She offers more than my coworkers whom I seldom see since I'm alone during the evening and weekend shifts. There are moments when Ms. Smith is present and then sitting in the lobby, always with the appearance of waiting—waiting for someone who will never come—she'll mentally disappear, and the tape reruns.

'You work here, right?'

Oh brother. I answer politely, 'Yes.'

• • •

Swung by Wendy's. The same guy I went to school with, Michael, was working at the window. He's been at the same job six years. We were in Mrs. Sparroh's drawing class senior year. He never wanted to do any work, mostly sat, making excuses, dabbling here and there. To think this is what he is still doing. He's dedicated, very polite. I'll give him that. It made me feel much better. Things could be worse. I have to keep this in mind for those moments of weakness when the depression or sadness unleashes itself. *Now that's depressing. How can he stand it? Day in day out, passing bags through windows.* I wonder if he recognized me. I ate in my truck—dashboard dining they call it—enjoying the grilled chicken sandwich, savoring the freedom of being outside, not closed away in a tiny cubicle of an office.

Regn's swearing-in for citizenship was scheduled for 2:00 p.m. Why did she tell me if she knew Jay would be there and I couldn't attend? I would later learn, when Regn showed me an attractive pendant, a congratulatory gift, that Magda had been there in support, as had Jay.

If it was raining, which it had been all morning, the proceedings would be held indoors. But now the sun was out, the streets dry; I was sweating in my jacket.

The proceedings were conducted in the Old, single building courthouse on Duke of Gloucester Street. The Historic Courthouse. I waited outside. Five minutes later I saw Regn in her strong sure-footed stride coming down the courthouse steps, a yellow envelope in hand. She wore a lively skirt with a mild pattern, Tuscan and summer like, and a peach-colored blouse. I had on sunglasses and a baseball cap, incognito should Jay be close by. There was no reason for Regn to look over or even notice me. As she walked in my direction, as though she knew she was being watched, she looked over. I nodded; she partially waved. A fair distance passed before I followed. Still she did not stop, crossing the street in her refined step, much quicker than the ambling bustle of tourists. She was picturesque with the sun out and the lilt and air of her facade of confidence, her skirt elegant with each determined step. I stayed on the opposite side of the street keeping a watch on her vibrant blouse so as not to lose her in the distance. But she was too far already and then she turned the corner. She did not so much as glance over her shoulder. Pressed for time, she did not look back. When I arrived to the same place I saw her way down the road heading to the parking lot. In that brief second of passing, watching her briskly trail away—that ever increasing distance between us, I felt the heavy sorrow. I held that image of her crossing the antiquated street, in step to her own beautiful time and forever walking away.

The afternoon haunted me.

I wanted my Lady to be there with me—to walk side-by-side, even if the world would not see us or condone us as a couple. I wanted the one person to be there who I could quietly sit next to in some obscure shade.

It was so nice having had the day off and not going into work that evening. I was greatly disappointed by the opening show at The Art Gallery. I'd anticipated seeing my picture displayed with all the other members'. Mother and I went upstairs first. Up the landing I turned right and scanned the walls. Nothing. I looked in the small hall with the black back-drop. And then the little room just off of it. I was mortified, absolutely disheartened to see "Her resting Place" displayed at knee-level beneath a loud purple and orange oil painting. It was just stuck there, as though they'd run out of room. Here was my 18x24 sepia photograph clashing with these colors. There were beautiful paintings around, but my picture did not belong in this genre.

It needed to be at eye level. It was a letdown to an already hurtful afternoon. At that very moment Regn was either heading to, or just arriving at, the Shenandoah with Rebecca.

I was foolish and like a typical man wanting to kill something inside. I went out that same evening. A part of me wanted sex at any price, another part was too deflated. I disclosed my most personal knowledge, of what I am to Juliette. It was only our second walk together. She took the knowledge almost like Sméagol in *Lord of the Rings*. Immediately I regretted saying anything. I only saw the first film in the series. I'd fallen asleep in it, but I clearly remembered Sméagol. Juliette received the information, squirreling it away like some precious gem of a secret, smiling and thanking me. She listened, then began rocking back and forth on her heels. We'd been sitting in a field. I was mildly disturbed, picturing her in a straitjacket. But I didn't care if I hurt myself. I wanted something. To be taken and brought down? There wasn't going to be any sex and all the better as I began to see as the night wore on that Juliette had problems and took medication. Besides, had something ensued, guilt would have consumed me.

I'd held myself so long in reserve. I feared given the right opportunity the flood-gates would open and I'd act on my physical needs. Not in spite to Regn, but from sheer unquenchable loneliness. Even though my body suffered its desires, I knew sex was not the answer. I still needed it, but somehow I knew in the absence of true affection and with a stranger, it would not work. I was safer and better off having myself.

A LIGHT DUSTING of harmless powder, talcum-like; a diabolical mouth, thinly grinning its dahlia grin—the long slits of metted, stainless steel depressors. It even has a style name—there are different types, and logically, various sizes. How simplistic a device yet masterfully engineered, articulating vulnerability, foreboding anxiety, depraved scrutiny. Quite imaginative really, a backless throat, the 'O' of observation. Looking out from the back, applying mild pressure, looking in. Curtains folded. A slender slip through the black thread—darkness spreads. A tilt of the shoulder clockwise, the curtain falling round procedure's shape. The director pushes himself up from his seat, thoughtful of critique. Halts. Rolls his pencil between thumb and index. Pressure of delay, pressure of what he expects him to say. The director opens his mouth slowly, yawning, holding his yawn. He exhales for him. In that moment he can't remember his lines. He pantomimes in silence, the directives sound so far away, though they fill him, raise him, dictate his role, his place, his purpose. The curtain stretches, parts yet. He bows, dew of flowers, gently pressed upon the stage. Thornless stem, nameless stream, a single rose viewed between two feet. His two feet.

He looks in the mirror that looks inside of him. Now he knows. Beautifully revolting. *I never knew a more pleasurable sex than with myself.*

• • •

18 June 20—

A young man is pacing. He wears navy blue slacks, Puritan brand purchased for $14.00 at Wal-Mart. His long sleeved olive green dress shirt is tucked within the proper fitting pants. His shoes are a leather brown; they quite nicely, but unintentionally, match his belt. The same belt he's worn for five years. A navy blue elastic band, leather on the fastening ends, and a small tarnished gold buckle. Very modest. His appearance is clean. His dress and manner formal. He is pacing up and down the leaf-carpeted hallway, hands occasionally akimbo. His pants are strangling him, riding up onto his waist. He pulls at the pockets to slacken them around his waist. He is as thin as a zipper. Dark brown hair, pale skin of an

Irish complexion, blue-gray eyes—of a brooding storm. He is pacing. He paces not merely to pace the time, but for the pure sensation of going somewhere. His frontal lobe feels like the zeppelin shaped weights attached to fishing lines, pulling, submerging themselves into greater depths of obscurity. The monotony wins every time. He is trying to keep busy. He is paid to fill time. It is no easy task to others who would argue otherwise.

He'd washed his detachable part in watermelon scented soap. His drawers strangle him; his artificial sex is uncomfortable, moderate. Sometimes he forgets it is even there—.

He wants to make love again. No, he wants to be made love to—have her undress him; a body compressing his own, his sistered limbs white in their silent and untouched trembling, slowly pushed out so as to look in. The landscape is dark, mysterious. It cries to the touch—barely wet at first. He yearns for a hard rain.

He turns from such thoughts and paces another length. At the end of the hall a hunched body shuffles perpendicular down the wing, supported by her walker. It is like passing in slow motion. He sees himself in this woman—it frightens him because his sadness devastates.

He's too young in body to be so old in mind. He's too tired in mind to be so wanting in body.

Elinor Davis said to him the other day, through the small window into his office, 'Old people like to get things in the mail.'

Indeed they do; the element of a singular surprise. Does that mean I'm old? I love letters in the mail.

The other day when he got back from Trader Joe's, his mother asked, 'How much was it?'

'Half a century,' he replied. It had cost him half a century.

He knew she meant the staple items. He was somewhere else. He looked through her, around her. He felt sorry, but he was long gone. Beyond her reach.

Westcott?

Yes, my Lady?

· · ·

I must try to make use of the time—though the isolating hours of the present job are tasking. Idleness is more exhausting than being busy. The front door in the lobby is obnoxious. Anytime someone enters or exits it slams with a heavy jank of metal gears. Nothing delicate—very irritating. I always make a point of closing it softly. It's a jolt to the senses when everything else is so still and quiet here.

The wind is beautiful today. And because of it the temperature is not as hot as yesterday, that and the sky is a haze; a degree higher in brightness and it would surely pain the unprotected eyes.

I come to work for no one.

It occurred to me while reading that the woman is created to give, whereas man takes. One might think by coming inside a woman he is giving to her; it is the opposite. The woman gives of her body to be taken. I miss that—I don't want to be the one making love—for once I want to be made love to. I confess it here to the confidence of silent words—I had always been afraid to let myself be loved in that respect. Regn slipped inside me once, but that I could be loved as I have loved her—completely exposed, shameless—to lie there as she has, atop the covers unafraid. To have the intimacy I withheld from myself. These thoughts are a chimera, endlessly circling back. No resolution, no alleviation. Tic marks on the granite wall. Waiting, planning, seeking an escape. I was talking to one of the residents. Gertrude Smith.

'You live here, right? You're 24? I'd like to be 24 again.'

'And what would you do?' I said.

'I don't know, marry someone else.'

She ran a restaurant while living in Germany. There will be a few seconds of clarity in conversation followed by long silence as she looks out the front windows, spills a packet of sugar on her lap, and then relapses. 'You live here, right? You live with your mother?' All of a sudden she'll throw her pink shawl over the handlebars of her walker, stand and shuffle away, humming softly. 'See you later, alligator,' she said for no particular reason this time. 'After a while crocodile,' I called to her back. I engaged in a long conversation with Elinor Davis. She has four children, not one will take her in. She consoles herself by saying, 'Oh they're good, they do things for me, but it hurts.' I know she's afraid to stand up to them—what choice has she? She was talking of riding a horse again—she could do it; if she were my mother I'd make it a point to let her ride once more in this life. Makes me think of the line in *Stealing Athena:* "Strange where we all end our days."

• • •

I had myself. There is a difference between masturbation and having oneself. The latter involves true intercourse. I didn't need it, but I'd been reading a book, *The Changeling of Finnistuath.* Certain passages were arousing and lingered in mind.

I undressed and stood in front of the mirror. My untoned nethers jiggled when I walked—the loose flesh of a P.O.W. I flexed my legs. *That's better.* I wasn't afraid to look at myself down there. My scarred chest, but a woman's body. In the shower I stood back so the head would spout water at the precise location desired. I washed up with soap—to be clean beforehand. It was a quick shower. As I dried I felt myself getting wet by my own presence, facing my clothes-less skin. I went into the empty room and lay down on the sleeping bag and towels. My head rested on pillows beneath the windows. I took my time. I was some-where else. I felt tentatively with the tip of my finger to ready for larger penetration. I'd bled lately, my hormone levels askew. Stress does it sometimes, even in spite of the testosterone injections, the hormone levels are a rollercoaster. I began to think I wasn't feeling erotically inclined, but it had been quite a while. I wanted *something* inside me, something to fill the emptiness. I rolled the lubricated prophylactic on the hardened phallus, placing its head between my legs. I pushed gently, wondering if I was in fact still physically considered a virgin—always gentle with myself—taking time until my body was accepting. Were a true penis with thrust to come inside in one ardent push, would it not rip me open?

I felt a sting in the threshold, it gave way and slid further, the slight discomfort a reverse pleasure. I pushed deeper, withdrawing and sliding to get used to its presence until it filled me. Then I pushed harder. How did it compare with a true erection? I bent my knees, I extended them flat and moved onto my side to comfort myself, withdrawing almost completely and then pushing, trying different angles. My pelvis, innately rhythmic, was like a step pedal one depresses automatically while at the loom, a seamstress and the old sewing machines.

I sat up, a rod lodged within, watched it pulled by gravity from my body. I gazed up at the sky, the few clouds, briefly at peace with just myself. Who was I hurting? Why be ashamed? I pulled a chair down on top of me—held *him* close against my chest. Hard contour of legs. I was not afraid of myself, to lie there openly with myself, and I began to think one can only know himself this way—to be alone.

Could another body please me, as I knew? Would I let her? It's not sex I wanted with another. I missed physical company—*to be held* as I was entered upon and held after, as any woman desires. I am a woman, but live as a man. How strange.

After coming twice—the second time more powerfully with the firm member removed, allowing for an open passage, free to constrict and contract in blissful spasm—I was exhausted, bored with sexual inclinations.

~

It is Wednesday. I'm writing about my physical forays with Self and here comes Gertrude Smith again. She walked by earlier. On her way back to her room I say, 'Did you get your hair cut?'

'Hmm?'

'Did you get your hair cut?'

From the expression in her eyes, I know no one has complimented or noticed her in a long time.

'Yes, does it look good?'

'Yes.' And it does.

• • •

Thursday 25 June 20—

Gertrude sat in the lobby again. She'd rolled by, several times and each time, 'How long are you here? You work 'til eight, no?' When a person born in another country learns to speak English and asks a yes or no question, he or she always ends it with, 'no?' I find it endearing.

She wore a light silk nightgown with a postcard pattern. She asked for my name though I wear a badge and have been here a month. I asked her middle name. 'Anna. Gertrude Anna Smith.' She pronounced it with her German accent, Schmidt.

I spoke a few words in German to her. '*Guten Abend, Frau Schmidt. Wie geht es einen?*'

She pointed out my beard. 'You have lots of hair. You shave?' Then she raised herself in the chair and broke wind. All of a sudden she decides to go to bed. I tell her I have to mow the lawn when I get home. 'Don't work too hard.' She pushes her walker down the hall leaving as abruptly as she'd come. Ever searching the hallways of her mind.

• • •

Friday 26 June 20—

I'm wiped. 2:25 Regn calls. She is on her way to Waller Mill Park. I head out, manage to get there before her. It's been so long since we've had time to take a walk. Regn parked near the entrance. She had on capris pants, and as she calls it her baby blue tank top. It looked so good against her tan skin and rich hair. Tamerlane "Laney" is very tiny, smaller than Liam, cute. A tea pot poodle, not frou-frou or anything, just petite and sweet. I picked Laney up and pet her. For a fleeting moment looking at Regn and Laney, her skin free to breathe while I shrouded myself in jeans and a long sleeved shirt—seeing her so content with herself—I imagined she truly was free. For a moment I saw us there together as though she were a free woman and we could share each other's company without pain. Such a thought was so happy and yet I dared not consider it long—it quickly flew. Why did it have to be this way, if only she weren't—. I pushed the thought away determined to enjoy the time we had. It was good to be somewhere isolated, no colleagues or ears to hide from. We took a small trail and wrapped around.

Regn pulled a raspberry from a bush. There were blackberries as well. 'Too sweet,' she said. I saw some tree stumps—two in the shape of chairs. I'd have to get a picture of those. We walked past the swing set. I stared off towards the baseball diamond remembering that fall evening so long ago—it had been very cold and we'd sat on the bench beside one another. I'd struggled to disclose the truth about myself, still unsure, and we'd walked down the same path we took this afternoon. Regn had turned to me then, we'd hugged, and she'd said, 'You can tell me anything if you want to.' It was like old times again today. We were stilted, argued a bit, then calm with each other. We sat on a bench just before leaving. Regn gently touched my face and let the tension go from her, pulling me close. Then we walked across the bridge, to live somehow.

Regn would have kept on walking; I had to be into work by 4:30. I wanted to stay.

Standing by her car, having loaded Laney in and given her water, I took a sip from Regn's water. 'I gotta go,' I said. 'Now you're saying it.' She smiled. We hugged, she came to me and kissed—though people in the dog park could see us. It felt good being open. For a split moment I imagined, I pretended she was free.

I must be careful not to relish the time too much or I'll make myself depressed or fidgety with want for more time. I am grateful to have had the afternoon. I must try and look forward to the next time—though we cannot say when that will be.

Elinor gave me a deck of cards this evening. I brought Miss Gilly to work with me. She stayed in the office for an hour after Mother came by.

I don't mind talking to Elinor, but sometimes the idle chatter wears on me, especially when I'm already drained. I know she is lonely. It made her day to see and pet Gilly.

· · ·

Saturday 27 June 20—

It's only ten and already I am afraid. I don't say anything to anyone, not mother anyways, but from the minute I awake a sickness takes hold of my stomach, a sickness of worry. I do not speak about these things to anyone. To talk about what can't be changed or helped only serves to frustrate more. I must find something within myself to counter the fear. I must depend upon myself for comfort, or any peace to be had. This morning getting into my truck I saw the bed was filled with petals from the blooming crepe myrtle. Taking Gilly out the early wind felt tranquil—how I wanted the whole day off—to leisurely take a bike ride. I will one day long for these days of work when I have time enough—too much time to do as

I please and yet now it seems a burden trying to keep busy. Never a balance.

At times I'm afraid to be alone within myself, knowing the sorrow can easily come in the silence of just myself. Other times I feel the only solace to be found is in just being with myself, for when I am around others there is a distance, as though I am always somewhere else, which could be true. It's Saturday and I can't run from myself, though I'd like to go somewhere.

I think of that line in the book I just finished, *The Changeling of Finnistuath*. She is afraid of the grief. And yet, another character tells Gray—you are continuing to live in spite of it. I eat, sleep, bathe, clean the house, work. A lady just came in with bright green hair. I wish I could enjoy the summer. I am afraid of my own sadness.

My body is a battleground; there can be no peace when it is occupied by opposing forces. And when the male tendencies kick in a part of me is conscious of this. I fear I am not a male trapped in the wrong body, rather I am both and I have not the freedom to live one way or the other. I try very hard to remove myself from the typical needs of a body. I know I am loved by a select few, but the irony of it is sometimes I just want to feel the 'contact' of love. I can satisfy myself with little shame knowing I am not hurting anyone by being alone. It is not love though that I give to myself, it is sex, as detached as the organ of delivery I may hold, virgin to the touch of a true erection.

THE FREEDOM *of your own skin, I cherish how easily you embrace yourself. What was I to begin with? Could I have endured as a woman? I do not regret my surgeries or course of action but sometimes I wish I'd experienced things first as a woman. I never was a woman, Regn. It's all too much to think about, I wish it could be straightforward. I don't want to explain anymore. I'm tired of hiding what I am.*

I must find solace in knowing that within this skin is a consciousness to be freed one day. In the absence of ejaculation I often cry upon having myself as though one liquid substance must serve for the other. Pain is my comfort, I sleep beside Her and were she not there I'd be lost without Her. I think of this not in vulgarity but want to know myself. I am not a man sexually frustrated, but a woman in tempered longing, as it were, for as I once laid a hand to you, I am no longer afraid to want it for myself.

~

He combed back the full coarse hair with his fingers and holding his hands in an upside down V, used both indexes to press the tiny engorged flap into view. It appeared very much like the armrest of a wingback chair, that is if you are looking at the curled arm and inner arched stitching face forward. By all aesthetics it was a miniature penis with no capability of penetration. The head was erect, and fully exposed it was maybe an inch and a half in height. A balled knob, a bud-like eye of skin sat in the head of the two folds. To think something so small, if searched out slowly and patiently, could send a shudder of rocketing ecstasy the entire lateral length of the body, exploding within the frontal lobe, a calm lake of temporary release mixed with everlasting remorse. Not remorse of shame, but the constant reminder. The private knowledge that this wasn't what he needed.

~

Sometimes I feel if I just keep writing and don't stop I'll be all right. I took an hour-and-a-half lunch break. Mother picked me up. We went to the diner. It was delicious. She had the open faced turkey and I ordered the pork BBQ sandwich. It is 3:35 and damn quiet. Why did I bother coming back to work? The limbo of everything is taking its toll and I'm exhausted. I cannot be calm, I just want to throw up. I eat and things go right through me. But enough about that. I try to focus on what things bring me pleasure, however small. No one said life was happy or supposed to be fun. It's that old adage—who ever said life was fair? I'm just overcome with sadness and the prospect of a *career* seems daunting. I keep going though, what choice have I? Heck, if I had my bike I'd take it to the Island and come back in an hour. There's no point in my being here at this job. What good is it to complain?

~

Well, I just got back from the Settlement. I think the phone rang only twice today. Each time the voice on the other end asked to be transferred to such-and-such Wing. If I don't pick up it automatically is relayed. So what's the point? I'm just a middle-man. Yes I'm getting paid, but God, let me do something productive! I left for an hour again. It was about 4:10. When I arrived to the Settlement Regn was on register 4 and Sharon behind her at 5. Regn occasionally fills in downstairs on the weekends. Eva and Tillie were on the main desk. I tried to act nonchalant; I over-compensated. I was glad to see the Supervisors weren't in. Conversation was polite, superficial, filler, a re-hash of the same-old-same-old, but it was good talking with them again, good to hear another voice, engage, interact. True, I went because I wanted to see Regn, but the Settlement is a comfort in another way. I missed it, though I can see politics have only digressed and the morale is as bad as ever. I forgot they close at 6—they're on summer hours—starting June 15th. I quickly went down to the rotunda and spent a legitimate amount of time in the upstairs exhibit. It didn't interest me, but I couldn't make it obvious that I came for no reason other than to see Regn and something to fill time. My phone rang. I was nervous. I considered it might be Regn, but assumed otherwise. We'd just seen each other. Why would she call? It was Juliette returning my message. I knew I was on camera, I spoke casually, feigning interest in the exhibit.

I stepped to the restroom where so often I used to go and break down. Standing in the dim and close museum I realized I was running from myself—I wanted more in life; it's too small and quiet. I've lived old so long. I was sad, so very sad as I looked upon the four glass and wood encasements holding parchments and literary documents. For all the grief—a job with no room to move upwards—those were still wonderful days in Visitor Services and I missed them. Days of wearing a shirt and tie, bantering among coworkers whom I enjoyed, and yet I cannot forget the hardship, the pain of Regn and I being so close all day, not able to freely embrace—it was a beautiful torture.

On my way out I gave a thin veil of 'everything's all right' in response to Tillie's polite inquiries. It felt good hiding the truth of details, pretending all was fine. She was the same old Tillie, 106 dollars short and looking for the discrepancy. Deborah came out from the supply closet. We exchanged a congenial greeting that felt obligatory.

Back at Contradite there's a breeze outside; the flag on the support pillar is waving and the sprinklers slowly fan the lawn and driveway. It is my window on the world for the moment as I sit in the cranberry wing-backed chair with its leaf pattern. Miss Smith's chair I think of it; were she to come down the hallway and see me in it there'd be a moment's hesitation as though she were searching for her place. Aren't I a contradiction—the noise of the lobby at the Settlement was welcomed by me—in contrast to the sheer silence of isolation. It really is one extreme or the other, never a peaceful meeting ground. *Now* I understand why Regn could never stand the silence. Silence gives time, breeds reminiscing. Silence does not distract as easily as noise. Vacant white rocking chairs wait on the patio; I can see my truck from where I sit. A little ways from here so much activity is going on, just down the road, and yet here, in this place, in this hour, Time as it were, stands still—recorded by a tap-tap-tap of gray-green keys.

Regn and I had exchanged a few words—I knew Sharon was watching, for the slightest of looks or gestures. At one point Regn stepped behind me on her way to put a key in the closet from one of the scooters. My back was to her as I engaged Sharon. I wanted to feel the slightest of touches, but I knew she couldn't—not there, after all that has happened. Sharon would see. I felt her close though. Just before heading out she said, 'Take care, Westcott.' Walking through the glass doors I took my sunglasses from my left breast pocket and slipped them on. I slightly turned wanting to look back over my shoulder. I knew better and pressed on, not wanting to be examined, made a lovesick fool by those silent watchmen in the lobby cameras or Sharon. I walked into the afternoon, Regn's gaze perhaps upon me. I was glad to have shared some part of each other's day. She had gone in early not realizing she was scheduled for the late shift.

I want to go places, see things. I wish Regn could come; it's no good to go alone. I'd like a male friend—to go horseback riding, hiking, some camaraderie, casual friendship. There is no quick way; yes I want to live. If I think too much on it all I'll go crazy. A visitor just left, a black man, and the strong odor of sunscreen lingers—it's comforting to the cracked spirit. Certain odors embody a temperature or texture. This one is warm and soft, like the sun.

This evening I drove into Regn's neighborhood. I was going to Juliette's house on the opposite side of the neighborhood. What were the odds? The entire town and Juliette lived with her mother just down the road from Regn. Juliette claimed she'd moved back, it was temporary, she'd move in with roommates soon. I took Mother's car to be safe; it was still light out even at 8:30 p.m. I wasn't sure if I'd pass Regn's house. It's a well-kept and lush neighborhood—a large circle.

When Juliette introduced me to her mother I read the expression on her face intended for her daughter. *So you've brought another one home? Does he know? What have you told him about yourself? How long will he stay before he runs?* Juliette's mother was a psychologist. She looked tired. Standing on the back deck I listened to the evening birds, increasingly wistful. Little did Regn know I was so close. Did that same bird ever light in Regn's tree? We watched a movie—the remake of *Journey to the Center of the Earth*. It didn't interest me; I'd have preferred the original. I grew tired from the already mindless day of work. Leaving shortly after eleven I decided to circle round, drive by Regn's house—the first time since last summer—the last time I'd been in her home. It was dark, well shrouded by trees, nestled, and the only apt word 'cozy.' I understood how she wouldn't give up such a life. I was only hurting myself by being there—it was so quiet, late, and peaceful. Somewhere she was inside, most likely in bed with a book and Tamerlane nearby. I turned and passed by on my way out—I had less of a view, but the moon was a crescent, rich and goldish brown, slightly veiled. It was warm out and I had the windows down. A wave of sadness came over me; I felt excruciatingly alone. My tiredness was made all the more clear. Regn has felt a child within her, had a man's erection inside her, experienced the gravity of death, been taken care of financially, and it is her right to rest, she has earned it. I love her all the more for it, though I envy the security.

It hurts because I wish someone was there to take care of my mother, to share the hardship. My mother needs me, I know that, and I myself fear being completely alone.

• • •

Sunday 30 June 20—

I asked to leave work an hour early. I got off at 5:30 to take advantage of the time. A storm appeared to be getting ready to open up the skies. I drove down to the Parkway, went for a long bike ride. A few drops fell. I expected a hard rain; it held off. The egret was on his post—standing still as a mirror on the log cutting across the enchantedly framed pond. I rode all the way to the beach overlook. I stopped and crouched down by a large gathering of Canadian geese. (I say Canadian, not 'Canada' geese because the latter sounds like literacy amputation). As a single entity they all shifted toward the shoreline, leery of my presence. The landscape was my company—the geese, the scenery.

• • •

MYSELF AND I

What's wrong?
That's what's wrong, the fact that you continue to ask me the 'why' of everything?
Aren't we edgy today.
Go to hell. I don't want to hear you anymore. It doesn't matter a hill of beans. It god damn doesn't matter.
What now?
The A's, 3.9 grade point average. Damn if this mosquito bite won't stop itching.
It's not so bleak. Imagine working your ass off in some third world country from sun-up to dusk.
I don't know—the whole world over—it's too much, just too much. Ya hear that?
I know. Someone just died.
Yes, right this minute, this second someone is dead, something is born, a dress is being bought in a store, a grocery bag is quickly filled, a body moves against another while the ceiling fan chinks, a hunter shoots his prey, a ship capsizes, a painter draws a stroke across the canvas, a picture is snapped, an aluminum can is kicked in the street, divorce papers are served, a priest holds his rosary, a lone traveler eats in the dining car of the jostling train, and so it is.
Yes, I suppose you're right. All the books that won't be gotten to, the places never seen. What's in a life you ask without saying?
Chasing yourself round in circles like one of those irritating cartoons, spiraling up and up and up—no end in sight.
I feel it coming—could I run—should we run?
Why do it, you know you don't need it.
No. But displacement.
Displacement?
Yes. Input one pain and output the other.
It hurts—
You fuck hard enough you find that relief—
It's not crude.
No, it could split me in half—
Are you not mad when you do it—bitter?
I keep myself isolated, what of it—give it a rest would you.
You want to be raped?
Sometimes—to cry out in a lover's raping—the pain—vacuum the emptiness and explode within.
Don't cry.
No worry, you cry enough for the both of us.
Tell you what.
Um?
Slow dance with me and I'll gently rock with you in the closet.
Forgive me.
You hurt no one but us.
Let's go up and never come down.

• • •

Regn cared for Jay as the father of her children. Appreciated the things he did. But she no longer loved him for the person he was—had she ever?

• • •

Magda knew of the affair. I composed a letter. Painfully circumspect. For some time I had wanted to talk. Magda was a female ally to Regn. Magda was financially independent in ways Regn envied. Maybe Magda could help Regn by offering reassurance, sound counsel from someone who had been there. I knew Magda had told Regn she needed to 'think about herself first,' that is Regn needed to think of her own future, not mine at the moment.

Magda spoke a bit garrulously as though she were forever nervous and couldn't help herself. To be quiet would cause an awkward hesitation. Silence left room for inquiries. She had a lovely voice, charming, but it was hard speaking to her as a peer. Magda was older than Regn by 13 or 15 years. We went to lunch, Magda picked me up and then we came back to the Fleisch's where I was petsitting.

'I think if Regn hadn't lost her full-time position things would have been different and she'd have gone on her own,' Magda offered.

Of all the things said that day, none of which I remember except that single statement, it was what wasn't spoken that made the air heavy. I was clearly distraught, gaunt. Lovesick and yet I remained dignified. I considered myself Regn's strongest ally. Magda did not know about me. Like everyone else I worked with, up to that point Regn was the only one who knew I wasn't born male. I knew Magda was religious. How religious I cannot say. Regn had suggested I not tell her, what purpose would there be in it? But, Magda never struck me as having any homosexual prejudices. So what would my gender matter to her? Would she not see my relationship with Regn in an entirely different light? The same could be said of Regn's husband.

Often I wanted Regn to tell him. Maybe then he'd feel less threatened. Maybe we could see each other freely. Regn said it wouldn't make any difference. But how could she know? She didn't try. My secret didn't bother me. The burden was our relationship. My gender was merely the runner-up.

JUNE. SENIOR YEAR

Westcott exits into the hallway. Had he not glanced at the clock in Mrs. Sparroh's classroom prior to departing, he'd still know from the shadows and angled light it is 4:30. He has stayed after school to wrap up some final assignments. It is down to the wire and everyone in Photography scrambles to get their work done. Westcott assumed more students would have joined him in his dedicated effort to satisfy any loose ends; after all they had committed to coming earlier that day in third block. He justifies Spring fever on this particular Friday afternoon is rampant. With graduation just one week away and only three more days of actual school remaining, who in his right mind felt obligated to keep diligence in check? To ignore the warm breeze at one's own discretion, to resist answering the beckoning weekend ushered forth through clear panes and main entrance doors mirroring blue skies, proved relatively easy for Westcott. His hourglass shows a mounting dune of sand occupying its bottom capsule, the funnel dropping steadily. Every extra minute to linger he cherishes.

Turning right from the corridor, he enters the main hallway detecting an unusual calmness in the air. Not a single soul; the entire building is silent, strangely still.

A conscious knowledge reflects itself in his plodding step and solemn face. He continues unnoticed toward the double set of doors at the other end. This will be his last Friday. Strolling parallel to the cafeteria, he feels the melancholy of recollection—countless lunches marked by self-conversations. The same sensation as when he listens to the crickets trill, the wind rustling through the trees. Approaching the meso-stairwell on his right he hears something. For a split moment, only a moment, he sees himself and everything for what it is, in its simplest terms. He wonders how he has come to be so queer. The tiles below him are awash in a subtle light; the sun cascades upon the landing, bathing all it touches with a lukewarm restful content. Understanding the rarity of such fleeting instances a chill passes up his spine, twitching his shoulder to attention. Any other faculty member or student might just as well dismiss such an aura as a nice day, too rushed to glimpse the truth beyond. It is a silent passing, he knows, the music of his life. Unlike any song played on the radio that might be heard or even felt, he *sees* the backdrop of his self-selected chorus. It's as though a one-shot frame has been taken in a movie and now the instruments are called in to create the appropriate feeling. A score from his *Out of Africa* motion picture soundtrack plays in his mind. He walks to the tune that defines him, a plaintive gait. In part, it is for this reason he never wears a headset. He prefers to play his favorite songs over and over mentally. He imagines his life playing out as a movie, not in a fancy of grandiosity or self-enthusiasm. Though he suffers, it is a selfless duty so that others might take comfort. A hint of martyrdom. But then what director could capture the breaking stillness? Silence. No melodrama of sound. Stillness is silence. No one ever cares about the afterwards. In a movie things just end, the audience takes it for what it is. He always wondered though—about the afterwards.

Westcott does not stop walking, but shuffles deliberately slower, hesitant to crossover the invisible line. No choice withstanding, he relinquishes himself once more to Time and heads outside into the pleasant afternoon.

~

Standing on the track making his presence known long enough for Mr. Allowick to check his name off, Westcott waits for some sign that the clusters of faculty and students encircling the football field can return to their air conditioned classrooms. It is Monday, late in the day when the month's mandatory fire drill has been issued. Since the school has yet to have its June excursion outside, Westcott anticipated the high-pitched chirping to fill the hallways and his eardrums at any time. He misses the traditional bell; the kind he'd had in elementary school. The new alarms are hazardous, a pressurized fluttering on the stapes and anvil. His ears have always been acutely sensitive.

Feeling beads of sweat roll down his back beneath the layers of duct tape, navy shirt, and cotton jacket, Westcott rests his arms on the chain-link fence, his back to the crowd. The still forest stretches out beyond the soccer and hockey field. He sees the insignificance. Each of them, himself included, standing there, mere capsules against the backdrop of the world, marking time. A hundred years and who would remember this day, these lives? Does it matter? How can he just leave *it* all behind, something that has been so much a part of him, for so long?

JULY

The camera takes a panoramic view of a grassy hill leading to a thin thread of shoreline. There are some shady trees on the hilltop. We see a man in a red kayak demonstrating tactical maneuvers to his small children. A few yards away a heavy set woman in her late thirties wades in the shallows with her four-year-old in dress. In the paved parking area on the left, facing the river, is a man resting in the driver's seat, a woman next to him. He stirs, adjusts his seat a little. The windows are down. It is a blue Honda SUV. He puts his prescription glasses on, takes his time coming to from a restful state. He is in his thirties or early forties. Thin and fit.

Just outside the vehicle, another empty car between, stands a young man straddling his Schwinn bicycle. It is blue-gray. He wears navy shorts to the knees, a proper length and fit, and a green t-shirt. His ankles are bare inside his denim blue and beige loafer, deck shoes. He is alone, standing with legs mildly apart, a bar between his thighs, observing the scene. To his right in a Nissan is another man and woman—heavier set, late forties perhaps, the man maybe early fifties. The woman is in the driver's seat in this car. They pay no mind to the man on the bicycle, assume he's there for the same reason—to enjoy the evening. Further down, buffered by hill, the head of a couple can be seen. They are close to each other, exchanging mild affections. Cars drive by, you can hear them long before they are visible. Which of these will it be? The camera sweeps from one to the other. In the distance a small boat jets across the water.

It does not occur to the one on the bike until he turns to pedal back, that he is the only solitary character in the scene. *Was I?* He speaks to the geese. The egret had waited, unmoving in his stance, perched atop a felled log.

~

A museum, he himself has become. All these places and lives once looked upon fill him, exist within. A private tour. Closed. Open on a rare holiday, a brief changing of the guards.

He wants to tell Regn what he can never tell her. That she has it made. Her whole life a security—a security that at times suffocated, dis-serviced, but a firmness of belonging all the same.

• • •

Fourth of July. Twelve years ago today we arrived in Virginia. I was dog walking this morning—Taki and Shimo—a pair of Shebas. They look like little foxes; the fur on their neck is so thick. They have pointed ears and curled tails. They're a russet color on top with the underbelly blondish. Every house has its own odor. Theirs is strong, pungent. Asian in its origin lending to the owner's heritage. It penetrates the fabric of my clothes, but in no way distastefully. It was not mere coincidence that I met Nancy. I'd been working at the Veterinary Clinic one morning with a colleague beside me, a young girl who also did pet sitting on the side. The telephone rang. I just happened to be prompt in reaching for it, picking up the line before my coworker. The woman wanted to know if there was anyone in our office that knew of a good pet sitter. Nancy became my third, longstanding client. When I hung up the phone that day I could tell my coworker was curious, perhaps disappointed she'd missed getting a new client. In years to come I would be able to say she'd never have lasted, never have gotten to know Nancy. Her critters, as Nancy liked to call them, were high-maintenance.

I arrived early to work today.

The office is hot—air conditioning not working. It's so quiet—the day's just heating up. Morning had a nice cool breeze, but now I hear the summer insects, the clock, an automated tone that sounds incessantly every second-and-a-half somewhere from the nurse's unit. It is Saturday. The clock on the wall is ticking. Mother and I drove down to Colonial Williamsburg for the fireworks. We parked in a back lot. My responses to her comments were nothing short of perfunctory. She'd picked me up at lunch, and returning to work it struck me. I hadn't even looked at her—I'd been so absorbed within my mind.

As we sat watching the lights in the sky, she didn't notice the wetness in the corner of my eyes. I stifled the hurt knowing it was no good to indulge; it changed nothing and was selfish.

Earlier, before leaving work, Regn had come by. I'd been distantly looking forward to it—I kept busy most of the day. My mind's been so tired lately I wasn't prepared to think on my feet. I wondered did she have the early or late shift. Elinor came to the front and was talking; I hoped she'd have left by the time Regn arrived. I should have given full attention to Elinor. The nurse came up and brought Elinor back to her room. I saw Regn's bug. She came with something in her hand—a book. I'd turned off the lights in the office—they hurt my eyes and it kept the place cooler; I'd meant to switch one on again—it was too dim and depressing.

She sat down; I perched myself on the edge of the desk. Her mood was not at all what I had expected. I should have known. It had been a bad day, she was tired, said she just wanted to pack a bag and move to the mountains. She said all she had to do was say the word and Jay would pick up with her and move. Would she really go? A part of me wants to fade into oblivion. Not say another word. Just disappear, walk away for once, and leave her to be the one to wonder. Whatever happened to—?

She was edgy, untouchable. 'I shouldn't have come,' she said uptight. I was too limp to argue. Why did you come then, I wanted to say. The book she brought was the one I'd loaned to Magda, which she in turn gave to Regn—*Pillars of the Earth*. Dad mailed it to me after he read it. I finished it over Thanksgiving—despite its girth it's a remarkably fast read. Regn hadn't enjoyed it—she didn't like the author's crude depiction of the men's sexual appetites and lewdness. 'What about the story?' I asked. *A few descriptions and you chuck the entire novel? I loved it.* 'Everything's so gloomy to you,' she answered. *Gloomy? You're being gloomy.* I told her not to take her bad day out on me. I wish she hadn't come. I was trying to think of something to save the conversation, when it became clear. 'It's just not getting through to you, you're just not listening,' she said. She was hurt and tired. Sometimes when I said something it seemed to register. She did not respond, which meant she couldn't contest.

'It is a constant strain.' Her words filled the silence of the office. Her hands were limp on me, afraid to touch. Hug me like you mean it, I wanted to say. It was worse this way, much worse. I moved to kiss her. 'It can't be too much, lightly,' she said as we kissed. She touched my face as she always does and the fool that I am I followed her out. She ran from me—never turning. She noticed the parched hydrangeas. 'How sad it is no one is watering them.'

What a thing to observe at such a moment—it struck me as remarkable, coldly detached. To her bug she rushed. I called out to her. She looked back, said nothing. I stood under the portico and advanced as her bug pulled onto the drive-out road. She stopped. Her top was down.

'You didn't say it,' I tried.

'Don't make it harder,' she said. 'Don't make me.'

Her foot began to let up off the brake and as the car moved, at a loss for the right words, I said, 'Ich Liebe Dich.'

She drove away, always the one to go—to run. And I was left watching. I was angry at myself. I keep the emotions within all week and then she brings them forth from me.

Tuesday 7 July 20—

He walks into the restroom steps on the scale. 124. He steps off and moves to the toilet. He pulls down his shorts, sits down. Sometimes he forgets to remember there is a reason for the vent in his drawers, the open slit running the length of his groin. It is habit.

He lightly treads back to his room and opens the closet. Ties upon ties rest on a hooked bar mounted to the wall above a map of the world. There is at least one for each day of the month. He used to wear a tie to work; mornings he'd stand in front of the mirror flipping it over not once, not twice, but three times, else it would be too long round his slender neck. He feels the silk of one between thumb and index. His mother had given him so many, all of which he loves. But this one had been a surprise, slipped inside his briefcase while at work by the hand he longed to take gently into his own.

Now he has no place to wear them, no one for whom to dress, except himself. The memory brings the slightest movement between his legs and a pain in his chest.

• • •

Friday 10 July 20—

Ellis picked me up at the Fleisch's. We headed toward VA Beach. We hit the 5 o'clock rush hour traffic on 64; it took two hours to get down to the oceanfront. Dinner was very good. We perused a few of the tourist strips and walked on the beach after dark. We took our shoes off, waded in the shallows when the tide rolled in ankle high. It was nice doing something different for a change. I thought about walking this same place a January day that seemed so long ago. I remember the wind blowing Regn's hair against the side of her face, her blue jeans, mulberry sweater and black boots pressing into the sand. We'd spoken of my dreams and one that, at the time, seemed impossible. Of the five items I listed the one I thought would be hardest to come had been fulfilled. I wished to go back to that afternoon, if only to avoid foolish errors for which I am still paying. We were safe then, not only from Jay, but from each other.

We'd had the entire day and she'd hugged me before we got into her car to head home. She'd hugged me outside of the Edgar Cayce Museum, and that's all we'd done. Even when we arrived back, I hadn't yet learned to touch her. In all that's come to pass, the security and pureness of that day whispers sanctuary.

As Ellis and I walked the shoreline I climbed up one of the lifeguard lookout chairs. It was white and wide. Ellis took a picture. Climbing down, standing beside the giant chair I thought about sitting up there, in the dark, with the woman I love beside me, looking out together into the darkness and imperceptible line—the night ocean as black as the summer sky.

• • •

Sunday 12 July 20—

I asked Mother to stop by work today—I wanted to talk. I realized there's nothing she can do—she's not even there for herself—the strength I need right now must come from someplace else. I truly feel alone and if I don't keep typing—there is no one with whom to turn—in person. Right now, this minute, I'm giving way to weakness. It does no good to think of the hours I have left to work in solitary confinement. God help me. Regn's right. I don't want to change, I'm too fucking afraid. Must have a plan. This is a most solitary endeavor.

This morning I awoke from a bizarre dream. A monument at Jamestown, a cylindrical water tank collapsed. There was an implosion as the structure fell and an instant of adrenaline as shrapnel pushed outward. Large pieces of tile flew through the air and I knew before they even hit I would have to dodge them; I felt the fatal force they would inflict if struck. I moved just in time to miss being hit.

At one point I looked over to my right to see if Regn was still standing. She was; I do not recall seeing her look back at me; I believe I was watching her fight the debris, I did see her face though. The rest of the details are hazy. The air was thick with storm and fury. I often have a vision of returning to the Settlement and finding it completely overgrown. Abandoned, an old outpost on a *jungled* island. Remnants of some great palace, some heroic testament, now fallen. Ozymandias. I will walk alone through the Great Hall, the outside world will have moved inside. Nothing will be the same. Everything will be the same if I look closely. If I close my eyes I will be able to smell the carpet and wood in the Rotunda, feel the coolness of ancient days—days when I looked up and saw Regn standing at the balcony or coming down the hall to relieve me. To take my place. The vision looks something like the picture on the next page.

Fragility of Order by Joseph Stashkevetch

I was going to read for a little bit tonight, but the book's in my truck and I'm not going all the way downstairs and outside to get it. The rain is pattering the roof, a subtle companion, but now even that is quiet. O'Grady is plumped at the foot of the bed. This bed with the red throw comforter and white frond pattern.

The walls are yellow in this room and it's a four poster, lavish compared to my convenient twin-sized mattress, which serves its function—'a small bed,' Regn once commented affectionately. In the darkness beneath these fresh sheets and white emptiness, a ghost on top of me, a slight tremor through the body of solitary climax may find me there. No evidence, no witness but the walls, the face of none other than the clock, and a dog's nose if he be keen. But this body is dry—a dry quake of the spirit before slumber's relief.

• • •

Tuesday 13 July 20—

What does it mean? I stood in the York unit. A woman in a wheelchair pleaded, 'Will you take me home? Please take me home!'

'I can't. I wish I could.'

'Wishing does no good.'

'I know,' I told her.

'I'll give you the address so you can find it and then I'll have the money ready when you get back. *Please*, take me home.'

I was feeling ill; an excruciating headache and my joints ached. I'd like to tell you I went to her, took her hand and said, 'Be strong and someone will come for you.' All she needed was a word of comfort. Not even the nurses nearby offered one; they looked at me speculatively, anesthetized to her rants. Did she recognize a familiar pain in my paleness? An elderly man passed by wheeling a resident, presumably his wife. 'Sorry, sweetie,' he said to her imploring wail.

I hesitated. As she looked away to find solace in someone who might help her I turned and walked down the wing.

She was desperate; if I'd only taken her hand in mine. If I could have driven her down the street, to get her out for a little while; I think death for her would be the kindest release.

I was looking at a magazine with pictures of the 1940s and Pearl Harbor—advertisements of a bygone era. Looking at their faces our wants are still very much the same. The basic human needs and hopes have not changed. I felt I could slip into one of the pictures and easily converse with them. What does it mean?

The sum of goodness I suppose. All the days of our life. I no longer have the energy or inclination to photograph a scene lest it be truly rare. I'd much rather take it in and keep it that way than try to preserve it all. What does she know that I don't; this woman who has no need to write or record of herself. I exhaust myself in trying to capture every breath of life; she just breathes with it. Regn flows with it. I am a stone in the river which the current breaks itself against, the energy is forked and I am drained.

• • •

Saturday 18 July 20—

One more hour 'til I partake of my freedom in getting the hell out of here, work that is, at the front desk.

There is a sorrow in me, a sorrow so deep that were I to give myself over to it now, I would want to go down in a corner and never crawl out. Why should I lament of my own pain?

It is so damn cold in the office and to step outside there is a warmth that penetrates the bones. Nothing I say here truly captures all that I am feeling right now. Maybe it's enough just to think it. I only wish the strength to comfort myself would pillarize within me.

The front door is obnoxious and needs repairing. It slams with a heavy, cold ruckus. Few bother to slowly close it, even those who are familiar with its ways. And when it slams I hear it as a punctuation. 'Humph! You are alone, humph!'

This morning a woman I'd spoken with the other evening—she has a broken arm and is here for rehabilitation—Mrs. Nahmmo, came to the front shaking in tears. One of the nurses scared her. She was afraid of falling in the restroom with only the use of her one good arm. This woman came to me, she came and told me, 'I think the world of you—I don't know you, but I—I say a prayer for you.' She blew me a kiss.

'If you need anything or to talk—'

'I was afraid I'd fall. She just left me in there—'

As she wheeled around the corner something inside couldn't wait. I stepped through to the back office, opened the door as she was coming.

'You all right?' I knew she wasn't. It wasn't a question, but it was the only way I could breach the pain.

She gave way and cried.

It could not wait. I bent down and hugged her.

•••

Saturday 25 July 20—

I am sitting in bed, I wear no shirt it is so hot, and why should I? If I can't even sit with myself shirtless then what's to become of me? I could be anywhere, anywhere, but I was put here. The world is too big, too much—one could disappear and never come back. It is too quiet, much too small and stifling here. My family is downstairs, the cat is about to launch himself on the bed, the lamp is a soft ambience. Wanting to turn to someone, anyone, and be assured everything will be all right. They can't answer. It leaves me alone in the dark beseeching a void-less unknown to tell me something. I find myself calling upon souls departed, relatives I never met—for strength—a comfort to see me through. Do I ask too much? Chores are actually a respite—something to do, productive. I wish a vision, an entity would come to me. I'm afraid of my sadness. I wake up to myself—I'm on a separate plane watching all of them. I enjoy a small glass of orange juice. Drying off and the routine of getting dressed. Sometimes I look at my completely unclothed body in the mirror before and after getting into the shower. I am aroused by the openness—not to be mistaken for vanity, but awe. No one looks upon this body. I love the wind as I drive, folding towels, french fries from Wendy's, baking a perfect cake.

Sunday 26 July 20—

I think about a year ago. Those few days of freedom were at our door. I asked Regn the other day when we met for lunch what she believes it's all about.

Her answer was so sure. Or rather, she was sure of it. 'Our souls are here to learn. We have plenty of time.' It was no comfort to me. We comfort ourselves with whatever explanation works at the moment. I'm tired of feeling the human condition—whatever it may be. I wish I could fly above it, but one must let go of everything and I cannot. I've become cold, distant in nature, for we can hold nothing of permanence.

• • •

Thursday 30 July 20—

Elinor called me over. I was walking down the corridor—a change of scenery from the silence of the front office. She hugged me while playing bingo and thanked me for the rolls I'd brought her from the Red Lobster. She loves their rolls. As the evening went on she came back up to the front and was speaking to a nurse, clearly distressed. She approached my window. Bill, the friend she'd been trying to call for several days, had passed away. As she wheeled around the corner I opened the office door, 'Are you going to be all right?' She started to cry again. I couldn't let her go in such state. Something gave way inside, maybe it was a second chance. I still remembered the woman in the hall tearless but crying, 'Wishing does no good.' And I thought of Mrs. Nahmmo. I hugged Elinor. 'It will be all right.' I squeezed her hand. 'I'll be here tomorrow evening if you need to talk.'

• • •

Friday 31 July 20—

A year ago this very evening we were in ecstasy. Regn and I were at home at this time and then we would be heading to her house. It seems a dream, so long ago. But I must not dwell on such thoughts. Tonight it is gray and dreary out, after a hard rain.

We met for lunch this afternoon—12:30 at the Glasshouse. The wind was captivating as I sat in the heated cab of my truck, windows down, waiting a few minutes. I watched the wind play with the light in the trees. I imagined the blank spaces winking in little Fort Apache, a silent witness to those minutes I spent alone. The painful loneliness after Regn departed and the bittersweet anticipation of her all too brief arrival. Regn was never the one who waited. I listened to the restroom door close. Hopefully no one would come for the next half hour so Regn and I could have privacy. The musket from the Settlement next door reported.

Regn wore a knit sweater of lime green with blue wing-shaped designs like birds and a white under shell, with beige capris and her white sandals. She had on her ivory dragon pendant necklace and silver rectangular earrings. She'd brought only a yogurt to eat. 'You could make me crazy.'

I told her I took it as a compliment. 'We need each other, we both do, but it's a constant see-saw of emotion,' I observed. 'When you're up I'm down and when I'm up you're down.'

'We help each other through it,' she replied.

'I think so. No. I know so.'

AUGUST

I went with Ellis to Kings Dominion. We arrived around 2:30. In the latter part of our fun, in the cooler hours of the 90 degree day, we rode the Ferris Wheel. I'd never been on one. The moon was out and every so often we'd halt high above the grounds as passengers unloaded and loaded. I felt I was already gone. And I told myself to try and be there—present that is—enjoy the time. I allowed my mind to drift to Regn and how we'd ridden the Skyride and softly kissed, once, some night long ago.

A mother and her little four year-old son sat in the basket behind us. She had a Season Pass. Waiting in line she told us she comes every weekend; her boy, Grant, loves the Ferris Wheel. I watched her hold him and the summer night breeze blow through our open compartments. Ellis and I sat across from each other. She took pictures on her camera. Each time I blinked, I too, was taking pictures.

I wish I could live within the stanzas of a poem—in that moment when it's read and the comfort it restores. We had fun yesterday, but I still found myself watching the day.

On a side note—for the last week or so the front door in the lobby has been closing quietly. My notice to please shut the door quietly paid off. I've been making more name badges since the last batch walked off with visitors.

It's drizzling now, a soft rain, and as I said, frickin' cold in here—I just stepped out to roll up my windows and the dampness has me even colder.

I'm not a huge fan of contemporary theme parks with their bombardment of mindless amusements. That's not to say I don't enjoy the rush of a rollercoaster I've never ridden before, but the concept of "amusement" has expanded beyond the point of charm to such a corporate level as to be distasteful. Every few years a new ride must be installed to keep the customer satisfied. More shows, more gimmicks, and where does it end? When is it just too much? Busch Gardens has always been known for its beautiful plants and landscaping. When I'd gone with Regn it wasn't the park that enlivened me. Being with Regn—experiencing the sensory details together—transformed the usual sights and sounds into something extraordinary, irreplaceable. When you get right down to it, it does not matter where you go or how you get there. The moment hinges on those who are there beside you. Regn made the park seem new. I realized this even in those hours with her. I was seeing it for the first time through her eyes.

I've always favored the timeless rides. The quiet graceful ones born from the original country fairgrounds of long ago. When diversion and amusement stemmed not from the desire for bigger, better, and more, but the inherent need to get away, share in a familial outing, and truly taste a caramel apple. The Ferris Wheel and Carousel are fine examples of "rides" meant to stimulate and engage the senses, not drown them away. Have you ever noticed upon leaving an amusement park as you're sitting in your car, the sheer crisp contrast of noiselessness? That is if you don't have a cranky toddler with you. The silence is like warm water bathing the eardrums. You can hear yourself think again.

The Ferris Wheel has long been ensconced in theme park lore as the couples' amorous escape into romantic heights. Is it the danger of proximity? The false sense of seclusion within the private basket and the restrained desire for more as a couple begins to kiss, knowing that just 5 feet above and 5 feet below dangle prurient others with stories unfolding side-by-side, in the quiet night, next to their own? The moment occurs again and again, yet it remains wholly original for the couple experiencing it for the very first time.

I felt the breezy night through my shirt, wondering if Ellis was pondering similar thoughts. Wouldn't she prefer the body of a beloved next to her as opposed to the polite, familiar company of her brother? We were both stranded, silenced by the great emotional divide—the chasm of our personalities—that had always lain between us.

Last night, reposed in the Ferris Wheel, I began to consider would I ever, or rather, would my life ever serve to mean to someone what Sophie Scholl is to me? Or in the books I read, will my words someday, long after I'm gone, comfort and give hope? It's all so sad to me—that's what had me down yesterday—the non-permanence of life itself and that moment and this moment. An allusive disquietude. There are instances of peace—so short-lived—but a moment of existing bliss wherein I feel a reasonable ease. (Excuse me one second while I relay this fact—the odor of diaper wipes, a fragrant powder, emanates in the lobby. I dislike it. And when the phone rings I find it most bothersome, especially when visitors open the door and the chattering of staff coming and going). Some have children to carry on their legacy. This is what I leave of myself.

• • •

Wednesday 5 August 20—

Magdalene came to the front. 'I have to get out of my 2x4. I don't like my roommate. She watches TV all the time and through the night! I come up here for "the view." It's nice.' She looked around. 'People coming and going. What more could you ask for?'

I didn't answer. *My misery is her place of relief—*

A storm is thundering. Somehow it comforts me—the heaviness in the air, close, and the rolling bellows of somewhere far away, sonorous to stir the body. I understand why Regn turned to her books so long ago for strength. My heart is strong; I can feel its strength even though at times I wish it would give way on me. I do not feel it is my time to go. I am not afraid of death—I see it as the ultimate relief.

• • •

Saturday 8 August 20—

I gave Elinor her birthday card and a present, which I'd wrapped. She loved the pink set of pens. She's always misplacing hers. I know these will be lost as well.

She asked me to her room where she had two cakes and offered me a piece. I sliced from the chocolate. In a dish just a few inches from our plates lay a pair of dentures. I made an effort not to wince, pretending not to notice.

———

The speedometer edges past 70. Ol' Reliable's transmission lurches. Westcott pounds the steering wheel with his fist. It is dusk. No one is around. No one can see. He screams as loud as he can. Holding the wheel, how easy it would be, a little turn and he'd be in the ditch or hit a tree. 'Aaaaaah! Aaaah!' His vocal chords are raw. The deer grazing on the side of the road can't hear him. He is afraid to shout in the presence of others. Now it doesn't matter. Only once did he scream for Regn. He screamed in agonized affection. He'd prepared her. 'I just want to holler.' 'Then scream,' she'd said. As her bug pulled away, he'd done just that. He'd tilted his head back and let himself go before turning on his bicycle down the hill.

Now, there is no witness. Only Hudson and Kinkaid. *How absurd. Absurd!* The pool of frustration within his chest erupts. The hardness spends itself.

What had triggered it this time? His mother wanted to know where he was going, when he'd be back. Why couldn't he go with her to drop something off for the flea market on Saturday? He shakes his head, irritated. Exhausted. And of course, Regn. She is always the twin of his discontent. If he is fighting for his own liberation, then it is Regn who reminds him at every corner of his frustration.

By the time she was his age now, she'd been married 5 years. How normal. How predictable. Comfortable. Her life was already flowing out from her. When, when would his begin!

The sign post reads 35 MPH. Who cares. No one is on the road. The only life he risks is his own. He can't wait another second. He wants out. The egret never ruffles a feather as he speeds by. Its stillness feels like mockery. Its austere whiteness and refusal to be moved is a virginal display, taunting. Its indifference blinds Westcott with resentment. *Why couldn't things have been different? Straightforward. Like Jay's life?* The explosion of energy peters out. His body has been depleted. It is good to scream. Is that why people sometimes cry out while making love? It seems crude, extraneous to Westcott. He favors the intensity of silence, for *the body* to scream out. He does not want to hear what it is doing. He wants to see and feel the movements. 'Huffing and puffing,' as Regn calls it, or moaning and crooning makes the act unbearably ridiculous. Alex and Daria cross his mind. The Russian exchange students. It hurts. They were 20. 20! Just when he was ready to be picked he'd been cast to the ground, left to perish and dry, half-bitten, cold, and wounded. The wound spread like a poison, thwarting his mind, clamping off all healthy, youthful appetites.

He feels like an apricot that has fallen. Yes, an apricot. *Westcott the apricot.* And the fruit of his youth is spoiling. The seeds are becoming sterilized; his passion wasting away in the peak of its ripeness.

He pulls over and parks beneath the trees. *Not again, not again.* He will not cry.

It changes nothing. He imagines being *taken* in his own truck. Being made love to, spreading his legs as Regn has spread hers. At the same time he envisions penetrating Regn, protecting her naked form with his body.

He knows it is dangerous to ponder such ideas. How else can he fulfill such longings? He makes love to the memory and idea of endless affection. Night is coming on. She alone will hold him.

———

Friday 14 August 20—

I'm bleeding again. I see it as a punishment for my self-pitying. I know it is stress-related. Must alter the injection dosage. I remember the last time I had a full out course. After the initial injection my system was shutting down and the pain—never had I experienced such cramps. Fortunately there is no real return of flow. I am not so much concerned as I am irritated—something else to quietly endure, another reminder of what I am. I have no right to be sad when I see the living conditions of those at work who are "waiting to die."

These cramps hurt when I move, best to sit still.

I hold no one accountable for my present state of unhappiness but myself.

Why put any of this down? As persecution unto my own person? I wish many things, I wish I had someone to confide in—but these things ought not to be spoken of. And I would suffer the more for it. Best to keep these things to one's self. I don't dare to love myself.

...

Saturday 15 August 20—

A man, a resident by the name of Miguel, pushed with his walker right into the office. He came to the desk. His language full of salivatory slurring, I struggled to decode his question. He does not hear well; I faced him directly so he could see my mouth and maybe read my words. It was hard to understand what he wanted. 'Ping,' he said. 'They've all gone.' Finally I gesticulated in the air as though I were writing. 'Pen?' I pulled one from a box and gave it to him. He was grateful. From the conversation he told me his things go missing; he'll have them and someone takes the pens. *I believed him.* 'Thank you, Sir,' he said with gratitude extending beyond the pen. There was dribble or something on his chin; it was difficult to look without becoming queasy. He asked my name and if I knew his. The accent made it equally difficult to discern his language. He thanked me again and pushed out. I was glad I'd been there to give him what he needed when no one else would. Was he allowed sharp objects? Surely, he was too feeble to be a threat. I was amused at the way he'd just come right in, cornering me without realizing it. He was desperate in a way. A furry beetle flipped on his back who just needed to be momentarily rescued and set straight in order to go contentedly on his way throughout the day.

I just called Waller Mill Park and I hung up most irritated. I'm so sick of it—can't have fun anywhere. I called asking about their policy on launching your own boat since we—Ellis and I—recently bought an inflatable one on clearance. Inflatable ones aren't permitted. If not on the lake then where the fuck can you go? The river? Too dangerous with currents. If we rent a canoe or row boat from the park, then dogs aren't allowed on board. Why not? They might jump ship? Oh, please! It's ridiculous, all the infringements and regulations.

A woman came by for the second time in her wheelchair. 'Has she called? Is she coming?!' I sometimes hear her wailing from one of the units. Her daughter was supposed to come today. 'Today *is* Sunday?' I'm to see my grandchildren!' She started to cry, staring out the front windows, helpless.

I pray I die than ever arrive to such a state. Elinor, sweet lady, repeats herself. How could she not? This environment would make anyone lose their mind. The facility donated her an electric wheelchair. Yesterday she offered me some more candy. She said, 'You're sweet enough already, but I always have some if you want. How come you're not married? I would think you should be.'

This morning I finished mowing the backyard at 7:45 a.m. The engine kept cutting out because the grass was so tall and wet from dew; the blade clogged up with cuttings. I had to reach my hand in and dislodge the divots from the slicing propeller.

It is nigh 5 o'clock I estimate. I do not consider the time and refrain looking at the clock—else I'll go mad. I'm stuck working today, don't fight it. There are too many unknowns, too many questions that can't be answered and so I try to find comfort in the simplest of acts. Sliding into bed at night—the feel mattress and softness of pillow. The coolness of the sink water after I wash my face with the warm. Eating a meal slowly and savoring it. Looking at the lawn and the hard work it took to mow it. A quiet drive with the window rolled down and a gentle breeze. Anything.

Yesterday when Ellis and Mother picked me up for lunch we went down to Powhatan Creek. If trees could talk—all the times they've watched Regn and I at that very place. Ellis and Liam were by the water's edge. I walked on the jagged stones. The water was so calm; it was mild out, and I imagined doing as Virginia Woolf. How much easier it would be to just slip into that water and not emerge.

All but for those few seconds of struggle as the lungs fill—such a beautiful day, why couldn't I enjoy it? Forgive me for taking so much for granted. I only hurt myself.

...

Tuesday 25 August 20—

My last day at Contradite Health Care. 3 months. I have to leave. It's too depressing. I spoke to the administrator. She said my absences would constitute a voluntary resignation if I wasn't back by the following Monday. I didn't care. I was angry, frustrated, confined. I met with a panel. Nothing they said would keep me. One woman who'd been particularly nice to me asked if there was anything they could do to get me to stay. A new manager is coming on soon, maybe things will change? I knew they had a hard time keeping employees. And I was always reliable. Always on time. All I wanted was to get the hell out of the place. I half-listened, mentally clambering to get up and literally run! I didn't want to sit still a second longer. I gave them notice that I was going out of town on an emergency and left it at that. I'm fleeing with Ellis and Rodge for a few days to Boston—need to get away. Need, or I will be in the sanitarium. None of the residents seemed to care except Elinor. None of them would remember. I went to her room at 7:15. She kept talking until 8:00. When I told her I'd be leaving she took it hard. I got her purse from her night table; she pulled out a dollar. She'd wanted a Milky Way from the vending machine, but didn't want to wheel all the way to get it. I volunteered to pick one up when I clocked out. I hugged her. 'I get lonely at times.' Her conversation skipped from one subject to the next, anything to keep me there. 'I know I'm always bothering you.' Then I'd say I have to get going and then she'd segue into another conversation. I was tired and had much to do, but I stayed a half hour after clocking out and we talked. She was desperate, I know. I was someone she enjoyed coming up to the front to see or hearing on the loud speaker. Her one good leg propelling her along with her arm as she glided down the hall. She told me how sweet a person I am. Her words were genuine.

She said I had a nice voice, not like some of the others who were too loud. 'Take some more candy.' I stuffed my pocket with the lollipops—flavors she didn't want, and bid her take care, promising to return. As I walked out this evening—later than customary, a crescent moon hung in the summer sky. It's funny I thought, walking down the hall, how you stop looking at a person, I mean really looking at person—what they wear and such when they get so old. I understand Elinor's pain and here I was out in the night air—mildly liberated but too tired and weary to enjoy it. Elinor had prattled on, kindly I'd listened, all the while trying to politely excuse myself. She will be downsizing to a non-private room. It is dying to end up in such a way. And I'd rather die young.

· · ·

I walked out on that warm August night. The moon was bright and the feeling of leaving filled me with absolute liberation. I had to go. Behind the doors of Contradite death waited in every corridor. The position had been morosely depressing. A few times I'd come into the front lobby—a small room—and fallen on the floor. My mind restless. Walking away, knowing I wouldn't be back (except to see Elinor), for that brief interval, I felt exhilarated. I did not have another job lined up—something would come; it had to—I couldn't stop, couldn't wait and watch the walls peel, see people in wheelchairs asleep, the dense odor of urine, no matter how often sheets and Depends adult diapers were changed. The occupants needed to be turned loose. Let them wander into oblivion, let them feel alive once more before exiting, even if that exit meant stumbling into oncoming traffic. At least they'd die out in the day, in the open, not shut away, cut-off. And Elinor! Oh God, the woman still had her faculties and was left to count minutes. I fled.

I kept my promise. Three months later I took Elinor out to lunch and for a drive around the Island. I would have kept on driving us to the old family orange grove she so loved to regale me on if only to set her free. I sent cards on her birthday and Christmas. I continued to stop by periodically. We'd play Yahtzee. She'd show me a new calendar her kids had sent with pictures of her great-grandchildren. She had flowers in her room and crossword puzzle books strewn over her bed and side table. My visits over time became less and less. One day I disappeared.

· · ·

Thursday 27 August 20—

I was surprised Regn called. She asked if I was getting ready, packing, when I'd be heading out? She knew I was going up to Boston. And then the kindest words, a certain peace to calm me—'You fulfill me as a woman—in all ways, I just wanted you to know that. I'll miss you, I do miss you.'

It was the greatest compliment of absolute sincerity. No words in return could suffice. I was temporarily put to rest, a peace filled me—all my anger and self-resentment lightened. The past weeks of turmoil, the months of our constant unrest, towing the line, coming so close, backing away, feeling goodbye, holding on. It was a gift. I didn't want to say or do anything—I wished we could leave it at that—a conversation to endure, no other words. To live just then.

SEPTEMBER

A beautiful day—cool and breezy. We had lunch at 12:30, the Glasshouse. I brought a vanilla cupcake, a candle, and a lighter. She held it in her hand and made a wish before blowing it out. I gave her the pewter keychain from the House of the Seven Gables, the Nathanial Hawthorne Museum in Boston where I'd been the week before. We sat with each other quietly for a long time—

'I wish I could take a walk right now.'

'By yourself?' I asked.

'No, with you.'

We spoke of the mountains—our going there together. Someday. I rested on her breast, I could hear her heartbeat. The air elicited a tinge of wood burning from the nearby fort. Every so often a musket would go off—the men would holler in preparation; I'd cover my ears. I watched the trees, sad that nothing stays. We all must go. Regn felt me shift and pushed me off—her lunch was almost up. 'Hold me,' she said. I felt her tongue enter, plunge with a force that stirred a tremor between my legs. I was calm, but it was herself she wished to keep in check. And then she took my hand, moved it to the place where her black skirt with the white roses concaved delicately in her lap. She brought it to her leg, letting me know it was all right to slip beneath, up to the warmth between. I felt her under garment, all too briefly. 'For my birthday,' she said more to herself as an explanation. 'Oh, Regn,' I whispered in mild protest of subdued frustration.

'I shouldn't have done that,' she said regretfully.

'It's okay,' I reassured. 'I just want it—to be slow.' I looked out the window—it seemed so clear, I was being careful of myself. I couldn't let myself go so easily—not here.

'I could just cry now,' she spoke from behind her sunglasses. But there would be no tears from either of us. We hugged again, decently. Kissed.

'Thank you,' she said, 'for the cupcake. I'll be with you—here and here'—she touched her breast. 'I love you.'

'I don't say it anymore, I don't know how else to,' I replied. And then stepping from the bug I leaned in. 'Regn, I do love you.' I kissed her on the forehead. 'Happy Birthday.'

That same evening I went for a bike ride on the Island. It was beautiful. Five mile loop. I don't know the last time I'd been there—

I called Regn at ten to five. We spoke for the last part of her shift. 'One of these days,' she said.

We briefly met at Powhatan Creek. She got out of her car and we walked down towards the river.

It was just for a minute—but she said she'd wanted to come.

I took her picture by her bug—they matched—her in black and white—the silver bug with its top down.

'You saw me twice today.'

'Don't count,' I scoffed.

'No,' she said.

'*You* saw *me* twice today,' I rebuked.

After biking Mother said, 'You smell like the sun.' Is that what Regn smells like?

None of this satisfies on paper. It was anything but crude today. We sat looking at the trees. Regn said, 'Look, the sun just peeked through the clouds.'

That's what I want to remember.

• • •

It's a Monday, Labor Day; the seventh of September. The skies are white, the day overcast. Amidst this silence the fear returns. I wish I was going somewhere—. Going far away for a while. If I do get this other job, it's not where I want to be— I want to get out, escape myself. I am damn glad not to be working at Contradite anymore.

A beautiful house, soon to be left, a vehicle, a full stomach, the love of animals— I should be satisfied. I'm anything but. I want to get out—to breathe. I won't tell anyone these things.

• • •

Regn—

I should shut up before I hurt us in a way that won't repair itself. I must be honest.

I resent things for which you have every right and never had any control over. That you married with little thought—that it just came to you and sex was just a part of life, children the next step—it is what we do. I'm torn and bitter and I apologize but I will not ask your pardon for what is only natural and cannot be quelled—something you yourself never had to endure—my youthful frustrations giving way to anger.

Sometimes I want to be hurt—to really have something to cry about; pain is what I know—it is who I've become—like it or not. I'm tired of love and 'wants' too long deferred. What good are these feelings if they have nowhere to go? Knowledge is not bliss, my Lady. Knowledge is pain! Maybe I don't believe in words anymore, they become as transparent as the breath it takes to speak them. There is a frustration in me so deep, a rod that anchors me, as though I were a flag and the wind whips it till the edges fray and the tear gradually splits in two. You're a positive thinker. Anything I say is gloom upon your day. It brings you down. Pick myself up—the anger is winning. I need the cold so's not to be hurt anymore. Let me fulfill my duties, collect a paycheck, pay the bills. I only hurt those I touch.

I'm a foolish romantic who never lived. I wish I could have a getaway weekend, have someone to share it with. I cannot forgive all that has come to pass. I cannot forgive myself. And don't, please don't sit there and say, 'I'm a good person, don't be so hard on yourself.' Regn, Regn, Regn, I wish you would hold me down and 'rape' me calm. You don't think I look at myself and sometimes hear the voice of youth in what I say? I just wish my life was done and settled, this is it, so-to-speak. Contradictory to this statement, I am like a horse that 'refuses' to be broken, but the lone horse dies slowly alone. It's like that song 'I could be satisfied knowing you love me.' I wish my desires would remain dormant—if not for your sake, than God knows for mine. I'm sick of these matters of the heart. I gave another dimension, mystery, character to your otherwise simple and ordinary life. I don't mean that in a bad way, as though your life was trivial—but you married, had children, did the 'norm' and it's all rather concise if put into a paragraph. But we changed each other's lives, created a beautiful pain.

I always wanted to be the soldier who meets the girl while on leave and shares a dance. A romantic I am, and why cast such passions into a body so reserved? I can't question, I can't analyze, I can wring an arm at the sky, but no one answers. We don't choose our sufferings—<u>I think we get complacent and something within us comes out.</u> I can't win. There's too much pain in this body. And I don't doubt we will have some time, other opportunities, but I have sadness that one or both of us will have gone to a place where we can't bear the strain and so go about our ways. I'm not like you—I was left starving. I tell myself I don't 'need' these things, what choice do I have? I'm turning into a quiet cynic—don't let these things show to those who don't know me. You had a life, some life, Regn. And me, don't go there, Regn, don't go there.

Studies show someone my age should be having sex several times a month, and rare though it may be, however distantly infrequent, you still do. And I do not ask, though I sense it. Even if it's not what you want—it's there, you have the option, the choice, and on the surface the world is on your side. It's your right, Regn, and wouldn't I do the same? How can I criticize? I should be going to group concerts, getting a drink with the guys every weekend, considering marriage and eventually children. Isn't that what we're born to do—isn't that what society has prescribed as mainstream? I don't want all these things—really I don't, but I did miss being young—what it meant to be young once upon a time. It's as though I slipped undetected through the cracks. I was a soldier. I did quietly ask a girl to dance some night in a town and time I know not. And we did make young love in a flat, some quiet room, hers perhaps, across the seas—long, long ago. I feel these places and things inside me and I miss them. That song "Dream a Little Dream" brings me back to an era I somehow know, as though I were there again. I miss these things.

I miss the virgin's innocence; I miss a freedom I never had. I miss the "idea" of what should be so easy—to just walk in anytime and be able to kiss lightly, hold gently and let go—the woman—the person you cherish, for whatever reason.

Have a safe trip, Regn. Stay safe. And please, think little on me. Have your mountains. I won't take them away from you.

• • •

Thursday afternoon I called Regn as she would be going to the mountains Friday and through the weekend. She said she'd read the letter and cried. Her heart was bleeding, she said. At her suggestion, since I told her I was taking Gilly for a run, we met at Powhatan after she left work. I parked my truck in the glasshouse lot and left Gilly in the cab with a window cracked. I'd gone through the park's Exit since the Entrance gate was already closed. I didn't want my truck seen near Regn's.

I hoisted my bicycle from the bed liner and pedaled a few hundred yards up the windabout to the right. I waited on my bike. I loved the feeling of expectation.

Just seeing her silver car quickened something inside me. Regn pulled her bug in diagonally. She asked to ride my bike for a second. 'It's a little high for me, my legs are so short,' she laughed. She was test driving it since she was planning on getting a new bike herself. 'Watch the kick-stand,' I said and pushed it up with my foot before letting her go. 'All right, now take off,' I said. She circled back, leaned to the side and hopped off. A car was parked far to the left—we couldn't tell if someone was in it. We walked down through the trees, approaching the river. I saw some people and signaled Regn to halt. We stayed where we were and held one another. 'It's cool,' she said.

'What's going to happen to us?' I looked at her.

'I don't know.'

'Jay will never accept me and I'll never accept him?'

'No.'

She pulled my tweed cap down and forward a little bit.

'I'll take you with me, in my backpack,' she said. 'This one'—she felt her breast.

I pulled the back of my cap down, raising the bill and repositioning it so's to see.

'I love you,' she said.

'I know, but maybe I don't believe it.'

We kissed—I held her at wait, stopping, silently telling her *let it come gently*, slowly—then she pushed inside. I kissed her forehead, pushed her hair back and looked at the gray roots of her dyed hair and the widow's peak affectionately, without a word. We started to walk back. We stopped again and hugged. I stepped back. 'Goodbye, my luv,' I said more in a whisper. The car had left—obviously it was not the people by the riverbank—had they watched us? It didn't matter.

'I love you, keep that.'

'I wish I could,' I said.

In her car, the door open, I remember looking at her as though that image would remain. The pain in her eyes. We squeezed each other's hand. I shut her door with her, she waved and I quickly tore down the ramp on my bike in the opposite direction towards the Island. I did not look back, but casually glanced to the side; her bug was already out of view.

On the Island with Gilly I drove to the visitor parking lot, I saw a mother deer and her two young. It was slightly overcast out, cooler, but beautiful. I was riding away. I biked the 3 miles—let Gilly loose on the bridge. She peered over the edge, her front legs on the wooden rail. And so it was. I pedaled as though in farewell, for the moment anyhow.

• • •

It's a Sunday, the 20th of September 20—. My life consists of the birds and squirrels in the trees, the post in the mailbox. I guess I thought for sure I was going to get that job. The unemployment doldrums have returned. I'd gladly go to work in place of my mother. I'm not so good to her, rather bitter if you want to know the truth, a regular bastard at times who tries not to snap but always does in tempered frustration. I'm angry *for* her. Nothing's turned out the way she wanted, nor I.

I wish, at least, she was in a better place—content with a job she reasonably enjoyed and someone with whom she could turn, besides me. I wish she was strong on her own and physically sound. I wish my sister—. All right if she isn't up for the whole marriage and family bit, but if she were independently happy. I'm sad because I wonder what happened to us. As for myself, I cast no blame but take full responsibility for my present state. I'm drowning in a sea of unknowns. This isn't how I envisioned things. What did I envision?

The silence is deafening, but I prefer it to the noise that has no distinct voice, little consequence.

The only person besides Mother who consistently emails is Jill Conway, and Regn. No one else—not Parson. Parson—twenty-five, married, traveling the world—was in Africa not too long ago. I'm happy for him. What happened to me? Doesn't it always go back to that core of separation? Of what I am? I wanted that day in Washington D.C. to lie on my back in the dark, except for a sphere of light, spread my legs apart, and be looked upon, probed, palpitated, touched there—what must you think of me? Am I nuts? No. I must not think of these things.

Too much time here alone. I dare not, dare not, no, open my mouth in silent protest.

Yesterday I went for a bike ride. I passed what appeared to be a pinecone and then on closer inspection a stone in the middle of the path. I was about to continue pedaling. It was too ovular. I stepped from my bike, removed my sunglasses and picked the shelled creature up. The turtle retracted his head. His shell would have fit nicely in my palm, but he had relieved himself so I only gripped the edges from the top. I set him in the gullied brush in the direction he'd been pointed. I took Miss Gilly for a walk last evening. How many more times will I circle this neighborhood? I came upon our home—the color is cheerful—not another combination like it. Cream yellow with burgundy shutters and a navy blue door.

I miss putting on a shirt and tie. Nigh a year since I last worked a day in Visitor Services. I don't miss the work—the repetition that is, but the place does fill me with nostalgia and the camaraderie and banter we all shared.

Do I feel sorry for myself—? At times. Ah, sex for a more peaceful disposition—it's a human need for balance. On the rarest occasion it leaves me empty and to tell the truth it's more of a hassle with all the preparation. I have to assume both roles, do double the 'work.' And I don't think it's proper to self-indulge. Yes, it's a basic human need, but alone— however slow and gentle I take it, the solitary act, pleasure by one's own, is mildly vulgar. I—

Oh to just be an animal or a plant. I wish I could exist purely.

Can anyone hear me? Can anyone hear me? I'm cold though it's comfortable outside. I wish I could turn to someone, tell someone who does understand and without hurting anyone around me. I don't want a body to *just* listen, I want him to understand. Many a time I consider heading to a counselor. It is an insult. I cannot shell out 45 dollars a pop for the *sake* of being heard. Some things must be carried alone. I need to get out. A person can only go for so many walks. Oh yes, a beautiful day it is, but I need to leave myself. Mother will get home soon; I should be good to her. It's not her fault. I could scream right now—I wish I were going somewhere. I wish I could tell somebody. A whole afternoon—no restraints on time—no "Oh, I'm sorry your hour's up," or "I'd really better get going," or "I wish there was something I could do." What can you do? Breathe hard you blubbering fool, you have to stand it alone. No one's coming to pick you up. Feel that coldness, it's coming from within.

• • •

Met Regn at Powhatan Creek. I knew she couldn't stay long. It was too much of a risk.

I hugged her, told her I wasn't angry at her. And I'm not. We kissed. I restrained her, if she let herself go she would go crazy—I could feel it.

'Are you going to be all right?'

'I'm not going to answer that,' I said.

We were passionately still. 'I love you. I mean that.'

'I never doubt you. It's not you I doubt,' I told her. 'How to keep it alive, I don't know how, that's why I'm so afraid.'

'I've learned some things always stay alive, though you keep them in these sealed places.'

OCTOBER

Nothing makes sense. My life fell apart and I want to fly, fly far away and not look back—not think back. I am sad because not one thing is right. Is our love? It is a good love, but with far too grave a pain. I want an easy love. Such is a contradiction. The other night I had a dream—a long dream. Even so throughout it was the feeling of Time—you could not stay and I felt you slipping away. What I remember most and this is not to romance, but the truth—we were alone and I said now no one's here to see us—and so we danced, really danced and it was good to take you in my hands and lead each other. You, the woman and I—I can't think of myself as a man, Regn. I told you that once, else I could not approve of what we share—I could not respect it. It is sad and it quite possibly will be sad longer than I wish to know or remember. Something was taken from me—a freedom—not by you directly—but little by little. I can laugh, be there in person amongst others, but I am always somewhere else, always distant. I don't think you recall the patience it took— the anguished patience for that wall within me that trembled before you, to come down. That's what I will always miss and I never want to become so comfortable that I forget the simple pleasure, that first solitary break when the years gave way within me, and I realized how much I'd missed "it." The innocence of my hand on your face and how I know our affections are good, more powerful in their decent restraint.

That is my wish, Regn. A dream? Dreams vanish with our waking—it is my wish, my endeavor with you, for us to dance and the world not care. A dance to displace the years of silence. What happened to me, Regn, to you, my lady?

• • •

Sometimes he thinks about his cousin. His cousin he met, but does not remember meeting because he was two or three at the time. The cousin that went to the University of Columbia. The one fluent in German who'd been studying medicine. His cousin. The cousin who'd killed himself, burned within his room—that cousin. Why had he done it and not himself, Westcott? *Why do I hang on to life?*

• • •

Big Meadows Campground
Shenandoah Valley, VA

They were ghosts wavering in the dawning mists. A platoon in the tropics. Banyan trees

428

signaling to him. His father had lived in Hawaii once, as a boy on a military base. Westcott would have liked the discipline of being a cadet at West Point, as once his grandfather had been. He walked back towards the tent; the morning frost within him. The shrubs and bushes distantly taunted; tangible shadows amidst the shadowed reel of pictures in his mind. He knew he shouldn't but his mind gave way and he pondered at the absence of that space inside. It was soon becoming a cavity, sealed—just a vessel he carried inside—letting nothing in or out. How many times had *he*—Jay—looked upon her, the one who took for granted the details, having had them within hand's grasp for the better half of his life? And Westcott had trembled, waited interminable hours for a moment's touch. He'd gotten used to these thoughts and stepped away.

~

His eyes briefly catch a tarnished reflection on the second shelf. The encasement is old, the items it holds—artifacts, keepsakes, memorabilia from a time not long ago but too far to recapture.

Somehow each piece bears a stamp of craftsmanship; an era when tokens were made to endure. Solid, heavy—nothing tinny, cinchy, or god-forbid, plastic. Solely authentic. A plate, postcard. He peers at the knick-knacks timelessly stored. The wooden floorboards—

Sitting in a rocking chair, listening to the fire crackle. He scans the old registries stacked on the entrance table. Ellis conceals Liam under her jacket and blanket. Earlier, when he'd gone downstairs to use the lodge lavatory, the flared mortar of burgundy cement and wooden handrails showed themselves as they'd always been—nothing had changed in sixty years. Westcott held his damp shoes under the hand dryer. It was cold outside and the hike had gotten his shoes wet. Stepping into the men's stall and sitting down on the commode, the facility was clean. He studied faint etchings, inscriptions, initials carved out of the paint. He wondered, pants on thighs, shirt covering groin despite the privacy of the enclosure, had Jay once sat here as any man would just going about his business? This timeless restroom inside Skyland's lodge. It was cooler in the basement and his exposed skin began to chill. He wished he could know him, know him as Regn did. Jay was a concept, an abstraction. Why, why did it have to be like this? *I wish I knew you so you couldn't hate me for what you merely think I am. Worse, you have dismissed me and choose to forget.* How can a thing not fully understood be laid to rest? Such is not peace. It is preferred blindness.

Wait for me. He read the private book behind her eyes.
How long? He did not ask her. He did not ask himself.
Just long enough.
I'll return, her tenderness promised.
Return for good some day? The gentle intensity of his touch *kneaded* to know.
He'd kissed her on the forehead. His way of telling her *I will.*

She'd pulled his tweed cap down over his eyes.

• • •

It is the third week in October and the skies have that uncanny clarity about them during the evening hours. The leaves have been bowing out for quite some time and on this particular night a mild breeze sends the summer's besieged cavalry falling in masses. Those dead and waterlooed soldiers in the corner inlet—sent flying upwards in a sudden whirlwind fury of yellow and orange.

16 months earlier, Westcott had gone to the Shenandoah with Ellis. It was June. The full breadth of spring. Regn was there as well—with only her granddaughter, Rebecca. They'd been doing circles round each other, not realizing their proximity. Regn had left Westcott a voicemail on his mobile phone, but in the mountains his phone did not get reception. It wasn't until he was home that he listened to the message. He was sad at the missed opportunity, but equally glad that Regn had called, that she had wanted so much to be with him, or at least see him in the one place she loved above all—her mountains. And what if they had met up? How would Ellis have reacted? The brief excursion had been wonderful. He and Ellis had camped. But the nights were still freezing. His joints ached from shivering the night through. Ellis and he shared a sleeping bag to keep warmer. Inside something hurt, something he tried hard to conceal. Yes, he was having fun, but a part of him wished he could be alone with just Regn in the mountains. No Ellis, no Rebecca. Was it wrong to want something so natural?

For his birthday, the next year, he and Ellis had gone again to the Shenandoah. This time in the full bloom of fall. He liked it equally as in the spring, if not more. The cold and damp, the somberness mixed with depth of color gnawed on his unsatiated desire. He wanted the warmth of Regn's body to hunker down next to, to take into the cabin, and make endless, endless love.

Returning from the mountains, it is a Friday, Westcott meets Regn at Powhatan Creek that very same evening. His birthday. He can't wait another day. Neither can Regn. 'I brought you something,' he tells her on the phone. 'See you in a few minutes.' He leaves Bob's and Patsy's house—his neighbor's—where he, his mother, and Ellis have been "camping out" for the last week until the townhouse is ready for them to move into and all the papers processed through the realtor. Things are happening. And fast. But not the things he needs most. Not the things he wants to happen.

It is cool, fall enraptures his senses. His life is in limbo.
'So, what did you bring me—what's the gift?'
'You're looking at it.'
She takes him in her arms. 'I love my gift. Thank you.'

PART III

HOW I LIVE NOW

CRICKETS IN NOVEMBER

"...intelligence and passion born of living, the ability to move and be moved by subtleties of the mind and spirit, were what really counted. That's why he found young women unattractive...they had not lived long enough or hard enough to possess those qualities that interested him." —The Bridges of Madison County, Robert James Waller

I like to go to cemeteries. They are very calming. I don't feel alone. I never speak of this—I never did to anyone. I couldn't bear to hurt the woman I loved, for her to think she wasn't enough. But there is a distance inside, a part that remains impenetrable.

I was at the cemetery one afternoon. I read the headstones, some dating to the 1800s. I came to a Thomas B. Nottingham. b. September 1939 d. March 1947.

I suspected a casualty of the Second World War. But on American soil and two years after the German surrender in '45? I reconsidered my initial notion and wondered the cause of his death. Perhaps a freak accident. Had his father served overseas only to return and lose his son? Did the boy's mother lose her husband, then her son? How devastating. The headstone offered no answers. Only questions.

Were you a Tom? I asked in silence. What were you like? Did your friends call you Tommy or Thomas? How long has it been since someone said your name? I spoke his name aloud.

To this day the sound of a solitary bagpipe followed by the strength of multitudinous baggers piping in sends a wistful chill through my bones. It would be grand, of that I was sure. I wanted a respectful procession, something out of *Imitation of Life*. If you're not familiar with the Lana Turner film, let me tell you that Ms. Annie Johnson, Laura Meredith's friend and maid, has the horse-drawn carriage and the main street filled. In death I will not be obscure. I've made certain of this.

CHAPTER 5

I, NO LONGER

WHEN HE WAS YOUNG THE SHADOWS spoke to him more. The way the light danced on the wall and pierced the panes, leaves sashaying across the floor. The long evening shadows, twilight mysterium, obscure but friendly. The laundry room was always his favorite. A small window from another era, 2 1/2 feet, a foot and a half when opened horizontally. It didn't push, it slid to the left. Hide and seek in the wicker hamper. Tall white cabinets that held the scent of paint chips. He'd climb both ways through the window, a walnut tree conveniently hugging the house within arm's grasp. He'd hang from its bough, much too high for his short legs, and drop to the lava rocks below. A tingling pain in his heels and ankles upon impact. Hours on end he filled his days playing. He was never bored. The house spoke to him, though he'd yet to know what it was saying. He and Ellis would crawl under the deck, trenches from when the rains fell through the slatted wood. Cobwebs, all manner of intriguing adventures.

Into the cement—much cooler—basement, a little doorway without a door, a rectangular hole in the corner wall under the deck. Wallpaper in its original form dating to the 1800s. The very foundations. They crept along on all fours. He'd yet to discover fear. All the way to the front steps, an earthy, dusky secret place. The creaking stairs. How high could he jump from them? Sometimes he flung himself from the topmost, the porch itself, 8 steps high, landing, toppling onto the red bricks below. A green boxwood on either side. Wrought iron fence, white and glistening. The click of the gate. Balancing atop the two-inch railing and the elaborate gate with curling detail. It wobbled violently. One foot danced in the air, two arms out, a bird steadying before flight. The shudder would pass and he'd walk on, having gulfed the hardest three feet.

Magnolia cones, and ever the shedding leaves. An avenue that when you're young looks bigger, longer, truly remarkable in span. It *is* one of the longest streets in the city. A ceiling made of real leaves. Gold and green, lacquered, a mosaic, forever sealed. A turret with bay windows. A balcony from which to pick up broken tiles from the never finished floor and cast to the gravel below, a chink on the red aluminum fence. The sole purpose of hearing that clink. And the attic with birds, an occasional scurrying in the night, a rodent amidst the insulation. Always warm, so high up. And the tree that called to him most. The fig tree where once when Westcott was five Ellis dared him to kiss a boy. Bobby. He was six. His mother was younger then, though he could not see it.

• • •

Sheets from Ellis' room—white with Care Bears. Light blue sheets with fronds and fairies with great bushy manes for hair. He liked those linens. The ponds and dragonflies. Saying prayers with no need to question. Ding dong pillows, long tubular decorative pillows. Playing horse with them and sword fights. One morning he discovered a stuffed elephant tucked beside him. Beneath his pillow the Babar tape. An elephant in a green tux. He had no reason not to be happy. He just was. A Christmas when his mother sat beside the tree, crying. Dad had bought a basketball hoop and ping pong table for them. It was years later that he realized he'd bought them to wheedle his mother.

Climbing the pantry shelves. Locking the door and going up from the inside, stepping over to the refrigerator and jumping down. A gas stove. What need had he for a dishwasher, a microwave, when there wasn't one? The world was about to change. He didn't know he'd miss it. How fortunate to have experienced life just before it found wires, signals, chips—a network of partition. Links, not of hands and voices, but airwaves. He'd watched without watching, taking account. And then that other life stayed and he—yet trusting—went ahead, but never, no never along.

• • •

Gedny held him, rocked him. The waves broke and drifted—shhhhhhh. He tried to look at the sand, it hurt to look. His head pounded. To walk was agony, a drum to the skull. At first a blur, more muffled. The sights began to stab, light, too much light and then the nausea. Rolling with his head, a lulling dull constant ache deep within and the pangs of the frontal lobe. Migraine. He'd thrown up in a brown bag in the car. 'I hear the cottonwoods whisperin' low—' his mother gently sang. He liked that song for its tune and smoothness. He knew the diction of the words, but their romantic sentiment evaded him—it was but a song he liked, the song his mother would sing. She held him on her lap. Eleven, twelve years old, a moment of vulnerability. Migraines. Could be related to hormones, onset of puberty, the doctor speculated. It wasn't so. Four maybe five episodes in all. The last when he was in the 8th grade at Walsingham Academy in Virginia. He was fourteen. And then as mysteriously as one comes, they vanished altogether.

• • •

Funny what sticks in one's mind. I know our realtor's name—Lucy Gunn, a nice old woman—in her 70s. She steered us in the direction of the better neighborhoods. We settled on a new housing development that still left trees and ample room between the homes. Our model was to be built on the last cul-de-sac with a forest preserve as the backyard. This last point being most vital, as it indicated the trees could never be torn down for further development. My family loves trees. Ours was to be a beautiful, brand new home. The ground hadn't even been broken when we picked out our style, the floor plan, add-ons, vaulted ceiling or unvaulted. Mother wanted the little extras and I was glad of it. Instead of a flat post for the banister out front, she picked a balled style. Inside in the foyer our banister curled rather than coming down straight and ending abruptly. It was the small things that I remember, though at the time I hadn't been much concerned with such aesthetics. I was busy considering the move east, eager for the change. I felt no attachment to California. I did not feel as though anything was being left behind. I—we, were excited to go. It also helped that the man in the model, representing the building site, liked my mother. He was handsome. Maybe he was married and just being polite. I don't remember. But I do know he made sure our dining room had an extra four feet—an entire glass panel more for no charge. He gave Ellis a summer job as the receptionist. But mother would never go down that road again. Never date. At 53 she started over, although a part of her never recovered.

We would visit Virginia one more time before our move and at this point building was well underway. There's something exciting about seeing your home built. Everything new. Walls not yet saturated in memories or the voices of those lives it contains. A house has a character all its own and of our house on Shackleton Lane what I can say for sure is this: it was warm and full of light. Always physically warm.

We pulled up on the 4th of July 199—. Our new neighbors had a cake in celebration of the holiday. I would be 14 in three months.

Ellis graduated from Notre Dame High School the year before we made the trek eastward. Mother clearly asked if I wanted to stay in California for one more year so I could graduate with my classmates from St. Martin's. I had no reservations in declining. I have no diploma from elementary school. My 8th grade year I attended Walsingham Academy. It had an upper and lower school. K-7 comprised one side of the grassy knoll. And 8-12th the other. Graduation at Walsingham occurred in 7th grade so I was done out of one altogether. But I had no sense of loss. I wish I'd remained at Walsingham Academy for the curriculum, if nothing else. But I decided to give public school a go. At the time I made the mistake of thinking that by changing my environment things would right themselves.

Drummond's Field High School was only two years old when I entered its doors. To this day I can still smell the brand new linoleum and the way the light entered the many windows. Though I did not realize it at the time, I'd come to miss the discipline of donning a uniform as I'd done in elementary school. At Walsingham we were permitted to wear black or brown shoes but no sneakers, except for gym when we could change our shoes. Our sweaters were maroon with a small embroidered insignia. Yes, it's true as I sit and reflect on those days, little stands out anymore, but leaving Walsingham was a mistake. The first one, at any rate. Some nights when everyone was in bed—Mother and Ellis—I'd steal down to the living room and sit in the quiet dark looking around at the furniture and out the lace drapes of the front window. I cried. The grandfather clock from my childhood on Magnolia Avenue, once sentried on the landing, now stood in the foyer. Like a metronome, its pendulum marked the silence. A silent witness to my inextinguishable, unidentified grief. I felt the weight of confinement. Having tired myself alone in the dark, my eyes heavy, I would steal back upstairs and slide into bed. Somehow I hadn't planned on this—I hadn't planned on any of it. What had I been planning on?

As a young kid of 8 or 12 I imagined living on a farm, working with wild animals—a zoo in Africa, of children. I pretended I'd name them Lorelei and Thaddeus. But never, never did I consider the course to these things or what I really wanted. If I'd been seeking direction there was none to be found. I lived in a self-erected world, and for a while I became the characters I read about or occasionally watched on television. My favorite books at the time were the *Shiloh Trilogy* and *Where the Red Fern Grows*. I wanted so much to be Marty Preston or Billy Coleman that I adopted their form of dress; I even received an imitation coon-skin cap for Christmas one year. I remember the smell of fall coming and the security of my thicker clothes. Plaid jackets, corduroy pants. And my beloved, oh yes, my green corduroy overalls, which I wore until they could no longer be stitched. The time I wasted in pretending. I thought by sitting still nothing would change. I seldom spoke in school. My diligence never slackened, instead it increased. Coming home I'd have a snack, take the dog for a walk, then retire to my room to do homework before dinner and the beautiful evening hours.

The evening hours. How it aged me sitting in my room on wonderful spring eves, hearing the neighbor's young children playing just outside. I would be reading or scrolling something, studying the very sunlight on the wall, silently wishing. Waiting. There was no one to call and no one who called me. I did not have a single friend on the weekends to invite for fun. Saturdays always seemed restless. Once I made it to Sunday things became hopeful. The next day meant school, activity, kinetic energy. Even in the absence of conversation during the week, the feeling and movement of bodies around me unconsciously eased some of the loneliness. I did not speak of the future, I did not consider it. I listened to the crickets, always waiting for their return each spring, for the first sound of the chirping, and the last, sometimes holding on into November. I often looked up to the moon on chilled nights and with open palm held its cool, penetrating light as it illuminated the carpet of my bedroom. I remember the grass on my blue Converse Keds after the lawn was freshly cut, and the sweat, the layers of clothes. One night, I was 15 or maybe 16, I got the notion to lie on my chest and try to sleep. I believed if I laid on my breasts long enough, and every night, it would keep them flat, or at least prevent them from growing further. This idea lasted only 45 minutes as I never could sleep on my stomach; my neck grew uncomfortable from being turned to the side.

My wallpaper had a 12" border. A very picturesque, antiquated country scene of a cottage on an isle—it looked watered down in beige and green—it was lovely, inviting. Sometimes I'd study it—at night it was cast in shadow. During the day all warm.

———

I would rather not bring attention to those four wasted years. High school. An exercise in denial. Sadness. Pathetic drollery. Strong character manifests gradually. My mother had no confidence in herself. My sister was insecure. I didn't know this at the time. I had nowhere to turn but inward. I was passive, preoccupied, cut off. My strength hung on the evening star even though the morning star burned bright. Patience forced oldness upon me. Endurance and silence gave me strength. That short interval wrapped around my persona so tightly that the discontent became me—the tendrils of unspent youth arrested me in a state of despair, longing, and unanswered speculation. Those were the lost years. The days of no one and nothing but myself and a hope so strong, a resolve so patient, hanging on the notion that one day I would be liberated from my body and that liberation was the key to happiness. Foolish youth that I was. I was not ready to become a man. I wanted to be a boy. But childhood was gone. I lived in a fantasy. I will not waste much time here because the past is done with, unalterable, but the events bear evidence to what came after.

~

In that interval intended for self-exploration and the examination of the body, I looked out the window and studied the seasons. I loved spring and in March I would press my face near the screen, late at night or in the evening, smell the cold air and listen for the first cricket. But I also hated spring. I dreaded the rising temperatures, the Virginia humidity, the still closeness of endless days. It was not the heat I hated; it was what it represented. In my flannel jacket, dark shirt and loose jeans I would feel swaddled, conspicuous, layered in concealment. In an effort to hide my body I succeeded in standing out. And so it was fall that I cherished most. I could smell its approach on an early September afternoon—that crisp coolness. The sun made the late afternoon shadows sharper and colors distinctly laden with impending color. In the fall I was safe.

———

There had been the possibility of friendship at Walsingham Academy. Being a much smaller school and a new student, Westcott attracted many a congenial peer. At that time he wore the plaid skirt and burgundy sweater donned by his female counterparts. He did not exhibit any sexuality. No breasts showed. He remained unisex in body, so putting on a skirt didn't bother him nearly as much in those days. Though relatively shy, he could blend in. His teachers liked him. He received all A's his 8th grade year.

At lunch he sat with Allison, Jonathan, and Michael. He found Michael cute. All the girls called him Simba. Lunch was difficult. Westcott listened to the others talk. He didn't like his appearance and never wished to draw attention to himself.

One January afternoon it began to snow. The school closed early. Elizabeth Wilcox, a friendly bespectacled classmate, who was in many of the same classes as Westcott, asked if he needed a ride home. He remembers the occasion because it was the only time a classmate ever pulled into his driveway, came to his house, even though Elizabeth never actually went inside. In recollection it signified yet another moment when life might have assumed a different course. What if Westcott had made a friend after moving to Virginia? What if in time he'd confided in another girl or boy about his distress? His compulsive rituals seized him that year so that sometimes he'd have to get in and out of bed 15 times at night. He couldn't sleep unless certain books were under his pillow. He washed his hands until they were raw and started to crack and bleed in the dry winter.

Many students transferred to Drummond's Field High School, rejoicing in the freedom to wear any clothes they liked and not have to attend church ceremonies or take religion courses. None of this had bothered Westcott. He left Walsingham to escape himself. Elizabeth stayed. At the end of the year, in his yearbook she wrote:

Please don't leave. I hope to see you this summer!
Your Friend,
    Elizabeth

Tuition was going up for private school, but the education was still worth it. What if his mother had insisted he stay? What if he'd been forced to confront himself? Westcott honestly had no definitive answer as to what was bothering him. There were hints, but the truth had yet to actualize itself. Even to him.

Another time, when he was 14 or 15, he'd gone to the doctor. On his way out one of the nurses said, 'Put your shoulders back, keep your head up and be proud.' She'd witnessed a timid, young woman with rounded shoulders desperately wanting to hide. As a "young woman" Westcott never felt confident or proud. He was ashamed of his body and the budding flesh that could no longer be ignored. He did not look at his naked form with curiosity and expectation as many pubescent females tend to do. Instead he maintained a chaste, self-imposed blind ignorance. What he chose not to see didn't exist.

———

He hadn't a name for it. As he watched Timmy in the modern day Lassie series, crawling on the ground in a pair of jeans and T-shirt, he felt himself sitting there in his corduroy overalls with the stitched knees and twisty-ties used in place of buttons to hold the clasp of the suspenders. He felt himself through his mind and envied Timmy, the character playing him. Something wasn't fair. Whatever it was he wasn't going to think about it.

He was fifteen years old. She sat in her chair, the little machine blowing air by the door—a sound barrier. 'Do your breasts bother you?' He would not, could not look at her and indignantly clenched his jaw in silence. *Breasts*, what was she talking about? He didn't have breasts! She was the first therapist who mentioned gender dysphoria to his mother.

His sixteenth birthday. Skinny as a bean pole, it seemed the theory posed by Frisch and Revelle was accurate. He did not have enough body fat to elicit the advent of monthly hardships. He was lean muscle. But it couldn't last. October. He'd come home from the dentist and like any other day gone into the restroom. Gathering some paper, he looked down, discovering the faintest streak of pink. Knowing without wanting to know.

That night he fell to his knees in supplication; bewildered, angry, vehement protest. *I want to die, this isn't fair. This isn't right!*

His mother said, 'Put something on.' He did not want any part of it—a cumbersome layer between his legs. The feeling of slow crawling from within.

He refused to enter the facilities at school, lest his sex be confirmed. Gradually, flow increased and on heavy days he wore black pants. A single napkin saturated. He sat on the edge of his chair, feeling the dampness seep to the fringes of absorbency. When he stood a reservoir of abhorrence gushed forth. The feminine scent—spoiled fish fried in an unventilated kitchen. One day it showed on the dark green plastic chair at his desk. His black cords protected him. With his knee he tried to wipe the blood off. It was the end of the day, the bell about to ring. He rested his knee, scrupulously. The stain only smeared. He could feel the wetness of his pants. His plaid jacket covered his netherlands. When no one was looking he nonchalantly moved the position of his chair, placing its truth at another's desk.

Tampon. The word was appalling. Nothing was going inside him. He would not use one. That part didn't exist. No one could see what was occurring below the waist. Up top— his breasts—that was something he must hide.

How I Lived Then

Flickerin' Firefly

The boy dragged himself upstairs to his room. Sank into his chair. Outside spring permeated the senses. The boy sat completely still, gazing at a picture. *O' God!* He pleaded in silence. His head dropped down between his arms, resting against his hands, his palms.

How pathetic I am, how pathetic! His body visibly shook beneath his skin. He couldn't help it.

What can I do, can't run away, no place to go, no one. How wonderful—just go into a picture. Disappear into a picture on the wall—become a character in a book. God, oh God. *O' God!*

His face grew tight, ached. His eyes stung, his head throbbed. He got ready for bed, threw the blanket aside, fell in, welcoming the hearse-drawn night. His heart remained restless while his mind was exhausted. He turned toward the wall. Resigned from pain. After a while he rolled onto his back and looked at the gentle light cast on his wall from the distant world—the moon.

His eyes smiled. Sifting over his room in the shadows, he focused his attention on the wall directly in front of him. There hung a picture of an old lane with shadows of great Magnolia trees blowing over its sidewalk. It was a painting of the street where he grew up. The boy lay still, studying every detail of the place before him, such content. His heart sighed.

~

It had been a long time since that night—a year or more. Again the boy found himself alone in his room, sitting limply at his desk gazing out the window to his right. He couldn't cry anymore that day, his spirit was tired. The argument had unfolded downstairs when he proclaimed, 'I have an idea of the kind of day I'll die on.'

Westcott now stared out the panes, his eyes falling upon a pinwheel in his neighbor's yard. It was in the form of a bird, with wings built to catch the wind and spin in opposite directions. Every so often the sun would hit the metal appendages as they turned and a glint of light would catch the boy's eyes.

Round and round the wings go yet the bird never moves, it is forever treading the same winds… *Neither you nor I am free to go where we want.*

The past few months the light had been dimming in the boy. A lime green iridescence. A breathing lantern—like fireflies. It was late April 200—.

Graduation was just around the corner. Westcott felt the little security he had slowly begin to drift away. He dreaded the day a diploma would be placed in his hands as he and his fellow classmates marched to the tune of "Pomp and Circumstance." He did not like the thought of leaving the only place he knew. Despite his isolation from the other students, he had come to cherish his years spent at Drummond's Field High School. He didn't care about the loneliness, the endless lunches passed in silence. It was the routine, the simple assurance that tomorrow would be the same. He had grown fond of his teachers; the likelihood of seeing them again would be remote. The social misfit he had become was no less a part of something greater. For all his seclusion, his phantom-like presence *did* fill a void in the entirety of his class. Westcott knew a test was at hand. His ability to adjust and continue was a question he could not yet answer.

A yellow light jumped about on the wall, its origin far away. An obstruction in the form of a swaying tree forced the light to separate, spreading across the white canvas with the wind as its guide. A spring eve painted itself before his eyes. The golden warmth comforted and brought a distant sorrow upon his face. It reminded him the days were ever longer and the tortures of summer idleness just a few short weeks away. And the heat. He thought back over the past five years. Moving clear across country to the east coast; the year he got his license; his sister's graduation from college; changing his name. And the day he told his mother. He wished he'd told her sooner. How could he? He didn't know what was wrong. The term for the condition was foreign to him, as were the implications.

The American Dream

It was the first day of his junior year at Drummond's Field High School. His straggly brown hair was long, falling just below his shoulders. He wore gray khakis, a long-sleeved green and beige plaid shirt. His gray shoes with the blue trim complemented the outfit nicely. Below the classroom windows running parallel to the drop-off area, tucked away in the shrubbery and bushes, a chirping vibrated. At such young hours of the day, 7:25, 7:30 a.m., crickets had yet to fall silent beneath the blazing sun. Many a morning would come to pass wherein the boy would plod alongside the bed of invisible musicians, a slight sweat beading from his neck and forehead soon to be quenched by the air conditioned interior of his school. He always listened for them.

Eleventh grade marked the time before Westcott became *Westcott*. He thought and spoke of himself as 'the boy.' For the past sixteen years he had been known by another name. A name he preferred not to mention.

The first few weeks of school sailed by. Westcott settled down for the long haul, glad the summer was over. At last he would have something to occupy his time, even if it meant studying, taking tests, and reading books—he enjoyed learning. It was in his third year of high school when he met Mrs. Talmedge and Mrs. McCormick. They shared the role of teacher for 4th block American Studies. Westcott quickly grew to like them and took well to their style of team-teaching. He'd signed up for Honors English 11, fully capable of its challenging nature. Upon learning the details of the course workload, however, he realized he had no energy for rigorous curriculum. His mother did not urge or tell him, 'You must.' She supported his not taking it, which later disappointed him. 'Summer should be about relaxation, a break, not having to do all sorts of assignments. All right, maybe read some books and do a report, but this other stuff—it's too much,' she agreed. His denial drained all stamina to the point of weary existence. Summers he stayed inside. He did not want to be seen out and about shrouded in his coat, concealing his body. Even though his breasts were bound, his features betrayed him—soft skin, wide hips. Not the least hint of facial hair. He hated being cooped up.

Rather than take the next class down, Advanced American Studies with its entourage of summer assignments, Westcott opted for the general basement course where no labels of higher achievement were attached to the class title. His teachers told him they sorely regretted his not being in a more academically elevated atmosphere—even in their advanced classes they had never seen work like his. Modest, or perhaps it was just shyness, it embarrassed him to hear them say such things. Westcott, though disappointed for not pushing himself higher, was devoid of the concern shared by Mrs. T, as she liked to be called, and

Mrs. McCormick. Taking plain American Studies gave him more than any college preparatory class could hope to—he had the freedom to observe because he found the work effortless.

Mrs. McCormick was a plump lady with a round face, bright blue eyes, and red kinky hair full and fluffed, indicative of her Irish descent. She was married to an accountant. The boy speculated she wore her hair so bushy in hopes of concealing some of her weight. At times she would push it back with a headband. She dressed thriftily and practically, but stylishly despite her weight, often wearing a salmon and beige striped or solid amber sweater. Mrs. McCormick was responsible for the historical aspect of the class, bringing her students through the settling of Jamestown and the colonial era. From there it was on to the shot heard round the world, the Emancipation Proclamation, the crash of '29, the dropping of the atomic bomb, Little Man, the Baatan Death March, and to round things out, Nine-Eleven.

For a woman also in her late twenties, Mrs. Talmedge was of average height with dirty blond hair styled to reflect the trends of the time. It was cut short in the front with bangs that fell slanted across her forehead and eye, flaring out on both sides and behind the neck. By studying the roots her natural hair color was a mousy brown. She was not what one would call heavy; she wasn't at her optimal weight level either. She was voluptuous with a Meryl Streep complexion and eyes very much like the actress's. Her hands and feet were exceptionally small and her nose ran long and straight; on closer inspection it curled ever so slightly at the end. She resembled Susan Lewis of TV's *ER* series. The boy found her titillating to look at without being conscious of it.

She had a strong voice that would transform without warning into a remarkably loud instrument used to get the class' attention. There was a gruffness in its tone, which the boy liked, nothing delicate or fragile hindering its pitch. Her most pronounced physical characteristic was her rear end, accentuated by her taste in form-fitting clothes. She did not always wear the most flattering attire. On certain occasions when not wearing a skirt or the stereotypical teacher's jumper, but cotton thin pants, Westcott would bet money on it that she was free as a breeze without underwear, or a thong. She didn't possess the slightest hint of a line even along the seams of her thighs and dimpled rear. The problem with Mrs. Talmedge was that nothing ever fit her voluptuous body properly. She was simply curved peculiarly and there wasn't anything she could do about it. He liked that she was unusual and he liked watching her. The feature that interested him the most was her eyes, which in most circumstances deliver the brunt of body language. He could never hold her gaze or anyone's. He was afraid to look a person in the eye.

Westcott respected his teachers and looked up to them. They were far from any status of senators, kings, or gods, but he always aimed to please them. He didn't want to let them down. Was he seeking their approval? School was all he had, he worked diligently. He wanted anything to divert attention from thinking about himself.

The second week of school the class received its first major assignment. Each student was to write a paper on what he or she believed to be the American Dream. He wrote his paper the evening of September 11th, 2001. He had just left Journalism class the morning of the terrorist attack and was heading to Algebra II when the world learned the towers had been struck. For the rest of the day normal classroom activities were suspended. Teachers and students watched the news channels. During fourth block Mrs. McCormick scrolled a dubious name on the dry-eraser board, underscoring that it would probably be the most dramatic event ever witnessed in the course of their lives, if not the most horrific assault on U.S. soil *thus* far.

Westcott feels no reaction one way or the other. He watches everyone's reaction. Keeps seeing the way the towers symmetrically fall. They cascade perfectly. They don't topple. Something is amiss. He'd dined in *Windows on the World* when he was 11. The way the media shows the same clips over and over. Truth is being supplanted. Everyone watches the screen. One girl cries. Westcott looks out the window.

Like so many things in his life, he unwittingly possesses the ability to defer emotional impact. It is the small things that shake him greatest. The horrific event proves far removed from the immediate war he is facing.

In years to follow he will often look upon his fellow man as matchstick figures. He hates war, it is the stupidest thing next to the invention of the "car bra." Little men blowing each other up, destroying beautiful architecture. Destruction, wasted resources, conflict. All for power, control, money—manmade entities. Since the dawn of time man has been killing himself.

In light of the recent events shaking America from its slumbering state of false security, Westcott recognizes the supreme paradox between reality and dream. The envisioned homeland, as described in his essay, is obsolete.

Westcott A. Rowan
American Studies
11 September 20—

The American Dream drives us, as a body, to continue going forth. It is disguised by many faces and cannot be carved to fit a single definition. It lives in the mind, which it calls home, and drums in the hearts of its creators. Each individual's hopes and dreams entail different pieces. These pieces, when put together, form a kaleidoscope of ideals; it's the point at which complete satisfaction and contentment arise, and for a brief second the bars of reality fail to hold that person back. A glimpse of the dream emerges from the distant horizon; the wall of bills, debts, worry and fear, concern for more money, more time, fall away. There is no right or wrong answer for *what* the Dream is or should be. It stands as a symbol of longing and hope waiting to be grasped before succumbing to a captor: hindsight, regret. How one decides to depict his/her dream and defend it against all others is singular, but in the end all human beings share a common ground—the need, the desire to have a dream.

I define the American Dream as living in the country. The roar of cars is gently displaced by soft winds, buildings and cement quietly give way to rolling fields, and the land with trees from generations past, lies still. The dream sways in the breeze of some distant home. The sun pierces through the tall branches of a tired oak, casting a gentle light on the leaves and dusty ground. Beyond the tree, the tall grass sighs in the wind and still further there rests an old farm with a small house nearby. A dog from long ago sleeps silently on the worn porch at the foot of a rocking chair. Every once in a while the paw twitches or the black nose quivers, perhaps the tall grass beckoning him. At the edge of the porch sits a rusted lantern. Like the flame of the lantern the dream flickers, yearning to be heard.

Today money is an essential part of the American Dream. New houses are erected, more parking space made available, and old businesses are bought out—all for the sake of the silver dollar. I find a rickety old fence along a dirt road to be of more importance, intrigue, than a new shopping center. The old fence is a remnant of the original American Dream; it stands in silent defiance, a testament of a story long ago, a dream that once was, but has somehow faded. The dream dims in the old country stores, hidden in the shadows of earlier American times, and in the fields not yet destroyed by tractors. Eventually, when the last bit of free land is taken, the country roads paved, and one too many trees cut down, piled onto trucks, then the illusion will cease to exist. Only in the minds of those whose dream it is still a part of will the stories be heard and the places remembered.

The majority of people I surveyed and some of those discussed in class said their American Dream means having financial stability, being well established with good opportunities. Mine, it would seem, is obsolete. The opinions of others support how they discern the world at present. I agree with many of their views as well as their desire for money and wealth—one must—but these aspects are not paramount.

Most, if not all, yearn for the idealistic utopia—the earth to be a place of peace. As human beings, we strive to make our dreams a reality. Something we created long ago, so that even in times of terror or sorrow it keeps us searching ahead for something better, a hand to catch us lest we fall and never regain strength. Too many forget their dream in the chaos of everyday and by the time they look up, look back to recapture the flicker of recognition, their life is but a memory of dream and opportunity. There are others yet, who find fragments, only to discover they still miss the crucial links. As for those few who do succeed in fulfilling their highest hopes and dreams, they are the blessed lucky ones—a fortunate few. Whether mere chance or by their own toiling hand, the walls are mounted. It is what we base our expectations on, set our goals to, and find refuge in from everyday mishaps and the mundane. The American Dream is any dream. She can be seen in the rising sun and glowing moon, her words echoing from some distant train whistle, carried on the winds. She seems to whisper what we all want and always will, the freedom to—

GETTING TO KNOW HIM

As the days drew on it became apparent to Mrs. Talmedge and Mrs. McCormick Westcott was a shy, quiet student. *Westcott* ascribed his introverted personality and nervous behavior to isolation, which he believed was the direct result of his "situation." He was never at ease with himself—his body—so naturally how could he be comfortable around others? He avoided eye contact. He might glance at someone—catch his or her eye for a brief second. At times he felt he came across as aloof or maybe out to lunch. Afterwards he felt foolish for giving the wrong impression. An excellent student, he had no friends. There were the occasional classmates he'd talk to or joke with, but he perceived them as mere acquaintances. There were no weekend get-togethers. No friendly phone calls. Other students were consistently nice to him. He was polite in turn. That's where it stopped. He didn't know himself. How could he let them get close?

Most days Westcott would go all through fourth block, and most of the day, without uttering a word. He'd sit at his desk taking notes or listening to one of the teachers lecture. His nervousness was at its height during his junior year. At times his hands shook, his eyes darted about suspiciously. 'Are those boys bothering you?' Mrs. T asked one afternoon. They weren't of course, they were idly chatting, just minding their own. And here was Westcott, evidently unnerved, a basket case of jitters.

Just great, now she probably thinks I'm being sexually abused at home. He couldn't tell her, it's not them. It's me. Yes, the boys are bothering me, but it's not their fault. Their mere freedom is an affront.

'No,' Westcott tells her plainly.

His bangs are long and pushed to the side—he likes to hide under them. Sometimes he is too afraid to move and push them back so he can see out of his left eye.

Finding arrogance and conceitedness to be unappealing attributes, he did not think very highly of himself for fear that such confidence might lead to certain undesirable traits. There were other days in contrast when he managed to muster up enough courage to relax *slightly* and his mind settled. It angered him not to be able to just sit back and enjoy the class as he wanted. These times would forever affect him—even then he knew it; they marked the best part of his life and he could not be involved in each moment nor could he live through each day as he yearned. He was imprisoned within his mind, his flesh and bones the bars of his cell. At the present hour action could not be taken to relieve the discomfort. He would have to wait. He did not know how to belong so he was forced to remain in the background, a silent observer, conspicuous because of his strange qualities.

Westcott's undying loneliness—and that's just what it was—became a companion to the boy; it was the one constant that would never abandon him. Even in his hardest hours, particularly in those moments of self-reckoning, *it* remained loyal. Westcott did not wish to conform. He simply wanted the privilege of normalcy.

Fortunately, there are a few advantages of being on the outside looking in, which Westcott internalized. Owing to his quiet nature, he would never raise his hand. He relied on himself to solve a problem or come to a conclusion. On the rare occasions he did seek a necessary answer, he first devised a plan on how to approach the teacher. He'd go over in his mind what he was going to say, there was a process to follow; he had to work himself up to asking the question. He then considered how easy things would have been if only he had... The thought angered him so he buried it in his heart with the knowledge that tomorrow, the next day, the day after, and always he would have to confront the cause of his despair.

Aside from strengthening self-reliance, his isolation provided ample opportunity to observe. He loved to sit and study people. He'd watch Mrs. Talmedge and Mrs. McCormick as they taught, taking in their gestures and body language, their confidence and self-assurance. There was something to be learned from them. He took notice of what they wore each day and listened intently to their daily teachings. At times Westcott would unintentionally make eye contact with one of the teachers as he looked about the room absorbing everything. Mrs. T might wink at him. He'd offer a discomfited blush in return, quickly glancing away. For some reason he felt less threatened when his eyes met with another's at a distance. Their gaze seemed less penetrating and damaging from afar.

~

Westcott stood at 5' 8" with spindly arms and dusky blue eyes hammocked in shadows of weariness. He had a straggly appearance. Rather than retreat at the sign of any bad weather he'd stay his ground, even if it meant weathering the storm. Ellis teased him. He reminded her of the characters in *The Dark Crystal*. His ears always poking through his untamed hair. His unkempt look was owing to the long, ratty hair stuck snarled down in his shirt collar and his shaggy bangs he liked to think curtained him from the world. By avoiding touching and looking at himself he did not have to confront the matter.

Others questioned him and wondered, sometimes being brazen enough to go up and ask, 'Are you a boy or a girl?' He'd fumble to answer, retorting, 'What do you think?' If anything they assumed he must be gay. This irritated him.

He almost wished he had been born a homosexual *boy*. Damn if it wouldn't have been easier for everyone. His paradox was still relatively unknown. The average person was unable, or more likely, unwilling to comprehend all of its medical factors. For the moment he had no choice but to live a lie and hope his patience could sustain him. His grief was just beginning.

———

Shortly after reading the boy's American Dream essay, Mrs. T and Mrs. McCormick prompted Westcott to join the Literary Magazine. A year earlier his 10th grade English teacher, Mr. Lambden, had urged him to do the same; however, his timidness inhibited his ability to assert such a proposal. Fully aware of Westcott's unobtrusive personality and impaired social skills, Mrs. Talmedge took it upon herself to introduce the boy to the club's leader; a position she once held but had recently relinquished to a close colleague. He didn't have the confidence to undertake the initiative of seeking out any meetings on his own. Mrs. T understood this and to her credit went the extra distance, making an effort to get him involved rather than have him fall by the wayside yet another year.

It was Monday afternoon, the last week of September. The 2:40 bell sounded its tone. He missed the "bells" of his youth. The automated tone seemed cold.

'Ms. Garlow, this is the student I was telling you about.' Mrs. T motioned towards the boy. She had not used the term *the student* to identify him, but rather his *former* name.

Ms. Garlow held out her hand, receiving a sweaty palm to shake.

COMING HOME TO A BROTHER

Early in the semester, Mrs. McCormick was discussing George Washington's pre-war hero life and his role in the Revolutionary Battle against England. Mrs. T indicated Washington was purported to have been sterile.

'How come?' The class wanted details.

'Let's just say he was an avid horseman!'

There was an eruption of laughter.

On another occasion, prior to the unveiling of the first president's virility, around the time they were getting ready to watch *The Last of the Mohicans*, Mrs. T told an old Indian legend about how the celestial bodies—the stars, came to fill the sky. Although the details of the story have become quite hazy, Westcott recalls something about a pack of wolves being chased out of an Indian village and a froth-white saliva streaming from their mouths, filling the darkness as they tore back into the night. The tale always stuck with him, perhaps because he loved how Mrs. T narrated it and captivated his intrigue. Perhaps because it reminded him of Jackie Moss and her love of Siberian Huskies. Perhaps because of his connection to Indian culture and beliefs. In that moment she ceased to just be teaching; she was giving them something, something to hold onto. Westcott felt compelled to listen.

In early October Westcott went with his American Studies class downstairs to the auditorium. It was picture day for the yearbook. Knowing he'd have another mug shot opportunity the following morning during Journalism class, he, along with a few other students, decided to postpone it. Mrs. T idly chided the boy.

'How come you're not getting your photo taken today...want to groom yourself first, right?'

'No. I hate taking pictures.'

'I know what you mean. I don't think it always captures my best features either.'

He was surprised. She didn't seem the self-conscious type. The kind of person who cared what others thought, that is, in a fair-minded sense. Could it be that the confidence and self-assurance she displayed when teaching was a facade?

~

The winds turned cold. Leaves cart-wheeled across the roads. Darkness fell upon the land shortly after five. Each year he always waited. Waited for the first breath of crisp chill in the air, an indication of fall—a haven of concealment. With the dropping temperatures he could wear his plaid jackets more comfortably. He did not stand out when the weather warranted layers of clothing. He hated summer for the sparseness of clothing and hiding himself away in his room. Spring was different. Spring always tugged at something inside—a wistful pull, a desperate ache—to just wake up, pull on a t-shirt and walk outside. No tape, no jacket, no discomfort. Everything was always so sharp in October. Was it the lighting? He loved the cool scent in the air, evenings when he'd savor the perfection of the lawn he'd just mowed, the residue of sweet blades and soil flecks dusting his clothes.

His birthday came and went for the seventeenth time, pumpkin rinds were carved, Thanksgiving rolled by without any visiting relatives. It was Westcott and his mother that year sitting around the dining room table with his two dogs, Thomas and Cricket, and his cat, Strum. Thomas was a Golden Retriever with deep russet-gold fur like wheat.

Ellis had been gone since August on her trip around the world. The previous spring she'd signed up to go on *Semester at Sea*, an educational program sponsored by the University of Pittsburgh. For four months she would be sailing to different ports across the globe while taking classes aboard the ship. Westcott had waved goodbye to his sister from the dock in Vancouver. He watched the little tugboat pull the S.S. Explorer out to sea. She was lucky and it had nothing to do with her leaving on a "Voyage of Discovery," the program's motto. He did not resent her for going off to experience the world; she was a senior at William & Mary and had every right to leave her family. All he wanted was the freedom. The freedom she took for granted. She didn't know what it was to scream in silence, 'This isn't right! For God's sake, why?' He couldn't do the things he yearned to—run, swim, throw on a t-shirt. Dating never occurred to him. His situation *was* crippling. Physically. Socially. And spiritually.

~

During Ellis' absence Gedny was the only person he had for company. He had Thomas and Cricket, but they had started to get on his nerves. They were another reminder of what he couldn't, or wouldn't do. He wanted to run with them at the park, go for long walks, wrestle with them in his backyard or even *the front*. What if the neighbor's saw him? What if something showed? He hated the feel of distended flesh whenever he ran, despite the use of a sports bra. Westcott had always been close to his mother. As a child plagued by psoriasis, growing up with her stepfather, Mel—the *cause* of Gedny's breakouts—she had been afraid, insecure, emotionally abandoned by her own mother. Gedny knew her son's insecurities in a separate way, sharing his pain of what it meant to be different. But she gave no guidance. He needed a firm hand. She was never hard on him. Ellis was not so forgiving. She accepted Westcott for what he was, but she grew annoyed with his inability to function. She could be hurtful, impatient, uncompromising. But this side would have been more effective. Westcott needed someone to throw him up against a wall and say, 'Look! Look at what you are. Deal with it, then if you still want to change, then change!' There were times Westcott's mother became exasperated, raising her voice out of sheer exhaustion and frustration. He knew it hurt her to do so. His sister was wounding in the beginning. She called him a freak. She was right. He *wasn't* simply a tomboy, nor was he socially adjusted. Ellis wasn't calling him a freak because of his body or ideas about gender. It was the way he was handling, or rather *not* handling the issue, that angered her. His distorted shoulders, stringy hair, shifty eyes. But Ellis had her own life. Without his mother Westcott had no one else—

He wishes his mother had been harder on him. Maybe then he wouldn't have resented her. Over time, in years to come, it no longer mattered.

———

For third block, Westcott had Driver's Ed held in a makeshift classroom, a trailer, behind the school. He didn't particularly like the class, but it would be better to take the course and test at school than with a DMV instructor. He'd never driven a car in his life, not even at home. He remembered what it was like getting into the student vehicle for the first time. In the beginning he distrusted himself behind the wheel and disliked the responsibility involved in driving. He held no desire to drive—it was just another sign of the advent of adulthood. First some adjustments would have to be made before he could grow up. It was at his mother's request that he unwillingly signed up for the course.

Every two weeks his class went outside to the rear parking lot for an exercise. Often the Drummond's FHS marching band stood on the field running through its half-time repertoire. Westcott listened to the hollow knock of the wooden block setting the rhythm for the other instruments to follow. He felt the wind play with his loose hair. He is standing, tempering the physical pain. He needs to use the restroom. He is wet. Something between his legs aches. The day is heavy. The sanitary napkin is oversaturated. He feels dampness on the seat of his pants.

He's deciding what to do when his instructor calls him over. 'Your turn!'

The interior of the car is tan upholstery. Westcott tries to pull the hem of his jacket down, far enough to sit on without actually removing his jacket. He holds himself up with his legs fully extended under the dash, still able to press the pedals. His instructor gets in beside him. Can he tell Westcott isn't sitting fully in the seat?

He maneuvers between the cones, hurries. If it doesn't touch the seat—

He waits for his instructor to get out, in case there is evidence. He wants to see it first. He quickly steps out, looks hastily at the driver's seat. Thank god.

His lower abdomen has cramps. He wants to change his clothes, relieve the fullness inside him. The warm dampness is disgusting. He will sit on his jacket all through fourth block. 90 minutes. 115 minutes until he can change. Until he can go to the restroom. Until he is safe at home.

~

In late November a series of bomb threats scrolled on notes or telephoned into the school disrupted the class block schedule. Westcott was denied the pleasure of American Studies for several days. A strict policy of supervision was put into action. An investigation to find the culprits ensued; students were no longer permitted to leave the classroom without being escorted by a teacher. He never asked to be excused. On one occasion, having waited out on the track field for 45 minutes the students were subjected to a backpack search upon reentering the building. Westcott hastily unzipped the small front compartment on his olive green backpack. What if they asked to see what was wrapped in the folded toilet paper? He crumpled the square in his fist, stuffing it in his pants' pocket. Why he kept the sanitary napkin on reserve he didn't know. He'd never dare to enter the restroom to use it. With the interruptions stopped, things returned to normal. Then one afternoon during fourth period Mrs. T called the boy over.

Mrs. McCormick was in the middle of discussing the annexation of Texas. Westcott knew he was not in trouble, but he hated to be singled out. For a while Mrs. T had been trying to come up with some extra assignment that would better challenge the boy; in her opinion he did not belong in a basic history course. She gave him a copy of Henry Thoreau's *Walden*. He should take notes on it so they could discuss it weekly. Fidgeting in his chair, ears bright red, Westcott twiddled with his pen unable to make eye contact because of her proximity. He returned to his desk looking reamed out, dejected, too concerned others were watching him to let on that something positive was the reason behind his being taken aside. Despite reading a quarter of the book, Westcott felt little desire to finish it. He found the presentation of it boring. He devoted all energy to his regular assignments going far and beyond the expectations set forth in the syllabus. He regretted not meeting Mrs. T halfway in her own devised independent reading project and missing the opportunity to exchange words with her regularly on his suggested Thursday afternoons. He let himself down, wondering at times how high he could have gone had it not been for his depressive, stifled emotions.

December arrived. Ellis would be coming home. Westcott and his mother planned to be waiting for her on the dock in Miami where the students would disembark. It was four a.m. on Friday the seventh when the boy left with his mother. The night before they went to Colonial Williamsburg for the annual Grand Illumination, a fireworks extravaganza. Afterward, Westcott finished reading a short play, *The Night Thoreau Spent in Jail*. His class would be completing it the next day when he was gone. For his own benefit he took it upon himself to read the ending. All together he'd be missing six days of school. Unlike most teenagers who rejoiced at the chance to escape the daily grind, it bothered him not to be there. His American Studies class was just beginning to study about the Civil War, an event that enormously intrigued him. It's not that he wasn't looking forward to seeing his sister. He just wished she was returning two weeks later when it would be Christmas break.

After sleeping over one night in northern Florida, they set out early the next morning along I-95 in hopes of reaching the state's southern tip before nightfall. On Sunday, before dawn had yet to stir the city streets, they made their way down to the harbor. Berets scoured the port with large firearms in hand, compliments of September eleventh's attack (Ellis' ship had been in the Pacific preparing to dock in Japan the morning that all hell broke loose. The Japanese welcomed them with open arms). Westcott was amazed by the 75-degree weather, stymied as to how anyone living there could believe it was nearly Christmas. Mother had lived in Miami 20 years and never adapted.

For his Journalism class Westcott described the events of the day in an article:

The figure hung out of the porthole, unnoticeable among the 600 some odd students who crowded the decks. Banners were strewn over the rails painted with words of thanks. Across the port, behind a metal fence, families waited eagerly searching the ship from stern to bow for their children. The figure called out excitedly over and over down to the dock, but the very people from whom she had parted three-and-a-half months earlier couldn't hear her. There she stood, just another face, watching the people ashore. It was a day much longed for. Now that it had arrived she was reluctant to leave the ship, which she'd come to call home.

Back inside, the students' luggage and belongings were prepared for unloading. Vietnam rice hats found themselves tied on backpacks—too awkward and fragile to pack. Keepsakes to remember the voyage lay tucked away in boxes piled ceiling high. Semester At Sea bumper stickers could be read through clear plastic storage bins, and t-shirts with the letters SAS were donned by many students.

The morning was young, eight a.m. The Miami sky was quickly warming. Stratus clouds illuminated gold against the faint blue and the rising humidity. The figure stood leaning out the window for quite awhile before withdrawing into the ship's bowels. It would be another two hours before students could begin disembarking. For the last time the figure made her way to the dining hall to breakfast. Her mind filled with experiences of 100 days past. It had been a voyage of discovery into lives unknown, cultures seas apart, and across oceans traversed by ancient explorers.

The semester had ended and the floating university was docked at its final port.

In Miami, Gedny showed her children the old places of her youth. The house on 16th Street. Her high school. Somehow they found the cemetery plot where her mother was buried. She should have been buried in New York.

~

Ellis learned of Westcott's dilemma a short time after departing on her semester-long voyage. Had his mother written a letter? It was a major adjustment, one she could defer while drifting away—literally. Ever since his family had moved back east, and even long before when they were still living in California, Westcott was forced to put in time with a therapist. Originally his mother sought counseling for him and his sister due to the 'long and bitter divorce.' His mother's phrase. In the end his father was awarded their 1880s Victorian, the only home he'd lived in. He, his mother, and Ellis were forced to rent for a year. They planned on moving out of the state just as soon as Ellis graduated from Notre Dame High.

It wasn't until they moved to Virginia that Westcott's issues surfaced.

A gradual revealing. No fireworks bursting out of a crate sending woodchips everywhere. It was like the leaves in fall—every day you look at the forest—a trick to the eye, the process so subtle. Then one day you look up and all green has given way. Westcott didn't have the courage to tell his mother directly. He wasn't sure what it would mean. He relied on a letter. Even then he alluded to the situation. Gedny sought additional help and advice. This meant more trips to the therapist's office. He had already seen three psychologists and a psychiatrist—not one of them succeeded in getting him to open up. Westcott hated going. If he couldn't confront his mother, or himself, how was he supposed to discuss it with a complete stranger? He disliked the atmosphere created by the waiting rooms. They were all the same with annoying pictures of sailboats, still life images of fruit baskets, flowers on the wall, the dim lighting, the stupid incense, the fake trees in the corner of the room, and the receptionist's irritatingly pleasant personality. Westcott spent the sessions in complete silence waiting placidly for the clock on the wall or table to tell him he was free to go. What aggravated him the most was when the therapist would greet him and ask how he was doing. Small talk. He'd yet to assert himself and take command of the conversation. He remained resolutely taciturn. They each recommended an anti-depressant to ease his mind. No surprise there. Westcott adamantly refused, soundly justifying it would not cure the cause of his anguish, it would be suppressing the issue—masking it, not solving it. Thankfully, he never took a single pill. Meanwhile classmates swallowed all manner of "controlling agents"—Adderral, Zoloft, Prozac, and god knows what else. Westcott hadn't the confidence yet to actualize his assessment, but even then he knew society was going down a slippery slope.

~

Westcott and his mother arrived back in Virginia the following Saturday with Ellis, having just celebrated her 22nd birthday. A trunk load of souvenirs and valuables from all corners of the world: Vietnam, China, Japan, Africa, Cuba, India—waited to be unpacked. Westcott was squashed in the back amidst all the bags and treasures. He didn't mind. He was glad to be getting home—a week was a long time away. Too long. The night sky was cool and still when they pulled into the driveway. It had been an eight-hour trek from their last stopover in Georgia; his legs were restless. Westcott stumbled out of the car, the bones in his knees snapped. He was beginning to atrophy from his self-imposed sedentary routine. Two years earlier he'd loved to run. How he loved running.

He pulled himself up the porch steps and entered the house with his mother and sister, then returned to begin the grim task of unpacking the trunk. Trip after trip they continued to carry in more. Westcott watched as his sister hauled her authentic 2-foot Kagga drum, all the way from South Africa, up the stairs into the front hall. What an ordeal. He was excited to have his sister back.

A semblance of order restored, the boy turned off the light and sat down in the porch rocking chair. Unconsciously aging. The air was crisp and refreshing with its chill. Despite his green corduroy pants and brown jacket he shook a bit. He could not see it from where he was situated, but he knew the moon was out. A luminous light flooded the lawn, the flagpole glistened. He studied the red, white, and blue rectangular cloth secured in its holster attached to the banister. There was something content in it, so absolutely free. A sorrow overcame the boy, a sorrow he would eventually regard as commonplace, no longer a mood but a personality.

COURAGE STAND BY

Over winter break Westcott had a list of assignments to catch up on. Some he could not complete until school resumed, like his Civil War test. For leisure that Christmas he watched the eighteen hour mini-series *North and South*. After viewing the first episode he was hooked. Not only were the shows entertaining, they were helpful in reinforcing his historical knowledge. He found the opening theme music enrapturing, powerful. And Orry Main played by Patrick Swayze. All the years he waited for Madeleine. At the time Westcott paid little attention to this aspect of the series.

In mid-January Westcott stayed after school to make up his pre-Reconstruction era test. Mrs. McCormick asked if he'd mind taking it in the office. He offered no objection. Shuffling behind her down the hall, he hesitated at the door like a true gentleman, waiting for his teacher to enter the faculty quarters first. Mrs. McCormick stopped, her skinny black two-shelf cart in front of her. Instead of taking the boy up on his courteous gesture, she motioned for him to go ahead. Sitting down at a circular table occupied by a radio and other faculty clutter, Mrs. McCormick went into the staff restroom. A moment later the toilet flushed. She came out and looked at him. Of course he hadn't heard anything. Fighting to stay awake, Westcott strained his mind to coherence. A little past four he rose, walked by the cubicles, and found Mrs. McCormick grading papers at the conference desk.

'Thanks.'

He handed over the question sheet.

'Have a good night.'

'Yeah,' he stammered. Plodding down the hallway in his jeans, blue Converse tennis shoes, and brown plaid jacket, he mulled over his answers. A day or two later, his passion for American history, specifically the Civil War, showed true. He received a hundred on the test, having missed one which he shouldn't have because he knew it. He got the extra credit question right in its place.

In early February Westcott began seeing a specialized therapist down in Norfolk. Of those infrequent visits he remembers one word. Celibacy. Maggie Chubb asked him about his ideas on the word. Did she feel it her civic duty? Was she trying to tell him not to experiment or be promiscuous? No problem there, he wanted to tell her. She made him uncomfortable. The idea of sex had never entered his mind. It was just a word. Meaningless. And celibacy? He'd heard the term; its definition escaped him when she asked. How young and innocent. If he'd only known. How that word would come to torment him. And what of *involuntary* celibacy?

Driving back one evening, Ellis was in the front passenger seat of their candy apple red Explorer, she turned around and asked, 'So, if you could be a boy or girl which would you *rather* be?' 'A boy,' Westcott replied, looking out the window. After two or three visits all seemed futile, leaving his mother no choice but to have him join a local support group. Meetings were held every Wednesday for an hour-and-a-half in a church rectory across from the College of William & Mary.

The SLANT youth organization renamed P.R.Y.D.E., a tentative acronym for Peninsula Regional Youth Doing Excellently, served as a safe environment bent on acceptance, offering young gays, lesbians, and anyone in between, a place to talk openly about their situation. Members ranged from the obviously out and confident homosexual to the borderline closet cases.

Westcott felt excluded and apart. His condition did not parallel the struggles of the other attendees. The ninety-minute discussions were a wash to the boy. He sat in silence on one of the sofa's edges, unrelaxed, disinterested, stiff. He never sat back. Never relaxed. His plaid jacket was kept closed in front. He made use of the weekly afternoon ennui, studying for a Word of the Day vocabulary quiz, as they were termed by Mrs. T, reviewing notes and textbook information mentally in his head. Often though, Wednesdays culminated with a much desired midday nap. He fought to stay awake during many a session. At home he would have dozed off with Thomas and Cricket on their mat. Longing to be doing something else, he found diversion in studying the gray-blue carpeted floor, discerning pictures and faces among the sole-scuffed threads going every which way, while the quivering beams of light cast from the descending sun relentlessly needled his patience. He could not know it then, nor could he see that in those hours he had everything. Everything except himself.

Of the five to six members who regularly attended, Westcott knew one of them. Dave also attended Drummond's Field High as a junior. In the spring of ninth grade he and Westcott had shared a World History class together, but failed to see their common thread of difference. Compared with Dave's outgoing and personable disposition, Westcott flailed like a cat dropped off the side of a boat into a lake, sputtering to keep his head above water in the social stream. Dave's life preserver of friends sustained him through good and difficult times while Westcott faced each day alone in the absence of any peer relationships. Westcott witnessed an indelible stigma of perversion tied to his condition as a result of misunderstanding and ignorance. The concept of what it meant to be 'gay' or 'bisexual' paled with Westcott's alternative lifestyle. Dave was bisexual. How fortunate.

Once second semester rolled around Westcott had to adjust to his new classes. American Studies was one of the few yearlong courses required to graduate. Westcott scheduled it so he could remain in Mrs. McCormick's and Mrs. Talmedge's fourth block class. Some students were forced to take the second half of the course during another time slot with different teachers. He would have hated to transfer to an entirely new class with unfamiliar teaching styles. He was extremely glad to stay with his two most beloved teachers.

As the winter months dragged on Westcott grew to like Mrs. McCormick and Mrs. T more and more. In March he went to the courthouse and received his driver's license. His lack of enthusiasm and excitement placed him in stark contrast with the whole teenage race who were ecstatic because of a new found independence. Westcott did not care. What was the point of having a driver's license if you had nowhere to go and no one to see? The 2x3 inch card was just another sign to the boy of how isolated he really was.

Once more spring arrived. Westcott stood in front of the mirror, an authentic beige and eucalyptus green Kagga Kamma hat all the way from Africa atop his head (a souvenir from Ellis' round the world excursion). He placed a pair of unused prescription glasses over his eyes and a felt mustache above his top lip. He looked ridiculous. Peering at himself, he grasped a rubber band, pulling his long brown hair into a tail as he used to wear it in younger years. He tied it back, tucking it under the safari hat. He liked what he saw, the short hair. Should he cut his hair before the end of the school year or wait 'til summer?

On Friday March 22nd Ernest Hemingway lived again with legends Al Capone, Elliot Ness, Tallulah Bangkok, Mae West, Louis the Satch, and the likes sitting round the same table. The classroom had been refashioned to recreate the 1920s Cotton Club. Several days prior to the event Westcott and his classmates made seating cards, painted a banner with all their pictures posted on it, and taped together paper bags to hang over the windows for a softer, lounge-like atmosphere. Mrs. T and Mrs. McCormick were unsure how things would turn out. They hoped to use such an experience as a launching pad for future American Studies classes.

An hour drifted by. Students snacked on dishes provided by themselves, their teachers, and the cafeteria. Some even got up the nerve to dance a few steps of the Charleston. Westcott sat at his desk taking in everything. He did not rise to fill a plate with hors d'oeuvres immediately. Everything looked delicious. He made the pretense of looking occupied. When he felt no one was watching he picked up a plate and a single piece of chicken. He didn't like eating in front of people.

Mrs. T and Mrs. McCormick, dressed in white shirts and ties as the MCs, directed the activities to a close and began calling on volunteers to go first in their presentations. Due to time constraints Westcott did not have to give his speech until the following Tuesday. Mrs. T spared him as long as possible until there was no one left to go but him.

Westcott waited at his desk, half listening to what the student before him was saying; his palms sweated. He remembered nothing of their biographies. Mrs. T stood up, glancing sideways at the boy. Everyone clapped as the other student sat back down.

'It's been a long night. I'd like to welcome our last visitor to the stage; he's come a long way to be here with us this evening, so...please welcome *Mr.* Ernest Hemingway.' Mrs. T concluded her introduction. Detecting the boy's distress she and Mrs. McCormick said,

'Don't worry, you'll be fine.'

'Yeah right,' his voice cracked, undulating with doubt.

Head bent down, holding onto the paper with his speech neatly scrolled, the boy mumbled through the presentation. He wore his usual blue carpenter jeans, Converse tennis shoes with rims green from mowing the lawn, navy plaid shirt, and a red and black-check-ered lumberjack coat. Surely his layer of clothes would protect him. Feeling a tremor about to become visible in one of his lower limbs he shifted weight from leg to leg. Hearing his own voice shake, knowing his head quivered, he could think of nothing but to keep going. He flipped to a page dog-eared in *The Sun Also Rises*, read it aloud, then rambled off a quote about courage. He clumsily returned to his seat still trembling. Placing his chin on the cool desktop, he rhythmically rolled his pen back and forth.

~

Ellis graduated from The College of William & Mary in May. It was Mother's Day, as is the customary commencement date. As he sat in the Great Hall, high up in the stands watching the entire class graduation, he was cognizant that in just one year he'd be down in the arena for his own commencement. Local high schools utilized the wonderful space provided by The College of William and Mary's sports activity building. He could not possibly know in that hour, that day, that moment, that some 5 years later another Great Hall would make for a pivotal turning point in his life.

Later that day they would attend the departmental graduation designated by each student's major—a much smaller, intimate, and more enjoyable event. Afterward they had a pleasant reception back at the house. Ellis' boyfriend, a nice young man by the name of Rodger Feldone, joined in the occasion and came to the house with his family.

~

Tuesday 10 June 20—

Westcott stands precariously, both hands encumbered. Rather than pull his backpack on to free up his arms, he carries it half off his right shoulder, the bulk of the weight falling in his palm and forearm, allowing him to press his knuckles against his coat collar, keeping it semi-closed. The strap never actually rests on his shoulder, making his load of books and binders awkward and tiresome to lug around. He never saw any point in reserving a locker. In his left arm lays a box lid filled with heavy ceramic artwork wrapped in brown paper. His arm runs underneath the middle section with the crook of his elbow as a lever of support while his fingers press against the front lip to secure his figurines. Below the box lid he holds his yearbook. He lets the lactic acid of strained, atrophied muscles in his arm and shoulder burn—unwilling to concede to a more practical mode of transporting his belongings. He stammers for a moment, the bell about to ring, vacillates whether or not to ask. Fondness triumphs over trepidation. Without ever having looked at her, he knows Mrs. T's eyes are upon him; he feels the question behind the gaze. Turning towards her, raising his head to glance into her face, he speaks in his low husky voice.

'What…what?' Probing her silent inquiry with a question of his own. Before she can reply, like a boy who's just become fascinated with the world of girls and attempts to speak to one for the first time he rattles off—'Would you sign this?'

She takes the book, flips to a page in the back and sits on one of the desks to write. Westcott moves slightly away not wanting to make her feel rushed.

Maybe he shouldn't have—such foolish sentimentality.

Finished, Mrs. T hands the yearbook back. He takes it with a delicate grasp.

'You be here tomorrow, kiddo?'

• • •

Wednesday 11 June 20—

The last day of full classes. Westcott rests in the back of the room straining his eyes to read the clock high above the left door. The red digital numbers show the time to be 1:24. He waits. Mrs. McCormick and Mrs. T ask the students to move their chairs into a circle for one final discussion that inevitably will bring fourth block American Studies to a close. They talk about major events comprising the 80s and 90s—all the way up to present day events. Each is asked to name a song that defines the era. When it comes to Westcott's turn he mumbles "Streets of Philadelphia" and is content to fall quiet again. His head throbs, he feels exhausted, attributing his fatigue to the past few restless nights he's experienced.

Before the students leave, Mrs. T distributes progress reports. Unconcerned with the grade printout, Westcott stands off to the side as a fellow classmate, Gardner, wearing an obscene shirt "Big Willy's Condoms," shakes hands with Mrs. McCormick. It is the last day, improper slogans are overlooked. When Mrs. T finishes, Westcott looks for a window and approaches with a folded piece of binder paper. He quickly shies away. The bell rings. As he walks out the door into the dank hallway, a 104 average creased in hand, he looks back with fondness at Mrs. T. She is sitting on her desk with the creased leaf.

He'd thanked his teachers, both Mrs. T and Mrs. McCormick, for such a wonderful year. He refrained from use of anything embellishing—it wasn't too nice or overly-thought oriented, but intentionally sincere and simple. The following morning, Thursday, he returns to school to take his two required exams for first and second block. Unfortunately, those classes did not have SOLs so he could not test out of the exams. After his ceramics test, still in awe as to how a class that dealt with clay modeling could have a *written* exam, he moves onto Law in Society with Mr. Allowick, a black man who Westcott remembers best for his stylish attire. Seventy questions and twenty minutes later, he is done. Both exams proved relatively easy, all the same he is amazed to learn he received a hundred on the latter. Prior to exam day Mr. Allowick went through the semester's packets revealing to his students *every* question with which to familiarize themselves. The test would appear verbatim. So it was truly just a matter of memorizing the answers. Since the class finished earlier than expected, Mr. Allowick had time enough to run the scantrons through the machine and reveal their grades. Afterwards, with no one to talk to, Westcott sits for the remainder of the school day in silence. Apathetic to study the night before—he really didn't need to at length—Westcott finishes the year on top, academically. After an evanescent feeling of accomplishment, his discontent attacks full force.

He remembers the feel of spring inside his room. The knot in his stomach. He wasn't ready for the year to end. He did not like summer. He longed to; he simply couldn't enjoy it. At exactly 10:50 a.m. summer officially begins. With not a hint of haste or spry in his step, he plods down the stairs and boards one of the many yellow buses. All the way home a desolate emptiness burns in him. Getting off the bus that day, Melvin Jenkins, the driver, pulls the lever closed, shutting the final door on Westcott's junior year.

~

The first day of summer Westcott goes with his mother to have an heirloom appraised. It is a particularly warm morning. His mother insisted he wear a short sleeved button down shirt and shed his 'security blanket' jacket. The dispute escalated into a drag out argument.

Exasperated, Gedny yelled violently. She couldn't take seeing him in the same outfit day in and day out. Westcott stays in the car while the man surveys their 18th century spinning wheel. The first day of summer. His ninety-odd days of freedom are viewed with disgust. Miserable, he scrunches down in the backseat, resting his head on the door, wanting to disappear. He thinks about the Magazine he had put together—an assignment for Law and Society. Mr. Allowick had written 'Dynamite!' on the front, given him an A. Westcott had taken pleasure in the creative assignment. What did it mean now? Nothing. Absolutely nothing.

In late June, Westcott's father comes out to visit from California. Both he and his mother help to buy him a truck. The boy had rebuked the idea of getting his own car. His mother argued he had to gain some independence and responsibility. Due to its age, Ol' Reliable required a little bit of fixing up. He named him Ol' Reliable because of what Trusty the Bloodhound always said in *Lady and the Tramp*. By the end of August the truck had a new paint job and personalized license plates. The boy loved the GMC indigo blue he'd chosen to replace the chipping teal, and the gold pinstripe running along either side added a nice touch. Except for a small nickel-sized crack in the windshield, probably from a kicked up stone, aesthetically it is in relatively good condition. And if he squints just right, the splintered glass looks like a distant bird, flying high in the sky. With ten years to its name, Westcott is pleased how well Ol' Reliable runs. He finds one of those small dogs with the bobbing heads—a German Shepherd—and attaches it to his dashboard with two-way tape. The little black and tan 'navigator' he names Hudson. He laughs to himself seeing Hudson's head, out of the corner of his eye, quiver left to right, jiggle up and down. Movement. He rummages through an old drawer. Finds his large blue rabbit's foot keychain. His Ford is complete.

On July 12th, shortly before vacationing in Niagara Falls, the Canadian side, Westcott takes the plunge and cuts his hair. He does not know it, but twenty-seven months later he'll be crossing the border into Canada again. Recreational tourism will not be in mind. In cutting his hair he is apprehensive. With a more masculine appearance, he hopes the questions will stop. The summer lulls his recently active mind to sleep; he enters a state of restless idleness. With the exception of one reading assignment, requiring completion before the start of school, he is otherwise unpressed and takes to watching TV, mostly *The Waltons, Andy Griffith,* and *Animal Planet.* Sometimes when Ellis has the day off she and her boyfriend, Rodger, will go to Water Country. Westcott sits on the stairwell, watches as his sister heads out—a towel slung around her neck, Rodge in his shorts and t-shirt following behind. He hears the front door pull shut, listens as Ellis' car backs away. A desolate force hits him—the silence of his own thoughts. Ellis would gladly extend the invitation for him to come along. The answer is always the same. He couldn't go out, wouldn't, especially scant of clothes. He stares out the window above the landing, catches a glimpse of the pinwheel in his neighbor's yard. The bird is motionless in the still and close heat of summer. C-lick. C-lick. C-lick. The solemn pendulum of the grandfather clock swinging back and forth in the foyer, constant as his yearning—exploiting a most devastating sense of separateness—

Westcott feels the resolute patience wall up within. Solidify.

ANGUISH

A greatness like standing on the crest of a valley,
an immobilizing realization of brief content
a despair drifting then drawing back
a void kept company by its friend loneliness—
Away, Away, Away

A chimney's smoke was never meant to be captured
a strength inexplicable, lacking an equalizing opponent
why deal such cards
courage—

Stand by, Stand by, Stand by

When All is Quiet, Dimming Wheat Fields

The sound of loneliness rang clear in his ears the summer before his senior year. It was a much different breed of loneliness than the type he'd come to know in years to follow. His loneliness did not have an object. He did not miss anyone or anything specifically. The loneliness had no face or name. He longed for the idea of what it meant to be biologically male and a boy, he had illusions and wanted to fit in, but who doesn't at that age? The loneliness was bearable because he had yet to taste its opposite.

Nothing is more deafening than the noise of a door being pulled shut as a person leaves. The hollowness penetrates, descends as a great force upon the soul. It's the realization that you are alone, no one can hear you. Isolation has such a way of injuring a human spirit as to steadily break it. And when, upon its shattering a far greater force is needed to revive it, the heart has not the will to seek one. It is too weary. Westcott ran his fingers through his short full hair.

As the days dragged by, Westcott became more and more restless. The summer lulled his recently active mind to sleep. Unlike most kids his age, he did not seek a summer job. It had nothing to do with laziness. He did not like being around people and being looked at, studied, questioned. The previous year he managed to work for a local theme park, Busch Gardens. He hated it, not for the obvious reasons. He didn't mind the work. A classmate of his worked in Das Fest Haus. Michael. A tall skinny boy, cute. Westcott enjoyed doing the heavy work.

Picking up trays on the dolly, pulling them back to the large dishwasher, expeditiously loading them with fire-speed into the washer. He didn't like to be seen out on the floor with the women, wiping down tables, sweeping. It was the connotation, not the act that bothered him. During the show he'd take a break or move into the corner recesses like his fellow coworkers. He learned a few German phrases and the oompah band was quite good, but after seeing the show more than five times, the charm wore off. At the entrance to the great building were the open doors showing small rectangular white lights, letting in the day. His only opposition to the job stemmed from the fact that he was forced to present himself inaccurately, as a girl, with a name tag proclaiming his legal name. His body, not the job, tormented him. One day he was wiping down a table in the cool, massive Fest Haus. Two teenage boys were passing by. 'My friend thinks you're hot,' one of them said and kept walking, smiling because he'd hoped to embarrass his friend. If only that had been enough.

If only Westcott felt like a woman. He refused to make a repeat of the summer before. *Anything* had to be better than working there again. Even if that meant being alone.

Late at night when all was quiet and the room still, the boy would lay awake in bed with just his thoughts to comfort him and the rhythmic cadence of crickets. He gazed at the painting on the wall in front of him. Sometimes the July moon would enter the window to the right of his desk and a silent peace fell across the floor. Streaks of wetness dried along the boy's skin; pain welled from his eyes and rolled down the sides of his face. He had an acute sense of hearing, which he prided himself on. He could hear the train whistle as it passed by the local station five miles away, beckoning. A constant loneliness plagued its cool metallic cry.

And then he envisioned what it would be like. The absolute freedom. Running through fields. Tall grass. Wheat dimming in the waning sunlight of a careless afternoon. Legs spry, heart pounding, the wind breaking against his forehead. Not far behind his dog trailed to catch up with him. The boy fell to his knees in the shadows beneath a giant oak, breathing heavily, exhausted from the jaunt. He could feel the throb of his pulse in his throat. It made him a bit nauseous; the pounding drummed in his ears. He leaned back against the trunk, his dog flopping down beside him with a grunt that interrupted his panting metronome. The wind would blow, the field would arc, and the boy would be cooled. There he would rest, always, for it was home. Westcott shook the vision from his mind like an etch-a-sketch board. It devastated him to consider he might never see the place he longed for in this life. By degrees this rigidity of mood became his temperament.

ON GO THE DAYS

There was something about the smell of the interior of a school on the first day Westcott always loved. He couldn't quite identify its intangible qualities. Maybe it was the scent of possibility, the prospect of success, the promise of a fresh start that comforted him. The idea of taking in knowledge was a wonderful thought to the boy after another brainless summer. He felt better when busy, working, studying—all his faculties being put to good use rather than rusting. Whatever it was he held it close. He enjoyed the afternoons where he'd come home from school, go upstairs, drop his book-bag on the floor, change his clothes, take Thomas out, eat a snack, retire upstairs for a session of homework. He knew all too well the sleep deprivation that comes with staying up late and rising at half past six five days straight. He welcomed such exhaustion. The more tuckered out he became, the better he felt; his head unclouded. At times his endurance was made infallible by such routine.

~

A September air filled the boy's nose. It was Tuesday morning after Labor Day, the beginning of his senior year, the start of 181 classroom stays.

Westcott was dressed in a bright yellow rugby shirt with a band of blue striping across the chest. He wore a new pair of the same blue jeans and leather brown shoes he had come to love the spring before. He had a much cleaner look compared to his appearance as a junior. His hair was short and neatly combed. Seeing him in the hallway, Ms. Garlow remarked how 'cute' it was. 'Cute' was not the adjective he was going for. Hygienically he remained gritty except for his teeth. He took pride in brushing them to avoid a visit to the dentist. Sometimes he'd go a month without showering. He hated getting undressed and would wash only his hair to create a clean impression and conceal any dirt. He bore the likeness of a young, *quite* young, ordinary boy. To those who did not know him from previous years he was passing. Concern for what students and teachers who knew him from before would think consumed him. They would arrive at conclusions, speculate in quiet, assuming that to dig for the truth would be an imposition to Westcott. No one asked how he felt. Everyone left him alone.

Westcott didn't find any enjoyment in his fall classes. For first block he had Nutrition and Wellness, cleverly titled in an attempt to get male students to take the course. It was your typical Home Ec. Class. Westcott was relieved to find other boys enrolled in the course. Followed by English and Yearbook Multi-Media. His day ended with an hour-and-a-half session of Anatomy. Westcott longed for a return to Mrs. Talmedge's and Mrs. McCormick's

American Studies class. By and by, as it is at that age, his interest was spurred and revived by second block literature. The class was taught by Ms. Hutchens, a good friend of Mrs. Talmedge. Westcott came to like her much in the same way he did Mrs. T. His fondness for Mrs. T wouldn't be replaced though and it dawned on him why he missed her. He'd had a crush on her and still did.

Ms. Hutchens stood in stark contrast to her colleague with her soft voice devoid of any fierceness. If she and Mrs. T had been in a hollering match you could bet your life Mrs. T would effortlessly prevail. Originally a math major in college, Ms. Hutchens switched to English, but she did not have passion for the subject. Ms. Hutchens was a tall, slender woman with a petite chest, which he liked, and lean stature. Her hair, a pallored blonde, and the manner in which it was styled resembled how Mrs. T's had been the year before. She had long, slim lips that spread wide when she smiled so she appeared all mouth. Westcott found it hard to believe she was still single. He falsely fantasized she was a lesbian. Her eyes were a faint and extraordinary light shade of blue, almost faded. The pupils created a piercing quality due to the surrounding pale iris, making the eyes more pronounced against her tan complexion. She reminded him of a character from his favorite miniseries, *North and South*. It was something in her eyes and skin, her smile and gentle voice that caused the boy to detect in her a hint of George Hazard's Irish wife, Constance Flynn. She wasn't as pretty as the actress, but she was still attractive.

By the time October rolled around a routine was well-established. The scent of new had been worn away from the classrooms and hallways. Westcott depended on Ms. Hutchens' English class to see him through the rest of the afternoon. He increasingly looked forward to it every day just as he had done with American Studies. During third block he often had the pleasure of absconding to the library while his absentee teacher, Mrs. Littich, managed to spend more time everywhere else but in her classroom. After devoting a short half hour to his assigned section of the yearbook, the other members of his group called it quits. Westcott, with the permission of Mrs. Littich, if he could find her, would venture upstairs submerging himself in a pensive state. If he wasn't studying or working on a packet for Mrs. Medley's Anatomy class, which to his solemn delight he now found respite in, he enjoyed paging through a series of Civil War books, reviewing its major events, remembering the reenactment he attended the March before. Sometimes he wrote.

The librarians came to recognize *the boy* by his frequent visits and anticipated his surfacing to their designated area of the school a few afternoons per week. As a rule students entering the facility were instructed to sign in at the check-out counter. He always signed in as Westcott.

Mrs. Medley proved to be a sweet lady, a true maiden of the South with her thick drawl. Despite being in her early forties and the mother of a thirteen-year old son, she was energetic, always in a jovial mood. Her thoroughness and attention to detail made it impossible not to succeed. Westcott wondered if such perfection and repetition of material was linked to some minute case of OCD. The way she reiterated items prompted him to speculate. When not taking notes from the projections on the overhead, students paired up to complete the surplus of worksheets distributed with each chapter. Westcott happily corroborated answers with another boy, Brandon. Although accustomed to working alone, Westcott enjoyed being partnered with a guy. Brandon was easy to get along with and considerate. He was one of those all-around nice guys, even calling *the boy* by his nickname since he'd yet to legally change it. Brandon was bone skinny and always had a packet of candy to tide him over for the last class of the day. He was the only boy with whom Westcott interacted in high school. He would have made for a decent friend. Slowly he was crossing over.

On Tuesdays he religiously attended the after school Lit. Mag meetings still headed by Ms. Garlow and seldom spoke a word. Throughout the year he never missed one, in large part because he now had his own mode of transportation. During the hours outside of the educational system he fought to keep himself going. He made it a point to take things in stride remembering the old tale about the tortoise—steady in his pace. He had no choice. This tempering and chronic self-control had side-effects he could not know, long into the future. Westcott's family—his mother, sister, and visiting grandma, celebrated his eighteenth birthday by going up to the Shenandoah Valley and staying in The Three Sisters cabin.

Shortly after his birthday he began the dull process of applying to colleges. He had two applications to complete. It was assumed he would not be going away to school and dorming. His first choice was the college his sister had attended. He asked Mrs. T and Mrs. McCormick if they would write him a letter of recommendation. The boy was glad to have a reason to go and see his two favorite teachers again; he still dreaded approaching them. The morning he went to see them Mrs. T was in the classroom working on some papers at her desk. Westcott entered the door diagonally from her on the far side, attempting to be as obscure as possible. She was wearing an orange shirt and black pants—indicative of the approaching holiday. Her hair was no longer blonde and flared. She'd let it go to its natural brown tone and style. Mrs. T said she wouldn't mind at all, but he'd have to come back the next morning to see Mrs. McCormick; she wasn't in that day.

Relieved, Westcott still felt foolish for the way he acted. Why couldn't he be normal, look at a person when he spoke, instead of shifting his feet, turning his eyes away? Carry on a conversation without mumbling, getting sweaty hands.

~

For the rest of November Ms. Hutchens had her class, down to fifteen students, delving into the work of Shakespeare. The three girls MIA had been pulled over for drinking and driving the night of the Homecoming Dance and were suspended for the remainder of the semester. Westcott was glad to have the class downsized. The smallest course he'd ever taken was Spanish IV, comprised of only six students. He liked the atmosphere generated by a small class. Westcott was content to be reading and studying the tragedy of Hamlet.

Early on the morning of the 22nd the boy pulled on his yellow rugby shirt, his green lumberjack coat, and made his way downstairs. He smiled at Thomas sleeping lazily on his mat in the kitchen.

'C'mon, Ponyboy,' one of his nicknames among many, something Westcott adopted for him after reading Hinton's book years earlier. The two walked out back, down the steps, over to the edge of the forest. Countless daybreaks and afternoons the boy had spent doing the same thing. This morning was the last time. Westcott watched his companion nose through the grass snapping up the moist blades, dampening his snout. Unsuspecting. Tommy-Gun was a good dog, a great dog; it wasn't his fault his owner was a mess. Westcott fed Tom his meal with additional treats. Gedny came downstairs and had Westcott kneel down next to Thomas in front of the fireplace. One last picture. It was for the better, he had to consider Thomas' quality of life. His decision to give Tom up, send him to live with his father, was solely based on the dog's welfare; he needed attention—someone to play and enjoy life with.

Westcott ceased to be capable of partaking in any delightful activities, however small. It was all he could do to keep on breathing.

Westcott and Ellis loaded Thomas into the crate, fastened it to the truck's bed. They piled into the cab of the truck with their mother at the wheel. It was a very long, cramped drive to Norfolk. All the way through the tunnel and along the commuter-filled highways Westcott was too tired to speak. Despite his drowsiness his mind wouldn't let him doze off. The morning was still young when they arrived at the shipping quadrant of the airport. Westcott let Tom out of his confines, slapped his side lovingly with pats, talking to him soothingly. He took the dog for one more bathroom break before the long haul. It was time to go. Westcott put him back in his cage and closed the door securely. The man in charge of the loading area placed a sticker on top of the crate. LIVE ANIMAL. Westcott looked at his mother.

Unlike his mother he internalized his pain. He gazed at his dog through the metal bars. *Goodbye, ol' boy.* Nobody heard him.

His void deepened.

Ponyboy would come back to Virginia and return to California once more. Three times he survived flying without tranquilizers of any kind, without familiar voices.

He made the journey on his own.

~

Westcott went to school late that day, arriving in time not to miss 2nd block entirely which ended at 10:50. The lights were off; the students had their attention directed at the television screen. They were watching a short clip from the authentic film version of *Hamlet* starring Kenneth Bragnah. He handed Ms. Hutchens his late pass before sitting down. He identified the scene from the book and tried to get interested in the dialogue, but his thoughts couldn't be lassoed. There was no one to tell, nobody cared why he had been late. The isolation was a wine-bottle opener; these instances of quiet separateness spiraled continuously, burrowing deeper and deeper into his heart, creating a hollow cavity in his spirit. The tighter the screw twisted the stronger the pain became. Eventually it would grasp the very will of his existence; the cork of control would someday give way to the pressures of despair, exploding. He would fall, his will emptied forth—able to shoulder the burden no longer.

A few days after Ponyboy's trip westward, Thanksgiving break started. Wednesday was a half-day. Leaving school Westcott went with his mother directly to the local courthouse. The afternoon weather was foretelling of the approaching winter. The air was chilled with rain and the dank sky appeared ominous in its gray and white blankness. The boy and his mother proceeded into the building, passed through the metal detectors and headed down the hallway to the clerk's desk. They handed the teller a typed document. As the lady skimmed over it, Westcott edged to the side anticipating a strange look.

'You're filing for a name change, is that correct?'

'*He's* changing his name, that's right,' Gedny answered.

Westcott was grateful his mother hadn't slipped up.

The lady turned to Westcott. 'How old are you?'

'Eighteen.'

He didn't need any parental or guardian signatures on the form. The lady took the paper to be processed. It would be four to six weeks before they heard back.

Mother and son walked side-by-side down the tiled floor. Gedny put her hand on the back of his head and neck, tousling his short hair.

'C'mon, son.' No one was there to hear. She was just letting the world know her acceptance. Westcott was her child. She would never stop loving him.

Crickets in November

The boy stared up at the vastness above, a distant cold was about. He stood with no chance to move or strike attention elsewhere. The moon he studied; desperately searching in the silent light and swaying trees beneath, but nothing, nothing could he find. All that once was had languished. He was lost. Terror overcame the boy.

It was the same as earlier when he'd gone with his dog outside. He remembered, waiting upon his dog to fill his nose and wants sufficiently, looking about the forest at the leaves of descending brittle and more sailing by winds to their graves. The wind—a peculiar warmth. The boy thought it strange the crickets were still out in November. How their beating resonance vanishes with a chill in the air. He absorbed all this, but saw nothing more beyond. Empty, aroused his thoughts could not be. He was simply there; it plagued him deeply.

The boy teetered on the anguished embankment that rested just so, beneath a cape of shaggy brown hair. That which he carefully planted his life and balanced his static ways on, turned to mud. Thus, he began to sink. At the bank's end water held conversation. It is much easier, the boy considered, if consumed by roaring waters, to release one's grip. He fell to his knees, immersing his trousers in an impossible resolution. Tired. Resolved. How easy to stop treading the waters, let the mind go, without laborious effort, sail under.

'What point is it?' the boy cried out. 'It's not fair, no way to escape, and yet to cast such a weight of anguish with no cure to abide it—it isn't fair! Oh, what could have been. What could have been.' He dropped his head in angry torment. His eyes fell upon a much tranquil creature; its home the riverbanks.

'That frog *is* that frog, if nothing else he has himself to fall back on. My mind does not fit.' The boy launched his attention forward.

'These waters,' he went on, 'these waters—the heart of the beds, soaring and pumping into the river veins—they do not question their being; they are content to be. I pity not myself, but yearn for an end, a faraway freedom from this plight...'

Am I to serve as an example, tested, for the sake of those commonly afflicted in times to come?

I don't think so.

Judge me how you may, but understand that my regard of *this situation* is that of no decision, it is not a choice—no, it is a dealing, a torturous hand.

You don't question, so I have no reason to answer, but I would be all right to explain. You fear my demeanor, hold back, say nothing. I've been told.

I walk the days apart in presence, always careful not to jar the balance of my unending despair. If it tilts and yields to one pole, I will die. Either way I don't welcome easily.

The boy rose and so he thought, I will live in agony, but may my hope and persistence recall my sight to the trees and moon, and the more behind them—a strength to endure. Then I will resume my spirit, work to harden the bank further and further, and recede the waters until at last I am home.

BECOMING WESTCOTT

All through Thanksgiving the boy worked diligently on his Senior Research Paper for English. While the turkey was in the oven, Westcott wrapped up the rough draft due the following week. He'd have the rest of the weekend to enjoy. The thesis of his essay focused on three of John Steinbeck's works. *Tortilla Flat, The Red Pony,* and *Of Mice and Men.* His claim: the novels reflect a sense of uncertainty. Constancy is a dream that can never be fulfilled. All things good must come to an end.

He does not know that his own claims will one day be tested.

The first Thursday back from Thanksgiving Westcott is in second block staring down at his wristwatch. 9:19; forty more seconds and the bell will ring to announce the beginning of class. He does not pull out any notebook or pen. Jaded silence. Ms. Hutchens stands in the doorjamb, facing the hallway, twirling her required set of keys on one of those soft straps that fits around the neck. Slowly, back and forth the keys sway and when the motion stops the teeth clink as they all crash to the bottom of the loop. The noise comforts him. When he walks about the halls in the early hours, he knows when a teacher is behind him by listening to the jingling of their keys. Westcott cocks his head to the left just enough so that he can study her. The tone of the bell sounds four times and the brief conversing between Ms. Hutchens and a fellow colleague draws to a close; she shuffles into the room and shuts the door. Another 90 minutes of intrigue. Westcott shakes the tiredness from his eyes in anticipation for the reading of Act IV in Hamlet. Ms. Hutchens is wearing his favorite outfit this morning—black slacks, a long-sleeved blue denim blouse, a black alligator patterned belt with a silver buckle, and low-heeled "duck shoes." He calls them duck shoes in response to their squared front and long flap-like appearance; her height and slender stature fit in accordance with the shoes nicely. She possesses an air of executiveness about her, refined but soft, and in his eyes she is ever so handsome.

In December the class finishes their Shakespearian tragedy. "Not to be" had been Hamlet's fate, but not of his own hand. Westcott finds the play's denouement climactic, abrupt—easy. It disappoints him. All the preceding acts have been told with shrewd, circumspect suspense. The action conserved. Suddenly it erupts in one tumultuous explosion of events. Although this makes for a more dramatic scene, it declines too quickly. Having all the main characters die is—idealistic? Death had been the resolution threaded throughout the majority of last year's literary selections and, so too, had been the case with Advanced World

Lit. If not the demise of an epic hero such as Beowulf or the tragic fall of Hamlet, then it is suicide as later demonstrated when they read Achebe's *Things Fall Apart*. Not particularly encouraging for a boy experiencing a spiritual stroke. *Memorable stories involve a struggle in which the main character incurs some level of injury or mental anguish. Happy endings are best left up to the realm of fairy tales...are they? Sometimes staring life in the face is more terrifying than death itself any writer, poet, or sage might tell us, but then why would man have a thing called courage if not to live? Maybe there is an alternative to death after all; would it be worth it? Had Anne Frank not died, would her life have been so eminent?*

As the semester drew to a close, Ms. Hutchens addressed the final assignment. A mandatory speech with a running time of ten minutes would be given by each student on a topic of his or her choice. Westcott knew from the course syllabus a required stand-up presentation was expected. The announcement did not take him by surprise. He devoted little time to selecting a topic. He would deliver a speech on the television show *Leave It To Beaver*. Ms. Hutchens wrote on his proposal 'love it!'

Over the weekend a cold front moved in, blanketing rooftops, cars, and streets with a delicate sheath of snow. On Monday roads had yet to adequately thaw. School was cancelled. Tuesday Westcott found himself back in Ms. Hutchens class; half the students had already done their presentations. The remaining would go the next day. Before the clock read 10:50, Westcott packed up his bag with his pen and notebook—the same navy blue three-ringed binder with the laminated picture of a beagle on its cover he'd used for American Studies. He approached Ms. Hutchens' desk to turn in a homework assignment pertaining to the novel they just finished by Chinua Achebe, *Things Fall Apart*. He'd read the novel on his own in two nights.

'All right if I wear a bag over my head tomorrow?'

'What?—I'm sure you'll do *just fine*.'

Moving toward the door, he smiled. 'I remember last year.'

It hadn't been that bad. He still hated to get up and talk in front of people. That all attention would be on him was something he strongly disliked. On Wednesday Ms. Hutchens sent Westcott to the media center in the library for the television and VCR. She asked him to go alone. Did she sense calling on someone to accompany him would be assaulting his masculine ability to handle it on his own? Whether she had consciously intended to be considerate or naturally assumed he would prefer to go by himself, he did not know. He asked her if somebody could come along for company's sake. Elaine, who reminded him of Joanne Woodward, went with him. He liked Elaine.

'Is this for *his* presentation?' The lady gestured toward Westcott.

Embarrassed, he spoke up. 'Yes, it's for mine.'

Elaine knew he wasn't a boy. She made no comment or peculiar looks.

'All right, just make sure to bring it back when you're done,' Ms. Burns instructed.

Wheeling the cart and T.V. to Ms. Hutchens classroom, he saw Mrs. T walking down the hallway.

'I hate having to do this,' he said to Elaine, referencing the speech, not the manual labor.

Mrs. T turned halfway around to see if the voice she'd heard matched the face. She moved on towards her office. She'd probably mention it to Ms. Hutchens later, ask how the speech went for the student she knew was painfully shy.

Westcott waited, much as he had done ten months ago. One by one the line of students standing between him and distress chipped away.

He rose, passed out a sheet of paper printed with classic pictures from the *Leave It To Beaver* series.

'You can look at these if you want...you don't have to,' he told the person he handed the sheet to, miserably. He hoped they would look at them. That was the point! Divert their attention.

Placing his page of notes on the podium he began. He did not need a guide sheet, the paper gave him an excuse to look down. Keeping his right hand in his pocket, shifting weight from leg to leg, he relaxed. While showing the short 3-minute clip from the very first episode, he moved back to the safety of his desk. There was a knock at the door. It was Ashley. *I guess I won't be the last to go after all.* He was disappointed.

After bringing the television and VCR back to the media center, Westcott returned to Ms. Hutchens' room and retrieved his backpack, eager to know what grade he'd received on his speech. She told the other students shortly after they were done what their grade was, but now she was speaking with someone from another class. Rather than interrupt or hang by annoyingly he quietly left. Later that afternoon, with Mrs. Littich temporarily off school premises, the boy took a long stroll up to the library. Choosing an out of the way route, he headed down the English Hall and was rounding the corner when Ms. Hutchens came out of the xerox room.

'How are you?'

'All right.'

'Just walking?'

'Yes. Our teacher's gone from the classroom.'

'What? You mean she just left you?'

'She had to go to Ukrop's...pick up something for the yearbook,' he said skeptically.

'That's rough...' she meant the teacher being gone. 'By the way you got a 48 out of 50 on the presentation.'

'Thanks.' He was pleased she remembered to tell him without his having to ask.

'How do you think it went?'

'I—don't know.'

'Did you feel better this time?'

'I guess so.'

'Then that's good. Well, have a good day. Take care.'

'Bye.' He called after her feeling like he had that afternoon last June when he left American Studies, room 223 and 225, for the final time. And just like that she was gone. Never again would he have the pleasure of being her student, watching her teach, looking forward to class each day. The soreness stirred. Slowly he continued to the library with Charles Frazier's *Cold Mountain* in hand.

In mid-January Westcott went to see his guidance counselor, Mrs. Pyke, as was customary for all students prior to the start of a new semester. Waiting outside her door he skimmed over the flyers posted on the bulletin board across from him. They were all about success in the technological field of computers, SATs, how to find a career. *How blind the world is.* Bored he recited a song in his head to pass the time.

Fujiyama was a drinking man
He drank his beer from an old tin can,
Fujiyama, Fujiyama, Fujiyama…

The door opens, Mrs. Pyke steps out, tells him to go ahead and take a seat, she'll be right with him. He goes into her small 6 X 8 ft office and sits down in a middle chair distanced from her desk. *Three and a half years gone by. This will be the last time I ever set foot in here to discuss my upcoming schedule... never again.* He scrolls his eyes about the room. Flags from colleges all over the east coast line the interior wall on a string. To his left hangs a painting of a fence leading up to a barn. It appears the artwork is that of a Pyke relative. The brush has yet to be perfected—the colors are too bold, unnatural, gloppy. He views the picture as quality for its pastoral content. Mrs. Pyke enters the room; he grows stiff very quickly. She is the type that will smile and greet him but as soon as his back is turned say to herself what a basket case freak. She is a double-edged sword; someone who has her favorites and evidently Westcott does not qualify as one of those few. Although a brunette, she looks like Ms. Peacock from the movie *Clue* with her large goggly glasses accentuating her dark brown eyes and digger ado voice. Her hair is cut shoulder length and humorously curls outward to a point on each side. Her feet are big. Her appearance doesn't disturb him quite as much as her subtle condescending air. Mrs. Pyke opens his file in the computer system. A photograph taken in the ninth grade for the yearbook pops up along with all his spring classes. He shudders. He wishes they would have updated the pictures; staring at the image he realizes the person before him, forever captured in time, is a stranger.

He tries to remember what he was thinking in that photograph, unable to fully grasp his own reasons for the prolonged latency of his revelation. He had always known something was wrong, but could never put his finger on it.

'So, how are things going...classes all right?'

Pulling himself back from the recesses of his mind, he blandly gives a stock answer. 'Yeah...fine.'

'Well, from what we have here it looks like you'll be taking Government, Drawing, Photography, and Keyboarding next semester...does that sit well with you?'

He doesn't see any legitimate reason why he should have to take three elective classes when Government is the *only* required credit standing between him and graduation. He's already fulfilled his computer technology course, regretfully having taken AutoCAD sophomore year. His teacher unfairly gave him an 'F' on the exam, which conspired to be a C+ for the course—his first ever! He could have cared less if he knew how to type numbers and formulas into a computer and construct blueprint designs scaled to perfection. He deplored computer technology; his teacher should have at least considered his dauntless effort for an hour-and-half, 13 weeks straight, to toggle through material he absolutely hated and deemed utterly irrelevant. How Mr. Kainer arrived at an F for the final was arguable in itself! Really the joke was on him—if he took one glance at Westcott's academic record it would show the fault obviously rested with his instructing methods and personal assessment. Westcott wasn't up for refuting it. He always completed the blueprints, even if they were of incorrect measurements. He even stayed after school once to understand the configurations and entering of data, but Mr. Kainer was neglectful to remember this. It didn't matter; anyone could look at his transcript and deduce the error. Keyboarding Applications would prove to be nothing short of busy work, although it would later help to rub salt in Mr. Kainer's unfitting mark when Westcott received an A+. By then all would have been forgotten— it mattered little to him. Considering his options, or lack thereof, Westcott halfheartedly pursued a dead end.

'Is there any way I can just take three classes and spend a block in the library?'

Mrs. Pyke explained students weren't allowed to have a study hall. He couldn't believe his ears. No study hall! He would have been more than glad to take a History or English elective. Nothing was offered. Reluctantly he had Mrs. Pyke print out a copy of his schedule. He knew his mother addressed the issue of his name change with her. Rising to leave he knew he must speak.

'About my name. It's okay with me if *you* tell my teachers.'

It never occurred to him Mrs. Talmedge and Mrs. McCormick would be included in her informant list.

Selecting a new name had been a lengthy process. For the fall semester Westcott tried out all sorts, using his unisex, self-invented nickname, "Tugger," until he settled on a permanent name. Only his family referred to him by Tugger, but at his own request teachers made the shift from the unmentionable female name to Tugger. Mrs. Medley, Ms. Hutchens, and Brandon called him Tugger. Mrs. Littich never did. Searching through his mother's old baby book of names—the one with storks flying across the cover and peach-colored bundles wrapped in folded sheets, he made a list to keep track of those he favored most.

Timothy Thatcher; Timothy Townshend; Andrew; Mason; Joseph; Jake; Jay; Marshall; Heremon; Rheid; Rheidman; Abraham; Myrikai; Tuck; Trey; Redford; Sullivan; Barringer; Stillman; Conway; Yorich; Theseus; Thadeus; Orry (after Orry Main in North and South), Trenton; Byron; Wheat; Ford; Easton; Shepherd; Rhye...

He was drawn to Timothy. His mother could only think of Tiny Tim. She preferred a stronger name. But ultimately, it was her *son's* choice. It was agreed that Westcott A. Rowan, with its stalwart and uncommon nature, fulfilled such a quality. In later years his middle name prompted conversation. Why Aloysius? Westcott was drawn to its "agedness." Later, upon research he was intrigued to find that 'Aloysius' is a Teutonic name meaning: famous in war. According to history, people with this name "have a deep value for truth, justice, and discipline, and may be quick-tempered with those who do not. Their practical nature makes them good at managing and saving money...because of their focus on order and practicality, they may seem overly cautious and conservative at times." *Wow*, Westcott thought many years later. The proof was in the pudding of his own life. *And to think I'd picked it because of the way it sounds.*

In mid-January, prior to the semester roll-over, Westcott was doing his routine walk around the second floor before class. It was 7:37 a.m. Mrs. T came up behind him, put her hand on his back to let him know she was there. 'Mornin'.' She walked on. In retrospect he believed Mrs. Pyke had been to see her around that time.

~

Westcott stared back at his computer screen in fourth block Keyboarding. He felt weak, tired, his head throbbed amidst the rising temperature between his ears. His body was chilled in cold sweat. Sluggishly, knowing the rapid deterioration of strength that accompanies illness, he lifted himself. A wave of pain thronged in his frontal lobe. His actions seemed in slow motion. He was pushing through water when he approached Mr. Allowick.

'Can I go to the nurse?' In that moment a precedent came to pass. Not once in his high school career had the boy ever sought a trip to the infirmary. To seek such permission Westcott knew the extent of his sickness was beyond tempering.

'Do you mind waiting a minute?' the same Mr. Allowick who had been his teacher for Law in Society a year before replied. 'I just sent someone to the restroom, when he gets back you can go...I don't want too many people out of the room at once.' Since the semester's start Mr. Allowick had made nothing of the boy's gender transformation. The fact that the student he once knew now bore a masculine name and manly appearance did not arouse any outward prejudices, which, coupled with a class where everyone was a new face to Westcott, made for an amicable environment.

Without the energy to object, Westcott returned to his seat, closed the Microsoft program he'd been working on, and let his hands remain listless. Drawing his black Route 66 coat with the brown striping on the collar and sleeves closer, he bent his head down, resigned to ride out the remainder of class in silent ailment. Closing his eyes, he longed for sleep. The afternoon announcements came over the loud speaker, interrupted by the 2:40 bell. Westcott labored toward his truck. Once home he fell on the couch. Half past noon the next day he had his mother write him a note to get into school late. Deciding the evening before not to miss his last spirit jam at Drummond's Field High, Westcott forced himself to feel better.

It was Valentine's Day; the SCA had rescheduled its pep rally for today, Friday the 14th, after the fire alarm had been pulled as a prank last fall, the 1st of November.

During the last thirty minutes of Photography Westcott developed only one print from his negatives. His fever rising, he couldn't concentrate, let alone focus his eyes long enough to manipulate the enlarger. On his way to fourth block he had the where-with-all to make his routine glance at the faculty photographs pinned up on the main hallway's bulletin board, secure behind a locked door of sliding glass. He caught a glimpse of Mrs. T in her red pull-over sweater and Ms. Hutchens. Both pictures were flattering from what the boy could tell in his mere seconds of passing. He wished to stop and study them on many an occasion, to locate Mrs. McCormick and Ms. Garlow. That would have been too obvious. By the time his keyboarding class was summoned to the gym, he could hardly walk; every step elicited pain in his joints. Entering the gymnasium he passed Mrs. Talmedge and Ms. Hutchens decked with green and white face paint. Ms. Hutchens wore a silver tinsel wig; Mrs. T her caterpillar hat. He rasped a sore throat-laden, 'Hi.'

He veered right, heading for the designated senior section—a mass of red. Everybody showed their spirit wearing senior t-shirts, spray painting hair, writing their class year across forehead and cheeks. He wore his blue and black checkered coat, navy short-sleeved button down shirt, denim carpenter jeans, and brown shoes. He climbed the bleachers about five rows, plunked down by himself. For a little over an hour he tried to find amusement in the activities going on before him. Some of the guys were pretending to be transvestites. Cruel irony. Westcott's determination not to be sick ran dry. His face was ghastly pale. He was in the stages of full-blown contagiousness. He isolated himself from the other students on the bleachers and was careful not to speak to anyone throughout the day. He did not aim to be the instigator of a slew of absences nor could he be blamed for such a thing. Sickness was already rampant as evident by his being taken ill.

Come Monday another bout of snow had fallen prompting school cancellations. By Wednesday Westcott made a comeback, was able to hold down a meal without flu induced vomiting. For six days plain toast, water, and occasional soup were all that comprised his diet.

~

In February Westcott discovered the many uses of duct tape. He had been using a waist cincher *to do the job*. It worked well, visually. But wearing the cincher stretched the material; over time it lost what he called its Motion Inhibiting Ability, something Westcott could not tolerate. He was forced to take drastic measures. To his delight the new method proved adequate, killing two birds with one stone. The only drawback: the cost of having to stock up and the discomfort of an aching back and sore ribs if bound too tightly or a wild itching from regions of oxygen-deprived skin. Duct tape does not breathe. Such pain and discomfort were the price he was willing to pay. It wasn't a choice. It was a necessity. Maturation hormones hadn't kicked in until the latter part of his teenage years, well after he was sixteen, providing him a stay of liberty from the confines of masking tape. His mother bound him. He would not touch himself, would not look at his breasts, did not want to risk running a hand into one of *them*. In her defense, Gedny only wanted to help her child. She didn't want to cause him further distress. What she didn't realize was that by not making him do it himself and forcing him to acknowledge the issue, she was fueling his denial.

Later that same month he called on Mrs. McCormick and Mrs. T for a favor. He needed copies of their recommendations to mail in with the scholarship applications he was in the process of filling out. Mrs. T was across the room sitting on top of her gray office desk.

'West!'

Had he actually heard his name? As she approached it became clear she was directing her attention at him. He couldn't believe his ears; his heart beamed. Just a few short months ago he had walked into a men's public restroom for the first time and here he was being called his male name by *her*; now he was absolutely sure she knew. But how much and what had she been told? Could he trust Mrs. Pyke had explained his situation accurately? He wanted to ask, what *exactly* did Mrs. Pyke tell you? He abandoned the notion, hoping to derive an answer from her attitude towards him.

Tongue-tied Westcott could not clarify his motives for seeking out her and Mrs. McCormick. He returned the next day for a second attempt. Mrs. T exhibited a postulating expression. The boy told her reassuringly, 'I swear I'm not trying to bother you. I think you misunderstood me yesterday.' He realized his error in saying *you misunderstood*. He meant to place the blame on himself, but the words mangled themselves as they always did.

His brief encounter with Mrs. T that first morning was the one and only time she ever referred to him as West. Consequently, he began to doubt her acceptance. She avoided using any pronouns. He realized her image of him was shattered. Perhaps she had seen a part of her younger self in him. Anecdotes and class stories revealed she had been a tomboy growing up on a farm with three brothers. Maybe it disappointed, or worse, disdained her to discover she was mistaken—that the Plain Jane she'd taught for an entire year and likened to herself turned out to be a plain John. It was all speculation. Maybe she didn't detect any similarity except for the fact her student favored the subject she taught and loved. Then again, maybe he was reading too much into her actions. Troubling as his conjectures were, his partialness for her remained.

Holding Steadfast

Rigid he does stand
Rigid he so walks
Where is his envisioned homeland
Where're his timid eyes when he talks

Slow is his gait
Slow are the days
There is no shortcut 'round thy born fate
His bones spear him like needles and stays

Trapped like Hamlet, a boy of all words
This much is unquestionably true
Seal up his coffin, nail down the boards
This life of his is forever through

STATIONS

For Government Westcott had Mrs. Webber. Again he failed to challenge his capabilities, opting not to take the more advanced course with Mr. Ambrose. As a new mother, Mrs. Webber was in that interval where women are forced to juggle between career and motherhood. It quickly became apparent that her attention was devoted to her home life and infant son. She taught the class what it needed to know, fulfilling the teacher's mandatory state proscribed quota, and that was the extent of it. There was nothing special or exceptional about her, unless one considers having a child extraordinary. She was typical, plain, and forgettable. A few of the students Westcott knew from American Studies were in her class, including Brandon from Anatomy. Since so many were previously acquainted with him, he debated what name to use, ultimately telling Mrs. Webber to call him by his nickname, "Tugger." Eventually he stopped caring and went by Westcott as he did in all his other classes.

Instead of sitting next to Brandon, he resided in the back of the room next to a habitually absent, troubled, but amicable girl he knew from eleventh grade Journalism. The aisle ran between them so his desk was paired on the left with a rather tall and stocky boy. Craig was best described as a "Lumpy Rutherford" from *Leave It To Beaver*. They were night and day to one another. He often stole glances at Westcott's papers for answers and served to be the class dunce, receiving the brunt of many hopeless looks. He never realized the truth about Westcott when the rest of the class knew. At times Westcott felt sorry for him, shaking his head helplessly, foreseeing instances where he set himself up to look like a buffoon. Teachers will often say no question is ever stupid. To his misfortune Craig had the knack of proving them wrong. Craig played chess and asked Westcott to join the club. This discrepancy did not go unnoticed. Did Craig really play Chess? Chess was no game for fools. Was Craig an underachiever? No, that couldn't justify his inept questions. Was he just not tuned in?

Westcott, who hadn't played in years, politely said he'd think about it. He knew he wouldn't go. All the same, Westcott thought Craig was a nice kid, becoming gravely disgusted one day by a fellow student's mistreatment of him.

She was a snobbish princess, short, with a two-inch waist band, dirty blonde hair grazing the top of her rear, a pug nose, bright blue eyes, bean-pole legs, doll-like wrists, and a head swelled as large as a watermelon. She was insecure. She was one of the three drunkard girls who had been involved in the intoxicated driving incident, incurring a three-month suspension from Advanced World Lit. and all other courses. Her name was Meagan, a self-centered drama queen who thought she was the hottest thing since Nicole Kidman. She wore skin-plastered clothes with all the popular brand names, letting everyone see her petite, sterling figure. Westcott would watch in the morning as she placed her hands on her hips in the middle of the hall with a look of deft irritation. It was of her superior opinion that she had the right to debase such lowly creatures as Craig; he was a swampy toad to her and did not deserve to breathe the same clean air. She told him, 'Move out of my way, you useless waste of life.' Upon hearing this derogatory remark that day, a nearby girl mouthed to Westcott, 'What a bitch.' The boy nodded in sound agreement, still taken aback by Meagan's harsh statement. With the heel of her shoe she squished the toad without the least sign of remorse. He told Craig he didn't know what her problem was. He had no choice but to be on his side, an ally fighting rejection. He, too, was vulnerable to vehement verbal attacks of a different kind. God only knows what Meagan thought of him. And so went Government. Westcott thrived. Meagan flaunted. And Craig floundered.

Mrs. Webber showed a forced understanding for the boy, not sure what to make of him, and that's how things stayed.

Most days Westcott spent his half hour break for lunch watching the minutes on the clock or using his wristwatch to time how long he could hold his breath. A few seats down from him three boys and a girl shared his table. Sometimes he'd eavesdrop on their conversation; it came as a surprise one day when one of the boys turned to his friend and said rhetorically, 'Don't you think Mrs. T's hot?'

Westcott's ears perked up. The other boy agreed. Mrs. Talmedge only taught tenth and eleventh grade. Westcott assumed from their appearance and immature voices they were most likely sophomores. Comforted that he wasn't the only guy partial towards his old teacher, he felt more assured of his masculinity; his affection for her was only natural. When not listening-in, he stared into space, studied his soda can, mentally worked on a poem, hummed a tune, watched other students. Sometimes he'd see Mr. Methodical, a boy with blonde hair tucked behind his ears, who struck Westcott's attention because of his meticulous, homicidal stride. When he walked he moved slowly as if to be pushing through thick liquid. Often Westcott traced his eyes over a purse printed with an Italian scene the girl down from him carried to lunch. She'd set it on the table to her right, perfect for his observational motives. A Venetian gondola was pictured against a cramped but quaint backdrop of a little town. Portions of the illustration were outlined in rectangular beads, which steadily diminished in number from wear. The boy enjoyed looking at it. Hearing the bell signaling it was time for third block Westcott would rise, dutifully throw away his trash, continue on to photography, a shadow passing among his peers.

Mrs. Sparroh was a tall woman, even surpassing Westcott in height, with a long face outlined by wavy brown hair that fell below her shoulders. Her light blue eyes spoke a kindness, peering out from behind a pair of wire-rimmed glasses. Judging by her lean body and trim limbs one would not take her to be thirty-nine going on forty. She exhibited incredible fitness for her age, and on top of that she was mother to a teenager. Westcott observed a difference between teachers who were mothers and those who were not. Somehow they seemed less untouchable and threatening, treating the students as they would their own children. There existed a pronounced line of division; they resided on the more established half. Westcott was not intimidated by their femininity like he was with Mrs. Talmedge and Ms. Hutchens.

The boy was appreciative of Mrs. Sparroh for her understanding and careful use of correct pronouns during his three-hour stint in her class. She taught Drawing and Photography. Since he signed up for both courses in consecutive order—that's all Mrs. Pyke could come up with—Westcott spent the better part of his days in good company. Mrs. Sparroh made a point to refer to him with the pronouns "his" or "he." He did not sense even the slightest hint of animosity; her acceptance was visibly genuine and allowed him to be more open. He was nicknamed "QB," Quiet Boy, by one of his classmates in 2nd block. John, the label's creator, had fallen victim to Westcott's much wanted gender deception. He was a sophomore and knew nothing of the boy. Art courses were not grade-delineated. Students in 10th, 11th and 12th were all represented. Amazingly, only three of his classmates were aware of his secret, one of whom was a closet homosexual. Westcott gathered from the few things Alan had said that he could never come out to his family. His parents wanted him to be a doctor; Alan wanted to be an artist. Unfortunately, such obliviousness was not the case in 3rd block where many a peer had previously been in classes with Westcott when he was still a tomboy. Claudia, for example, a tall, trim, athlete who played for the DFH's basketball team, knew Westcott from Advanced World Lit. There was Lindsay, a very sweet girl next door. She had been a member of the yearbook staff; seldom if ever did any words pass between them. Once in Photography all that changed when Westcott politely began engaging in conversation while sitting next to her. He'd tell her lame jokes. 'What is a cat's favorite dish to order at a Mexican restaurant?' Finally he'd answer his own riddle. 'A catsadilla.' It gave him a reason to interact, a chance to try and connect, maybe even belong.

One afternoon a girl approached Westcott asking him to unscrew the cap off a glass jar that was sealed securely by the black ink it contained. The boy obliged her, leery, doubting his own strength. To his surprise and relief he effortlessly twisted the baby jar cap until it popped loose. With pride he handed it back to the girl, proud of his newfound chivalry. She had sought him out on the basis of his masculine abilities. He would come to realize as time went on that the train he'd boarded housed a cargo of gender-tied expectations. Society's perception of the male equated to superior physical strength. Westcott, atrophied and sedentary for the past two years, needed to *rebuild* himself.

The other boys ignored Westcott's efforts to be one of the guys. He was at the starting gate of his transition, fighting to shed the stigma of his old name. True males—biological males—proved intimidating and threatening to him. He didn't know how to be a guy in certain areas, but by no means did that make him female. He'd ridden the fence for so long, blurring his identity until time and pain brought forth a suppressed realization throttled by unconscious denial. He couldn't lie to himself anymore. Soon it became clear that achieving harmony between being and living would be impossible without surgical intervention. It was like the trans-woman had said at the PFLAG meeting he attended a year ago. There is tremendous variation along the gender spectrum and within each individual's transformation. The process is similar to a train. One can keep on riding to the end or get off at any station along the way. How far you decide to go, your comfort level, is guided by one's own discretion. Westcott did not choose his lifestyle. It grasped hold of him. *If only they could perform head transplants.* He laughed painfully at such a wild idea. Being and living are two separate yet interconnected concepts, which the boy forced himself to understand. He could live and pass sufficiently as the opposite sex, but the personal knowledge that mentally and physically his gender was at odds compromised this sense of being. He refused to look at himself in the shower for fear of shattering his internal, cognitive self-concept, and he got dressed with a gaze fixed ahead and in the dark.

~

Westcott stared down at the double creased letter held limply in his hands. Skimming, his eyes fell upon the dreaded words.

'We're sorry to inform you that we are unable to offer you a seat…'

The knowledge hit him with a great force. His future was now determined. Foolishly he'd still maintained a slight hope of receiving admittance to W&M as a freshmen, and yet, distantly, he felt such wistful naiveté could only be met with certain disappointment. It was March 25th, the eve of his mother's birthday. Notices weren't supposed to be received until mid-April. He suspected a possible rejection prior to opening the thin envelope. To his dismay his assumptions were proved right. It disgruntled him immensely; four years of hard work and a 3.9 GPA. Where was the payoff? He had a sibling alumna, which always bears weight. His second choice of schools didn't even require a 3.0 for acceptance. He should have played up the community service bit. He begrudged the use of SAT's to measure an individual's prospective success in college. The scores could not measure a person's abilities; he wasn't a timed-test taker. Nothing seemed fair. Mrs. Pyke had been against him trying for W&M from the beginning. She would most likely be pleased with the outcome. After all, the idea of Westcott attending her alma mater would be intolerable. The terminology she used in her recommendation sealed the boy's disdain. He wasn't supposed to open her letter, but he had an extra copy, temptation got the best of him. Reading the words "young woman," Westcott's anger broiled with bitterness. Was she completely deaf and blind? Did she think his situation was some kind of a hoax, a phase? The audacity to write such a lie. What she thought of him didn't matter, he reminded himself. There were others, he knew, like Mrs. Sparroh, the librarians, and his old 10th grade Biology teacher, Mrs. Wesson, who were on his side.

The first week of April, Westcott, his mother, and "girlfriend," went to a tuxedo rental store. Although prom was over a month away, it was thought that reserving a tux early would prevent any hassle down the road, not to mention offer a greater array from which to select. Westcott decided on a traditional style tailored to his size and frame. The shoulders were still too big. After picking out a vest and black bow tie, the oriental lady in charge of the store took his measurements. Everything was going fine until she got to his neck.

'12 1/2 inches,' the lady spoke in disbelief.

'You have a scrawny neck, girl…boy!' Ellis slipped, tried to recover.

Westcott shot Ellis a murderous look, but was relieved when the lady made nothing of it. Nothing infuriated him more than to be passing and have his cover blown. He wondered what had caused Ellis' memory to relapse. Learning to say something one way after programming oneself to say it another for sixteen years must take time. She, too, had some serious adjusting to do, a fact Westcott often neglected to remember.

Sometime in April, having digested his rejection letter, Westcott was doing his morning stroll around the hall when Mrs. T, approaching from the opposite direction, initiated a conversation.

'Hey, darlin',' she began. Often when talking with students, male or female, she would refer to them as such, and for an instant her southern tongue was employed by dropping the "g" on the second syllable. Although a rather endearing term, the boy thought nothing of it for it was just another character trait by which he came to know her.

Instead of stopping like any normal person would so she could speak with him, Westcott continued a few paces in his plodding gait. Mrs. T turned around, walking with him in the direction she had just come.

'So, have you heard back from W&M yet?' she asked.

'Yes, I, uh, didn't get in,' Westcott replied in his low voice. Hastily, not wanting to show any disappointment he added, 'But that's okay!'

'Well, don't worry, it's always more difficult applying as a freshman. Transferring is a lot easier. I mean you can always try that route next year, that is unless you find out you like it at CNU. Whatever makes you happy. It's *your* choice.'

'Yes,' he acknowledged, coming to a halt.

'What about the scholarships? Did they say when you might hear somethin'?'

'No I haven't heard anything...they said probably in early June.'

'I'm sure things will work themselves out.' There was an air of withholding in her voice, as though she knew something. 'Have a good day.' Resuming her Thai sales rep gait, she only had to double back a few feet before advancing further due to the fact that the boy's incredibly slow and steady tortoise pace had caused her to backtrack just a couple of steps.

The Ardent Wind

The boy rested on the pale boards of the steps. Fourth up from the dusty ground, six down from the swinging gate above. And so he was situated. The shadows were ascending, nearing what—if a tree were human—would be its shoulders. The birds were settling in, another day gone—their words seemed almost fragile. So at ease was that world among the trees; he feared any movement or shifting on his part would shatter all he cherished.

~

The boy turned his attention to a branch—a ruler he often used to measure time. The leaves were no longer shielded by their coats of renewed, valiant green. A tint of yellow had emptied forth, giving the sense that turkeys were soon due to be on tables.

The dry counterparts of the branches surrendered to the wind and thus departed. The days grew long and the boy's patience short.

The boy studied the ruler before him. The tints of gray within the bark appeared somehow more alive, welcoming. He knew that soon the day's light would draw on and darkness would be forced away by an unyielding sun, lingering at times beyond eight at night. Far off he heard the engine of a lawn mower. *How can it be? Just yesterday I was taking down Christmas lights.* He stared down at his dilapidated shoes, waiting. A few minutes and then the roaring ended as the boy had silently anticipated. He loved and dreaded the sound of its reverberating engine; he distinctly knew the scent with which the owner of the mower was filled. A dusty warm, dirt-ridden redolence from the cuttings would invade the stranger's nose. His olfactory, most undoubtedly, would be driven crazy; although, it would be a happy, content crazy. The boy glanced back at the tree. The shadows were now upon its neck. A gentle wind arose and the boy's heart quietly began to die. All hope withered away. Despair overtook him and was quickly replaced with insurgent anger. An absolute agony of misfortune. The boy moved his mouth, chewing on his spit. Desperately, he tried to release the tautness of the muscles in his legs; his mind refused to let him. And so he remained. Still. Trapped. Unable to escape. Running provided no cure for his pain.

One cannot break down the bars of his own skin and bones. The spirit shakes the sinewed poles, throws itself up against the bones of imprisonment, but inevitably falls—resolved once more.

The boy yelled. No one except for himself and the wind heard the cry. There was an emptiness, a void grasping him—like the sound of chain flapping against the flagpole, lonely and hollow—heard on occasion only in the background. Once, before school, he recalled sitting in the parking lot listening to the noise of melted ice as it sailed through a drain's grate, into the depths of nothing.

The tops of the trees swayed; the slabs of wood beneath the boy transformed like a chameleon into a desolate, faint tinge of blue. The light was dimming. So, too, was the boy's spirit. The wind brushed across his forehead—a distant comfort.

'What is it that you want?' Wind seemed to ask.

Boy thought for a moment then replied, 'Not to die alone.'

'Why burden yourself with death,' Wind continued, 'when you have yet to live?'

'I cannot.'

'Cannot what?'

'Live. Long have I endured. My spirit can withstand not another torrent of rain. Like the gloom cast upon a day by a pathetic rain, I am my own constant tormentor of relentless despair. The sky is never completely free, the storm is nearby, always home.'

'What is it that you yearn?' Wind questioned.

'Not to spend this life alone.'

'Aren't I company enough to satisfy your wants?'

'The wind doesn't always beckon so dearly. And when it does its warmth taunts unmercifully, for I cannot enjoy wholly the eves of its spring and breeze of its summer. How cold the wind can be, even mocking at times. Ah, but you're not the enemy. It is simply animosity between a question with no answer, a situation lacking a resolution, and a heart inflicted with hope battling anguish, which causes bitterness toward your ways.'

~

Soon the leaves will emerge from their dormant months, the evenings will no longer bring slight shiverings, and the birds will be busy all day accompanied by insects droning away the afternoon. As for the boy, the boy will watch. The needle of his spirit waiting to jump another hour. Long are the days, short is his patience. The wind is forever free, standing by. A friend to the boy. Until. At last. He can come home.

THE EVENING VISITOR

Westcott rested complacently in his chair, the pinwheel in his neighbor's yard stopped. He studied his Civil War calendar tacked on the corner wall, the sun slanting across its dates. April 27th. It pained him to think another month was just about finished. Time was so fragile, simultaneously fleeting and stagnant, it didn't make any sense. His mind drifted to earlier that afternoon when he'd gone to purchase the tickets for prom and was asked to show his driver's license; he hated showing it for fear their attention would be drawn to the damning 'F' partially hidden by the Virginia seal, giving way to his cursed biology. Fortunately, it was neither Mrs. T's nor Ms. Hutchens' turn as SCA chairmen to sell any tickets. A more innocuous teacher, Mrs. Malladore, had been put in charge during the particular time slot in which Westcott decided to shell out the seventy dollars his mother had given him. Returning his thoughts to the present, all was quiet in the room except for the rhythmic trill of some invisible force shrouded beneath the overgrown tufts of grass outside. The crickets were alive with a beating resonance that defined the twilight atmosphere in terms of music. Dusk was the boy's favorite time of day and there was something particularly striking to him about a spring eve. He could never explain it; words didn't exist for the feeling or aura that accompanied the hours from four to seven p.m. The world transformed into a symphony of sights and sounds: wind chimes blowing in the gentle wind, children laughing and playing on the next street over, dinners being cooked, the sun setting in the west flickering through forest branches, the ducks in the pond, the bullfrogs honking like wild moose, lawn mowers reverberating, four-legged friends going for walks with flush tails and jovial barks, home-work being scratched down in notebooks, conversations in porch rocking chairs, and ever the cricket's muse. Together they culminated a sense of content for the boy, epitomizing the aura of happiness. Such times were wonderful and the boy hated to be shut away in his room, alone. He felt the visitor pull at his heart, calling him. Unable to appease his ardent desires, he did not answer, but watched as another year was lost to his condition. And denial.

I am like the crickets.

One did not have to see the musical insects to know they were present. Inversely, Westcott need not be heard in order to be seen; his silence set him apart. Both were a background accustomed to, overlooked by others. He stepped to the small double windows behind him. The sky was incredible; lavender stratus clouds streaked the domed ceiling aglow with a tinge of bright orange cascading upward from beneath the treetops and illu-minating the land as the golden sphere dipped into a state of slumber. The scene coiled around the boy's spirit, his will strangled, it was killing him—the sorrow, always the sorrow and the steady patience. He couldn't endure any more waiting. Too long, he had been alone too many years. The emptiness of watching another day go by and knowing tomorrow, the day after, and the next shared a common thread of isolation was too much. He turned to his right and gazed at home—the painting, a sanctuary of imagination combined with reality, given life by a scarce unknown, January Hooker, copyrighted in 1984. Perspective dominated the picture; a lane assumed the role of railroad tracks in a drawing exercise. It stretched endlessly, narrowing into the horizon with giant trees of spring foliage on one side casting shadows upon the pavement. The boy became transfixed, his eyes marveling at the patches of sunlight and blue sky peeking through the branches. He was reminded of his carefree childhood days spent on Magnolia Avenue in California.

Westcott staggered downstairs to find his mother in a sitting position with her arms crossed and her head down, napping. He moved into the kitchen with deliberate lightness of steps and opened the refrigerator door. Scanning the shelves, nothing appealed to him. Behind him there was a rustling. He sighed inaudibly.

'I was going to call you soon. Did you fall asleep?' she spoke in a hoarse, half-groggy voice.

The boy shook his head.

'What do you feel like eating?'

'Whatever you want.'

'How 'bout our favorite restaurant,' his mother suggested. 'Quiet table for two in the back.'

The boy managed a slight smile. His mother was acting out the lines from a movie she was obsessed with. Knowing the dialogue just as well he replied, ' "Very quiet." We taking my truck?'

'If you want...bring me the phone so I can call in the order.'

On their way over to pick up the dinners Westcott remained quiet. His mother's eyes were red from crying. He didn't want to upset her further. After getting their take-out meals his mother took a slow drive to the park. They looked out on the open field. Another few minutes and the skies would be dark. His mother looked over at him.

'You're such a good kid...I can't stand getting angry with you. I know how much you suffer already.' She placed her hand on the back of his head and rubbed it. 'I'm not mad...I just wish things could be right for you. It hurts me to see you like this.'

He stopped eating, he felt guilty and annoyed. True, he didn't smoke, drink, or shoot up, and seldom did he ever cuss, but what he was seemed to supersede such parental heartaches. Sometimes he wished she'd stop loving him.

'Don't you love how the trees are silhouetted against the sky, it's beautiful.'

Westcott studied the cobalt blue dome, the black arms of oaks and dogwoods stretching skyward in the dusk light, glad his mother had changed the subject.

'We pals again Mudge?' Mudgie or Mudge was her pet name for him.

He did not answer.

A long silence followed.

Westcott turned his head and looked into his mother's eyes. In those days she was the only person he could do that with outside of Ellis.

It will be a Thursday. He thought about the kind of day he'd like to die on. A fall or spring eve. The wind will be blowing through the forest leaves. If it is fall, the day will be a rare sight for that time of year, something to behold. The sun will shine and warm the land.

Autumn colors will be defined in such crispness complimented by the rich blue sky. Trees that have taken root next to houses will tap their brittle appendages against nearby window-panes, stirring all to come outside. If it is a spring day shadows will slice lawns and rooftop eves. Waning sunlight will flicker across the forest floor with cattails by the water's edge disintegrating in the sweet breeze. Reeds will arc over; the lush green foliage shall whisper farewell. The flag on the front porch will wave gallantly while great cumulus clouds drift slowly across glass panes, mere reflections in the window. The grandfather clock will chime as the crickets prepare their serenade.

He imagined the scent of the day...sights, sounds...everything.

Returning home, the boy went upstairs with the sole purpose of killing time before his nightly episodes of *Leave It To Beaver* came on. Though completely dark, he hesitated to turn on any lights and proceeded into his room, straining his eyes to see. The blinds were still up, permitting the moon to shine across the floor. Outside, the crickets were in full harmony. Their resonance had grown louder as the noise of routine excursions—trips to the grocery store, eating out, local sport events, yard work—a whole litany of activities died down, ending with garage doors shutting, porch lamps being switched on, living rooms becoming illuminated in blue from the blare of televisions, and young children coming in from playing only to wash up and be sent off to bed. The boy looked at the painting again. Day had departed, the sun's yellow flickerings through the trees had transformed into its brother's light. The moon's grace radiated through branches casting a white lace along the sidewalk. Westcott felt the warmth of spring around him, forgetting his worries for a moment. Reluctantly he pulled himself away from that place before him, his sorrow ushering back. Leaving the room he glanced at the wall in front of his desk. The evening visitor, his only companion, had gone. And with it all splendor and despair.

That same night, after an hour or more of lying awake in the dark with his thoughts to keep him company, the boy fell asleep. He slipped into a deep slumber and dreamt. In his dream he awoke early in the morning. The sun had yet to reach altitude enough to shine in his window. He speculated that the time was roughly 6:15 a.m. Of the three hanging clocks in his room, all on separate walls, each needed a battery and told a different time. Westcott intentionally fixed them so they wouldn't run. Their ticking disturbed him when he was reading and doing homework. Now they were mere aesthetic pieces. A bird tapped at his window. He pulled his legs out of bed and planted his feet on the floor, keeping his eyes half shut so's not to wake up immediately, savor another moment of sleep. As was his habit for the past two years, he pulled his shirt collar up and clenched it in his teeth, not wanting to be disgusted by seeing the rise of his breasts. He held the collar of his shirt in his mouth like a tent. He slowly staggered his way into the laundry room, shut the door, dressing in the dark. While grasping for his pants on top of the dryer, his jaws accidentally loosened their grip, his saliva-wet collar fell from his mouth and a very strange thing happened. Something was different. He took the collar in his hand, pulled it up and dropped it again. Something was different. Afraid he was mistaken, Westcott jumped gently twice. Nothing. He couldn't believe it! God, was it true? No movement of distended flesh bounced when he jumped. He ran into the bathroom, positioning himself in front of the mirror. His stomach grew nauseous, numb with hope. He stared at his reflection in the dim lighting, there were no words for what he saw. Sheer elation welled in his heart; he turned sideways to be positive he wasn't dreaming. *Dear God is it true, am I really free? Oh God let it be so and not my eyes deceiving me. Oh God, I'm free, I'm free...free, free!* He tugged the shirt over his head, threw it to the floor and in that instant was born.

A boy stared back at him from within the mirror; Westcott's mind was still shaken with disbelief. His heart rejoiced as he checked himself out from every angle. The content was too great; for sure his chest would split right open with happiness.

After the initial shock, Westcott placed his hand atop his heart in such a manner as to say the pledge of allegiance. Never again, he thought, never again. All the little things he wanted to do but wouldn't, all the restrictions, all of them gone, not ever again. The boy finished getting dressed, picked out a short-sleeved greenish-beige plaid shirt, the excitement overwhelming. He entered his sister's room as he often did in the early morning, envying her prolonged state of slumber. Strum was curled up at the foot of her bed. He sat down on the edge of the mattress, careful not to disturb Ellis, and roughed up Strum's fur lovingly—rubbing her belly. She yawned and rolled playfully on her back, her gray tail swishing. He looked out the windows that opened onto the forest. The sun was young in its ascent; an antique sundial with a crystal sphere on Ellis' table caught the light and cast a prism on her closet doors. Glancing at her Bombay clock, Westcott realized it was getting late. Standing, he turned to the wall opposite the windows. A Kodak collage covered the whitewash; Ellis had stylishly arranged a sort of family photograph mosaic-timeline, spanning five years. He saw a picture of himself with long hair taken a few years earlier. Staring at the snapshot, he felt it was another person's life.

He went into his mother's bedroom.

'Ma,' his voice hushed. 'Ma, I'm leaving now.'

'All right, come here let me give you a neck kiss.'

The boy leaned over the bed bending his head down. 'Have a good day....and don't forget to call me.' She always had him call when he arrived to school.

'I know, Thelma. Have I forgotten to yet?' He was perturbed she reminded him. It was her OCD. He called her Thelma (after Thelma Lou from *The Andy Griffith Show*) whenever he felt nagged lovingly or she slipped up on his new name. She hated the name Thelma, it sounded so country bumpkin, so Westcott used it to get back at her with joking affection. Even Ellis would occasionally chide in, substituting 'Thelma' with 'To-hell-ma.'

All the way to school Westcott was beaming. He rolled the window down halfway, a warm spring breeze ran through his short brown hair, filling his nose with the sweet scent of fresh cut grass as he drove by a pasture. Everything seemed alive with goodness to him, for once he was a part of that other world. He pulled into his usual space by the island with the tree and switched the engine off. He proceeded to do as he had always done. After three or four minutes of people watching, he slid out of the truck, faced eastward. The sun shined upon his face as it had done every morning. Today it was somehow brighter. Its rays didn't just warm the surface of his skin. They impaled him with a surge of energy and will. As his heart ignited, the sorrow languished and the desolate sickness of his existence melted beneath the light.

Westcott grabbed his backpack from the passenger seat, hoisted it to his right side as he had habitually done, then realized...he flung the other strap to his left arm, placing the pack completely on his back. For once his arms and hands were allowed to hang loosely at his sides, unencumbered. His posture was impeccable, his back felt strong. He sneaked a glance at the driver's window to see if he looked all right, still in disbelief. It was just as he always imagined. No more paranoia, no more duct tape...he was home. Westcott walked into school nonchalantly, devoid of any nervousness or fear. He treaded down the halls with a sure gait, experiencing what it was like to be normal. While making his rounds about the second floor he ran into Mrs. Talmedge who greeted him cheerfully.

'Morning Westcott, how are ya?'

The boy was shocked, she had actually acknowledged his name without hesitation, as if he had always been as she saw him that very day. He smiled with deep appreciation.

'Good.'

This was all he had ever wanted, the simple, commonplace things most people take for granted, a knowledge that he belonged. Westcott stopped at the balcony, peered over at the students below, no longer envious. As he stood gazing out at the treetops aback the building, a distant roaring sound caught his ear. All the while he was trying to figure out where the noise was coming from, it grew steadily louder. And louder. Perhaps one of the maintenance crew was mowing the lawn outside, but surely it wouldn't be that loud? Suddenly everything blurred and began to swirl around him. His mother was calling him, 'Son, son.' He saw himself turning off the ignition to his truck. Mrs. Talmedge's voice rang in his ears repetitiously, 'How are ya, how are ya, how are ya?' Nothing made sense anymore. The boy observed his morning in replay. The last thing he remembered was seeing himself, hand over heart, looking in the mirror. He collapsed.

Westcott opened his eyes to find himself alone in his room. Outside a neighbor was cutting the lawn. *No, it can't be...it was so real. God let me wake up, let me wake up!* He lay still for a long time, speculating. Torturing himself with such fantasies only made things worse.

As the sun shone in on the floor and birds awoke from their nests with beckoning songs of joy, Westcott stared at the ceiling, his eyes clouding over.

THE RAIN CAME DOWN

Westcott stood in line for his yearbook, eating away at his half hour break for lunch. Fifteen minutes later when he was fourth from the window, Mrs. Littich explained in a moderately exasperated tone, 'You'll all have to come back later. We're not handing out any more right now. Get back to your classes.'

The boy was reluctant to move, even a bit agitated. Why shouldn't he be? Aside from completely wasting his time, he *had been* a member of the staff assisting in putting the yearbook together! It was the one and only time he hoped for a shred of favoritism. Mrs. Littich appeared not to have noticed him. He should have been persistent. Westcott slowly headed back to the cafeteria. Alas, third block came. Mrs. Sparroh demonstrated her usual kindness by letting the boy and a few others head down to the yearbook (multimedia) room. Receiving the book with his nickname, Tugger, engraved in the lower right hand corner, he returned to Photography class eager to look through the finished product. He flipped to the senior portrait section, scanning for R's, his fingers slipping on the slick pages. His eyes came to Rowan. Something inside stopped. His heart floored. It wasn't cliché. He actually felt it go light and fall—it skipped a beat. The contents of his stomach churned. He felt numb.

No. How could she? Westcott was mortified, crestfallen. *How? There can't be any excuse! I spoke to her in person, specifically told her what name to use!*

He couldn't think straight. Once the initial shock wore off he shifted his attention to the pictures.

At least that's right. Damn good thing they didn't put the one in of me with long hair—that would have done it!

The very idea of getting back to work was too impossible to entertain. He desperately wanted to stand up and tell the world, 'This isn't right, they made a terrible mistake, that's not my name, that's not who I am, it's a mistake, a God damn mistake!' He wished over and over the books could be recalled, the name whited-out, or at least for a correction of the ones still in boxes yet to be passed out.

It is just a name. But when you're 18 such moments embody everything. In time the yearbook would be archived. It would always be there. Evidence of his lie. This was something permanent. His cover had been obliterated. He was exposed. He wanted to crawl under the table, although slipping into the darkroom would serve to hide his pain just as well. In the dim lighting the boy tried to crank the enlarger into place bringing the negative into focus. Flipping the switch, he exposed his photo paper for a pre-tested amount of time, then placed the blank sheet in the developing tray. His hands shaking, he couldn't bring himself to concentrate. An anger started diluting the disbelief, bringing to the surface a distant notion that Mrs. Littich had deliberately and facetiously wronged him. What would those who only knew him as male think? The boy considered this with deep concern. He did not have to wait long before confrontation ensued.

Walking into Keyboarding class, a fellow student, a freshman, bombarded him.

'Have you seen the yearbook yet? It says you're...'

Westcott cut him off hearing *the name*. Mr. Allowick stood close enough to be listening. 'I know, I'm furious...can't believe they mixed up the names.' Stammering, he kept cool. 'I guess they must have confused me with someone else on the roster.'

'Yeah, but three times?!' Harrison pointed out.

Westcott realized how far-fetched his concocted excuse sounded. There was no way in hell he was about to tell the truth.

'I suppose they just read it wrong on the list, that's what Mrs. Littich told me,' he lied convincingly.

Later that afternoon, after being released early for an appointment, Westcott returned to school, his mother with him. Westcott opted not to accompany her to see Mrs. Littich; instead, he went back to fourth block to face the muse. He regretted not confronting her on his own. Why didn't his mother tell him, 'Go in there and demand an explanation? *You* need to face her.'

Westcott dried his eyes as he watched his mother coming back to the car.

'She assured me it was an oversight on her part and apologized profusely.'

Westcott listened to his mother recount her conversation with Mrs. Littich, half caring because any reason she gave had no bearing on the situation now at hand. Nothing his teacher said, or might say, mattered; what was done was done and he alone would have to endure the next eight days of school under a microscope. For a little while he gave Mrs. Littich the benefit of the doubt, presupposing that her actions were not of a malicious nature, but a product of sheer negligence. As the final week-and-a-half rolled by, Westcott had yet to hear any apology from Mrs. Littich. She told his mother that if she saw the boy she'd be sure to take responsibility for her error and tell him she was sorry. The fact that no such words were ever offered condemned all doubt in Westcott's mind. She had intentionally slandered him. More damning, like Harrison had said, how could someone make the same mistake three times! It was bad enough to be identified with a female name once—a reasonable margin of error, but *three* times? It could never be justified. Most intolerable were the Senior Superlatives. Everyone, both upper and lower classmen, enjoyed finding out who had been voted "most what." Westcott was nominated most shy and regretted ever accepting the title. He thought he was voted most shy *boy*. But no. All the superlatives had one guy and one girl. And *his* picture mate was a boy. At least in the formal photograph with his cap and robe he was harder to find, far less noticeable, but being pictured among a few select students on a two-page spread invited debauchery.

Only one other guy wore the robe instead of a tux, adding insult to injury. Thankfully not a single girl donned it either. Westcott had simply wanted to be photographed in a coat and bowtie. Mrs. Littich came up with the lame excuse that it might cause a ruckus and offered a solution by having the entire senior class take their picture in robes. The decision backfired with upheaval from parents and students alike. Some girls complained they looked like judges in the outfits. Westcott never asked to have policy changed on his behalf, nor did he intend to cause fluster to his peers. Later he knew he should have just gone ahead and taken the picture in the tux; the photographer would never have questioned him. He looked male. Mrs. Littich made it a problem. Westcott would not forgive her. Only an incompetent imbecile could make an oversight three times; she had been the first to learn of his condition the previous summer when he met with her to discuss wearing a tux and not the traditional senior girl's garb. She knew full-well the extent of his condition. How many gender-different individuals does a school have? It's not like he could easily be missed among the body of average students.

Mrs. Littich had done more to injure Westcott in one day than all four years of high school together. All his efforts to come out and be seen for who he really was were instantly shot down. In ten, twenty, or fifty years no one would recall his new name. She had ruined his attempt to be remembered in his self-identified sex. He could not pardon her. The book would live on as testimony to the past, and it would be a lie. He wanted to come out, casting the mask aside, tell them his story—explain why he had acted as he did, the silence, the miserable expression, the longing gaze.

That night Ellis repaired the *mistakes* in her brother's yearbook. Carefully matching the gray pigment of the senior pages and script font, she typed Westcott A. Rowan then pasted it down. For the other two corrections only white paper was necessary. Westcott appreciated his sister's efforts to restore his true identity in the yearbook. His mother had asked Ellis to do it.

Besides the slanderous typos, Westcott was disgruntled to find that part of what he wrote for the Academic section of the yearbook had been omitted. He was also sorely disappointed not to have submitted a quote to be printed below his name. Scanning through all the pictures, he noticed that just about every senior had included a few defining words and a list of their extracurricular activities. He thought it ironically comical how he had only been in Ms. Littich's class and failed to receive any sheet for recording such information. In hindsight he knew the perfect quote to sum up his high school career, "There is no prosthetic for an amputated spirit." Or perhaps, "I hope somebody, sometime will recognize the agony of spirit I have undergone," William Howard Taft. Or maybe, "So you know." Yes, he liked that—his own words.

It made no difference. The past could not be changed. This he understood quite well yet refused to accept. Westcott wished his mother had asked him what photographs he preferred to be used in the Senior Ads section designated for parents and family tributes to their children. Westcott detected an air of softness about his features in the pictures his mother selected, especially around his face. He disliked the droopy bangs. It's not that he wasn't grateful for what his mother had done, but he was bitter towards Ms. Littich. Now he had to prove he was male all over again. Had it not been for her defamation of him, then the pictures offered by his mother would not have dismayed him so.

Over the weekend the boy considered wearing a tie on Monday in the hopes of disproving the damning pictures.

John, from Drawing class, never spoke to him again.

———

Wednesday. June the 4th. Westcott wore a nicely pressed long-sleeved brown shirt and his carpenter jeans. Making his way into the half-filled auditorium, his nerves unleashed a certain intestinal sickness. With head down and eyes to the floor he quickly found an empty seat in the last aisle. Behind him were the rows of tiered seats offering an unobstructed view of the stage; they appeared relatively packed from his quick glance. He opted to sit somewhere that was easily accessible. As the junior and senior classes continued to pile in no one else sat in his row, creating the false impression that he had been quarantined. Westcott felt very uncomfortable and sensed a hundred pair of eyes burning into the back of his skull, but there was nothing he could do. To get up and move after everyone had settled would bring attention to him, an alternative worse than a burning neck. He remained seated.

Although he suspected he might receive some sort of recognition at the Awards Assembly, from his mother's less than obvious fuss the night before that he wear a nice shirt, upon hearing his name announced it startled him. Scholarships granted by the high school were being distributed to students with commendable academic performance. When they called out Westcott Rowan, the boy froze, his heart sank, and his hands were clammy. He hugged his seat with the back of his knees. Ellis appeared from behind, sat down in his lap, put her arms around his neck, as though she was his girlfriend.

'So, what's this? You're not going to go up there?'

Before he could answer a teacher came over, told Ellis to get off him, clearly displeased by the untimely display of public affection. Little did she know Ellis was not his girlfriend. Terrified, Westcott rose and walked to the stage. Unhappily he received an envelope and returned to his seat with relief. When it came time for the English Department Awards the boy grew numb, fidgeting his elbow on the armrest, moving his hand back and forth between mouth and lap. It was then that the news of Ms. Hutchens' departure from Drummond's Field High was formally announced and a farewell gift imparted to her by close colleagues and friends. Mrs. T ran her hand under her eyes a few times, the sadness of Ms. Hutchens fate visible. Westcott was unhappy to hear she would be leaving. Distantly he hoped to hear his name again. After the last honor chord had been given away a silent disappointment filled the boy. To justify the let-down, he reasoned that since he had not taken any Honors classes or the course proficiency SAT test, perhaps he wasn't eligible for nomination. He was appreciative of the sum of money granted by his school, but a token of recognition from his most beloved teachers would have been of more sentimental value to him than any check. The money would be spent, gone. It was impersonal. An Honor chord is something he could have kept. Thinking back to the morning when Mrs. T had told him she was "sure things would work out," the boy questioned if she had played a hand in ensuring that he not be passed over. Why didn't she support his receiving an award that better reflected his love and dedication for a specific field of academics? Deflated, Westcott remained defensive of Mrs. T in the face of his reservations.

Once the assembly broke Westcott left his mother and sister momentarily to go back upstairs to first block as instructed earlier that morning. Mrs. Webber had yet to return with the keys. The class was locked-out, unable to retrieve their belongings. Leaning back against the wall, the boy waited patiently off to one side, envelope in hand. For no apparent reason Mrs. Talmedge came strolling down the hall to his left. Halting in front of the room directly across from him, Westcott tried to discern why she was there—none of the teachers she usually corresponded with would be over here. Furthermore, her calling on this particular classroom was obviously not of any urgency or important subject matter as demonstrated by her casual attitude. The boy glanced at her with the slightest anticipation of an acknowledgment. Instead, Mrs. Talmedge reciprocated his gaze. The subtle warmth that was usually there had vanished. He didn't know how to describe the look. There was something unspoken, he couldn't put his finger on it. In no way was it disdainful. But it was indifferent. Yes, indifferent he decided. He had taken note of her seemingly stand-offish disposition ever since prom and began considering the idea that she did not approve of his lifestyle. It hurt and disappointed him to think of her as un-accepting or even prejudiced. Studying her, he hoped for his assumptions to be disproved. He liked her too much to let a derogatory strike, a shadow of doubt in character, destroy his fondness for her. It never occurred to him that maybe she was preoccupied with thoughts of Ms. Hutchens.

Behind the gym a special lunch was held for the seniors. After reuniting with his mother and sister, the three wandered out to the lunch area. The boy's paranoia shifted into high gear. He unobtrusively slipped through the crowd of students, peppered with a few faculty members and parents. He no longer felt hungry.

'You guys can leave you know,' he explained with a pang of guilt. Not many parents were around, which made him very awkward. He wanted to blend in and his award didn't seem praiseworthy enough for them to stay. He hadn't expected them to sit through two hours of scholarship announcements. The boy knew his mother wouldn't have missed it for anything, she was always there for him and Ellis, however trivial the occasion.

Westcott entered the gym. His mother and Ellis departed shortly thereafter.

'See ya when you get home,' his mother told him.

The boy said goodbye sadly and was alone, left by the folded up bleachers watching everyone exchange yearbooks to sign. After analyzing the situation, determining who to ask for their John Hancock, he got up the nerve to trade books. Soon students were seeking him out, even ones he had never met, there being 231 seniors in the class. Some put email addresses; an idea to do the same completely escaped the boy. He saw Ms. Hutchens standing in the middle of the gym, considered whether or not to approach her. Another student from Westcott's American Studies class walked over and by his gesticulations the boy knew he had asked her to sign. Reassured, Westcott waited until she was done before timidly going up to her. He came from her backside to avoid being seen approaching, then veered to her left. Not looking at her, he mumbled, 'Would you sign my yearbook?'

Westcott lifted his head, glancing over her face. She was staring at his shirt and masculine chest, it was so flat—the silent questioning. Did she want to tell him something else? A word of reassurance.

Yes, I'm a guy he wanted to say.

'Of course,' she replied, holding out her hand for the book.

The final scheduled activity for the senior class was a compilation of pictures spanning from babyhood to teenagers in the form of a life progression slide show; a walk down memory lane. Claudia and another girl asked Westcott to sit with them in the auditorium. He politely declined. Why? His response had become automatic. He wanted nothing to do with females—even just sitting with them made him feel conspicuous. Claudia had dark brown hair and soft brown eyes. She was thin and played basketball. She'd always been nice to Westcott. 'Hey, I see you have Chuck's on,' she'd said once. She meant his Chuck Taylor Converse tennis shoes. He would have liked her as a friend. He was attracted to her. Why did he wait so long? Their persistence finally forced him to take a seat beside them in one of the front rows. He did not want to be identified as sitting with *the girls*, regardless of their kind intentions. It couldn't make up for lost time. The second to last week of school and someone had decided to befriend him; it was too little too late.

—

WINDOWSILL CAT

A BOY'S OBSERVATION

The cat rested on the dusty ledge accompanied by a lifeless fly in the corner sill. Drenched in a stream of motionless light, its fur looked like watermarks on a granite face—as ridged and divided as platelets. It was a scene meant for capturing by a skilled craftsman with needle and hand. The picture was something to behold, an image one would think to see on a Japanese tapestry or decorative screen.

The afternoon had been sultry and in the evening the cat watched the heat rise from the dark pavement as rain fell over its bevels and into the side gutters. Now the cat listened intently to the rhythmic drip of water as it sailed down a drainpipe, quenching the thirst of the parched grass. A slight wind brushed through the forest opposite the window, the half-drawn blind tapped against the pane. The cat's tail fell limply over the ledge and gently swished back and forth to the pace of the wind.

Something could be heard in the rustling of the green beings—the cat's ear twitched—its eyes mirrored the spring leaves in color. The cat leaned up against the screen and peered out one of the many rectangles within the permeable wall of crossed wire. The cat's heart was lifted in that brief moment, then it fluttered and died. The cat looked over at the brittle body in the corner—its wings twittered against the incoming breeze. The cat dropped its head and studied the floor. Shadows jumped back and forth with the wind.

The frogs were out on this night; their backs silver for the time being. The cat drew its neck up, turning its face to the wattage-less light Edison could never replace.

There was something to be said of that moment. For in that second, time did not exist. It was as though the cat had always been there, if not in the windowsill then on some city rooftop, in the loft door of a country farm, or in some lonely tree beside the road. It didn't matter the day, it didn't matter the year. What one man or beast saw 40,000 moons ago could still be seen this night, in its same form. One could live in any place or time for that instant. It was the only constant to hold onto. The boy held it close.

Often, the boy had thought, that cats were reincarnates of individuals who'd worked hard in some past life. What else could explain the carefree ease of their existence?

The boy walked over to the window, stared up at the chalk-white path, and spoke. If only I had been a cat, things would have been different. If only I had been—. He stopped and turned to the being upon four legs. He whispered with an edge of resentment, 'I cannot kill myself, but this condition surely will. For God's sake, break down the wall and jump to your freedom, cat! I must fight to live in this world as I want, you do not, and I will die trying. What ledge of security have I to stand on?' The boy threw himself against the wall and fell to the floor.

A sheet of gray clouds drifted across the moon. The cat jumped down from the windowsill with a thump and left. The boy watched the sky closely.

The gray above passed and the distant constancy slowly re-emerged. The boy's mouth moved; his words were inaudible. He glanced at the fly's corpse, then back at the starred ceiling. Knowing there'd be no reply, he said, 'When will I see the other side?'

The Letter

Westcott turned the light switch off as he always did before stepping to the front porch and sitting in the wicker rocking chair. The vinyl along the doorjamb made a crackling sound as the handle was pulled. Never had he known such sorrow contradicted by a calm, tranquil night. The wind was resting, ever mild. The moon unveiled itself; the earth was dimming. And despite the hour, the sky wore colors of twilight. Westcott was bridled with sickness. He gazed up at the sky and watched as a lone star flickered, fought against a gray sheath of clouds, surrendered, then disappeared. He saw it as a farewell. Once again, immense reservations consumed him; the future he feared. The boy rested quietly and came to realize he was not alone. A small shadow with sides that bulged as it inhaled sat nearby; the frog listened intently from the porch stairwell. The outside cat, Thistleonious, weaved between his calves. Westcott hunched forward, placed his arms on his knees, and brought his hands together with interlocked fingers. Inside something was heavy. He felt completely helpless and alone in his pain. He knew this was his last night. His heart was tired; he did not know how to move on. His constant was no longer and to turn away from it—the flickering was dying; *the lantern on the porch* had been blown out by the sighing wind.

Westcott thought back to earlier that morning when he'd gone to give Mrs. Talmedge and Mrs. McCormick his thank you letter. He'd circled the hall once only to discover the classroom doors were locked. On his second attempt he found them open. Without trying to be noticed he entered. Neither teacher was present however. He patiently rested against the low counter near Mrs. T's desk, waiting for someone to arrive. The room was dark on the half where he stood, rather befitting of his despairing mood. Opposite him the lights were on, a lone student was at a desk getting ready for class. Westcott studied the line where the dark converged with the light. He set his life parallel to it and saw what no one else could possibly have known.

The boy did not have to wait long before someone came and that someone was Mrs. Talmedge. She seemed a bit surprised to see him standing there, so Westcott quickly explained his reasons for coming.

'I know it's a little after the fact, but I never got a chance to thank you for the letter of recommendation you wrote.' 'It was my pleasure,' Mrs. T responded.

Westcott jerked his hand up to give her the envelope. Slowly he drew his head up, his eyes brushed over her face, he tried. He couldn't do it. He wanted to look her in the eye, to see a glimpse of what she was thinking. For so long he relied solely on his ears to determine how others felt about him, he listened to the tone of their voice. He gave people so much power. He feared she might see the sorrow and pain within him. He was afraid of what he might see in her, contempt or understanding? The face of prejudice, however well she tried to conceal it. The boy yearned to know and to ask, 'Do you hate me for what I am?' He wanted to find in her eyes the answer. His courage failed. He stepped away.

'Here...here,' Westcott rasped stretching his arm out with the letter. Mrs. T seemed apprehensive to receive it.

'So where ya off to?'

Westcott, unable to think clearly, responded with the name of the college he was to be attending in the fall. He was so preoccupied thinking about how to avoid making eye contact he missed the point of the question. Mrs. T already knew where he was going to college. Westcott felt he created the wrong image, one in which he was intelligent, but lacking in common sense. It bothered him that she would not see him in his true form. He knew how strange he came across. He wanted *her* to know that he knew what a complete oddity and conversational wreck he was. He felt her eyes studying him. At last she said, 'Enjoy the rest of your day.'

He would revisit the morning often and look back upon it with sorrow. Once again his silence had prevailed, his fear had conquered; he had surrendered to himself at the expense of a tortured and flawed image.

That same afternoon Westcott entered the makeshift schoolroom in back of the school for the last time. Since the very first meeting held eight months ago, the Literary Magazine's participants had significantly dwindled in number. For quite some time only three students loyally returned each week. Westcott was one of them. Ms. Garlow arrived at 3 o'clock and without delay, informing her loyal trio of attendants that she hadn't planned to read or discuss any new submissions. They were free to stay and chat for a few minutes or leave if they liked. Not in any rush to get home, Westcott remained seated, savoring his only source of so-called camaraderie. He was disappointed that in two years a new edition of the magazine had failed to be produced. He wondered how things might have been different had Mrs. Talmedge remained club leader. There never seemed to be a plan with Ms. Garlow, no goals or active sponsorship, He supposed in a way that was better, keeping things just between each other. She served as a listener more than a guide. That's what they needed. They were misfits.

He remembered their last meeting a year ago. The subject matter of his prose had undergone a dramatic shift from the abstract to the concrete. In contrast to his old style, he no longer used metaphors to dissemble his pain. He began writing himself into the poems, mindful to keep them in third person. As the months progressed he revealed a little more of his story. He never came right out and said what he was. The boy on the paper carried the burden of disclosure, speaking a language decipherable to Westcott only in silence. He used 'the boy' to tell the world, the three readers—Ms. Garlow and his two peers—the source of his misery.

Westcott regretted his own silence and sparseness of words. He wondered if his quietness was misconstrued as arrogance or disinterest. He never shared his opinions of Reanne and Andrew's work. At times he was so concerned with maintaining his silent persona, favoring his nervousness, that manners and thought escaped him. It wasn't that he didn't appreciate or deem important what they had to say; he just couldn't shed the image he had become. They were misfits, but of a different kind. Even in such an atmosphere of unobserved understanding, he felt apart. All of them suffered in some form, using a variant style to convey their sorrow. He wrote out of necessity until there could be nothing more to tell. The Literary Magazine offered him a place to be when, in every other aspect, he did not belong. For posterity purposes he could say he was involved with a club, though his role was the equivalent of a fly on the wall. Once when Ms. Garlow had ventured to critique something in the boy's poem and was met with opposition by the other students, she withdrew the notion. Westcott would like to have known her suggestion, but failed to voice his own position. He hoped that she did not think poorly of him for this, assuming that he viewed himself or his work as superior and was indignant of criticism. It was just his way; surely she wouldn't hold it against his character. Back then he wished he could have explained, but there were bigger issues at hand already in the process of elucidating.

Ms. Garlow handed each of the three students a book—a gift bought with her own money and carefully selected to match each reader's taste. The boy could not make out the title of Reanne or Andrew's present, and foolishly he would never ask. In his own hands he held a paperback copy of *The Last Unicorn*. He'd seen the movie when he was younger and enjoyed it. Of all the literary genres to consider, it surprised him that Ms. Garlow would choose a fantasy tale for him. He disliked fairy tales and the fanciful, but after reading the summary on the back cover it occurred to him that maybe she had picked a book paralleling his situation. He wasn't the only FTM in the world, but he was on a quest, as holistic as it may sound, a journey to find and become himself or others like him. He appreciated the thought Ms. Garlow had given it—an unexpected gesture of acknowledgment, a silent thank you to each of them for always showing up, laying open certain truths, putting into words what made them tick. By the time Westcott discovered the inscription Ms. Garlow had left him on one of the pages, he would be well into college. More than a year would have passed. It was one of those rare surprises. Like putting your hand inside a coat pocket and discovering a 10 or 20 dollar bill you'd left there eons ago.

'What do you all plan on majoring in?' she asked after allowing them a quick scan of the book sleeves. A unanimous hesitation. Drew replied first.

'Engineering.'

'I hope to be a professional writer,' Reanne followed.

Then Westcott confessed. 'Probably education,' he answered plainly.

Her interest spurred, Ms. Garlow pressed further. 'What subject?'

'English or History. I'm not quite sure how that's going to work though.' Everyone in the room knew his private nature. Perhaps they interpreted it on a different level, which he had not intended. He was only making reference to his shyness not his gender. Looking at the political aspects of his situation rather than the social phobic element, they must have thought how *would he* pull it off in a system that still showed bias toward the silenced, gay professional. Little did they understand that in two years when he went to apply for a position, nobody would know he'd ever been anything but male. All traces would be gone.

Before calling it a day, a man opened the door and stepped inside the makeshift classroom. His hair was a rich dark brown. 'This is my brother.' Ms. Garlow gestured toward the unfamiliar visitor; he had come to give her a ride. Westcott suspected Ms. Garlow did not own a car. She was always catching a lift with someone, be it colleague or in this case, kin. She gave his name then introduced each of the students. Getting to Westcott she looked right at him, was met with an equally telling gaze. She paused ever so briefly, a hesitation only the boy and she could detect. For once he looked her in the eye, his words unspoken. Heard all the same. She said the kindest thing possible.

'This is Westcott Rowan.'

When the three students and one teacher rose to leave that day, exchanging sincere parting words, Westcott hoarsely mumbled goodbye, trailing off down the ramp. Ms. Garlow placed her hand on his gray plaid jacket. June and the boy still wore his security blanket.

'Take care,' she said.

And off he went.

Westcott hunches forward in the rocking chair, the pain insuppressible. *It isn't fair*, he cries in silence.

A mysterious light bobbing down the road. A hush of voices. He stiffens automatically. His neighbors across the way are on their nightly. An orange glow three inches from Patsy's faceless person. Her cigarette. She's in her sixties. Bob's pure snow white hair shines in the darkness. He waits for them to walk up their drive, dissolve into their own lives. Leave him in peace. Another part of him wants them to hear. To look over at the unlit porch, see the unmovable figure rocking like an old man, remembering the youth he never had.

He listens as Bob and Patsy shut their front door. The night belongs to him again. The trunk of his body shakes violently. He waits for the convulsions to rupture a major vessel, render him dead. He does not want to die; he just wants out. To escape.

He remembers one line, a casual statement Mr. Allowick had said. Westcott was always diligent in Keyboarding class. It was easy, busy work. Mr. Allowick told him, 'You will go far.'

Yes far. Far, far, far. But how? When?

The note he gave to Mrs. T and Mrs. McCormick included a poem.

A Simple Reason

Do you hear me,
do you hear me?
I fear not—
'See you tomorrow,'
'Have a good weekend,'
that's what they say.
Are their words sincere,
perhaps they speak only
a gesture of kindness.
A desolate sickness—
I yearn for your words
to be laden with truth.
It is a void, a breaking—
incapable of description,

a consuming emptiness to
which your words descend.
Insignificant from your
standpoint it may be,
but a reason to continue,
to endure is thus given,
and on my part received.
Would it matter to you
if I did not return the next day?
Your words are evidence, alone,
—indeed it would.

Small acknowledgments not
forgotten—

The boy walked away following his
plaintive step and in quiet said,
    For this I thank you most gratefully.

~

Westcott exits into the hallway. Had he not glanced at the clock in Mrs. Sparroh's classroom prior to departing, he'd still know from the shadows and angled light it is 4:30. He has stayed after school to wrap up some final assignments. It is down to the wire and everyone in Photography scrambles to get their work done. Westcott assumed more students would have joined him in his dedicated effort to satisfy any loose ends; after all, they had committed to coming earlier that day in third block. He justifies Spring fever on this particular Friday afternoon is rampant. With graduation just one week away and only three more days of actual school remaining, who in their right mind felt obligated to keep diligence in check? To ignore the warm breeze at one's own discretion, to resist answering the beckoning weekend ushered forth through clear panes and main entrance doors mirroring blue skies, proved relatively easy for Westcott. His hourglass shows a mounting dune of sand occupying its bottom capsule, the funnel dropping steadily. Every extra minute to linger he cherishes.

Turning right from the corridor, he enters the main hallway detecting an unusual calmness in the air. Not a single soul; the entire building is silent, strangely still. A conscious knowledge reflects itself in his plodding step and solemn face. He continues unnoticed toward the double set of doors at the other end. This will be his last Friday. Strolling parallel to the cafeteria, he feels the melancholy of recollection—countless lunches marked by self-conversations. The same sensation as when he listens to the crickets trill, the wind rustling through the trees. Approaching the meso-stairwell on his right he hears something. For a split moment, only a moment, he sees himself and everything for what it is, in its simplest terms. He wonders how he has come to be so queer. The tiles below him are awash in a subtle light; the sun cascades upon the landing, bathing all it touches with a lukewarm restful content. Understanding the rarity of such fleeting instances a chill passes up his spine, twitching his shoulder to attention. Any other faculty member or student might just as well dismiss such an aura as a nice day, too rushed to glimpse the truth beyond. It is a silent passing, he knows, the music of his life. Unlike any song played on the radio that might be heard or even felt, he *sees* the backdrop of his self-selected chorus. It's as though a one-shot frame has been taken in a movie and now the instruments are called in to create the appropriate feeling. A score from his *Out of Africa* motion picture soundtrack plays in his mind. He walks to the tune that defines him, a plaintive gait. In part, it is for this reason he never wears a headset. He prefers to play his favorite songs over and over mentally. He imagines his life playing out as a movie, not in a fancy of grandiosity or self-enthusiasm. Though he suffers it is a selfless duty so that others might take comfort. A hint of martyrdom. But then what director could capture the breaking stillness? Silence. No melodrama of sound. Stillness is silence. No one ever cares about the afterwards. In a movie things just end, the audience takes it for what it is. He always wondered though—about the afterwards.

Westcott does not stop walking, but shuffles deliberately slower, hesitant to cross over the invisible line. No choice withstanding, he relinquishes himself once more to Time and heads outside into the pleasant afternoon.

~

Standing on the track making his presence known long enough for Mr. Allowick to check his name off, Westcott waits for some sign that the clusters of faculty and students encircling the football field can return to their air conditioned classrooms. It is Monday, late in the day when the month's mandatory fire drill has been issued. Since the school has yet to have its June excursion outside, Westcott anticipated the high-pitched chirping to fill the hallways and his eardrums at any time. He misses the traditional bell; the kind he'd had in elementary. The new alarms are hazardous, a pressurized fluttering on the stapes and anvil. His ears have always been acutely sensitive.

Feeling beads of sweat roll down his back beneath the layers of duct tape, navy shirt, and cotton jacket, Westcott rests his arms on the chain-link fence, his back to the crowd. The still forest stretches out beyond the soccer and hockey field. He sees the insignificance. Each of them, himself included, standing there, mere capsules against the backdrop of the world, marking time. A hundred years and who would remember this day, these lives? Does it matter? How can he just leave *it* all behind, something that has been so much a part of him, for so long?

THE HORSE

Westcott awoke to the sound of his mother's voice. 'It's time.' For a brief moment, before the effects of sleep wore off, Westcott's mind was at ease. Then he *remembered*. It was Wednesday, June 11. His mother would not be calling him to get up tomorrow. This morning marked the end of his high school days.

~

Westcott pulls back the covers, lifts himself out of bed. A heavy load weighs him down. As he ties his shoes, combs his hair and packs his book bag, poignancy resounds. His actions this morning are insignificant, commonplace, but today the ordinary becomes something to cherish, to behold in its simplicity. Hearing a persistent tapping noise, he follows the sound into his room. Outside a familiar bird pecks at his pane wanting in; calling to him?

He stands in the kitchen peering out the back window at the life emerging from its hours of slumber. He savors these times when all is silent except for the early morning breeze through the trees and the birds have yet to vocalize their joy for such a splendid day. The world is still, calm, and somehow less painful to him. He checks the clock on the stove. 7:11. It is time to go. He hesitates. He knows that once he picks up his keys and backpack the day's events will be set in motion, he will be unable to stop the minutes and hours from unfolding, and soon it will be over. This time forever gone. He glances back at the forest and the rising sunlight, reluctantly grasps his blue rabbit's foot keychain off the counter, lifts his book bag from the floor, and steps out the door into the garage. Nothing stirs in the house.

He drives without hurry. He looks at the cows in the pasture milling atop the cornbread meadow of poplars. He comes to the stoplight at the intersection, turns right. He studies the shadow of his truck on the pavement, watching the shade from trees on either side swallow him up as he drives onward. He looks for Jake—the boy in his Keyboarding class whose bus stop is on his route. Many a time Westcott has waved to him, questioning whether or not he should stop and offer a ride. After all, the school is maybe a mile down the road from this point. Jake is not out there this morning; the bus probably hasn't come yet. Westcott often arrives to school before the buses. He misses the friendly exchange of howdy-do. Following the winding road, he passes the church parking lot where he first learned to drive. Easing down on the brake, he comes to the final traffic light before turning left into the school, remembering the mornings when he'd see Mrs. T's or Ms. Hutchens' car pass before him coming from his right. Westcott wishes he'd ventured to take their route at least once during the year. It is probably a shorter way to go according to the Hypotenuse Theorem's formula since it cuts through and wraps around diagonally from his house to Drummond's Field. In that time, in those years, he didn't like traveling unfamiliar roads with uncertain turns and stops. He stuck to his own course, not wanting to overstep into their private territory. At 7:18 he pulls into his parking space by the small grassy island, turns the ignition key off, listens to the engine grow quiet. He looks to his left, his eyes falling upon one of the many constants. The tree's young bark is white, its fronds sway gently in the morning breeze. He smiles. Countless days endured in silence and to think this is it.

Lunch comes and goes. The boy slowly makes his way to third block Photography. With his bin all cleaned out and his artwork gathered on the desk for him to take home, Westcott, along with many of the other students, has Mrs. Sparroh sign him a pass to the library. To his delight, a few pieces of his work have been misplaced; Mrs. Sparroh says she'll try to locate them while he is gone. Secretly he hopes she won't; it gives him a legitimate reason to return next fall after August cleaning and preparations for a new school year have unearthed them. He heads upstairs. He veers left from the corridor rather than going straight past the cafeteria; he doesn't want to attract attention. Reminiscing, he disgustedly smiles, tired-like, thinking about the time he'd tried to pay for his lunch using his pin number. When the account holder's name came up the lunch attendant had looked at the boy in front of her— 'This is you?' Westcott responded with a strained yes; hungry as he was he'd had no other choice. 'Yeah, right,' the attendant smiled reading the old name—his female name—on the screen, not buying it. And then there was the time a student from his World Literature class, one of the girls, had come up to him and said, 'So and so thinks you're a nice *guy*.' All the little things. He smiles at this last thought.

Westcott is nearing the end of what he estimates to be his thirteenth lap around the second floor, feeling a bit delinquent for not being in class, when the bell for third lunch sounds. Instantly, doors are ajar, students pile out—the austere solitude of his journey abruptly comes to a halt. A din of voices, lockers slamming, brown lunch bags crumpling, and shoes screeching atop the tiles, replaces the still quietness. He sees a couple of girls with pacifiers attached to nylon cords around their necks. One playfully pops the rubber bulb in her mouth like an infant. He shakes his head without actually shaking it. He never could understand that—how can such sexual solicitation be tolerated. *And I'm weird?* No one sees him; they are too busy. Soon he will be a shadow to them, just another face in the yearbook, a name among thousands, a classmate they once knew, a student they once taught. Little do they know how much he'd received from them in receiving nothing.

After the halls vacate, still on his rounds he passes by a black girl.

'How are you?' she asks too nicely.

What's this? Do I know you?

'Fine.'

'Are you a boy or a girl…girl, right?'

'No.' His repugnance hangs in the air.

'Oh, you're not…cuz' someone said you were?'

'No.' And then it comes to him, the confidence of what he must say. 'I'm a boy.'

Westcott returns to the art room only to find there is still nothing to do. Mrs. Sparroh is reviewing course material with students who are not exempt from the final exam. As a senior and because of his high marks, Westcott doesn't have to take the exam. So with a quick glance, he takes this as an opportunity to make one last stroll around the second floor. As fate would have it he runs into Mrs. Talmedge. He starts down the English hallway and is headed towards the foreign language department when he notices a teacher in a nearby doorjamb stooping to grab a paper. The next thing he knows Mrs. Talmedge is staring in his direction, startled to find him there, alone. Mrs. T walks a few paces with the boy. Passing the girl's bathroom an unpleasant odor emanates from within, spoiling the moment. Neither one makes any reference to it. She speaks in an obligatory fashion; her words are kind, he is appreciative of her acknowledgment of his being there, but she is distant.

'Thank you for your letter. It really meant a lot to both of us.' She's searching for the right words.

'You're welcome,' Westcott responds mechanically more than thoughtfully. As she enters a classroom to retrieve something, the boy plods onward. Looking at his watch there is time enough to make one last trip around before his fourth class. It is quite unexpected when he runs into Mrs. T for the second time while she is en route back to her office. He is glad he hasn't missed her. He has the impression the delight isn't mutual. And why not? She must be thinking, what in god's name is he doing trodding about when he should be in class? Luckily, security had yet to detect his classroom truancy on their surveillance cameras. Had they seen him making his rounds, why, he may never have run into her that day. Westcott keeps his head down, is about to say something, when Mrs. T offers rhetorically, 'So, ya just doing laps?'

The boy simpers guiltily, unable to look at her. 'Yep.' He wants to say goodbye the right way. So many opportunities. Had he known this would be the last time he'd ever talk to her he'd have spoken earnestly. And just like that Mrs. Talmedge is gone.

The clock on the wall reads 1:15. Westcott is in the library. Despite receiving an early release slip from the attendance office that morning, he opted not to leave the school premises until the 2:40 bell mandated his departure. Giving his pass to Mr. Allowick that afternoon, he meandered back upstairs. He sits in a wooden chair at one of the tables in the library mulling over his recent and brief conversation with Mrs. T. There is something about it that bothers him terribly. In some way he has been disappointed, let down by her. He holds himself accountable for this disappointment. Perhaps his expectations were too high, but was a simple 'see you at graduation, best of luck, farewell, or have a great life,' a lot to ask for? Up 'til now Mrs. T had always initiated an acknowledgment. It hurt him that she had not told him goodbye. Maybe he is being too harsh in his judgment, unforgiving, ridiculously analytical. Mrs. T's actions were likely unintentional; she had a lot on her mind especially with Mrs. Hutchens leaving. There are any number of possible reasons for the oversight. The remoteness and underlying prepossession that had seemed to be in her voice gnaws on his fondness towards her. Then again hadn't he been drawn to her praise more than Mrs. T herself? The boy examines his emotions. The not knowing is what crushes him most. He still wonders if Mrs. T refused a farewell because of some restrained animosity toward his condition. Does she hate him for what he is? This single recurring question, an inquiry he was too afraid to ask, pains him. It is not only Mrs. T who let him down, he realizes. It was himself. He had every chance and said nothing. Even in his brief letter he avoided the one, urgent, question. He resigns himself to not knowing. It is better that way.

Westcott glances left. Directly above the glass cubicle enclosing the librarians' office is a digital clock inlayed in the wall. 1:45. Strange how dread has a certain tendency to bite at the heels of time, send the minutes flying. He sits waiting, his mind laden with reticent grief, and watches as his final hour chips away. He looks out the window before him, studies how the light cutting across the roof places half the school in a cool shade.

Putting aside a book about the Old West and Indians he haphazardly selected from the shelf, Westcott pulls out his notebook, flips to a blank leaf of paper. Begins.

A sickness fell upon the boy—a deep loneliness. His stomach was hollow, not a morsel could he maintain. His heart had collapsed; the horse gained on him. His time was drawing to an end. He couldn't help it—the pain trampled him. His spirit sank to the earth beneath the iron shoes. The beast reared up on its hind legs; the boy lifted his head, hesitated. Their eyes met. A flash of fear passed over the boy's face. What did the beast see?

Was it the anguish, the anger, or perhaps the despair?

'Please,' he pleaded in silence, 'bring down your hooves. I gave you my eyes for a moment, now give me my freedom!'

The horse brought his legs down gently and stepped back. It appeared frightened. The boy studied the beast before him.

'This is it,' he understood. 'If I let you defeat me through death then I have...' the thought hurt him. 'Failed.'

The boy saw the challenge at hand; yesterday was no more. He had but one choice. Could he—did he remember what it was like to live? He jerked his head away, unable to withstand the beast's glare.

The beast whinnied, charged the boy, stopped, came at him again. A cloud of dust choking him, the boy lowered his head in submission. The beast snorted, stamping the floor with his hooves.

'I don't know how to go on,' he protested. 'I don't know how, I'm so damn tired. Take me for God's sake! Fast!'

The horse stilled himself. His eyes were patient, strangely understanding.

'Don't you see,' the boy cried, 'you are all I have; you are all I know. I know not how to return to the beginning. Long have I lived at the fringes of the end. To start over would kill me. I'm too far in to go back.'

A slight wind arose. The horse's mane waved gently. His ears tilted forward in waiting, listening for the answer.

The sun was dipping.

The horse looked to the horizon and back to the boy.

Silence.

The boy spoke.

'I can follow the sun on its present voyage to darkness—' He grew quiet. Something flickered in his heart. He recalled a reason, a hope. He looked at the horse—its gaze penetrated. The boy's words were soft and drifted up to the twitching ears with the breeze.

At last he saw the horse for what it was. Once more the beast REARED, slammed its hooves down in front of the boy, grunted. Turned. And galloped away.

The boy watched the dust bellow up, slowly clear. He uttered a last farewell.

'You must go,' he called after, 'you must go,' he whispered.

The wind was calm.

The beast—the horse—was no longer.

His heart, as it often had, sighed and the emptiness faded. Leaving the spirit to be scarred.

~

Westcott understands this is the last time he will ever sit in this chair. The last time he will ever walk these halls. He does not like the thought of not being able to return. Never again to see these people as he does now. Never again will he walk the halls in silent torment. Never again will he hear the security guards open the doors in the morning as the school buses arrive or see the early sun cast its light upon the empty corridors. Nor will he stand rigidly looking over the second floor balcony at all the happenings (a front he used in hopes of catching a glimpse of Mrs. T and Ms. Hutchens coming down the upstairs hallway). There is a breaking inside him; he does not want to leave. A desolate sickness. How could he have known goodbye would hurt. He's never had to say goodbye. But it isn't just goodbye. It is the absolute knowledge that he can never, never go back. Somehow he isn't ready. The clock turns 2:40.

He feels the chair. The bell sounds. Slowly, with commanding precision, he rises from his seat. Returns it to its proper place under the table. Grabs his backpack. He quickly looks around the room. At the reference desk he scribbles the time of his departure in the librarian's log next to the name: *Westcott A. Rowan.*

He had no way of knowing it, but it was the easiest goodbye he would ever have to make.

I Heard a Cricket Trill
(not a fly buzz)

I heard a cricket trill when I died
Rigormortis constricted the Room
Like the storm-noosed eye
Of a hurricane's exponential wrath

The stillness within wrung *him* loud
While shadows gathered round
For that last exhale when life's soul
Levitated above the Room

I willed my possessions consigned by death
To the discretion of those left behind
And then it was
There sprung a cricket

With green-chitin rhythmic chirps
Between the silence and me
And then the tunnels closed and then—
I could not wait to leave

A FINAL FAREWELL

Graduation came and went. To Westcott's despair his heart never skipped a beat. It drummed on steadily refusing to let its master surrender. The challenge was finally at hand. Westcott was buckling. He yearned to go back.

The commencement ceremony took place on Saturday the 14th.

The skies were kind that morning; the possibility of rain kept at bay by a strong sun—perhaps a late shower. The onset of a slight wind promised relief from an otherwise still and mildly warm afternoon. Westcott stood in the upstairs bathroom straightening his blue silk tie patterned with Wile E. Coyotes. He tied and retied his Windsor knot. He sensed movement on the door. The Visitor. He listened to the motions. Patterns of light, leaf silhouettes vibrated. Is someone in there? A face. A golden warmth wavered in the early breeze. A graceful waltz across the door. He started over to the small window to his left. The sun yellow white. *He* is quiet in his ascent, subtly emptying forth an energy upon the day. The burning sphere's path upward beyond its own control. It did not choose its present standing; its course was predetermined. Right or wrong He was created to rise and fall. There was one aspect the sun did not possess. The ability to resist. Westcott had a solitary freedom. He aimed to alter the course of his fate. He would not betray himself for the sake of others.

Entering his room, he saw his father getting ready. He'd flown in from the west. Polo shirt, brown leather belt, and dark navy jeans. His father never wore a tie or suit, but offered to assist Westcott in a firmer knot. They stood that June morning in Westcott's room. For a moment Westcott felt in this strange man the slightest presence of a *father*. There was no origin, no connection, save this fleeting instance. They shared the same blood, but they did not know each other. Had never been close. He wanted to love him, but didn't know how. Little pieces of paper given to the wind which made no sense. He missed what never was.

~

After signing in, waiting for what seems to be only a fleck of grain in the hourglass, but in actuality is much longer, Westcott takes his place among the alphabetically aligned chitchat. He is close to Lindsay. Her last name begins with S. 'Hey, I saw the piece you wrote in Mrs. Sparroh's Senior Autograph album and the photograph. Maybe one day you'll write a book about—*everything*. My family's having a reception this afternoon. A group is coming over. You should stop by, if you want.'

He checks that his tassel is on the right side—it is, and makes his way into the auditorium. A slight chill. The riveting tune he has dreaded to hear encompasses him, echoing throughout the arena. Once situated in their seats, everyone is asked to rise for the playing of the national anthem. Dutifully, Westcott removes his black cap, placing it over his heart as he and all the boys have been instructed to do. For an instant, a gentle sweep fills his lungs. It is a much different kind of pride than that of his fellow classmates. His brief moment of happiness is not related to the feeling of hard-earned accomplishment, nor is it the recognition he and his peers are receiving. It is the sense, the sense for one fleeting second, of outward camaraderie—he belongs. He wears the black robe and tie. Deep mint among distinguished dark shoulders finds the girls in green gowns and high heels. Westcott fingers the silk tie about his thin neck.

Throughout the ceremony the boy remains still. He listens to the speakers offer their words of wisdom. Sitting among his peers Westcott appreciates that this is the peak of their lives and yet he is falling into a bottomless crevasse. The choir presents the audience with a rather nostalgic song. Despite being in key, the notes have an elementary recital quality about them, sounding just short of sour, like the vibrations of a single drawing of air on a harmonica, but the sentimental tune is beautiful simply because of what it represents. A few class officers give their speeches, and finally, the principal announces it is time to distribute the diplomas. Westcott watches row by row, the students rise. They stride up to the center stage, a necklace of green and black beads—his classmates. One by one a green leather folder is placed in his or her hand. He waits in sickened anticipation until it is his row's turn to stand. He thinks about Thoreau, and possibly doing the same thing, taking off his shoe, saluting the entire congregation. Ms. Cannon, the designated usher of his section, signals for them to rise. Walking by, advancing ever closer to the stage, she smiles at him kindly. During the spring of his junior year she had been his chemistry teacher. Standing in his tie and black robe, the girls wear green, he is glad Ms. Cannon knows. It always seemed to him that science educators were more understanding of his condition as reflected by Mrs. Wesson and Mrs. Medley during certain brief encounters. Maybe they had watched a program on Discovery Health about individuals like himself or had greater knowledge of chromosomes due to their field of study. Westcott detected a noticeable difference between them and other teachers. Ms. Cannon might even have been a lesbian, a conclusion he reached from studying her mannerisms. He moved up the line and stood at the base of the platform waiting to hear his name. Mr. Forbes shakes Westcott's hand, holding it in quiet instruction.

'Not yet. All right.'

'Westcott. Aloysius. Rowan.' A voice announces to the world of parents. Faculty. Peers.

He timidly reaches his arm out for his unwanted diploma, receives it from Mrs. Pyke and exchanges a handshake with his principal. He looks at the carpet on his way back to his seat to patiently wait for the rest of the students. At the end of the ceremony, Principal Joseph Canter, a terrible public speaker, stiffly proclaims the class of Twenty Hundred and— officially graduated. The auditorium erupts in a roar of cheers and jovial screams. Black and green caps flung high into the air in ecstatic affirmation, drop like stunned birds. Westcott slowly lifts his hat from his head. Thirteen months ago he sat up in the same surrounding bleachers, watching Ellis receive her Bachelor's from the College of William and Mary. The familiar tune resumes; a faculty member trips on the green roll-out carpet, completely pancakes on her face, helped to her feet by those nearest. The ceremony would have seemed incomplete had someone not borne the brunt of public humiliation. Aren't such mishaps always the case with social galas of this nature? Westcott, momentarily embarrassed for the woman, follows the train out through the back of the building to a ramp where the faculty stand lining both rails along the passageway to the sidewalk. Reanne steps nearby. Westcott issues a half-hearted best of luck. He must say goodbye to his teachers. Later he feels he should have extended more. And years later, it occurs to him how indifferent he'd been.

'Hi,' he acknowledged her hastily, still moving toward the door. She continued to talk. Westcott halted in his step. He listened as she explained that her family had not come to the graduation. Westcott tried to brush her off, preoccupied with getting outside and seeing his beloved teachers one last time. 'That's not good. Well, see ya.' Reanne had tried. And once more Westcott had pushed another away.

Later he felt guilty for not throwing Reanne a scrap of kind words. His disinterest in what she was saying stemmed from anxiousness, or was it? He had been selfish. If only he had picked up on her subtle pity plea—he wished to apologize for such abruptness. How terrible she must have felt for no one to be at her graduation, and then for him to act as though he didn't care. Once on the ramp, he had not intended to stop, but as he made his way through the crowd of voices he saw Mrs. McCormick and hesitated for a moment. He was debating whether or not to say anything. Instead, he held out his hand to shake hers, but she did not meet his offering. To the boy's surprise she went to hug him. Westcott became rigid; he wasn't one that could be easily embraced. Feeling her breast press against his chest he quickly pulled away. Nonetheless, he was glad that she had made the effort to return his gesture of farewell. Further down Westcott's eyes fell on Ms. Hutchens; despite his increasing nervousness he approached her. Again, he held out his left hand, unable to free up his right tightly gripping his diploma and cap; she shook it and wished him good luck the next year. He hoped she hadn't noticed the petite size of his class ring. Westcott discretely looked around for Mrs. Talmedge. After a quick search, he continued down the ramp where his old anatomy teacher, Mrs. Medley, wished him well and a former classmate, Craig, congratulated him with a hearty handshake. Before Westcott knew it, his sister was charging at him excitedly and about to sling her arm around him. The rest of his family was close behind. As they maneuvered their way through the sea of bitter-happy farewells Westcott's sorrow overwhelmed him, then he spotted Mrs. Talmedge. It was too late. Already she was walking away with Mrs. McCormick, Ms. Hutchens, and Ms. Garlow. The boy studied her for a second, realizing why he had not seen her earlier. Her appearance was different, she had worn her hair half up, unaccustomed to the way he was used to seeing her. Now he was beginning to wonder. Did he walk right past her? Was she observing him when he went to shake hands with Mrs. McCormick and Ms. Hutchens, secretly hoping he would not see her? He wished he had been able to say something to Mrs. T. He was still hurt by his last few words with her just days before. He had held out for this day, hoping- it was his final chance and he still longed to know in spite of what he told himself. At least with Mrs. McCormick and Ms. Hutchens he felt there had been a closing, that they did not hate him. He understood that to most the whole issue was seemingly trivial, perhaps he was making something out of nothing. That wasn't the point. He could not explain why it was so important with Mrs. T; all he asked for was a goodbye. Even the librarian, Ms. Binns, had given him this. A sign to let him know that someone objective, someone besides his family, on the outside gave a damn!

As commencement parties and receptions unfolded, as young men and women toasted to the future, as sweethearts embraced, as the young men patted each other on the back and the girls celebrated with a weekend away, and perhaps as Lindsay and Claudia looked for a familiar face of anguish amongst their peers, what no one could possibly have known was that somewhere in the world a boy was crying, for his past, present, and future circumstances had forced the flood gates open. There would be no closing them.

Holding him that afternoon on the edge of her bed, his mother wept for her son.

'What is it, West? You never cry. Something is bothering you. What is it?'

'Nothing.'

'Graduation?'

'No!'

'Then what is it?'

'I'm tired...of living.' The fluid in his nose began to drip into his throat. A coughing spasm ensued and a clear liquid smeared itself above his upper lip. Westcott wiped it with his hand.

His constancy, his routine, his security—all were gone. He was hopeless and looked forward to nothing.

'I know how tired you are. What can I do right now?'

'Nothing. Just leave me alone. You won't tell them, don't let them know?' He meant Ellis, his father, and adopted grandmother who'd flown in for the occasion.

'I won't say anything. Just come down when you're ready; we have reservations in a couple of hours. You sure you'll be all right?'

'I'll be fine.' He didn't mean it. He just wanted to be left alone.

THE CAUSE OF HIS DESPAIR

Westcott felt cheated. Tired. His anger gave way to bitterness. His unhappiness consumed him, but the boy could only stay in such a state of despair for so long. He knew there was nowhere to go from misery; he could not drop any further. Westcott was not living. His lungs were taking in oxygen and his heart was still pumping, but these were superficial indications of what it means to be alive. His hope was dwindling, he'd used up all reserves of patience, exhausting his sadness to no end. The wasted time. The silence. Four friendless years. Gone. Lost.

A body's soul cannot live in torment indefinitely. The boy knew this well.

It had taken Westcott more than four years to be seen for what he was. When, at last, he was getting somewhere—had established his true identity—it was too late. Just when he'd begun to refine his duct taping techniques and was starting to be more at ease in school and learning that others *would* accept him, he had to leave. It wasn't fair, but what could he do? There was no one to blame except for himself. *If I had only known and acted sooner!* The thought of having to start over, he could not face another four or five years of silence! He remembered the mornings when he'd be in hysterics because he didn't think he was adequately bound and his mother would argue with him not to wear a jacket. She said he saw himself like an anorexic. In his mind, even when flat as a wall, he thought something was visible. His paranoia was in full swing the spring of eleventh grade and the following fall. Standing in front of the mirror, making his routine check, he'd become enraged if something looked questionable. Even after his mother assured him there was nothing there, alone he'd thrust his fist against his chest, pounding it smooth, sickened, straining to keep himself from crying. While driving to school he'd bang the steering wheel, gripping its cover with sweaty palms, helplessly distraught. On one occasion he managed to sneak his jacket with him, but deception was not his game. So upon calling his mother that day to let her know he had arrived all right, he pleaded to wear his coat, more for security purposes than anything else. Of course he didn't always win and on those days he walked into school with his head much lower than usual, his misery discernible by a most hateful expression.

There was so much he had wanted to do in high school. Ordinary things the average person takes for granted bothered the boy. Like being able to place his hand over his heart to say the pledge of allegiance or using a public restroom freely. It wasn't until the November of his senior year that he finally acquired courage enough to walk into a male bathroom, but not at school. He remembered feeling awkward and immediately taken aback upon viewing some men standing at the urinals. Never before had he actually seen a guy piss in real life. Sure, there was television, but it wasn't the same.

Over time Westcott acquired boldness; it became second nature to enter the men's room. Facilities at school posed quite a problem. In his entire high school career never once had he *used* the restroom. On occasion, maybe four times at most, he entered the girl's washroom to rinse his hands or what not, but that was all. He conditioned himself to being a camel for fear of being identified, waiting nine, sometimes ten hours. During his senior year he'd gladly have used the boy's facilities, but too many people knew him from before. He figured it was a risk and avoided them all together. Looking back, he often wondered if his teachers thought it strange his not asking them to sign his passbook to go to the restroom. And the fear on certain days. A sanitary napkin becoming saturated. Beyond the restraints of bladder relief, Westcott would love to have played boys' soccer, baseball, or track. He would have had friends and not forgotten how to speak. What pained him the most was his quiet belief that he would have been happy, if not free. This regret for what could have, what might have been, prevented him from moving on. He was not ready for college. He had missed out on so many boyhood adventures and social rites of passage he dreamed of. Now he was expected to grow up. How could he be a man when he had yet to scratch the surface of being a boy?

In the remotest sense possible he feared losing his individuality and becoming ordinary. Once in college he'd be presented with a clean slate, no longer facing the stigma of two names. His secret would again be unknown, but this time he'd be on the other side of it. Yes, for two years Westcott had dreamed of nothing else except passing as male without any questions, but he did not want to be just another run-of-the-mill-guy. It would seem that his desire for something more made him a contradiction, but that is not the case for there is a fine line between normal and average. Westcott sought a degree of normalcy in his quest for sexual identity, but in all other respects, be it character, intellect, or physical ability, he did not wish to settle for mediocrity or being common. Even had he been born anatomically correct, there was a quality about him that was different, something more delineating than just his hybrid-genderism, an anachronistic trait that took form most acutely in his American Dream essay. More than just a physical and social misfit, generationally he did not belong. It was for this reason that he loved to watch and live, if only for an hour, in the era of *Father Knows Best*. Even as a more liberal apprentice of Thoreau, he relished the idea of simplicity, escaping through the television to a time when the world *appeared* wholesome and less chaotic.

Westcott wondered what, if anything, would set him apart once his transformation was complete.

O' my dear boy, you have miles to go before you sleep.

Then he realized, whether others knew or not, he would always be different. A rare opportunity to experience life had been lain at his feet. It's not everyone who gets to be born female and die a man.

The boy missed his teachers. Ironic, he thought, how Mrs. McCormick, Ms. Hutchens, and Ms. Garlow all had blue eyes and first names that ended in A, but not Mrs. T. Even more strange was the fact that in twenty years or less, when they were fifty and he was forty, society would group them in the same generation. Funny how to an eighteen-year-old boy they could seem so old and far away, but to a forty-year-old man there would be no difference. For quite some time he tried to identify the cause of his feeling so strongly towards them, but it was difficult to explain. He reasoned that he had revealed to them a certain truth about himself. They knew more of him than any of the students through his writing and taciturn behavior. What was it Ms. Hutchens had said? He gave them insight into what he was thinking. They were, unbeknownst to themselves, his promoters and constants. He worried they might fail to remember him or time would hasten a forgetfulness on his part. Somehow he knew it couldn't happen. He was a rare breed and he never forgot anything of consequence.

~

Looking through a pile of old papers, Westcott read what he had written two years before. The American Dream. Much of his dream had been perfected. He placed his life on it, trusting that it was attainable and there was only one way for sure to find out. But he no longer wanted to go off into the country and live alone; he was *alone*. He was already that rural farmhouse shrouded in some valley basin, that lantern rusted and weathered with little kerosene enough to burn, that oak hunched and weary, his shoulders arching in deformity like the tall grass blowing in the wind, an island unto himself. Westcott knew he had transcended into becoming his American Dream. What he wanted now was the proper hearth for his heart's flame. He needed to have people around him, voices to fill his desolate cabin; he'd been secluded for too long, rocking to and fro in his tempered misery.

Quietly he hoped one day he would see his endearing constants again. That one day he would meet Mrs. T or Mrs. Sparroh, all those who knew him from before, from those haggard days, look them in the eye, no longer a mousy, timid boy, but as a hard-earned man. And at that moment he'd know. He'd know on which side each of them fell. It wouldn't matter anymore who was for or against him. It wouldn't matter. He had told his story in silence and the few who bothered to listen and hear him had witnessed a glimpse of the truth within.

Someday he would be free to go home, he would belong, someday. It was so far.

~

Two months had passed since Westcott's departure from high school, yet the emptiness he felt that June morning was still there inside. The heartache he thought would have dissipated, but the time between failed to assuage his pain and succeeded only in making it stronger. He sat on the edge of his bed numbed by the persistent longing. He looked back on the summer, recalling the afternoon he pleaded to be taken. He just hadn't planned on living this far. College was a few weeks away. He thrust the thought out of his head, unable to accept the fact that four tedious years were gone and another set were on the horizon. It had seemed once that the present would never end. He had somehow distanced himself from the times before and the times ahead. He'd become detached in endless suspension, tasked. He simply did not want the future to be his, believing the best had already been, disappearing without his ever being able to enjoy it. *Why should I stay?* His quest for contentment had tested his spirits and tried his patience. He was so young. He just didn't know it.

Westcott slid off the bed and stepped into his adjoining closet. Crouching, he pulled out a small rectangular folder from the bookshelf then opened a wooden box with a river scene painted on the lid. Inside he retrieved a shiny gold pocket watch. He brought the items over to his desk and slowly sat down. Studying the green folder, he found it hard to believe that dust had accumulated on the leather cover in such a short time. Holding it in his hands, he flipped it open and read in silence.

Drummond's Field High School, Commonwealth of Virginia,
Department of Education
This certifies that Westcott A. Rowan has completed the requirements
for graduation and therefore is awarded this advanced studies diploma.
Given at Williamsburg, Virginia, this 14ᵗʰ day of June, 20—

A sadness welled in the boy. Looking at the silver seal. *How could they have known? What wouldn't I give to go back just for an instant and speak.* He valued more what they had given him, the intangible, over any sheet of paper. He understood it would be a great mistake to forget. All his hard work and dedication compiled into this one page, meaningless, in comparison to all he had learned from living.

Westcott closed the sleeve, his eyes moved to his right hand. The callous on his middle finger where he was accustomed to resting his pen had receded from lack of use and the half crescent of gray skin in the fork of his thumb and index finger ceased to be discolored by the persistent irritation of a backpack strap. Both were pricking signs, mere residues of time. A moment and then he reached for his pocket watch, a sentimental graduation gift from his mother. A train lay etched in silver on the outside shield surrounded by a gold rim. Alongside the steam engine was an engraving. His initials. W.A.R. The boy pressed down on the tiny knob and displayed the clock's face. He admired the sharpness of the Roman numerals and listened to the rhythmic tic-tic-ticking. If he looked at it very closely he could see the minute hand shift gently, almost a twitch. Drawing his eyes to the surface of the glass face, he detected a faint reflection of himself. With shaggy bangs drooping over the left side of his forehead, mouth turned down, and a steady gaze dark and quiet, the sadness was evident. After a long moment he clicked the case shut and lovingly studied the train again.

Somehow I'll find a way.

The boy looked down at his desk. A Ticonderoga pencil—his prized brand—with a dulled nib. Ticonderoga. Where his mother used to go in the summer, fishing with her Uncle Charlie on Lake George. Separate histories. Separate lives.

He peered at The Avenue. It was day again in the painting, sunlight streamed through the trees, casting shadows below. He jumped, shaken out of a trance.

'Ride to the bank with me, West...we'll get out for a bit!'

The boy did not answer. Distantly he heard his mother singing a familiar self-invented tune. The words drifted up to him.

Mudgie Mudgero. My little sparrow.

He rose. Stiffly. Knowing what he must do.

Outside his window the pinwheel was spinning.

Regret:

Had I known
I was a son

I would not have
Lived a lie for so very long

Had I known
I was a brother

I would have
Looked into your eyes despite
my unyielding fear

Had I known
The years were soon to be done

I would have
Spared my soul from a fate cast
unduly wrong

Had I known
This time there'd be no other

I would have
Spoke of loneliness and
kept my silence near

Had I known
I'd miss you so

I would have
Let be known my torment so the
assumptions could
finally end

Had I known
The days would surely fly

I would have
Clasped your palm—
sensing your contempt or
understanding for what I am

Had I known
The toll one's spirit takes from woe

I would have
Regarded you then as I do now—
an enduring strength,
an undying friend

Had I known
This would be a last goodbye

Then—

Lastly, I would have
Painted myself a boy to you,
Forever waiting upon
a sign of your accepting hand

How tedious, wasted, ridiculous were those years! Ah, the lamentation.

Journal Entry:
from the Book of West
August 20—
Summer before college

I'm back at Busch Gardens. In April I was let go from my job at Subway after only three days. The Asian manager said I didn't move fast enough, implying I was on drugs. I never can move fast for fear of not looking right, something showing. So I applied and was hired last May at Busch. At least I know the ropes here and it's virtually impossible to get fired. When I went to Human Resources to complete the paperwork, all the old and incriminating information was still in the computer file. I did have an updated license with a new name and picture—but—. The office agent was a black man. I told him I wanted to take a new picture for my employee ID. The one on file was appalling and outdated—of course I didn't tell him that! He didn't seem to care, for my sake it was a relief. Afterward, I went to the costume shop where I was given a small form to fill out—a blue receipt with four bold black letters in the upper right hand corner: M-A-L-E. As if the colored sheet wasn't enough. Next to the stack of blue papers rested a heap of pink; it was like having your sex announced by the blanket nurses swaddle you in when you're born—all very elementary and yet signing that blue sheet was a private affirmation. I worked for about a month in the England location as a park photographer, which did not go over too well. I was supposed to stroll around taking pictures in a presumptuous manner and hand guests a card—this demands an aggressive, extroverted personality. The supervisor transferred me because of my refusal to shed the fleece jacket—part of our uniform intended, naturally, for the cooler fall months. In ninety degree weather I'd be scouting about, digital camera slung over shoulder, a glass of ice water in hand. I kept the jacket zipped. It was conspicuous. I achieved the opposite end, attracting rather than diverting attention. My head supervisor inquired as to my reasoning behind such absurd attire; I offered up some lame response. 'I'm really not that hot.' Even now I know I will remember the scent of my sweat mingling with the distinctive odor of the park and how the heavy summer heat hangs around me, the perspiration rolling down my back in itching rivulets. The confinement, will it ever stop? I now work for the merchandise department in New France and I must say it's been quite nice, much better than hiking from here to there—I often used to ride the train—cooled by the breeze as the cars moved. Which reminds me of the time I saw a small Asian man, an umbrella stroller propped on end. Beside him a little girl; she was maybe five or six; presumably his daughter. She sat perched on the edge of the seat, her legs a foot above the floor—not dangling but held still, her posture utterly perfect, wide-eyed and obedient. She was having fun and she was being so good about it. For some reason she reminded me of Ellis at that age—though I was too small to remember. Her innocence and respectable curiosity. I often wonder, had mother not had the miscarriages and I'd have had a little brother or sister—. For a moment, it was nice seeing the world as the little girl must. She sat so small, dutiful. Unafraid. Self-possessed.

I still wear the fleece because the costume for this site is a white shirt. Even with an undershirt, sweat has a way of making tape lines visible, particularly when you stoop. There are five stores I rotate amongst: the beer, candy, flag, hat, and grand prix store. I especially enjoy the candy shop, soon to be Build-a-Bear. Judith is usually assigned to this location.

Judith is an older lady, maybe mid-fifties or early sixties. She has short, short gray hair and wears glasses. She's very nice; we get along great, bantering often. I suspect she knows. Working with her makes the shift easier to tolerate.

This evening I was in the hat shop. We sell all sorts, unbelievable hats—cheeseburgers, enormous Lone Star Cowboy hats made out of foam, hotdogs, jester and baseball caps, Uncle Sam and pimp hats, crowns, and then the traditional souvenir hats. I love the gentle music piped through the speakers of New France; it sure beats Das Fest Haus' Polka drums and its repetitive show. I did learn some German, but here the music is tranquil, light, a subtle background. And I can 'see' the day. Inside the dimly lit Fest Haus, the oomph made the atmosphere more compressing—the only light coming through tiny rectangles at the far entrance.

Mack was there tonight. He's a comedic guy, more big around than tall, who loves to give me the razz. He's studying flight engineering. Once he socked me in the shoulder. He's all the time asking why I look so young, how often, if ever, do I shave. None of the other employees in the area would be so forward. The rest of the guys are easy-going, not in the least confrontational. There's always that one wise-guy in the bunch and he is it. I constantly organize the rearranged hats. I enjoy cleaning the giant pixie stick machine. I use a paint brush to sweep the spilled sugar. One day a little boy, eight or nine, approached the register. 'How much is this?' Having sold enough of them to know the price by heart, I told him. He stepped away to his mother. 'Can I get it?' 'You don't really need that. Put it back. I'll let you get something later.' 'But the man said it—' 'That's not a man.' Her words were not unkind, but simply meant to correct. Did she know I was listening? I don't think so. 'Yes it is,' he defended.

Thank you, little boy.

I manage to sell a bit of damaged merchandise, hanging velcro-pawed monkeys with broken voice boxes. I make signs and place the plush toys on top of the register with their plea: 'My name is Herstchel. Please adopt me before I face the shredder. Please, please save me.' I can't believe people are actually moved to sympathy and rescue them. We're not allowed to sell damaged goods. The way I see it, as long as the customer knows they're defective, and I give it to them at half-price, President August Busch would be proud. Hell, I'm just bringing in more money. I was making one of these signs for a voiceless green and yellow monkey when Mack busts in through the door adjoining the race car store with the hat shop. He starts fooling around, issuing his barrage of questions. 'Why you always wear that jacket?' Before I could move he grabbed my arm and started patting my chest playfully. 'Ah yeah, cut it out.' I tried not to sound alarmed. Never having put my own hand atop my chest, I worried, could he detect anything? Tightly bound I still felt leery. He let me be for a bit. Boisterously the swinging door opened again.

He had a hot dog hat in his hand—one to be thrown away because it was ripped. Scrolled in marker across the foot-and-a-half long frank were three words: What Westcott Wants. 'Oh you're funny, Mack. That's reeeaaaal funny.' I quickly took my marker and scratched the sentence out before trashing the tasteless dog. Boy, does that guy like to razz me. I don't hate him or even dislike him, but it's the closest to being threatened that I've ever come. I wouldn't give him the satisfaction of letting him know he'd gotten to me. When I got off work and met Ellis, just as she was closing, I told her about it. She felt me up, patted my chest. 'Nah, you're fine.' I still had my reservations.

~

Addendum: I did not know that the following summer I would be back at Busch, this time working in the Wine Shop located in the area of the park designated Italy. Sometimes when I arrived into work I'd go behind the hole-in-the-wall shop and look out at the forest, checking to see if the black apron I wore over my white shirt was flat. If not for the discomfort of my body, I'd have experienced youthful, carefree pleasure on the job. I enjoyed making the smoothies, dicing oranges, decapitating strawberries, running the Frappuccino machine. We were a small crew. Many foreigners worked over the summer. Lex was Philippino. In front of the outdoor, open air shop, just to the left, stood a cotton candy vendor. Frequently, a young girl—Russian, would come over to the counter and ask me if I'd make her a cup of coffee with "lots of chocolate, please." After the first couple of times, I knew she was not waving me over just for coffee. When I handed her the paper cup— sometimes I brought it to her since she couldn't leave her post for long—she would smile and thank me. In years to come I'd yearn for such casual flirtation. The missed chances. Had things been in place, had it been two years later, maybe we'd have had a summer fling. My youthful appearance made me particularly cute to young women, but for a little while longer my attractions remained dormant.

Journal Entry:
from the Book of West
7 May 20—

To live for yesterday holds less esteem for all that is in the present. The tug-of-war between future and past tears the spirit; its mendings never as firmly knitted as the original bonds—more vulnerable and easier to rip—a lesser effort to repair?

*

Instead of being invigorated about college and a fresh start, I was in mourning. I'd gone from 12 to 18. I had no social experiences to call upon. No activities. I was not prepared. Besides, my attention had not been on: what do I want to do, what is the best school, where should I consider applying? My only focus was: how to get out of this body.

My grades and GPA were excellent but I had no extracurricular activities to show for it. Nor any AP classes to my name. I was without direction. When I applied to William & Mary it was under my given "birth" name; I'd yet to legally change it—that would occur a month after applications were due. Secondly, in my essays, I candidly explained that I was a social phobic. At the time that's how I felt. It wasn't true. My phobia wasn't everyone else. My phobia was running into myself! What was I thinking, honesty is the best policy?! My guidance counselor wrote a recommendation using female pronouns and saying 'a fine young woman.' Young woman! And then two of my teachers, Mrs. T and Mrs. McCormack, wrote their own letters of recommendation referring to me as 'Westcott,' avoiding any use of pronouns altogether. Well, it's not hard to imagine the end result: W&M did not want some social misfit entering their ranks.

I would apply again my freshman year at CNU. I had two professors who were taken with my performance and dedication. One of them was Professor Combes who I had for two different classes. He extolled my analysis and creation of a dialogue between Erasmus and Socrates. Plus, W&M had been his alma mater. Since Ellis was also an alumna, it seemed a shoe-in. I had the grades, the recommendations, associations. I never considered applying to any of the Ivy League schools. College had become a business and I knew being a Columbia graduate didn't make you anymore qualified to make an impact in the world. If anything it just made access up the corporate ladder easier. But no education could instill grit and determination. This came from inside. Untaught. The second time W&M turned me down my dismay was mildly alleviated by the knowledge that it was purely a matter of discrimination. I'd applied once as a female and then as a male.

It's one thing to transition after being admitted, but to attempt to impart understanding in the midst of an identity crisis screams no, no, no! to the selection committee. I was a minority population, but I did not want leniency or accommodation. I just wanted to be considered as a young man with scholarly potential. I was not discouraged. It had been more for convenience than desire that I should attend W&M, since it was just down the road. CNU had a far better English department. It seemed I was hung up on the principle of the matter. I was more than qualified for the rigorous curriculum. There was a reason I was not supposed to go to W&M and I put it down to this: I wanted more out of life. So much more. W&M was not the answer I was looking for. At this point I'd yet to be told I was a genius, tormented, but lovely. Did I believe them? Doctors, some holding PhDs, who pronounced me as exceptional? I knew the pain made something beautiful and I accepted that knowing too much alienated one. But was I a genius in the scientific sense of the term? That's not for me to answer.

Some years later I was working in Colonial Williamsburg. One of my colleagues, in her late 30s, had graduated from W&M. Her degree was in German. W&M is known for its supposedly strong business courses and its Law School. Majoring in German seemed suspicious to say the least. My colleague candidly confessed that she lacked ambition, was lazy. And so with a BA from William & Mary she contentedly made 14-15 dollars an hour working 40 hours a week for a company that lined the pockets of its executives and left its interpreters and laymen scrounging. I was an intern at the time, making a nice 10/hr with few duties requiring exertion. I had ample time to read and write, shred paper for various offices and assess the pure antiquity of the building in which I worked—the architecture being the only true thing that spoke to me besides my honest colleague. My colleague's father also paid off all of her student loans. He wanted to. She was, and to this day still is, a very smart, funny, and savvy woman. But is this what William & Mary and so many other "calling card" colleges have in mind when they scan prospective applications? Being a social butterfly, bright, and well-adjusted does not ensure iron-clad tenacity and dedication to one field. Sometimes the seemingly boring, quiet, introverted "scientists" of life pool their energy, generate new ideas. The inventors and artists possess something no textbook or math formula can instill: passion. Not crazed, fly by the seat of your pants passion, but a dedicated, lifelong drive to pursue an intrigue to its end.

• • •

Westcott was just beginning to taste the inconvenience of adversity. He was tired of story analysis, textbook knowledge and pure facts. What he needed was to know his purpose, to find and fulfill it.

Over the course of his life he'd meet many wonderful individuals who had walked into their current place, either because of family, choice, or security. As the years passed, Westcott came to value his unique freedom. Sometimes he wanted a sure, rock solid place to belong, but it was an illusion. A role. Everyone had his or her part to play. Westcott observed during those years after Regn and he came to realize what it was he *didn't* want. Something was alive inside. He didn't want to fall asleep. Or maybe, just maybe, he wanted to finally wake up and find himself right where he was supposed to be—on the crest where he'd worked so hard to get. The crest of humanity.

HOW I LIVE NOW

...

Nobody asked me 'why.' Not one of the psychologists who prepared the mandatory letters recommending surgery. You don't like your breasts? You want to be male? I hated those questions. Nobody asked *why* I wanted to become male, only *if*. Nobody mentioned the sexual repercussions. Did I know what I was getting myself into? What was a man's role as opposed to a woman's in society and how did I see myself in either role? Psychologically I remained asexual. It is *typical* to start on hormones prior to undergoing surgery; however, it is not required. I did just the opposite. I underwent surgery first. I had never seen myself. No doctor, therapist, family member had said, 'Look! Look at what you're removing. Fine if you want to do it, but look before you jump. Know what you are and where you're going. Be socially prepared.'

People often said it was a courageous thing to do. It annoyed me when they said this. I know they didn't intend for it to be received adversely, but what they always failed to understand was that it *wasn't* a choice. It's like a woman who's pregnant. She has no choice but to go through the labor; it must come out! Is she courageous? Brave? It's something one endures. No one in his or her right mind would choose the pain. Unlike childbirth, the act was not painful, nor was it a one-shot deal. In having a child a woman's physical pain and even emotional upheaval is temporary. My state of being was indefinite. It didn't just come out, separate from me, and go away. I remained divided. For life.

Journal Entry:
from the Book of West
13 October 20—

He put his hand on my chest, speculatively. Stiff as a board, I felt his fingers raise my breast. Mother was in the room. Not once did I look down as he described the procedure that would be taking place the following morning. He did not force me to look. There were two methods of action that could be done. Liposuction, he felt, would leave me displeased, which left only one alternative. Unraveling the gray strands of duct tape, unclasping the waist cincher I wore over my breasts, he told me he'd seen much worse, instances where patients had dead skin. He was unaware that Ellis had rigorously scrubbed me clean the night before. And taken a picture. I refused to ever look at myself, let alone touch the unwanted orbs. His words disappointed. I wanted him to know the severity of my fanaticism when it came to binding.

• • •

14 October 20—

'Madame, Madame, it is time.' Gedny rustles to get up. Unbeknownst to her, Westcott hasn't slept a full wink the entire night. His eyes sting with exhaustion. Francois, a short, pudgy, adorable white-haired lady, has been the night shift nurse at the convalescing Residence. She speaks very broken English. When she comes to wake them at five o'clock her thick accent stirs the silence warmly. A taxi picks them up at 6:00, arriving to the privately owned hospital at 6:27 a.m. How busy the highways are at such an ungodly hour. Driving by a huge cylindrical building on the right with giant chrome letters illuminated in the still dark morning, Gedny points to it. 'Look.' The block-print signage reads: COLLOSUS. Some sort of space museum he supposes. Ellis and Rodge follow in their car to save expenses. Gedny tips the driver generously. They wait on the cold sidewalk for Rodge and Ellis to park. They dawdle in their fatigue. Ellis presses the ringer on the side-wall so staff will let them in. A solitary man sits in the waiting area. Promptly, Westcott is shown into his room. He removes his Coleman wristwatch, sets it on the wooden dresser.

• • •

No one asked Westcott if he'd mind Rodger coming with them. It doesn't bother him. Years later he'll remember Rodge's kindness and interest in the whole matter. He never showed the least bit of prejudice or cruelty. He was always polite. When Ellis decides not to marry him and Rodge is heartbroken, Westcott will silently sympathize. Sometimes, to keep himself going, he will think of Rodge. In some unfair way, Rodge's sorrow made him feel better or, less alone. Rodge understood what it was to lose the person he most loved. Rodge understood what it was to be afflicted and hurt. Rodge was a good, decent man.

• • •

(Post-op)

The lady unhooked the I.V bag from its metal stand while Mother moved to keep the back of my gown shut, showing motherly awareness of my distress for being seen. The nurse helped to steady me. I cringed when she went into the bathroom with me, sat me down, so I wouldn't lose my balance in the process of voiding and topple over. I asked her as politely as I could in my woozy state to leave me. That was her intention. To my dismay, nerves and the recent hours of sedentary recuperation forced my bladder to be inert. I waited for nature to take its course. The more I focused on it, the more tense I became, terrified of a knock on the door. I was reminded of my *not* being able to fall asleep phobia.

The nurse came in, asked if I was all right, turned the faucet on, and left. I was glad for the liquid sound barrier; I wasn't thinking of waterfalls but privacy, now I could piss in solitude. It was a nuisance maneuvering with a needle in one hand and two drains fastened to my thoracic dressing. Relieved, I feebly made my way back to bed with escort. Visiting hours ended at eight p.m. Mom and Ellis said they'd see me tomorrow.

When I awoke I learned the unsettling news that it was only 9:30 p.m. The night was young; already I was exhausted from resting. Hourly a nurse continued to take our blood pressure and pulse, this time she suggested I take something to help me sleep. I said I preferred not to, I was sufficiently groggy. I tried to sleep, but was kept awake by my roommate's tendency to incessantly scratch her throat, making a salivary clicking noise that moved me to fidget in disgust. She wasn't conscious of it—I'd gladly have taken snoring over it. I found myself most content when she was awake, having the opportunity to talk and pass time.

Around ten I discovered I had to use the restroom again, as did Heather. Half past twelve (I asked the staff what time it was) we were hobbling to get there again. On one occasion, getting back into bed, a nurse went so far as to put cream on my back. I felt quite guilty for all she was doing. I didn't deserve such attention. I took some oral pain medicine in the form of two yellow pills and a large white one I had the nurse break in half. I managed to rest peacefully for a couple of hours but without sleep. I fell to studying the beige-green wall before me through the endless night. The shadows created an illusion in the corner. If you looked at it just right in the dim light, you'd think the wall depressed; on closer inspection it protruded like a single vertical stair—a trick of the eye that vanished with the rays of dawn. Peering out the slits between the blinds at the sparse number of yellow headlights traveling past the hospital in the late hours, I longed for morning, wishing I still had my watch so I could know the time. In my state of "sedated" euphoria it still hadn't hit me. In my mind I told myself, *You're free now.* The extent of what free meant branched endlessly from the paramount to the most simplistic of liberties. No more salivated collars before bed and in the morning as I held my shirt in mouth—a tent to avoid seeing the ever increasing protrusions. No more tugging on shirts, stretching them to the point of ripping a gape in the side, or refusing to go into a store because I didn't look right. Never again would I have to mow the lawn in 88 and 95-degrees in an oven of layers—jacket, overshirt, t-shirt, duct tape and wrap—a sweat suit, heat-stroke, death-trap. Two o'clock came, another excursion to the bathroom ensued. God did I want to pull that contemptible I.V. out. Damn saline fluids kept going through me. I sipped ice water to moisten my parched throat; a canker sore in my bottom gum had formed as a result of the breathing tube used during surgery, adding irritation. I could taste the abominable scent of my breath and felt sorry for any nurses who came too close.

• • •

15 October 20—

Early Friday, 6:30 I estimate, Dr. Brassard came in to check on my roommate and I, pulling the dividing sheet out for privacy. He wore a slightly modified mint green shirt, a burgundy tie and the typical white overcoat dabbed with his medical cologne—an undisguisable tempered latex glove odor that comforted. Looking down upon me, I felt severely intimidated, mentally fidgeting as he lowered the bed so I lay flat. The level of dim lighting he'd raised the switch to made him appear all the more menacing, defining his red-skinned features with a shadowy line. But he was a kind man. I wasn't used to anyone looking at me. He drew the cover and gown from my chest. Lifting it from the side, I was pleased to be wearing my boxers, which he didn't expect, judging by his cautious actions. 'I see you've been eating,' he said to my chagrin, 'there are crumbs all over.' Silently I caved in, mortified. I'd only had a lightly buttered slice of bread at 5:00 a.m. Bad enough he saw me sleeping, but now this! He cut the bandages up the middle along my sternum for inspection. 'Sorry,' he pulled the adhesive medical tape from my skin as slowly as possible. Satisfied with his inspection, he taped it back. 'Have you seen?' 'Not really.'

I didn't look at him, too ashamed of the complete bodily exposure the morning before. I cringed to think how much he'd seen on the operating table the instant I went out and they removed the gown beneath which I wore nothing. 'You have the bandages on right now, but there's nothing there,' he moved to convince. 'You'll have to keep the drains in until Monday.'

'Right,' I compliantly responded. Moving to leave, he placed his hand on my shoulder— a noble last effort. Speaking in a hushed voice. 'You're very flaut, *Sir.*'

I can still hear him in his French accent—his words soft and non-abrasive.

'You're very *flaut.*'

~

Many of the nurses, I've noticed, step outside for a smoking break. Sometimes I see Linda standing on the concrete step, opposite the kitchen—far away in her gaze.

Saturday I awoke with a gastrointestinal sickness. My neck with the black cross temporarily tattooed in its cleft, a remnant of the two-day old measurements, was sore and kinked. I still couldn't sleep on my side because of the sting/strain caused by the pulling of skin as I moved, and the drains running precariously along the sides of my torso. I asked for what would be my last painkiller. I didn't want to exploit their effects. The operation sight didn't warrant medication as I experienced little pain, mostly stiffness. My stomach bothered me most. Someone new arrived, a revisiting patient who had completed her operations in March. Her name was Diana. Male-to-Female. She wily told the nurses, 'I've come back to have "it" reattached.' We all laughed.

Paulette, the nurse with a voice truly as gentle and soft as a lamb, had the weekend night shifts. She showed us how to play *Monkeys in the Barrel.* She was endearing; an older woman, tall, slim, with short hair. 'I can see it in your eyes you're feeling better,' she said. I smiled. She must have been very attractive in her younger years. She had aged quite handsomely.

~

'So young man, are you ready?' Ambling side-by-side down the hall to my room, he turned to get something. His words were kind, but I didn't feel like a young man. It embarrassed me because I knew it was a lie. Breasts or no breasts, I wasn't a young man and never would be much as I desired.

While the doctor drew the blinds for some much-needed light, I took off my button down shirt as he yielded for me to do, an ever so subtle edge of agitation wringing his body language. In the absence of words I heard him say, *Come now, how can I possibly get to you with it on?* He was unequivocally commanded by a tight schedule and always on call; my inaction warranted his reasonable, imperative, though silent "remark." My mental processes had bottlenecked eliciting shy ineptness. Together I whipped off my coat and shirt—the same navy blue one I'd worn two years earlier, undoing the last button. Dr. Brassard hadn't anticipated such an instantaneous response; by the time he turned around a split second later, I was ready. He appeared a twinge compunctious for his hurried decorum, as hypothesized by the look on his face. What he didn't know was that beforehand I'd undone all of the buttons except the top-most. I understood he didn't have all day, my nerves were the subterfuge of initiative, slowing my reaction time so that I had to wait to be told to do something before acting. He must have thought me a strange one, stranger than most—reserved in my silent manner of jittery reproach. Standing taller than him, he asked but in essence really instructed, 'Do you want to sit down?'

Resting on the edge of the bed, hanging my head, I studied his black shoes again. Nice shoes. Squared in the front. Handsome shoes. He was a man. I still wasn't used to a man being so close. Underneath his clothes there was no doubt, he was a man.

'Are you all right?'

'Yes.'

Coyly staring at the floor, I noticed he came very near to stepping on my feet. I shuffled them back to avoid having him issue an extraneous apology.

While he carefully cut the bandages and pulled them away, mom walked in wanting to see how it came out. In that moment I was annoyed. Just once couldn't she wait? Let me have this time alone, time to digest the unveiling? She meant no harm, that I knew, and always would know. I still felt intruded upon.

After removing the blood congested drains, he placed a gauze over my grafted nipple, instructing me to hold it in place while he got another one out. Hesitating, leery of what might be felt, I put my hand on my chest. It wasn't shock. It wasn't euphoria. I was pleased to discover the truth, but it still hadn't penetrated. Nothing remained. Suddenly his phone rang. 'Oui?' Still keeping the one gauze in place with his free hand while speaking in French.

Detecting his precarious situation, I moved to press it, deaf to his conversation. Apologizing for the disruption, he finished his work, velcroing an abdominal binder around my chest for compression. 'You'll have to walk around like an old man for a couple of weeks,' he told me with a smile.

I moved about the house, sitting in different places, most favorably the comfy blue chair in the entrance hall. Keeping very still, deep in thought, I breathed rapidly, my stomach feeling mangled. I took in everything, much as I had done on that final drive to Jamestown High. I looked at the Halloween poster pinned to the wall, the red sticker atop the marble tile that read *Sortie*, indicating to watch your step on the small ramp. I counted the number of panes in the door, studied a picture commemorating Canada's founding anniversary back in the 1500s. I longed for everyone to go to bed so I could indulge the protection of darkness. Though Mother and I shared a room, I cried silently until sleep came.

Francois was the night nurse, our stay thus being circular. We spent our first night and would sleep our last with her awake by the light of the lamp, comforted to know that she was there for us.

Morning came; another man further along in his surgeries was scheduled to arrive later that day. Unfortunately we'd miss him. Not forsaking the ladies I'd warmed up to, three wise old broads, I still desired to meet someone going the same way as myself. Lise asked me for a peck on the face; I shyly declined. She asked if she could kiss me goodbye and planted one on each cheek—a friendly French custom; I felt like a little kid again. Getting into the car my chest burned with restraint. Life's metronome would never be the same. We followed the cul-de-sac to the left before traversing Time's bridge.

After filling up at a local gas station, we stopped at Wendy's for some light fare to tide us. I sat still, gripping my stomach. It started a day after the surgery; she came a week and a half too soon. This had happened before. In the past sometimes my level of worrying or heightened stress would trigger the onset of a monthly course. I constantly dreaded when she would come and wished to get it out of the way as soon as possible, always concerned what I'd be doing activity-wise during those times. No sooner would it stop, the reprieve all too short, and she'd slither back. The degree of intensity the last few days was a catalyst. I didn't want to move. I felt hot outside and wet inside. The aching always started on the second and third of the worst days. A dull, circular ache, situated on the threshold, as though the wound were cleansing itself. The only relief was using the restroom and shedding the heavy accumulation not already in the napkin. I was often amazed, though more disgusted, at the quantity of blood. I believe it is from this that a woman first masters endurance. Holding my sides in private discomfort, and with Rodge holding the wheel, we headed onto the highway, passing by the Colossus again. I took more careful notice of it this time, studying it hard.

The cold weather was bright and sunny in Montreal. Heading south into New York, the skies transformed, becoming overcast and drizzly. We were descending towards a most debilitating storm; the drive back seeming so much shorter than the one up.

Before having lunch at Johnny Rockets where I heard The Four Seasons hit "Walk Like a Man" on the radio, we went downstairs to the basement laundromat. I had on a t-shirt for the first time in years. Printed in white letters across the chest it read, 'Since I gave up hope, I feel much better.' Mom and Ellis loaded two washers. Still suffering from an upset stomach I sat in one of the chairs, watching the clothes spin round in the dryer. So, too, was the world spinning on its axis. Life, I realized, was continuing with its rhythm in spite of my grief and desperate desire to fix certain moments and place the skids on time. I saw myself tumbling about and knew I must break the cycle of the past four years. Watching my mother and sister from miles away, the distance between us seemed unyielding in its sorrow. Heartache swirled me in its cyclone of pain, hurling me into the abyss of despair. The little room permeated with heat, covering my open arms like a blanket. I was on the gurney again.

• • •

Wednesday 20 October 20—
Six days post-op

I would much rather live for a brief interval in clarity than for a lifetime blinded by everyday monotony and the right of society's routine. I'd like to live in that vista where I step back from it all, not afraid of living as I see fit and essential. I was awakened for a week's moment.

• • •

Eight days post-op
Friday 22 October 20—

The core of my existence, waiting, the solitary entity upon which my persona evolved, has been destroyed. The pain is mentally paralyzing. I'm scared of forgetting what I've just been through. I knew the night before I left how difficult life would be thereafter—just keeping myself going. I breathed in shallow gasps not wanting to wake Mom, constricting my chest, unable to inhale through my congested nose. The hurt wouldn't subside. What was before and after dissolved, perhaps shooed away by shock. Everything has been brought into focus and now I see the absurdity of continuing in an environment I hate—college. No matter what, regardless of aims and accomplishments, we're all here for the same thing and not a one of us knows why. I don't want to wake up 20 years from now and ask what was it all for? I'm not sure teaching is right for me anymore. How do you go on living when every second you feel like dying? I never thought I'd wish the surgery had yet to come. It was the right thing; God knows I have no regrets. I used to fantasize I could return to Drummond's Field High and finally belong, now I know I've become too old for that—another part of me has died and had I passed away all together I wouldn't have minded. The operation forced me to get over the sorrows surrounding high school, now the grief is another kind and far worse. Sometimes in my darkest hours I hope, dear God, I will be reunited with those who had a profound effect on my life.

I remember sitting on the edge of Ellis' bed in her apartment Thursday afternoon before heading back to Virginia. I stared out at the dank day much like I'd done a year before when she still lived at home; it brought me back to those high school mornings when I'd look at the forest, Strum sleeping peacefully on the sunned comforter. Presently, an enormous tree over two stories high sprawled before me, its bark coal black in the overcast afternoon. I picked up my watch from the bed-stand to see the time. Exactly one week ago I had just come-to from surgery.

Standing by the trunk of our double-parked car, hazard lights flashing, waiting for Ellis and Mom to bring the last of the bags down to the curb, I stared up at the bleak sky. It was the only non-delineating geographical thing I could think of to take me back. New York fell away; standing there, gazing above the apartment buildings, dismissing the sound of traffic, distant horns, and the gleeful yells of children in a nearby playground, I could have been anywhere in the world. Just me and the universal dome. Anywhere. But I pretended I was still in Montreal, peering out one of the many windows at the Residence. I hung on as a long as I could before Mom and Ellis appeared, and I was forced to withdraw myself from the sky.

~

All the way home, driving from New York to Virginia, I remained transfixed in silence, answering only when spoken to. Looking out the back seat window at highway landmarks signifying we were moving farther and farther away from my gateway to freedom, I noticed something written on the pane. At some time, probably when out sightseeing with Rodge, Ellis had scrolled with her finger the word *Sud = South*. I studied the yellowing bruise on the top of my left hand. Depending on who was sitting in the passenger seat, we'd have to get the EZ pass out and hold it up to the windshield for quick drive-by at the tollbooths. We detoured from the main highway for two rest stops. Neither of which I felt compelled to take advantage of, restroom-wise. Stretching my legs, pacing, I looked up again, far away. It was evening with warm colors sprawling the partially clouded skies and then night— cold, still, clear, spangled with stars. Around Washington and Maryland we put on the John Denver cd I'd received for my birthday. I half listened, my mind adrift. *There's nothing behind me and nothing that ties me to something that might have been true yesterday—all alone in the universe, sometimes that's how it seems, I get lost in the sadness and the screeeaaaams—*

Now that I'm home each morning when I awake with a flipped stomach, I keep my eyes shut, pretend I'm still at La Maison. I remember the floral patterned comforter with its fuchsia roses and beige design, the touch lamps on each bedside bureau, the loud squeaky, teeth-grinding noise of the tall-backed chair that the Doctor sat in to discuss risks and proce- dures and where I wrote my account of the operation. The smell of the wooden floors, the creak of the basement steps, the painting in Ellis and Rodge's room that looked like Mary, haunting. The abstract piece of "mud" artwork in the hall illustrating the merging of a light and dark puddle that I likened to a representation of the diffusion and metamorphosis of gender. Sometimes when I stare up at the sky I wonder if nurse Linda is gazing out at the same dome on her smoke break. I haven't been talking much lately. Mom said she's not angry with me, but concerned. It's not uncommon, I know, to have post-op depression. I keep reliving the past, going over every detail of that week, night and day. I recall signing the waivers for liability purposes that morning. 'Just initial in the left hand corner.'

. . .

Friday 26 November 20—

Today I went swimming for the first time in four years; I wore a beige t-shirt to hide the scars and a pair of trunks borrowed from Rodge who is down for Thanksgiving with Ellis. Walked through men's locker room. When I was little I came in on my father taking a bath, but that was so many years ago. For now browsing through home decor Toscano magazines selling Greek sculptures of David bodices must suffice to see the natural male body. Pulling the swimwear off, I kept my head down to avoid bringing attention to myself. I maintained a nonchalant composure, as though I'd been one of them all my life.

. . .

Wednesday 8 December 20—

Eight weeks ago we arrived at the Residence. The weather was warm and mild, much like it is today despite the approaching winter. It sounds like spring outside—a tantalizing disillusionment.

This evening I took my usual stroll at the park. The black barren trees silhouetted against the lavender, gray skies. I gazed off in a northerly direction. Birds chirped in the bamboo brush near the baseball diamond. I walked.

The time seems to be running a marathon despite my mental standstill. The fall of the operation is drawing to a close. It's hard to believe. I still rest in Montreal, my life's battleship marooned there, having reached the shore of my spirit's enterprise. I now see there's more to happiness than *just* being one or the other. Assimilating into the correct gender role is essential, but only part of it. I can't endure to be a self-banished Indian anymore.

• • •

December 20—
Two months post-op

I sit here on the edge of my bed listening to "Autumn Leaves." A little cabin ensconced in a glass globe with a lantern cap, hand-painted—a birthday gift. Ironic there should only be nineteen nostalgic notes to its tune. The age I was on the eve of transformation. Five, five, five, four, I count them to myself. I'm by the Schroon Lake historical sign at a rest stop, on the Canadian Parkway, in the hospital bed, looking out the basement window of the Residence, studying my bare chest long and hard in the bathroom mirror, and once again 'here,' about to get up and crank the music box and see where it takes me. Here will someday be a yesterday, falling into the middle of the tune and not embodying its end.

• • •

Three months post-op

Song of the Broken One
(Not all songs are exultations...)

He's tired—the silence of his own thoughts within his head. Rarely here—always so far away. At certain hours he's begged to die—yelling noiselessly, straining his vocal chords to a quiet burning whisper, "Take me, take me!" He looks up to the ceiling fan, his words ascending invisibly—momentary pleas of passion. Even when the dome is blue, the sun bright on him, it is raining, pouring. Sorrow is his violin— the bow invincible, unbreakable, unwilling to bend—all he knows... company enough—a weariness without end.

The future he wishes not to consult—the past he embraces.

Not long ago he went into his sister's old room, vacated now for more than a year. She'd flown home that night—he and mother had dropped her off at the Richmond Airport sometime in the evening. The moon on the ride up had been uncanny in its spherical magnitude, perhaps lunar evidence of the natural oceanic catastrophe halfway round the globe—so many innocent lives lost and yet his spared. Once home, he had walked over to the barren windows—in the dark. Gazing out at the blackened and similarly barren forest, he watched headlights streak through the trees, traveling along a young highway—to where who knows, a mile or so away. Bringing his focus a bit closer, he searched for a boy's reflection in the panes. His nose practically touched the glass. He tried to make out his eyes, but they were hollow—melting with the darkness of the night. A moment, then he pulled himself from the looking glass and lay down on the floor. He'd brought a plaid pillow in from his room. Resting on his back, something he seldom did, he positioned himself just right so as to have the crown molding connecting the double windows shadow his face from the moonlight. He lay motionless for a while before rolling onto his left side and creased arm. He studied his left hand, contorting it in such a way as to make an elongated shadow on the floor. His fingers assumed a disturbing length, his hand resembling the appendage of some Extra Terrestrial being.

He stopped; let his hand go limp, palm face up. He held a white beam, powerful in its ability to psychologically warm. He needed its light... so desperately...any light strong enough... The boy drew back his arm compressing it beneath the weight of his side, burying his face in the pillow—crying for his life with dry eyes. The ducts had long since been emptied during one ultimately tumultuous breakdown in the course of his heart's excavation. He was already exhausted—no one could hear him. His mother knew of his state, worrying herself sick—ever fearful of his hand rendering his own self-destruction. He assured her he would not. But nothing remained for her to comfort— he was numb—his will, or lack thereof, beyond penetrating, beyond resuscitation. Only he alone could boil the kettle back to life. Really. It was he against himself—a battle to be forever confronting.

Physically staid, listening to his own heart pulsating in his eardrums, wishing it no more, he heard the TV downstairs.

"Travel down the road and back again, your heart is true you're a pal and a confidante...and if you threw a party, invited everyone you knew, you would see—the greatest gift would be from me—and the card attached would say—thank you for being a friend..." His mother was watching The Golden Girls; the show had just begun—a half-hour mental respite from the pain of reality. He was too tired to join her that night, though he quite enjoyed the characters. He felt like crying even harder; who could hear him—no one—nothing mattered anymore.

- - - -

Evenings he occasionally takes strolls at the park—the black, stripped trees silhouetted against the lavender, cobalt skies...gazing off in a northerly direction...birds chirping in the bamboo brush near the baseball diamond...he paces alone. He used to watch his dog roll in the grass.

- - - -

He is an island tree...

He is a lighthouse on the bluff, sitting in expectation of the storm...his beacon shattered, his flesh eroded by the salty winds obscuring sight.

He is a ship drifting atop the whitecaps of the sea...

- - - -

The half-empty glass resting on the table—he knows its anticipation...hardship of seemingly absolute goodbyes...recollections of those he cares for—he knows the dolor...the bagger at the local grocery store that is physically disabled but whose smile is enough to make up for the one the boy doesn't wear—he knows not the trade of dissembling to display such masks...the railroad stations where trains never come...John Denver's songs in his head...wind chimes clanking in the gusts... cattails disintegrating by the pond's edge...the rims of his shoes green when he's just cut the grass...rocking his life away in the porch wicker chair, the desolate and voiding tone of keys in the ignition when the driver's door is ajar...and a million other details too numerous to recount...most important, his music box of hope that plays so softly only to wane and fall silent once again...Perhaps I've said too much.

- - - -

Nights he goes for walks—his gait, whether slow or brisk depending upon temperature, is of no consequence. He hasn't an urgent need to hurry. Plodding along, looking to the sky and the confines of life— the neighborhood below, a tink and jingling of a bell trails worriedly behind him. His shadow—a sweet, stri-ped, tumbleweed of a cat. Each is like the other...so lonely. From time to time she meows in a "kittenly" mew, "wait...wait." The cat gives up halfway into the walk, wriggles her body in the sandy, pebbled base of some stranger's driveway... waiting and knowing...he'll be back, he always comes back, she thinks. The boy continues on in the absence of a four-legged tag-along. To the entrance he marches, his step consistent—slow, steady. He sees the stop sign up ahead on the right—the cautionary reminder to look both ways before venturing onto the "main" road. He hesitates in his step, taking careful notice of the three giant, magnificent trees on his left, situated behind the white fence that displays his neighborhood's title. He stops, makes a 180 and goes the way he's just come. To the end and back he's been, his spirit whiplashed by the constant tug of war...he's tired of walking and getting nowhere, driving aimlessly only to return to the silence of his own isolation. Life. His life. He wants to be one of those streaking lights on the highway, going somewhere, anywhere. Even in moving, he is standing still. The stop sign has no authority over his mental wanderings...one day he knows he will not return. He's afraid of losing himself in living as a normal man would, sacrificing his securities for a simple measure of belonging. He does not like the blind man's world. He's afraid of going blind to save his life.

...

Five years post-op

He looks at his hair. A receding patch on each side above his temples as if two palms had gripped his head and poisoned the healthy roots. It used to be so full and shiny. It's oily and thin. Decaying.

'We never die,' she would say.

He tried to tell her—to explain, but Regn had her way of looking at it and he had his. It will never again be this beautiful. The circumstances. What I am, how you are. I wouldn't change anything about myself or you, only the circumstances. The pain, don't you see, the pain is what's so god damn beautiful.

~

Autumn Leaves. His musical lantern. The light burned out long ago. The cabin sits ensconced in glass; the key when turned still plays the familiar notes. It used to be a nice tune, without meaning. Now he knows.

PART IV

WHO HAS KNOWN HEIGHTS

THAT EVENING SUN

Had things been different. Had *things* been different, I'd have started young devoting myself to becoming a musical composer. If not a wunderkind then an actor. Even now I think about grabbing my single suitcase, boarding the train, finally going up to N.Y. and entering one of the masked buildings parading as just another suite of offices, while deep within chance or maybe just luck awaits. I'd audition. When the screening interviewer asks my experience and credentials I'd reply: 28 years. 28 years of living hard. I can't fail. I don't have time. Look, what do you want me to do? I'll do it. I'm here.

I am reminded of a passage in *Stealing Athena* where, to paraphrase, she writes: man wants to have his name chiseled into history, while the woman, such as Regn, remains faceless yet steeped in the grace of fulfilled being.

How wonderful, isn't it, what we all want at one time or another, to try on different masks, or rather, remove the masks and enjoy the freedom of finding who we truly are. Isn't this the luxury afforded an actor or actress? And yes I say 'actress.' Distinction of gender is no degradation. Men and women are not the same. Neither is better nor worse. Just different. I never came so close to my intended self as those years with Regn.

And then I remind myself: Where would actors be without their scripts? The real creators seldom are known; their names unrealized, the real characters who actually lived these stories are shanghaied and portrayed by a well-known Hollywood-ite. Filmmakers highjack the beautiful quality of an unknown physiognomy. I suppose that's why I enjoy independent films—'stars' that are still human, not airbrushed. Someone has to sit behind the typewriter while others soak up the warmth of limelight. The vast majority remain nameless, yet they are the ones who provide the most honest stories.

It is a burden living between both worlds.

Helen "Gedny" Cray
September 1975

Once more it has happened.
You're gone as quickly as you came.

Is there no end to the continuous
exits that are forever confronting
me?

The brief, but oh so meaningful
encounter we shared.
Did we really share it?

My heart and mind were yours entirely, but no seeds
did you plant to cultivate our being one.

All the words of kindness and comforting arms
about me cannot replace the emptiness within.

Now I must proceed to find my way home, but all is not lost,
for I have gained the irreplaceable memory of you.

Re: A Prayer for You {Ingenious Pain}

Of all the books and voices I have read—
Observing from my post the teeming day
Of all the burdened spirits gone ahead—

Sit me down, hand to breast, and soundless pray
To those whose lives are breaths upon a page
A passion can endure though reason doth allay

Strong be the blightened soul—though body serves to cage
Dance with the Dreamer, the dew of softened rain—
What of one's years when an hour bears no age?

Lilac's Whisper, Willow's Cry—each a name
We ask to know, we perplex to discern
Death be not afraid—it is ingenious pain!

                         —Westcott A. Rowan

CHAPTER 6

RUGGED GRACE

MAMA CASS IS PLAYING. He's listening to Mama Cass. Dream a little dream. An evening drive, summer heavy in the air, driving the southeast portion of the American continent. No. His imagination wanders. He's touring the English countryside, the Dark Forest, the pagan hills of Ireland. It's 1937. 1942. He's wearing breeches. Breeches is what they still call them and his tweed cap. Put-putting at 35 mph; a Sunday picnic of yesterday—this is what her words mean as she sings to him.

Stars shining bright above you
Night breezes seem to whisper, I love you...
I'm longin' to linger till dawn dear
Just saying this—
Sweet dreams till sunbeams find you
Sweet dreams that leave all worries behind you
But in your dreams whatever they be
Dream a little dream of me—

...

We should never have lost the house. It happened during the scramble, when banks threatened to seize and foreclose. Ellis had no attachment to our home. She was the one who had been so set on it when we looked at places to move—the location, style. Now she just wanted to wash her hands of it! She'd been away too long.

It was an August day, maybe September. Mother and I had come home. I'd recently mowed the lawn. The crepe myrtles blew gently in the summer breeze. All the ones we'd planted 11 years earlier. The windows were open. Everything was beautiful. Sharp in color. Immaculate. Fresh. I didn't want to lose the house, but the need to break free, to get out, seized me. I couldn't stand the confinement a moment longer. And Regn—my mind was consumed with plans, the process, the patience. "Bear with me," she'd said. This was it. The first break. The first step. I wanted Mother to stay in our home, for that to be her place of comfort, but she could never cover the mortgage on her own. She would always require tenants. It had become a burden, a sinking ship. I felt like the tugboat anchored to the vessel, straining to keep afloat. It would be easier to let it go. It would hurt, in time, because I knew my mother required roots, a place to call home. We'd already lost our first house. My father had stayed in the Victorian. This was my mother's creation—our creation—the house we'd designed and built. I was tired of holding on, tired. Tired. Tired. It was time.

———

I was the last to step inside our house. The night I pulled the door shut and turned the key in the Schlage lock, I pressed my palm against the patriot blue door. How I loved that door, even today. The porch light was off, we'd removed every last light bulb. I closed the door on the past eleven years, closed the door on whatever shred of childhood ideals remained.

Helmsley came to the thin vertical panel of glass, pressed his white muzzle to look out. The dimness inside illuminated his white fur, made him seem an apparition, locked within. *Don't worry*, I whispered, *I'll be back for ya, we're not leaving you*. I'd left him a dish of mix and a bowl of water, a makeshift litter box in the form of an aluminum turkey pan.

I walked down the porch steps, crossed the street and stepped into our neighbor's foyer.

Bob and Patsy were gone for two months. I'd taken over the clients for whom Bob mowed lawns.

They said we could stay in their house in the interim. A week passed. Our house stood there, six paces across the street to the driveway, untouched.

I found what I was looking for in Bob's well-ordered garage. I took the fishing knife, stole across the street, around the side to the deck. The stairs I'd climbed up and down so many times. Under the stairwell, on one of the support beams, I carved my initials. I'd never had that childhood rite of passage. I'd never left a permanent mark. I wanted to say goodbye the right way. I etched the following: *11 good years. Für Immer. W.A.R.* It took some doing. When I was satisfied I folded the knife, put it in my pocket to return to Bob's garage. I breathed the October air. I was neither sad nor happy.

Late one afternoon, a vehicle pulls into the drive. I make haste. Hurry across the street from my neighbor's house. The front door of our house is locked, of course. I don't want to let them know I have a key, that I am the owner. I walk around back, up the deck and into the kitchen. Two men are on their knees changing the locks.

'Have you seen a cat? I'm the neighbor across the street. The people that lived here told me to come and get him.'

'We were wondering about that. We bought some cat food and I was going to take him home,' one of them said.

I am a stranger in my own home. I hurry to collect Helmsley.

I fumble with his squirming body as I tote him across the way. We keep him in the garage so his fur won't shed on the furniture. He also has an occasional hankering—a restlessness—to scratch upholstery when confined too long. We've already invaded Bob and Patsy's house. Miss Gilly stays on their deck; it will be precarious for the next few weeks.

. . .

Ellis and Mother had a sudden and severe cold from all the dust unearthed in the haste of our moving. The distress of new surroundings, I sat on the stoop in our neighbor's garage. I undid the button of my jeans, slipping a hand between my legs—searching for calm.

As penance perhaps, a few days later the cold took hold of me. I lay in a daze on the small comfortable sofa of my neighbor's TV room. I gazed at an 11x14 painting of what appeared to be a mission. It seemed tropical in locale or, I conjectured, from Albuquerque. Patsy liked New Mexico and much of their décor was interspersed with midwestern paintings.

While closing proceedings took another few weeks on our soon to be 'new' place of residence, we were guests of our neighbor's. I would look out the window. Strange to see your life from the vantage of objectivity. All those years and this is what they 'saw.' Patsy went into her dark moods. 'The watcher' we called her. She'd sit in her front corner window and observe the goings-on, an ashtray of cigarettes at hand. Bipolar? Schizophrenic? Her behavior was eccentric, but she was a part of this street, a part of the years.

The scent of smoke permeated the otherwise clean and prettily decorated house. I liked the smell—it felt cool, indefinite, new. It was like staying in a hotel when you requested a nonsmoking room and had to make do. The scent of cigarette smoke would always bring back those days of waiting. I was without a job, a home, and the woman I loved. At least I still felt Regn's passion for me. That was still alive.

I stopped looking out the window. Only after we'd gone, the temporary storage unit emptied, some months later, did I begin to look. And when I did, I looked away. Not back, not forward, only inside.

A year after we'd settled into our new home I suggested to Mother that we invite Bob and Patsy for Christmas dinner.

OCTOBER

Boxes, boxes everywhere. A makeshift table and chair—the only items remaining, in what was the TV room. Ellis is drinking water from a leftover flute glass. Everything else is in storage. Westcott steps into the kitchen from the garage, returning from another run to the storage unit. Gunpowder.

'You haven't even helped! You could have at least told us you were taking him!' She means Liam, her Jack Russell. Westcott had taken him along in the truck. They were frantic looking for him. She unleashes a battery of remarks.

'Fuck you!' *Haven't helped!* What the hell did she think he was doing! He briefly met Regn the afternoon before—he needed a break, someone to confide in—the situation was so stressful. Leaving their home in 72 hours. A mad scramble to get everything out. He'd come back, he'd been moving the contents of their lives nonstop just like the rest of them. Mother, Ellis, Rodger and his Mother, Mrs. Feldone, who'd come down from Staten Island to help and offer emotional support to Gedny.

Westcott launches himself at his sister. The flute crashes to the floor. His arms fly out, contacting her chest. She grips his neck with her hand, goes for his eyes, digging, pressing her nails. She fights mean. He wants to throw her to the ground, he feels it coming, he will be on top of her.

Gedny and Mrs. Feldone watch in animated suspension.

'Knock it off!' A force throws him against the wall. He feels himself lift up and out of his body. Rodger underestimates the brunt of his push. Westcott is a rag doll experiencing the shove between two men. In physical strength he is still a boy. His small frame thuds against the wall. A piece of crown molding protrudes just missing Westcott's spine. A crazed look flares in his eyes. For a moment he is wild in disbelief—the jarring so surprising.

He turns and flees upstairs. Inside he feels alive. The pain is incredible, the impact has him trembling. Part of him would like to feel it again—to be lifted out of his body.

He goes to the farthest reaches of the house. Locks the bathroom door in his mother's room, slips onto his knees, hands on tub.

'You're an ungrateful bastard. You remember that. You're an ungrateful bastard. You remember that. You're an ungrateful bas—.' He scolds himself, stops abruptly, listening to their voices below. His mother's room—he still thinks of it as her room—is located above the garage and her bathroom directly above the kitchen.

'Good. You should have pushed him harder,' Ellis says through clenched teeth. He hears something in the garage then a crunch. Later he discovers she has smashed the nose on the left side of Ol' Reliable's hood and cracked the headlight.

Mrs. Feldone comes up. He hears her searching. Does not answer.

'West? Are you in here? West? Is your back all right? Rodger is sorry. He didn't mean to push you so hard.'

'Yes,' hoping she'll leave.

'You all right?'

'Yes.'

Ellis says he hits like a girl. Yes, he thinks. He can still feel the punches he threw. The rage was strongest, not the fist. And Rodger—for all his gentleness of character, decency of heart, he is physiological male and his forceful push proves it. Westcott will never be a hulk. He doesn't want that kind of power. Nor is he upset at Rodger. Four months. Not even Ellis anticipates she will separate from Rodge. Rodge would marry her in a minute. But Ellis is searching. Always searching and picking up and moving. In time, when Ellis has left Rodge, Westcott will feel akin to him. A brother in understanding, someone who knows what it is to lose someone you love most of all.

· · ·

Journal Entry:
from the Book of West
Friday 23 October 20—

My first night in our new house. I should be happy. It was beautiful this fall evening—in the 70s; and tonight a gentle breeze as we brought stuff into the townhouse. It's two stories. I've only ever lived in two story homes. It has 3 bedrooms, 2.5 baths. I decided on one of the two smaller bedrooms facing the backyard and easement so I can watch the sun set. *The sun setting. Yes. Always the denouement.* I should have been happy today. My mind was enveloped in pain—circling thoughts—anger, sorrow. I wanted to turn to someone; I wanted a friend to tell, someone who could understand. I looked at my mother, considered Ellis and even Rodge. No, I couldn't. I just couldn't. Regn can turn to no one. I feel like the character of Edgar in the book I'm reading, *The Tale of Edgar Sawtelle*. Magda loaned me her copy. I want to say something; on the verge, inside, something stops me and I know I can't tell them. I want to hide; I've become distant even when standing right beside them—life is going on around me. I am apart, trapped in silent brooding. Regn hurt me today. It wasn't anything she said or did, it was what she *didn't* say, didn't do. Our conversation lasted almost until six. She's upset and rightfully concerned about her mammogram report, but her lack of response to my letter and plans for the future—she still has no answers. I failed to gain the upper hand in our argument. I want to say all this out loud—I don't want the silence of it in my head. Who can I tell but these walls? These walls that are new and now my home. Ellis and Rodge went to the store for supplies. Mother is staying at our old neighbor's until we get the furniture and beds set up.

I saw a baby at the post office yesterday while picking up our mail that's being held in the transition. He looked just like Paul McCartney must have—what Regn doesn't want to hear or dislikes, she dismisses, grows quickly defensive. She will not let herself feel guilt where I'm concerned, else how could she live? It could have ended today—I could have ended it. I'm hungry again, didn't eat enough today. After our argument I had to go to O' Grady's and walk/feed him. Here I am, Helmsley's beside me, his chin on my elbow. I can hear Gilly breathing as she rests on her side. What's my father doing at this moment in California? I miss it being good with Regn. It's no longer good. I'm scared when Rodge leaves and then Ellis goes back to N.Y.—when everything's settled down and it's just Mom and I here—

I'm afraid of the walls closing in—the confinement becoming too much again. I wish I could have stayed in the mountains and not returned. Just gone to sleep, not awakened. Mother is on a waiting list for an apartment of her own. I want to get away from everyone and everything, just for a while. For a while.

• • •

Journal Entry:
from the Book of West

The other night, I can't remember which for they all are a puddle of running colors, my mother was heading back to Bob and Patsy's. She asked me to stand at the door, wait while she got to her car. As I watched my mother walk down the narrow strip of path, cane in one hand, legs bending inward at the knees and feet pointed out, I wondered how she came to be so old. Where was the woman I never met but know through stories? The woman who swam with crocodiles in the Everglades. The woman who went rock climbing and shot skeet. The woman who floored it when a cop in unmarked clothes and a plain vehicle came across her hood, pointing a gun at her—a car chase that lasted thirty minutes resulting in an APB being sent out for a supposedly 'stolen' vehicle. The judge gave the rookie cop hell and commended my mother for not stopping on such a lonely stretch of highway for a man out of uniform and with no police tags. The woman who wore stockings and high-heels and could dance all night. The woman who took her team to the Orange Bowl as Captain of the Majorettes.

Her hair rolled and pinned to her head to set, I watched her leave. My mother. A distant sorrow, a subtle echo traced through me. I knew I would tell no one of this—not even Regn. It was an instant reserved only for me.

I showed Ellis a huge spider hanging from a web outside the door—she grabbed a shoe and batted it into the dark, shrieking when she didn't know where it went. I waited and listened as mother's engine started before heading inside.

• • •

Journal Entry:
from the Book of West
Wednesday 28 October 20—

Last evening I let Regn have it—I would bar no words. She was scared. And I felt all right for once. I'd pulled myself together, I had some power. This morning there was a message on my phone. She worked all day—we could have lunch. I was curt and cool. The weather was beautiful—warm, low 70s high 60s, a gentle breeze, everything in fall colors. Ellis decided to take my truck to storage, so I drove her car. I was waiting at Powhatan Creek when Regn's bug drove by into the park. I thought she'd lost her mind—hadn't she remembered what I'd said? I called her as she tried to call me. 'Sharon was walking, I had to drive in—did you see her?' As she said this Sharon was strolling up the right incline taking her lunchtime walk. She looked the same as when we worked together. Khakis and short-sleeved navy blue form-fitting cotton blouse that stuck out a bit with her rear. It was good to see her. I wasn't mad—she had every right to be there. In that moment I realized how lucky it was I hadn't taken my truck. Sharon took no notice of the gold Saturn. I told Regn on the phone to hold and waited 'til Sharon was out of earshot, my window partially cracked. Sharon never looked in my direction—she was lost in her own thoughts. Even when I started the engine she continued on her way. I drove onto the Island. We parked at the first pull off. Regn got out of her bug. She was a wreck, seeing Sharon and then everything that was happening with her and Jay. We started to walk.

'Things are very tense at home.' Regn started talking about herself. I listened. Sensing I didn't want to walk, Regn suggested we sit in Ellis' car. She was upset that *I* was angry. Her defense-mechanism. Fear made her unreasonable, moody, angry. I proceeded cautiously, frustrated by her helplessness and lack of answers, no plan. After a few minutes of trying to defend herself she took my hand. 'Let us come inside each other,' I told her. She unbuckled my belt; I undid my button. She slipped her hand down and between my legs. Over-shooting, searching, feeling, she found entrance. I pulled her close. I should have let her hand rest on me longer—just me—instead I slid inside her slacks and tight underwear, gently pushing for access. A storm, serious and firm impaled us both. Everything let go. All her fear. My anger. Our tension. I bit her neck harder than she expected, held her so tightly my shoulder ached from the strain and awkwardness of being in the car. We'd stop; she'd bend her head down as a car drove by, my arm draped around her as though we were merely talking. She plunged her tongue inside me. I tasted her lips; I could have choked in silent acceptance. I wanted to swallow her. In the end we were left staring at each other, breathing audibly, trembling ever so slightly—my mouth quivering. We looked unraveled. 'Are you all right?' she asked. I didn't answer. 'Smile for me, I love your smile,' she tried. She had on her loose burgundy suit with the white blouse and sleeves she rolls over the cuffs of her jacket. She wore the white ivory rectangular pendant of the dragon necklace. One of her earrings had fallen off—a ping as it hit the consul and disappeared. She wore her boots. She would be late getting back. I didn't say what I needed to—I walked her to her bug—and we hugged outside of it.

'It's not the end,' she said. But somehow inside, for me, I was saying goodbye. A series of goodbyes.

We never found the earring.

NOVEMBER

My first day at the Goodwin Building as an intern found me sitting alone in an office sorting envelopes in silence for five hours.

In time the paid internship will generously be extended from six to ten months. Duties are varied and prove relatively mindless. I feel no pressure which is a relief. Another saving grace is the architecture of the building. The floors are a checkerboard marble with real wooden banisters and green leather chairs. Some of the chairs will be reupholstered with cheap imitation brown leather. There are four floors. The basement, where I stuff envelopes, is called "The Garden Level" because it's small rectangular windows are level with the sidewalk outside. I feed endless papers into an electronic shredder which consistently jams. Sometimes I enter donor gift information into the system database. I prepare packages.

The restrooms are a sight to behold. Green marble floors—beautiful, and black porcelain toilet seats mounted on white commodes. It exudes an air of refinement. I love the brass atomic clocks anchored to the walls on each floor. The antiquity serves as a friend amid the silence of my own thoughts. I can envision what the offices looked like before hard drives and monitors. I look for fountain pens and old banker's lamps, remnants of a not too distant way of life. The fourth floor is called "The Attic." Up there I file stacks of manila folders and perform endless data entry. I do not like working in "The Attic." My favorite floor is the 3rd floor, one above the main entrance. Here is where most of the high paid execs have their offices with large dark sturdy desks. Most of the building is quiet except for the sound of women's high heels, but somehow this floor is exceedingly still. I like to escape to the conference room and look at the painted portraits of all the past Presidents of Colonial Williamsburg. What would Mr. Goodwin think to see how run amuck things have gone?

There is a small closet just off to the side within the room. It is here that the expensive, electronic signature machine is stored. I prefer to sign the president's letters by employing my own penmanship. When there are over 200 generic letters to be signed, stamped, and mailed out, the signature machine becomes excruciatingly tedious. It is far more efficient to sign them manually. I forge the signature as seemly as possible. I am allowed a minimum of 20 hours per week. Eventually I put in 40 hours. There is not nearly enough work to fill 20 hours, let alone 8 ½ hours 5 days a week. Over time I get to know some of the staff; my position makes me readily available to anyone who might require something. Even so, it is lonely. I like to sit in the closet, obscured from the world, and look out the tiny latticed window. The glass is old and has a slightly rippled effect in its firing. I'm sure some of the building materials have lead and especially asbestos down in "The Garden." In months to come I will look out this window and once more ask myself what I'm about and where I am going. I miss Regn. I miss her terribly.

The building is circuitous, meaning there are stairwells on each end of the corridors so you can walk up or down the west side and come up or go down the east side. I can't imagine tinkering my life away in this place. I know I am merely passing through.

I wear a shirt and tie, of my own will, to shred papers, stuff envelopes, and compose poems while on my 1-2 hour lunch break. Sometimes I take long walks through the historic area, sit on a bench and read to fill the hours. What I will remember most about these days is the pain of killing time for the sake of a paycheck. A paycheck I need but don't want. Life is elsewhere. The spool of my youth is being threaded in geriatric pastimes, a heavy blanket of remembering. Longing. Reflecting.

· · ·

I'm sitting in bed at the Fleisch's, watching Mr. O'Grady for the weekend.

The Fleisch's are gone on an antique car show. I have to be up very early tomorrow morning, 5 a.m., just to get to work on time. There are yellowing bruises on my chest where I thrust my fist—did Tarzan ever get so frustrated he wanted to jump out of his skin? I hear the gentle wind outside skimming the leaves. It's been non-stop with the move, work, organizing boxes and storage—no time to think.

> *You're too young to be brooding in your aim—*
> *isn't that the name?*
> *When all that's good has gone away—*
> *And there's nothing left to say.*

I lowered my shirt, ashamed not of the bruises, but that I'd been driven to such lengths.

· · ·

Here he comes across the field. A little panther unknown. I am a wanderer, a traveler in mind.

Helmsley steps into the box. Westcott hunkers down on the porcelain chair.

Honestly, so Alpha. Helmsley gives no never mind, flattening his ears, tail raised at the tip, eyes slitted.

Must you, such a horse.

Helmsley paws around the sodden emulsified crystals having finished. Tending to business. Westcott flushes his own latrine. Two bachelors starting their daily routine. A man and his cat.

Westcott thinks of Elinor. He'd gone to see her last night. He lives even closer to Contradite Health Care since he moved. It seemed strange being there—had he really worked in the place for three months? And now he distantly wishes to be back there again.

How she held him when he bent down to hug her, skin slipping.

'They told me I'd never be able to move my left arm again.' She raised it ever so slightly—twenty years since the stroke. 'Hah,' she cheered, raising her good hand for emphasis—a final triumph.

He'd taken her hand and she'd held it—would have hung on, but he released his, after all he was no relation.

'See you next weekend.' Lunch and an outing.

Stir crazy. He'd come for her.

Elinor. He couldn't tell her he came not for her sake but to escape—himself.

~

The minute the words passed from his mouth, it would fail to come across. Some things were unutterable, ineffable and to speak of such privacies aloud, they transformed into a melodramatic apparition of self. An anticlimax leaving one all the more desolate. There are no words.

Strange how from nowhere except memory, the scent invaded his olfactory senses. Ancient depths unknown. The amygdala stirred with no apparent trigger and her scent returned. Correction. Not just her scent, but the scent of her in the early days. Always a warm scent. So warm and safe. Such rugged grace. The scent ushered forth within himself and the blankness inside flooded momentarily with color—too vibrant to let in but for a slight crack, a fault line in the rigidity of his stone.

• • •

He opens the door, steps into her room. His mother's room. He walks over to the glass case with four shelves—figurines, crystal, books, a collection of glassed wonder. Jack the mouse, birds of a fairytale, castles, music boxes, porcelain likenesses, Cinderella. He would never give it away. Looking at the pieces he lights upon his favorites. He would never give the collection away—

He lies down on the made-up bed with its coverlet, calm in scene alone. Bill, a tactile man he once worked with, comes to him—a memory—something he said. 'Hey, hand-some,' hand on the back and shoulder—too friendly, even around the ladies, hovering in, 'you're one of those birds on the lake—calm up here' he gesticulates, 'but underneath'—*yes, underneath.*

Why is it easier to love her, his mother, when she's not here? What is it in the absence—the expectation of personal effects, a brush on the vanity, clothes on a hook, items so often and gratefully taken for granted—his mother? He was safe from all but himself just lying there—no one could harm him more; no one knew best.

All the noises—hustle and bustle of the city—that's what he knew of New York; crazy, lonely—too much. He was glad to be so far away, *am I?* He was far away in himself—it didn't take being far from a large city. What are they doing in the streets of a German village this evening? He finds it easy to imagine *life*—lives playing out in the places he's been to without having been.

• • •

A strange remembrance.

He'd been sitting in the men's room at the University. Someone had sketched an obscene drawing in black pen. At first he didn't notice, it blended so well with the gray and white marble partition.

Is that so. It was well-proportioned and accurate in detail, but vulgar. A pair of legs spread and darkness between.

He wondered what the black woman must think who routinely cleaned the restroom.

Boys. A good education, parents paying to put them through college, and this is what they do? Maybe she'll pretend she doesn't see it. *You can't beat it out of them,* she shakes her head in disgust.

He doesn't know why, but some time later he was in another bathroom, the corner stall, safe in the drowning privation of thought. Was it boredom? Is this what *they* do? A statement of: I was here? With a black pen, he lightly etched a picture of similar content as the one he'd seen. A little water would take it off. You could hardly notice. He wasn't there to vandalize. Female genitalia. He pulled some paper from the dispenser, tidied up, bumped into the unmottled, bulgeless gristle of his sex. He repositioned the squishy imitation within his briefs, rinsed his hands, dried them as he ran fingers through his hair, pushing the bangs to the side.

What are you?

A woman feels with her mind.

———

ANNA WORKED IN THE CAFÉ AT JAMESTOWN SETTLEMENT. She was foreign, from Russia, maybe. She had brown hair. On days that I did not bring a lunch or just wanted an afternoon snack, I would get in line at the register to pay. Anna would wave me by, or if a coworker of hers was near, she'd ring up the cheapest item. I thanked her and would be on my way. Once, I think I told her, 'I don't want you to get in trouble.' Employees received a discount in the café regardless, but this was personal. An unspoken, unsolicited transaction. I never ate much and I never had to pay for a drink. Even when Anna wasn't working, I'd stroll into the café, as most employees did, grab a small 8 oz. styrofoam cup—the tiniest, fill it with a little soda—non-caffeinated. Anna worked through the summer of 2007. It wasn't until she was gone that I noticed her absence, and even this came a year or two later. I regretted not reciprocating her kindness, never pushing just beyond the bounds of everyday polite exchange. What if it had been her instead of Regn? Anna was probably between 19-22. A little shorter than me. Not small but delicately breasted much like Regn—a B presumably, which I always prefer. I liked her. There were a couple of other girls that year, and I say girls because we were all in the same age range, who passed my way. Each one slipped by and somehow all opportunities ceased altogether once I'd departed Jamestown.

In looking back, that year 2007-2008, was an axis of possibility. I'd already made my decision. Anna was cute, likeable, maybe even loveable, but something in her age kept me at bay. I was too *old* for her. Emotionally. I can't say for sure, but unconsciously I didn't want to hurt her. Maybe I sensed she wouldn't understand. Maybe having her like me without my ever having prompted it, was enough. I didn't want to shatter that genuine affinity. I didn't want to taint her memory of me with the truth. In a way Anna was a younger version of Regn. With her accent and sweet nature. Something in her gestures. Anna was nothing like the Russian exchange students who had stayed with us the summer before. How did I know this? Somehow one could tell. It was nice attracting the attention of a young woman. Maybe I couldn't reciprocate. I didn't know how. I didn't know what to feel. I had yet to confront myself, to embrace the role of masculinity. I was incredibly aged and yet so young all at the same time. I don't even know what her last name was. She is just Anna. She will always be Anna—so easy, so unfinished. So many things.

~

During that same interval of time Regn experienced many new things. She had so much going for her. A new car which she'd proudly bought in her name and was making payments on—the first car she'd ever purchased herself. A lover. She was being recognized personally *and* professionally—being selected employee of the month and becoming a classified salaried employee with state benefits. Things were looking up. She was experiencing the flavor of independence. A cruel flirtation. Everything had been in place, if only she'd reacted, responded. I had been consumed with determination. Regn had been blinded by self-doubt and fear. Her freedom became what Anna *is* to me.

• • •

This is my body. I will someday be gone from it.

He'd glanced at his mother asleep on the sofa. The quiet darkness—no lights turned on to pain the eyes. So tired. She looked peaceful. He wanted to bend down, kiss her good morning on the forehead. He didn't.

He got his lunch ready, finished dressing, took Miss Gilly out. Freezing, exhaustion in his limbs, just wanting to sleep so peacefully, hunker down beneath the warm covers, a body beside. His mother stirred.

'Has she been out? Make sure to put them in the kitchen. Pull the door tight. It sometimes opens when the heat comes on.'

Go back to sleep. Jesus. They're fine. Don't I always take her out?

'I'm not going to have them running around, waking me up.' She means Helmsley and Gilly.

'Why? You're down here!'

'Lock them up!'

It was a quality he disliked. She clung to life, just as she had, or so it seemed, always clung to what she could—unconsciously—as a result of the neglect and psychological abuse she'd experienced throughout childhood. In those days, before the knee surgery, it took her a while to get going; her joints were in constant pain. Every step an effort. As a house settles, and the foundations creak, he felt a tiredness—her tiredness—on top of his already tired disposition, settle into his bones. He was angry for her. Westcott's presence served as an emotional crutch. She didn't see it, she agreed with him perhaps to appease, but actions are the best teller. Sometimes he'd look at her with a side-glance, more like an aside to himself, a self-conversation. He gave her an injection twice a month for the joint discomfort. He'd overcome his aversion to administering injections. No one gave him his injections. He had to do it for himself. Why couldn't she give them to herself? When had this woman ceased to be the breathtaking pin-up in the photo albums of her prime? Where had she disappeared to? A languid voice. Even Regn had competition. Helen's charm had dissipated in the latter half of her marriage. Or most likely, Westcott could not see it because she was his mother. She had always been Gedny to him, not Helen Cray. He did not want to recognize it in her, to search her out. She'd aged well, considering. Others mistook her for being a decade to fifteen years younger than she actually was. She exhibited almost no wrinkles; she'd taken care of her face and always protected it from the sun. Maybe Westcott didn't want to look at his mother objectively. He was still trying to find himself. Gedny had borne him late, too late for either's convenience. He wanted to take her in arms, so many times to go to her, rest a hand on hers, reassure, and let her know a smattering, let her feel that intangible strength he'd received from Regn, if only momentarily, a conductor. A grace he knew but could not hold for himself. Not yet.

While growing up, his mother's car held the pleasant scent of oils from moisturizing creams and in the creases there could be found clean dried skin from her psoriasis. He took this for granted. It had never bothered him, but it cast a fine layer of crust on life. Her favorite perfume was White Shoulders, which Westcott admired. In her late sixties she couldn't find shoes that were attractive and comfortable. So she suffered in the ones that looked nice. Her feet swelled from arthritis. One had an unbearable corn that hurt with any friction. Westcott wryly offered to numb the protrusion and slice it off to save on the ridiculous price quoted by the doctor who wanted to perform the surgery. Gedny wasn't about to walk around in clod-hoppers or shoes that made it look like her feet arrived before she did. She tried the medical "boots" and dismissed them. Black, cushiony shoes designed for practicality and support, not aesthetics. 'All I need now is a pair of oars,' Gedny declared, and into the closet the shoes went only to be worn in the house. Westcott sometimes helped to find her a nice pair of stylish, modern shoes. Gedny had her pride and refinement. She remained attractive, quite so, strangers complimented her, but she had not survived unscathed. She'd gotten by, and her lack of self-love—her constant companion—showed from within. All her energy flung into her children. And it was for this that Westcott some-times resented her—resented circumstances. That she had not loved herself, taken care of herself. What strength was left she used to manage what remained. It would take years before he came to see how hard he'd judged her. Even then, he knew, he was so very much like his mother. Her grace was masked. She could change. And she did. Most people in old age don't. But she did.

And a good morning to you.
    Why couldn't she be still? Why couldn't she listen to him if awake, just lie silently without these ridiculous questions? And at such an ungodly hour!
    Had Gilly been out?! Fucking Christ! Of course! No, I'm just going to get up and not let the dog out, just go off to work while her bladder's full. Have I ever! Why doesn't she think before she asks? Always so impulsive.
    How did it get to this? No use questioning, must have a plan. No one going to help, on your own, *mi* boy. Trapped. The walls were somehow closer; he quickly grabbed his bagged lunch, zipped his jacket and stepped out the door; the cold taking away his breath. Damnably cold. Colder yet. Everyone nestled in their lives. The morning dimness a private show, a silent conversation. The trees dark and moorish; the world a deep blue, still. Tiredness at the corners of his eyes. He shivered inside. Driving the same roads along the untrafficked streets of his pre-masculinized condition. The heaviness was coming, he must out maneuver it—too early, much too early for such devastating introspection. All my life. As alone as ever before. Regn. So much we bear in silence. Truly on our own. Can't a single body do it for you. Keep going. *Contemptible bastard, you are as you chose*—oh please, shut up.

∙ ∙ ∙

Such a beautiful day.
    -What a shame to have to be stuck inside at work.
You don't like your job(s). Mindless tasks.
    -The sun's still shining.
Sophie Scholl's last words on her way to the chopping block.
    -So beautiful today.

I wish I had somewhere to go, someone to talk to.
    -The old mantra.
Yes. The mantra.
    -Amazing how easily we lie to ourselves. And just where would you go?
Don't—please.
    -You'd still be alone. Who'd you go with?

Just couldn't let it be, could you?

    -You wouldn't let me, you know it. She hurt you, didn't she?

Yes. No. She had the effect of making me feel foolish. That hurt. Just wanted a nice walk—I spoiled it.

    -Did you?

I hurt myself.

    -It felt good though. Didn't it?

The push; the soft scraping inside.

    -His gloved index.

Yes. Funny how you can say some things to yourself but the minute they become 'real' words, sounds to the ear, they acquire a new meaning. It can't be spoken.

    -No. But you did want him to stay inside.

It was just a procedure—he's used to it—second nature, all in a day's work.

    -But not for you. No one touches you and not—

You're a masochist. These words.

    -No, you are—they comfort you—these *words* as you so call them. Make love on paper. No one's—

Shut the fuck up. You're relentless.

    -Run, run fast as you can, can't catch me cuz I'm the nowhere man—hah!

I'll kill us both.

    -No you won't. You know 'I' know you won't.

Always something to consider.

    -How was it?

Vulgar.

    -No one to see, I mean no one was there.

Does a body have to be present for it to be—

    -cruel?

Yes, that too. I did feel—lighter.

    -A natural high.

Natural. Still—alone it—

    -My, my, aren't we pious.

I'd rather be held.

    -Ever the woman. My dear boy—

• • •

He wore his sunglasses as though even the trees were someone from whom he had to hide.

"Courage is when you know you're licked before you've even begun but you go ahead anyway." *O' Atticus Finch. Didn't you miss your wife? Those still, hot summer nights must have been awfully painful. But you had your children and your career, a reputation. You kept busy.*

Courage. I wonder about that. Must consider the context, yes, of course. Just foolishness. Not courage here, isn't that it. You're a coward.
    -But not to life. There are two sides to everything.
A coward to death then. Are you suggesting only the weak act against themselves in seeking absolution?
    -I was merely—
Suppose it does take more courage to face life. The familiar accepted, bargained with time and again over the unknown. One of these days though—
    -Gets the best of us all.
Doesn't it though.
    -And what did you think. Did you really believe you could waltz right through and dispel 35 years of marriage—
That's not fair—I—
    -What did you want; it changed and you wanted more, you wanted all.
I—
    -Say it.
I didn't want this.
He looked around.
    -No one's here.
Exactly. Precisely.
    -So soft the tears. "Be a man that way."
"O' Montana Skies," hmm? Can't a body cry?[5]
    -Course he can. Just don't let it show.
No, foolishness to let anyone see. All so foolish.
    -You really think so?
You know it.
    -Ah the spite; the hurt in you is what's talking. Carry on then.
Let someone of lighter spirit take up these pages.
    -And remember so.

• • •

---

[5] "Montana Skies" is a song by John Denver. One of the lyrics is: "Be a man that way."

Poets are fools
some will say.
Are they?

Fools because we dream
or fools because
we refuse
to die?

•••

Regn—

The other day having been put upon, as was mere procedure for any doctor, I couldn't tell anyone or speak the words aloud, that I welcomed being put inside of—that I am woman yet and wish to just be taken and not have to assume the effort of both sides. To know a male's organ. Something you can never give me. An emptiness which I created.

I wish I could feel life tremble within me. To lie there and be loved as was the original design.

Throughout your life responsibilities came with joys and pleasure—interspersed as such. My responsibilities are no such thing. Obligations I was born into and I continue to pay heavily for the need to break away from myself.

The loneliness pervades—a sensation that no solitary vice can ever assuage. To hold and be held—my heart cries in a woman's longing, though my spirit be divided in gender. 'Tis true my body aches for you at times, but it is the warmth of your contact that lightens the heart.

I can never truly penetrate you as a man and thereby feel you inside, but by knowing and sharing the knowledge of what it is you can and do feel, by knowing the woman's self, I feel closer somehow and it is through each other I come to rest inside you—a core knowledge and you upon me.

Wherever I am to go, however far or nearby, long or soon, it is a comfort knowing you will be there, that someone is waiting for me.

•••

Like so many arguments the cause is hard to remember. A few weeks after moving into the townhouse, Westcott snaps. He's standing on the stairwell.

He thrusts his fist against his chest as a man would thrust a woman. Again and again and again. Relishing the perverse pain, spittle flies through clenched teeth. 'I want to die, die, die—'

The hollow impact echoes his rage. Die. *Thud*. Die. *Thud*. Die! The confinement is too much. The uncertainty. The patience! God, he needs a body to hold him down when he gets like this, press him hard, love him until the coldness dissolves. He must feel something! If not affection then its opposite. His frustration reveals itself. Ellis and Gedny sit on the downstairs sofa, watching.

'You're sick. Get help! Or kill yourself.' Ellis responds with disgust.

'West, stop it!' his mother tries.

'I want to die!' He knows the pain is speaking. He is more alive than ever. In that moment he would choose death if only to escape the pain. He runs upstairs, shuts his door, turns the lock.

In the dark he falls to his knees in genuflection at the mercy of himself. The night is cold. Still. He wants to shatter the silence walled up inside his head. He hears Ellis' voice downstairs.

'Kick his ass out. Send him to a clinic. Stop defending him.'

'I'm not. I don't need you attacking me on top of everything.'

'I knew this was a mistake, both of you moving in here. You should have gone your separate ways.'

'I will. I'll be on a list for an apartment as soon as my knee surgery is over with. I'm doing everything I can. It's been a real transition for me. I know you don't care, but losing the house hurt. Those were my roots.'

'Well, you should have planned better.'

'Don't start on me. I can't take anymore!'

Silence.

'You always let him get his way.'

'What way? That's not true. I can see he's hurting. I don't know what to do.'

'That's the problem. Let *him* deal with it. And worry about yourself.'

'I can't do that. He's my child.'

'And I'm not?'

'Of course you are, Ellis. I love you both. Why do you always do this? Haven't I always been there for both of you?'

'Yeah, right.'

'What's that supposed to mean? Just because I'm concerned about him doesn't mean I don't worry about you. I've always wanted the best for you. For *both* my children.'

'But it isn't.'

'Don't walk away from me. Where are you going?'

'I can't wait to get out of here.'

Westcott hears his sister leave. He knows she'll be back. She's just going out to cool off. She *will* be leaving though as soon as Gedny has had time to recoup from her double-knee replacement. Until then emotions will be fraught. Westcott listens to his mother crying. He finds it exasperating. Why does she have to cry? Why can't she be rock solid? It angers him. And Ellis. She'll be gone. Gone.

Westcott stops listening. Stares at the cool night. The slightest thought of a warm body holding him, just feeling his back and torso—a calm hand running fingers through his hair—sends a jolt of ice through his body. Why torture himself? No one is there. Not in the way he needs—the silent, knowing way. In the quiet, in the dark, with only the moon and the large oak outside his window, he cries. All the wasted grief. And yet, the frustration must be released somehow.

He hears Helmsley treading up the wooden stairs. In a minute he'll be at the door. Westcott moves through the blue darkness, unlocks the door, opens it a sliver so Helmsley can slip in. He jumps on the bed, fur illuminated in the moonlight. He sits at perfect attention. Westcott kneels again. He knows that to fall into bed means the floodgates will open. Helmsley is not *just* a cat. Westcott has always known this is not Helmsley's first incarnation. There are cats and then those animals with something more, a consciousness of watching and knowing, a sage-like presence. Always sentient, Helmsley arcs his neck downward. Westcott bows his head. Their foreheads touch. A meeting of the minds.

DECEMBER

The night was rarely clear, so cool and still. The stars distinct; they were away from the city energy and light. They'd gone to Sharon's Christmas party.

From his post upon the wooden stool he watched. His velvet blazer was warm. To take it off and turn, turn, turn. A short distance, so slight. Why couldn't she have friends like this? She—his mother. He was sad again.

Regn danced alone, lost to herself amidst the House of the Rising Sun. In that moment, seeing her there alone, she did not need him as he did her, nor would she ever. For those few minutes she showed the joy of having oneself absolutely. It was just her and the music and the year of once was. He admired her for it. Watching her sweep alive in a solitary moment of self. Her solitude—a solitude he was too human not to envy—holding himself in contempt not only for the envy but the freedom he withheld from himself—a peace within he could not sustain alone. An empress of the forest; queen of the gypsies. She wore herself as though swept up in the rhythms of some Indian song unknown.

An anger overcame him. An anger at seeing her so content but for a passing sigh, and all she sacrificed. He wanted her to live—to taste the grandeur of first times always. So much was alive inside, quietly kept in a box—and he raged for the injustice, the absolute self-denial. The girl she'd been danced before him, still teetering between young and old. There was so much—so much—what was it—untapped life inside! All the years of what she was not allowed to be and there she was as though her form had simply expanded, not in physicality, but being. One encapsulated the other–an Egyptian sarcophagus–her true self preserved within—a Russian Matryoshka. He could not forgive her such selflessness.

~

He stood in just his briefs; the much too small protrusion removed itself when the gray cotton shield fell down. He stood utterly natural, and stepping up, came gently over her. With limbs intertwined and feeling the bareness of his own skin, his *shaftless* hearth pressed against her thigh—two women.

'Is that weird?' he whispered.

'No,' she answered softly.

He moved slowly down her length, coming inside the only way he could. Her woman's part was fastidiously trimmed, a light dusting next to his thickness and darkened hollow. He felt her body as if to examine every nuance. Flicking the clitoris with his tongue, sliding down, he slipped inside. Like his conch shell, just under his desk, were he to lift it to his mouth, viewing its apex of conispirals, her body offered itself to him.

He gently moved his head upward, nuzzling the softness of her face, finding his twin

with whom he danced a smooth slide-and-draw as soundlessly—breathway to breathway—
they gave voice to the perfect anguish while the winds of beseeched stardom found
themselves momentarily stirless, merciful.

~

He looked at her breasts while she held her bra in suspended motion, before they
would forever be lost to him. They drooped lovingly in age, ever so. 'They're just tits!' she
joked. He didn't like that word, but he did not tell her this.

Standing, she studied him. 'You look like you're in pain.' Dressed, they sat side-by-side
on the edge of his bed. She said, 'I saw you.'
'And—'
'And—you just don't have a willy.'
'I do.' He made to softly smile, glancing to the tan penis flumped on the floor. 'In short
order.'
'I love you.'
'I know.'
'Merry Christmas.'
'Merry Christmas, Regn. No regrets?'
'No regrets.'

He'd walked with her out into the freezing night in just his t-shirt and white dress shirt.
'Thank you, meine Dame.'
'Bitte schön. No regrets.'

He bent his head down, kissed her forehead. He walked back to the street lamp and the
path up to his door. Though he could not see her, he waved in the light of the street lamp.

• • •

In hindsight it was but a brief interval in his life, like so many things. He had cherished
it with every fiber, tried so hard to hold on, and now he wished he'd just been able to lightly
enjoy it. Not a second did he take for granted, loving and hating it all in one, apathetic to
the stagnancy, fearing change—whatever that would be. And when he could not, or rather
would not take action, it found its own way and an answer had been made for him.
He lay in bed, not wanting to move, but just lay there and consider.
Cuts were made, an informal resignation. Regn's full-time classified position dissolved
and feeling they at least owed her consolation, she was given part-time status in a separate
department.
Did he miss the work? No, not at all. His friends though—is that what they were—his
friends he missed, and of course the proximity of Regn.
All the places he thought to go. How nice to just cast himself to the wind.
*Be damned if I'm going to sit staring at 'mi' mug in Ireland and an empty chair across the way. No
point to it in going alone.*
Was it true, he wasn't proud of his parents? No, he was saddened. Both had worked
hard their whole lives, only to be unsettled. It pained him to think of Regn—her 'traditional'

situation. Both children reasonably happy *and* independently successful. Their jobs were by no means grand; there existed nothing extraordinary or exciting in their professions, but if they were content and didn't have to worry about their parents wasn't that enough? For some maybe. But not Westcott. He teetered between wanting the simple life and the exceptional one. The latter came with a slew of complexities. It became evident that his course was predestined. Regn's children were a reflection of her and Jay's good, but plain lifestyle. None of them had fulfilled their calling, if at any time they had actually known what it was. Jay loved history and Regn wanted to be a ballerina. As for their son and daughter, their jobs were replaceable. It seemed a tragedy and horror how few people identified and mastered what they were intended to do. The "perception" of life so often chained one's mind to the notion of "what is" as opposed to "what could be." Westcott was not at peace to *just* fill a job he was good at—something inside him would not be ignored. To turn away and attempt to live lightly, as he had tried on more than one occasion, was death to his soul. He knew he'd be wasting his life. He often imagined himself on his deathbed considering the paramount questions. Above all, he needed to be able to say, beyond a shadow of doubt, that he had never betrayed his own heart. He'd seen too many hopes in others pushed aside—shelved—until the gaze of longing settled upon a certain cabinet or chest long avoided. The minute one's eyes reviewed the contents of forgotten dreams, the soul would impale itself upon the dagger of regret, while the body continued to distract itself, finding "things" to do, to keep busy until—. To Westcott, *this* was madness. Regardless of age, passion needed to burn its host alive. Ashes to ashes, dust to dust—the earth enveloped by the sun.

Passion wasn't waiting for the next train to come when the last one had just pulled away. Passion was running ahead, inertia, chasing the urgency, running to meet "chance" at the next stop. With Regn, Westcott's body had matched his mind—he'd have run miles to meet her. But lately, his passion had been clamped; he was running the length of his mind arriving back at the same place.

As for his mother, she had no one to fall back on but himself. Ellis *had* had Rodge, but lost him by choice. Their father had remarried. And who did he, Westcott, have but a silent wall, a half-hearted prayer to turn to—his mother miles away, only a few feet from his caged sanctuary? He wanted to run, starve if need be, if only to live and be alive. Not be alive in slowly dying. But live *in* the feeling of being alive. He'd endure hunger and cold.

He imagined being undressed in the dead of winter. A bright day when the sun reflected from the packed powder and the air was crisply still. His bare back on the icy compact. His head at the base of a tree, staring up its narrow trunk—a pole to the skies and further still. A place that once was true but now known only in dream. Bared to the world, the hair stood on its end—his arms, his thighs, even the thick ground cover of his sex—so dark, darker more with the striking white, frightening even to his own eyes—bewitching in a forgotten way. A body pressed upon him; his shoulders forming an indentation. The warmth of this body sent a chill through his length. Her breasts touched upon him; he held her to his own breast. And then a hand between his legs and the body gently spreading them apart. A trickle of melted snow. The tree's root unearthed itself, cold and raw. It coursed, grew and extended in thirst. Barely inside, a traveler just handing his cloak and hat to the doorman, the interior walls began to breathe and the hallway became its own living entity. Her form expanded and contracted, beckoning the visitor, inviting her further within recesses of 'her'self. She somehow bore a penis, this forest gypsy. And he with the smooth butter chest showed no such instrument. The piece pushed inside. She held him down, smoothed the fallen hair on his forehead. Both arms pinioned by his ears. She lifted herself; the stone partially dislodged. Her eagle's talons grasped firm, a concentrated compassion, merciful. Each met the other's gaze. She waited as if to give him time. And with a sorcerer's glide she swooped down in one graceful move. Soared inside. He trembled, holding her tight, a burning freedom, a pleasant pain. He cried so. Not a sound could be heard as she enveloped his mouth, withdrawing the sorrow. A morsel of wetness in his corner eye, brimming and sliding to the ground, crystallized.

His head lulled to the side and dropped away.

He awoke; the room an echo of cold exhale. The winter firm in its grasp of the morning tree just outside his window. And now the pain inside thudded him, silently, the weight of many stones.

• • •

The woman turned with him.
He had never before danced.
Holding herself in his hands her
skin stirred. Until now she had ceased
to remember such a calm moment.

Back at the table he watched with discretion—
the woman discreetly handkerchief the corner
of her eyes.
He'd felt in her hold and that far away look—
someone—*something* in her still believed
in the expectations of long ago hopes.
He read it in her gaze—*it was her first time also.*

No one had ever *quite* found her stride.

MARCH

Jumping ahead. Strange things come to me from nowhere, a remembrance. Today—this evening is beautiful—it could hurt if I allowed it to—we left our other home five months ago.

Is it lofty arrogance or pure madness? No, it's what I am—life itself, a temporary condition, and even I must go. There is time and never time, no age but now.

I rode my bike. The scent of daffodils and the warmth of the approaching rain.

I gave up drinking caffeine—Pepsi and Coke altogether. On occasion I'll drink it if it's caffeine free or I may have a single sip if mother orders one, but for no rhyme or reason, I gave it up. I remember this occurring around that Christmas. The Christmas Regn and I danced at the Foundation holiday party. I no longer wanted to drink it. Soda adds weight, it really does, and caffeine. It was not a conscious decision; I just stopped. It was a drug and I didn't want it. Maybe it had to do with the testosterone injections. I don't know. Correlation—cause and effect is difficult to establish.

I recall the mornings and afternoons, should we be fortunate to both be assigned the main desk. Regn and myself, all day, working side-by-side. I got used to switching out the staplers, giving her the lighter modern one and taking the heavy metal Swingline. The weight hurt the effects of carpal tunnel in her wrists.

We'd give snacks to one another—she always liked her pieces of chocolate, as did we all.

I held off going, went after the ending parade of colors—every March the Foundation hosts *Military Through the Ages*, a weekend-long program filled with costumed reenactors. I walked into the restroom at the end of the Great Hall. Used it as a tourist would. Searching for some other part of me I left there. The times I'd waited in the restroom—longing and dreading those agonizing last minutes we'd have in the lobby before 'our' time was up for the day. There was no reason for me to hide and yet I wore my sunglasses and tweed cap. I felt an unspoken admission exhibited itself in my being there—to anyone who knew me. I'd shown too much that last year I worked in Visitor Services.

Regn had said I should stop by. We'd spoken the day before on the telephone. She was behind the main desk when I walked into the lobby. Like old times. What had changed? Millicent sat beside her. Rawlings locked up, even Mary was there—I asked polite questions, tried to equally distribute my attention to all present. But I fear I ignored her too obviously.

565

Eva was there, too. 'Well we're just getting everyone today.' Regn told me Jay had stopped by earlier. Obviously Eva had seen him and cordially offered her remark. Being there, I knew I could never go back, never work there again. I didn't want to—I had never enjoyed the work—it was my colleagues whom I enjoyed—the jokes, the camaraderie, the routine, and good welcome—

I have a picture of Regn taken that Anniversary Weekend a few years before. She looks lighter somehow—younger even? Or was it that I didn't know her then—the woman in 'that' particular picture was still untouchable? I remember imagining what she felt like, having never placed a hand, never really hugged. There is a lightness in her face in that picture, and I wonder—did I kill something inside her? Was our love so powerful, our passion so strong that it made her old? Yes. And yes. I know this because the same thing happened to me.

The evenings we'd all walk out together, side-by-side or sometimes just Regn and I— her keys clanking against her water bottle sounding like a cow's bell. The sun setting on the river, deliberately ignoring the eyes of security behind the camera. We walked harmlessly and yet speculation lay in any faltering or lingering step. We risked, trusted in the power of our affection to protect, and in the end, I was but the young boy to them, and she, she the woman who had misguided me and finally come to her senses. That's how *they* saw it. The truth I carry is more. Oh I was young, young in being afraid. How I'd suffered months to utter a single compliment. 'Those pants look nice on you.' I'd meant it. 'Thank you,' she'd said genuinely appreciative. And then months later—I'd sneaked up on her in the rotunda to relieve her so she could go to the lobby. The Christmas video was playing. I'd come right up on her and gently, cautiously, placed my left hand on her left shoulder. As she turned I strug- gled to stifle a smile of awkwardness—which she detected and I felt annoyed with myself.

Seeing her when we'd return from lunch, watching from my register across the way, her chest lightly heave as she stood behind the main desk one hand on her farmer's tanned breast, looking out the window, looking out but in essence lost within. Tempering. And I knew what she felt. The way her hand rested on her breastbone, a woman of grace and the unspoken desire. The energy of her respiration and the love therein, reserved passion and the very pulse of life in its restraint. That was her love. That is what I loved most. A true lady. And the grace to hold me inside.

———

"The Bloke"

"Thine"
20—

Helen Cray "Gedny" 1975

Where have you been for so long?

Never knowing, never caring,
just being.

Being so free and always running
from what you are.

How beautiful the realization of your existence
and what it is meant to be.

How quieting to find you made it through the revolving door
and met yourself on the other side.

It's so good to see you.

CHAPTER 7

STRANGE BREED OF HOPE

'**R**EPEAT TO YOURSELF OUT LOUD, *I will lose them.*'
'I will lose them. I will lose them. I will lose them.'
'Say the first thing that comes to mind.'
'The sky is blue.'
'What do you see?'
'Gray.'
'Where are you?'
'Outside. Everyone's gone.'
'What do you feel?'
'Empty.'
'Where do you feel this emptiness?'
'In my stomach and chest.'
'What are you wearing?'
'Just pants and a shirt. Brown shoes.'
'Do you wear a hat?'
'No.' The part of him that remains conscious and analytical knows this question is meant to determine if he *was* a Nazi soldier.
'Do you hear anything?'
'It is quiet. As though a leaving has occurred.'
'Where are you?'
'I'm standing on the road, looking right and left. I need to go.'
'Go where?'
'To find them.'
'Who?'
'My family.'
'Are you married? Do you have children?'
'My wife is gone.' She is Regn, before Regn exists.

569

Wife. The word hurts.
'What has happened?'
'I don't know.'
'Did you know this was going to happen? Did you plan to be away?'
'No.'
'What does it feel like to lose them?'
'Like nothing else. Like being punched in the back. Having the life thrust out of me.'
'Can you move forward in time? Where are you now?'
'In a flat.'
'How much time has passed?'
'A couple of years.'
'Did you find out what happened?'
'No. I am alone.'
'What do you see?'
'People in the street. Happy, going about their ways. I feel detached. How can they just go on as though nothing happened? I don't talk about it. I don't want to spoil their contentment.'
'Do you hear anything?'
'Just city noises.'
'How do you get out of here?'
Silence.
'Where are you? How did you leave this life?'
'I died.'
'How?'
Silence.
'What do you see?'
'I'm sitting on the floor in the bathroom. A tile floor.'
'Why are you sitting?'
'It's something I would never do.'
'What is?'
'I'm going to cut my wrists.'
'Is there anyone else there?'
'No. I am alone. I'm not afraid to die. It will be a relief.'
'What is the last thing you see?'
'The sunlight on the floor.' A wooden floor.
'Can you leave this place now?'
'I can try.'
'Do you see yourself?'
'Yes.'
'What have you learned from this life?'
'Pain.'
'Can you leave the pain behind?'
'I don't know.'
'Can you see your wife now that you've left your body? Does she tell you what happened?'
'She was taken. It was a quick death.'
'How?'

He knows but doesn't tell the woman beside him.

'What does she say to you?'
'She says it's not my fault.'
'Can you move on knowing she is with you?'
'I don't know.'
'Try.'
Silence.
'What does it feel like?'
'Free.'
'Can you move ahead to a different life?'
'Yes.'
'Why do you think these themes followed you into this life? What are you meant to learn from Regn this time that you didn't in the past?'
'Punishment.'
'For what?'
'Killing myself.'
'I'll let you in on a big secret. There is no punishment for suicide. That's a social construct. You will have to go through the same issues though if you take your life.'
'I know that. It's *me* who does the punishing.'
'Why?'
'I can't forgive myself.'
'Why can't you let go of that life?'
'We loved each other. It ended too soon. Before our time.'

Conscious of the woman beside him asking questions, Westcott restrains the tears. He doesn't want her to see him cry behind his sunglasses. He is reclined in a wingback chair with a blanket over him. This woman whom he's known for just an hour sits perched on a chair less than a foot away, free to study him, listen. It makes him uncomfortable. Vulnerable. He keeps his eyes closed. Thankful for his dark sunglasses. Before commencing the regression they'd talked for an hour about his current life history. She is a little older than Regn and has been doing this for over 25 years. She began working as a young woman, beside the pioneers of Past Life Regression. Every case is different.

Before they begin, she suggests he use the restroom. It is better not to interrupt the mood. He has to go, but there is no way he can. Her house is so still. So quiet. On the 3rd floor, the blue room where they sit is like a doll's room. Energy impregnating the walls. At one point during their discussion, prior to the regression, she'd asked him a question. About to respond, clouds moved over the sun. 'There's your answer.' The room dimmed gloomily—visually exhaling—before inhaling to a lighter state. It felt prophetic.

She's too close for him to use the privy just next store. She goes to the bathroom. He hears her water. Listens without meaning to as she gathers toilet paper. He even hears her wipe herself. The intimacy of a stranger. Now he knows he cannot use the bathroom. He listens as she washes her hands in the sink.

She returns. They begin.

Halfway through, his bladder wants to burst. He is too stiff to move, does not want to leave the past behind. He feels his body in the present, while his mind drifts; the sound of the woman's voice beside him is a clear bell.

When he comes out of his trance-like state, privacy or no privacy, Westcott *must* use the privy, immediately.

Coming back, the woman holds his rawhide tan jacket with the fleece collar. She has gathered his belongings—his notepad, snack of almonds, and sunglasses.

'My god, this is a heavy coat. What do you have in it?'

'Rocks.'

'To keep you grounded?'

'No. In case I decide to pull a Virginia Woolf.' He smiles morbidly. Utterly sarcastic. He would never—not that way.

In leaving, Westcott shakes her hand. The hand that wiped herself in that private place. He feels he knows her in more ways than one.

He is incredibly disappointed. The session opened a cavern.

Later, through email, he tells her the experience was toxic. Initially. She answers, 'I've never had a client use the term "toxic" to describe a session. In most cases the feelings I have quickly leave me, but with you they lingered.' She felt his pain and could not shake it.

The sense of loss is so firmly planted within him. She could not penetrate it. He'd come for answers, a shred of solace. He left only with affirmation of the cause of his suffering. The past followed him into this life.

*

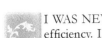 I WAS NEVER ONE WHO LIKED to be in a rush. I enjoy order in terms of efficiency. I believe punctuality is a form of respect as well as composure. I can't stand individuals who have things all the time falling out of their purse or bag, are looking for something, doing five things at once—a whirlwind of chaos. In carrying a single grocery bag out from the store, I am glad that my truck is a relic without automatic doors. I am glad that I am not spoiled and lazy thanks to instant gratification. I take pleasure in fingering the right key, putting it in the lock and manually turning it—I have control—not some gadget, no battery required. One bag of groceries is sufficient. I am amused when cars speed by and race to the light that has just turned red. I ease up about 10 or 15 seconds later, my accelerator keeping an easy pace, no grinding, touch and go, rush to get there. That's not to say there aren't times when I've been running late and need to amp it up, even so, in those moments, I am conscious of not wanting to run around like a chicken with its head cut off. That image always seemed hysterical, but in truth terrifying. Chickens really do continue to run after their heads have been chopped off. Life is fragile, and yet, humans, despite their frail stature, are resilient, multiply, crop up, take over, stake their claim. I find it pompous. I never wanted to control my environment, I knew it wasn't possible. I just wanted to live decently, productively, efficiently, contentedly. A full tank of petrol, groceries in the refrigerator, and a landline telephone were private victories. I would never succumb to the race.

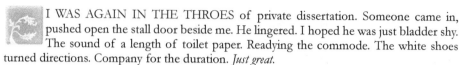 I WAS AGAIN IN THE THROES of private dissertation. Someone came in, pushed open the stall door beside me. He lingered. I hoped he was just bladder shy. The sound of a length of toilet paper. Readying the commode. The white shoes turned directions. Company for the duration. *Just great.*

I hesitated to turn my head should the least sound of movement—even the sinews of muscular pivoting—illicit the slightest detection.

We all do it. *The strains like me*, I wondered of my mate with the white shoes? I raised my index finger to my lips. The universal sign of silence to be observed; a precautionary. I looked at my blurred reflection on the black door. A skinny gent, receding hair, oily and disheveled for the moment—a free spirit was once the remark—a madman; eccentric artist she had said. I waited. And when I thought for sure due course had passed, I waited some more with bated breath for the tick-clack of the dispenser. Mr. Whitesole was quick to tidy up the nethers and with a flush the excruciating silence became peacefully undisturbed.

I returned to the business at hand. My business. Sometimes it would just come, naturally, but this morning it had to be coaxed. Guess it will have to be to the rocking horse. So forward and backward I hunched my torso, the force on the backward draw pushing down on the sphincter, compressing the waste into lifeless muddied mermaids, birthed to drown and be consumed within the black throat. Sometimes loose and spry, the mermaids streaked the sea, other hours their scales were belligerent, apathetic, and rebellious. The feeling of a complete bowel movement was almost holy. The things one overlooks.

DECEMBER

They had been in their new home a little more than a month. He was working two jobs: his paid internship with Colonial Williamsburg and as a concierge at a local timeshare.

Can you not feel the place from which it came? When you hear the music, do you nature see—a winter branch, the prairie grass, a distant shoreline, the mountains, a sparrow on the wing?

- You live on the crest.

It's fuckin' cold. Hey, Hud, how you doing? The plastic dog head wobbles. He's sitting in his truck, driving to work, some godawful hour so he can arrive to the lobby desk by 7:30 a.m.

I wasn't going to sit in a room and talk about it. He looks out his window to the east. *You and I.*

Living a lie. When they look at me. Yes, so do I.

- You want the freedom of—the young—

No—it's more than that—you damn well know it.

- What then—it's—
  that crest you live on—

You're right there beside me, don't forget.

- There are moments of—
  passion—

Yes—the very breath of life—it's what I am—

- You can't exist in a prolonged height—no one can—that's why you—funny the way you won't let the sun on your face.

You know why—it might cause pigment marks, skin blemishes.

- Well, if you were to look at it from the standpoint of symbolism.

Please.

- What haunted pallor—

I love natural light; how little time we had to bask in it.

- Cold, isn't it? Always just about.

Not about. *Within*—

- Don't give me semantics.

What gives warmth?
Peace.

- Like a dove.

Soft, gentle; in the breast pocket—safe—

- Such as a magician's act?

No act—

- Not as it would appear though—

No, nothing is at all what it seems.

- The great enigma.

Songs of—
Can't we just stay on subject?

- Listen—you know she's there—always in your mind.

But *they* don't and if you press just so with your arm—
shed the heavy coat of protection—let someone in.

What are you?

- Put it away—

That's just it—I can't. It never goes away. *You* never leave me.

He skips the third step on his way upstairs.

HE IS STANDING in the kitchen, looking into the night and the darkness of his surroundings. He thinks of his family. What he will say in the note. Ellis' birthday is coming up—how unfair to spoil it—cruel. Regn would hate him at first. His mother would blame—Regn. He steps into the dining room, hands on the shoulder wood of a chair, lights only from the lamppost squinting through the folded blinds. Never coming in the front door again. This is it. He missed himself, imagining leaving all behind and they would have to pick up—make sense of the pieces. *I'm too arrogant. You selfish son of a bitch. You were right, all right. No Regn, I'm not a good person.* All quiet, his mother upstairs. Alone in the frozen kitchen, the clock on the Emerson microwave, recently bought, 10:34. To be gone, game over, that's it, no more—*you selfish ungrateful bastard.* The tears fall silently, gently squeezed from a bottomless well. Shouldn't have called Ellis. Mother for sure hates me—no, she hates what I've become. Has every right to—*you selfish son of a bitch; horrible person, only think of yourself.*

He thrusts his fist against his chest—again, and again and again—the thoracic cavity— a hollow thud echoing the inaudible thud of his life's drum. A momentary wisp of spittle seethes through clenched teeth. There is no register of discomfort after the first wrap. After the eleventh he stops, his whole body shaking in a pantomime of yelling. His pulse continues amplified by the sudden stillness. 'You make yourself miserable.' The words stab him for everything Regn ever said was true. *You foolish bastard, such a fool. You deserve whatever happens to you. I blame myself entirely, for everything—no one else. I am.*

~

He read in his psychology textbook years before that statistics show most suicides occur in the spring. He has his own theory of explanation. Winter is predictable, what one would suppose to be a normal, likely choice. After all, it is the season of farewell, the world closes up, death among the branches, coldness in the air, gray skies, wet vicious days and short hours of light. Hibernation. That's what it does.

It hibernates until spring thaw and when the hope of the warm sunny days and long evenings—the sight of blossoms rejoicing in silent maturity—mocks unmercifully, then it seems the right time. Spring fever, the joy of it everywhere slaps the face flaunting in the eyes of your discontent. And so another signs away his life. A life for a number. A faceless, singular data amassed in a textbook.

In taking an Abnormal Behavior psych course, the professor once asked, 'How are you doing so well on my tests? I design them to be tricky.'

Yes, trap doors, ambiguity, correct answers, but not the right answer. The key was knowing the best of the right answers. A matter of weeding.

He seldom read the assigned pages for the week. He'd wait until a week before an exam. Take each chapter and begin the process of familiarizing. He liked studying.

Why, the answer's in front if you. Just have to pick the right one. It all makes perfect sense. There's only one true answer! So I answered the questions 'you' devised.

Mary, Mother of God, why are we here? Wait, you're the mother of the son of God. See how easily words change who we are. Who *are* you? I know your face from what the world has painted you, but who are you really? *Whoa there, come up—come down for some air.*

I WANT TO REST out in the day, take a walk, anything in the fresh air. My eyes hurt. From typing.

Do I miss my breasts? Sometimes I feel they moved inwards, pushed inside and grew, pressing my very being from the other side. I am glad they're gone though, tangibly. But the sensation lingers. I never felt myself. In touching Regn, in knowing precisely how to knead her breasts, it became an extension of me, in some strange way I could feel myself through her. The complacency of this job puts me in a malaise and I feel nothing. I feel dead and I am afraid. I write this to be calm, let it flow from me, flow down and out, else drown in the weight. It is insanity—the society to which I was born. I want to walk amongst the trees and converse. To run right now, run so fast. Where to?

Alone at this station.

HE LIES IN BED, thankful for the solitude. Miserable for the privacy. The warm flame melts; a calm emulsion, he lets it come. Happy for the voice of his sister downstairs. Saddened that he cannot turn to them who fill this house with him. The Christmas party mother held for her colleagues was fun, but now the quiet; the comfort of his own thoughts, free to give way, without facing himself.

Morning.

The painting; sketch. How perfectly symmetrical, unintentional how that worked. He'd just hung it on the wall in proportion to the other picture and the furniture, but here, from this angle it presents itself aptly placed. A faceless Eskimo, a Native American, squatting in ritual dance. An eagle swooping in and down. Caption: *Renewing his strength*. Gift from Jackie Moss. His teacher. Jackie. Now there was a tragic end. He looks at the drawing. *I need a real medicine man, a shaman.*

What happened to me? Or rather just, what happened?

Was it possible to miss something even in its *abhorration*? The sensation still lived where *they* once had been and in the touch of her, in every knead of her delicate breasts, he knew the faceless current of emotion. In touching Regn, he'd felt the touch through himself.

I am neither man nor woman.

And that's how it will always be—what they saw and what they didn't see of me. The injustice of never being known.

It was a dream, so soon a dream. Having waited so long it ceased to be real when at last it came. Had he not imagined it so long—loving in mind alone, a caress of pen to page, key to tap, and the silent rustle of lone wind. To the post and back he walks—junk mail, bills.

It's a terrifying thing coming face to face with yourself—who you are. Very few people ever do—the image of who they want others to believe they are becomes them—the things around them. But strip those away and—

Am I long for this world, this time, this place?

-    That's right. Question to your heart's content.

You mean discontent—

-    Yes, of course.

The only answer is the one that comforts.

-    Go easy on us—

I will go.

I sometimes miss being a woman.
Not that I'd *want* to be seen out in public as one.

-    Why are you looking that up—

Be quiet. You know why, stop nagging.

-    You crazy?

If I am then you're damn well, too!

-    You'd actually make an appointment and go to one—

Yes, just so's to be touched. Annihilated.

-    Ah the shame—the truth untold.

Yes a gynecologist.
There. I said it. Now are you pleased?!

-    No, my boy. It's ridiculous.

I know. Just upset is all.

-    I know.

Forgive me?

-    You know I won't.

Nor I.

IN THOSE DAYS, a year after being laid off from The Jamestown Yorktown Foundation, when I'd go into work (wherever that happened to be), or rather just before going into work, along my drive I'd try to hold onto the music to keep it in me to get through the shift. I wondered about Sophie Scholl. Would I be able to make such a sacrifice? It would hurt. But sometimes I would think it was the only way for peace. To lie down in the soft leaves and become them—my Being but a mere passing of sentimental thought. I engendered hurt. The anger was winning and I was only angered further by my own anger. It wasn't something that had passed and could be reasoned into peace. Standing in Target, somehow, it seemed smaller, the registers and check-out lines. I looked at the items of clothing on my way to buy cat mix. A little girl's sweater. A sadness distanced me from all those shopping. It would be nice to buy that sweater—a family, a niece, daughter, cousin—life, someone to share it with, to laugh with, anything. It was easier for Regn in that way.

What's to become of me? It's a part of who I am—every day and that is something she will never know. I took it all, took the years and a place to belong, traded one lie for another.

———

Did you think you could rewrite history? It was the way then, back in Regn's era, and to see it in the girls' eyes today—how romantic they say to each other—making it all those years together. I can't tell them what they must find out for themselves, that it is an ideal society—man—developed long ago. Even ideals are flawed. Quality not quantity. The girls are so much younger at twenty today than when Regn had grown up. So young. Too young. She'd never had the confidence. All the years.

I wish I could tell someone—who, who, who?
    -What are you an owl?
Yes, something like that. Ah but it doesn't matter. The walls will listen, that tree out there, the child laughing in the aisle. And all are mocking because their insensitivity ignores. It feels so good to be alone—no one can hurt me—I take care of that myself.
    -I'll be fine and if anyone asks we're happy as pie, remember.
Don't talk to me anymore. Fuck you again for all the lies. Just leave me be. You foolish boy, man, woman, thing.
    -That's what *you* are. I'm just a phantom—the endless ribbon inside you.
Like everything else. Reality is action. I don't believe in anything you say anymore.
    -One day it will all be over, settled, done, spent.
Yes.
    -So isn't there relief in that?
Yes. The finite solution. Absolute epilogue. Complete freedom. Such a strange breed of hope. Death. And in the meantime?

IN JANUARY, after their all too brief physical intimacy a month before, Regn's grand-children are born. She has two new granddaughters. It is her son's second child and her daughter's first. Little by little, over the next two years, Regn retreats, pushes Westcott away, wants nothing to do with him. And then, all of a sudden she is old.

• • •

Journal Entry:
from the Book of West
Saturday January Twenty Hundred and—

Regn spoke, most, how should I say, 'intimately' of her view on her daughter. Her second grandchild was born yesterday. Thursday Regn had gone to help Dee clean her house. The way she confided to me—as though she were telling a friend—a woman. She said she needed to talk to someone and there was no one she could tell *these* things to—she was clearly upset. 'There was this sting,' she explained, 'when Magda told me she was going away for 3 months. I was jealous of her and then I felt bad. I can't talk to her. There were times when I looked at my daughter and saw a puppy dog expression in her eyes as she looked at her husband. Ah, girl—' she shook her head. 'I almost envied her—she'll see, give it some more years. I just want her to be her own person.'

In that moment I realized how truly resentful Regn is of herself and the degree of regret for never being on her own. It was quiet and the sun brightly shone. We placed our foreheads together. 'Take the heaviness from me,' I said. 'Here,' she joked, 'take my vibes.' She put her hand to my skull. But she was tired, inside. And then it was time to go. So peaceful there; if I was sad I was too struck by Regn's openness. The complexity of the woman sitting beside me stunned. A split second glimpse of the side she hides so well—those two words 'ah, girl' —a heaviness of regret; the weight of what she carries. She turned to me—and I was glad to listen—never did I feel her love more, so indirectly.

• • •

He opens the pantry door, grasps for the pull chain. A light bulb without a globe comes on. He reminds himself later that he's become accustomed to light bulbs without a glass fixture to surround them. A striped creature slips from the lowest shelf, stretches, and hops down from her nest within a cardboard box storing odds and ends—remnants of the move.

Westcott lifts the item he'd wanted off the shelf, shuts the door. He scoops Thistlelonius into his arms. Her fur stands on end, the winter air abundant with static electricity. Her hind legs dangle like rabbits' feet. She is soft, yet rugged, a soldier in the outdoors. She merely comes and goes for room and board. Their outdoor cat. He kisses her flat head. Her ears scowl. He slides the back door open, nudges her with his foot. Into the evening she goes. She sits on the cool cement, curled and waiting. He has just returned home from visiting his mother in the hospital.

Westcott is standing. He looks at her in the hospital bed. Wishes he was there in place of her. For the wrong reasons. Both legs are wrapped. Her hair is damp with pained perspiration. He imagines being sick, so sick the only thing he could think about would be the discomfort. Slipping in and out from the pain. Free to think and be flooded. The way the light plays with his eyes. What time is it? The coolness of water in a paper cup with crushed ice. A bite of cheesecake leftover from dinner. She's just had both her knees replaced. He wants to lie down.

'I could tell you anything.'

'What?'

'You're so out of it you wouldn't remember.'

'Talk to me then.'

He is losing ground.

'Wakey-wake. If you sleep now you won't want to later.'

Her eyes flashed open. Was she seeing colors? 'I'm worried about you.'

'Oh, I'm fine. I don't need you to worry about me. You're in pain. Just rest.'

Of a sudden he felt old. Seeing her so—incapacitated. He didn't want to know about mortgages, interest rates, fixed rates, bankruptcies, life insurance, health insurance, deductibles. The slide from normalcy was gradual, distantly inevitable, and the waiting made living impossible to sit back and relax, enjoy. When everything went under he'd already wearied himself from treading. It occurred to him, the lack of normalcy in his life; had it ever been there, really? He felt let down, set up, as though his entire life he'd been led to believe in a certain way. He could handle dissatisfaction with himself; he could fight to save himself, but all around him—to be surrounded by it when growing up everything seemed ideal. Gedny was not happy now. His father never changed, had simply become more docile with age, and Ellis—. Ellis. Now she was the one who'd slipped into the shadow of her brother's condition.

He wanted that pain. Her pain would cease when the joints healed. She would get up and step-by-step walk again.

Plastic tubes, monitors. He could only imagine such absent-minded rest, and yet he'd been there once—watched the dim corners of a room the whole night through until restless boredom drifted into his reclined body and settled into his eyes.

He bent down and hugged his mother, touched his dry lips to her hairline. He could do that *only* when he was sure she didn't know who he was, wouldn't remember. The painkillers made her so loopy. She'd taken absolutely nothing in childbirth. Her pain threshold was high, but this—her knees—she needed something.

Why does he look so pale, so pale, so pale, standing there. West?

• • •

Westcott watched the man polish the carpet of the hospital lobby. Back and forth on his giant sliding machine. Smooth went the brushes. A calmness in its routine.

Ellis. Funny—not funny, dramatically ironic. My god, the sheer juxtaposition of it—everyone in the opposite place than where they ought to be—want to be. For all her boldness she'd been the one to cry—Ellis—when mother came out of surgery. Too afraid to question the doctor for details. What no one could know, but seeing her from the point of view of brother, sibling, she was the shy one—afraid of herself. She traveled, traveled, traveled—running from what? Westcott felt he knew and yet he knew also, he would never, could never, tell her these things. Rodge. Rodge was a good man, dependable, always locked up inside, the boy seeking approval. Westcott respected his person, but not his appeasing character. Rodge should have stood up to Ellis, taking the lead. He was young. Ellis was young. History can repeat itself in the next generation. Mother and Tony all over again. Minus the affair. Westcott made up for the affair part—the affair mother had with Bob. Ellis and Westcott were reliving their Mother's own history in separate ways.

Ellis. Many friends but no confidantes. Ellis. She will leave Rodge. Westcott would watch from a thousand miles away, sitting in the very room, walking down the street beside them—the bickering—constant bickering—squabbling, more often exasperation. Ellis would tell their mother her frustrations about Rodge, sometimes in front of Westcott, but he knew. And Ellis knew he knew the reasons—they all did. Why Ellis? She got angry at Westcott— his clandestine ways, accused him about Regn. What right did he have to accuse her or offer his opinion of her own relationships! No, Ellis, he wanted to tell her. It's not like that—I'm not perfect. But you and Rodge are more like roommates, siblings. Always *right there* within hand's reach of one another, and yet no desire. Ellis. You don't know what it means to love with every fiber inside you. Why are you *afraid* of me? We are not sisters. We are not brother and sister. What are we? Night and Day. Ellis. You resent me, I can feel it. Do I resent you?

• • •

That January Miss Gilly is given away. One of the nurses helping Gedny to rehabilitate and exercise her new knees loves dogs, has rescued two from shelters and given them a good home. Miss Gilly has become a fixture. Westcott walks her, feeds her, it is perfunctory. Miss Gilly is jealous of Helmsley. Always has been. Westcott's mother tells him about the offer. Westcott agrees. One day he comes home from work and Gilly is gone. Just like that. No formal goodbyes. Oh he can go visit her, see how she's settling in. He never does. All his affection is used up. He'd stopped touching Miss Gilly, petting her, showing love long ago. He didn't mistreat her; Gilly was always a little skittish, but he'd stopped *seeing* her. He looked around her, through her. All he could see was Regn. He knew Gilly was going to a good home with two older children who would give her the love she deserved. He did not mourn his own loss. It wasn't a loss, just a change. The only pain he felt anymore was Regn.

Two years later he would adopt another dog. This time a puppy. He'd raise him from the size of a potato in his hand, shower him with endless love. Was he making up for the lack of affection he gave to Gilly? He spoiled his little dachshund whom he called Robert. Robbie for short. But the void inside himself never filled. Westcott required human love. Romantic love. Without it life felt meaningless.

HE SAVES UP HIS MONEY, somehow, and that June, six months after last making love, Westcott boards a plane for Munich. He has booked a two-week program through EF tours. He finds a vintage suitcase, navy blue, with cream trim and cranberry satin lining. It is anything but practical for lugging. It has no wheels. Only a handle. Packed, it is quite heavy. How did they ever manage in the past? Hardiness. Westcott puts old-time stickers on the outside. He asks Regn to bring him one from the Shenandoah if she wouldn't mind. He also slips in his large double-belled alarm clock, which security asks to examine. He stays with a host family, takes language classes to build upon his self-taught skills. The Bavarians take him for one of them. He assimilates well. But inside, as he rides the S and U-bahns alone, to and from his host family who live in a small town outside of Munich, the loneliness descends. He'd always wanted to go to Germany. The language came naturally to him. The history engaged him—the composers, artists, long before the onslaught of the Holocaust. Everyone seems to forget about the writers and musicians. When they hear the word 'Germany,' the first thought is Hitler. Jews. Concentration Camps. Even Westcott finds it ironic, suspicious, that he should be drawn to a place where, half a century earlier, he'd have been executed.

Munich is clean. The subway system easy to navigate. Two weeks. Seven days into his vacation he uses the payphone call center at one of the stations. He speaks to his mother, briefly. And then configuring the time change, ensuring Regn will be at work back home, he dials her number at Jamestown Settlement.

'Regn? It's Westcott. I just wanted to say hi.'
'Aren't you in Germany? It's expensive to call. You shouldn't have—'
'It's not that expensive.'
'So what have you been doing?'
'Oh, different things. The stations are so clean, not like the subways in the U.S.'
'Yeah. Well—' a long pause.
'Actually, I'm somewhat bored.'
'What? What's wrong with you!' her voice is dismayed not concerned.
He feels scolded. 'Oh nothing, you know—' He wants her to say it, the one thing he's been waiting for—
'Well, have a nice time.'
'Yes, of course, I will.' He speaks enthusiastically to dissemble the emptiness spreading inside. He does not want her to know how much what she *hasn't* said hurts him.
'All right then. Bye.'

'Bye.' Her voice is flat. Nothing extra. Not a single personable word.

The only reason he'd called was to hear her say, 'I wish I could be there with you.' Like she used to.

He knows she still believes he came all this way—to Germany—because of her. He didn't come to Germany because of Regn. It wasn't about her being German. Westcott wanted to experience the culture, the history. He had no one else to go with. So he made a conscious decision not to sit around and to go by himself. She gave him credit for nothing.

He had no reason to return home—home across the great sea. What if he just disappeared into Europe? He would be out of money by the following week. What then? It didn't matter where he was in the world—he would still be lonely.

One evening, on the way back to his host family, he was riding the S-bahn. He looked out the window at the countryside, a terrible desolation gnawing at him despite his calm composure. He studied the other passengers. Listened to the pleasing automated announcement. *Bitte links aussteigen.* 'Please exit to the left.' At one stop a man and woman step on, take a seat directly across from him. They are close enough to touch Westcott, a little space of maybe 8 inches between their knees contacting each other. The man briefly looks at Westcott. Being polite, Westcott meets his eyes then turns his attention away as the couple proceed to kiss passionately. It is obvious they are in love and more is to come when they arrive home, wherever home is for them. What strikes Westcott though, is their age. Late forties, maybe, and they are engaging in a passionate public exchange. It isn't lewd. He has known exactly what they are feeling, once upon a time. He does not begrudge them their momentary happiness; he does, however, envy their freedom. When they leave the S-bahn, the rims of his eyes become wet. There is no one around to see. No one, except for his mother, who even cares where he is. It hurts. He shouldn't have called Regn, but how did he know she would be so distant, detached?

The highlight of his vacation came on the day he visited The Ludwig Maximilian University. It was drizzling. He wore the nice black raincoat with red stripes on the sleeves his host family had let him borrow. It was a little big, it belonged to the father, Urn.

He found the University easily enough. Wandering through the courtyard, he was about to leave, move on, when for no reason, no reason at all, he looked over at a large wooden door at the top of flat stone steps. He did not have a map of the campus, only the surrounding city streets. He decided to step inside, knowing he wouldn't be back to the town.

Pulling open the heavy door, the foyer gave way to beautiful marble floors. The vestibule gave way to an open hall—a Great Hall. A brass plaque indicated it was the Student Building. In disbelief that he'd found the very building he'd come to see, Westcott felt himself being pulled. A memorial to the Scholls hung on the wall. He listened to the echoing of footsteps. Students idling on the steps. He took the main stairwell up one floor and then a smaller one to the next level. Peering over the balcony he saw Sophie pushing the leaflets off the edge. A moment of certainty. 67 years ago she'd stood here, just a few years younger than he was now. There was nothing sinister about the place. It was beautiful, architecturally. Deep green marble pillars, wooden columns. He looked into one of the lecture halls. The wooden benches were tiered, with a balcony. He tried to imagine a more sinister time. On the lower level a museum had been installed specifically addressing *The White Rose* and the students who sacrificed their lives in the name of freedom.

He navigated the city efficiently. The S and U-bahns were immaculate. One afternoon, in a town whose name he can't remember, he had bread and a soda at an outdoor café. He'd just purchased a $300.00 authentic wooden music box. His one splurge. A beautiful carving on the lid. Three country musicians, two ladies dressed in skirts, and one man. Were they peasants? It didn't matter. They were happy, playing music.

~

Westcott gets up to leave the café, doesn't realize his coat is still over the back of the chair. He gets home. His stomach drops. His jacket! He wouldn't care, but this jacket means something. This gray, insulating, Columbia jacket was the one he'd lain on the forest floor. The one he'd made love to Regn on—it's foolish maybe, but no, it's all he has of love, of sex. Only reminders. He must call the restaurant, see if they have it. Urn, the father in his host family, gets the number. Westcott calls. They have it! Thank god. He'll go tomorrow to fetch it.

~

His last night in Munich Westcott dined with two fellow classmates. They were from Russia. Luiba was 16 and Olga 29. Both liked him. During their tour of the Alps each had grabbed onto his arm; he'd escorted both of them, politely. Had he been a different sort of man he might easily have persuaded one of them to go to bed with him. God knows his body was cold, and he ached inside. But the feelings weren't there. The words never came. And besides, how could he ever explain that he wasn't like other men down there—

Regn never called when he got back. After several days, Westcott phoned her at work.

'I was hoping you'd call.'
'I was going to—' she offered no explanation.
Now you say that. But when—
'How's work?'
'Oh fine. And your trip?'
'It was good. Lots to tell you. Maybe this weekend, if you have a chance?'
'I'll see.'
'All right then.'
'I have to go, another call's coming.'
He hears the line ringing in. But it's never urgent. He knows. He worked the desk. Can't it wait this once—they'll call back. She doesn't care that he called. If she did she'd keep him on the line, tell him to hold, then smother him with questions of interest.

'Talk to you later.'
'Yeah. Bye,' she hangs up.
So that was it.

They met that weekend.

'I got you something.'
'What? No, please. I don't want it. I can't!'
'You don't even know what it is.'

'I told you, I don't want to have to hide anymore things.'

'You don't. It's nothing like that.'

'Please—'

'You're spoiling it. I brought it all the way back with me.'

She takes the small bag reluctantly. Inside she pulls out a rectangular bar of chocolate wrapped in a beautiful museum print depicting *The Room of Ladies* from one of the castles he toured. It's almost too nice to open the paper wrapper. Also inside the bag is a postcard with an attractive scene.

'How will I explain these things?'

'What?'

'I don't know where I'll put them.' Her voice is rising.

'Regn, just put the chocolate bar in your purse and eat it at work. And the postcard—it's a bookmark.'

Her expression shows agitation. Westcott is annoyed. He wants to say, *It's a damn chocolate bar for god's sake! Eat it. Enjoy it. Savor it for once! Could you show the slightest thanks? You're welcome. I drive all the way over here, we agree to meet, could you try even a little!*

The mood has been spoiled. The entire gift and idea behind it ruined. He'd managed to get the candy all the way home without it melting in the plane or ever breaking. She couldn't even receive it with kindness. Westcott is disgusted by her helplessness, irritated. Most of all, hurt.

———

Regn had, several months before, changed her hair color to blonde. Westcott joked to himself painfully that the hair dye altered her brain chemistry—her personality. She changed her license plate, too. She never asked his opinion or even cared to know his two cents on either matter. He politely told her the blonde hair made her look faded. 'Well this is how it's staying!' Her license plate was something her granddaughter came up with. Had she asked him he'd have suggested DOODLBG or LYTNBUG. By changing things outside of herself she believed she was making a fresh start.

AND NOW THE FISH WOMAN MAKES HER DEBUT. We met in a reading group that convened every Tuesday at the local library. She was frazzled in appearance, by my regards, despite the veneer of productivity. Her profession was in 'wellness.' She'd been a personality analyst and worked in many places. I mistrusted her from the beginning, but I had no one else to turn to; besides, she was interesting. We met once, privately at the library and one other time at a Starbucks. I wanted to meet in the beautiful cemetery by the William & Mary Law School. I suppose the seclusion of the location proved too mysterious for comfort, so The Fish Woman said Starbucks.

'You're right on track for something like *this* to happen.'

Her single statement to me.

Something like this. I'm not bipolar, schizophrenic, or manic depressive—mental illnesses which rear their heads in one's mid to late 20s. I listened, knowing full-well my apathy for life and my depressed state was owing entirely to 'other' causes. Other: Emotional devastation. Sexual frustration. Social isolation. Physical dichotomy. She asked about my diet and swore that if I took several fish oil capsules a day in time my symptoms would disappear along with a planned diet. None of this really hooked me. It was our conversation at the library that meant the most.

'You're the type of personality that whatever you do you have to do it all the way or it's not worth it to you. It has to be the best or nothing. You do nothing halfway. You're not content to dabble in anything. When you decide to undertake a skill or pursuit, you master it. But—'

Yes, always the BUT.

'—It will take you a lot longer to get from here to there, A to B. Maybe a decade or two, whereas other personality types speed along, maybe in mere weeks or a few months. You're highly contemplative. Each person has a blueprint. Your intelligence and creativity puts you way out here. I'm going to need you to stop analyzing me if I'm to help.'

When she got up from the table she was faint. She asked if I'd mind giving her my arm and walking her to the water fountain. I couldn't help thinking this was another one of her character tests, to see if I'd be open enough to touch her, help her to the water. I found it manipulative. Was I over-analyzing? Two years later would I not receive a generic mass forwarded email saying that she had been in the hospital recovering from a quadruple bypass? And then another year later I'd hear that she'd died. Ironic for a woman so health-conscious. She took several fish oil capsules herself and in our group meetings I'd often notice her silently hiccupping, a quieted belch—side-effect of the fish oil. Her observations were intriguing, no doubt she possessed certain expertise, but—

In a phone conversation we had she said, 'You can count on me.'

I came clean in a post-telephone email. I told her I'd been born female.

'Your secret is safe with me,' she replied.

And our *relationship* concluded.

Neither of us contacted one another. I had other matters to tend to—working, which prevented me from attending future literary meetings at the local library.

She'd met her match. No amount of fish oil could fix my gender-bender. She backed away. The implications clear. She didn't want to touch that issue—it was out of her field.

She wrote me a recommendation for an internship with National Geographic. She said,

'One day I'm going to be able to say I knew Westcott *when*.' She meant before I was well-known and famous.

Long before The Fish Woman, I never believed (and still don't), anyone who says, 'You can trust me,' or 'You can count on me.' Such truths are never spoken. They are always demonstrated. She was right though. About one thing. I do fly very close to the sun.

• • •

The closest Westcott ever comes to meeting his favorite actress is the day Mamie Gummer performs in the gardens of Colonial Williamsburg. Her visit is only for the afternoon. Westcott knows from her voice and yes, even her appearance, there is no mistaking it, Mamie is the daughter of Meryl Streep. He is more interested in detecting similarities in mannerisms between mother and daughter than following the performance itself. The day is hot. Westcott wears his shirt and tie. He is still on the clock, but staff have been permitted to attend the live performance.

• • •

His internship at the Goodwin Building is winding down. It is mid-August. Westcott stands in Shannon's doorway. Shannon is a casual acquaintance, a friendly face, who makes coming into work tolerable. He looks forward to their conversations. Shannon is secretary for the head chairman of Special Gifts and Tour Planning. High paying donors are invited to go on excursions to places faintly related to colonialism. Shannon is a responsible, cordial worker, but self-admittedly she possesses no ambition. Having graduated from William and Mary, she makes a few extra dollars more per hour than Westcott. She is married, in her late thirties, and staunchly opposed to having children of her own. She's big-boned; her height at 5'10" evenly distributes the few extra pounds she carries. She's stalky but attractive. Her personality exudes laughter. Westcott often hears her before he sees her. Despite her lackluster for a grand career, Shannon is intelligent, savvy, a wordsmithee, and on the level. Westcott finds her company natural, easy to get along with, and in time he sheds a little light on his own past and personality. Shannon had been to Germany and other places abroad during her college years, so she was pleased about his excursion to Munich.

She finds projects for Westcott to do, whether it's preparing luggage tags, or carrying packages to the mailroom. Through the course of one of their late afternoon conversations, Shannon said she'd been to a psychic years ago.

'Was she authentic?'

'Well, what she said came true.'

Westcott was willing to try most anything at least once. What could it hurt? If nothing else, it might prove entertaining, if not enlightening. Fodder for his writing.

'Where was this?'

'In D.C. She might still be there. I think her name was Crystal.'

'Stage name?'

'I don't think so.'

'Well, I'll see. You know, if you're still here in four or five years I'm going to have to come back and give you a kick in the ass to move on. You need to get out of here. Like me, you're too creative.'

'Thank you for the lovely compliment,' Shannon laughed.

'It's refreshing to know that someone else consistently uses the word 'lovely' in her vocabulary. It's a good word.'

'I like it.'

'I mean it—a rolling stone gathers no moss. Don't stay here. You'll become a fixture, a relic. Standards are something different. And you have them.'

'You know who you remind me of? Have you seen the movie *Feast of Love*? You're like Harry, old and wise beyond your years.'

'If you say so.' Westcott smiled. 'Enjoy the afternoon. Now, if you don't mind I have *important things* to do for the next hour.' They both smiled. She knew the work was shiftless for him, idle. Hardly stimulating. He'd be moving on.

Westcott started to unpeel the banana he'd been holding in his right hand.

'I can never eat bananas,' Shannon laughed. 'They're too phallic.'

Amused, Westcott finished unpeeling the third flap and took a generous bite. He loved the scent of a fresh banana. 'Hey, frozen chocolate banana nips are really great.'

'I'm sure.'

'It's true. I'm referring to the fruit!'

'I just can't do it.'

Westcott shakes his head. 'You just don't know what you're missing.' He takes another, more delicate bite. 'Now I'm really going.'

Heading down the corridor, he looks at the sunlight on the tile, remembering that time he'd been eating his chocolate doughnuts during Anniversary Weekend. Regn's wry comment had prompted him to take another savory bite and he'd silently smiled back, 'Delicious.' Three years and three months it had been since that evening. It seemed like yesterday and yet, it felt like a lifetime ago.

• • •

Fortunately, Westcott never had to give Shannon that swift kick. Several years later he discovered she had found another job. After his internship concluded, their contact tapered off, then stopped altogether.

• • •

He waited until October before taking a Greyhound up to the nation's capital. The train would take too long and driving was an added expense. He'd need a rental car. Ol' Reliable couldn't make it that far on the highway. He might get there, but not be able to return.

The day was spent in anticipation. He'd been able to locate Crystal rather easily and he'd spoken to her on the phone to set the appointment. He maintained a level of skepticism. But he also knew there were individuals throughout the world who genuinely possessed a keen sensibility beyond mere intuition. However, those who were "real" usually did not advertise in bright neon letters. They offered their services only if they picked up on something. They did the approaching. Westcott made the journey with an open-mind. Not everyone who put-up a sign was a charlatan.

Her office was also her home, located on the main street, up a flight of stairs. The appointment was for late afternoon. Westcott didn't have to knock. She simply came to the door, knowing. That or she had a hidden surveillance camera. He still had a hard time reconciling the believability of Crystal's name.

She invited him inside and they sat down. She offered to read his palm or have him split a deck of cards. He chose the latter.

Westcott made sure not to supply any information and to let Crystal perform the reading.

Her price was reasonable and she was interesting to look at—one of her eyes was slightly turned in—not unattractively, but it gave the appearance that she was truly looking inward. This was not a ploy. Medically, her eye had something wrong with it.

Westcott listened.

'Is there anything specific you'd like to know?'

'Will I always be alone? Is Regn gone from my life?'

'Just wait. Maybe two or three years.'

Crystal had gone on to say other things that didn't line up. But she did offer this: 'You're very intense and you attract many people, of both genders, whether you try to or not.'

As they parted, Westcott extended his hand. It wasn't anything she'd said that made an impression on him. Truthfully, it had all been rather vague. What struck him was the warmth of her touch. After his hand released hers, it was *still* warm—a calm energy held only in his hand.

'Come back and see me sometime. And get something to eat.' She offered genuine concern.

Westcott didn't remember anything about the long walk back to the station. Streets passed by, but it seemed like he arrived in a matter of minutes. Even as he entered the depot, his hand remained peaceful. He didn't feel alone. It wasn't an ointment, there had been no such residue imparted to his skin. The psychic hadn't been the one to offer a handshake. Westcott had. This is how he knew there was nothing false about it. Eventually, as he stopped for dinner and waited for the greyhound to take him home, the sensation dissipated.

Two or three years. Well, he didn't have to kill himself yet. He'd see if what she said came true. Little did he know that *exactly* three years later a woman by the name of Birçan would enter his life like a cyclone.

Westcott never went back to see Crystal. He thought of sending a note. But there was really only one way to know the future for sure. And that was living long enough to see it.

• • •

The winter after his summer trip to Germany, Westcott finds himself meeting Regn one evening in Colonial Williamsburg. They take a brief walk. The dark streets protect them. They head back to her car. Standing in the cool night they embrace. As she kisses him he feels the old Regn alive again.

'You never know,' she says.

She is telling him with just those few words that yes, anything is possible. And this is how it has been and continues to be for the next two years. A seesaw of emotions, cold and hot. Her moodiness has him on pins and needles. He never knows how she'll be the next time they speak. He becomes afraid of telling her how he feels, afraid of upsetting her. He knows it is wrong to compromise himself, he feels frustrated, angry, resentful. For a while they might be on good terms, but then the need to voice his feelings, his true emotions brims. He can't pretend everything's just fine, that life is going along. He needs concrete answers.

Regn won't have to lift a finger. All she'll have to do is say "go away." She can stay at her job, stay in her home. Her life does not change. It is not really upended. Her tone begins to suggest that Westcott is an irritant. She turns on him. And something inside him cannot shoulder the hurt.

• • •

HE NO LONGER TRUSTS MUSIC. It makes you remember—enlivens—too soon a feeling comes to pass—you can't keep Her—when the noise of getting by rushes in—and the truth becomes maudlin.

No. He trusts the voice, the sound—the wind's many tones. Natural noise. That initial scene in *Copying Beethoven*—the music of everyday. Nothing contrived. Music in its poetry of motion. Everything. Everything. And what does it say? It speaks to him but never answers and so he feels *I am yet alone*.

I RECALL HER WORDS and how I'd rebelled against them, vehement disbelief at such resignation. I now understand. 'Make the best of it,' Regn had said.

And yet much, much later I replied, 'That's where you were wrong. Years and years ago. What I don't like I don't accept. I *change* it.' *Your whole life, Regn, you accepted. I'm too young to make the best of it. You were once, but you—*

Looking back I realize I hadn't been aware that I was missing something. I knew how much I needed it and tried to hold onto it for dear life, knowing the significance, cherishing the opportunity with every fiber of my being. The coldness of isolation allowed me to feel the need, but until that moment I was not conscious of how long I'd waited. We sat on the wooden bench overlooking the James. It was a slight cold with the wind off the river, but we stayed. Painfully I asked her, 'No one says these things and I know it's off subject, but could, would you mind if I—felt your face?'

'You can feel my face.'

I didn't move. 'I don't know how.'

She took my hand and pressed it to her face. I can still feel it, even now, that initial touch. How warm her skin, or was it that my hand was so cold from the inside? I wanted to feel her face completely. She moved my wrist to her neck. 'You can feel my ear,' she said smiling. 'My leg, it's *just* a leg.'

And then we'd driven together to Waller Mill. I'd divulged that I had scars. She'd run her finger across them through my white shirt. She let me hug her, taking my arms and placing them around her waist. I sat there, not moving my limbs, but leaving them just where she'd put them. I could hear her heart. 'I'm not looking down your shirt, so don't worry,' but I was looking down, searching for a glimpse of the hummingbird atop her breast.

• • •

He imagines it, standing with his sister beside their mother's grave. She would cry and think to herself, 'How cold, insensitive, snide and arrogant, impassive, imperturbable, untouchable he is.' Her grief would brim to her eyes and spill forth. He couldn't tell Ellis you don't have to show tears to cry. Inches apart they were miles away from each other. More alone together, she'd said. Yes, true so.

IMPECCABLE TIMING. I didn't know what I was about.

We had all the time in the world and no time at all. Regn and I.

All these places and lives once looked upon fill him, exist within.
A private tour. Closed. The changing of the guards.

WHAT HAPPENED?

-You're quite the snob, aren't you?

Is that what you think? Then you don't know me at all.

-But I am you. Remember? Anyway, where were we? Oh yes, miserable. Not the sort to hide it, if you're miserable you want someone to share in it with you. Never could pretend long enough. You can hide it away to a point but then it builds. Weak I 'spose. Feel you keep enough to yourself, hide so much, cheated of so much, it's your right to be miserable, angry. Is that it?

Maybe. No. Just leave it alone. Leave me be.

-It's your freedom, sorrow, the one thing you can openly exercise anytime and anyplace—well, you still have to put on a front.

Always. Never. 'Til I can't stand it a minute longer.

-You have a nice smile.

Yes. If only it would last.

————

We could have loved each other for years—made love. I thought a lot about *Same Time, Next Year* and *Brokeback Mountain*. But Regn wasn't cut out to be a lover.

I could have survived on once a year. On some level she wanted Jay to know, else she would never have let him find out. Her age was a refuge, it would protect her. Everything was already in place. My age was a sentence to endure. It was something Regn would never understand. She'd been waiting without knowing it, her whole life sailing by. It was a luxury to pass the years without having a name or face to place on what was missing. But much too soon, far too soon, I became conscious of the void. It had a name, a scent, a feel, and a form. The knowledge was mine to carry. I was not sailing into the horizon seeking; rather, I was a few miles offshore, unable to reach land again. Anchored on the reef, tousled by the breakers. No longer in the depths or the shallows but listing in the mesostream.

WHEN DO YOU PULL AWAY and stop looking out the window? In the years between I would sometimes stand in my room, unclothed after a shower or in getting dressed. I'd look in the mirror, look at my naked form and something would start to hurt. I'd been this open with Regn only once. Only once. Any other time we had slipped a hand beneath our clothes. I'd confronted myself just that one night.

'I saw you.'

'And?'

'And—you just don't have a willy.'

How funny the words sound, but at what cost they came. Regn could never know, did not want to know what I felt inside. The emptiness.

I wish it had always been this way—each of us completely exposed to one another. The warmth of her body beneath mine—no barriers.

Standing alone I began to know myself. My body is nice, young, slender. The waste in hiding it—the startling contrast of such pale skin, hidden from the sun with the dark creases of underbrush. The mirror in front of me does not extend to my face and so the body I see, in shape and stature alone, resembles a woman's minus the orbs of men's passions.

There is an emptiness between my legs—a space never fulfilled or filled. At this point I've never touched or even looked at a real human penis up close. I've never felt its hard ardency push up against me and into me—nothing fills the emptiness. It's not the same as having yourself with some fake 'thing' that you have to press up inside of you—the nuisance of having to assume both roles. Regn never had to 'work' for it—sex that is, or love. She's had so much love.

———

Somehow the tables turned. Somehow. And the strength with which she needed him faded. She no longer needed him at all. He could not fathom, or rather it was not in his nature to do so, how to compartmentalize emotions. She operated like a switch. Nothing he said or did mattered—his opinion, his efforts to persuade, collided with a fortress. She pulled up the drawbridge, shut all the windows and covered her ears to avoid his eyes. She spewed a barrage of destruction. The woman who would never think of uttering an unkind word turned cold, cruel—in a vain attempt to drive him away. Westcott knew better. It wouldn't work. Then she began to mean what she said. The damage caused by those words could never be completely undone. What Regn failed to understand was what Westcott acknowledged to himself—the greater the resistance the stronger his resolve.

Regn had thirty extra years—a lifetime to be broken in—Westcott had to be strong, to muster strength of equal or greater substance in the span of five years.

———

Sometimes to torment, to punish myself, in some perverse way it makes me feel better, I imagine Regn and what it must feel like—all the years. I know she still has sex with Jay. She said it wasn't that often. For a while I believed her. Too shy to press for details I left it at that. But then I had to know. What did "not that often" equate to? Every few months? Two, three times a year? I asked in a diplomatic way, presenting the inquiry in the form of a scale—a range. 'Is it less than six or less than ten times a year?' There was silence on the other end of the phone. 'It's much more than that!' She said it with an air of pride as though my thinking it could possibly be anything less was absurd. She gave a rough estimate. Had she slapped me across the face full force, it wouldn't have stung. I'd never have felt the pain compared to the sting unleashed inside. Like a house of cards, everything collapsed and backed up inside of me. I quickly did the simple math. X amount of times per month multiplied by 12. Regn had more sex in a single year than I'd ever enjoyed in my entire life! It was clear. Regn's definition of "not that often" greatly conflicted with the true definition. I was in shock. *So that's what she considers infrequent? My god, what would she say about my life?* 'Believe me, I get what I need. I am not frustrated in that way,' she added for emphasis. (She would later confess she'd said it to hurt me, that she'd exaggerated. All I could think was, how cruel. Love will hurt but it should never be unkind. Regn had become unrecognizable).

It may not excite her anymore—it doesn't—that's what she told me—but even so, should a frustration waver through, all she has to do is lie there in her king bed and wait for the body she knows so well to compress her. Compress. Nobody compresses my body. Nobody. I wonder how they go about it. After so many years. No words. Does he reach for her, a kiss, a movement of the hand, and instinctively she will know that tonight he needs her? Does he always come to her or does she ever solicit him? I know it is fast, the release of frustration, not passion. I can see her legs handle-barred out beneath the sheet—like that time I saw her beneath the tree in the forest when we made love.

I lie inside her, waiting for *his* organ to advance. I imagine his weight on top of me, feeling it as Regn must. And then his hardened sex pressing inward, Regn's pelvis preparing, as I know it can, and her body accepting his organ, his right to enter her by nature and decree, she never turns away—. Him pushing more, feeling her wrap round him and pull him inside, and then the rhythmic thrust as Regn seeks the peace of climax for her own sake—not for the satisfaction of their two bodies, but merely for hers and Jay's separate relief. And then beneath the sheet Regn will feel spent, calm, at peace. But empty. Perhaps she wears no underwear this night. She is free to bask in the mild afterglow of physical satisfaction—how familiar it has become over the years. For those few minutes she is not alone. A body that is safe, clean, and loves her, is free to come inside her. He is 65 and she knows him as well as he knows himself. But as she moves to her side of the bed she is far away. Emotionally spent, closed off. Jay knows this. He will not dwell on it. He pushes the thought aside. Lets his calmed body ease the doubts in his mind. And in the morning she will do her meditation. Some remnants of fluid will discharge themselves through the day or the next. She'll see her grandchildren on the weekend—pick them up—hug them—they'll hug her, they love their *Oma*—she has a place to be—she does not have to go searching for affection—it just is—and it comes to her. This is enough for her—it has to be.

Even when Regn and I were intimate she said she could not enter me. Not in those words, but she indicated the organ I used with her she would not press inside of me. Oh she loved me and touched me—a part of her hand came inside, but I was never fulfilled. The summit was not my greatest source of pleasure with her. This I could achieve alone and rapturously. *I wanted* to be felt—long and lovingly, to be pressed upon, held close, to slumber side-by-side—it was Regn who always wanted to come so quickly. I favored the prelude and the aftermath. My passion came from love, not love from passion.

All the love spent and all the affection tempered. It seems a shame to grow old before one's time.

———

Looking at himself he was ashamed—not of his body but of his desires. He knew the prowess of his love and how he had given all, completely. He hated himself for loving Regn, for needing her still, when all she had to do was continue doing what she'd always done. He had her love, but it wasn't enough, it could not comfort. Regn didn't suffer as he did; her purpose as a woman had been fulfilled. Ironically, *she'd* known the best of both worlds. Westcott told himself it is better to be a decent man than a gratified one. But he didn't want greatness. For once he just wanted an easy way.

———

Sometimes I long for the days of Regn. When the only things on my mind were when we'd see each other again and what tie to wear to work the next day. There was no concern for bills, no worry about my balding crown, no thought of grocery lists or when to schedule taking the pets to the vet. There was no focus on my back pain or when will my truck have another major repair. No thoughts of how mother is getting older and my sister hasn't settled down and married though she would like a child—somehow she must carry on the lineage; although I think it's best if we stop it here. Everything *then* seemed manageable and the only discomfort was being away from Regn. Having said this you might think I am pushing 70, longing for the days of my early manhood. O' I did long for those days, but that was before when I *was* still young.

I paid 500 dollars to touch a woman. I told her I'd just come back from the Peace Corps and it had *been a long time*—. Did she believe me? She asked if I'd marry her and then she said, 'You're nice.' She shook her naked ass in my face, which I thought was ridiculous. I didn't like it, but I did get to feel her breasts and when she told me not to put my hand inside her, I listened and just ran my hands over her skin.

I made love and undressed myself in the presence of one woman without ever having gone on a date with her. Yes, Regn and I. We never actually dated. But we did make love—a love that would outlast all others.

My first year of college, a girl sat down at my table in the dining hall. She struck up a conversation and in no subtle way included the topic on her mind. 'My bad boys,' she said, looking down at her breasts. 'Do you want to take a walk?' No doubt I must have looked prime for the picking, fresh, pure meat for her loins, green and right off the stock. She didn't seem offended when I told her, 'No, I have some work to do.' Her name was Kellsey.

The next year I received a note from a young woman. I'd been absent from class a few days for reasons of a surgical nature. The note read:

I hope you're all right, Westcott. I've missed you in class. See you soon. Tess

A mutual friend of Tess', actually her most recent boyfriend, asked me to give him a ride up to Williamsburg one afternoon. He lived on campus. I said sure, though I maintained a nervous tenseness the entire way. Ian was nice, we spoke of many things, though I don't remember any of them but one. He told me, 'Therese is nice. I took some pills after we split and that really helped. If you're interested in her go for it. I had never experienced *that* sort of thing before—' I caught his drift. She was his first sexual exploration I assessed by the way he said 'that sort of thing.' He needed to talk, perhaps he was waiting for me to shed light on my first time or my own experiences. I had none to speak of. I don't remember what I said other than 'oh.'

And thus concludes the 'social' sexual episodes of my life up to the age of 29. All other experiences have but one witness—myself, and those moments which in the span of one's life add up to hours, remain with me. I will say this though—I was twenty years and two months old when I felt sexually aroused for the very first time. After that there was no turning back. Like a young boy of 14 whose testicles are descending and whose stand is lengthening—I can only imagine, the hormones I'd recently begun injecting took over. That bud of intense sensation became a source of shamed pleasure. In all the years before, never, not once, had I touched myself. I approached it tentatively and the more I probed the more I yearned. It was that first sensation, when I was attempting to urinate while standing, that signified the point of no return. I remember where I was and the guilty desire. Feeling the initial stimulus, having grazed the tiny organ, unintentionally coaxing the clitoris to attention, I quickly finished up, zipped my pants and left the dangerous privacy of the privy with all its waiting possibilities. I tried to forget the feeling, but it nagged, and a need all on its own came alive between my legs—a relentless throb, boldly making its presence known, demanding attention. Even were it not on my mind, the physical symptoms would elicit a reminder and I would relieve the breaking tension. The anticipation building, building. I always took my time, relishing the tease. The foreplay of coming so close and backing away, letting things rise and fall and then—then the euphoric release of calm as limbs shuddered and the eyes closed.

Penetration started with small objects. At first I used Q-tips and then I wanted something to 'push' inside. Never having seen one up close or unwrapped one I tried a tampon. A nifty little apparatus. I knew well that it was considered hazardous to use a tampon when not menstruating, but I took my chances. I wasn't planning on leaving it inside me—I just needed something soft and large, but not too large, to fill up that space. My body received the small cylindrical spool of cotton without complaint—it felt snug and kept me in a state of arousal until I removed it. I then began adapting items around the kitchen into home-made devices for potency of penetration. I took a small travel size tube of toothpaste and wrapped it thoroughly with toilet paper to smooth out any sharp or uncomfortable edges. I taped the paper down. I then inserted it into a latex free examination glove and placed its head at my body's warming threshold. The tube worked well because of its malleable contents. I tried this with a small dill pickle. I even used a plastic spoon on occasion. In time I became more and more curious about the real thing. Seeing as how there was no means of procuring a genuine, fully-functional phallus, I sought the next best thing—a silicone penis.
As the hormones took hold and time passed, the intensity dwindled and the starving season began. It wasn't the act of sex for which my body longed anymore.
I was tired of satisfying both roles—having to do double the work. I missed the

physical intimacy of another's presence, of being held and feeling myself through her. Sex became a chore, and after Regn, I shoved it under the bed for a while, back into the closet. The high was no longer a pleasure but a constant torment, a reminder of the isolation that had pervaded my existence for the last decade and a half.

———

He had no guilt for the love. There could be no guilt for something so earnestly and honestly sought. Instead, he was guilty of something he had no control over. Something he could never forgive himself for—of being young. He would not lose Regn to her marriage. In the end, he knew, he'd lose her to age. Yes, maybe, down the road, many years to come, Westcott would find himself in a marriage—a loving, amicable, affectionate exchange. But the passions of his true desires would always remain with Regn. Even after she was gone. It was characteristic of him—a deep-rooted melancholic nostalgia—to miss those whom he loved even in the present moment, when they were standing right before him or in the same room. An anticipatory loss. For this very reason he wanted to die young. He did not want to witness losing everyone he loved. Why did he have to be the one left to remember?

It was not so much that he resented her for having someone to fall back on. He resented her for not admitting it. If something went wrong with her car, Jay would call and make the appointment. Regn would just have to drive it to the shop. She paid her credit cards and some minor bills—her own bills—for shopping expenses, but Jay took care of the mortgage, the utilities, even the grocery shopping. If something went wrong with her car, Regn didn't have to figure it out. She had Jay to turn to—it's not that she couldn't depend on herself. She didn't have to. Westcott always had to rely on himself. Always.

———

HE REMEMBERS THAT DAY, long ago. August. And the evening sun. That evening sun as he pulled out of the lot in her trail and began the longest drive of his life. He'd driven on interstates he'd never before traveled, turned around in trying to find the Botanical Gardens. He hears his own words. 'All I want, I just want, is to be good. And maybe that's the test.' His recorder was not on, he'd been saving the reel.

'What do you mean?'
'*Staying* good.'

He can feel each in its turn—anger, contempt, resentment, frustration, apathy, malaise, comfort, complacency, second-wind.......That evening sun.

THE LEAVES—I SEE MYSELF turning in the leaves as they fall,

    turning,
        turning,
    turning.

Suo Gan, how pure the voice. Master and Commander…Movement Three…*Corelli's Adagio…Christmas Concerto Grosso Op. 6. No. 8 in G Minor.*

Regn—

How do you write grace?

You may still know a cumbersome, bungling, quick sex in the night. A body slides over you, strains, a body so familiar, an old shoe. A mild huffing and puffing, as you would say, of domesticity. The body is relieved. You have that human contact. The element of touch. Of having been touched. It relieves, you fall into sleep, welcome it so's not to think. But then you're alone 'in yourself' in the dark of the day when you awake.

I have to be earnest here—in the past, always, I would often leave exhausted inside as though an energy, an unspoken cable of 'being' was transferred. As though in gentle, dignified loving of a simple kiss, a trembling hug, I gave myself. And my body was left devoid of 'real' physical strength. It was making love—the same effect of restful bliss in the absence of anything carnal. And my heart would somehow be lighter. Somehow replenished for a short while before turning hard again. Who would believe me? In the absence of a penis my heart yearns to expel itself. And when it does the tears are substitute for a more crass, distasteful bodily fluid. The tears are for the happiness I cannot keep and so little shared with a woman—an ordinary woman you think to yourself. 'There are others, I'm not so damn special? Let yourself go. Be happy,' you may say. I didn't choose you and were your love not true, only then would I be free inside to go. But you have honor and we experience 'love' differently. That doesn't make it any less true. Perhaps because I go so much without it is stronger.

Physically you were always wanting to move so quickly. I could stand in restraint of you were you to be perfectly unclothed before me. I could look at you, touch you, and nothing more. It was always, and still remains, your fear of Self. I've seen it in your expression. I would never spill out—it comes gently, slowly, as though lifetimes before travel down in currents and I've waited so long, why hurry, why rush? I've experienced the sexual highs, and it is nothing compared to the satiating feeling of an intimate kiss, an unspoken transfer.

I wish for you to take me into the forest somewhere. Press me down into the cold earth, and to feel the hand of love. Not for you to 'be' loved, for you have been spoiled in that realm—all your life—the world embraces you. But I want your hands to love me, not sexually, but physically. To be pressed upon, held down, mildly restrained beneath your weight and feel 'my' body loved. To feel that love and the coldness inside warmed. My heart aches to be loved as a woman—the intimacy of an embrace, to just lie there and 'receive' the affections for which I was born. It's not youth that would have me speak this way. It's being human.

...

So what are you going to do, my dear boy?

Because of her he loves gray days. Maybe he always did and just didn't know it.

• • •

He looks down. Realizes he's wearing the light gray jacket.

The one he'd lain on the forest floor when they made love beneath the tree.

• • •

He stands at the window in the dark, looking at the great acorn tree.

My Peter the Swan.[6]

He stands. I stand. He stood. I stood.....I'm so sorry, to you all. I'm sorry. I'm—
Take my hand—You. I. Me. I leave you to the wind.

See you at the *finishing* line.

• • •

---

[6] Reference to a scene in Radclyffe Hall's, The Well of Loneliness, in which Stephen is alone by the lake, filled with sorrow, and the only witness to her grief is the peaceful swan on the water who is named Peter.

HE WATCHES AS THOUGH he is conscious *for* them. A bicyclist. Up and down, how funny the leg looks. A conversation at the register, an over-exuberance, a spur of engagement—the way a person would tell more about his or her life than is necessary. *Oh well, I can't do it that day, I have to go get my haircut* or some added detail—how many listened? All the details.

He lies on his stomach. One leg rests atop the 8-inch wooden rail. His other is below on the bridge itself. Both arms loosely hug the girth, his neck twists right, cheek to wood. A cat basking in the sun. He watches through sunglasses, watches the gentle wind wisp the strands of hair falling from his forehead. Corrugated ridges, grooves, a topographic map, DNA in the wood. He looks at the lines running like fossils, silt residue, and the horizontal lines of the flat slabs comprising the walkway. The arched line of the railing disappearing within the trees, the mowed line of marsh thistle, tractor lines, girding each side of the wooden trestle. The distant horizon line of faint lavender. All these lines running and intersecting, passing, perpendicular, parallel, crisscrossing, converging in a thousand minute intricacies. He feels the sun through the back of his shirt. His buckle digs into his stomach and a button on his shirt sharply presses his ribs. He pushes himself up. Walks to his bike. Swerves a line. Cold in the shade. His faintly hands, chilled. Colder inside than out. He pedals with arms outstretched. Pedals fierce. Pedals to breathe. The sun warms the tops of his hands, bars of shadow from the towering trees. He grips the handlebars to brace against the breaking cool air. He comes out into the lot. Stops where he had begun. The line of the curb. A line across his gaze, staring from the windshield, resting in the warmth of the winter sun.

• • •

He watches himself do it—going downstairs, finding tablets, many, many and like tic-tacs or little chicklet gum, orange flavored, swallowing a palm full. *This is it.* The Fleisches would pull into the driveway. At first they'd wonder why his truck was still there—but no alarm, maybe he stayed to say hello. Then they'd call his name. No answer. O' Grady glad to see them. So silent amidst his excitement of paws on wooden floor and jovial yap. He needs to go out. Maybe *he* went for a walk. Odd though, not to take O'Grady. I'll check out back. Maybe he's reading, or fell asleep. Looks out the window. No sign. Something's not right. It's too quiet, an odd feeling, a presence in the house. But everything's in its proper place. That's what Westcott had always appreciated about the Fleisch's. Pens in a vase on the counter. Soap in the dish. Even a glass medicinal jar housing cottonballs. A squeegee for the shower. Everything thought of, within grasp, at the ready. *I'll check upstairs.* 'Westcott?' The door partially open, not enough to see walking up the steps. Pushing open the door. 'Westcott?' He looks to be sleeping, and then the alarm sets in—*my God!* The Fleisch's will call an ambulance. His mother will be destroyed. Regn will hate him. Ellis will resent him later on, but first she'll cry so easily. The news would spread slowly. It didn't matter. He wouldn't be there to hear it, see it. He wondered, who would record it, if he wasn't there? His own death and he wanted to write it. He looks around the room; feels the warm wire-haired body scrunched up beside him, taking it all in for the last time. Never to brush his teeth again—the Fleisches return tomorrow.

Alas, exhaustion finds him still to the world. Dampness lines his face.

The day triumphs. He wakes. Walking O' Grady. The sun on the back of his own neck. The cool morning air numbing his aching, swollen face—he was glad he hadn't missed this.

...

I'm afraid of the years.

You mean the pain.

Yes.

Follow in that line—to get married, have children, and, and—I never considered it.
I just figured—

Doesn't matter now, does it?

No. Can't go back and sometimes I wonder.

We'll never know.

Would it have been any worse? Would I have been less miserable?

My dear boy, what's done is done.

Yes, but had I remained as nature borned, endured—at least on the outside nothing would
need explaining. True to self or not—things would match. Might I have become a wife,
been taken care of in that way, had a child and then—

They will misunderstand. Think you're saying your decision was a mistake. But I know.

No, I don't regret the surgery. I just wonder. I never knew what made a man a man, a woman
a woman—the roles. I—

Had you known the power a woman has—

Yes, a woman is so much stronger and I didn't know, I—but I love putting on my shirt and
tie.

But you don't want to be male?

Silence.

Do you?

Yes, but it can't be. I know too much. I'll never *truly* be male. It's a lie. A lie!

Then—

I just wonder would it have been any less hard had I stayed the way I was?

You didn't function. Remember? Wouldn't go out of the house. Wouldn't shower. Never looked at yourself. Never!

Denial.

You were never a woman.

No I wasn't. And you were never a boy.

True enough.

You can analyze every which way. It's a funny thing.

Hmm.

In becoming masculine on the outside, a desire to be woman, to remain woman—breathed within.

• • •

The distinct scent of fabric softener in the air.

I feel so alone inside. Stranded. Absolutely alone. I despise myself for it. I'm ashamed to say it. I can tell you, but then we won't tell anyone.

I don't—

Forgive—

I can't. I might have been married by now, had children, blended—

Instead you're out here—

Yes. And *I* did it. I don't want to talk about it anymore. I really don't. I let them see too much and not enough. Sometimes I think it would be best if I went away. Punish myself, punish them.

They let you down—?

It's easier to believe that—everything I believed.

Then who's to—

You are. *You are!*

Went to the mailbox. A letter for me. It felt good holding it in my hand, expectation yet opened.

Well—

A John Dear from a magazine editor—

Keep fighting, my boy.

Go to hell.
I just miss—her.

I know. So do I.

I really miss—. Regn doesn't have to do anything if she so chooses. Jay doesn't have to—why do *I*?

It's what you are.

It's not fair.

No, my boy, it isn't.

Sometimes I think it'd be best if I wasn't here anymore, just went away.

Best for whom?

You and I.

And your mother?

Ah. Phhhhhh. My Mother. Yes. She just wants what every good mother wants for her child. For me to be happy. She deserved someone like *him*—Jay. It's what she always wanted. Security.

I know.
And Regn.

Don't. I sometimes see that dependent naiveté, that school girl yet.

She never had to—can't blame her for that.

No, I don't blame. I'm—I'm fucking angry. Don't you see! Can't I be angry, can't I? Don't take away that right. No, I'm fucking angry *for* them! So much, wasted—potential—yes and life! My god, she tried, my mother did. I'm sure she did. I know she did. But Regn. It's herself she tries to forgive for never standing on her own. The resentment. Self-resentment.

Have to forgive yourself.

That's what she meant. But I won't let myself off that easy. No Sir, No.

No one needed to die more.
    *Florentina[7] Ariza is it?

Yes. I mean Jay's lived a good life. Seen his children born—the legacy of who he is— watched them have children of their own.

It's not up to you. Not your decision.

I know. I just—I'm not trying to play God. I wish him no harm.

But he's lived his life.

Yes. And a reasonably enjoyable one. *She* still has life untapped. Something inside to live.

He just wants things kept a certain way.

All to himself he wants it. Scared.

7*Florentina Ariza of Garcia's *Love in the Time of Cholera*.

What right have you to judge?

Such a hypocrite, am I? But he stands in the way of her—her—
    Identity?

Always. And to think. Just think, I have him to thank for what—who—she is not. He brought her here—here to this foreign land. Such irony. It's just—

    Not fair.

She's sacrificed so much and isn't it her turn, now? Isn't she entitled?

    With you?

No! She! Of her own! She doesn't belong to me or anyone. We aren't put here as each other's. That's what's so unfair. I'm not trying to take her away—why must I carry it—the knowledge, the truth—she was gone long ago, long before me!

    Silence.

Silence.

• • •

SHE'D TRIED. His mother had. She'd done her best. It wasn't what he needed. But it didn't make her a bad person or a failure. Jay had tried. But it wasn't what Regn needed. Love is not enough.

· · ·

I'm going to a place where you can't come in—I'm going and I will leave without mention. Privacy abounds without privacy. It is unforgivable. I hung myself and I must never look back at the corpse dangling from the tree. I may hate the hours of toil to come, I will endure as punishment unto myself.

I am going to a place—address—no human language can discern so I leave without one. Do not try and find me. I will bide my life serving and then my body will stop. I won't tell another soul. I forgive myself nothing. One day I will pass away.

She always claimed I didn't know her. Maybe that's so. She'd say, 'I don't think you can ever truly know a person unless you're them.' It's utterly profound, but poignantly true.

· · ·

For most often it comes at night. The onslaught, heavy swarm of endless thinking so you can't sleep. It wasn't the case with him. Mornings he'd awake with a start—a knot in his stomach the instant the day found him conscious to it. He'd lie there, considering the enormity of the task at hand; the years leading up to that point. All his life. He missed their house, the navy blue door and warm cream color. The climbing vine had been removed. *Sonny's Blues.* He'd been playing for his life. But this was no feat against heroin or race. *His was, and remained a tenacious fight against the drug of the drones—and go, go, go.*

· · ·

Everything I ever loved only hurt me.

These kids today—do they know what they're about? Trying on sex for size, something vulgar, crass, loss of the moment, unbridled physical lust, curiosity. My god, and the unwanted pregnancies. Get a hold of yourself man—grab that wad between your legs and know what it's about—what you're about—before you think to use it. There are responsibilities, you fucking kids—welcome to the real world. Don't grow up too fast, but you can't help it—they shove it down your throats—magazines, television, computers—how can you miss what you never knew?

But *it* was inside me—and I miss it every day—a place, a time, a body, that made sense.

The indecency. Things said. Phrases today. It means nothing. So trite. So—so—my god there exists an intimacy far beyond any sexual mingling—the term 'I love you' flippantly tossed around, interjected after every sentence, becoming a common phrase.

Ask yourself this question upon the altar—would you stay with the same person all the days of your life if the element of sexual gratification was removed completely? Life is getting longer.

Oh it's but a trend. And the girls today still have that ideal, that ideal in their eyes—

It's an illusion society implants—<u>and not always</u>, but more often than not, it disappoints—grows complacent, familiar, convenient, an old shoe you just put on because you've worn it so long and it's broken in—you know how to manage it. So it is with myself. But these treads are running thin on 'sole.'

They say the young are selfish. Aye, 'tis true.

I'll turn my back, because if I follow the masses I can't see the direction I'm going. By god screw your neck on tight, they don't want you to know.

I miss you all. Judge me. JUDGE ME. What do I care? Your words run off from this hardened granite.

Death. I wouldn't cry. Though I may hurt, we keep going, we keep going. Life does not stop, the insensitivity of such indifference. Lie down and die. It still goes on—make the best of it?

Is this bleak? Do others attack my assessment, arguing it's depression-induced monologue—or are they—You—afraid what I say is actually true—afraid of looking life so earnestly in the face? Hold it by the shoulders, love it, crush it in your palm, but know in the end, life will get its way.

I was thinking just yesterday driving home—here we are all in our little cars doing our thing. The world could be hurled into the universe, swallowed up in a second, flicked from its axis—we have no control. And yet we believe we do. I could sit and *have* sat in an office, but to talk about these things—it's so comical! We seek help, go to a doctor—but they're only human, they're not gods, they don't 'have' the answers. Yes there are experts in fields of science, mathematics, nuclear physics, but we're all the same. They can't comfort in the way I need. They can't answer what I seek to know. I saw a picture of a huge executive office— the sun shining in on empty chairs where big decisions are made—man asserting his power. Power is a funny thing—you alone give it to someone. It's not arrogance—but I don't have reverence for any figureheads as to their title. I will respect a body if I feel his/her 'person' is gracious and deserving.

You can have a billion dollar bank account—you're still going to die. We make sense of as much as we can—what else can you do? I seek a greater Truth, and perhaps I am blinded. I want the blood of life to flow through my fingers and to bleed out. I cannot live in a state of complacency—day in and day out going to work—a splash of calm, looking forward to the weekend. Let me go out fighting rather than meekly treading the shallows. <u>I will venture to the depths. And this is why I feel so alone. I am alone. No one wants to venture so far out and let go of everything</u>, to abandon that security all for a fleeting moment. And that makes sense. But all I have to lose is what I must bid farewell to in the end—my life. It's my life. And if I die suffering inside, feeling something is better than feeling nothing. <u>I have known happiness in experiencing pain's contrast.</u>

My dreams were taken away—dreams I never knew I had. And you didn't take them away directly—but You "symbolically."

The innocence of that first time—it's supposed to be—having one's age—that camaraderie of growing up side-by-side.

The camaraderie of a sex, an age, a dream. None of these—NOT A ONE was mine. I am indeed a solitary being inside.

I am apart. You are different in your own way, unique, and distinct, but you belong—you've worn many names—woman, mother, wife, grandmother, sister. I am simply 'Westcott.'

Not even these words mean anything were the world to implode. In the end you have it just right. In the end, Regn, you take it inside and that's all that matters.

My heart hurts, it is tired, it yearns, it has died many times over, and yet it still holds me conscious. I loved life, Regn. Every breadth, the green leaves and I want to go out 'feeling' it so alive. Don't you see? They all would think I'm mad. Can you understand? I 'lived' and I loved—you are light—pure, a breath of fresh air—I am heavy, rich, and explosive. I want you to hold me down, pinion my arms and tell me it's all right—that I'm not crazy. To say, 'Go. Go. I'll see you when I get there, god willing. You go on ahead.'

Some things are between myself and myself. And a god unknown. Ice on fire. The artificial lights of society. Give me the natural sun *without* its silent solitude.

· · ·

TIME PASSED. It had been five years since they danced that first time at the Foundation Christmas Social.

Regn said, 'You'll have to find someone else.'

'And what about everything you said—you break every promise.'

'Oh don't start or I'm going to leave. You're so childish—you and your promises—like a toddler, whining, why, why, why!'

He looks at her in disbelief, fighting to remain stern, to conceal the hurt. Inside he is dying. She shows no hint of regard, no understanding.

'A promise is not childish. A person's word is all he has. You betrayed me.'

'Don't you dare! I'm leaving if you use *that* word one more time—' She means betrayed.

'Have you no guilt?'

'I hurt Jay. You'll never understand.'

'I meant guilt where I'm concerned.'

'There you go again. You'll never understand.'

'Stop saying that. I do un—'

'No you don't. You'll never. It's all about you—you, you!'

'How can you say that?! Regn let me—'

'That's never going to be again. You have to make peace with it.'

'I get so frustrated. Not only sexually, but physically. I don't get to touch anyone. And I don't want it to be *just* anyone.'

'I can't help you there. That's your problem. You have to deal with it on your own.'

'You take me for granted.'

'You're an arrogant, pompous, selfish, big shit, you know that?'

'Those aren't the right words. You need to look up—'

'Shhhut up!' Her voice is a guillotine, swift and blunt, remorseless. 'I'm not going to listen, I'm not going to hear this. Now *you* listen to *me*, you're going to listen to me!'

'—The definition—*arrogant* is the wrong term.'

'It's always about you, only you—'

'Can I say something?' He tries to interject.

Her voice is ranting. Hysterical.

'Are you done? Can I say something?'

'What?'

He stares at her.

'What? Say it!'
'Arrogant is the wrong word.'
'No it's not.'
'In what way am I arrogant?'
'For expecting me to see you.'

He can't believe his ears.

'I thought you wanted to—no one made you come.'
'You—you manipulated me, I was vulnerable—'

So that's what your therapist's been filling your head with. You who said you'd never go to one.

'How can you say that—I always listen and have been there—all I *ever* did was love you.'
'Yes, yes, poor you, and I'm the horrible one that did this all to "you." '
'You are hurting me so much.'
'Don't you even—*you listen* to me, don't you threaten me—you hurt *me* so often.'
'I beg your pardon? In what way *am I* threatening you—'
'All these things you say in your letters—attacking me.'

Westcott is in shock. He is not defeated, but it is pointless to argue. Regn has completely shut herself away. There is no penetrating her line of thinking.

'Don't turn this on me'— her voice becoming shrill again. Westcott wishes he had a camera so he could film her and let her see how absurd she is behaving. Helpless, ranting. It is useless for him to speak; she hears only her own thoughts, panicking. Westcott thinks of a raccoon slipping its black-gloved hand into a can pierced with nails. Inside, at the bottom, is the reward, a shiny gem of a treasure. The raccoon carefully maneuvers its hand around the spikes, clutches the treasure and refuses to relax its grip. Realizing she can't escape, the raccoon becomes frenzied, thrashing about. The fight and flight response takes hold, but neither side will give. The raccoon needlessly perpetuates its wounds.

Westcott wants to tell Regn to relax, let go, ease up. The hand can slowly be retracted. But he knows any attempt to calm her will only succeed in angering her more. On some level she knows he's right, logical, but the truth terrifies her. She cannot admit it openly. She has not the courage to tell him, 'You're right. I'm a coward.' Instead, Westcott says,

'You're turning it onto me. How can I respect you, Regn? You were dishonest to Jay, to me, and now yourself.'

'I hurt Jay. And what about you? You feel no guilt?'

'If Jay sat down with me right now I'd speak the truth. I'm not afraid.'

'You think it's so easy, you have nothing to lose!'

'I have everything to lose, Regn.'

'He's been hurt enough.'

'The shame of it is he doesn't even know the real truth. He only thinks he knows. Maybe if he knew *about* me he'd feel less threatened. What if I spoke to him or wrote a letter—'

'Don't you dare, don't you dare! I'd never forgive you.'

'You said you told him I was a part of your life and that wasn't going to change.'

'I have to go. This is going nowhere.'

'Regn—do you care about me at all?'

'Right now, no.'

'That says so much about who you are as a person.'

'Don't you dare analyze me! Look at the time! Oh God, if I get home what am I going to say, what will I tell him? He'll know I'm lying.' She begins to cry, not in sorrow but frustration. She wants to get away as fast as possible. Inside Westcott feels the hurt, holds it, and knows she doesn't even see him sitting there. Something inside quietly wilts. He doesn't want Jay to hurt, but why are his own feelings discounted? Why are they any less important? He wants to yell, 'Love isn't a possession. Regn belongs to no one. She is free. Free.' But Regn is too scared.

'Look at you, Regn. Just look at yourself. It doesn't have to be like this.'

'I have to go. ' She is not addressing him, but herself. She is telling herself. Westcott knows this.

'Yes, that's right. Run when you don't like what's being said. Ignore it. I know you.'

'No one's going to tell *me* what to do. I've lived 33 more years. You don't know me!'

Then why are you so angry, so defensive, he thinks.

'If you don't get out of the car I'm going to screeaam!'

Now who's childish?

Westcott reaches for her arm—'Regn, please. What has happened to you, why are you making it like this?'

She jerks her arm back—refusing to let him hold it. Her agitation is amazing. He's never seen anyone work herself up so quickly. She is spewing remarks. He is finally struck silent.

'If you don't stop this I'm not going to talk you again. I'll call your mother.'

Now who's threatening whom?

'And tell her what? She knows. Regn, listen to yourself. You're out of control.'

'You just won't take no for an answer.'

'I don't believe in 'no'—it's a defeatist's term.'

'I tried to make it easy. I said I was sorry.'

'Sometimes sorry isn't enough, or it's too late. Sorry is when you break a plate or step on someone's foot. You told me to bear with you. That it was never the end.'

'I changed.'

'Then it was never true.'

'It was true at that time.'

'No, Regn. There isn't a switch. We had absolute certainty. I'm not like you—you can't just flip something like that and turn it off. You used me.'

'We used each other.'

'No. I. Did not. Use you. I didn't change.'

She looks out the window. A National Park security car comes up the ramp, making its rounds. 'You see, I'll call security over there if you don't stop.'

'And tell him what? That we're sitting here having a conversation.' *Does she know how foolish she sounds? Again the threats.* 'You just insulted the integrity of our relationship. Go ahead, wave him over. The only one worked up is you, Regn.' He calls her bluff. The last thing Regn wants to do is draw attention to the situation. Westcott knows Regn too well. She says nothing, continuing to stare straight ahead.

The security vehicle passes behind Regn's car, exiting down the opposite side of the pullout.

'You know, I haven't even once raised my voice to you. And you've screamed at me. Why won't you even look at me—?'

'Yes, you're so perfect.'

'Stop reading your thoughts into my words. Nowhere did I say I was perfect.'

'I have to go.'

'The other night I cried until I fell asleep.'

'That's what a teenager does,' Regn shakes her head.

'No, it's what a normal person does when he or she is hurt. I'm telling you how I feel—'

'Yes, but you have to move on.'

'And what, pretend? Lie to ourselves, say everything's just fine when clearly it's not. I'm too young to live a lie for the rest of my life.'

'You knew what you were getting into—'

Did I? 'I am here for you, Regn, no matter what. I told you whatever it takes—'

'I don't want it anymore.'

'I don't believe you.'

'I can't go on living like this.'

'No, you can't, and I don't want you to. Neither can I. We agreed you'd work towards being on your own.'

'I can't make it.'

'It takes time, Regn. You can't do it alone. You'll need support in many ways.'

'I have to go.'

'You're a coward.'

'Get out of my car!'

'I loved you, Regn. I still do.'

'I know.'

Inside something tightens—hurts—he wants her to say—

He waits for a second, it seems endless, hoping without reason for her to reach for him, bring him close, hug him like she has so many times.

'Have you nothing else to say?'

'What should I say?' She continues to look straight ahead, waiting for him to go.

Westcott looks at her blonde hair. Grabs the door handle. One foot out—'I kept my word.'

'Well—' Regn shakes her head as if to say, *There's nothing I can do.* 'Take care of yourself.'

Can you spare it? He softly shuts her door. She backs away, does not look to the side or behind her. Her car speeds off. He listens to the engine accelerate and the tires trundle away.

Westcott slips into his cab, lets the pain he's been restraining give way.

~

That night a curious memory comes to him. The Visitor Services staff had gone out to dinner a few years before. Regn always got up to go to the restroom once or twice. During one such occasion a colleague had turned to Sharon and said, 'I guess we're boring Regn. We're not talking about *her*.' The colleague who'd spoken had looked at Westcott to see his reaction, knowing he was Regn's closest ally. Sharon made light of it. 'Oh, stop.'

But now it seemed obvious. If she didn't like something, Regn up and left. If she didn't want to hear the truth she'd always run, zoom away—trailing hurt, or hang up the phone. Silence impaled like a knife. Did Regn know what it was to be vetoed, dismissed, cut-off in mid-sentence? No. She was passive-aggressive. Ignoring an issue made it go away, in her mind. For years she'd kept herself busy. That's how she coped. She hadn't changed.

• • •

'I lived in reverse.' He stares out the window. 'Yes, when you're young you should go headlong into it, ride into the horizon. Of course there will be hard times, but that's a part of growing up. I lived for those things—the trees, I lived it to the nth, too long in those places. You were distracted your whole life and now you have time, so it's fresh and new, but I've known these places—the years have been so long. I look forward to nothing. Oh the sun is out, the birds are chirping, but I lived for these things—it's a different perspective. I outlived myself,' Westcott tries to help Regn understand.

He was angry at the wasted potential. He could not forgive her for being so selfless, so damn good and the grace of life itself.

'You live as poetry was meant to be read. It's—do I relish it, or admire it about you— you live lightly—you can take it and then let it go. It's always so heavy with me.'

'I know.' Her voice on the receiver.

'You never ask me about my views on death.'

'Well, you're often so very dark in what you write.'

It's as though everyone's somewhere else, the juxtaposition.

'I'm so angry. Sometimes I feel I'm the only one who has to swallow hard.'

'You're not the only one.'

I just—

'Listen, this is very difficult for me to say. I love you, I always will, Westcott. You're part of my soul.'

'Then give me the peace I need so I can give you your peace.'

'No! Please don't.'

'That's all I want. Peace. Closure. You've shut me out emotionally, completely. It's a two-way road, Regn.'

• • •

Two images. That's all he has. He'd shaken his hand—a tall man. Taller than himself, much taller than Regn. And a picture he remembered. The one he'd briefly looked at so long ago in her dining room. She and Jay stepping from the church. The latter in a suit. Germany 196—

Jay was a pilot. She was the third born, a sister, a girl and the years stretched out ahead. They didn't really know each other when they got married. How could they? They were so young. She didn't even know herself.

He'd asked time and again for Regn to send him a picture of Jay. 'Why?' she snapped. She always snapped now, was never gentle. 'Because it's just natural. I want to know what he looks like. I don't remember. He's seen me. I know so little about him.' This went on for months. And finally Regn emailed a picture. Not a flattering one either. He thought she'd send one of herself with Jay. Instead she'd attached a photograph of Jay with his grand-daughter, Rebecca. His one eye was squinting, which made him look unfairly dweeby. He wasn't bad looking, but he was not handsome in a traditional sense.

And then one day, maybe a year later, it happened.

He sees an old man and a little dog walking out from the back entrance of the Visitor's Center—he'd been on the Island with their gray teacup poodle. Westcott creases the note.

His plan to leave it on his windshield then go walking, chance to run into Jay, engage a conversation—is dashed. The time has run out. Here he is. Westcott waits in his truck to see if Jay recognizes the blue vehicle. He doesn't look over. It's more of a 'doesn't want to look' gesture. *So that's how it's going to be.* Westcott steps quickly, a tree between his view and Jay's. He lightly lets the door fall shut—doesn't want to startle him. As Westcott opens his parasol (it is quite sunny), Jay is closing his own door. He sees a skinny man holding an umbrella approach. At least he's not wearing his straw hat, the one with the practical drawstring he can tighten under his chin on sunny, windy days. 'Hey, Pancho Villa,' Gedny sometimes calls him, affectionately. Westcott comes to Jay's window, a respectful step or two between. Closing the umbrella, he waits for him to look up or drive away. He does not even consider his own boldness. He has waited too long for this chance. He must speak. Jay doesn't want to acknowledge him. Cornered, he rolls the window down.

Westcott stands, exposed without the protection of his sunglasses. He is wearing his prescription glasses so he can take in every detail. The little dog is sitting beside Jay. Calm. He could needle him and say, 'Hi Tamerlane, Tammy,' or 'Laney,' just to let him know *he* knows his dog's name. But Westcott doesn't want to agitate him further. That's not why he's here.

No names are used—no 'Hello Jay, I'm Westcott, as you know.' Not once does either mention Regn's name. Jay knows exactly who he is and wants to get away. Regn is an abstraction and yet she is the very reason for this confrontation. Confrontation? No, how can that be, Jay is waiting to see what he wants—it isn't a confrontation. A reconciliation? No. No. No! But that's what Jay thinks. Why don't they speak her name? Why can't he say it? Westcott asks himself. *Why can't I speak her name to him?*

'I was out and saw you, a coincidence—I've wanted for so long to tell you—I never meant any harm.'

All the scenarios he's imagined, the words, telling Jay, *You don't possess Regn! You don't know the truth. She never told you about me. You think I'm her boy-toy, but you're wrong. You don't know the pain you've caused me. You think I hurt you, but it's Regn—she hurt us both.* There is so much he wants to say. He isn't ready. Instead:

'I wanted you to have this—'

Jay is reluctant to take the folded paper. 'A nice day out, isn't it.' It is a statement. The only thing he's said. He wants to dispel—what? Does he think Westcott has come to fight for Regn? Has he?

'Yes. I just wanted to say something, so often, but I didn't want to—'

'Well'—filling in the spaces, the silence, the awkwardness, *'we've* moved passed that.' Westcott doesn't have time to process the words. He responds to put Jay at ease.

'That makes me feel better.'

It is a lie. Something he will regret in a few minutes. It doesn't make him feel better. He feels worse. It's as though he never existed. They just swept him under the carpet. Moved on.

Westcott hesitates, lingers. He does not know what he wants at that *precise* moment. He thinks of extending his hand—

Jay offers his own before he can initiate.

They shake hands. Both have soft skin.

They are both cowards. Or they are both heroes.

It is brief. Much too brief. He wants time. To sit down, collect his thoughts, have it out with this man. He wants Jay to get upset. He wants Jay to move to strike him. Punch him. Slug him. Interrogate him! Anything to acknowledge what happened! Jay shows no desire to say anything further. He is running away from Westcott.

He looks just like the picture from four years ago—the one Regn finally sent after months and even a year of his asking for one. He is nerdy, bearing a vapid expression of flaccidity. A nose that looks like a gavel upended. A bolt on each side of the stem. Such nice, full white hair though. His hair is handsome. He is an old man. Westcott feels sorry and outraged all in one. Not sorry for what was done, but for the ridiculousness of the human condition. Really. He wants Jay to hear the truth from his own mouth and yet he doesn't. Why should he know? Let him wonder. Let him believe it was about sex with a younger more vibrant man—let him think it was a midlife crisis, let him think—

The not knowing, the speculation does more harm. How can a person just 'choose' to forget?

Here is this window, by god, an actual "window" rolled down, and then this window of opportunity—He wants to tell him, *It doesn't have to be like this. No one's going to take her away. If anything, you are the one taking her away, you're afraid. I understand that. But you don't know me.* The moment of reckoning and it falls flat. He hopes Jay will tell Regn he saw him today. What then?

For so long Westcott wanted to get him alone—to encounter him. And at that Westcott was the one who initiated. Never, not once did *he* ever confront Westcott. The cowardice of it all. Not a single harsh word. No menacing advance. Just a handshake as if to say, *Well, it's done, now please let me go.* The satisfaction does not come. If he had not approached, Jay would have fled, said nothing. Nothing.

He'd walked away from Jay into the Visitor Center to use the restroom. Now he feels limp, numb, his mind high in disbelief. Or is it shock? He never looked back over his shoulder. He'd wanted to—not enough had been said. But there is the note—isn't there? And what had he said in it? Westcott can't remember. It had been so hurried. That one line bothers him though. Why did I have to tell him, 'That makes me feel better?' Why, I wish so many other things—other words. He imagines the right words. Everything he wanted and needed to say. *Regn and I still love each other, you can never change that; she is not yours to own—* That's what he should have said, not angrily, but simply. He should have fought for her. Why didn't he?

He felt Regn no longer wanted him to fight for her. She was tired. She'd resigned. Turned old. He hadn't time to go home, look on the computer, and read the letter he'd prepared for such a meeting. The letter he didn't want to mail. He wanted to address Jay in person. This had been it. He'd never run into him around town. Here was a neutral, safe chance. Perhaps the only one. *Regn wants to be on her own. It isn't about you. It's not about me. It is about 'Regn.' She doesn't want to hurt you, she's afraid. 'Long before me' she wasn't true to herself. She is compromising for your sake.* The truth was Jay had asked Regn if she wanted his help to be on her own. Regn was scared of what her children would think, how she would survive. She stayed not out of love, but security, comfort. Westcott looks out the glass from the Visitor Center. Jay's truck is gone. The momentary content he felt in speaking to him immediately leaves him. He feels terrible. Alone. Worse than had he said nothing at all.

What does he think? It's all over? *We've moved passed that*—the words wounded.

More than anything Westcott feels his own statement, 'That makes me feel better,' is an admission of guilt. He *wasn't* apologizing for what happened. His words were intended as an explanation. 'I never meant to harm you'—the sentence *should* have gone on, 'but had I to do it again, it would still be the same.'

He hadn't lied. He hadn't said the truth either. He wasn't afraid. But for once he felt defeated. Not by Jay, but emotion. Free will. It wasn't his place to tell Jay. Regn had to. It was Regn's choice. She'd been too afraid and said nothing. He no longer trusted the strength of Regn's love. Nor could he put her in the position to choose knowing she'd stay out of duty. He'd been prepared to stand by her no matter the strain; she'd given him hope, raised it so high. Inside he was chalk-white with grief and he could speak of it to no one. Not even Jay had cared to know. Regn would go on pretending, making do, just as she had throughout her life. For her getting by was enough. She'd tasted possibility. Over time her words ceased to mean anything. He could only hear and remember her hurtful voice, the coldness and irritation. In the end she had taken Westcott for granted. Her actions contradicted her words. Not one of her promises did she keep.

Meanwhile Jay drives down the road, parks and unfolds the paper.

Jay Tompkins-

I never meant to hurt you. I've wanted to tell you that for a long time. There are many things I wanted to say. I never possessed, nor do I, any ill-will towards you. Life is painful enough. Never forget that.

A Quiet Man

The image of him walking out with Tamerlane made him harmless, no competition, just an old man enjoying the day. This man who's been married to the same woman for 42 years, this man who's worked hard and provided for his family, this man who's never done without sex and was fortunate enough to pick a fluidous woman in that department. This man who's only fault is existing at all.

He tries to put it in its place. Somehow Westcott wanted more from him—he wanted a heated argument, he wanted a 'jarring.' He'd have taken a punch gladly, anger, anything in place of nothing. Jay's passivity angers him. He said, 'They've moved passed it.' That means he just wants to forget. *Well, I can't.*

Driving by the Settlement Westcott passes an old man on a bike. It is him. Apparently he'd parked in the visitor area of the Settlement and pulled out his bike. Is he waiting until Regn gets off work, to meet her? Discuss his chance meeting. Perhaps he'll say nothing of it.

So much hurt. He comforts himself with the notion that he's done the right thing. If Jay keels over tomorrow at least he'll know Westcott doesn't hate him, which is true. Westcott hates his passiveness and Regn's coldness, but he does not hate "him." Jay hates him, Regn said as much, which is foolish. He doesn't even know him. How can you hate someone you don't even know? Silence does more harm. Now is not the time. Will Jay ever know? Or will it be too late?

———

WHEN I WAS 29 I cried and cried. When I thought I could cry no more, I cried again. My cheekbones ached, swelled. My eyes looked bald—stretched. I cried until I could cry no longer—for the time being. It felt good to hurt so much.

The lightness came afterward. A day after. The inconsolable grief spent, the heart felt light. The retching of the spirit, momentarily purged of sorrow.

I stood on the shore. It was fall and blue upon blue upon blue—a trifecta of shades ran together—the water of the James, the sky, and the blue dusk. I stared upward, trancelike—still inside. Still to the world. I did not want to move. I let the expanse fill me, enter me—the sky was endless—no parameters, the world below the firmament could wait—would always wait. I felt nothing inside, nothing but calm. The sky took me in—its infinite view became me—or I became it. I was now the sky looking upon myself and the shore. I saw the scene as a painting—the immovable figure—myself—in blue plaid wool coat, fixedly standing, gazing. The night before I'd imagined what it is to die. I went through the process of release, of suicide. My own. And the moment of confronting myself. That final moment of no tomorrows. I stood on the shore as though the act had already been rendered. The horizon was inside me—the full scope inside. Nothing attached me to this strand of beach—this patch of time. Nothing. The freedom was without end. I thought of the Indian tale, the boy who swallowed the universe. All earthly sentiments dissolved. I was high—far above and within, not tethered but struck. Not violently or boldly, but powerfully still. My eyes drank, I did not want to ever lose this window. Pain no longer existed. Everything, everyone I ever loved no longer hurt me—they filled me—a series of copper coils—thin wire threads bundled together—when twisted they become one and that conducting energy flows. Often the sky grounds us. I was everywhere all at once. It was peace. All desires, all needs dissolved. I was happy. The sadness had made me happy.

This was after Birçan and I had made love.

OTHERS SAW ME as a quiet young man. Often and throughout my later life, I had the unintentional propensity to attract individuals who loved to regale me about this and that. In short I often listened out of mere politeness when inside I was reeling and clamoring to run away. No one listened to me for I chose my listeners only when I knew they wanted to hear me. I felt like Nick Carraway, (or even Gatsby), forever a witness, but without another as witness to my own life.

After Regn's complete withdrawal even from a simple embrace, my body reeled. Coldness entered my bones. The starvation would come in waves. Restless. I focused on being useful. I drifted from job-to-job, taking what I could find, what I could get. Treading to stay afloat financially when, emotionally, I didn't care; to just stop fighting would be easier, quieter. To escape the confinement of Self, I sprinted, trying to outrun the pain, the frustration, the icy sensation holding up inside my chest. I hoped jump-starting my heart would result in cardiac arrest. It wasn't sex by itself that I missed, for sex was always limited and never actualized where I was concerned, even at the peak of our amorous affair. What I missed was closeness. The intimacy and warmth of holding Regn and being hugged. The ecstasy of our kissing. The warmth of her face, the squeeze of her hand. Regn still had the presence of a body next to her at night. She'd never been alone. From sharing a room with her sister straight to getting married, she'd spent all of her life sharing a room or a bed. A person emits energy, the mere proximity of another, even in the absence of actual contact, warms the body, affects the mindset. On top of this Regn was still having sex with Jay. A safe, easy-to-come-by relief. She could not know, nor would she ever fathom, what it was to never be touched. I resented her for telling me, 'Many people go through this; they have broken hearts and move on.' Her words were an added assault, as though it were nothing more than a trifle scrape of the knee. 'Many survive on their own.' Well Regn, I wanted to say, until you have been alone don't claim to be an authority on it. She was never on her own—dependent solely on herself. My body had been taken up and up and up, only to be cast aside at the most critical turning point. I had yet to come to terms with *it*. I was at the very cusp of confronting myself with Regn. We never really studied each other. Regn didn't like to be looked at—I longed to know every inch of her as any husband does, but over the years he takes for granted the sights he's seen and may no longer take account of. It wasn't the sex I was after. It was intimacy. The fact that I was coming into my own, finally feeling free to assert my desires, only to have the door slammed, resulted in trauma. I asked Regn many times to let us have peace. For us to have the closure my heart needed. Sex with another woman, finding another viable body to sleep with, was not the solution.

Regn refused. *She* didn't want that anymore. In spite of all her promises. She wouldn't acknowledge any form of affection. The worst part was she *did* want it. Her only way of coping was to deny it, erect a mental and emotional barrier. Tell herself a lie. She'd returned to Jay, not in love, but absolute guilt. Her weakness and helplessness frustrated me. I had been betrayed, just like Jay. I continued to sprint. One cold March night I went into the backyard, laid down on the frosty grass in my thin t-shirt. The cold of the night was nothing compared to the freeze inside. We'd never actually slept together—never spent the night and woken up side-by-side. I wanted to feel her on top of me, take in her scent, the warmth of her skin again. I wanted her to love me as she claimed she did, to feel her hands on my skin. I wasn't expecting, nor was I hoping anymore, that she'd have the courage to leave Jay. 'Bear with me, wait for me, I have to do it the right way'—all the words spoken. I just wanted a little time—the time we never had except for that one weekend when we'd tried to fit a lifetime into four days. Even then our lovemaking had been tentative because of me. I wasn't yet free. There was no throwing each other down, tearing off of clothes. All the months of sustained lust had rendered the time we had that weekend surreal.

I needed her more than Jay—he'd had her for over 40 years. In the course of a lifetime I didn't feel a few hours was asking or wanting too much, considering all that had come to pass. I wanted the peace of knowing every inch of the woman I loved. To have that memory and be able to call it up in years to come. It was the wondering, the imagined unfulfilled that left me writhing. The physical part of the affair had lasted three years and in all we only ever undressed and lay down together 8 times at most. The emotions of the affair had been stronger than any actual relief. I saw Regn completely naked 7 times. Of these times she saw me unclothed only once. Just once. The affair was hardly what one would call indulgent. In that final year we were intimate one time and for just twenty minutes. She'd come on her lunch break, which was only 45 minutes. I had not undressed. I touched and loved her. The rest of our lovemaking had always been released in slipping a hand under clothes in Regn's car.

On the outside I appeared calm, if not weary. My body was more gaunt than ever. I attempted to starve myself; this lasted only a day. But I was already emaciated. Nothing helped. The loneliness was complete. Mother knew certain things. The full extent I shouldered alone. She could not help these frustrations; why make it worse by telling her?

In high school and into my early college years I did not long, nor did I miss, physical affection. There had been no such desires. After Regn my body never got used to being alone. My reliefs were few and often too little. I'd take long hot showers—the water couldn't be warm enough—I'd let it penetrate into my bones. It temporarily soothed the coldness. I thought (and hoped) the loneliness would be merciful enough to finally take its toll and render me dead. I masked my desperation in tempered reserve. The absence of contact was magnified all the more by having had it so intensely but conservatively. By the time I knew what I wanted to do with Regn and felt safe to actualize my own desires, she was already gone. The frustration of unfinished affection was inconsolable. The void was worst when, on a crisp fall evening or a bitterly cold winter day, I'd step in my front door, the side lamp on, the warmth of heat. The house would be empty. I'd look at everything neat and in its proper place. In these moments the loneliness hit me hardest. Everything was right—on the outside. A good home, nicely furnished, clean, a pleasant warm scent. I've been told I can be charming. But it wasn't me or anything I was doing. No one knew where I was and even if they did, they weren't the right women. I felt cut off from the world. My solace was a nice soft pillow and sinking into it, hunkering down and escaping through sleep. Leaving the coldness behind, if just for those brief blessed hours of slumber. I'd put a cassette tape on—a recording of crickets, a habit I still maintain. It reminded me of spring, summer, and warmth. The rhythmic trill, soft and pulsating eased the deafening silence. The constant winter inside. My dreams were rarely vivid, but when they were they always embodied pain. I remember one—the physical pain in the dream took such hold of me that to this day I believe I suffered a myocardial infarction. In the dream there was a woman—it was not Regn. She claimed to be Virginia Woolf—although she didn't quite look like her. This woman—in the dream—was more attractive. We were in a dimly lit room and a large bed. She took me in her arms and a terrific pain, a jolt, paralyzed my left arm and spread intensely through my chest where the heart is—I felt my body seize up and convulse in constriction. It hurt beyond the point of hurting; striking with such shocking force. She was not trying to kill me; there was nothing sinister about it—quite the opposite. But the pain she inflicted was arresting—why the pain? I have never felt anything of its equivalent. And though I was asleep I knew my body was experiencing it.

HE HAD NO ACQUAINTANCES his own age. No friends. No pals. No one in whom to confide. He was a contradiction and knew it. He lied to himself, pretended sex didn't matter. He wanted sex. Lots and lots of meaningless flings to kill the physical starvation. He needed what was natural, what was wholly *un*natural to suppress, deny, be cut off from—intercourse. He knew as well that sex would not cure him, only relieve the restless, pounding frustration. He'd never had easy sex. Never had fun. Pleasure in himself with someone. His heart would not be healed, but something, someone had to break his yearning for Regn. It fell heavy and did not leave. It never left. He awoke with it, slept with it. On the other hand, he didn't want sex with a stranger. He didn't want just anyone. He wanted someone who cared, who did not ask, but quietly knew—the unspoken understanding. He didn't want to mechanically kiss someone—a mouth who had been god knows where. A mouth without real want and desire stirred. It would hurt more to indulge in casual sex because it meant nothing, gave nothing. He could give himself sexual relief. The thoughts were endless and always circled back to the same point of departure: *I am completely alone in this feeling and Regn is dead emotionally.*

Sometimes he let the mail accumulate for two, three days. The excitement of a large bundle. The hopes of something to delight him beyond mere advertisements and bills. He started keeping a paper clip in his palm at night or slipping one into his pocket. The firm wire made him feel safe. It was something reliable, something tangible. He traced it with his thumb. As long as he followed the curves he could withstand the moment. Its contours reminded him of a micro track field. To ease the emptiness he felt the hardness, followed along the wiry path of certainty and then back. Sometimes when he awoke the paper clip was loose within his sheets. He'd let go in sleep. Was free in sleep.

The only sound was the voice of his own thoughts. Eventually he tried to meet someone. The need was there but the desire betrayed him. He remained loyal to Regn. He was not free inside to pursue another. Thankfully, those he encountered were either the wrong type or not seeking a relationship. There were six or seven women he had mentally fiddled with. Anca was not one of them. There had been the woman he worked with at the veterinary hospital. She'd only been a friend and he was not attracted to her. She was rough looking with piercings and tattoos. He briefly joined a lindy dance group, which he did not like. One of the women there was a teacher, in her late twenties. One holiday dance he found himself in a local restaurant dancing with her at 3:30 a.m. He was so afraid of feeling something for her, afraid of betraying Regn. He needn't have been afraid. Laurel was not interested. She invited him to a small bonfire get together at her house the following summer. He'd arrived promptly on time, too on time. He'd baked a cake for her birthday. Inside he was dying of loneliness. She wasn't married. He didn't know her story. He just knew she taught at a local elementary school and was single. No apparent boyfriend, but many friends. Was she a lesbian? She didn't seem like it. He asked to go on a picnic, nothing came of it. Another door politely shut. He didn't pursue. There was no reason to, his heart wasn't in it. He still wanted Regn and maybe it showed. (Later he found out Laurel had been in a relationship and soon married). Why not say so? Then there was Ana, another Ana apart from the one at the Jamestown Settlement café. The young woman whom he'd played chess with in the park two or three times. She was 22 or 24, separated from her husband. She was in the military. Had he been a real man he'd have been aggressive, acknowledged that she probably just wanted to test the waters, maybe have a casual tumble in the hay, reevaluate her priorities. Discover if she truly wanted to get back with her husband. She was nice, attractive. But she, too, disappeared.

Anca liked him. She was the teller at his local bank. She was not flirtatious. She was married, but she did small things for Westcott like always putting his balance on the back of his slip regardless of whether he asked or not. She always wished him a pleasant day. Anca was foreign—Russian maybe? Westcott knew that had Anca been single and he'd asked her out she'd have accepted. For a few years the pleasant window exchange had occurred. So fleeting. Westcott never showed anything improper. How could he? She was shut away behind the plate glass. He had no earthly desire to know her any more than their casual passing. It was decent, kind. He valued her genuine kindness. She was not simply doing her perfunctory, 'How are you today?' She meant it when she asked. And maybe she wondered what his life was like. Then one day she was gone—had moved away. Westcott sent a card, left it with one of the tellers at his bank, asking it be forwarded as he had no address for Anca. Did she receive it?

There was the young lady at the Colonial Dance group. She reminded him of a young, not quite as alluring, but cute version of Kate Winslet, minus any accent. He'd asked her out in February. It took a few times of seeing her at the weekly dances to get up the nerve; he didn't want anyone else knowing. He managed to quietly ask. They met at a local coffee shop. Aromas. Where Parson used to go all the time. Parson—the nice young guy he'd worked with at the Settlement. He'd been married what was it—3, 4 years now? Westcott and the girl talked for a good two hours or more and then they'd walked out to the parking lot. Amanda, that was her name. She kept prattling on—Westcott was exhausted. He wasn't used to so much interaction. He wouldn't dare consider asking her over, not on the first date. Even had he wanted to, which he didn't. Not yet. Is that what she had in mind? They left it open, cordially. See you at dance Tuesday. Well, she did not come to dance. They spoke once more on the phone. That was it. No answers. No reason. She wasn't his type anyway. Her voice was too young. Besides, she talked on and on about her dog. He liked animals, but after a while it was boring.

Then there was the woman who worked at the library. He met her through the colonial dance group as well. She was in her early forties. A skittish creature. Italian. Nice eyes. But disturbed in some way, excruciatingly shy. He was intrigued by the mystery, though put off by an older woman being so nervous. Was she in the Witness Protection Program? Had she been raped quite young? Did she have some disease? Being desperate he decided to give it a try. He gave her a note asking in a polite, arcane, but no bones about it way, if she'd like to be his lover. Part of him anticipated a chase and ultimately a 'no.' He would be relieved when she said no, because then he could satisfy himself with the knowledge that he'd tried to date other women and move past Regn, but each time had met with failure. The Librarian said she was too old. He wanted to laugh. She was only 41. But then he wasn't really trying. These weren't the sort of women he would ever want or even consider marrying. No. No.

No. He was the dark horse. He deserved someone refined, full of life, charming, elegant, attractive, intelligent.

June was one of those kinds of women. She was married. In her forties. Thin, quite attractive in a simple way. She'd married young, married her teacher while in grad school. Had 4 children. Her eyes were beautiful. A soft, crisp honey brown. He'd had dinner at her house once. They'd driven to one of the dances together—June, her husband, Phil, and Westcott. She'd never lived anywhere else. Always in the same small town except for a stint away at a women's college in Maryland before getting married. She had a quietness in her. Westcott recognized the quality. She wasn't in any way unhappy. She was actually quite content and well loved. She loved her husband. It wasn't that, but somehow she felt she was missing something. She wanted just once a taste of power, passionate abandonment. She'd read his book of poetry, short stories with his photographs. A professor at William and Mary had told Westcott, 'This is quite impressive. You published the book all yourself? This is excellent.' June had asked if it was appropriate for children. He said to use some discretion. Certain pieces were not. What had the story, *The Blue Line*, meant to her? Westcott had met her husband, seen him at the weekly dances. Phil followed her through the figure eights, sharp sidings, circle rounds, like a puppy. Sweet but without grace. He must have been in his early fifties. He imagined the kind of man he was. He looked like Jim Anderson played by Robert Young on *Father Knows Best*. Phil could be romantic, loving, eager to please, a fine, respectable man and husband, but June's expression, something in her eyes betrayed the truth: she'd never been tested sexually. She'd never been taken by erotic, boundless passion. Phil could be eager, virile, and sweet, but he would never be powerful or intense. He could never offer her mystery.

June had given him a lift one time, her son had been with her. Westcott's truck was being repaired. She also checked on Robbie one afternoon when he had a long day at work and needed someone to let him out.

Every year the Colonial Dancers hosted a local ball. On the day of the ball a refresher class was offered. Apparently Phil had dropped June at the dance hall. At the end of the session she asked Westcott politely, 'Do you mind driving me home?' There was no intent on her part, Westcott was sure. But he was willing to reciprocate her previous favors in giving him a ride.

She wore a nice skirt and blouse. He quickly dusted off the passenger seat, rumpled up the towel Robbie sat on. He apologized. 'I hate for you to get your nice skirt covered with dog hair.'

'Oh, it's fine, don't worry,' she assured.

The drive was causal. Polite. She looked at the tan and black German Shepherd mounted on his dash and the 3-inch knight anchored beside Hudson.

'So why do you have a knight?'

It was an innocent question. She'd read his book. But which pieces? Had she read the one about the deer hunter and the woman about to be raped? Surely she must have. And yet he sensed something in her wanted to know more about *his* personal story.

'Oh, I just always had a fondness for the idea of knights and their codes.'

He didn't tell her his name was Kincaid.

Had he been another sort of man he'd have asked her questions, nothing dangerous, but something to let her know he knew that expression. That smile she had when she looked at Phil on the dance floor. A mixture of love, but also a portion of humoring thrown in—she'd married young, perhaps too young. No time to experiment, falling head over heels for her professor, her mentor who admired her singing voice. He taught music.

He saw her one other time as he was loading groceries into his truck. She was out with two of her children. They said hello. The night he'd come for dinner he'd met her daughter—she must have been 16. Susanna was going to turn out beautiful just like her mother. For a brief time Westcott had wondered if June was trying to set him up with her daughter. There was an obvious age gap between herself and Phil, but Susanna was too young. And maybe in reading his book, June felt Westcott was too experienced, a little too old for her innocent daughter. Westcott felt the squeeze again. He was too old and too young. Never the right age. Rare was it that he ever felt attracted to a young lady, let alone a girl of 16. But seeing mother and daughter side-by-side, comparing the two, knowing how the daughter would mature, he felt an attraction. Susanna had brown hair and eyes. She struck him as intelligent, sweet, and yes, too innocent. The family would want children. They had home-schooled theirs. Westcott could never give June and Phil grandchildren. Besides, he didn't feel they'd be able to accept his situation. They were good people. Down to earth. But it would never work even were it in the cards. Westcott did not believe in organized religion. He'd grown up going to Sunday school, but he felt no religious ties. Religion divided. It was a crutch. He believed in the wind to carry an answer more than any sermon.

A few years later he saw Phil coming out of a local grocery store. It was slightly windy. Phil's hair blew up. The top of his head was balding rapidly. He smiled carrying his bags. He walked alone. But he was smiling through his glasses, smiling effortlessly at the fine weather. Such a fine day. Westcott was glad the day made Phil happy. Glad he was a decent man and took care of his family. Glad there were good people in the world.

Why did his mother have to be alone? Why couldn't he have been male from day one? These questions could never be answered, he knew. But throughout his life Westcott could never avoid gazing—considering the ramifications. What if his mother had been truly loved as a child? What if she had stayed with Tony? What if Westcott's father had been a gentleman in every sense of the word? Would it really have been so beautiful looking at these things from the inside? Did they not become apparent only when standing on the periphery, removed from the joy of family, contentment, completeness? Westcott was Robert Kincaid in some very clear ways. He was alone. Obsolete. A passionate individual from another time, infused with intensity that only pain enriches.

———

Needing to tell someone, he went to six new counselors over the course of four years. When the anger and silence got to be too much, he didn't care who he told within the confines of a small office. But, he resented it. Resented having to pay someone to listen. In the end not one of them did a damn thing for him. He knew they could not. He would go in with an open mind; it always ended the same. The women counselors were the least helpful. He had naturally assumed they'd be more understanding, but it was the men who understood. It didn't matter. Understanding was useless. Accomplished nothing. He still had to walk out the door, 30 bucks lighter and live each day. Not one of them recognized what he needed most. Not a single one took the initiative, the brave boundary breaker, to simply grab him, hold him close, and hug him. His paleness and emaciated presence were unmistakable, he was starving from the inside out. Dr. Bessa said it most plainly. In fact, he had seen Regn and Jay on one occasion. Did he know who Westcott was? It didn't appear so. Regn hadn't liked Dr. Bessa—said he saw things from a male point of view. But what he said to Westcott, what he acknowledged as no other person had was this: you have a broken heart.

To think the statement to one's self was safe. But to say it out loud seemed stupid. Hearing him say it though, sounded direct, complete, absolute. Knowing the cause did not provide a solution. What neither could know at that junction was the extent of its being broken. The reason seemed simple enough. The end of a relationship, the loss of his one and only true confidante. His best friend. But Westcott sensed with fear it was something worse, something more complex, something Regn *represented*. Life would never again be the same, not only because Regn had decided to distance herself, but because of who he was. Life would never be a straightforward process. He hated it. Resented it. Hated what he was. He wondered, when the loneliness got to be too much, if in time, had he stayed female, if he'd been able to get used to it, accept becoming a woman. It was simple. Always the first question when someone got pregnant. So what is it? Do you know yet? Over time he knew the answer, but knowing the answer didn't change the situation. He wanted to be male. Completely. He hated his sensitivity, despised what others praised as a gentleness, a goodness in him not because it made him less masculine. No. But because it seemed a lie; a façade. He wasn't a good man. He wasn't a man. He was cut off from both sides. He felt socially more at ease in the presence of women—but seldom *at ease*—he always found it natural to converse with the ladies. With men he was conscious of what he should and should not say. He did not speak of women in the same manner they spoke about them.

Dr. Bessa was the only therapist who did not know about his gender dichotomy. It was better that way. It was no one's business any more than his affair with Regn. It was private. Even so, the burden of secrecy became too much from time to time.

Upon his suggestion, Westcott joined a support group held by Dr. Bessa once a week. There were about six attendees. Dr. Bessa said little. Westcott wondered if he, too, questioned the usefulness of these sessions. One man, quite heavyset, often stole the floor. He would dribble on and on—he didn't have a speech impediment, but a way of uhhmming chronically. Westcott tried to be understanding. He watched the Dr. and the other attendees. He didn't mind speaking about himself. But it didn't alleviate the discomfort. One boy was required to come; he'd been expelled from the College of William & Mary. This interested Westcott. Secretly he laughed in sad disbelief. *So this is the model student William & Mary admits through its doors. Obviously good character is not what makes good citizens of the world. Oh no, just those SATs, club affiliations, and impeccable grade report. How sad it's become.* He asked the boy if he felt bad about what he'd done or what had happened. Dr. Bessa moderated, curious to know Westcott's angle. It was subtle enough. Without saying it directly, Westcott wanted to know if this kid was genuinely remorseful for what he'd done, stealing equipment from the computer lab, or was he just upset that he'd been apprehended? What a waste, Westcott thought. All the work, money, even prestige. And he threw it away. His parents must have been reeling yet. One girl was on medication, said she didn't cry now, felt numb. Another young woman was clearly obsessed with illness and paranoid about death and becoming sick. There was a middle-aged man, interesting fellow, and a woman in a t-shirt and jeans who was lonely and had her dogs for company. At 30 bucks a pop Westcott looked around the room. This wasn't going anywhere. He didn't want to talk about things that couldn't be helped. Airing private matters would not change them. After the second or third meeting he did not return. A bill arrived in the mail. Westcott composed a formal letter indicating he'd sought support to alleviate stress *not* add to it and that another bill coming at the moment of unemployment, was not helpful. Dr. Bessa was gracious enough to waive the remaining fee for sessions not attended. And with that Westcott washed his hands of western therapy. For the moment. *As Good as it Gets*, that's all he could imagine. When Jack Nicholson walks into his therapist's waiting room and declares, "What if this is as good as it gets!" No sir, he wasn't going to shuffle in and out of some office, talking. Action. Movement. Westcott *needed* to move. The emotional suppression masked the underlying sexual and physical tension. What he needed was affection. The heart does not heal, it simply continues in its involuntary processes. No one came.

A year later, yes an entire year, he stopped by Nancy's. They sometimes spoke, infrequent though it was. They drank tea and Taki barked in his old way. After 3 years of petsitting he still never warmed up to outsiders. It was his breed. Standing in the foyer Nancy did what no therapist had had the courage to do. She hugged Westcott. Really hugged him. She was not afraid to hold on, press him close, run a hand up and down his back to soothe the cold. She'd reached for him, knowing what he would not ask. He couldn't remember the last time someone had hugged him. With Jill, Jill Conway, it was always a quick embrace. Westcott needed to be held.

Nancy was an introvert. A self-proclaimed eccentric. No children, a widow. She understood what it was to be on the polar extremes. She told Westcott he possessed exquisite torment. They discussed the difference between 'exquisite pain' and 'exquisite torment.' As Westcott explained it, 'The latter was something that had become crystallized. Torment was evidence of the pain that *had been*. It made him think of a stalactite. Frozen in time. And how it had formed. Whereas exquisite pain was being in the throes of agony—still *feeling* it.'

He had no lasting relief, no social light-heartedness, no friends to divert his attention, keep him from turning inward, further and further. After Regn the idea of love was drowned in shame. It was a weakness to need affection. He hated it in himself, his loyalty, because it did nothing but torment him.

———

After Regn, by degrees, the withdrawal *intensified*. There was no one to hold me down, warm the coldness sliding over my skin. I didn't care if I was raped, beaten, or even killed, just so long as someone touched me. No one reached for me. And a hug from Mother made it worse.

I no longer existed. If we happened to pass on the road, Regn didn't wave or even smile. If she saw me out for a walk on her way home, she didn't honk, or make a U-turn so we could speak. The emotional alienation was inconceivable. She wanted no reminders. Seeing me was proof of everything that had happened. To be erased, forgotten, dismissed, and ignored is far worse than being told off. Regn's refusal to even speak of intimate emotions suggested she was ashamed. In reality, it was the only way she could cope. But the heart knows only what it feels and my mind could not rationalize the deliberate pain she caused when a mere phone call, a hug, a meaningful kiss had the power to change everything. How one word can save the day.

I despised myself for needing anyone, for ever having let myself become attached to Regn. I felt like a goddamn fool; often I was angry, for feeling anything. Most of all I was alone. She was to my body as air is to the lungs. The simplest pleasure. A body who loved me and whom I loved. A broken record. A broken reel. No one came. I investigated different avenues, my standards temporarily blinded; I was willing to concede if only to lighten the hardness in my chest. It was a constant erection hulled up inside. In the absence of a tradi-tional male erection, I led with my heart instead of a prick. It became so hard and heavy. The only way to expel it was to exhaust it. But it still remained cold, hard, unstroked. After running I'd drop to my knees, ill and nauseous, a ringing in my ears, a light-headedness, a soreness in my throat. I'd put my hands on top of my head to elevate—the heart didn't give out, it only burned.

And the cycle resumed. I had not been relieved—merely spent—momentarily arrested, exhausted. The heart was still full, hardening ever more.

At night I'd feel a cold sensation shoot through my groin. I'd hold my arms at my side as though they were bound firmly. I did not want to touch myself anymore. It changed nothing. Meant nothing. My body needed what I alone could never satisfy or give myself—contact, the presence of another, to feel myself alive through another's body.

It didn't matter how long or hard I writhed. My comfort was privately indulging in the dark night, indulging in the pain. By this I mean crying, quietly, without restraint. But never loud as though I was afraid of hearing my own distress. No one could see me and so what was the harm? No one had to know; I wasn't being selfish or burdening others. Alone at night, the pain was mine. All mine. It was not self-pity but sheer, undeniable frustration. My body was so tight and rigid from restraint. My mind passed the brink of patience. My heart obliterated. I worked, I maintained, I moved about, but inside the weight was immovable. I not only needed a friend. I required a lover. Were I a ready-made man, a one night stand would not have satisfied. I'd have been all the *more* lonely. The void inside was spreading and the more I sought to fill it, the greater it expanded.

I pressed the paper clip in my pocket, tracing the endless elliptical curve of wire thread. It always circled back. No beginning. No end.

Because of my chronic uptightness and loose bowels, my general practitioner at the time, whom I rarely saw, asked to do an impromptu exam. He knew about my other "condi-tion," but he'd never *seen* me. I knew he was only being thorough and to his credit, cautious. He wanted to ensure there was no blood in my eliminating processes.

As he politely pushed on my clothed abdomen, feeling for any signs of discomfort, he could not know the sensation his casual, professional contact imparted. I wanted him to search further, to feel under my shirt, if just to listen to my heart and lungs, if only to feel a bare hand on the bare skin of my back and chest. His hands felt and exuded the scent of exam gloves and antibacterial soap, though he wore no gloves.

'Do you mind if I do a quick check of your stool?'

I blushed at the word, the private ablutions of my body. But again he could not know that my flush face was really a quickening inside, an ashamed eager desire to be probed, examined, touched. He was safe, clean. And this proposition was so unexpected I wanted to leap at the chance before he took it off the table. He mistook my excitement for mild alarm. 'And just what does that entail?' I knew very well the in-and-out procedure, but I was buying time, feigning deliberation.

After his colloquial description—I would have preferred to let the statement stand in its clinical, more formal and polite definition—I gave my answer.

'If it will make you feel better.'

He laughed. I realized the choice words I'd offered and their pseudo-sexual connota-tion. It was not deliberate. A Freudian slip one might argue.

Impending penetration, the lack thereof, aroused me, *emotionally*. Though my body felt no such stirrings.

I asked him not to have anyone else attend. It has become ridiculously customary for a witness to be present. A nice young lady joined us in the room. Younger than me. I declined removing my pants and covering myself with a sheet for something that would take less than 30 seconds. The doctor put on a blue glove, blue, my favorite color when green is not a choice. I lowered my trousers and drawers. My shirt hanging down to conceal my bare netherlands. Nothing in front was visible. Shouldn't something in front have been visible?

'I feel just like a horse at the vet.' I wanted to ease his embarrassment, dissuade any notion that I might in fact be relishing the procedure. I leaned over the exam table.

He was a decent man, genuinely concerned. He could have raped me and I wouldn't have protested. I had messed with nature. By changing genders I had defied the natural order and the only one to blame was myself. The repercussions were mine. I had not realized I was consigning myself to a prolonged sentence of involuntary celibacy.

He alerted me to the moment of penetration. His blue index slid inside, scraped for a moment to collect the desired specimen, and removed itself. *Why not use a swab? I could have swabbed myself?* There was no trace of any blood. And why would there be? I knew why I awoke every morning with a knot in my stomach. The cold sweats. I ate, but nothing stuck to my ribs. Nothing filled the void. It was done within 3 seconds. The disappointment descended. I knew it was all procedure to him, and I was disgusted that my sexual forays were reduced to a singular clinical examination. I never imagined it being this way. I did not anticipate the loneliness of belonging to neither gender. As a young man of 19, 20, I foolishly believed all matters would peaceably resolve themselves once the surgeries had been completed. I never entertained the social ramifications.

———

On a separate occasion, two years later, a woman touched me—the one and only time I requested a frontal exam. She preferred to have an assisting nurse. I succeeded this time in persuading her otherwise. I felt ashamed all over again. I'd made the appointment as a hybrid solution for my frustration. I was subjecting myself to the one thing I'd most feared and never dreamed I'd ever consent to—but here I'd *requested* the exam. Yes I. My desperation had led me to the one situation that for years I'd shunned. No one was going to look at me down there. No one.

It was through a regular doctor's office and she was very discreet, carrying the probing instruments in a small gift bag so no one would know.

'I'm very natural down there.'

I'd never shaved, had no aesthetic reason to—no one ever saw me; besides, I didn't particularly want to see me and be reminded of what was and wasn't there. The front foliage would have been enough, but testosterone does not discriminate—it ensures ample ground cover. I sometimes joked I had a monkey's ass and it kept me warm in the winter. It was an exaggeration, but the netherland's ravine needed a good slathering of Nair. I was ashamed and annoyed; had I been more groomed, she would have probed me further. I'd momentarily obliterated all barriers—undressing, opening my legs to a complete stranger. So why not get the full experience, the full treatment of routine examination.

'Oh you're funny, you have a sense of humor I can tell!' She was nervous, not sure what to expect, talking to ease the situation. I knew what to expect. It was her reaction I waited to know. 'I always thought feet were ridiculous,' she went on, making small talk. Tense with anticipation, her comment still registered in my mind. So, I had an ally in my prejudice against feet. Nice to know. I was thankful for my black socks. God, how I hated the soles of feet, however nice or clean. I would make an exception for one person and one person only. Regn.

In a moment I would be spreading my legs. The word alone, "spread," aroused me. The doctor was kind and if she held any prejudices, she hid them well enough. She performed a manual exam only, despite our brief discussion of a pap smear and rectal exam prior to beginning the process. No sample was collected.

She asked if I wanted to see the instrument. I knew very well what a speculum was, how it felt, and what it looked like. I owned a stainless steel one. She held a plastic disposable one. I feigned innocence, and politely said, 'No.' Afterwards she left so I could get dressed. Returning she said, 'It has been an honor, Mr. Rowan.' She shook my hand. There was no mockery. It was simple, honest. But I knew this was going to be one for the books. Her discussion over dinner to her spouse or perhaps a colleague. 'You'll never imagine what I saw today—'

On my chart she wrote among other single words: *hirsute*. It was amusing, but then I was upset with myself. What if I was in an accident and then died? Would I really want to be seen in all my glory ungroomed below the equator? Hygiene was not the issue; I'd always been fastidious—except for those marinating years of high school, but I could let that go—pretend I was just going through a grunge phase instead of severe denial. A refusal to look at or even touch my body, let alone wash it.

My how I had changed after *they* were gone. And showers became a comfort, one of the few. I couldn't believe the lengths I'd been driven to for contact. I had changed, but I knew I would never be reckless or promiscuous. I was careful, patient. The expectation of the exam had been an exercise in mental masturbation. No one had been hurt, nothing lost. I'd wanted to know. I'd wanted to lay prostrate and exposed if only to escape myself. Punish myself. Gratify—. I'd been aroused by the idea but not the act. Even as she palpated and felt, all I could imagine was, *What must she be thinking?* She'd looked at me more closely than Regn ever had. Regn had mostly just felt me; even then it was sparingly. And that was it. Dormancy descended. Regn had experienced a lifetime of carnal intimacy. I'd only had stolen moments, an accumulation of some odd hours.

My body was still cold. And my heart withdrew into its private asylum. I had no choice but to endure.

I yearned for someone, anyone to come inside me, to rest inside me, to feel the other's hands encompass me. I could not yet know that it was too late. The emptiness could not be filled. It was no longer a matter of intimacy and feeling, of being loved. The emptiness had become me.

———

Having nothing left to lose and needing human contact, I went to a massage therapist two or three times. She was Croatian. Her name, Tanja. I told her I had scars and as I lay on my back in the dark room listening to the soothing music, feeling her professional hands move up and down my skin, I remained tense. Wondering what she thought. She said she felt like she'd always known me. I confided that I was trying to get over my past relationship. She didn't wear shoes, I noticed when lying face down. I was completely unclothed except for my briefs beneath the blanket on the massage table and my black socks. I looked at Tanja's left hand. No ring. I was careful, weighing the dynamics listening for some clue, some indication. Too shy to ask in person, I wrote her a thank you letter and asked if she'd like to get together and talk. She was grateful but informed me that she was married. And why wouldn't she be? I figured as much, but I'd hoped nonetheless that the absence of a gold band signaled her freedom. Foreigners don't much like to wear wedding bands. I well knew from Regn that no ring means nothing. I'd tried not to get my hopes up with Tanja, but after the news I felt too embarrassed to go back for another session. Why were the good ones always taken? Or at least the ones I felt a connection to and who related to me? Why was the timing never perfect? I'd have easily dated Tanja.

———

By the time I reached my late 20s sex by itself no longer interested me. It was merely a relief valve, a reset. Often I couldn't be bothered with a momentary high. With Regn carnal intimacy had come at such a price that I gave up on it altogether for a while. Further, the burden of disclosure, of again disrobing my past by degrees to someone, was too tedious to undertake. There was an occasional woman here and there who I told upfront, almost too soon. I couldn't see the point in wasting time getting to know one another if the major issue of gender was to stand in the way. I didn't have time to wait. Not anymore. I was in dry dock and with the exception of Regn, I had started to rust in dry dock during the prime of my life. Naturally this bothered me, but there was nothing to be done about it. One's personality doesn't change in one sweeping night. I may have wanted things to be different, but that didn't mean they "would" be different. I attracted attention, but never of the type that I could see myself pursuing a relationship and growing old with. I'd look at them and imagine them old. And then I'd listen closely to the voice. Without an accent I felt nothing, especially if she was young. I wanted a rich voice. I always felt ancient, miles away. Love shouldn't be learned; if it isn't natural then why force it.

Eventually I came to value the necessity of self-maintenance concerning sex. Sensual by nature, I wasn't about to let my coveted organs atrophy. My heart was imprisoned, but my body didn't have to be. With the same approach to brushing one's teeth, showering, and exercising, I engaged intercourse. It became a safe, clean, free part of my routine. With proven health benefits, I knew I had to maintain and prepare for whatever the future held. I was keeping myself, in more ways than one. Sexually, yes, but *more* importantly, emotionally I was holding out, waiting for the right woman to come along. I would not give myself to just anyone. So went the years.

———

That spring and summer long ago a new routine had taken hold. After work I'd come home and record the day's events. My only thoughts were of the moment and the next time we would see each other. During this time Miss Gilly became a fixture in my life—I fed her, walked her, but any and all affection was needed for Regn. Every ounce of my energy was consumed with analyzing, going over the day's exchange of discourse, the simplest detail meant everything. I turned inward, further and further away from Mother, entering an ever more private life. Ellis was gone—she came for periodic visits, around the holidays, Mother had her work, there were our tenants—but I felt no need to be specifically interested in everyone else's life. After the stifled years of high school and even college, I felt it was finally my turn to have my own life. How could it be selfish? I had no family—no wife or children that depended on me. I was working, contributing to the home and bills. Mother would continue as she always had. The time seemed perfect—a window of possibility. To this day that time is looked upon as an insular capsule. Nothing before or after has ever fulfilled me—it pales in comparison. I look upon the loss of my youth as a parent who loses a child. At 27 I lost the will to live.

IT WAS AS THOUGH ALL TIME POSSESSED HIM and he didn't want that beauty to go—to be disrupted, mulled over, forgotten, marred, tainted by the trivialities of the day. He was alive and wished to die as such—utterly sensed, imbued with the universal. A singular realization within his own. Feeling the weight of his impermanence, he became infinite.

Walking by the tourists, he took causal notice with his sights. He listened. 'Let me get you now, oh Denise, come Bijou'—just by their mannerisms, the politeness about the whole thing, he knew they were from far away, the Atlantic between. Yet he, just like them, could have been them. Just taking a picture while on holiday, sitting on a bench, dipping for the right angle. He held his fedora to the side of his face, holding a receiver, the suggestion of conversing with the insert of his hat. The East was on his left, the sun dipping. He felt he knew them. Was happy without showing it, that they were happy and enjoying themselves. He walked on, turned left at the obelisk spearing the firmament. He headed into the quaint church. Fifty feet in length? He looked at the panes with cross-meshed wire of antiquated design. Ancient. Timeless, he felt the years all the way back, back and back, to the origin— he'd always been there somehow, and looking out he wished to take leave of his form, he felt suspended within, a levitation as cool steam, a transparent energy rose just above the fixed framery of muscle, calcium, silvery conductors. It was not consciously manifested, something external bound to that within, soundless, the drum returning to its maker. Not knowing why it resounds, just knowing that it must. All the memories that ever were, he held, for he was of the universal thread. The darning needle of the vaulted horizon was but a stitch for each life. To see it all would bombard the senses into torment. To be swallowed, enveloped. He did not speak. Did not need to—for in this brief ever other he had known a most certain peace.

• • •

It is quiet in this room
    this room
        this room.

Those words spoken so long ago echo through him. *That can never be.*

And yet it had. Anything is possible.

There's something terrible and wonderful in knowing it's up to me.

There are but only two choices. He'd made to lie down and not get up. Lying in limbo it seemed motionless, yet things still happened. Even in standing still, change took place. He had waited for peaceful release, an absolute answer to all, but it did not come. Something inside had yet to finish its purpose. Slowly he came back from the heights, the stencil of what he once was. Either way it was up to him. An impractical course, an insurmountable impossibility of patience, sheer madness. But knowing what he wanted and having that same vision returned—

And just like that, Regn was gone.

•••

Westcott lies on the floor. He is watching the day outside the sliding door in the kitchen. The wind is playing with the branches. The curtain is warm from the light. He lies on his smooth chest, his neck turned to the side, his face taking on the impression of the carpet. The back of the chair, from this angle, looks like an owl. Yes, distinctly an owl—there are the eyes and the beak. Box lids against the table. A thready design—beetles, they could be beetles. Are we ever fully conscious? I will die someday, but do I believe it? Do you?

Stay with me.

　　I'm not leaving.

How time, long or soon makes it but a dream
the cold distance sets in—though near and by
Do not dwell long on these things
for in being alone the true loves more
It is a bargain, a gift—wrapped in brown paper
or festooned with design—were it an easy truth—
a lighter way—might I have aged when grown old?
I *see* you at the *finishing* line

• • •

And then came Birçan.

I'VE ALWAYS MISSED THOSE I LOVE, even when they are still alive. It is the knowledge that, inevitably, one day they will be gone. I never could show this love to my mother, to the immediate members of my family. But to Regn and Birçan, I laid myself open Completely. I loved each as though tomorrow she, or I, would be gone.

I often questioned why I could be so loving to these older women while resenting my mother so much. I could not hug my mother willingly even though I knew she ached for the contact. I knew the pain she felt, having experienced it myself for many years, but I could not freely hug her unless I knew it was for the last time. Alone, I imagined bringing her close, hugging her with everything in me. She'd been alone much longer than I had. But it was as though I didn't want to catch her loneliness, which was impossible, for it was already born in me through her. I couldn't lie, I couldn't pretend even for her sake. In hugging her I would be doing it for her and not of my own selfless inclination. It angered, frustrated, and annoyed me that I could not help my mother. But I knew I couldn't, just as I knew she could not help me. After Regn I could not allow myself to ever depend on or need anyone again. Even with Birçan the love was different. I told myself I would never let my heart be commandeered. It comes quietly, enters into you, cannot be blockaded. I wanted to give way to absolute abandonment, but inside something was tired, too old for unbridled, racing emotions. A private cynicism, a sense that it would not last. I knew as well, and for a long time I feared the day when she might be gone—that I would break all over again. You imagine that with one loss anything else after is easier. We wish. The shock isn't new, but it's no less devastating. It is never easy. And as a young man I wanted more than anything to be old for the sole purpose of not being left behind, of not having to be there to watch those I loved leave this plane. I knew it was selfish, but I couldn't help it, I did not want to be left alone, emotionally. Not even a handful of individuals ever reached me. Of those few it was enough to satiate the heart's need and desire. I was content to die young. In fact, it was what I waited for.

• • •

Everyone has his or her own music. We may keep this part of ourselves behind panels, opening such private vaults in moments when we are sure no one is listening. Others flaunt their music. And others still you would never guess at, never suppose the tune they carried. I don't mean the songs or melodies you may hum in your mind. I'm referring to the symphonies that silently propel the hours. The tune you set your life by, whether consciously or unconsciously. Music that would bring you to your knees were you to find yourself with a gun pointed at your head and the instant of crisis waved in front of your gaze—a tattered white cloth, windblown in the distance. The final truce with yourself. The music is a reminder. In the chaos of living it is often drowned away, but for those like myself who have made a life's work out of watching, the music appears, in overlooked instances, when no one is there but yourself, and it would seem that it is playing just for you. It isn't of course, but you acknowledge it, for in being alone, your senses are keenly open, and human relationships seem an endless exertion. In these rare, minutely passing windows of contentment, I have found myself wanting for nothing. It may last 5 seconds, 10 at most, but in having been loved so deeply, and having loved, the breeze across the field, the commentator on the radio, the routine of pulling on clothes—the transience of being here—in these moments, life seems achingly beautiful and cruel at the same time.

Birçan's symphony, a cinematographic masterpiece of composition, was Ennio Morricone's *Once Upon a Time in the West*. She had always possessed a pioneering aspect, an elegant tomboyish charge. Our song was, by my regards, and let's not be shy or bashful about it—every couple has a song—ours was "Wand'rin Star" and the instrumental-operatic hybrid, "Aria," by Paul Schwartz. Three cds were produced. On the second one: Aria 2, were "Ebben" and "Ave Maria"—an amazing rendition. It reminded him for some unknown reason of that image, Fragility of Order. The voice became the antithesis of destruction. The toppled marble pillars, the jungle invaded Great Hall of Jamestown in Westcott's mind, salvaged itself, was bathed in pure goodness. Aria's "Ave Maria" was the voice of burning hope and trust, the redemption of pain. He wanted to fall asleep inside that voice. The belief that something so powerful was blessed and could not die in the end. The feeling was bigger than himself. All the emotions of love, waiting. Her voice signified an advancing, a turning of the tides, peace cresting the horizon. Whenever he listened to the foreign voice sing, his heart swelled and he wanted more than anything to have his belief in the impossible restored. Good things come to those who wait, he reminded himself. But how long? How does one live knowing he is waiting?

The other song, "Ebben," translated from the Greek, says this:

"Well then, you must travel a little ways
Just as the echo flies over the blessed countryside
There in the white snow
There, in golden clouds."

Westcott was the countryside and sometimes his past seemed like the golden clouds of youth.

Birçan was the white snow.

• • •

She had ashen hair. Beautiful really, short, thick with a natural wave. And the front was a dark damp gray, so that her bangs always looked wet. It reminded me of a pigeon. And that's how I referred to her, in my mind. She was my Pidge. She never wore makeup. I studied her expressions in all their varying aspects. I'd look at the lines that would eventually deepen with old age. The small hash strokes above her upper lip, the creases by her eyes—subtle. I saw the woman she'd been—and the woman she'd become. And I didn't want to change her. I wanted to change myself. I wanted to grow old with her.

There are images of Birçan, even then I knew, I would remember the whole of my life, just as I have moments of recollection for Regn, my mother, and those few individuals who knew me best.

There is the proud Birçan.

We were walking at the Island. She was telling me about one of the highest points in her life—when she made the top score on the college math examination in Izmir. She was an anomaly being a girl in the field of mathematics and geophysics. She hadn't prepared for the test; on a last minute whim she took it to increase her chances of receiving a scholarship and thereby continue her studies in America.

Her fiancé was jealous, but her advisor encouraging. 'I didn't even find out right away. It had been posted for a day or two and then my advisor called me.' We were walking and Birçan, like an ad from early Americana, stops on the path, kicks her foreleg—a thrust across the other, swings her bent elbow in the same direction, smiling. I envision her being nine years old. "And I just told him, 'What do you think of them apples!' " I was always amazed at her grasp of our colloquial expressions. It far exceeded that of Regn's and her vocabulary was quite broad considering she didn't begin learning the English language until she was 27.

There is the laughing Birçan.

I straddle her waist. She is lying on the carpet in my entrance. We are being playful. I have her body pinned, I hold each wrist down on either side of her head and talk to her in foolish, light-hearted amorous profusion, like I would a cat or dog. 'I'm going to ravage you!'

'I've never heard anyone put it that way before.' She laughs and can't stop laughing. The more she laughs, the more I squeeze her, pinch her stomach through her cotton shirt. She sounds like a squirrel laughing if I can imagine what a squirrel's chattering would sound like in a moment of hilarity. Her laugh is contagious. Still pinioned, she finally quiets. I release her wrists, my legs loosen around her waist. Gently bending my head down, I kiss her. We are becoming serious again. Then she says the curiousest thing. 'Never give your heart to someone *completely.*' As though it's a choice. I know the heart can be suppressed, but the truth never dies. The heart does not *choose* to love absolutely. It just does. It knows by what it feels. Our pasts brought Birçan and I to this moment. She lets me stay, sitting on top of her. She puts her arms under her head, not caring that she is lying on the main thoroughfare of my living room where my two roommates track their shoes. It is not dirty. I vacuum, but I always remove my shoes when coming in—but Birçan doesn't mind. And I am glad it doesn't bother her. She doesn't want everything perfect. It takes enormous energy to constantly maintain and control everything, more energy than a little chaos of things left strewn here and there. Nothing is, but sometimes I ask myself, why bother? To what end the vacuuming or tidying up? Isn't it more important that a place be lived in? I look at the woman beneath me. She is comfortable, feels safe. I am glad she trusts me. I wonder if being in this position reminds her of something terrible, another place, another time. She was young, in her early twenties. When an acquaintance raped her.

Her laugh had me smiling and laughing in turn in a way I hadn't felt in years. We laughed so hard. And this time in laughing it wasn't to stave off crying. I was truly laughing, enjoying it, her, this ridiculous but wonderful segment. There were many times I just wanted to rest my nose in the crook of her neck, my head on her shoulder, and fall asleep.

And there is the strong Birçan.

I stand in her foyer. It is an early March night. Snow melting, what remains, outside. She takes my brown leather jacket from the back of the chair, holds it for me to slip on—even in my sadness I recognize the irony of reversal. She is holding my jacket. It is I who wants to protect her. To be strong for her, to go away for her. Protect her. From me.

Before opening the door we hug. I kiss her forehead, run my fingers through her ashen hair. It's too short again—she cut it the week before, but that's how she likes it.

We hug once more and step back.

'I'm just so afraid.'

'Afraid of what?' Her voice is quiet.

'Of being alone. It's my greatest fear.'

'But I'm here right now, aren't I?'

I nod. *Right now. But you won't be here forever. Nothing's permanent.*

'You'll write a bestseller, become famous and then women will come flocking to you.'

'That sounds nice, but it's wishful thinking. Besides, one woman is all I want.' *And even if they did come, would I, could I love one of them, as I did Regn? As I love you?*

She stands at the door, watching me go, waiting for me to get down the path.

• • •

Birçan was often oblivious and knew it. Isn't that funny. She knew she could be oblivious. She'd often say, 'I pay no attention to details.'

'You're an easy target then. I could hide in a bush and jump out, attack you.'

She laughed, obviously imagining the scenario.

'Really. You're lucky I'm not someone diabolical. You're easy prey and should watch it.'

'Oh when I get into my work, even as a kid, I wouldn't even look up, I'd be so busy.'

• • •

Birçan was excellent at cutting hair. She'd never had any training, it came naturally. Like my sister before, who would cut my hair, Birçan said she didn't mind. Cutting hair is very intimate. Anyone working that close to your head, privy to the vulnerable, thinning scalp. Trimming delicately around the ears. Standing at the back of your head with scissors. Having someone cut your hair requires extreme trust.

• • •

She often walked with her face mildly askance as though she were pushing through the world with her cheek.

• • •

Birçan was a great cook. We sometimes cooked together. She taught me how to make Borek. I went with her to the gym. I felt safer swimming with her company. Birçan would come out in her swimsuit and a t-shirt. She was self-conscious of her body, particularly her ample breasts. She'd slip the t-shirt off just before slipping into the tepid water. I like swimming. I am not a strong swimmer. It often feels like a brick is pressing down on my lower back and I do not kick in stride. I hold myself in reserve. I hate that I wear a t-shirt anytime I go into the pool. More than swimming, I love the locker room. Watching the various men, each displaying a unique approach to personal hygiene, etiquette, and grooming. Some men just walk about, free as the breeze, bare bone naked, immodest as the day they were born—no thought of discretion, no need. It amazes me and yet at the same time I know I would never have been one of those types of men. Others keep a towel wrapped about the waist. The aisles have an air of casualness about them. We all have the same parts, right? Why the shame in showing what's natural? I am sad when I look at these men and also amused. How insignificant the male organ really is—a jiggling appendage, too short to call it dangling. And yet the power it represents. I don't know why but the sound of a man stepping into his trousers with a belt already looped through them, and the clinking of the buckle, always strikes me as masculine. The chink-chink-chink of the buckle is not delicate. It is heavy, heavy with the force of the hands that pull the trousers up, swiftly, precisely, zip the fly, and pull the leather strap to the secure notch. Everything is held in place. The body secure.

It is not a sexual sensation, but it speaks to the senses nonetheless. Something rugged. Good. Strong. Equipped.

• • •

Birçan was independent, resourceful and above all, capable in spite of her small stature. I often thought if the situation ever arose where the vast majority of the human population was forced to hunt their own dinner, Birçan would be prepared. I imagined her raising a rifle to her shoulder, steady with the trigger, following down the sight. She would not take pleasure in the kill, but if it was necessary she'd get the job done. Regn, having become the extreme vegetarian that she is, would be content to scour for mushrooms and berries. I love mushrooms, but sometimes a mouth and stomach need fortifying. Lettuce leaves wouldn't be enough. I liked that Birçan wasn't a fragile woman and yet, she was still a woman with her gentler charms, whether she acknowledged it or not. Which she didn't. She never did anything to draw out her softer side.

I loved hugging her from behind. Draping my arms around her small frame, nuzzling her ear. Embracing her from behind, I felt protective. Strong. A person is vulnerable from behind, and I was there to hold her, even if she didn't require it. The endearment of it was more important than the necessity.

Birçan loved learning new things for the sake of learning. Up to a point I'd always been that way myself. In high school I devoured facts, but it was more a memorization. Yes, I was excellent at critical analysis in my papers, but after a while the idea of learning something, something I would never use, seemed wasted. What's the point in knowing something if it will serve no purpose? It's like a computer hard drive—empty facts filling up space. I say this because I knew a gentleman—a friend, or rather former colleague of my mother's. This guy was brimming with facts, the most obscure trivia, and yet he did nothing with it! What could one do? Go on Jeopardy or become a professor? It wasn't *useful* knowledge. Even in a social gathering it had its limits. It might impress for a little while, but then one would see that all the information he was doling out had no core. They were just fibers passing through time, filling space for the duration of an hour or two. Birçan undertook projects like someone learning purposeless facts. She filled time.

Birçan had a way of looking at things. If, say I was to walk by a patch of flowers I'd take in their color and their shape. I might even look at the geometrical form of their petals and imagine them looking like a certain thing—an animal's face maybe, or sexual genitalia, perhaps. I looked at the thing from a poetic creative standpoint. Birçan, on the other hand, were she to look at these many flowers, would analyze what the shape of the petal meant—how it might aid in the accumulation of rainwater, what the different shades of color suggested. How the shoots pointed in a specific direction. She looked upon the scene in an entirely scientific matter. Oh yes, she'd admire the color, say they were beautiful, but she liked to take into account the structure of something and its functionality.

· · ·

Birçan and I were more academically matched. Regn and I had been more emotionally, spiritually matched. Experience had taught Birçan many things, some she'd rather have done without. Birçan was wise in having survived the loss of her most beloved. Her second husband—they never formally married—but what is a ceremony when the heart has already fused—had committed suicide, shooting himself in the head.

That's not to say Regn didn't possess her own wisdom. She was not an academic nor would she ever be. Her intelligence didn't come from manmade textbooks and a long list of analytical fodder. Formal schooling had ended at 16 before she worked a year or two in a doctor's office. The world of academia made her self-conscious, more vulnerable. She was a housewife who regretted the unanswerable what-ifs. Westcott had tried to draw out her talents and strengths, but one does not change her ways lest she has the courage herself.

Birçan never had children; in fact, she'd had a minor operation, ensuring no accidents could occur. Her tubes were tied.

Their similarities were cruelly and remarkably uncanny at the same time. Both were 5'2". Both had accents and had emigrated to the U.S. When Westcott and Birçan met, the latter was the same age Regn had been when Westcott and she had first met—53. He questioned in later years if Birçan's and Regn's initial inclination towards a physical affair linked itself to some post-menopausal influx of hormones. Birçan's husband's name was the same as Regn's. It was too unbelievable to even make up. Birçan had a niece the same age as Regn's granddaughter, Rebecca. Though similarities and parallels abounded, the differences were striking, enough so that after a brief deliberation with himself, Westcott entered the relationship headlong. It was death by loneliness or enjoy the moment and live with the consequences. Starved for affection, he opened by degrees. In the beginning he was cautious never to lay himself bare as he had with Regn, but all too soon caution blew away.

Birçan was domineering. Regn was passive. Birçan's need to control everything made life seem regimented, mechanical, whereas Regn's spirituality and open desire to just go with the flow made her sensuality and sexuality enveloping. Regn wanted to be loved. She was alive inside. Birçan didn't want love. Something inside her had died, or perhaps, never was.

· · ·

She'd take my hand and hold it as we walked. I'd hold her hand in turn. We were not grabbing for each other as the young do or holding on. We were remembering how nice it is to have contact. The love of her life, the man she loved romantically (for she had loved her father more than anyone), had put a gun to his head and as she always said, in a matter of fact tone, 'blown his brains out.' She'd loved him as I'd loved Regn. A passion so strong, relentless, that it could only end in destruction. Twenty years before, when they'd met, Birçan had been married. Snowball was just a friend. But her marriage to her first husband had already gone cold. Before anything actualized itself, so she claimed, Birçan took Ahmet aside and told him she was in love with Snowball, that she wanted a divorce. They separated and during that time Birçan and Snowball experienced three years of seesawing emotions.

A person does not kill himself for just one simple reason. I know. There is a triggering point, a moment which sets the need off and permits the individual to finally put into motion his plans. But that singular impetus is never the true reason for a person's decision to kill himself. In the case of Snowball he had suffered a work-related back injury. Everyone called him by his nickname. As a boy he had the blondest hair. They'd see him playing outside, walking by the deck or porch, just the top of his head showing, the sun shining off it, a levitating snowball. He was an engineer. Over time his injury worsened. The doctors offered the prognosis: in a few years or less the condition very likely would render him paralyzed. He did not ask Birçan if she was prepared to take care of him. It was not an option in his book. Instead, one night, in his apartment, while Birçan was downstairs in her own apartment, he got himself staggering drunk.

• • •

There is a knock on her door. Birçan opens it.

'I've told you, you're not coming in here when you're like this. Now go to bed and rest. We'll talk in the morning.'

Snowball was never unkind. He was a talented engineer, but sometimes memories of his childhood found him vulnerable and now that his back was out—

He quietly leaves her door.

A few minutes later he returns.

'I told you! Enough,' she calls through the divide.

She opens the door. For the last time.

'I love you. Take care of my sister, will you.' He is pressing something against the side of his upper thigh. The black barrel, the piece is loose in his hand, like a kid scratching an itch through his clothes.

He turns quickly, runs up the stairs, locks his door.

'Snowball? Snowball!'

Birçan pounds on his door. Several shots go off. Even in her panic, she thinks to count them. She is a mathematician. Everything is an equation. 1-2-3.

Another. Four.

A neighbor comes out.

'Help me! Snowball has his gun. I can't get in.'

Five.

The man and woman are grad students. They know Birçan and Snowball from college.

Robert is a friend. He goes to the door. 'C'mon, buddy. Open up. Let us in. We can talk this through. Don't be foolish.'

Silence.

'I'm going to call his sister.' Birçan hurries downstairs to her apartment.

The corridor is quiet. Only the smell of carpet. The sound of electricity. The air heavy with intention, cigarette smoke.

And then—

The sound of metal.

The bolt in the door turns over. Snowball has unlocked the door but not opened it.

Robert turns the knob. He enters with Sonja behind him.

'Take it easy. Give me the gun. Don't do this. We can have a drink, just sit, talk about it. All right?'

Snowball's grip on the gun loosens.

Robert looks to Sonja. He's fairly certain the chamber is empty. How many shots did he fire?

'Where's Beer-jahn?' Snowball's voice is remarkably steady. Calm. He says her name with the proper accent on the second syllable. His voice rises.

'She's trying to get your sister on the phone. Do you want to talk to Charlotte?'

Snowball looks to the side, at Sonja.

'It's all right, Snowball. Why don't you and Rob go in the living room, sit down.' She moves towards him, feeling no threat. He would never hurt any of them.

'I'll get us a drink.' Robert steps away, just for a moment, to the kitchen.

Sonja hugs Snowball, gently, to comfort. Before she can push away, register the upward motion of his own arm, a crack so loud, so powerful in its proximity, shatters the tenseness in her skin. She snaps backward, the noise volatile, instinctively her body recoils, but the reaction is too late. Her response after the fact. She hears a loud humming.

Sonja wants to scream. She cannot hear her own voice. She cannot think. Her senses have been blasted through the ceiling, the floor has given way, or so it seems, leaving her no foothold. She does not think to touch her face. Why is it wet? She sees red, dark red. On the peripheral. Flecks of paint decorating her cotton shirt.

'Snowball? Snowball!' her voice gives way, wailing. He is on the floor. Smoke from the barrel burns the inside of her nose. Not because it hurts, but because of its intention. She knows what it means. Her nose tells her a shot has been fired. But her mind cannot get a handle on it. Her mind has not caught up. The action is done, but it isn't registering.

'Oh God!' Robert kneels on the floor. A pool of blood is leaking from the small cavity in Snowball's skull.

Robert grabs Sonja, tries to pull her away. Protect her, knowing it's too late. He looks down, following the line of her vision. He feels the acid in his stomach rise to his throat. It is too real to contemplate. It's not, it can't be—a piece of matter, blood-spackled is on the hard floor. The way Sonja won't stop staring, as though she is tied by an invisible current to that beautiful head, no longer spurting, but leaking its personage—Robert knows without wanting to, what he is seeing.

There is movement in the hallway. The door opens.

'Don't, come-in-here!' He stumbles to his feet. 'You don't want to see! Do you hear me! Birçan! Snowball's gone.' As he says this Robert feels his own emotions slipping. He must protect Birçan. Right now. A sense of order. 'We need to call an ambulance. I will if you can't.'

'Someone already did. I want to see him! Let me see Snowball. I don't care. I don't care!'

Robert fills the doorway. She is only 5' 2", but incredibly strong in her will. She ducks to run under his arm. He catches her, restrains her. Holds her as she fights and gives way. Screaming in frustration, then crying. Crying. She doesn't believe him. Why won't they let her in? She is bewildered. Snowball isn't dead. He isn't dead!

'Where's Sonja?'

He doesn't want her to see Sonja's shirt. 'She's in shock. Wait for the police to get here. I'll take you downstairs.' He calls into the other room. 'Sonja?' His voice is quiet but firm. 'Go back to our apartment. I'll be there in a few minutes with Birçan.'

He knows he needs to get Sonja away from the body. Why destroy Birçan's last image of Snowball, too? He spared her. Snowball did. That's why he asked, 'Where's Birçan?' God damn it! He hopes Sonja understood him. He wants her to change out of her shirt, for her own state of mind and to protect Birçan.

'Sonja?!' Still no answer.

Birçan hears whimpering, muffled crying, coming from the other room. The way it sounds, closer then farther, closer, then away, it reminds her of someone swaying. She knows because she is gripping her own stomach. No longer crying. But letting herself be drawn downstairs. Robert has his arm around her back, pushing her, not letting her stop.

Why didn't I let him in? Why didn't I let him in! WHY DIDN'T I LET HIM IN!? Birçan sees a red and blue light through the window on the landing between the floors. Why didn't I let him in?

She hears the footfall of urgency, formality in the paramedics ascending the stairs. Maybe it's not too late. Maybe Robert is protecting me. Just give them a minute. Just let them go in and see. Tomorrow we can talk about it.

'Robert—'

He looks at the stairs. For balance.

She's already forgotten what it is she wants to say.

Snowball *was* 36 years old. Birçan is 33. I am 9 years old and living in California. Birçan does not know I exist. Nor do I know that her life will never again be the same.

———

REGN ONCE TOLD ME, 'I love you, isn't that enough of a guarantee?'
But as Birçan justified, look what Snowball did. *Love* is not enough of a guarantee. Birçan took an interest in me, in my situation, in a way Regn had never cared to probe. Her face and ears were flat and her neck squat, indicative of her Turkish heritage, and her eyes had no brow to shadow them, no shelf to hide under and behind. Her expression was always open, pools of gray-blue; a shade lighter than mine. Clear and beautiful. When telling a story she was long-winded as though searching for the right words. She looked up without moving her head. Her eyes would just look up, engaged in thought. When she became agitated or adamant about a subject, even if she wasn't upset, her eyes took on a sly slitted appearance; she was adorable when she got upset. She hated to be told this. She looked like some caper on a mission, intent at succeeding. Her energy abounded so that throughout her life others had bestowed her with the nicknames 'hummingbird' and 'fireball.' Though highly approachable and friendly, Birçan was intensely alone inside. She hated boring chitchat and shallow people. It's no wonder we felt inclined toward one another.

• • •

Birçan called me her 2x4, two-by-four, because of my gaunt almost sickly skinniness. Sometimes my hip jutted into her, a sharp edge. She'd always been attracted to the string bean type, so it was surprising when she fell for Jay. He was her Pillsbury Doughboy. By no means fat, he had a paunchy stomach but carried it well given his immense height and broad bones.

Birçan and Jay were no longer intimate and hadn't been for six years. Arguably ten. But they loved each other deeply. Jay was asexual. In his younger years long before he met Birçan he took advantage of youth's sprightful libido, but he was more interested in matters of intellect than sexual satisfaction. Physically he was not one for plentiful affection. He did not need to be touched. He enjoyed his own company and had an intensely active mind. Birçan confessed he'd always been somewhat selfish when it came to sex. Once every six months, maybe. Birçan was direct, blunt. Were she and Jay still intimate an affair would have been out of the question. And under no uncertain terms would she ever leave or abandon Jay. Westcott accepted this. Birçan was open from the beginning. He respected her and he respected Jay. What Westcott and Birçan built was an intimacy founded on friendship. Sex, when and if it happened, would just be the icing. Each in his and her own way gave something to the other that could not be given to one's self or provided solely by just one person.

Birçan had larger breasts than Regn. And, she said, they were too large for her body. She carried them well though. To his surprise, Westcott found their larger-than-Regn's size appealing. Jay was not one for tactile affection. It did not matter to him whether she had breasts or not. He tended to look at his wife not as a woman, but as a professional colleague. Jay existed within himself.

Birçan only liked showers. Regn loved her baths, to submerge her whole body and head, listen to the calm. Regn could be still in a way Birçan never could. I'd bathed with Regn only that once, that late night, early morning, with the lights off in her bathtub. I wish we'd kept the lights dimly lit. I wish I'd looked at Regn and let her look at me. Birçan and I showered together a few times. Neither of us liked to be naked in front of anyone; we were both self-conscious of our bodies. Somehow our intimacy allowed us to feel comfortable with each other—the physical freedom I'd just barely tasted with Regn. Birçan's movements were seldom slow or sensual, even in the shower. It was always quick, kinetic energy, however pleasant. Like Jay, Birçan lived inside her mind. She frequently forgot things—dates, appointments, names. She'd lock her keys in her car, leave her purse or reading glasses at home, in a restaurant, at work. One time she even missed her flight! She thought it was the next day. It cost $800.00 to change it! Being of a personality that appreciates precision, accuracy, and order, Birçan's scattered tendencies were not always to my liking.

Regn liked her own company. And Birçan enjoyed her own company as well. She could get lost within herself for hours, live in past memories, remember people she loved without it affecting her mood. I, unfortunately, disdained my own company. I didn't mind being somewhere alone though; I found most people irritating, exhausting. I was the type that was content to have one person or maybe just two or three strong, lifelong connections. I would happily go with a woman into solitude—if we were well-connected. I didn't require many people. But of those one or two that I did require, they were rare indeed and the way we felt for one another was and would have to be founded on an affection seldom seen nowadays. It wasn't suffocating. It would be comfortable. I'd tasted that comfort in my life with Regn and Birçan but it never became comfortable because circumstances forbid it. Regn had her own life. Birçan had her own life. I had only myself. I hated it.

I had no friends, acquaintances yes, ample acquaintances, but no one I could call upon in an emergency. Birçan had been it for awhile. She was my only true friend. I knew that wasn't healthy—having all your eggs in one basket, but that's just the way it was. No one else came along. No lasting friendships.

Birçan, like Regn, spent most of her time keeping busy. Neither thought of themselves in relation to others. Their role had already been established. Was long-ingrained. I spent most time thinking about how alone I was, and how I couldn't stand it. Well then, you or any person might criticize, do something about it. I made efforts, but I wasn't interested in the run-of-the-mill, nor a woman on the fast track. Birçan had finished her Ph.D. at 39. She wandered through life. There was no plan and I liked that. It made for insecurity, but in reality, it was more honest because security is an illusion. Birçan and I both recognized this. However, there were times when Birçan's confidence seemed too much. She'd adopted a take it or leave it attitude over the years, and could be unconsciously insensitive, which hurt at times. Regn clung to her sense of security, her sanctuary, her nest of domesticity. With Regn I had felt the masculine side in me assert itself. She made me feel like a man. With Birçan the role had already been assumed—by her. I felt unnecessary and not because she was married. She didn't need anyone to protect her—that's what she believed. With Regn I had felt the need and knowing she needed me made me stronger.

• • •

Even after Snowball, Birçan had found love. She didn't go looking for it. It found her. So I knew, much in the way Birçan and I had met, that genuine passion and affection were not something advertised. It was subtle and came from the side when you least expected it, but, and it's miserable to consider, for some it never comes. On one level I was grateful. On another, haunted, tormented, alone in the knowledge of how great my love was, and how great to be alive it "could" be, and how unfair and impermanent the object of love is. The love may persist, will never leave, but the person—the object of life's most crucial emotion—will, inevitably depart. This is why I knew it was better to die first, and if necessary to die young.

Being a woman came naturally to Regn. She was a woman through and through. Regn was sensual; emotionally Birçan was more like a man. When I forgot about all the hurt and stepped back from Birçan, I often missed Regn.

Birçan was comfortable in her body, but had she been a man she wouldn't have minded. Sexuality was not the forefront of her concerns. Regn checked her appearance periodically throughout the day; she would be mortified if even a hair was out of place—that is if one was to be discovered protruding from her nose. Birçan could not have cared less. Birçan had a lot of hair. I told her that she took no interest in bringing out her womanly attractiveness. I didn't want to hurt her. I ended up doing just that. There was no reason for the hair in her nose, specifically the single strand that curled out. Who wouldn't want to pluck it, zap it? Didn't every woman (most people for that matter—men and women)—look at herself in the mirror every morning, presuming she had access to a looking glass or even a pool of water? A causal once over to ensure things were in the right place, so-to-speak.

No eye crust, fuzz above the upper lip, clean teeth, hair combed. Finally, after our first argument, Birçan said I'd offended her. She did start trimming the nose hair, however. I never brought it up again. But it was so simple. She was quite beautiful if she only put in a little time. That's not to say she didn't care about her body. Quite the opposite. She worked out, was in good shape, but makeup, even a light foundation, was something she never deemed essential. She didn't know how to use it she said. I remembered Regn putting on her lipstick or pulling out her small compact, she was never without it. Her little case. It stirred something in me, the confidence with which she performed such everyday, female rituals. Regn possessed the female knowledge—she knew how to accentuate her natural beauty.

Birçan carried a can of WD-40 in the console of her car and a paring knife in her change cup for slicing apples. Birçan's charm and attractiveness was kept just beneath the surface while Regn's elegance and womanliness floated on top. Regn always loved hummingbirds, why else would someone have a tattoo of one stenciled atop her breast? But Birçan was the real hummingbird—so much energy, her eyes always cast about. Her movements fast, efficient; she never seemed to be at rest. She was sectioning, quartering, busy preparing something in her mind. Above all she was logical. Regn was a dreamer more inclined to romanticism; as such it was easier for me to relate to her. But neither she nor Birçan were true romantics. I was the romantic. Each had told me so. I wasn't romantic in the cheesy chocolates and candlelight-incense way. It wasn't the things I did—I wasn't a supporter of commercialized holidays like Valentine's Day. I preferred random acts, pleasant surprises on the most ordinary of days. My romanticism had more to do with my nature and character than my actions.

After making love, Birçan did not like to linger more than a few minutes. 'I feel like the guy,' she would say. 'I'm done and then I just want to go…I feel selfish not giving you what you want.'

'I enjoy the feel of your skin and your presence, just being close,' I said. And it was true. I relished the foreplay and aftermath more than any climax. I didn't need to come with someone. It was my heart that needed release. That much hadn't changed.

I kept a count of how many times we made love. There was no risk of losing track because the act of such inherent pleasure was never excessive. I'd never known an easy sex or a free love.

One time after we'd made love I immediately wrote the following:

Tuesday—

I wish I could hold onto these feelings and thoughts. The exact way I feel right now. Birçan and I made love. It had been awhile, several weeks. We never had any love-making in March. B wasn't even wanting it, but knowing I did she opened up. It was wonderful. The contact. I was "packing." I left my drawers on and undressed B completely. It worked better this way. If she didn't see me down there, if we could both imagine that the bulge in my drawers was really me—it was almost perfect. Even I pretended. It is a beautiful warm day. We spent just an hour together. I've been looking at her in a way I never had a chance to with Regn. I want to remember every detail. I told her I was attracted to her because her body is natural. I don't like air-brushed, perfect figures, or fake breasts. The subtle imperfections are what make something genuine. Beautiful.

• • •

All too soon Birçan felt guilty. I didn't understand why, I told her so and for this reason: Jay had no interest in carnal intimacy, even were he in a physically more virile state. An earlier bout of cancer had left him entirely without those natural desires. I knew they would lie down together, completely clothed and maybe kiss, but nothing else. This was fine. He was her husband. I didn't want to take her away. In loving each other Birçan wasn't denying Jay something he needed or wanted. Birçan was the one frustrated, who controlled herself. It was the ideal situation. Me—a "man" who didn't have strings attached, who didn't demand sex *for* himself but received my own pleasure in giving it to the woman. My pleasure was seeing her body, feeling her bare skin next to mine. I didn't need or care about orgasms anymore. I could lie completely naked and not be aroused. Birçan said she could never do that. She always became aroused. Birçan was the one mandating, putting the skids on a natural process. She realized she could not handle a double life, could not trust herself not to show something, evidence, in front of Jay. So she pulled back. Eliminated sex. To me it felt like Regn all over again, only a sped-up version. I understood Jay would be hurt if he found out, but even if he had the slightest inkling he would never ask Birçan. What he didn't want to know he shied away from inside. For such a big, tall man, he was gentle, lost somehow, helpless emotionally. If he couldn't deal with something he went into his room, cloistered away with books, his computers, gadgets. Or he took to the open road, going for a drive. But, I wanted to say, what did Jay expect? Birçan had needs that he no longer fulfilled. It wasn't an excuse. Just a fact. It didn't mean she loved her husband any less. I did not want to hurt Jay anymore than I wanted to hide my feelings.

Birçan would one day tell me, 'What we had was a hay fire. Not an oak fire.' I didn't feel that way. Fires can spread. She snuffed it out. With Regn it was an oak fire.

WE ALL COULD BE HAPPY. I suggested Birçan tell Jay or let me introduce the subject in a delicate way and under no circumstances was he to feel undermined, betrayed. It wasn't about possession. Birçan belonged to no one. One of Jay's favorite books was Heinlein's *Stranger in a Strange Land*. Even I felt certain ideas in the novel were too progressive, too uncivilized. Fraternizing, making sexual advances in the presence of multiple people, group sex. Out of the question. A sacred act best kept private. However, if there existed a meeting of the minds amongst three isolated individuals, three respectful, understanding, civilized people, what was the harm? Why couldn't we live happily? It was always about love. Sex just came as a natural expression of that love—it could never be the other way around. Jay had no desire to even look at Birçan's body. I thought it sad. She was no longer 'woman.' He didn't look at her as a woman. It wasn't her body that stirred me. It was who she was and the glint in her bright eyes, her rare personality that attracted. Sometimes her ceaseless analytical mind got on my nerves; she never rested, but her company was stimulating and I craved stimulating, engaging conversation. In being opposites we offered each other variety; we looked upon the world in completely different ways. Birçan looked at its shape; I would look at its colors. My mind was creative, visionary. Hers was logical, functional.

Birçan's first loyalty was to Jay. I respected this and did not want to dismantle their commitment. I could not have respected or trusted a woman who threw her husband over, just walked out after years together. With Regn it had been different. We'd both entered uncharted waters for the first time. And we agreed the separation had to be gone about in the right way when she decided to leave her Jay. Birçan had a past. I had a past. We'd loved and lost in great ways. It wasn't that we were simply wiser. Our hardships had also made us more aware. I just wanted us all to be happy. No anger, no jealousy, no heartache. We could help each other in different ways. Myself. Jay. And Birçan. I wanted that openness more than anything.

I could not feel guilty for something that came so naturally. I'd read Khaled Hosseini's *A Thousand Splendid Suns* and all I could think was—look at the terrible lives those women lived and the men—the brutality, the selfishness. Some of the men had multiple wives for their own disposal. Love was not the motive. Convenience, producing a male heir at whatever price was. I didn't want to own these women—Birçan, Regn. Yes, a part of me wanted to stake our claim together, to be recognized as a couple—married, but if we could be together and simply happy, then that would be enough. I wasn't put on the earth to take. My intentions were never to take Birçan or Regn from Jay. All I wanted was to give them my love, to bask in the goodness of it, to share in it. In some self-skewed way I wanted to believe Jay and Jay were the selfish ones for keeping these women all to themselves. There is but one thing in this world you can never deceive. The heart. Love has never been a choice, and when that feeling is mutual, god help you. It comes of its own. There is no asking or uncertainty, no manmade designs. It advances side-long, absorbs you, then hits you up-side the head like a 2x4 and you realize despite all your cautious measures, your store of experience, your age, you can never be prepared. The emotions take you into a corner and like a lover crazed with passion, seize you. One does not go looking for these things. They find you. In these fleeting moments of circumstantial examination, Westcott tried to be happy. Grateful. Not once but twice he'd known the true motive for living. It was society's parameters, not nature's, that Westcott bucked. When he loved it was always for the first and last time. He brought to the table all the years of waiting. The private vigil of anguished patience.

REGN WAS FANATICAL about three things: her car, the protection of animals, and being a vegetarian. I was relieved Birçan was not a vegetarian. I was glad the floor of her car had leaves along the sideboard. Birçan was fanatical about her kitchen. Eating with Birçan and Jay was different. I went to their house several times. I say house because it wasn't a home. They were merely living there, renting; it was temporary.

Being the great cook, Birçan whipped up all manner of dishes as though it took her no time at all. She busied herself away. Come dinnertime, Jay, the tall, broad shouldered man that he was, quickly wolfed it all down. Birçan ate quickly as well. It seemed a shame not to savor the meal, the work that had gone into preparing it. Birçan may not have considered cooking "work," she loved to do it, but it felt rushed. Dessert often followed. A home-baked cake, anything delectable.

The minute Jay was done eating, and I mean the minute, Birçan was up clearing plates. She would never set her own plate down on the table, let dinner digest and consider seconds. It was straight to the kitchen to pack everything up, rinse the dishes before putting them in the dishwasher. I often wanted to clean my one plate and fork in the sink and then dry it off, put it away. Birçan insisted I put it in the dishwasher. Even if we were in the middle of a movie, the three of us, Birçan was up and clearing. I did not find it relaxing. Jay had learned never to interfere in the kitchen. The kitchen was entirely Birçan's domain.

Birçan almost always packed a container of leftovers for me, but the feeling of indigestion often sat in my stomach. Jay said little to nothing at all, two feet away as I ate. There was no real sense of pleasure in him. Sometimes it seemed to me a process. Okay, we have to eat, it tastes good, but let's get it done, out of the way. Having been raised to socialize at dinner and let the meal settle, it was an experience dining with this productive rapidity. I understood it to a point. I never liked to linger, even as a young kid, the minute I'd finished eating—though I took my time—when I was done I needed to get up and walk. It helped me to digest. But neither Jay nor Birçan hurried to get up and walk. Birçan seldom, if ever, did any physical activities in the late afternoon or evening. I often wanted to go for a pleasant bike ride some evening. We never did. Birçan always said by that time of day she was tired and after Jay came home from work—he usually went in around 3 or 4 a.m. to one of NASA's satellite offices and came back early afternoon, 12 or 1 o'clock—she had to plan for dinner. Other times Birçan said all she'd been doing the last few days was reading and reading. 'Trash novels'—easy reading, crime action adventures—mindless things. She went through these periods. 'You can't always read the heavy stuff. Sometimes you need a break.' So she turned to her 'trash novels'—not romance or sex, just fast-paced reads. Birçan read words. Jay read whole sentences at a time—she said he read voraciously.

• • •

My favorite activity with Birçan was The Shopping Run. Once a month or perhaps every two weeks, we'd go to several grocery stores. One or two for produce and then Costco for bulk items. I love the lunch counter at Costco. Such a wonderful menu, fair portions, at a remarkably economical price. I would always get a chicken bake—a foot-long piece of bread stuffed with chicken, ham, and cheese. And then a slice of pizza. An enormous wedge. All for under $6.00. I always had leftovers for dinner. Sometimes we'd eat at one of the tables. I would take my time enjoying every bite. There was nothing extraordinary about grocery shopping, but this was made special by her company. A whole morning spent together. Jay knew we went together. No one on my home front knew where I was. It was so casual, mundane to any outside observer, but in its simplicity it was wonderful. We were out together, enjoying the day not for its errands, but the pleasure of each other's company. The task became enjoyable. I appreciated the efficiency with which Birçan shopped, how she positioned her items in the cart and in her trunk. The energy it took. She just kept going. Got in and got out. Unlike Regn's Jay, Birçan's Jay hated grocery shopping. Birçan did all the shopping and cooking. She didn't care what store she went to so long as the produce was fresh and presumably healthy and a good price. Regn could be a snob. To my knowledge she never went into a thrift store. Her childhood had been poor. Post-World War II in Germany during the '50s had its multitude of hardships. But Birçan's early years were rustic to the extreme. No indoor plumbing. Birçan was practical, thrifty, and great at unearthing finds. I valued her economizing mind. She was never superficial. I knew both she and Regn had had tough childhoods in Germany and Turkey, money was never in abundance, but Regn seemed never to want to associate herself with those memories, whereas Birçan accepted them for being a part of her. She was happy—could make something out of anything if necessary, but self-admittedly she had no artistic skills. Regn, on the other hand, was a great drawer, sketch artist. With the exception of "Aria," Birçan and I never listened to music while driving, which I preferred. Music evokes false moods. With Regn there had always been music. So much music, internalized.

The juxtaposition of these two women often filled my mind.

...

On one of our shopping runs to Costco I ran into someone from my past.

Birçan and I had just finished in the checkout line. She was grinding the two bags of coffee beans she'd purchased. I was speaking to an attendant regarding an adjustment to Birçan's receipt. She'd been overcharged $100.00. When I turned around there was Magda.

We started talking. Magda still looked great, her hair was more fine, white, but handsomely so. She didn't exude oldness at all. She talked rapidly. Many questions. And then Birçan came over.

'Magda this is Birçan. Birçan, Magda.'

I saw Magda looking from one to the other, trying to ascertain were we an item. 'We work together,' I answered her silent inquiry, wanting to leave her with some speculation.

'I'm stocking up before I leave to go home this summer to Turkey,' Birçan offered.

'Oh. Are you going?' Magda turned to me.

'I wish. No.'

'My husband's an imbecile when it comes to cooking, I need to leave him some things for when I'm away.'

Inside I was disappointed. A part of me hadn't wanted Birçan to reveal she was married. I wanted Magda to believe I'd moved past Regn and was getting along just fine. Did she and Regn still go for an occasional walk? What would she tell her? And the way Birçan had said 'imbecile.' Like two women idly, harmlessly chiding about men. But Jay could fend for himself. He could cook if he wanted or needed. However playful the comment, I did not like the emphasis Birçan had placed on the word. But what bothered me most came later.

The grinder stopped, Birçan turned back to collect her coffee.

'You look so good, Westcott. Really. You do. I'm so glad. You're getting along all right. I know for a while there was a rough patch, but we all go through that I guess.'

'Yes.' What was Magda seeing? Me, well!? How could she know. My emotions were still raw and Birçan was temporary. I didn't exactly love my job. The people were nice, the environment pristine, the work easy, and the pay a relief. But—

'It's so good to see you.'

'Yes. The last time was at the theatre. *The Impossible*,' I said.

'That's right.'

Birçan was done.

'We'll have to talk again.'

'Yes.' I knew we wouldn't, not unless we chanced to run into one another again.

As Birçan and I left, she pushing the heavy cart, me directing it, pulling for more momentum, she did not ask how Magda and I knew each other. She did not ask anything about her. Not a word. Once in the car on the drive home I volunteered this information, but the fact that she never made any comment showed me something about Birçan's character I did not like. She lived in her own world. Detached.

She did not thank me for catching the error in the charges rung up. The item scanned as $100.00 had been something I got from the deli counter. If you've never been to a Costco you pay for deli items at the main register or else you need cash. I didn't have cash on me that day. Birçan said playfully, but for all intentions she was serious, that had I not bought anything from the lunch counter the mistake would never have been made in the first place so why should she thank me. In essence, it was my fault she was overcharged. I couldn't believe how flippant she was in spending $400.00 dollars and not even checking the receipt! Somehow we started laughing again and the matter was dropped, but I never forgot it. Another hurt, another transgression shouldered, alone. Birçan could be very blunt and uncompromising.

• • •

HE GOT A JOB working for the local community college. He'd done a short stint with the College of William & Mary. After a month he was ready to check himself into a sanitarium. He came close. The work had meant nothing. He'd been a file clerk. 8-5 M-F. He'd have been able to make a career out of it, the salary was enough, but the duties the position entailed meant nothing to him. He wanted passion to surround him. He resigned. Besides, the hierarchy in the office was so heavy the work space felt pregnant with stagnation.

Everyone at the community college was, or seemed, happy. Westcott enjoyed the laid-back atmosphere. He was to be the Evening Facilitator 4 days a week. This meant that aside from security, he was the head administrator on campus, the last man to make a call should anything go down or arise. He exchanged polite niceties with the adjuncts and professors. But that is where the familiarity stopped. It proved to be a lonely position. The pay was remarkable considering it was part-time; it was a state job and therefore, decent. In actuality duties were few to none. The position hindered on 'If.' If this happened, or if so-and-so needed something.

———

Regn stayed on at the Settlement until she retired—however many years that was. We no longer communicated. I was so relieved, so glad I'd never gone back. How depressing, how sad, I thought, that day-in-day-out she did the same things—nothing to challenge her mind. She'd never broken her own ceiling. And she regretted this. I of all people knew.

I'd applied a few times to go back and work with The Foundation, but strangely I was never hired—not even in Visitor Services. I had an interview with Celia, what was I thinking! But I was not offered my old position. Celia made sure of it. After Eva retired Celia became the lead supervisor until she, too, was forced out by younger blood. A few years after Jill made her exit, she told me Celia had moved to Phoenix to be closer to family and to do God only knows what. No one liked her—we never had. Those who remained, like Jill, either avoided or tolerated her petty antics. Jill and the other ladies didn't "need" the paycheck. When the time came they would, and did, leave of their own volition.

Celia was in her late forties, married, with a teenage step-daughter. She never had any children of her own. If you were the type of person who studied others, you knew her laugh was a front, the smile a façade. Her short palomino, practically white hair, displayed itself in tight ringlets making the contrast of her deep blue eyes off-putting. Had she been bestowed with dark wavy hair and green eyes she would have resembled an exotic plant. Enchanting, though potentially poisonous if one came too close. She was also missing the first joint of her left index finger. A childhood accident as she explained it. I saw her at eight years old and imagined one of her siblings pinning her on the floor after she'd tattled and chomping down on the finger for revenge, then running outside and disposing of the evidence for good. It was gruesome to think about, but far more entertaining than the likelihood that Celia had chopped it off while dicing vegetables or stooping to feed a snapping turtle. Perhaps this is why she overextended her social skills to the point of being meddlesome—it was her way of compensating. She masked her discontent behind a perky personality that proved irritating. Celia was the sort who liked to make the lives of others hell; unconsciously it gave her a sense of control, validation, for whatever her life was lacking. Those who feigned to like her were keeping their positions secure.

After my last time applying—we'd spoken on the phone and I'd given Celia a heads up that I was interested in coming back part-time (it was easy work and I could use the money, and the chance to see Regn would be a comfort)—I sent a letter and left a voice-mail admonishing her rude, unprofessional behavior in never responding to my message regarding summer work in Visitor Services. I did not anticipate a response. Nor did I ever receive one. All she had to do was call over to HR and say, 'Hey, pull this guy's app. He worked here before.' I was desperate for familiar work and my pride was gone. This was the second time I'd applied for re-hire in the VS department. On an earlier occasion, about 2 years after being laid off, I'd been given an interview. It went fine. I was never given the position though. Celia did not like me. I also wondered if Rose Marie had any say in it. Did she think it best that Regn and I remain distant? Regn only ever worked upstairs anymore, but maybe eliminating any chance of temptation was in Rose Marie's mind. Then again, maybe she had absolutely no say in the matter. Like the others, except for Jill, no one stayed in contact. Being young they probably figured I had more important things to move onto. I couldn't tell them those "other things" meant a lot less when the person you love isn't there to share in them with you.

Finally, to close off that part of my life for good, I sent one last, terse note:

Celia-

Thank you for your lack of acknowledgment regarding my letter and phone message. It speaks so well of your social etiquette.

The world operates on a much higher caliber when human relations and common sense are combined, subordinating the robotic handbook policies you so love to thrust about. I see through people's superficialities—if a person has something to hide he/she usually takes offense to those who display a genuine attitude. I have bigger fish to fry, as I am never petty. I'm sorry you do not.

Good day to you and farewell!

Regards,

Westcott A. Rowan

———

IT IS LATE JULY. Westcott has been with his new job just over two months. He climbs to the tower—the third stairwell where he is obscured from all line of vision, though he can see others walking up the pathway outside. The sun is cresting the horizon—it's almost 9:00 p.m. He lays his forehead on his arms which rest on his bent knees. Sitting on the steps he gives way again. Yes, again. He's been stealing away more often to the restroom and the stairwell for privacy. He smiles as he walks the hallways, smiles to his colleagues and students alike. 'And how are you?' They may ask. 'Oh fine, very well thank you.' He walks on. It is easy to pretend. He smiles without effort despite the sorrow in his eyes about to spill over. He's learned to hide his pain. He listens now to the silence. No one comes up to the third stairwell. It leads onto the roof which is locked. Only maintenance needs access. Westcott does not worry about being seen. He does not wish to jeopardize his job by being discovered, a blathering basketcase on the third floor. Here he is relatively safe. He shudders quietly, cries silently. His chest heaves, soundlessly. He can't stop. *What if this was it? My last day here—on Earth? What difference does staying make? No one's coming—it's not their responsibility anyway. It's always me—always up to me—all the wasted energy—none of them helped. Not a one. In the end I'm as alone as I ever was. It doesn't matter who I tell. Changes nothing.*

He wears himself out, watches the evening blue darken. Students coming and going. *What does it all mean?* He knows he can't stay here forever. He wipes his eyes, composes himself, leaves his post as watchman. Down from 'the tower' he steps, enters the third floor landing. Listens to an instructor teach as he passes classrooms with open doors. Only one class on the third floor at this time of night. All GE courses. He doesn't listen to the words, only the sound of a voice. He stops at the window that looks out at the giant empty field below. Presses forehead to pane. Studies his reflection. There is a forest across the way, giants in the coming night. *Where to from here, my boy?* He is tired of looking out windows. Tired of living inside. He walks on. The corridors empty. The floors sterile. He must run, wants to feel the fresh air outside. He races to the nearest stairwell on the opposite side of the building. Down and down, pushes the door open. Inhales. It is summer. A beautiful night. He has no one to tell. No one to share his life with. No one who needs him. He tells the night. Walks out to the parking lot and continues on his evening jaunt. He's allowed a break. He walks through the night. Passing time. Again. Always the sense of waiting without waiting.

———

They'd met before. In the spring. She taught chemistry, mathematics, and statistics. She was an adjunct. Over-qualified for the position, but taking what was available. Since he was in charge of faculty mailboxes he asked her about her name and its meaning. She started to laugh. 'When I first *come* to this country everyone calls me "beer can" or "burr can." Occasionally someone would say Bir*sen*. I didn't mind that. It means 'only you.' Birçan is similar in meaning and Sevgi means 'love.' I tell my students the 'c' is pronounced as 'j' and the 'a' is soft, not hard, more like an 'o' sound. For a while I used to spell it Birjahn on the syllabus. I still laugh when someone says, "Professor Beer Can, I have a question." How about you? What did you think when you saw it?' He tells her the truth. He figured it was either bur-kahn or birsehn. 'Well, now you learned something new. And what about your name? I've never met a Westcott before.'

In time Westcott looks up other names. 'You should have been called Behice (*Beh-hee-Juh*),' he tells her. 'Why Behice?' 'Because it translates to *always smiling*.'

Birçan did not teach during the summer. She returned in the fall. She'd asked him about Turkish poetry—bought him a book of Hikmet's work and gave him excerpts to look up— he being a writer and all. Sometimes she wanted him to check her writing. She was taking a computer class for certification to teach online courses if need be. The assignments she had to fulfill were busy work and her mechanics in written responses demanded extensive revising. Westcott more than cleaned up her syntax, not because he enjoyed it, but because he felt he was doing something nice for her. Then Birçan asked if he'd like to join her in bicycling. Cautious, Westcott didn't see the harm in a shared activity. He'd been a taxi driver. Received his CDL so he could drive a 30-foot bus full of seniors to the bank, grocery store, events. He'd emptied waste-paper baskets and vacuumed offices in clean executive buildings as a janitor for cash under the table. He'd worked in the Dean of Students Office for the College of William & Mary. He took any position that paid, but didn't demand his soul. And through it all—on breaks, in restrooms, in empty corridors—he paced and was writing. Writing for his life.

In the Campus Center of W&M there was a piano in the basement. On his lunch he'd steal down to the empty auditorium and play. It made him feel alive. It countered the drone activities upstairs—sitting behind a desk in a windowless office, answering phone calls, sorting files, preparing confidential paperwork. The music imparted freedom. Shy, he played with the lights off. It was an attempt to stave off the restlessness inside. He looked at the old print room where the college's newspaper was published. Life, his life, was elsewhere—not to be lived as a sentence in any of these places. So time and time again he left, moved on, relishing the freedom of not being tied down to a traditional career. It had taken him 14 jobs in the last four years. 14 wandering lacklust jobs for someone to look up and to ask, 'Would you like to—'

He'd grown tired of entertaining himself. A person can only read so much, go for so many walks, watch the sunset oh so many times. After a while it loses its appeal. Without someone to discuss these events with, time slowed down. Meant little to nothing.

Those years of ricocheting like a pinball from one job to the next had made him weary. He'd taken just about any job he could find. He needed the money, but on some level he also knew he had been punishing himself. No job was too terrible. He deserved it. He'd been a fool, a fool for ever trusting in love. He shook his head in disbelief—how he'd brandished the necklace (he still wore tucked away) by wearing it on the outside of his shirt when he worked at Jamestown, inviting gossip. But he'd been so proud, so alive. The feelings of love had made him want to proclaim it to the world. At the time it didn't feel foolish. He remembers Rodge declaring one time that the gold band reminded him of Frodo. Yes, Westcott had smiled to himself, I'm on a perilous quest. In time the symbol of indomitable resolve became a familiar yoke. Banishing the ring into a drawer would mean the capitulation of all his hopes and desires, so he persevered in wearing it—his talisman—close to his skin. From job to job he moved, trying to shake free of the loss, the heartbreak. *Heartbreak*. He scoffed. It was just a word, but God it packed a wallop. Sometimes the simplest word is enough. Like a broken compass, the needle of his ambitions just kept spinning, spinning, spinning until he was tired. Above all he could not forgive himself for having been so young. For believing love conquers all. For trusting Regn. For exposing his most private self to another.

———

I stand at the window looking out and down at the expansive field spread before the sterile, pristine building where I man a desk, dare I not say actually do work. For 'work' requires mental and/or physical exertion. I study my Timex face with the leather band. No digital watches on this wrist. 30 seconds…35….40. The sit-down lawn mower passes before my gaze—rows upon rows—a green rectangular cutout. The forest just beyond. No real falcons circling in the sky here. Inside this vestibule of artificiality I see the fresh cut green blades shooting out the side. A cloud of dust rolls across the field. Students on the walkway. How lovely it is from this viewpoint. Perfect and trim. Removed. No one sees me though I am in full view at the window—forehead pressed to pane. As I run away down the hall, I look over my shoulder and see the smudge of oil from my skin left on the window. And I just showered this morning. Testosterone makes the skin oily.

Back in my office people talk to me. I am forced to listen. Feign true interest or mild attention. 'I value your opinion,' the professor tells me. But I never get to speak—not really. The things most important. Like that man on the mower. I've been there—literally. I know what he feels as the sun warms his arms and the sweat mixes with dust. The sweet odor of decapitated blades. Back and forth, futile endeavors, but beautiful, satisfying for that split moment when the job is done.

IN BICYCLING I LET BIRÇAN TALK. I listened to her stories, content in not having to think or talk about myself. We biked sometimes 16 miles. The pain in my knees made me too tired to do much else but listen. Those first few excursions we'd finish up by pedaling into the Jamestown Settlement parking lot, where we'd parked. One morning, our 3rd time riding together, Birçan said she needed to use the restroom. We pedaled up to the front, the entrance. I said I'd wait outside with the bikes. I wore my straw hat and sunglasses. It was the weekend. Chances were no one would be in, no one who might recognize me. Even so, the irony was too great. I stood against the wall, right where I'd snapped Regn's picture 6 years earlier. Birçan didn't know any of this. I didn't want to disclose my past. I just wanted to enjoy the day, the company. I expected nothing. When, a few times later, she parked at my house I was careful to make sure I was ready and outside, that way I didn't have to tell her to wait, or politely invite her inside. Then, one morning, after a long ride, she said, 'Can I use your bathroom, I really need to go, I drank a lot of water and coffee this morning.' I didn't mind, nor could I very well say no. It would be rude. Birçan was taken back by how nicely decorated the restroom and interior of my place was. 'I've never had a place to really make my own,' she said. 'We moved a lot and Jay spreads out.'

The process with Regn had been excruciatingly long, but the affair quite short. With Birçan it was the opposite. The process of elucidation—of us getting to know one another, was amazingly fast, and the affair longer. I did with Birçan everything I never could with Regn. Dinner, dancing, going to the grocery store, having fun together, gardening. It was too good to be true.

After our 5th bike ride it seemed we'd hit a wall. Birçan could talk forever. She knew I'd been hurt, but she did not know any of the details. I didn't want to push her away. I felt it best to be silent, but some things didn't add up. She was missing large pieces about my life and it made conversation one-sided. I wanted to tell her certain things. She'd been completely open about her hard times. One morning as we were returning from our ride, I told her about Regn and then I said, 'Wait, there's more. That's not all'— and I came out with it. 'When I was 20 I underwent GRS. I was born female—'

I thought about Hannah in *The Reader*, and how Michael Berg had watched her dress flow as they went bicycling on a weekend holiday. Birçan wasn't sensual in that way, but her voice was. I'd study her body as we pedaled. She'd cock her head like a bird, mentally talking to herself, remembering something.

• • •

We carved pumpkins at my house. Birçan had never carved a pumpkin. I always love the smell of pumpkin rind and the hollow sound of scraping the inside clean. We discussed the ramifications of having an affair. I was the one who laid it out a week before. 'Can I ask you a hypothetical question? Could you see yourself having an affair with me?' Birçan had said, 'That's not a hypothetical question.' We walked the parking lot of the campus at noontime. Students heading into the building, everyday goings-on, all the while a grave conversation was unfolding. Should other faculty or staff see us about I was conscious of maintaining a nonchalant expression. I had not expected that she'd be open to it. I'd made the advance, politely. I'd taken the risk. I had to know. A part of me would be relieved when she said she couldn't. In a million years I didn't allow myself to believe intimacy had found its way to me.

• • •

One remarkably warm December day we bicycled around Jamestowne Island. We took a break and propped our bikes against the trees on Black Man's Point. The wind was mild, the tall reeds lightly rustling. We sat on the ground. Birçan against the tree, and I between her arms and outstretched legs. She wore her frontiersman's hat. A couple saw us. What did we look like to them? Birçan in her wide brimmed hat and the slender body she held? Could they tell it was a woman and a young man? It was innocent and affectionate at the same time. Two individuals reposed. The couple had every right to be there, but somehow I felt intruded upon. In leaving I looked at the place where 6 years before I'd snapped the picture I later titled 'Stay.' The stump was still there. I never told Birçan the Island had been Regn's favorite place. I looked at Regn's Seven Sisters—her group of trees all gathered together, as we pedaled on by. I was making new memories, and they were just as good.

Regn never went to the Island anymore. In the years before meeting Birçan I never ran into Regn or Jay biking. She no longer biked. She no longer went swimming. She'd pulled the branches in, tucked herself away inside her nest of safe domesticity and waited for old age. I sometimes wondered if the Island was just too painful for her to visit. Maybe she went some winter afternoon with Tamerlane, but if she did we must have been slipping past each other. I never ran into her in any store—she didn't do the grocery shopping, I knew that, but even just around town, I never bumped into her. On occasion I passed her Volkswagen on the road. That was all.

Another time Birçan and I biked along the Parkway. I took her down a grassy incline marked by a cropping of three large trees. It sloped gently and our bikes bumped along until we reached the river's edge. In the corner of this little area was a convenient place to sit on some rocks. A few years before I'd come out here alone. Some winter day when I was laid off, no prospects of work, and needed to escape. I'd sat and read for two hours imagining making love on the hill. Cars driving by couldn't see you if you were lying flat. But down here, if you looked carefully, you could see someone sitting—probably fishermen a passerby might say.

We kissed and I held Birçan with one arm, looking at the water. I was in disbelief to be sitting there, sharing the time with someone who felt the same way I did. I thought of the movie *Falling in Love* with a young Meryl Streep and Robert DeNiro. It was a movie my mother loved and one Birçan had seen. Our being there, relaxed, open to the world, felt right. It came so naturally.

'You kiss like Michael Smith. You know what it says—in *Stranger in a Strange Land.*'

'Yes. With me, Birçan, it's always for the first and last time.'

Birçan had to use the bathroom. Like Regn she stepped behind some foliage. Unlike Regn she asked me not to look.

We would kiss many times more.

MY HAPPIEST, PEACEFUL MOMENT with Birçan among so many, unfolded on a Tuesday morning. She wore her red fleece jacket, dark jeans, and jade necklace. I asked her to turn on her side so her back was to me. Taking her in my arms, she held my hand in hers against her breast. The traditional spooning position. But spooning sounded foolish. We were holding one another, resting, not fondling. My cheek lay against her shoulder and head. We were completely still. 10, 15 minutes. I wasn't tired. Didn't sleep. I took stock of all the sounds, mentally itemizing them. I listened to: my double-belled alarm clock ticking. A crow outside. And in the background nameless other birds, softly busy in the trees, countless activities out the window. The sound of our stomachs—an occasional liquid spasm, a gurgling in Birçan's abdomen—some Martian spiral freezing gun—the noise—that's what it sounded like. The sound of my own breathing. And the silence. A light pressure on the ears—the energy itself—of things at rest—a noise. For even "quiet" is a sound, a wave-length. We held each other, and then she turned. We just looked at one another. I kissed her after a moment, long, deep. Our tongues searching, playing, sliding, becoming one. I lay on top of her. She lay on top of me. Removing her fleece so that I saw her sandy-tan colored t-shirt. Staring into her gaze she said, 'I could never win in a staring contest. I always look away.' She was right. She looked away.

She held my hands down beside my head. 'Do as you like,' I told her. 'Do anything. Everything. Smother me as you will.' We just smiled. Today wasn't about sex.

When we'd been lying silently I'd looked at my walls, my room, felt the presence of Birçan—her thoughts so near. I wondered what she was thinking. Her mind pressed beneath mine. So close, yet a world away. Each of us in our separate universe. I'd spoken to her, silently. *Do you hear me? Can you hear me? I love you*—but mostly it was a feeling, a willing. I was sending more than words.

On top of her I said, looking directly into her gaze, 'Seni seviyorem.'

She pulled me closer.

My body did not feel tasked, worn out like it does after sex. It felt complete, replenished. The energy was slower, quieter, no wasted exertion on expectations or needs. Just being there, holding each other, feeling the warmth, the connection—physically and emotionally, was enough. *And* even better than sex. It's what I'd always missed, for so long. Without dramatizing, without exaggeration, it is how I'd prefer to die—in such an embrace. It was happiness.

We rolled onto our sides.

'Sometimes you remind me of a child.'

I looked at her skeptically.

'Don't take that the wrong way—I don't mean you *are* a child. I just mean you're so vulnerable, so fragile, and alone.'

I nestled my face into her neck, her warmth. I was, for the time, at peace.

———

During the first winter of our relationship the weather brought more snow than usual to the area. Nothing like Birçan was accustomed to in Colorado, but enough so that campuses and businesses were closed on more than one occasion. A slight dusting of powder and schools shut up like clams. I found it absolutely absurd. I also wanted to work. I needed the hours. On one such morning Birçan and I went to breakfast at a Pancake House. Williamsburg has something in the range of 80 Waffle and Pancake Restaurants. Due to the *less* than inclement weather, most people stayed home to play it safe believing the weatherman's hyperbolic forecast. We were the only patrons of Astronomical Pancakes. The sun was out, and the snow had not been sticking to the roads. We sat at a booth. Birçan removed her scarf. I took off her gloves from my hands, which she'd let me borrow. She sipped her coffee. We shared a breakfast sampler. The meal was always good. Birçan had never been before, I wanted to share it with her. We held hands across the table. It was a quiet wintry morning and I could see in her eyes she was content to be nowhere else at the moment. I had her full attention and she had mine.

• • •

Even while enjoying Birçan's company, the emptiness never went away. I was merely tasting, once more, something wonderful, but that something could not stay, was not mine to keep. Even in our moments of content and happiness, the sorrow was just on the other side of the coin. Birçan did not need me, did not require my presence to get along in life. She might not have been rip roaring happy, but she was content. She was to Regn as Regn was to Francesca Johnson—a wife, a woman with a place to be, a role to fill, a life established, someone to go home to. Of the three, Birçan was the most fiercely independent, but it made no difference. I had no one to turn to freely. With or without her the pain was the same. The ache unrequited. Nothing was required or needed of me. I could just slip in and out of these women's lives. I could come in but never stay. Nap but never sleep.

I held myself accountable. But it did not change the fact that I had loved these women, and loved them still and they loved me.

For a long time I was angry at Regn. I would give over to moments of bitterness. Not bitterness towards anyone, but towards myself, and life. Underneath I knew she had been right to break away.

She should not have made promises she *wouldn't* keep nor spoken such harsh sentiments—but in the end it made perfect sense. I was the piece that didn't fit. It was not the loss of Regn by itself but what the loss signified—the dissolving of illusions, the prospect, or even just the idea of a regular life. The cold reality was: Life would never be easy. Regn and others after her would argue that I "chose" this course. Such is a cop-out. No one chooses pain anymore than he chooses to be straight. You just are—it's ingrained. Inherent, a part of one's make-up. Pain is what I'd come to expect and anticipate. Pain is something I could count on—the one thing that would not abandon or disappoint. Pain was a companion. I thrived upon, and drowned, with it. Moments of happiness were possible, but always shadowed by the knowledge that it could not last. Nothing and no one is permanent.

One of the last things Regn ever wrote me was this: "My love made you a stronger person." A person believes what comforts the most. It's what Regn had to believe. She was wrong. Her love didn't make me stronger; it hardened me, which is not the same as strength. And just beneath the distant unavailable exterior persona, I was increasingly vulnerable. Any prospect of actualizing my desires and receiving affection required a certain amount of thawing and then traversing thin ice. Hoping, trusting the other person would still be there, waiting to embrace me on solid ground.

In meeting Birçan it was like a switch had been turned off. I'd loved Regn, even in spite of the hurt, I'd loved her for 6 years and 9 months. The night we'd danced at the Foundation Christmas social, the pilot light had been lit; it never went out, even in the hours of doubt, anger, and yes, moments of hatred. But I would not have hurt so much had I not still loved her. And then, quietly, without ceremony, a soft wind came through, call it the tailwinds from Birçan's bicycle, and Regn ceased to be the axis of my desires, pain, and ambition. All the years I'd loved Regn I had been in mourning, yearning to be hers and her to be mine. But we were not right for one another. And age had nothing to do with it. Our views on most everything were opposite. You could say I traded one grief for another. Birçan and I offered each other a challenge. Birçan had confidence. She saw the world as an equation. I was afraid when she did *not* run away from me. Afraid that one day, inevitably she, too, would turn. That she would change. Two things were certain: she would never make any promises and she would never abandon me, emotionally. It took a long time for me to believe this, to trust that she was in my life to stay.

Going into the relationship with Birçan I brought along my slough of insecurities. It was not easy, but the moments of grandeur were all the more rewarding, pleasurable, with the contrast—knowing what it took for me to stay alive. We spoke often enough of death and suicide. Possible options down the road. Neither of us feared death—it was just a crossing over—but Birçan still had things she felt she should do. I was content to leave upon the hour.

There were times the detachment from life rendered me morosely unbearable, but Birçan never gave up nor did she cut me loose. She could not weather the storm *for* me, but she could endure it *with* me. It was admirable. I never took her, not for a single second, for granted.

· · ·

Birçan once asked, 'Have you ever considered why you're attracted to married women? Maybe it's because you don't want to be committed, so you choose these situations.'

'No. It's not that. I've analyzed the reasons, many times. I'm very committed. I'd have been there for the other woman. I am loyal. If you were reading this in a book anyone would say, "You god damn fool, didn't you learn your lesson the first time? You get what you deserve." But it's not like that.'

'I know, but you set yourself up to be hurt.'

'I don't choose who I'm attracted to, I can't help it. It's just natural. Yes, I choose to act on how I feel, but the attraction is not a choice. And controlling it always takes more energy and suppression. It just ends up that the person I'm drawn to and feel right with is already taken. I wish it weren't the case, but when I make a connection with someone it is so rare and to pass it by—I told you the alternative before we became close. It was have something and take the consequences, or have nothing at all. I'd waited a long time.'

'You're doomed!' She mildly laughed.

'It's not funny.'

'I know!'

· · ·

Jay neither liked nor disliked me. He simply didn't care. OR if he did, he didn't show it. He and I shared a minimal relationship other than being linked through Birçan. He never asked anything about me—to me. It didn't concern him. Birçan had confided my gender situation, but he never asked about my job, my desires, my former relationships even in a polite manner. What he knew was completely volunteered by Birçan. When I came for dinner to their house his presence was uncomfortable. Not intimidating, but a silent awkwardness. It was obvious that my being there was irrelevant to him. Go, stay. It made no difference. His only concern was how Birçan would be affected if something happened to me.

Sometimes I brought Robert along with me. Birçan loved Robbie; she often wanted a dog of her own, but knew her lifestyle was ill-suited to anything requiring constant attention. Jay never touched Robbie, never showed a gesture of affection. Anyone who saw Robbie immediately fawned over him. Birçan said, 'He's so cute.' Robbie would look at Jay, then dismiss him. Sometimes Birçan would say, 'Can't you give him a little attention?' Jay liked animals, he photographed them enough, but he wanted them to remain outside. He did not like any animal in the house. Even Birçan would not let a dog or cat sleep in her bed. Regn never minded. She loved all animals, even insects. Robbie was irresistible, clean, handsome, well-mannered. I didn't understand how a man could show no interest in such a sweet presence. He made jokes, sometimes baited Robbie, harmless little things, but nothing else. He was particular and grew quietly agitated if Robbie whined or barked at the groundhogs through the glass door that opened out onto their backyard. Jay loved his groundhogs.

Jay looked like Albert Einstein around the eyes and mouth. His eyes were brown and though his hair was short, it was grayish white. His stature was imposing. He had only a mustache. But it was definitely in the eyes—that quality of looking through something. Unlike Einstein, who loved his women and vivaciously lived life, Jay was a true Scotsman, a closed off man. Over the years his abruptness and antisocial behavior had reacted with Birçan's autonomous drive. They considered themselves nomads and loved to travel, just go for drives. They'd been in their current home for almost a year. Few wall decorations were hung—everything was still in boxes or in the attic. What few pictures were displayed showed themselves haphazardly thrown on the wall wherever old nails happened to be. One evening I helped Birçan decorate. Rearranging, aligning, and designing the artwork. Jay sat in the living room on his computer. We asked for his eye. 'Is this straight? What do you think?' Birçan asked. 'It's fine.' There was no reaction, no voluntary input. Whether the place seemed like home, Jay didn't care. He collected things, too many things kept in storage, but didn't do anything with them. I immediately realized my efforts were recognized by Birçan. It was for her that I made the place more livable with domestic appeal. She'd never had a room to really make her own, she said. Jay was always spreading out, leaving things here or there.

On the day Birçan went to get their Christmas tree she had to *tell* Jay he should go with her, that it was something special they should do together. I helped Birçan decorate her tree after I'd put my own up. Jay made the point of putting on a single ornament. He loved the tree, always wanted one, but in the past they'd find one the day before Christmas when barely anything was left. They'd enjoy it just for a day or two and then out it went. I thought it sad and absurd. I understood Jay's behavior was not intentional. He was very much like Sheldon Cooper in behavior, the fictitious Sheldon on television's critically acclaimed *The Big Bang Theory*. He could be oblivious to his own antisocialness; that was still no excuse. He was a good man, an odd man. He knew it. Birçan commented often about it. 'How many men would let their wife have friends and go do things with another man and not worry?' Sometimes Jay struck me as a sad man with no way to express it.

Jay and Birçan had a partnership. It was not romance they shared. It was a meeting of the minds. Westcott knew Birçan had chosen to make many concessions in her life. Jay said that when he announced they were getting married friends didn't think Jay was crazy. They said Birçan must be the one out of her mind.

Jay had his depressions and Birçan was quite adept at distancing herself so she wouldn't be pulled into his mood. Birçan did not like to be taken care of or smothered. She liked to have someone to care for, it made her feel needed. In many ways she operated from a man's mindset. She was always logical and seldom let her emotions get the best of her, lest she was angry. Often she seemed to be elsewhere in her mind.

· · ·

For Christmas she gave Westcott her father's beautiful necktie. Jay certainly never wore a tie, and she wanted such an important keepsake to go to someone she felt would take care of it and his memory. Her father had been a teacher. They made love by Westcott's Christmas tree; it had been spontaneous. They lay completely unclothed on the cranberry wine sofa before walking upstairs to shower. Westcott had never known such freedom. It cost him more. He didn't know they only had two months left. That Birçan, like Regn, would pull the rug out from under him where sex was concerned. A trifle sampling. The memory would remain.

•••

There was one thing Jay and Westcott did have in common outside of the obvious Birçan. Jay enjoyed photography. However, his analytical interest in the methodology and composition of the process had the effect, by Westcott's regard, of killing the passion. Jay never photographed people. He had in excess of 80,000 photographs and never threw away the bad shots. He kept *everything*. His approach was scientific and his pictures were well-executed, but for years he didn't do anything with him. He printed some samples, though for the most part, he stored all the files.

Westcott helped Birçan frame one of Jay's pictures as a Christmas present. It was the one and only time he saw Jay enthusiastic and overtly pleased. He'd shaken Westcott's hand and in return given him a picture Westcott had commented on, one he found particularly interesting.

On a later occasion Westcott was eager to show Birçan some photographs he'd recently had printed on canvas. Beautiful landscapes of the mountains. He was pleased by the craftsmanship and the price. The canvases came with the wire on back, ready to hang. The photographs were easily marketable and ready to be sold. Jay made little comment about the photographs themselves. His primary interest was comparing the quality of the material it was printed on to the company he'd used. They'd discussed starting up their own business, Westcott and Jay, but they operated so differently. Westcott would love to sell his photographs and Jay's, work in a studio. He also knew Jay would be the primary investor in starting up the business. They would not be financial partners. It was all musing, things to consider down the road. In the end, Jay assessed that the quality of wrapping on his prints was of higher-grade than the company Westcott had used just to see if he liked the product. Westcott had been exceedingly pleased with the product. He knew people were lazy. They wanted something ready to put on the wall. They didn't want to have to spend more money for framing and mounting brackets, wires. Jay's lack of interest in the subject of Westcott's photographs initially disappointed but then irritated him. Most viewers would ask, 'So, where was that taken? I like the composition,' something. Birçan had to tell him to look; even *she* showed minimal interest in their aesthetics, examining the material they were printed on, scrutinizing the canvas more than the subject. There was no way she could go into frame work. The way she flew about. She had no patience for details, intricacies of dexterity. Westcott later wondered if she was the slightest bit jealous.

After he started teaching at the college, holding the same rank as Birçan as an adjunct, she showed little interest in his class. Westcott knew all too well how proud Birçan was of her Ph.D. And yet, she didn't use it. She defended herself by saying she taught because she loved it. Maybe she did, but the pay per credit hour was meager. Westcott was aghast to find he made more with his evening position alone. He also knew Jay was the breadwinner and Birçan and he had gone broke more than once in their time together. But when Jay landed another government contract it paid big, roughly what Westcott earned in 5 years Jay grossed in a single year. Birçan's income covered groceries, petrol, little odds and ends, and sometimes an electronic extravagance like noise blocking headphones for a tidy sum of $110.00. Birçan could be very thrifty, but she had the habit of speaking out of turn.

One time at work, nearing the demise of their relationship, Westcott was eager to show her a photograph he'd had printed on driftwood. There was a holiday sale and so he felt it was a great deal. The product turned out beautifully. Other colleagues stopped to look at it, admire the tones and composition. Birçan picked it up, without asking. No harm, it was wood, but a polite, 'May I,' would have gone a long way. She turned it over, scrutinizing the quality and make, asked how much he'd spent for it. Another adjunct was within earshot. Birçan was oblivious and continued talking. She never complimented the piece. What she did say was, 'Your priorities.' Westcott was too annoyed and then hurt to immediately respond, but after she'd left for class, his ire was immediately up. Who was she to tell him how to spend his money? Hah, she was hardly a fine example. He paid his bills, maintained good credit, always paid his own way. He was also upset that the psychology instructor had overheard. Why did everything with Birçan have to be an analysis? Her response had meant more to him and she'd offered the least. It was rude, is what it was. Rude and inconsiderate. Her life in review seemed to leave a trail of hurt. A storm that just moved on. Westcott didn't see this at the time. He was still hoping for the kind and sweet Birçan to come back.

———

Trees, parades, and the Empire State Building will always remind me of my mother. Great big trees—ancient ones, especially oaks and magnolias, which she loved. Even the trees she disliked remind me of her—palms, cacti. The scent of wood shavings and the sound of an electric saw, the scuffing of shoes on the sandpapery floor of a Home Depot, a man in a purple shirt, will always remind me of my father. Whenever I eat spinach pizza I think of my sister. Volkswagens bring back images of Regn. No matter where I am in the world or how old the style, any Volkswagen bug triggers a second look in me. The sound of a jet and the sight of its contrail remind me of the times we sat in her car, analyzing the future. The scent of a mountain wood fire makes my heart yearn for the passions it once knew with her. And snow. Yes, snow will always bring back the memory of Birçan and that January evening when we sat inside her home, the snow falling outside beyond the closed curtains. Birçan loved snow with that childlike curiosity and spirit of excitement she carried with her throughout her life. An earmark of her personality and resilience—the capacity to remain curious and still possess wonder. We'd sat, each of us on one arm of the soft chair, talking into the night in hushed voices. Her husband was sleeping. We did not wish to disturb him. She listened and looked at me. The years I'd waited. The hours for such a confidante. We exchanged truths and the details of our lives. 'We'll never abandon you, you know.' She meant herself and Jay. 'You can come with us.'

'And if I get sick would you take care of me?'

'Yes.'

• • •

I didn't mean to fall in love with her.

OUR LAST TIME WORKING TOGETHER, or rather, our being at the campus at the same time, was exam week. She came just before 7:00 p.m. I went into one of the empty classrooms on my floor—the second floor—and looked out the west windows. I didn't know when she was coming. I had nothing to tend to at the moment. The blinds were down but the slats open. I saw her car on the main road, watched it all the way. She took the long route, always making an 'L' along the perimeter of the parking area instead of cutting down and into it. I saw her get out, no loitering, and start walking toward the building. She looked just like a student with her backpack. She was pulling on her blue fleece jacket as she walked. That moment was good, happy. I wanted to stay in that short interval. It wasn't creepy or voyeuristic. I just liked seeing her, knowing she was on her way up. Watching her as she really is. Had she known I was watching, which on occasion she did—she'd see me at the main window or downstairs ready to open the door for her on rainy days—it wouldn't have been nearly as intimate.

I left the classroom and made my round, started walking the hallway. I ran into Birçan just as she was coming up the main stairwell. Her eyes were happy, her face always with its smile. She noticed my blue shirt, asked if it was new. Told me about her fun time on Tuesday—how she locked herself out of the house and how she'd thought I'd laugh my ass off when she told me. 'I can be such a space cadet! I leave my purse all the time. I'm becoming like my mother.' I wish I could be happy with just that friendliness, but the memory of our making love tormented me. Being so near her and not being able to express what was deepest only hurt more.

In the beginning she had touched me all the time. Even out in public. A casual hand on the hip. A warm desire in the eyes. She wanted my company. Much too soon that all changed. I told her I didn't do anything wrong. She said, 'You're right, it's nothing you did. You need to find someone who deserves you. I just don't want it anymore.' Birçan realized she wasn't cut out for having an affair. It made me very sad. The last time we made love I wish she'd told me, 'This is it.' I wish we'd gone into that final act with a meeting of the minds, a joint decision. Instead she ripped the rug out from under me. The decision didn't bother me as much. The way she went about it did. We had many arguments. Brutal to the point of saying goodbye forever. She gave me back my stone blue teacup and matching saucer, which she kept in her cupboard for times when I visited. For some odd months she was cool, distant. But with time and the approach of her departure, her ultimate leaving, their moving away from Virginia, Birçan opened her door again. Never in the same way as those first wonderful two months we'd shared. Her pending leaving made it bittersweet for me. I preferred something as opposed to nothing. Why spoil the time we still had with thoughts of the future?

———

It was like living a version of *Paint Your Wagon*, starring Lee Marvin and a young Clint Eastwood. A woman who loved two men and the men were friends *and* Jay knew about Westcott's physical situation. One older, one a bit younger. It was easy. No hardship of emotions, just an understanding. And love enough for everyone. That's how I *imagined* it could have been. Birçan loved her Western movies for their musical scores.

• • •

Like the villains of her westerns, Birçan had a terrible temper. The second Christmas of knowing each other I left a note in her mailbox before taking winter break. She didn't get it until the New Year when classes started up again. Not having seen each other for a month she was amicable 10 seconds and then she proceeded to chastise me. She tore the letter in fourths, emphatically threw it into the garbage can. Inside something hurt. I couldn't believe it. What was the matter with her? She didn't want any reminders. I'd simply said what we'd shared had meant something important and to have a Happy New Year.

'Birçan, why'— my tone was even, cool.
'Don't say my name!'
Saying her name, having her name inside my mouth was too much for her, a violation. An attachment. Had I no say? No rights?
A normal person would have said, 'Thank you for your sentiments. They mean a lot.' Not Birçan. Birçan made everything about *her*. She demanded I not bring up the past and what good times, affectionately speaking, we'd shared. She didn't want to be reminded. Her way of coping.
We were standing outside her classroom, the room full. She whispered in the corridor, but her body language said enough and any student near the door could easily hear.
'You are a selfish woman,' I said calmly.
'Yes, I am.' She nodded for punctuation. 'Fuck off! Go away.'
And just like that I'd been dismissed.
The rudeness, the hostility. All because I cared and at one time even loved her, a woman with whom I'd shared affections and who, at one time had felt the same, 'I do love you, Westcott.'
My mind could not reconcile the two Birçans. The one who had been so warm and sweet, always being the first to reach for my hand, hold it in hers, eagerly kiss me as she stepped into my foyer.
I felt used.

I did not want to see or speak to Birçan. I had to. I had to confront her. A week later after her evening class, I entered the room. 'I deserve an apology. Coming from you I don't expect to get one, but I deserve one. There is no justification for your behavior. It made me so angry and hurt. Birçan—'
'You are demanding.'

Me. The one who didn't even ask for sex or require it? All I wanted was the emotional closeness we'd enjoyed. A nice kiss. To hug one another. If anyone was demanding it was Birçan. She never compromised. At times I felt very sad for her. I knew she was broken. She'd denied so many things for so long she could no longer tell the difference. She was the woman who filled her life with odd-job projects that amounted to nothing except her own personal pride. No other audience but her own. One time she spent all day washing, rewashing, soaking an antique set of bed linens that belonged to Jay's mother. She would never use them. But she took the time to clean and bleach the brown mildew away. Another time we went to Home Depot for paint. She wanted to freshen up the little vanity drawers in her room. The furniture belonged to the house they rented, nonetheless she decided to paint them. Her job was not gratifying. She had a Ph.D. she seldom used. The students she taught came and went. She had no children to her name, no sex life, an emotionally detached husband who, if she became sick, wouldn't know what to do in terms of bedside manner and would call a friend to stand in for him. Bírçan filled her life with rare finds from thrift shops. Little things that gave her momentary delight. A new used pot, a ceramic cow, iron trivets, several nice shirts. This is how Bírçan lived. Always staying busy. Cooking and quickly packing it away. Nights she sat in bed alone, her room. Reading until sleep. She was the epitome of aloneness.

Bírçan became hysterical. A class was starting next door. I moved to close our door. I kept my tone modulated trying to keep the situation together all the more as Bírçan flew off the handle.

She apologized, but she wanted to know if I'd apologize for giving her another letter. I found it ridiculous, petty. Tit for tat. Write whenever you need to she used to say. My only fault was ever giving a damn. Caring about her. Bírçan didn't want to be obligated to anyone. She wanted no attachments to anyone or anything living. Pets were even too much of a responsibility. Robbie had started to irritate her. Everything about me was a nuisance. Despite her "active" life, it seemed hollow. Hollow in a separate way from my emptiness. My life, though lonely, felt rich, alive in its yearning. Bírçan's felt dry, like a fossilized wound. The feeling gone from it; only hardened dusty facts. No juice. No marrow. Only painful decay of the soul.

I was glad I hadn't bought her birthday present. The one I'd planned on for some months. Bírçan would have received it for its usefulness, but her gratitude would have been forced. Not only would the money be wasted, but the sentiment would go unacknowledged. The thought of making Bírçan happy had made me happy, but the same could not be said for her.

After a while it just didn't matter. The anger flared up now and again, but I knew Bírçan did not care. I missed Regn anew. Bírçan made my emotions surrounding Regn seem so long ago, like a walk in the park. Regn had been cold and harsh out of fear not selfishness. Bírçan had nothing left to give. She was ruthless. My presence reminded Bírçan that her life wasn't perfect—far from it—and being a woman who wanted to forget, who needed to shut the past out, I challenged her coping mechanisms. And so it was her or me. She didn't have to hurt me, that's what bothered me the most. She only saw her side. I was too tired to tell her otherwise anymore. I could talk until I was blue in the face. I would not want Bírçan on a jury. Once she'd made up her mind that was it. Being right or wrong had nothing to do with it. Proving a point was the impetus. The issue of control. Bírçan would not be persuaded. It had to be her decision. Her say. Otherwise she was being forced and the whole idea behind that one word, 'forced,' traced itself to having been raped long ago. The more you pressed, the more vehement she became. Bírçan was incapable of seeing my side. She believed harshness would get the job done. Her life was so self-managed it felt trivial.

One day she'd feel it. The lack of being noticed. If she bought something new Jay might be prompted to respond. And if he did it might be one of two responses. 'Yep, that's new!' Or 'That's a blue skirt all right.' His remark would reiterate the obvious. No compliment would be paid. No, 'That looks great on you, it really works well with your eyes.' Nothing personal would be attached. Over time Bírçan got used to this. Bírçan seldom paid compliments of her own. I'd decorate the office at work for the holidays. Everyone would compliment it or make a kind remark. Not Bírçan. It made no difference. Once I went with Bírçan to buy a new winter jacket she needed. She wanted my company and opinion. A pleasant day. In a causal encounter Birçan came across annoying, fluttering, brusque, and even rude. I looked past these flaws once I discovered them. When getting out of the car at the grocery store (she always parked far away and I suspected it was because she wasn't a good driver and didn't want to mess with other cars nearby) she'd quickly walk away, never wait to walk in together. At school I'd sometimes see her cut across the corner of grass when, for 2 or 3 extra steps, she could have stayed on the bricks and set a proper example for students. These "things" weren't important to her and to point them out would only provoke a sulky defense from her. She didn't have to answer to anyone. And criticism would not be tolerated. One might question how I could have been drawn to her. I searched for the person inside her and found a sad woman. A woman who just kept on going, come hell or high water. A hardened woman. I'd been so careful with my trust. Reluctant to show anything, give back. At first it had all been fine. But then Birçan abused my goodness. Stomped on it. I wanted so much to forgive her before we parted. To hear her say, 'I did you wrong. The love was wonderful. Thank you for what we shared, I'll cherish it.' In the end, she gave me no reason to forgive.

. . .

Birçan was a woman who gave the impression she was always passing through. Not anchored. No attachments. 'Here' meant anywhere she was at that particular moment. She would move back to Colorado with Jay. Neither liked the Virginia climate and work was simply that: work. Birçan relocated first while Jay finished out his contract in Virginia. Roughly a span of six months. They were used to living separate lives. They'd found a home in Colorado so Birçan went ahead to fix things up. During the time Jay remained in town, 4 miles from where I lived, we never spoke or saw one another again. No goodbye was ever offered. I wondered what Birçan's excuse to him had been. Why I suddenly just stopped coming over, was no longer invited. Even if Jay asked, Birçan wouldn't tell the truth. Just like that I was deleted from their lives. Blip. I was more angry than sad. Jay's behavior was slightly excusable. Birçan had mentioned once that he might have a form of Asperger's. It was never confirmed. Whereas Jay *might* not have been able to help his indifferent behavior, Birçan had no justification. She did as she pleased without an ounce of regard. 'Don't you care what I think of you, Birçan?' 'No,' she said. 'It doesn't matter.' I'd come to her steps, knocked, anticipating a polite exchange. Birçan was disagreeable, slammed the door in my face, and dead-bolted it for emphasis. I called and left a message explaining how rude her behavior was. Amazingly she called back. I tried to speak, but Birçan kept talking over me. 'You said I could turn to you.' 'You can't count on me! I take it back! Bye, bye, bye, bye!' She said it over and over with disgust. My system was in shock. I hadn't done anything to warrant this wretchedness. Where was the woman who had given me her bottle of perfume?

I began to look back over the last year, the last 6 months and all the selfish instances. Birçan had traveled home the past summer, undergoing cosmetic surgery. For a much fairer price than the States, she'd had a breast reduction. When she came back 10 weeks later I was curious to see the results. After all, I had a personal interest in the matter. I'd been through a similar, albeit more drastic procedure. I'll never forget Birçan's ridiculous modesty. I'd come to her house. She'd just gotten out of the shower and was wearing a pink bathrobe. I mentioned that sometime I'd like to see how things turned out. She wasn't completely satisfied. She'd wanted the surgeon to take more. Standing in her living room, she slips a breast out being sure to keep the nipple covered. She reveals just a slight incision line on the side.

It felt like a tease. I wasn't going to fondle her. I wanted to see the results, a profile of both breasts, to visually examine them. Not this absurd peep-show with her acting as though I'd never laid eyes on, let alone, ever touched her breasts. It was foolish. Childish. And felt unfair. She'd showed them to Jay on Skype—a man who couldn't have cared whether she was flat as a pine board or otherwise. And yet, there I stood, a man with a vested interest. Yes, I wanted to look upon her with restrained desire. Didn't that count for something to her? Were her breasts nothing more than organs? Was she really so frigid? She begrudged me even the smallest affections. I'd anticipated the unveiling. It felt like a flash.

One time before we'd made love Birçan and I had showered together. I was pet sitting at the Fleisch's. I loved Mr. Fleisch's shower. The tiled red and black walk-in shower. It was hard water and often dried your skin out, but the heat made the windows steam up quickly. We'd rubbed each other with soap. I was rinsing my hair while Birçan dried off. I had the sensation of being watched and opened my eyes to see Birçan peering around the corner, smiling, looking at my naked form. How long had she been taking me in? She didn't pull back, she wasn't trying to hide the fact that she'd been looking.

Now as I stood in her living room, just as the sun crested and the night lifted into morning blue, that image of Birçan's smiling face appeared before my eyes. It angered me. She'd been spying on me. Yes, we'd been about to make love, but why was it all right for her to see me? To study me? And now, this very moment, she covers herself like some pious matron, resigned to self-mandated celibacy. It hurt. I'd never told Birçan she couldn't see or touch me because she never really asked. She moved in response to my moves, touched me because I touched her. That moment in the shower was the only time she'd stolen a view. In retrospect, it wasn't an erotic episode; she'd acted from impulsive curiosity. I was an oddity.

Another time, the day before my birthday, we went for a long bike ride. 20 miles. I had a new backpack. Swiss brand, black, comfortable and durable. Birçan complimented it in a way she had never complimented me. 'I *really* like your backpack,' she said as we stood on the concrete bridge looking at the Chickahominy River. I secretly decided that for her birthday I'd surprise Birçan with her own backpack. The one I had cost $45.00, but it was built to last. I might even have hers monogrammed with a bee buzzing around. I imagined her delight when I surprised her with it in January. Lifting the pack onto my shoulders, sometimes I had to remind myself that just 10 years ago such a simple act would have been impossible. 10 years ago I had breasts. The surgery was supposed to cure my unhappiness. It wasn't enough. Birçan and I got back on our bikes and continued the long ride. It was easier for me going up the hills. Birçan made an excuse. Said she just needed to warm up. If I wanted, I could easily out-pedal her even though she believed I had no endurance. I just didn't like marathon bike rides. They became boring. My body had the stamina; if it were a race that would be a different matter. Birçan had forgotten my birthday was the next day until I said, 'Tomorrow's the day your father died on.' I knew that would get her attention. We hadn't been close since April. Six months. I just wanted to lie down together, completely clothed. To feel another's warmth. Birçan exploded. No one was going to force her to do anything! 'This relationship is over!' She started pedaling away. 'Leave me alone!' I couldn't believe her callousness. She behaved as though she were being raped. Just as we were pedaling up to my house I played the only card left. At the mention of her father she quickly came inside. We laid on my sofa. Why was this so hard? She wasn't losing anything.

Could she really give nothing of herself to anyone? What had happened to the Birçan from a year ago? Surely she could be brought back to life. I desired scraps and even *that* was too much for her. For a split moment the old Birçan returned. The tactile sensation, the warmth of her body next to mine soothed like no other. But the lengths she'd made me go to, her ferocious refusal, for something as simple and decent as a long embrace—had destroyed my pride. I didn't want to hold a stranger. Birçan and I had shared much more in the past, we had a certain history. Why couldn't she just let me—us—enjoy this moment. Why did she have to spoil it with anger and meanness? I tried not to blame her. I tried to excuse her hang-ups as being post-traumatic symptoms. She'd never recovered from her past.

One month later we were driving to Costco. Birçan became enraged. I'd merely spoken of the past. She threatened to leave me on the side of the road. 'I should have left you to kill yourself!' Her cruelty was like a shoe stepping on the last flower of summer. Without remorse. She started to veer into the other lane. Somehow we arrived at the first stop, Kroger's grocery store for produce. Her car lurched to a halt. She pinched my cheek hard. I truly believed she'd strike me next. 'Birçan, if you ever do that again, I will not speak to you. That is it. Do not ever lay a hand on me,' I said. She went into the store alone, demanded I not follow her.

Something inside caved. I knew I had to hold it together. I'd be damned if I was going to be dumped on the road in Newport News. Later that same day we were driving into the Costco parking lot. 'You're broken, you know that?'

Birçan started to laugh. It was a chuckle, disturbing in its tone. 'No one's ever told me that before,' she said.

Another time I'd asked Birçan, 'How do you think I think of you?' She'd answered, 'With admiration.' Everything in me backed up. No, no, no. She'd used the wrong word. It was a slip of the tongue. She'd meant another similar sounding word. But I knew Birçan was well-versed with the English language. She'd intended the term 'admiration.' We'd been in bed, just resting. I pulled away. 'No, Birçan. I don't admire you. Adoration maybe.'

I wanted to forgive Birçan. I gave her every opportunity. But, in the end, she gave me no reason to. I tried to forget the bad things and yet, anytime a good memory came back it became a lie. The loving Birçan wasn't real. To remember anything nice was to be reminded of how you can never know someone. The Birçan I'd loved no longer existed. She killed everything wonderful. And I couldn't fathom why anyone would choose anger over happiness. Hostility over reconciliation. Hate over love. Birçan had built a wall, a cell. A computer cell. Input new date. New studies, facts, more things to keep busy. Delete the old hardware. But at night, yes at night, her clear blue eyes, the prettiest blue, so open and exposed—an irony, for her personality was just the opposite—at night guilt clouded her dreams. Guilt that followed her from one person to the next. The knowledge that she'd been violated. She blamed herself. And then 10 years later Snowball's suicide, and finally, Westcott. The way he'd looked at her, the way his words reduced her life to shit. He'd struck a chord. The emotional loneliness chased her. Westcott had felt too much. Been able to see too much and that insight required reciprocation. She could no longer give, for to give of herself would expose her. She'd started to open up, she'd come close, but the feeling of vulnerability in herself was too great. She would not let anything or anyone hurt her again even if it caused others to suffer. The kind of affection she'd shared with Westcott led to passion. And passion had brought her to her knees once before and nearly taken her life. She could not go back.

So she willingly and knowingly slammed the door. Westcott's offense? He'd loved her. He'd showed affection to this woman and she didn't want it. Westcott hadn't wanted pure sex. He'd wanted love. Her womb was empty.

Once more *I* stood alone, on the threshold of the world.

$$\bullet \bullet \bullet$$

Eventually it was time. Time to venture out. Westcott had come to know Birçan in such a way that he wouldn't miss her. He knew her life, her routine. He would miss her presence and embracing one another, but he'd missed that when Birçan was nearby. It was the internal distance that still stung. He did not feel he was missing out on anything in her life or experiencing things together. They'd shared so much—everyday little things. He could be anywhere in the world and he felt he would know what she was doing. He could envision her cooking, reading her textbooks for her class lecture, watching a movie, bicycling alone or with Jay. He felt free inside and so he went. He put his belongings in storage, dismantled his small wooden bed and wrapped his mattress. These he would never sell. They represented for him what the formica table represented to Francesca in *The Bridges of Madison County*. He stowed his pictures and paintings. He asked his mother to please take care of Tomás, Tereza, and Binoche—his three houseplants named after *The Unbearable Lightness of Being*. All the items of his life compartmentalized, he pulled the door closed for an unknown duration of time.

For old time's sake, he drove by Birçan's house some night late in summer. Jay's truck was gone. The place was completely dark. The light in "Birçan's window" was extinguished. Westcott noticed a trailer hitch in the driveway with a contractor's name on it. The outside looked freshened up, nicely kept. Cleaner than it had ever been while Birçan and Jay lived there. The owner of the place was obviously getting it ready for new tenants. It was sad somehow. To know that the lives that had momentarily existed within those walls were now vanished. Nothing remained. Westcott would never again step inside that house, smell Birçan's cooking, feel her adoring embrace. Those memories were dead. Birçan and Jay had up and left in the night without so much as a trace. It was as though they'd never existed at all. And if they hadn't been there, then neither had Westcott. He'd been erased. He'd held out for a proper goodbye. For something. It was startling to just be forgotten. For the lights of hope to be turned off while he was still searching within.

$$\bullet \bullet \bullet$$

AFTER MUCH DEBATE, practicality triumphed over sentimentality. For a while Westcott considered leaving Ol' Reliable with his mother. She could use the truck for little errands around town. But he didn't want to pay insurance on a vehicle that would barely be used. And Ol' Reliable needed work. If left to sit, the truck would quickly rust. So Westcott placed an ad in the classifieds. Under no circumstances would he sell Ol' Reliable to someone who wanted spare parts. The truck was fast becoming a "classic." The type of vehicle you could still work on under the hood with just your own hands and no computer scanner. He sold the only vehicle he'd ever owned for $1,500. Not bad considering his parents had purchased it for two grand 16 years earlier. The gentleman who bought it promised to restore Ol' Reliable. He loved cars. Westcott told him that if he ever decided to sell, or wanted to unload the truck, to please call him and he'd buy it back. He doubted the likelihood of this scenario, but the idea gave him consolation. He didn't want to sever all ties. He didn't want to let go completely even when he knew a clean break is most often the best.

It was a hot summer day when Westcott stepped into Ol' Reliable for the last time. He drove by his old house, looping around the cul-de-sac. The small tree they'd planted on the east side of the house, a year before moving, towered over the windows that looked upon the stairwell. Westcott glanced at the window to the left that used to be his room. The leaves were higher than the roof now. The tree had grown up. How many times had he looked *out* that window?

In one full swoop, a matter of seconds, never having stepped on the brake pedal, Westcott remembered every detail of those hope-filled days. God had he changed. He felt weary, old. He was only 31. Something inside stirred. All the emotions unraveled, like the wooden planes with rubber band propellers. He watched himself go. How beautiful it had been. How beautiful it might have stayed. He wanted to go back. He knew he could never return.

Westcott had continued on his drive, making his way to the Powhatan Creek overlook. He'd taken a picture with his beloved truck. The heat made the interior alive with scents. His amygdala had always been keen and attuned to nostalgia. The original scent was still there— the "new" smell of a car, which he always loved, and yes, the scent of youth—of how things had been when he was just a "kid" of 18. He'd taken Hudson, Kinkaid—his knight—and Maureen, the hummingbird that hung from his rearview mirror, and put them in a box. Last, he removed the Scooby-Doo steering wheel cover he hardly ever noticed anymore. He told himself not to look at the situation as a loss, but a beginning. Ol' Reliable had served him well and in turn he'd taken care of his truck. More than just a vehicle, Ol' Reliable was an extension of Westcott—a tether to a certain time, place, and perspective. The color shined in the sunlight. Now everyone wanted black, silver, or white cars. How sad, how boring, uniform. Ol' Reliable's patriot blue was vibrant even when his owner had faded. Westcott took him down to Powhatan Creek for one last afternoon drive. With no one around he got out, placed his hands on the hood, and yes, bent his head, kissing Ol' Reliable farewell.

There was only one thing left to do. The time had come. He'd waited long enough.

On *the* hottest evening in June, Westcott leaves work. The moment of reckoning. Why hadn't he done this sooner? Years ago? He knows why.

He drives into Regn's neighborhood, following the circle of road. It still registers uncanny with him, just as it had the first time he read the name of the housing community.

The marker bears the first part of his own name and the rest of it makes it sound bucolic, as though you are entering the site of a horse derby. Regn lives on the backside of the loop. He parks across the narrow street. One of the white garage doors is open. Striding up the driveway, Westcott sees that both Jay and Regn's cars are parked inside. He can't think about it anymore. Who will answer the door? How will he be received? Will he be received? Up the front steps he goes, fully aware that he has never stood on this porch. Even in that summer of love seven years ago, he never entered Regn's front door. They'd gone in through the garage. Westcott now waits. He studies the flowerpot. How clean, how immaculate the porch is. No bench to sit in, but no debris either. Not a single scrap of bark or leaf. He wants to remember the details, to put off the inevitable. His heart is light with sick anticipation. His mind floating. He presses the doorbell, grips the small package wrapped in brown paper in his right hand. Jay opens the door.

He is wearing a bright yellow t-shirt. He no longer seems imposing. He really isn't that tall.

Westcott's confidence wanes. Rather than bravado, he displays an ingratiating brevity.

'I've wanted to say something for a long time. I have this book to give to Regn and I don't want her to have to hide it. It's for both of you.'

Jay opens the door wider, indicating for Westcott to come in.

'Regn's in the kitchen.'

Jay does not lead the way. The entire house is dim to keep it cooler. Westcott cuts through the small dining room, remembering it like it was yesterday.

'She doesn't know I'm coming,' Westcott adds for reassurance.

Regn's back is to him. She is at the sink, turns.

Even without his glasses he detects a mild concern in her expression. Alarm, masked in the guise of dismay.

'Hi Regn, I wanted to give this to you and I didn't want you to hide it.'

'Is it your new book?'

'No. I've had this one a while. It's my poetry and short stories. It's for both of you to read.' He wonders what Jay will feel when he gets to *The Blue Line*. 'This,' he turns to Jay who has entered the kitchen and is standing quite close, 'is for you.' He holds out a white envelope.

He wants the three of them to sit down and talk. He doesn't want to rely on a letter. But he didn't know how things were going to play out. The letter had been a back-up. A safety net in case Jay refused to hear him speak.

Jay shakes his hand and Regn hugs Westcott.

Westcott does not feel like a man fighting for the woman he loves. He feels timid. Overly-polite. And begins to back away. He wants to say more, do more. But the letter. Jay has the letter. It says everything he cannot at the moment.

Westcott retreats to the front door without being asked. They all walk onto the front porch.

'I have to say, you keep an immaculate home.'

'That's all thanks to Regn's doing,' Jay answers.

'It's a hot one today, for sure. The hottest yet.'

'How's your truck doing?' Regn asks.

'No air conditioning. But I'm used to it.' Westcott is sweating profusely in his long-sleeved olive shirt and navy slacks.

Regn reaches for him again. Hugs him under the scrutiny of Jay. Westcott wants more than anything to squeeze her, to look Jay in the eye, to display his intent. Instead he feels like a guest, a token embrace safely received because Jay is there to witness nothing inappropriate.

Oh it hurts. But at least he has the letter! And the book. His book of poetry.

'No hard feelings,' Westcott calls back to Jay as he walks down the driveway.

He pulls away in a fog, on a high, in disbelief. Now things will change. They must. Westcott drives to the nearby shopping center, parks, and lets the emotions spill over. What had Jay been thinking as Regn's lover hugged his wife? Seeing the gaunt and forever adolescent body standing before him, did Jay notice how much hair Westcott had lost? Had he taken delight in the fullness of his own? And just think, he'd once hidden behind his long bangs. A dark brown curtain. He no longer has bangs to speak of. The Greeks associated virility with a full head of hair. Did Jay say to himself, *Go ahead, hug her all you want, I still get to sleep with her?* Westcott knew the virility of their sex life. But frequency has nothing to do with potency. When Westcott made love, it was potent.

His nerves give way. He'd finally confronted Jay. Again, he had been the one to initiate it. He is taking control of his life.

The next morning there is a message in his inbox from Regn. 'What did you do, Westcott? What was in your letter?'

Westcott does not respond. How many times had he sent Regn a note and she never answered. Besides, didn't Jay show Regn the letter? He'd expected that they'd sit down together, look through the book, and Jay would naturally confront Regn over the contents of said letter.

Regn calls.

'Why didn't you answer my email?'

'I don't always check it. I have a lot to do.' He gives Regn the answer she'd give him.

'Didn't you read the letter?'

'No. I don't want to know what's in it.'

'What!'

'I do admire your courage though. It took courage to come like you did. But—'

He wants to tell her, *I've always had the courage. I stayed away, I waited all this time for your sake, Regn. You were always too afraid. You never believed me. You were scared. But I stopped listening to you. I did what I should have done a long time ago. Because you didn't have the strength.*

'It's not going to change anything.'

'How can you say that? You don't even know what was in it. Did you even look through the book?'

'I will.'

'And Jay?'

'You've really caused a problem. He's very upset. But I don't ask. I let him deal with it in his own way.'

'You mean you don't even talk about it?'

'If something happens to him I'll never forgive you. Leave him out of this!'

'Regn'— *are you out of your mind! He's a part of it.* 'You can't blame me. Stop with the guilt. If Jay all of a sudden dies tomorrow it's no one's fault.'

'You're ruining my life! You're torturing me.'

'*I'm* torturing *you?*'

• • •

20 June 20—

Jay-

I should have done this a long time ago. Some might consider my coming here suicide. I don't think so. I come in peace. I look at what humans are capable of, what we have done to each other throughout history. It saddens and disturbs me. The capacity for such horrors, even now. The truth is, were you to put a gun to my chest and pull the trigger, I would thank you for your mercy. Of course, I don't encourage, nor do I want you to do this. I am not here to upset you.

I do not hate you, Jay. I don't even know you so how could I possibly dislike someone without firsthand knowledge? That day I ran into you 3, maybe 4 years ago at Jamestowne Island, we were both cowards. We never even spoke Regn's name. The issue was skirted. Things went unsaid. The truth is, you and I have something very much in common and that is Regn. What is between you and her I can never take away any more than you can take away what she and I share.

It was never my intention to steal Regn. We cannot possess other human beings. Everyone has free will. The heart cannot be commandeered. I had two choices. You could either receive a note someday soon that I had died, of natural causes, or I come here and speak plainly. Again, I am not here to cause hurt, but to bring peace all around.

If you think Regn's involvement with me was simply about a midlife crisis you're gravely mistaken. I am not your typical man and if need be I will explain this.

There is nothing (within reason) that I wouldn't do for Regn's well-being. No one knows with certainty why we are on this earth. But I can tell you this. There is a reason you, Regn, and I, share this time and place. And how we deal with it is our epitaph.

I am not angry at you Jay, only frustrated. My anger is at Regn. She betrayed both of us. But I cannot dwell on the negative.

It is possible, and it has happened throughout history, that one person can love two people at the same time. Regn loves each of us in different ways, for different reasons. And love should never be viewed as something bad. Love is rare. It is a gift. I will tell you one more thing; I have never loved another woman as unconditionally as I do Regn. I want you and I to talk, to know one another. Instead of hating me, or god forbid, being jealous, I ask what seems impossible, but really it isn't. I ask you to accept me, as I accept you as part of Regn's life. I ask you to try to see that I bring goodness. Refusing this doesn't hurt just me, it hurts Regn and places her in a compromising position.

I try to put myself in your shoes. If I'd lived with Regn as long as you have, then I'd trust her heart and know that emotions are complicated, but life is short and should not be spent pretending. They say the truth shall set you free. I believe this, from a spiritual standpoint.

I have beautiful pictures of Regn in nature—pictures your children and grand- children would one day cherish. It would be a shame if you let anger blind you and refused to look upon these manifestations of perfection. Also, I didn't want Regn to have to hide this book or future publications of mine.

Again, I mean you no harm and I want to believe the same is true of you, but I know how strong conflicting emotions can be. And so I hope, for Regn's sake, your family's, and even your well-being, you will understand this is not about winning or losing Regn, but compromising. Regn doesn't want to hurt anyone. Don't put her in the position to choose. She shouldn't have to. I am actually conservative and very traditional in my values, but if I knew that someone I loved deeply was hurting, I'd do everything I could to make her happy. Neither one us, me nor you Jay, should be sacrificed. Everyone can be happy; it just requires a meeting of the minds.

Have you ever read Stranger in a Strange Land?

So now, the hard questions. Why Regn? In your eyes I am a young man. But I come from another place and time (hogwash maybe to you). It is true. I have never felt a human connection so strong and natural as with Regn and she will tell you the same. Maybe you don't care, but where Regn's concerned, I hope you do. I also know she cares for you; she's said you're a good man. Your life has been fulfilled, Jay. I will never have children and grandchildren. From a physiological standpoint I can't. I am not asking for your sympathy. But you love Regn and as such, you share my pain and fear of losing someone dear. It is empathy you and I have as common ground. I am an ally not your enemy. I want and need more than anything in life—more than money, fame, success— your acceptance of me in Regn's life. Without this, everyone suffers. Maybe not visibly, but silently.

In peace-

Westcott

• • •

After six weeks and no word, Westcott called Jay's mobile. He'd left one polite voice-mail on their home line two weeks before. Jay never replied. So Westcott decided to call his mobile. He knew the number because it used to be Regn's phone before she acquired a new one.

'Is this Jay?'

'Yes.'

'This is Westcott.' He feels the mood change without even one word spoken from the other end. Jay is short and determined to get off the phone as quickly as possible. Though his voice is calm and collected, as is Westcott's, he clearly has no desire to prolong their conversation.

'I got your other message and I have nothing to say to you.'

'There are things you need to know. They would shed some light and help you to understand.'

'I'm not going to be an enabler.'

'That's an odd choice of words. I would just like us to talk.'

'I'm very busy right now.'

'I want to make one point very clear. I mean you absolutely no harm. I'm not on this earth to hurt anyone.'

'If I have something to say I will contact you.'

'All right. Goodbye then.'

'Goodbye.'

Jay never responded. No, 'Go to hell.' Or, 'Yes, let's speak.' His denial was spectacular if not unbelievable. And Regn never pushed for details. Westcott couldn't believe it. The absolute passivity. They lived their lives pretending. Westcott had done everything he could. The truth had been spoken. Jay wasn't ready to listen.

 ONE OF THE LAST TIMES Westcott saw Regn, before he slipped into the world, was at the library. It had been early fall. He remembers the details so well. It unfolded like this:

Westcott takes Robbie with him. The parking lot at the library is full. The weather's been stormy lately, everyone wants to get out and enjoy the reprieve of sun. Westcott sees a Volkswagen. His eyes automatically dart to the license plate. It's Regn. In all the years they've known each other, he has never run into her by chance. Why now? It is not mere happenstance. There are rare moments in life when he knows the meeting is intended. Westcott casually searches inside the library. He finds Regn in the children's section. She does not see him. She is crouched on the carpet reading to her granddaughter. Westcott stands on the ramp running between the youth and adult sections. There is a glass window. He wants to watch the two of them, to take in Regn's gestures and her granddaughter's reactions to the story they're reading. At the same time he does not want to be noticed. It doesn't look quite right for a man to be staring into the children's section. What would the attendant at the circulation desk think? He sits down at a table, perusing the local newspaper. Should he say hello? In that moment, seeing Regn with her legacy, Westcott understood her life more than he ever had. There he was, looking through the glass, forever on the outside. Banned from the regularity of life. He would never have children or grandchildren. It hurt. Regn looked so young. She was in her early 60s then, but 60 was fast becoming the new 40. The way she just sat on the floor. His own mother, some odd years older, could never get into that position anymore, not without immense effort. She was afraid of injuring her new knees. Sure, Regn had arthritis in her hands, but it didn't show too much. With Gedny there was no hiding it. Regn was the epitome of physical health, at least that's the impression she gave.

Gedny let things out, whereas Regn had always kept them bottled up until she erupted. Having become a vegetarian so late in life, Regn was often deprived of the protein and nutrients her body was conditioned to and needed. She took vitamins, so did Gedny, but Regn's characteristic tendency to ignore an issue—push it away—as opposed to Gedny's aggressive, sometimes demanding, 'Let's get this off the table and clear the air' approach to life, had far reaching physical effects. To suppress emotions for a prolonged period, as Regn succeeded in doing, is toxic to the system. Then again, so is chronic worrying in Gedny's case. Nonetheless, throughout her life, Gedny addressed the emotional hardships. In Regn's culture one was expected to bear her burden silently and without recourse. The body cannot be made whole if the mind is constantly trying to avoid the heart. For all her emotional insecurities, Gedny spoke her heart. Both she and Regn could be impulsive. Regn's short fuse came out as horrific anger, a tantrum. Gedny's impatience displayed itself as a need to know 'right now' quality. Gedny would linger. Regn would flee from the scene. Gedny needed resolution. Regn preferred unfinished business, broken conversations, pending heartache, passive silence. Regn gave the hurt. Gedny received the pain. The amazing thing was, in spite of all their differences, both women's behavior in response to Westcott stemmed from the same emotion, albeit for separate reasons: Insecurity.

Westcott walks down the ramp and into the little cubby area where Regn and her granddaughter are now standing, selecting books.

'Hi, you.' Westcott is almost to Regn's arm before she even notices him; she is so caught up in the books.

'Oh my gosh, you startled me. What are you doing here?'

'Just returning some books. I'm going to take Robbie for a walk after all the rain. Now which one is this? Cara?'

'No, this is Loren. Cara is all blonde.'

'I've never met Loren before.' She is Dee's only child. Regn's son has two daughters. One by his first marriage, Rebecca, and then Cara. He also has a stepdaughter by his second wife. *All the dynamics. How easy it seems. Divorce. Marriage. Children.* Westcott keeps looking at Loren.

'Yes you did, didn't you?'

'No. I held Cara. I never met Loren. This is the first time.'

Regn is silently struck by this realization.

'What's your name?' Loren asks with the openness of a happy child.

Regn introduces him. 'This is Westcott.'

'She's so cute. She's how old—5?'

'Yes. Tell him when your birthday is.'

'I'll be 6 on January 15th,' she says proudly.

She hops around, jumping from circle to circle on the patterned carpet.

'Look, I have my permanent teeth in front.' She comes right up, smiles.

Westcott smiles back, enjoying the interaction. Little kids are something he knows little about. He'd held Cara once when she was a few months old and then one last time when she was two. He'd picked her tiny body up. It felt good to hold something so dear. Regn did it all the time, without a second thought. They'd been standing by the horses in Colonial Williamsburg. He'd always wanted to see Loren.

She is precocious, beautiful, and sweet. Westcott knows Loren will never forget these times with her Oma. He still remembers his own mother reading to him. All the fun stories and wonderful pictures. Loren is lucky to have Regn.

'Well, have fun.'

'Bye,' Loren waves.

'Enjoy your walk,' Regn tells him.

Westcott takes Robbie out of his truck. He walks him around the fountain in front of the library and under the lattice where the wisteria blooms in spring. Regn and Loren have exited the building. Loren is balancing along the perimeter of the fountain. Westcott lets Robbie have free rein on his leash. Eight feet and he's at Regn's ankles. She doesn't even notice she's so lost in her thoughts. *Running into Westcott like that. Now he's gone.*

Westcott is right on top of her.

'Hey.'

'I didn't even see you.'

'Cute finds cute.' He points to Robbie then Loren.

'He is cute. What's his name?' Loren asks.

'Robert. He sometimes goes by Robbie.'

'That's a nice name. Is he still a puppy?'

'No. His birthday is September 8th. He's 4.'

Westcott looks at Regn's shoes. White low-top Converse. So young, hip. Her jeans, too, are rolled up like capris.

'I thought Loren would like to meet him.'

Robbie noses Loren's ankles.

'He probably smells Tamerlane or Loren's Pugsie.'

'There's something going on over there.' Westcott nods at the group across the way. 'I think it's a wedding. I saw a few bridesmaids earlier.'

'Yes, but those men are just standing there. Like they're waiting for a command.'

A line of 10 men dressed in black stand across the road in front of the community building. Regn keeps looking around. Westcott knows she is worried. What if someone sees them? Surely Jay is at home. And who cares? There's a discrepancy. Regn doesn't realize this. Why, Westcott wonders, had Regn told Loren his name inside the library? He'd been surprised the moment she'd said his name.

If she is so worried about someone seeing them now, isn't she equally concerned that Loren might slip-up and accidentally mention Westcott's name when they arrive home? What if her Grandpa asks, 'So, what did you two get into at the library? Did you have fun?' And then Loren, just being an honest child responds, 'We talked to Westcott.' Did Regn honestly not see the contradictory state of her words and actions? No, she didn't. She could be so innocently naïve one minute and unreasonably paranoid the next. Westcott knew this and had suffered many a time because of it. As had Regn. The tragedy being this: It was always avoidable, but Regn panicked and let fear blind logic. All these things Westcott sees, but will never tell her. The parts of this woman, what makes Regn who she is.

'Well, I'll let you go. Have fun,' he tells Regn and Loren once more.

'Bye.

'Bye, bye, bye,' Loren calls after Robbie whose nose has him wandering back in her direction.

So that's life, Westcott thinks. It makes perfect sense. Regn would not have been any worse off had she left Jay to be with him, financially speaking. In fact, she would have experienced far more with Westcott. Money—security—was a constant concern in Regn's life. But in seeing Loren, Westcott felt the truth. It was her image more than anything that she wished to preserve for the sake of her children. And yes, her three granddaughters.

The gravity of such a rare encounter. Westcott never saw Loren again. Years later he would wonder what she looked like. What were her talents? What did she want to be? What had her Oma instilled in her? Could she possibly remember a 5-minute exchange in the library a decade past? Children file away odd little details. Would the name 'Westcott' mean anything to her if she heard it again? And if by sheer odds she did remember, would she say that he had been a nice man? As the eldest grandchild, Rebecca might seek to know who he was. What he was about.

• • •

I gave Regn a letter.

Regn-

Jealousy and frustration are a lethal combination. I am not jealous of Jay. You and Jay are married by contract and years together. A marriage bestowed by society. But you and I, Regn, are married in soul.

If this were all about me, I'd have left long ago, married, and said the hell with it. But I am loyal, and I love you because we recognize something in each other that no one can take away. I am the only man who has ever made love to you all night. Part of me does have pride knowing this. I am grateful that I gave you passion and ecstasy. Everything will be all right in the end. I never stop believing in you.

There are times I'd give my life for the feel of your hands and taste of your lips. I nourish your spirit and you replenish my heart. This is what it means to make love. And when I touch you or you feel me, it enters the body into the bloodstream of remembrance.

I don't want to take you away from Jay. 'I just want to enjoy you as well.' There's the difference. I am a giving man. Let your love for both of us be your strength.

Enjoy, embrace the love of Jay and me. Life is about flowing, not damming or blockading. It's when we refuse the truth that we suffer greatly. Loving makes us kinder, stronger.

I don't view your loving two men as a betrayal. I see it as an asset. A strength. What is a betrayal is suppressing natural desires, wants, and needs. We love each other, Regn. Such connection doesn't come every day. No one needs to be sacrificed. When you look at Jay think of the life you gave him. And still do. When you look at me, think of the love and happiness your presence gives me, just like him.

You don't belong to either of us. So why deny either one? Just because Jay came first? He's had so much of your time, life, and love. And I can never take that away. Nor do I want to. Loving each other should not be painful. It should always be beautiful and open.

You once said, 'We're so lucky. Some never find this. There are a lot of sad, sad people in the world.' By "this" you meant the level of our love. You loved me with everything in you and expressed that I was your true love. 'Now' I am one of those sad people.

Your love, Regn, made me feel like a man. I was so happy and alive. Oh, I felt alive inside. My life had meaning—a certainty of purpose. No one before or since has ever moved me in the same way. It's not for lack of trying. Our love ran over the brim and there is no substitute. I don't want our affection to be a tragedy, for our lives to be sad. You are the other half of this pain and it takes <u>both</u> of us to make it beautiful and leave it that way, return it to a level of goodness.

Why, Regn? Why is it so hard for you to face the truth? I may not have balls, but at least "I have the balls" to look at these feelings head on and embrace them as opposed to denying them. The truth always finds a way. Our love is good because it is natural. Humans are created to love. Society is what creates barriers in the mind, but never the heart. Look me in the eye and tell me there aren't times when you just want to be held, to have a hand run through your hair and to be told, 'Everything will be all right.' It is better to be wanted than needed. And I wanted to know you before I ever learned to need you.

You called me unverbesserlich. Yes. A person who does not give up changes the world. Ich liebe dich. I say this because it's nice to hear those words and to mean them. Sometimes it gets to be too long not speaking what is kept silent in the heart. I can travel the world. But you were, and remain, my greatest adventure.

I survive on my own. We found true love. That is rare. A gift. I know deep down within you the Regn I fell in love with still burns—a soft

ember. You're Meine Dame and I will never see you as an old woman.
It doesn't become you if it restrains the spirit. You may have gray hair,
but to me I see you in all your stages—the sum person.

...

December 20—

'You're abusing my love!'

'Regn, how dare you. Stop yelling. Get a grip. Would you let me tal—'

'Get a grip? Yes, yes, poor you. Always so calm. Maybe you should let it out sometime!'

'I try—'

'It's all about you. I don't want to hear about your problems!'

'There are important things to discuss.'

'Important to you, maybe.'

'When you love someone, what's important to that person should be of interest to you, especially when it concerns *you*.'

'Don't fuck with me!'

'You never let me spe—'

'I'm spent, I can't take anymore!'

Westcott moves the receiver away from his ear.

'You always go off half-cocked. Make it worse than it needs to be.'

'Why can't you use normal words? Half-cocked—I can't even understand you.'

'I'm trying to speak and you won't let—'

'You never listen—'

'Regn, I'm going to hang up—'

'I've listened to you so often—'

'—if you don't stop screaming. How can you say that?'

'If you ever—I will never talk to you again. You selfish son-of-a-bitch!'

C-lick.

Westcott stares at the phone. Feels the wave of injustice envelope him. Just like that—vetoed. Silenced. Dismissed. The rudeness. How childish. The poison of her words courses through him. He laughs and can't stop laughing. Laughs loud and long, and as he laughs he cries so that the two become one. The pain is too great. He knows Regn is just scared. When she's scared she behaves impulsively. The image of the raccoon lashing out in defense returns. Frightened. Her words are reactionary, not responsive. This is no justification for her lack of respect.

A week or two later having passed her cool, Regn comes to Westcott's home.

'You know, sometimes I wish I could just tie you to a chair and tape your mouth shut. You cause such needless pain. And don't tell me it's your temper and you've always been this way. That's a cop-out.'

'A cop-out!' Regn stands to leave.

'There you go again. Half-cocked.'

'And there you go with your big words!'

'Half-cocked is a common phrase. You don't know it because it's not your native tongue, but I would think after all the years you've been here you'd know what it means. I'd explain—'

'I don't care.'

'You treat me like shit. All I ever wanted was to bring out the best in you.'

'So I'm not a good person?'

'I didn't say that.'

'I'm a horrible person, is that what you think?'

'Regn, everyone has room for improvement. Everyone. But your behavior—'

'And you're perfect!'

'No. You are so critical of yourself you always put those criticisms onto others and think they're accusing you. You never hear me.'

'Don't you analyze me! I've heard enough.'

'Haven't we been here before? I deserve an apology for what you said the other night. The only one being a selfish son-of-a-bitch is you.'

'I've apologized to you so many times. And you've never once apologized to me.'

'For what? All I've ever done is love you. I've been there no matter what. I would do everything in my power to support you. How dare you! I gave you books, and music, and poetry. I tried to make you a stronger person. I've *always* listened when you needed to talk. I gave you everything inside of me.' Miraculously, Regn is still quiet. Westcott continues to study her until she turns from looking outside and meets his gaze. 'When I am at fault I do apologize. But not this—. Maybe if I really said what I thought and told you to fuck off, then you'd respect me again.'

'Maybe you should.'

'I squandered my youth over you.'

'What do you mean, squandered?'

'Wasted. I deserve better than you.'

'Thanks a lot. That really hurts. So I'm shit, is that it? Well, if you can do better—' Regn moves for the door.

Westcott stands to move between her and the door. 'I am not letting you run out of here like this so you can sit and stew at your desk all day. It solves nothing. You *always* run or hang up when I try to speak. It's dismissive. If I let it out and get mad you call me crazy. It's a double standard.' He grabs her firmly, one hand on each shoulder, so she can get a grip on herself. 'I'm not holding you in affection. You need to calm down.' She mildly tries to disengage before turning. She paces up and down the foyer.

'I was referring to your character, Regn, not your looks. You are so damn self-critical you project *your* thoughts onto me.'

'Don't talk to me like a therapist.'

'God damn it, Regn, stop this! You snap at everything I say!'

The grandfather clock on the landing chimes 1:00 o'clock.

'Is that right?'

'It's a little fast.'

She walks into the kitchen taking into account Westcott's home. She looks out Westcott's back sliding door at the yard and fallen leaves, made somber by the gray day.

For the last two months they've periodically been seeing each other. Just sitting and talking. Regn had said they'd make peace. But she refuses to say *when*, to make any plans.

'I pray to god for help.'

'Regn, you can't pray to the gods. You *can* pray for strength from them, but only you can make things happen. No one can do it for you. There will never be a right or ideal time.'

'It's easy for you. You're free.'

'No, Regn, that's where you're wrong. The only restrictions are those placed upon us by ourselves and man's conventions. Not any God's decree. We are born free.'

'Yes, yes, you're so wise, you and your words!'

'It's not about wisdom, it's a self-evident fact. Stop taking your self-resentment out on me—'

'Don't you—'

Seeing she's about to fly off the handle, he diverts her fury. 'You never even asked why I called. You didn't have to call right back, the same night. You chose to.'

'You were pressuring me.'

'I've waited years! That's pressuring? The day before Thanksgiving when we kissed, it was so hard coming close. I just wanted us to be able to give way, to have everything right then and there—but having to pull away—the restraint it took. The frustration—I had nowhere to go with it. I could tell no one. I don't want to end up hating each other.'

'I could never hate you, Westcott. It may come out that way, but it's not you.'

'It does so much damage. Your words.'

'They're just words—'

'How you use them makes all the difference.'

'Yes, that's true.'

'If I really thought you were shit do you think I'd be wasting my time standing here talking to you?'

The truth registers. She turns. 'I can be a real bitch sometimes. I can't help it. Listen to me,' she pulls Westcott to her, holding him as they stand. 'I'm sorry. It just had to come out. Can you forgive me?'

'I love you, Regn, but I don't like who you are—your character. You can be passive, vain, volatile—'

'That's how I am. I always was.'

'That doesn't make it right.'

Regn is silent.

'I don't know if I can forgive you. God knows, I'll try.'

'I just erupt.'

'It isn't right or fair, Regn. You are so hard on me.'

'I love *you*, Westcott. I will love you until the day I die.'

'I just wish I could protect us—' he searches for the words.

'We will make peace.'

He isn't ready to make amends. All the times she's blown her top and destroyed him. He maintains composure.

'I'm shaking, I need to sit down,' she is conciliatory.

They walk back into the living room, sit on the sofa. Regn reaches for Westcott's hand. Squeezes it and doesn't let go.

'Please, forgive me, Westcott.'

'It goes nowhere. All the anger—it does real damage. It's toxic.'

'You're right. It's not healthy.'

'No. All the wasted hurt and energy. For nothing. If you'd just waited, not called at all, or at least said, "I don't feel liking talking now, I'm going to hang up, we'll speak later." You always leave me hanging.'

'I'm sorry.'

'I'm not like men. My emotions are that of a woman.'

'That's probably why we have this tension.' Regn grabs Westcott. Kisses him, cups his face, and presses him close. 'Here, turn. I'll massage your back.'

Through the flannel of his shirt Westcott feels Regn touching him. How often, how long he'd waited. And she dared to call him selfish.

'How do I look? Do I look like a mess? I don't want anyone to see anything back at work.'

'Regn, even on your worst day you could never look bad.'

'Thank you.'

She has to go. She must get back to her desk. 'Smile, I love to see you smile. I want you to laugh. Here, you can hit me,' she tells him.

Westcott would love to slap her with force for all the times she's abused his love. He lightly flicks her cheek. They both know she deserves a sting. 'I want to kick your ass,' he says. Instead he squeezes it. But he is not giving in. The wound is still open and he will not forgive her so soon. All the weeks, months, years she's kept him waiting. His pride and dignity were attacked. Affection alone will not secure a reconciliation. Respect cannot be enticed through passion and outpouring, but consistency. Westcott guards himself. Regn is not calculating. She is simply being Regn. Impetuous. Tempestuous. But the tone of her voice still rings in his ears. *You selfish son-of-a-bitch!* Regn is sincerely remorseful. Something inside Westcott still wants her to suffer. For whatever her pains, he knows she has not experienced the duration of his suffering. He would shield Regn with his own life if the situation ever arose. The ultimate sacrifice. For once, he is shielding himself.

 WE MADE LOVE once more. For the first time in several years.

I told Regn about the past life regression I'd undergone. In turn, she revealed something I'd never known.

'I want to explain why I love you so much, Regn. It's not because I believe or think you're the only woman in the world. It was never an obsession. It is loyalty. Simply put, I just love you because I've known you before. You were taken from me and the guilt was too much. I killed myself in a way I would never consider doing in this life.'

'How? Hanging?'

'No. Cutting my wrists. Maybe this is why I can't stand anything to do with the veins and blood tests.'

'How did I die?'

'You were taken away. I believe to Birkenau. You died in a gas chamber.'

'Oh, wonderful! You know something, anytime I'm in the car or a room that's completely closed, I start to feel trapped. I have to open a window. I can't breathe.'

It made perfect sense. I had not known this detail. It was not implanted before the past life regression. It served to confirm what I already knew, in a reverse way. I'd always felt that I'd died and been the one taken away during World War II. Not the other way around. But the bizarre circumstances were just that—too bizarre for me to unconsciously make up. The way I had died so opposed my current life views that I knew it had happened.

'It explains your mild asthma.' I'd known Regn had minor symptoms, but nothing like the sensations she just described to me. 'And the time frame is right. You were reborn rather quickly. Seven, eight years after the war. But I—I couldn't forgive myself for not being there when you were taken away. Some call it survivors' guilt. This goes beyond. Even if I couldn't have prevented it, I wanted to die with you, to know exactly what happened. Not knowing is far worse than any truth. I lost you once before; my heart can't bear to lose you again. This time the situation *is* in our hands.'

'You don't have to be afraid. We'll always have each other. You're never alone. I didn't mean to hurt you. I always love you.'

'But when this life is gone you'll never again know me as Westcott. And I'll never see you again as Regn.'

'No. But our souls will always recognize each other.'

The stakes were no longer so high. We entered the act of making love with the understanding that it would liberate our hearts, not cage them, as it had for so long.

• • •

It was a gray night, warm, in December. Rain made the glow of streetlamps hazy. Just before Regn arrived a cardinal left its body at my front door. I did not bury it until the next day. Regn wore the scarf I'd brought back for her from Ireland. I had on a red t-shirt that read: Wrangler, Since 1947. It depicted an outdoor scene, the outline of a tent and trees. I wore it for the year. I felt the 'Since 1947' represented me.

That night as we sat on the sofa downstairs, having exhausted our affection upstairs, I turned to Regn.

'There are two things I want to know. I was too nervous years ago to ask at the time, but does the prosthetic feel real to you?'

'No. I don't think it's natural—I—'

'In what way?'

'I think it's perverted.'

He'd meant did it feel like a *real* penis to her; this new comment derailed his train of thought. She'd wounded him again. 'So you think *I'm* a pervert, now?'

'No.'

'That's pretty much what you said.'

'I just don't find it necessary. I don't think *that* should be used.'

'And what about women whose husbands go off to war? What are they supposed to do? Go out and have affairs?'

Regn was nonplussed. Her expression revealed she'd never thought about the idea in such terms. Her perspective had expanded. She said nothing.

'It's not perverted. It can be crude if exploited; you know I don't care for tawdry fetishes. Like everything it depends on the context.'

'I didn't mean you—I know you're not like that.'

He was still injured by her statement in a way she could not know. It hurt because in some private chamber he *agreed* with Regn. He wished he never had to use one, on himself or anyone. Of course he preferred a real p——. Anatomically, he would never be a true man. Her words had left him stranded, once more. He did not belong to the male breed of species nor did he belong to Regn's sex.

'But it's a part of me, Regn, and you, our history. So, yes, you did mean it.'

'You don't need *it* to give me love, that's what I meant. We just made beautiful love—'

Westcott nods.

'What was the other thing you wanted to ask me?'

'It always preys on my mind. What is the one reason why you stayed with Jay?'

'I couldn't make it on my own, financially. How would I afford my prescriptions? I need good health insurance.'

'Don't you know you will collect social security and there are plenty of health programs? You'd also receive alimony from Jay.'

'Alimony?'

'Yes—'

'It doesn't matter. I'm not leaving my home.'

'No one said you were. We're just talking. But you never even tried. That's what bothers me the most.'

'What do you mean I didn't try? I've worked my whole life to get what I have and so has Jay.'

'I meant you never even tried to be on your own.'

'It's not possible. Maybe if I'd been twenty years younger.'

'Regn, you might live another twenty or thirty years. I know security is essential as you get older, but don't make it your excuse.'

'I might die tomorrow.'

'Exactly. You never know.'

'I'm not leaving. Nothing you say will change that. I couldn't make it on my own. I'd be miserable.'

'When you think like that—'

'Besides, Jay's good to me. He did nothing wrong.'

'No one said he did.'

'Leave Jay out of this.'

'Regn—'

'I don't want to talk about it anymore.'

'But he's a big part of it. And you brought him up just now. Not me. You *have* choices.'

'So do you. You're free. You can do what you want.'

'We all have free will, Regn.'

'You're not going to change my mind.'

'It's not my intention to, but I'd think you'd listen to your own heart.'

'Love isn't enough.'

'That's where you're wrong. It *is* enough. It has to be.'

'I need to go soon.'

'Don't you know by now I'd take care of you? My roommate is getting married and moving out soon, there's plenty of room.' I half-smiled.

'Oh sure. If we lived together we'd argue every day.'

'Healthy arguments. What I call affectionate banter.'

'I could never live with someone again. I'd want to be on my own. I don't want to be dependent.'

'But Regn, you are depen—'

'Not in the way you think.'

'Well, it sure appears that way.'

'I should go.' Even as she spoke, Regn remained sitting.

'The difference in circumstances is this. You ruined love for me. I exemplified it for you. Your life was leading up to me.' I looked at Regn. She didn't know what to say so I continued. 'You crave solitude in a life that isn't your own. You always have. I've known mostly solitude. Though convenient and pleasing at times, it has become an asylum. Marriage is your cage and silence mine. Perhaps we noticed this quiet melancholy in each other. The longing to be turned loose.'

'Yes, maybe.'

'I don't want to die. I *need* to. I've always felt I was left here and I'm waiting to go home. I never felt attached to this plane. I'll be glad when I'm gone.'

'Oh, my darling,' her voice was even lighter than usual, 'you will die. One day, and you'll know.'

'But what's the point of living if you aren't with the ones you love?'

'You make the best of it.'

'That's where you and I are in disagreement. I don't believe in making the best of things. There shouldn't be a gray area. It is all or nothing. I live on the extremes, whereas most people live right here,' he used his hands to draw a line. 'I don't dream of things. I make them happen.'

'Then live for that.' Regn took another sip of the Riesling I'd poured her. She'd needed a warm, mild buzz before going home and dissembling all that happened in three hours. No one in the entire world shared our knowledge of that evening and what it meant. What it took from each of us. 'Thank you, Westcott.'

As Regn stepped into the drizzling evening, the cardinal could no longer feel the wetness as it lay on its side on the stoop, looking up. I did not want to examine the symbolism. Instead I gently shut the door and started to pace, monitoring my emotions, letting myself feel them, hoping frustration would not be one of them. Everything had taken place. Everything for which I'd waited so long.

· · ·

We saw each other once more on the eve of New Year's Eve. Regn stopped by. Having enjoyed love only a week before, Regn was back to her jittery ways. She wouldn't look at me. She was anxious and edgy. I'd bought two miniature cartons of Glee chewing gum for her.

'What's that? I always chew the whitening kind.'

'This is better for you. There's no aspartame.'

'I like mine.'

'How do you know, you haven't tried this.'

After a brief visit we stood at my door. She was going to leave and say nothing.

'Take your gum,' I handed her the small gift bag it was in with the note.'
'I don't think I even want it. I don't want to read anything.'
'Here. Take it. Well, have a Happy New Year.'
'Yes. We'll talk soon, again. I need time by myself for now.' Regn wanted no reminders. Taking the bag was an incrimination of everything that had taken place a week prior. I sensed she'd been intimate with Jay since then. Her emotions always revealed themselves as cool whenever she was conflicted and didn't want to deal with the issue.

'Bye.' As I pushed the door shut, I felt a change inside me. The heartache had grown old. And Regn had become boring. Nothing changed with her. She'd stood in my kitchen two weeks ago, asking for my forgiveness. Her peevishness had returned. The simple fact was, Regn had chosen to go back to "sleep." She didn't want to change and I was tired of caring. I realized, as Regn left that afternoon, how uninteresting she had become. She never tried anything new.

We didn't talk "soon." Months passed. It was typical of her to say one thing and do another. She thought she knew me so well, but the sad part was she knew so little. Were someone to ask her for the details of my life, she wouldn't have responded correctly. My favorite song, favorite scent, color. I had asked Regn and I knew these intimate details about her. She had no idea that I had been a bell ringer and that one of the reasons I enjoyed it, as well as formal colonial dancing, was because of the group commitment. Everyone had to be precise, right on, and working together for things to run smoothly. The coordination exemplified a sense of necessity and camaraderie. Each person, each part, was crucial to the whole. Regn never asked what I did socially. Her excuse was, 'You never want to answer or tell me.' But in reality she seldom asked. She failed to see that a single night of passion, a spontaneous Christmas gift like the journal and calendar, however well-intentioned, could not make up for all the months and years of cold silence and small trespasses that added up. It boiled down to consistency. Regn, over time, had proved herself to be predictably unreliable, consistently disappointing.

● ● ●

I knew I could not stay. To linger is to dwell in the past. I'd sacrificed enough years. The happiness would wear off if I remained. The only way to keep perfection alive is to leave it be. I was at peace. I no longer required Regn, and with that knowledge, I departed.

My existence kept Regn alive. Regn's existence kept Jay alive. And the Truth kept me alive.

———

WESTCOTT LANDED A JOB TEACHING IN EUROPE. He traveled to Budapest. By now he had an MFA. He'd been bored and felt it was something to do, to have. He'd finished it in the span of time he'd known Birçan. His peers and mentors had extolled his work, couldn't wait to read his book. But there were things he had to do, to experience, before it could all be laid to rest.

It was intensely lonely at first, being in Budapest, not speaking the language, a completely different environment, but he wanted to get some track under his feet, increase his teaching experience. This had been his first real international assignment. After six months he made it to Germany. His first time back since that time when he'd still been passionately in love with Regn. To his surprise he made acquaintances fast, and from there even a friend or two, or at least colleagues with whom he went out to dinner and did things in the evenings and on the weekends. He was busy, always adjusting. The language was coming more fluidly. In three months he felt comfortable carrying on a prolonged conversation. At night though, going back to his small apartment room, alone, the old feeling and panic would turn in his stomach. He did his best to avoid it, to quickly pick up a book, grade some assignments, or write a letter home. Eventually his travels took him to Russia.

He often missed Robbie. But traveling in new places and moving about frequently wasn't practical with a dog in tow, however portable his size. Despite her self-admitted black thumb, Gedny informed him whenever he asked that his miniature fern, Binoche, was still thriving, and Tomás and Tereza were doing fine. Anytime he visited on holiday he made sure to repot them, all the while touching their leaves and talking to them. A link to the past.

After three years it was time to come home for good. In the meantime he'd enjoyed and said goodbye to one relationship and then another. He'd met Lorraine while teaching in Munich. She was from Sweden, working on a Master's program and taking English language courses. She spoke fluent German. They could teach each other. She both looked and behaved much older than she was. Westcott had never dated anyone younger than him. Lorraine was 4 years older. He enjoyed the feeling of belonging and knowing the feeling was genuine. It had always been genuine with Regn and Birçan, but the difference in age had always made him feel like an outsider.

Lorraine was an attractive woman, but the type who didn't place much value in it, that or she was unaware of her own attractiveness. He liked to hear about what she was studying. They'd ask each other about their lives back home. Westcott thought it would be nice to visit Sweden, but he never suggested it. After two months and still no physical advances Lorraine asked him one evening, 'Do you have someone back home—are you here trying to sort things out or maybe you're planning on going back to her?'

Westcott looked at Lorraine fixedly. He was thankful for her directness. He could not have broached the topic. He was still too reserved. Not until that first brick was removed, that initial question asked, would he volunteer to give it up. He did not want to impose upon her, much as he enjoyed her company.

Westcott weighed his emotions for a moment. Was he still waiting, planning on going back? If Regn came walking up the sidewalk in front of them now would he go with her? He knew the answer and was relieved. Regn wanted him to be happy. Always happy. Regn had dissociated herself from Visitor Services after her position "downstairs" dissolved. She worked upstairs as a receptionist for Development—cloistered away. How boring, was all Westcott could think. How absolutely, horribly mundane. Thank god he'd never been hired back in any of the departments. Even the "product" did not interest him. A museum. Where everything is stored, still. Silently turning stale. It wasn't the Settlement he missed. It was his youth and that's what the Settlement would always represent to him—the peak of his youth; the feeling of being in love—the ardor of passion and a young body. A full head of hair. It was the feelings and the place which had held those feelings, witnessed them, which he looked upon with nostalgia, but no longer sadness. Sure, visiting the site would evoke memories, but he had no desire to go back. The memories had feelings—meaning attached to them because they were linked to Regn. The excitement was gone from the Settlement. At the time of his employment things had been imminent, preparations for the 400th—there was hubbub.

It was not flattery unto himself. It was a fact. The most interesting and exciting thing that had ever happened to Regn was Westcott. He knew she would be very unhappy if he ever told Regn directly, but he felt sorry for her. Such a little life she'd lead. Small part-time positions before staying at the Jamestown-Yorktown Foundation all those years. It wasn't as though she'd had 5, or even 7 kids demanding her attention. She claimed she was a rather uninvolved mother with just the two children she raised. So what was she doing all those years?

Dreaming her life away? Just making ends meet? She had true artistic skills. She did nothing with them. She could have been a picture book illustrator. Westcott wrote a couple of children's books and asked her to make some proofs. He received two small sketches, quite good, and that was it. She might have painted in her spare time. She could have taught German in a local school. Did her life consist solely of cleaning, managing, tinkering around the house and reading? She had no inward confidence. Westcott knew she liked mystery novels, stories which he found quite dull and boring in language. She did read material by mystics and Madame Blavatsky, but what else and to what end? She didn't belong to any book club, she had no close friends. She may have, on occasion, gone out to breakfast with a colleague. That was all. Towards the end of the affair, for the relationship itself would never end, Regn had confided in Westcott that Rose Marie had become 'cold and ignored her. She used to be my friend. I feel so bad about it.' He'd tried to warn Regn about Rose Marie, but Regn had to find out for herself. And how do you think I feel, he wanted to say, losing you? I am reliable, always there. Regn didn't see the double-standard in her statement. Westcott couldn't sympathize with Regn about Rose Marie. Nonetheless, he tried to comfort her by listening. On some level Rose Marie and the other ladies, even Magda with whom Regn took walks, privately criticized her relationship with Westcott. They blamed her. An older woman; a young impressionable man. In the end it was Regn they held accountable. A part of him wanted to tell them it isn't true. Yes, she did me wrong, but I started it, I was the one who pursued her with relentless determination. He sometimes wondered if Rose Marie was angry at Regn for breaking her promises to him. After all Rose Marie knew what it was to live with a broken heart; she knew the depth and strength of Westcott's affection, which Regn just threw away. Regn had no one outside of Jay and her grandchildren. No one in whom to confide after Westcott and she stopped speaking. Her stubbornness was her weakness. Every year they went a few times to the same place in the Shenandoah Mountains. Why not try something different? All right if a place is beautiful and you like it, but throw in a dash of variety. The country is enormous. There are so many mountain ranges and trails to hike. Regn stayed in her comfort zone, her own little world of things she felt she could control. It would never be enough. She convinced herself it had to be. All the unlived life. Her story was the tragedy. It was hard to believe, but Westcott's mother had experienced more adventure than Regn ever had. His mother had lived a lifetime before he ever came into being.

'No, Lorraine, that is not the case. I want very much to be close with you, but I'm just afraid. I'm afraid of losing you before it's even begun. Isn't that funny or maybe it's sad.'

'You're a very serious man. And I sense you've been hurt in some way you don't want or can't express yet. And that's okay. I won't make you. But if what you said is true and you want to be close, then what's there to lose? We only lose if we never try.'

'I know that. All I ask is that you remember how we are and what we have said in this day, in this moment.'

'You are a funny man, but I know you don't mean it to be at all funny.'

'It's been a long time since I—may I kiss you?'

'You don't have to ask.'

'Until I know it's all right, I always do.'

She smiled a little, said nothing else.

'Close your eyes.' His ways had not changed, the process was the same. First he touched her face, took in its warmth, its softness. He made sure no one was looking, came closer, kissed her softly. Feeling her acceptance, he pressed firmer, longer.

Pulling away they both looked at one another. He knew it would not be long before she would be moved to take him to bed. He feared her reaction. Would he let her find out like Regn did, or tell her as he had Birçan? What if she ran out, yelled, tore him apart, accused him of being a liar and worse? He knew it would come to this. It always did. He wanted to enjoy this simple pleasure, this moment of perfection and mutual fondness for just a little while. It might be all he took away from their two months of knowing each other. He wouldn't wait too long. Waiting would only make it worse, harder. He would let them have this day, but soon she would know.

Westcott looked at his watch. 5:05 p.m. *You have to be able to look and feel ahead.* His whole life that's what he'd done. He'd always anticipated tomorrow. He remembered the days of Regn. When 5 o'clock carried the weight of the world.

'Lorraine?'

'Hmm?'

They stood to start walking again.

'Should we make love, before we ever do, there is something I must tell you. But not now. Not today. Today is wonderful. Shall I take us to dinner—we can sit outside, enjoy the fair weather.'

That evening as they dined, sitting in the warm summer evening on wrought iron chairs at an outdoor café, music from a nearby performance mingled with the pigeons and sound of social life. It was an outdoor symphony of 5 musicians. Westcott counted the different instruments he heard though he could not see the players. The violin. For a moment he remembered the harpist and dulcimer player who had played at Jamestown Settlement on rare occasions. He recognized the tune. "Meditation Thais." Regn's favorite song. It always sounded like a phoenix flying from the ash. Westcott told himself to be present. He did not want Lorraine to see the momentary catch, the hesitation in his restive state, the feeling of being alone while sitting with someone. Lorraine hadn't noticed, she'd looked at her plate for that split second and in that infinite breadth of time, Regn returned to him as she would throughout the years when he least expected it. She always managed to find him, even when he told himself he'd put her away. She once told him it was the song she wanted played at her funeral. Westcott listened, resumed eating, his appetite restored the moment he looked at Lorraine and saw that she was glad. Not smiling glad, but a quiet, peaceful glad.

———

When he started to feel really depressed he would apply for a new host location. En route to a post in Poland, he once enjoyed a 2-day excursion through the Bialowieza Forest. One of the last primeval forests in Europe. Regn had said she no longer needed to travel or see faraway places. She had experienced them in former lives and when she was younger. Westcott knew she was making excuses, staving off her own brand of longing. As he looked about the old growth trees and breathed the scent of old earth dampness into his lungs, his mind became intoxicated with peace and a sorrow that had petrified itself within him. He looked upon the world not only for his own benefit, but also taking it in for Regn who would never lay eyes on such original grandeur. Her favorite scent was the smell of a forest. For this reason Westcott had wisely avoided going into seclusion, living and working in the remote countryside, cut-off from social opportunities. To be alone with just the land as he had imagined when young, would mean endless torment. For nature itself—the shade of clouds on the mountains, trees and pine needles—each of these was a trigger. A synapse formed long ago. Any beautiful sight, however simplistic or even rustic, evoked affection. It was not only an exquisite cathedral with its tintinnabulation of bells at dusk that moved him; it was the meaning behind those stimulated senses. One kind of affection always begets another. He often saw himself standing in a room full of shuttered windows and watching, hearing them unlaced. The room becoming impaled with streams of light. A zip-line of wooden chorus as the slats flipped open one after the other as quickly as all the notes on a xylophone can be played to resonate. This is how fast it takes for a memory to awaken.

Westcott stood in the imagined room, enjoying the warmth on his skin and face. He was *remembering* who he was.

It was late afternoon and the sunlight streamed chalky through the trees and heavy underbrush, not far from the borders of Belarus. For some unknown reason, Westcott felt a familiarity to the land, a sense of returning as if he'd always known it, somehow, or been there long ago. That afternoon, like other moments in his history, was worth all the discontent he'd ever experienced. The pain had enabled him to love far more than had he never suffered at all.

He visited his mother and saw Ellis during the holidays—either Thanksgiving or Christmas, and he wrote hand-written letters to Jill Conway. Sometimes he felt guilty staying away so long. His mother wasn't getting any younger. He knew she missed him and she always told him how lonely Robbie and Helmsley were, waiting for his return. She'd moved to be closer to Ellis. But he also remembered his presence wouldn't change anything. He'd go into a decline. He'd always been restless inside. He knew why.

ONE SUMMER DAY, OUT OF THE BLUE, he heard from Birçan. Jay was not doing well and on the decline. A few years ago, when they were close, Westcott had offered to be there or give his support in any way he could should she ever need or want it. He hadn't expected Birçan to ask him to return. Nor did she. He understood it was a private matter and really there was nothing he could do. Besides, the audacity. After all this time. That double standard. It was all right for Birçan to hurt, to need him in a moment of pain or weakness, but when the shoe had been on the other foot, when he'd needed her, she'd left Westcott to freeze. 'So what!' That's what she'd said over and over. It was the way she said it. With no remorse. 'Birçan, you're hurting me. Can't we make this right? Why are you being like this? I'm not demanding. You are. I wanted so little.' 'So what. Get over it. People get hurt.' 'You're so rude.' 'So what. I am.' Westcott was in disbelief. He'd been careful, trust had come gradually. How could someone turn so easily? Furthermore, he'd done nothing to wrong her.

Her note was brief. Cautious. He printed it out and read it several times. 'I never meant to hurt you. I don't expect you to come, but if you're traveling you're welcome to stop by.' She gave him her newest address. *And what*, he thought? Drop in? Her being sorry couldn't erase the hours and months of anger; pain she'd ignited in him. He wasn't a dog that could be kicked and would limp back. His pride rose in him, then disdain, and last—loneliness. He crumpled the note in his fist. Then unfolded and tore it in disgust. Just like she had done with his Christmas greeting years before. How dare she reach out to me, *now*! *What am I, a trick pony?* All the hostility came back. The broken pieces. He must be strong. *I'll pretend I never got it. She'll never know what happened. Let her feel the same sting of being shut out, ignored, dismissed as she gave me*, he convinced himself. It wasn't enough. Six words. What about the rest?

He did not want to intrude in her last days with Jay. When it became critical she sent news and said it would mean a lot if he was there. Had the recent years made her feel more vulnerable? Birçan vulnerable? Hah! He laughed at that notion. He didn't have to do anything, say anything. He could send a card? No. Why did she have to show up out of the blue and like this? What was her angle? Birçan was always direct. So why not be direct. This wasn't about Westcott or making amends, was it? This was about *Birçan and her* feeling alone. Westcott must not delude himself into believing anything else. *How dare she!* He wanted to yell at her and hold her all at once. Why, why did he still feel affection for her? She didn't deserve his love. Was this a test? Some last chance offered by Providence? Death had finally elicited compassion from Birçan again? Westcott didn't know what he wanted. What was right. Pride, anger, sympathy…he let the emotions filter through. Waited days, hoping the answer would come to him.

For four days he deliberated. The memory of hurt made fresh. He knew Birçan would never tell him, 'I need your support. I need you here.' It wasn't her way. What was more important was this: she wanted him nearby. Okay, then what? He flies in spends a few days and—what next? If he went it was his decision. She did not offer him any promise. Would he be going for Birçan or for himself? But where was she when he had needed her? Again, the resentment. He wouldn't go. He'd asked for nothing more than genuine affection. She'd given him only so much and then, nothing. How the cold devoured him. She was apologizing again, this time of her own will, in so many words '…I didn't mean to hurt you.' Oh, but you did Birçan and only because I loved you. Yes, I did at one time and you wanted to remain unlovable. I paid the price for your own guilt. Westcott was tired inside. What was selfishness, guilt, love, passion, understanding anymore? At its best it always led to the same end: pain. Even exquisite pain. The door had been opened to him once more. He had to find out what it meant, where it led.

Westcott flew back. Not home, but back. For home seemed miles away and without a concrete location.

Jay passed away two days after Birçan met Westcott at the airport. He'd accompanied her to the hospital. Jay was awake but heavily medicated. Westcott was afraid Jay would misinterpret the reason for his being there. He didn't want Jay thinking, 'So, this is what he's been waiting for all this time. Well, now she's yours.' Not knowing if he followed, Westcott knew he had to say something.

'Well Jay—neither of us ever went in for small talk, but it's been a while. I'm going to be honest. I'm not here to see you off into the next world. Birçan asked me to come; it's going to be hard on her—you know. I hope in your life you have no regrets.'

Jay just stared at Westcott, that same old stare he used to give him when they'd first known each other. They'd be joking, and Jay would just look over, disturbingly silent, and a smile would form in the corners of his mouth. He wasn't smiling now, but somehow Westcott felt Jay's beneficence. Jay was not angry or jealous. He was relieved. Someone would be there for Birçan.

•••

In the days after Jay's death, Westcott said very little. He listened, did what things he could to comfort Birçan. He held her close when she cried and let her go when she didn't want to keep still. Staying busy was key to her recovery, her grieving process. At night he read. He thought of all the places he'd been, the people with whom he'd exchanged words whether for a few minutes, an hour, or days. He volunteered nothing. He understood when the time was right, Birçan would ask. And if she didn't, that was fine also. He felt no urgency even though he didn't know what his next move would be. For the moment he was content to rest. Westcott did not go with Birçan to scatter Jay's ashes. Birçan had invited him to come, in fact she wanted him along. Westcott had wanted to go as well, but somehow it was a private affair. He wanted Birçan to have that final goodbye all to herself. Over the years Westcott had become very good at goodbyes.

The day after Birçan returned from the mountains and placed the empty urn in an appropriate place in her home, she immediately started dinner. It had been nine days since Jay died. They sat across from each other at dinner. 'So tell me,' her voice startled him they'd been so quiet the past week, 'what have you been up to?'

Westcott started with the places he'd been, the students he'd taught, the sights he'd seen. He was in no rush. Eventually the subject would lead to more personal matters. Finally, Birçan knew she'd have to pull it from him.

'Did you meet anyone? Are you seeing anyone?'

Westcott looked up, directly at Birçan. He then scanned the room. Some items he remembered from years before in her old house, most were new.

'Are you tired?' he asked her.

'No.'

'Good, because I'm going to tell you a story. Just like you always used to tell me stories. Remember our bike rides?'

'Of course. I haven't gone bicycling for a couple of years now. My balance.'

'We'll get that bicycle for two we always joked about, and I'll pedal.'

She smiled.

'Now, as I was saying, a story.'

He told her all about his love affairs. Love affairs—the words sounded funny. He could count on one hand the women he'd loved and with whom he'd *made* love.

Twice more love had failed. Twice more love was not enough. What he did not tell Birçan was that when the time came to end his relationships with Lorraine and later, Augustine, he was not so much sad as he was relieved. The truth was he had not ended them. Each time the other had. Nor did he tell Birçan about Josh, the young man he'd slept with a few times while in Germany. Westcott welcomed the experience. He'd felt a rare, brotherly kinship. Josh had been the one to initiate contact. He was an unexpected friend, an expat, completing his internship in Agricultural Studies. Were he himself gay, Westcott would have found Josh ideal. It had been a memorable interlude of camaraderie and exploration, not love.

'Lorraine and I had talked of marriage. Fantasizing I suppose. After she knew about me we proceeded tentatively. She said, 'We'll have to see. I don't know how I'll feel after we sleep together.'

'We made love. Beautiful love, but ultimately sex was more important to Lorraine. She told me I was a decent, kind man, and deserved someone who could give me what I needed. It wouldn't be fair to either of us, she said. 'You're a wonderful, passionate, and sensitive lover, but I desire a *real* penis. I don't want those words to hurt you. But we can't give each other what the other needs.'

'And what about *wants*,' I said. 'Isn't it better to be wanted than needed? Sex is just the icing.'

'You've always been too old for me even though I'm just a few years older than you, but I admit, you're right. That's how it *should be*. I'm not ready. I still want—maybe one day I'll look back and regret it, but that's the choice I'll have to live with.'

Recounting the conversation, Westcott suddenly realized how Lorraine's words paralleled Regn's and in a way Birçan's—though the latter had never spoken them. He wondered for a moment if all women were the same.

'Anyway, Lorraine and I parted amicably. We wished each other a happy life. And just like that a little sliver of 5 months was set up on the shelf, a little sleeve in the vast history of one's life.'

'How old was she?'

'39.'

'Do you miss her?'

'No. In fact, though I was more attracted to her physically, if I had to say I missed one or the other, it would be Augustine.'

'Augustine?'

'Yes. Quite a name to carry, don't you think? No one's a saint, but she came close. She was, well—is—Russian. She's probably married now. How ironic.'

• • •

Over the years Regn sometimes crossed his mind, but not in a longing way. He knew what she was doing. The weekends she had her grandchildren. During the week she worked part-time answering phones and printing shipping labels. Before work she would be cleaning, doing laundry, perhaps spraying down the deck, washing her car. Everything had to be in order and clean. Evenings she'd come home, maybe fix some dinner—whatever Jay had bought at the grocery store. They'd watch the news or a Mystery on PBS. She'd read for a little while, take a bath. And then it would all start again the next day. Every year, two or three times at most, they'd go up to the mountains—the same general area, hike familiar trails. How very boring Westcott would think. How absolutely uneventful, even pedestrian. The things people do with their lives. Their lives. At such moments he was grateful to have been dealt the wild card. Life, though sometimes mundane, was never ordinary. It may not have always proved eventful, but even in the placid aloneness, walking the aisles of the grocery store, straightening his home, the source of his isolation was anything but dull. The silence made it loud. It created speculation. Why was a young man, reasonably handsome, so alone? Was he gay and leading a private life? He knew Regn would be angry if he ever said it, but she couldn't stop him from thinking it—at times he felt sad for her—what a boring, domestic life she led. Predictable, practical, ordered to the point of madness. But, he had to remind himself, it was her life. Her choices. For a second he'd think what year it was and quickly do the math—she'd be 71 soon. 71. He was afraid to ever see her again; afraid a very old woman would appear before him and he could not trust himself not to betray an expression of sorrow and yes, disappointment. Better to remember her in her prime.

One day a new realization occurred. His working at Jamestown Settlement hadn't changed anything. It could have been anyone in his place. His being there changed the course of no one's life but his own. Regn would still have stayed on and worked for the Office of Development after her layoff from Visitor Services regardless of whether or not they'd met. Nothing about her life permanently changed. She was static. The experience had been a vacuum of passion for her, whereas the direction he would take was forever altered. The memory of the passion never left him. Regn had her life. Westcott's had been bisected, in every way, just as it was beginning. So what had it all come to, what did it mean in the end? He'd always believed in the adage, *Love conquers all.* But Regn had chosen the path of least opposition. Her fear confined her to the safety of familiarity. Her entire life had been spent in the realm of wife, mother, grandmother.

Augustine would sometimes look at Westcott, waiting for him to come back. 'Where do you go? You sometimes stare off, but I know you're not looking at anything out there—' her hand would gently gesticulate towards the horizon—'you go somewhere else, deep within, and I sometimes get the feeling there are places in you where I can never come in.'

'Oh, it's just me getting old. It's better to have some things for one's self. I'm not trying to keep you out. We each have a private life and sometimes I like to remember so I can trace the route it took to get here.'

At last, with Augustine, Westcott found a partner willing to do "things" to him. They did everything and experimented. At 34 she was the youngest woman he'd ever slept with.

Sitting across from Birçan it was hard not to get aroused thinking of all he had done with Augustine.

'Auggie—that's what she wanted me to call her. Can you believe that? A beautiful strong name like Augustine and she preferred Auggie.'

They'd made love from behind and traditionally. She'd penetrated him with a fake penis and he'd pushed inside of her. It was wonderful to have her tongue between his legs. Augustine was bisexual. She respected that Westcott never had anything alcoholic to drink. She herself was by no means a drunk, but it was ingrained in her blood, a social custom she'd been brought up with and surrounded by since her earliest years. Often when they'd lie back on the sheets he'd smell the spirits on her breath. They didn't have the same scent; he could never define them by their beverage name. He just knew ones were richer or more pronounced, others soft and lithe. It didn't bother him to smell it on her breath—he actually found it to be a turn-on—more importantly, Augustine was never drunk.

He remembered the way she'd studied his left shoulder, the one with the skin engraving. 'When did you get that?' 'Oh, when I was 24.' He'd gone with Ellis on his birthday to a professional tattoo parlor. He never called it that—a tattoo—all he could think of was military bands when he heard the word. "Skin engraving" sounded cleaner, more holistic. He'd only wanted the one. Augustine had looked at the knight, kneeling, sword down, a gesture of respect. The color shading had not faded. It was blue and the detail was nicely rendered. It was not a stock template. Also, a few words in German were added to frame the image. 'What are the initials for?' Augustine asked. Everyone assumed the SW on the shield signified Sir Westcott. But the S was actually for Scatterbird. He knew better than to ever use real names when doing something permanent to the body. He had never, not once, regretted the image on his arm. He'd enjoyed the process. It had taken a good 2 ½ hours and he remembered vividly the sensation. It was like a burning zipper slowly, methodically being pulled as the tattoo artist engraved away. The part that hurt more was when the color was added. A day or two later, when he showed Regn, she had said, 'No one has ever done that for me. It's nice.' As Augustine admired the Teutonic image, Westcott wondered if Regn even remembered he had the image on his arm. She had chosen to forget so many things. He thought of the colorless hummingbird on her breast.

Birçan brought him back from his reverie. 'So, what happened? She sounds perfect.'

'Augustine wanted children. Her parents also wanted grandchildren and soon. I told her there's adoption. But that was out of the question. I suggested invitro fertilization. We could choose the father together. She considered this for a month or more. In the end she started to cry. 'I want to carry the child of the man I marry. You are a man, I only think of you as being a man, but we both know we can never have children together.' Until Augustine, as you know, I'd always been rather opposed to having children—that is bringing them up. But I wouldn't have minded becoming a father and coming home to Augustine every night. Not surprisingly, there was another man eager to pounce once opportunity presented itself. He was Russian and once he knew I was out of the picture—well—I left at the end of the semester—found another post in South America. Besides, her parents, whom I'd met and liked, didn't know about me, my situation. They were enamored with the idea of their daughter marrying an American, but also afraid their only daughter would be whisked away for good. They didn't want that to happen. So the Russian suitor wasn't *un*welcomed, I can only suppose. South America was a nice break from the climate in Russia. And the culture— I was surprised how hospitable they are. But to tell you the truth, I was tired, maybe even burned out by the time I reached Brazil. I was surprised when you wrote me. Not glad of the news. Glad for a reason to come back, I suppose.' Inside something tightens. He didn't mean he was glad to see her. Birçan always assumed he was paying her a compliment even when he wasn't.

Birçan looked older all of a sudden. It was as though he hadn't really taken stock of her looks since arriving 9 days ago. But the old Birçan was still there. Her voice had not changed as voices sometimes do with age. Hers was not frail or lighter. And she still smelled irresistible. He'd noticed this the moment they'd hugged outside the pick-up area at the airport.

'What are your plans now? Will you go back to Europe? Does your family know where you are?'

'At the moment, no. Last I told them I was in South America. They don't know I came here. I didn't want to have to explain right away. I'll see them though. Birçan?—'

'Yes?'

'Why did you ask me to come? Really?'

'Well, I knew it was going to be hard losing Jay. And I remember you always telling me you'd be there if I needed you—maybe it was selfish.'

'Is that all?'

'Oh Westcott. I don't expect you to stay. You have your whole life ahead of you—'

'Would everyone stop staying that! They've been telling me the same thing for the last 15 years. If you haven't noticed I'm getting older not younger. Soon my life won't be ahead of me. I'll have lived through it.'

'I didn't mean to upset you.'

'I'm not upset, just—well, annoyed. Did you ever consider that maybe I *do* know what I want and I have for a long time? I always knew. I just couldn't enjoy going after it. I had to—' He stops himself before the word drops. *Wait.* Yes, he knows, it's true. He'd been waiting all along. He didn't want Jay to suffer or be hurt, but death is a part of life. His body had said it was time. Westcott had stayed away. And as for Regn? Was she even alive? What about her Jay? Somehow the years had finally passed. All the waiting seemed worthwhile. But—

'Birçan? I'm going to say this and you think it over carefully. I loved you once. Loved you in those earliest days bicycling together, before we even made love and you did love me. You just pulled away. Wanted no attachments. You wrote in your note I was always welcome here. I don't want to be welcome anymore. I want to belong. You hurt me so much and if all you can offer me again is more hurt, then it was wrong of you to ask me here. Quite selfish.'

'Westcott, I'm sorry. I had enough of my own problems and so did you, I didn't want any more back then. I didn't want to hurt you.'

'You say that now, but the smallest of gestures. There is so much you could have done to ease the pain. You were cruel. You lost my trust. When I needed you most you slammed the door.'

'What is it you want?'

'Don't you know? What everyone does. What we touched upon so briefly and you threw in my face. What felt so natural and secure. I want your love.'

'But what will you do with this old woman?' Her hand flies up in a demonstrative gesture, casting her arms down as if to display her aging body.

'Oh, B. Have you not learned anything from me? It is "you," who you *are*, not what. And it doesn't bother me, I can still love you.'

'But you're still young, I don't want you to be tied down or feel obligated to me.'

'Birçan, I hate to break this to you,' a slight smile in his voice and then with grave maturity, letting her know he alone has control over his life he says, 'I can walk out that door anytime I want. I don't want to. There's love enough in this room and the kind I've been wanting all my life. The best kind. I love you and I want to be with you and take care of you.'

'It isn't fair to you—I'll get older, and—'

'We all will.'

'You are an anomaly. You know that?'

'Call me a rare breed. We both knew this years ago when we met. Did you think I would get any younger in my travels?'

'I'm glad you're—home.'

'Yes. *Yes.*' The words descend slowly, the single expression. Home. He hugs her, places his chin on her shoulder, and rests. Her hands press him firmly. She is free to give affection, to show it without guilt. But she does feel guilt of another kind. Guilt for having hurt him years before. She'd suffered in silence, let pride carry her away. She could not admit that she had missed him, though she did. Many times, inside. He had been good to her. What she could not know and he would never tell her was that as they hugged something inside himself knew it was compromising. He could never fully forgive her. She never asked for it. She never felt she needed his forgiveness. If she did, she was incapable of expressing it in words.

That same night Westcott takes his wallet and does something he hasn't done in a long, long time. He reviews its contents. He looks at the pictures. One has blurred beyond recognition from heat and moisture, but he still knows where and of who it is. Regn. The other ones are clear. He flips the page. He sees himself with Regn embracing him. It is a profile of them kissing in front of his Christmas tree. He can tell even from the side that he is smiling and so is Regn. They are kissing affectionately, just by the way Regn's fingers hold his hip, touch his navy blue velvet coat. Had he not insisted on getting their picture it would never have been. Westcott looks at himself and Regn for a long time, then removes a tiny piece of paper from his wallet. Receipt paper from Jamestown Settlement. On it is scrolled: *Have a nice day, Regn* and a smiley face with eyelashes. All these years, he'd kept it. These are the things he wants to remember. He unfolds a larger piece of paper. Regn stands in profile inside her lodgings at Skyland. Jay had taken the picture. It is an everyday scene. The ordinary gesture forever captured. Regn is fixing something, standing at the foot of the bed, her sea green sweatered breasts in profile. She'd titled it: "Twilight Time" and wrote four words: *I am with you.* The picture makes something hurt inside, his heart stiffens. That woman no longer exists. But he still wants her, all of her. Her hair is no longer reddish brown, he knows. And there is one more thing. Another piece of paper folded many times to fit in the wallet. He never takes it out. He'd read it once so long ago and that was enough. But tonight of all nights, it seems right to consider old ghosts. He removes the paper slowly, reverently, taking pleasure in remembering. He unfolds once, twice, three times, and four. A slim paragraph, and yet, one of the longest passages Regn had ever written to him. He knows he has never loved Birçan in the same way he loved Regn anymore than Birçan loved him as she did Snowball, Jay, or even her father. What they share will be comfortable. The years of unspent passion made Westcott's heart rich and tired at the same time. Their love—Birçan's and Westcott's—is not founded on necessity. There is an element of practicality, but above all, desire. Throughout their lives, each had survived the loss of their greatest love and knew what it was to go on.

Westcott glimpses words and phrases from Regn's note which he still holds in his hand.

She'd titled it: *Sweet Obsession*

My Irishman, my Love,

I can't express myself in a letter the way you can. You have that gift. I have to tell you how much I love you. When I think or look at you I feel warm all over my body and I mean all over my body, and it aches to. I want so much for you to hold me and kiss me and touch me. I never said that to any other man, not even my husband. This must be special Westcott. It feels so right with you. I have said this many, many times before. We must be soul-mates!

Forever Scatterbird

He smiles at the missing 'o' in too and the short, circular sentences. He loves that she has stepped out of her comfort zone for him. Affection is, after all, ignited by the most overlooked, every day gestures. The ordinary becomes sublime only when someone is present to witness the subtlety of transformation. He feels the fervency alive on the page and in his hands. It is proof. Tangible proof of the most honest moment in each of their lives.

———

I HAD OFTEN IMAGINED the following scenario. Of course, it *is* too idealistic. Nonetheless, it was a harmless fantasy and a distant comfort. Instead of being in love with the idea of love, for the love was already present, I was in love with the idea of hope.

• • •

Time passed. At last the waiting subsided.

It was an early June day when Regn walked into her house, sat down on her screened in patio and sifted through the mail she'd just retrieved. Nothing exciting. Junk mail. Companies were still sending out notices addressed to Jay Tompkins. She'd thought she was done notifying all of them. He'd been gone almost four years now. Stuffed between an envelope for veterans with return address labels as a gift, and a credit card bill, Regn held a thin envelope, cream-colored. The handwriting looked familiar and yet it wasn't. She glanced at the return address.

For a split second something inside stuck, flitted. It was the first time in a long time she felt excited.

There was an official seal on the back. Carefully she broke it and pulled out a thick notecard—it was an invitation. A folded piece of paper came with it.

You are
cordially invited
to the wedding ceremony for
Westcott and Birçan Rowan
to be held on the 7th of September
in the year Twenty Hundred and—

Location: The Historic Church of
Jamestowne Island

Your attendance is anticipated on this private occasion.
Please respond in kind to—
as soon as possible.

Unexpectedly the tears came and she forgot for a moment the slip of folded paper. Opening it she recognized his handwriting. The script, it's privacy in being reserved, small, tightly refined.

She read:

Dear Regn,

May this find you well. Though we've not kept in touch over the years, we had our own lives, inside. It is my sacred request if you would give me away at my wedding. I don't need to tell you what this would mean to me. I hope you will come.

Immer-

Westcott

Regn reread his note. What had she expected? She sat completely still letting all her emotions come in waves. Had she been hoping—? She did not know, could not answer this. Westcott was getting married. Regn stared out her back porch. A bird was busy by its feeder. Do all old women have bird feeders? She laughed in spite of herself. No. She'd had those same feeders even back then—yes, back then. She suddenly missed Westcott and realized she'd been avoiding him for the last several years—avoiding the emotions surrounding him. But if he was happy, she would be happy for him. Yes. The feeling was overwhelming. It came up all of a sudden. She was happy he was getting married. But who was the woman? B—she picked up the invitation again. Birçan—pretty name, unusual. Origin? Well, in any case they'd meet soon enough. Why the church, though? She couldn't help smiling a little. Why travel all the way here, unless—was it his way of telling her—ridiculous. He was getting married. Maybe the Island had meant more to him than she ever supposed. Maybe it wasn't about her.

She pulled out a piece of notepad paper and wrote a few lines. Never one to write much, she was polite and to the point.

I would be delighted to give you away. Please send more details when the time is closer. I am very happy for you. Please say hello to Birçan for me. I look forward to seeing you both. It is good hearing from you.

Love,

Regn

Summer passed quickly. They'd spoken by telephone after Westcott arrived and had settled into his lodgings. He and Birçan were staying in a nice hotel until the day after tomorrow. The day of the wedding.

They planned a light lunch and to maybe take a pleasant walk afterwards. Regn could come to the hotel and they'd meet her in the lobby.

All morning Westcott had been in an anticipatory state. Actually, he'd been waiting for this day for several years now—how many? What did it matter. Often as he'd thought of the scenario, played it every which way in his mind over the years, he knew in reality it would most likely fall short of his imaginings. He'd been preparing for the moment he'd see Regn again followed by her introduction to Birçan, and yet there was no way to prepare. You could never get ready for something like this. It had been a quiet yearning, far off on the unknown horizon. He'd hoped but never quite believed it would land. But here he was. Smoothing his tie in the mirror he had to remind himself that in just a short while the woman he once loved with every fiber of his being would be before him. And by his side would be the woman he now loved and cherished.

What would Regn think of Birçan? He knew her vanity, but would he be able to detect even the slightest trace of the woman's satisfaction in feeling superiorly attractive? But then, how much had Regn changed? Maybe the last few years had taken their toll. He'd find out soon enough.

Birçan came into the room. 'Well—'

She was more charming than ever. She rarely donned a skirt. At heart she'd always be a tomboy. But today her underlying elegance matched itself in her attire. She wore no jewelry except a pendant of rare stone and a bracelet. He'd learned to tell the different minerals by their scientific names. Her short hair was still its attractive ashen gray interspersed with dark gray and a patch of white on top. Her eyes were like glass. A blue gray sometimes green. She smiled and laughed.

'Am I fit to be your wife?'

He wished she'd put a light coat of makeup on, just a hint. He loved her just as she was, but even a gentle brush of color brought her features to life. She was already in possession of natural charm and fine looks, so why not accent them just a tad? He'd seen pictures from her second wedding—years ago—and my, he'd have married her right then and there. The years had been good to her. She still retained a lovely vibrancy, which he knew was the product of her amicable, ever inquisitive personality.

11 o'clock arrived. Westcott and Birçan were already in the lobby waiting to receive Regn. It was three past 11 when a small figure stepped through the sliding doors. She was dressed casually, but not too casually, nor had she outdone herself. She did not see them at first and then Westcott called. 'Regn—'

She looked in his direction.

They embraced and in that flurry of long awaited union, flustered by anxious nervousness, he made sure it was a polite hug, not too long or too short. For a second he inhaled. It was Regn all right. Still the old Regn he remembered. Same scent. And why wouldn't it be? Had he worried her scent would change with age? Perhaps.

'Regn,' he stepped back, 'this is Birçan. Birçan this is Regn.'

The two women embraced, as women often feel compelled to do. Birçan took the lead—always the one to initiate. 'I'm so glad to finally meet you.'

Westcott watched Regn's face. Told himself not to take his eyes off of it. It betrayed no falseness. And he knew Regn's shortcomings when it came to hiding true emotions.

So she approved. But what did that matter anyway?

The two women continued to take each other in—

'Shall we go to lunch?' Westcott acted as diplomatic host, trying to avoid any lingering awkwardness. And then—'I still can't believe you're here.'

The eve before his wedding Westcott had asked Regn to come up to his room the next morning. He wanted time alone to talk with her. Birçan understood and was content to give him all the time he needed with his old flame. She'd lost her true love once. He'd shot himself. And some things never go away, even in pain and anger, the love is still there—else we wouldn't hurt so much.

Birçan was practical, logical, side-effect of an engineering intellect, but she also had passion. A passion so strong she could analyze things from a pragmatic viewpoint and an emotional one. He loved her for it.

Regn knocked on the door. He walked over, pretended he hadn't been sitting in anticipation ready to leap up at the faintest sound. He hesitated a reasonable amount of time, politely opened the door. 'Come in.'

'You look very handsome.'

'Thank you. And you—' He wanted to tell her, 'You haven't lost it, Regn. You still have it.' But the old hurt came back and he couldn't say it. He didn't want to encourage sweet talk. After all, what were words?

'So are you all ready to walk me down the aisle?'

'Yes. But isn't it a bit—um, out of the ordinary. The man being walked down the aisle—who's going to walk with Birçan?'

'Come now, Regn. You don't think I've considered that. I wouldn't leave her without an escort. Although she wouldn't have any qualms about walking herself. You reach a certain age and—'

He looked up, realizing Regn was not that much older than Birçan—9 years.

'Well, I mean, she doesn't need anyone to walk her to the altar. But I know she wants me to. And I want to.'

There'd been no rehearsal. It seemed pointless with such a small gathering.

'So you'll walk her down and then come back and I'll walk you?'

'No, Regn. I'll walk Birçan down. And you'll walk me down. All of us. Together.'

'I see.'

'You know, Regn'—now was the time for boldness. He was too old to be afraid of speaking his mind—'it could have been you.'

He looked up to meet her eyes. Before she could interject—

'Even then, young as I was, I was prepared to take care of you for the rest of your life.'

'I know—' her voice was soft. He'd always loved her voice.

'But I'm glad that's settled now. I have one last request.'

'Yes. What is it?'

He hesitated, felt the warmth of the room, the stiffness of his muscles, the cold clamminess of his hands. After all these years Regn still made him nervous—in a good way.

'Will you just lie down with me. For a little while.'

Was it surprise or relief that washed across her eyes?

'Of course, Westcott. You don't have to ask.'

In his white shirt and necktie he lay down. Regn had on a beautiful skirt and blouse. For the first time he noticed the bangle on her wrist. He rolled his finger across its silver thread. Letting her know he saw it. She'd worn it for him. They held each other. His hand brushed her face, cupped its warmth. He kissed her and she met his kiss. It was decent, not restrained or unbridled. And then he kissed her forehead. He reached for her hand, closed his eyes and rested his head on her breast while she pushed her fingers through his dark brown hair.

Inside he was at peace. Regn was still desirable, but the thronging passion had been replaced. In its place a richness, a calmness in himself had finally been borne. The test he was most afraid of, this moment had come to pass. He'd feared his heart would begin to doubt itself and his love for Birçan be lessened. But no. If anything Regn's presence strengthened it. They'd had their time. It would always be theirs. And he would never stop loving Regn anymore than she stopped loving him. But— Birçan was the woman he wanted to be with, to wake up next to, to take care of whatever the future held. Regn had made her choice years before. She'd turned him out, kept him away inside. And now he'd made his choice. They were equals.

Regn would never have married him. She never had the courage. She couldn't bear the remarks of society and her children—they'd never understand. What about her grandchildren? How old was Rebecca now? Was she married? She'd stayed married for the security, claiming, 'I could never make it on my own. I'd be a bag lady.' Did she not know anything about alimony and social security? Of course she didn't want to be cut off from Jay's will. And then her children might never forgive her. Westcott found this selfish. Regn had given her whole life to her family. She just wanted a little time to be herself. They did not know of, nor could they fathom the bond their mother had with this "young man." It broke Westcott's heart. Time and time again. The burden of a beautiful love, secreted from family.

Westcott thought of Birçan. In less than two hours he'd finally have the pleasure of calling himself a husband. He was giddy and calm all at once. He couldn't wait to call her his wife.

•••

At the church that day his mother had a moment with him, aside.

'Are you happy, West?' She meant where Regn was concerned. She knew they'd had time to talk this morning. She had to know if he had any doubts. Of course she wanted him to marry Birçan. She never forgot the pain Regn had caused him.

His mother always needed affirmation. Confirmation.

'How could I not be? All the women I ever loved will be in the same room today. I am happy. As happy as I ever want to be.'

His mother had her peace. She hugged him.

With only a handful of bystanders, the ceremony began at 9:30 a.m. Westcott and Birçan hadn't wanted fanfare and hoopla—it wasn't intended as a spectacle and only those who would not cast judgment had been invited. As for the rest of the world—what did it matter what they thought? The world was enormous and what did *It* know of this unlikely pair? Citizens of the world may ridicule the unorthodoxy of the union, but the earth itself would rejoice. Goodness borne of love, decency, can never be unnatural. Birçan was clearly old enough to be his mother and he her son, but as they exchanged vows that day what they'd always known between each other, became visible to those privileged to stand witness. He loved her and she loved him. What else was necessary? They were happy. Their love was a burden. Not unto themselves, but to those who would never understand. Such is the way of the world.

With Birçan on his right arm and Regn with her arm interlocking Westcott's left, man and *women* proceeded down the brick aisle. Such a short distance and yet in that span of twenty paces, 8 full stride, his life was coming full circle. He remembered for no particular reason the scent of places he'd been, places he'd worked, different ages. The clean sweaty scent of the uniforms at Busch Gardens—yes, the sweat was clean, it reminded him of youth, and the summers of discontent. All the years and places, each a notch in the twine, every experience buffering the ivory tusks of his heart. His dignity had been tested, his patience tried. He'd lived with suicide all his life—the notion of tomorrow being his last day. But finally, alas, the waiting was over. He had arrived.

Regn squeezed his arm and leaned close. 'She's a very lucky woman. Take care of her. I wish you all the happiness in the world.' Regn disengaged and stepped to the side. Westcott knew then how Regn felt. And knowing was enough. To be so loved. To be so wanted.

He looked at Regn who held tears in her eyes but did not let them come. He turned to Birçan, took her hand. He was home. Home.

• • •

What really happened.

For a long time I worried about her age, losing her too soon. But I had to remind myself that there is never a guarantee in life. My wife could have been 35 years old and died—I could not spoil today with speculations of "what-ifs." Keeping this perspective was difficult to say the least, an active effort. Sometimes a moment would be so wonderful that I'd feel a heavy sorrow descending, knowing I'd want to remember this fleeting contentment for the rest of my days. Images, expressions, statements, I could no longer ponder, but had to store away—living in, and only for, the present was hard work. It decreased with age—the emotions of youth leveled themselves—I somehow managed to become comfortable in my late 30s, early 40s. I said comfortable, not happy. Happiness, true happiness is fleeting. I'd known it once, in summer hours and blue fall skies. I'd known it with Regn. I'd held it with Birçan, and I'd known it as a child. Memories of my mother, the love she gave not knowing it would hurt us in the end. Just like Regn and Birçan's love.

Over the years I thought of my great, great uncle Charlie. Mother had told me about him, as much as she had been told. A picture of him always hung on her wall. Now there was a quiet, unspoken story. A man who never married. A man of utmost decorum, respectability, and propriety. He was made of old money, good money, hard-earned. But why the single life? Was he latently homosexual? Or was his heart irreparably broken by the one woman he had loved in his youth? His journals—reports of the day, logs describing routine—what time he woke, where he went—but contained nothing, absolutely nothing of a subjective tone. What did his life mean? What did it say? Sometimes I'd look at him in his suit, posed for the cameraman, one hand in pocket. Mother always said I would have loved Uncle Charlie. When the days stretched too long and too lonely I would study the photograph wanting to ask him, to know, 'How did you manage it—all those years?' Of course, no answer was ever given. I knew I'd have to leave my own answer—for someone else down the line who might find himself or herself staring at a stranger in an old photograph. I'd be damned if I was going to endure and then say nothing about the process.

I'd asked Birçan to marry me. I told her, 'Just once in my life I want to be able to call myself someone's husband.' And I wanted her to be my wife. At first she laughed kindly at the absurdity—a woman her age, but then she became serious. 'Yes, Westcott. Let's get married.'

One thing I imagined did become reality.

On an off-chance I called the last number I had for Regn. Her home number. If a man picked up I would claim I had the wrong number or maybe I'd just ask, 'Is Regn there?' Would Jay know it was me? What if Regn had died and Jay was left behind? I stopped speculating and dialed long distance. I pretended no one would answer. That the house was for sale. I could go for a visit, look at it as a prospective buyer. The cozy blue house I'd been in so many years before. But no. I didn't want to look upon empty rooms, to be reminded that Regn had moved on, forever. The memories belonged to a certain place and time, an age. To go back and see something different would destroy the sacredness of those two nights we shared in her home. Oh Regn. All the details of our lives we missed. I wanted to see again what was on her refrigerator, how she kept her kitchen, what went where. Everything was immaculate, no dust of disuse. The only thing that would feel dusty would be my heart. There had never been. Nor would there ever be again in my life, a greater love.

A woman's voice.
'Is Regn there?'
'Who?'
The voice had no accent.
'Regn Tompkins.'
'There's no one here by that name.'
'Oh, well, maybe you can help me then. This *is* 4735 Watercress Way?'
'Yes.'
'The Tompkins used to live there. I'm an old friend of Regn Tompkins. Can you tell me how long you've been there, or if you know where she moved to—'
'Well, we've been here 5 years. As for the Tompkins, I think I may still have our realtor's name and number. He might be able to help you.'
After a week, having left a message with the realtor in Virginia, there's a message.
'Ah yes, Mr. Rowan, this is Richard Prentice calling you back. If you can give me a call at my office—I believe I may be able to help you.'
After explaining who I was to the Tompkins, a harmless white lie, Richard Prentice was convinced he wouldn't be making an infraction of confidentiality in giving me the address on file of the Tompkins' last known address.
I kept the number in my wallet for several days. I was afraid the number would lead to another stranger. I was more afraid it wouldn't.
Regn had contacted me, a few times in those first few years, but after I moved away the line was severed. By me. She had my email. True, I had never given her my new address. We corresponded during the holidays and for birthdays. A rare phone call. I never told her the specifics of my location. It was easier that way. If she had a place and a name for my whereabouts then I'd begin to miss her terribly. I'd want her with me—to tell her all about the things I'd seen. In moving around, it softened the hurt. I knew my stakes were firmly planted far away and that my travels would one day end. Silence is the same as waiting.
What if Regn had tried to contact me? Maybe she thought I didn't want to be found, I didn't want to hear from her? One of us had to take a step and if I'd remembered anything from the past it was that Regn's stubbornness often caused more harm than good. She let fear get in the way. She gave up too easily.

On the third day, perspiring heavily, a hollowness of anticipation, I dialed the number. I had back-up plans in mind should she answer, should she not. If Jay answered. Then the ringing stopped.
'Hello?'
The voice was soft.
'Hello?'
She sounded more delicate than I remembered.
'Is this Regn?' I knew it was. I had to hear her say yes.
'Yes. Who's calling?'
Now I didn't know what to say. Everything I'd rehearsed sounded just that—rehearsed.
'Regn, it's Westcott Rowan.' So formal, I thought, why the last name—it's better that way, set the tone.

'Westcott—'

'Is this an all right time?'

'Yes, it's fine.'

I hear movement in the background, a chair, and then it sounds as though she is sitting down.

'How have you been, Westcott?'

'Good. Fine.'

'And you? How are things with you?'

'Oh fine. The grandchildren are about to go to college—the youngest ones—. And Rebecca's engaged. I still think she's too young even at 25, but she's happy.'

25. The last time I saw Rebecca she was 7 years old. And then I saw a picture of her at 13. Now she is a young woman. Beautiful no doubt. She'd always looked like Regn. Does she still have Talis, the rice-filled cat with the Converse tennis shoes? Perhaps she is sitting on a shelf waiting to be given to her own son or daughter one day. Another generation. Regn's great-grandchildren.

'Look, Regn, I'm going to be direct. How come you never said anything again? Not a word?'

'Oh Westcott—please don't bring all that up. It was a long time ago. It was for the best. I thought about sending you a letter again or calling from time to time, but I didn't want to hurt you more. And when I didn't hear from you—'

'Did you ever try to find me? Did you wonder if I was even alive?'

'Of course I did. But you told no one. And so that was it.'

'Who would I have told? We didn't share any mutual friends. And Jill passed away.'

'Jill—?'

'Yes, Jill *Conway*.' I thought about the lunches Jill and I had shared, the short walks we took every few months. The time always regimented as though she had to keep going. Jill had been a true friend. Lonely in her own way. She kept herself on track. A practical woman, not happy. Though married, she traveled with friends. Her husband had no desire to go anywhere. He'd retired at 50 from the Navy and in 25 years he just hunkered down, existed by routine. She admitted that she'd never been passionate about anything in her life. Was that the key to surviving to a ripe old age? I'd rather die young and absolutely alive, than old and feeling *just all right*. She believed that when we die it is lights out, eternal sleep. I knew Jill was my friend because she also needed a friend. Her brother had gone missing when she was in her 20s. She never found out what happened to him.

Jill didn't know *about me* until after I left the Settlement. I'd known her 5 years before I revealed the truth of my gender. Besides Regn she was the only person from the Settlement to know. She once said, 'I like Regn, but she and I could never be friends.' They were different types of women. Regn was the Siren. Jill had been the attractive secretary.

'Oh yes, yes. She retired from the Settlement a few years earlier before she died. I remember reading about it in the Gazette. Sharon told Fernus and Fernus told me.'

All the old names. Strange to hear them spoken. What was it now—17 years since I'd worked at the Settlement. I thought of Phil Emerson. The President of the Jamestown-Yorktown Foundation. Emerson. I'd wondered if there was any link to Ralph Waldo. Sometimes Phil would see me dining on the stairwell. 'Come to my office and eat,' he'd say. He was a nice man. I appreciated that he never said, 'You can't eat here. It doesn't look professional.' The truth was, no one could see me. It was the employee passageway, and I always sat to the side on one of the steps. The only individuals who might chance to run into me were fellow colleagues. It was subtle, but reflected Phil's old school policy. Like Eva, he spoke from himself, not a handbook. Maybe Phil also appreciated the way I dressed. He was not a tall or imposing man, and he struck me as being humble despite his title of President. I wish I'd taken Phil up on that offer, called his bluff. Surprised him by just dropping into the President's Office. All the lives we pass by, a moment's exchange or something more. People watch and listen. I knew that a few women, at least one in the Executive Offices, had suspected there was something more between Regn and myself. And then one day, just like that, the young man who always wore a shirt and tie in Visitor Services, the young man who caught the eye of others but was too intent upon one woman only, was gone. I was gone.

Hearing silence on the other end, Regn wonders.

'Please, Westcott, things haven't been easy for me.'

'How is the rest of your family?'

'They're good. My kids are doing well. Jay's health has declined. It's really been hard on him and me these last two years.'

'So you finally moved.'

'Yes, I was going to ask you, how did you get this number?'

'I hope you don't mind, I called your old house number and the woman there had it.' I didn't want to explain about the realtor.

'Really, that was lucky. You were always good at things like that. We never gave the new owners our number though, unless Jay did, maybe for questions.'

'Actually, the realtor had it.'

'Oh, okay. I loved that house. It tore me apart to move, but it was for the best. Too much maintenance.'

I envisioned Regn on the day they moved out, standing alone, taking one last look. And I knew she'd see the empty living room and a passing thought would waver through. She remembered. I saw her removing the photograph, Somber Passage, she'd bought from me, packing it in paper. So much of what remained was based upon creation in each of our minds. We no longer shared anything. Nothing in the present, until this phone call. All we had was the past. Her remembrances and mine. I missed not knowing what Regn had thought about every day for the past 10 years. How did she do it? Making the heart go blind.

'So, where is Jay?'

'He's resting—in a chair outside.'

'Well, I won't keep you.'

'It's all right, he just went out a few minutes ago. We have some time. Tell me, what have you been up to?'

'Before we talk about me, where are you now? I mean, where did you move?'

'Oh, we moved closer to my son. Jay's retired now and I still do a little part-time work at a gift shop nearby.'

'When did you leave the Settlement?'

'A few years ago. I was glad to be done.'

'I'm sure.'

'Nothing ever changes in that place. Except the people.' Her voice sounds tired.

'Of course not. It's a museum. What would you expect?'

She laughs. 'Now tell me about you.'

'I've been traveling and working quite a bit. I've seen a lot. Been to Russia, Budapest, Brazil, Africa, other parts of Europe'—I don't want to mention Munich.

'How's your mother? Is your sister married yet?'

'Yes. They're both doing fine. My sister is married.'

'And what about you?'

'Well, as a matter of fact, that's why I called.'

'No Westcott, please—Jay is right outside—I'd hoped you'd find someone—I really hoped you—'

'Regn, would you let. Me. Finish.'

'Go ahead.'

'I'm getting married in a week.'

Relief in her voice. Westcott is irritated. Still the same old Regn who goes off half-cocked.

'I let you go a long time ago, Regn.' It isn't true. That's why he called. The truth. To tell her the truth. This is it. 'Actually, Regn, that's a lie—the part about getting over you a long time ago. I am getting married, but that's also why I called. I want to say goodbye the right way this time.'

His mind wanders. He sees himself walking into the small warm office at Jamestown Settlement. All those years ago. It was a December. Fall filled his senses. The year of the quadricentennial. The big event over. He'd found three tiny flowers almost wilting, broken off on the ground. It was his day off. He'd come by specifically to see her. He entered the office. And though he was being watched from above, the camera anchored in its globe, he set the flowers by Regn's hand.

Her back was to him. She'd turned. He was in plain clothes. Relaxed looking, but anxious inside. 'I've made a decision,' he said evenly, with the bravado of unscathed youth, but his voice was quiet. 'And—' she waited. 'I've decided I will wait for you.' He'd been standing in the shower that morning when it hit him. The absoluteness of it. He didn't have to lose Regn. They never had to say goodbye. It filled him with energy, hope.

But the hours and days would become too long. Waiting was exhausting business. Pedestrian in its shiftless routine. A life spent being responsible, paying bills, eating, being polite, but otherwise meaningless. No highs. No excitement. No real joy. The pain of absence took its toll. He smiled, shook his head to himself at the preposterous declaration he'd made so long ago.

'Yes.' Her voice is very quiet. She hadn't expected him to say it. A part of her is sad. Somehow wondering where he was, what he was up to, had given her a strange sort of hope. Not that he would come back—she was an old woman now—but just the thought of him, knowing secretly that he loved her, was a comfort.

'Listen, Westcott, I want you to know I have missed you. Don't think that I didn't.' She feels it is safe now to let him know. He is getting married. It is not false hope. He is no longer waiting for her.

'Regn, before I hang up, most likely this will be the last time we speak unless you ever wish to call me, if you ever need anything—I just want you to know this: you hurt me greatly, more than anyone, but I never really ever stopped loving you. The first is always the best, right?'

'I know. So your fiancée—'

'Oh please, I don't think of her that way—'

'Well, do you want to tell me what she's like?'

'She's a beautiful woman. I love her. And she loves me.'

'I'm glad. I really am. Do you mind if I ask, how old—?'

'How old is she? I knew you'd want to know. Put it this way, she's younger than you.'

'Well, that's good, you're not still going for old crones, then!'

'It's all relative. I've never dated anyone younger than me.'

'Well, I wish you all the best. Both of you.'

'I told her about you, you know.'

'Oh—what did you tell her?'

'What was important. Anyway, the point is, she knows how close you and I were.'

'Does she know you called?'

'Yes.'

'Well, Westcott, I wish I could be at your wedding, I really do.'

'In a way you will be, Regn.'

'Yes.'

'She's foreign and has an accent.'

'Just like me.'

'Did you expect anything else?'

'Well maybe if you like you can send me a picture of you both at your wedding.'

'Maybe I will. But if not don't be disappointed. I live a private life.'

'So do I.'

'Regn. It was good to hear your voice.'

'Yes, yours too. Take care of yourself, you'll be in my thoughts.'

'Regn? Don't ever hesitate to contact me if you ever need anything. You won't disrupt my life.'

'Your new wife needs you more.'

'I know. That's not what I meant. I make alliances for life. And you're still one of them.'

'You were always too good. She is lucky to have you.'

'Yes, she is. And I am lucky to have her.'

'Take care, Westcott. I will always love you.'

'Goodbye, Regn. See you around.'

'Yes. See you around.'

IT WAS A PRIVATE OCCASION. Mother and Ellis attended and a few friends of Birçan's. I knew Ellis found the situation bizarre; she forced herself to be understanding, offering Birçan a warm welcome. I'd have told my sister just about anything, had she asked. But she never did. I did not need to prove anything to myself, whereas Ellis needed self-vindication. We seldom spoke intimately. I sensed my sincerity left her feeling disarmed. On the surface she exhibited acceptance, but I knew she had never come to terms with who I was. The wall between us was constructed of fundamental differences. We dealt with emotions in separate ways and silently judged each other. Through no intentional fault of her own, Mother had always stood between us, leaving me in the position of having to choose sides. But it was my wedding day and so I allowed such thoughts to sputter through without regret. The past could not be changed.

Although religion is something I put away long ago, leaving it to my days of Catholic school, I took the ceremony and oaths with great seriousness. When B slipped the gold band, the one I'd worn for years on a shoestring around my neck inscribed with the words *The Color of the Mountains*—over my finger, I felt an enormous burden lifted. The waiting was done. I knew B would not wear her ring, so the one I gave her was for the ceremony more than sentiment. As a gift, in private, I gave her a beautiful necklace with an oblong amethyst. I'd always been self-conscious about wearing a ring. In my mind it made my hands more delicate. Someone once said they were piano hands. They had done many things in the course of my life. I was aware of the gold weight on my forefinger, but I enjoyed the satisfaction of letting the world know I was spoken for, that my affections belonged *with* someone. 'And Birçan, do you take this man to be your husband—' Birçan smiled, an unspoken knowledge of what she and I shared. The truth of my person, the irony of his words. *This man.* When the priest formalized the matrimony with the concluding phrase, "You may kiss the woman"—I insisted he say woman and not bride—I picked Birçan up off her feet, kissing her long and gently. I felt her kiss back, a free, desired exchange.

Some things about Birçan had not changed. I knew better than to comment anytime she left her chair out in a restaurant or at home. I merely observed, no longer a critic. I watched the way others still perceived her natural brusqueness for rudeness. She was unaware; it was just her nature to be oblivious of these details. Sometimes I felt sorry for her. And yet, I, the sentimentalist, always the one left to see from both sides, envied her ability to be detached. It didn't bother Birçan because she didn't pay it any mind. It only bothered her if I brought her attention to it. We'd come to tolerate certain annoyances in each other, much in the way of any married couple who's been together longer than apart.

We were comfortable, content, complete. For a few years.

And then my wish came true. A fantastic notion I never actually, truly believed would happen.

I suffered a heart attack and then another one. The doctors were initially baffled. Here was a patient in relatively good health. Non-smoker, never drank, exceptionally clean, strong teeth, reasonable diet, good weight. And then they asked about medications. I never considered the testosterone a "medication," it was just a "habit." After a blood test to rule out anything serious, and an EKG, the physician attributed it to the years of testosterone usage. I'd been injecting the hormone for two decades. Certain forms of testosterone are more hazardous than others. But, the toll had arrived. I didn't refute the doctors' explanation; I'd always known the risks of a body divided—the suppression of "natural hormones." I didn't tell them the real cause. I wasn't in the business of telling anyone what had taken a lifetime to accumulate. Something had entered my heart, at an early age, the size of a weevil you might say. And it began to gnaw, to chew, to spread. It never went away and set up its chambers, lying down snug in its bunk.

Testosterone may have been the primer; the actual source was more elusive, not to be found in any medical encyclopedia. The years of hard-earned loving with no closure in sight had caused a strain. The weight of sorrow, like dampness hanging from the eaves of a roof, silently gave way. Fell in. I'd gone on, done many things, but the breakage had never been repaired.

~

The doctors tell me with ample rest and absolutely no strain, physical or otherwise, I will likely recover, especially since I am "still young with my life ahead of me." I just smile and say, 'No doubt. I'm feeling better already.' As I say this something inside hurts. It feels heavy and light at the same time. It takes every last reserve of energy to say the words. I smile so they feel they're doing a good job.

At first I was sad, a bit surprised but by no means shocked when they told me I'd nearly died. And then came the calmness of peace. Finally. No more waiting for the other shoe to drop. Finally I could make my exit without guilt—I was glad I wouldn't have to kill myself. I had accomplished what I'd come to do and I was ready to leave. I had known so much affection—I had given and received—my life felt fulfilled. And all I had left to do was lay down the ending. The conclusion had finally presented itself. I could stop worrying. I was, for the first time in years, free. No longer afraid.

Everyone I loved would be near and I could say goodbye. It had been a good life. The best life. As a young man in his twenties—if I had known then, what I do now, I'd have been able to embrace both the pain and pleasure of love without reservation.

Regn came. I no longer cared about the shock of seeing if she'd aged well or not. This was the last chance for farewell. She kissed me, I felt her face and in that moment I realized how much I'd missed her. All the years. How much I'd controlled, subdued. Something inside shifted, like a giant stone being pushed aside to gain entrance to the tomb. A hollow, cool, grating, the sound of scraping pottery, of earth and stone. Her eyes seemed tighter, her features smaller. Her scent would never leave me. Her Dior Essence was like breathing in the sunshine. So necessary, soothing, complete. I never thought of other women wearing the perfume. It was Regn's identifying scent and hers alone. Closing my eyes I felt the presence of the Regn I once knew. I asked her to sing quietly. And for once, without protest, she did. I saw her cry.

'You know, it could have been you, Regn. I would have married you in a second. All those years ago. But I know you didn't want to get married. You were afraid what others would say, and your children.'

'I had no choice.'

'Regn,' I sighed a long sigh inside. 'Have you learned nothing in all this time? Our entire lives are a series of choices. Even doing nothing is a choice. And yes, you did have a choice. And you made your choice as did I.'

'I loved you, I've always loved you. Isn't that enough?'

'No, Regn. It isn't. What matters now, right now, is that you are here. I missed you. I missed holding your body. All these years. The love we never shared.'

'You don't know how I missed you at times. You don't know.'

'And how could I? You let me wonder.'

'It was easier that way.'

'For you maybe.'

'You found Birçan, though. Didn't you? And you love her.'

'Regn, please don't patronize—I know that's not what you mean. I know that. You're just stating the obvious as though it were a walk in the park. Birçan *found me*. And I've loved each of you in different ways, both because of who you are. The *way* I love never changed. The hurt of you never went away—'

'Listen, Westcott. I wish I could have been there for you. I mean that from the bottom of my heart. You gave me something no one else ever has. And no one can take that away from us. No one.'

'Oh, Regn.' My head pressed back into the pillow. I felt I was going back and back—a feeling of absolute peace and release. An exhaustion so heavy. 'Sometimes it's nice to be reminded. Sometimes the silence gets to be too long. I tried often to imagine the outcome, this day. Would I be at your bedside when the time came? But this is better. I'm happy.'

'Can I lie down next to you?'

'You can try, not much room. But then you always were the perfect portable size.' I managed a trifle smile.

'Should I lock the door?'

'I don't think you can. Besides Regn, now is hardly the time for hiding. If someone comes they will only see the truth. And that is wonderful.'

'What if Birçan—'

'She already knows. Believe me, she would understand more than most.'

Regn slipped her shoes off and managed to slide in beside me. She cradled my head, ran her long fingers through my very short hair. I'd lost even more over the years. I took her hand, interlocked it with my own. Regn kissed me softly for the first time in 13 years. She pressed further and I opened my mouth to receive her. We held each other inside that way. Her tongue felt good and safe.

'I have an important question.'

Regn looked at me, waiting.

'Do you still have those silk mint night clothes of yours?'

Regn thinks for a second, then starts to laugh a little. 'You remember those? I always liked them. I think I have them somewhere. Why?'

'No reason. I liked the color so much on you. I just wanted to know if you remembered them—'

She understood. What I really meant was if she remembered that summer night long ago.

'I've never forgotten.' She held me closer.

All those years waiting for a moment of reckoning. For this hour of peace. It came hard. But it was worth it.

'I love you, Westcott. Never forget that.'

• • •

Mother and father came. Ellis. Mother was a mess, initially. I told her all would be fine. This was best. I'd go on ahead, check things out so-to-speak. She wouldn't have to be afraid when it was her time. I'd always feared being left behind. Knowing that when my mother was gone I'd have no one. There would be no one left on earth who loved me as she did or who empathized. I wanted to die first because I was a coward to the mourning of a loved one's death. I didn't want to experience that loss. And now I wouldn't. How very fortunate. I truly was content. 'Ellis needs you,' I explained to my mother not to give up. I'd no sooner calm Mother down than she'd leave the room crying again. I told Ellis to take care of her, but Ellis started crying. I didn't know what to say. None of them believed this was it. They sensed it was another depression and I'd pull out of it eventually. To take my mind off Ellis' grieving I told her, 'Don't be jealous because I beat you to it and I get to go first. Besides, *you* never wanted to die anyway.' She laughed then cried again all in the same breath. 'You're such a shithead'—her way of being loving—'you're my brother. Who else will I have to pick on?' 'If you're going to be all sentimental about it I left lots of reading for you. So, I won't really be gone. You'll have fun going through my things, won't you?' I wondered if she would ever listen to all the cassettes. What would she make of the one labeled "May

Suicide?" I hadn't forgotten that day. You never forget the hour when you have decided to conclude your life. My hormones had again spiked or plummeted, as they often did, sending me into a state of rabid morbidity. It had been a beautiful afternoon. I was going to take the gun from the only person I knew who kept one *loaded*, and drive to the Island. Without a word. No last phone calls. I'd step into the forest, place the barrel to my chest, and farewell! My tango with Death made Life all the more urgent. This was the reason for my restless spirit. I'd always known it was my heart. I needed to obliterate the place where the soul's memory dwelled. That day the gun's owner had been at home. I'd called. When the voice answered I was nonchalant, upbeat. I thought of stopping by, we could chat, I'd make an excuse to use the restroom and quickly slip into the bedroom, take the gun and stuff it in the back of my pants. But that wasn't part of the plan. I didn't want to see anyone. I'd have to wait. Rule No. 1 of mine was always stick to the *original* plan.

I looked at Ellis. Our separate lives, private lives. We create the lives we want others to believe. We are alone.

My father had been the most accepting. 'Do what your body tells you. Take a break. Just know we all want you here. I love you, West.' For a moment I felt guilty again. There was nothing left to say or do where my family was concerned. I wanted no loose ends. And this was it. A proper goodbye. My father and sister had always existed on the periphery of my life. Mother was the one who'd known the most details. We both always hoped for "happily ever after" endings, even though we knew it was seldom the case. We knew, but we never accepted.

There had been good times with my father. I remembered the lightweight wooden airplanes we'd get from the hobby store. A quick assembly, sliding pieces together, and a propeller attached to a metal clip with a rubber band. As you spun the propeller the rubber band became taut and then, swoosh. Let her go. Such a simple, fun contraption. Wooden airplanes in the park. I was 12. Another time my father came out to Virginia for a summer visit. We went to Ace Hardware for something. I saw a blue wheelbarrow. It was beautiful. My dad bought it and the attendant said she'd never seen a young "girl" so excited about a wheelbarrow. For me it was the color and structure. The expectation. William Carlos Williams. So much depends upon a red wheelbarrow. My father proceeded to spray paint my nickname on it in utilitarian letters. T-U-G-G-E-R. I told him not to. Afterward mother and I removed the white spray painted letters with alcohol. I wanted only the blue. And the cheery brown handlebars. I put a lot of yard clippings into that wheelbarrow, sweat permeating my layers of clothes.

Another memory was that summer on Martha's Vineyard. Kim's family had a reunion. Her father, my dad's father-in-law, had been born and raised on the island. Sharing the expenses between multiple families, we rented a house for a week and went round robin to different relatives for dinner. I had no blood relation to anyone but my father. Nonetheless, everyone was so nice. I missed large families. Community. A shared life. One morning we drove out to a remote part of the island, deep within, the road narrow and dirt. A place untouched. We came out onto a private beach. On the backside of the ocean, the overflow tide, I went swimming. Father was taking pictures. I was a good 100 feet out. The water warm unlike the chilly ocean. I removed my shirt. And then my trunks. I looked up at the sky and then down at my white nakedness. By myself I was not ashamed. How many children and later, adults, indulge in this freedom? I thought of the movie *The Reader*, based on Schlink's novel. The scene where Michael goes to the lake, removes his clothes, and swims as god intended. His right as a male. I always hid my body. I always parceled my emotions. This moment was mine and I knew I wouldn't talk about it. I was proud and deeply sad.

My family took shifts. And then I was alone. Birçan and I, almost like we'd planned years before. A dual suicide, only this time it wasn't a choice and only one of us was going on ahead. I was glad for her presence, her beautiful blue-gray eyes—still so clear. Could she see the obscure people standing in the room as she placed her warm hand on mine? These people didn't talk, their silence conveyed waiting. They were waiting. I was not. They were patient.

It would hurt, and yet I welcomed the going. I was not afraid. Just tired. Ready.

'You might have to be worried, B. This makes for your being a widow three times! Someone might think you're killing your husbands off.'

Birçan just laughed in her old way, and I laughed, too. I started to make lists, when I had the energy. Often I would drift off to sleep, a notebook on the flat of my stomach. I made important lists, things people ought to know about me.

The best inventions: paperclips; whipped crème in a can; wax paper
Favorite words: perspicacious; redolence; lambent; sauerkraut; caterwaul; glade
The phrase "you goose" or "you silly goose" always makes me smile.
I miss landline telephones. At least you felt connected to something.

My mind drifted and I thought of a fine memory. Years ago I'd seen two little boys—they were brothers—they had to be. I'd been standing in a line at Busch Gardens. Mother and I. We'd gone to Howl-O-Scream. I was 28, mother was 68. I had no one else with whom to go. Anyway, the color of their hair was mesmerizing. Shiny, thick, Scottish red hair. Carrot tops. It was beautiful. Little Opie Taylors, or rather Ron Howards playing Opie. I hoped they'd never lose their hair. The mere sight of such perfection left me in awe as I stood there absolutely blown away. Something so simple—hair—and yet theirs was extraordinary. Not just any typical red-headed little boys; no, this red was unblemished, striking. A rare sight to behold and I'd been there—but it wasn't my being there to observe them that was important.

What was key was the fact that not only was I present—I noticed *and* appreciated the pleasure of something so rare, so perfectly sublime while standing in the queue on an ordinary afternoon.

The things we take with us. The details we leave behind.

Another time it was evening. I was 29 years old standing in my blue kitchen, standing at the stove, eating an ear of boiled corn. Turning the cob slowly, feasting upon the sight of its gorgeous yellow sheen, it hit me. There are so many things in this world, thousands upon thousands of overlooked wonders. This ear of corn tasted like nothing else. Why did it taste the way it did? What made it the shape and color it was? How did so many things come into being? How was it possible? I knew the answer was in the corncob if I remained conscious enough to pursue it. I'd eaten corn, countless times before, but somehow, sharing it with the blue kitchen, the primal code of what it meant and felt to be alive sat down before me, presented itself on a red dinner plate with a rooster and an ear of corn, lightly slathered with butter. It was happiness tasting something so specific, individual, complete in itself.

•••

Over the years I've come to realize why I love *The Jungle Book* so much. As a kid, unconsciously, I related to not belonging, of being in the wrong society, separate from my own kind. That, and the desire for the rarest of adventures.

•••

All the things I could have been. A foreign officer, chief editor/photographer for National Geographic, a horse handler, a famous painter, musician, composer, astronomer. In the end I was, and remain, a lover. A poet by nature, and the world is not kind to poets while they are alive. I lay in bed thinking it makes sense for me to pass. I would like to believe that the Truth of what fills these pages and a closeted handbag of letters embodies purpose—and it is my desire that it be recorded. I listen to all the old songs, the music that stayed with me. A minute and 45 seconds into Dvorak's *Humoresque* it crescendos and I think of Van Gogh and understand why a man so impassioned could be driven to slice off his own ear. Relief. The pain. The emotion was too beautiful, so loud in his mind. He needed to flee. The gravity of truth comes so heavy at times. I think of the Irises. Note: Please have Irises at my funeral. And yellow roses, white roses, and a single gardenia, for my mother.

My list was complete. The list spoken many years before when Regn and I walked beside the Atlantic. An ordinary afternoon in January made memorable by our being there together. I've fulfilled each item. This, here, is the last.

'He's only 41—' I heard my mother's voice the other afternoon, starting to cry again. 'I know he's happy but—I can't be. Not about his death! They say there's no reason he shouldn't recover. He just doesn't want to. He's given up!' I couldn't answer her, I wanted to and to tell her this—

I haven't given up. I've arrived right where I want to be. The heart knows when to take its leave more than the body is willing to concede—this time *they've* made a truce. 90% of life is a pain in the ass. It's like panning for gold. Only 10% remains—the stardust of who I am, and only the share I may take, in the last farewell.

•••

I'd been too afraid to ask how Regn had managed the time away. I knew I had to ask.

'Regn?'

'It's Mother.'

'Is Regn still here? What day is it?'

'Do you need to see her again?'

'Is she still here?'

'Yes, I have the hotel number.'

'Please. Thank you. I want to see her again.'

Regn came into the room.

'Do you have to leave, so soon? What I mean is, how did you get the time away? What did you tell Jay?'

Regn sat in the chair near my bed.

'I wondered if you'd ask. Jay— He passed away almost two years ago now.'

Something inside me lurched. I wanted to bolt upright. My heart began to pound, the monitor showed the increased heart rate. I didn't want Regn to see. If she noticed she made no indication.

'Two years. You never said anything.'

'I couldn't—I didn't want to hurt you more. You were married and I wanted to let you be happy.'

'How poetic. One year after I get married you are—free. I don't mean that to sound—'

'No. It's true. I cared for Jay. And it was very hard the first year, but my kids helped me and I'm at peace now. Free like you said.'

'Regn?'

'What, Westcott?'

'I'm afraid to say this, but I must.'

'Don't be afraid.'

'There is something—all these years—I wanted—'

'Say it.'

'Let us have the mountains. We may not get another chance.'

'But you're in no condition—'

'It's just a drive and a gentle walk. I won't overdo it and if I do I die happy on top of a mountain. You once said that was bliss—standing on top of a mountain.'

'Yes.'

'Well—'

'When should we—'

'Soon. Do you still have your beloved bug?'

'I traded it in for a newer model, but it's still silver.'

'Can I drive? I'm kidding! I don't know who's more of a liability risk—me with two heart attacks or you at 73.' I smiled. 'And shrinking. How tall are you now? Can you still see over the steering wheel?'

'I have a cushion I use. Me the little old lady, the old crow,' she laughed.

'Oh Regn.'

'What?'

'It's been so long since I laughed with you.'

• • •

Birçan understood and let me go. She knew she couldn't keep me and if she'd had one last chance with Snowball she wouldn't have given it up for anything. Our marriage was founded on an affection born of companionship not passion. We were place holders for one another. With Regn the passion remained rich.

When I left I knew I would not be coming back. I wanted to spend what time remained with the one woman who unconditionally loved me. A part of me knew I'd married Birçan for the sake of being able to call myself a husband, just once.

In those years before our reuniting, the memory of pain had never let up. Birçan was cutthroat. How then, you may ask, could I have returned and taken her hand?

I owed her nothing. But I knew people changed. Once, Birçan had loved me, however brief. It was possible she could again. I was tired of drifting. I'd given the world a chance, tried to make a go of it and find a woman to call my own, a life to come home to every night and wake up to every day. In the end Birçan gave me a place to be, a role to fulfill. There were parts in me she could never again reach. I wouldn't let her. And I was glad. Glad to have so much hidden. It meant I didn't require as much from her. We both had shadows in our hearts.

The night before Regn and I left, Mother kissed me. 'Have a wonderful time. Don't overdo it, hiking. No backpack, no steep cliffs. You have so much left to do.'

'We all have to go sometime.'

'My Steppenwolf. It's not your time. I'm not ready for you to go.'

I smiled as if to say it's not in my hands anymore. 'It'll be fine.'

REGN DROVE US UP to the Shenandoah Mountains. It *is still* spring and those days of splendor linger yet inside me. We listened to endless music. When Corelli's "adagio" movement from Grosso Op. 6 No. 8 in G minor played, I knew the evening sun had come to take me home. The fervency of the cello answering the violin made me old and young at the same time. I remembered the music as I'd first heard it when a young man falling in love with Regn. *How nervous I'd been to even step near her car.* And now I heard it again. The music was the same. So was the passion.

A misty rain made the roads sharper, the mountains greener. We came out of the haze into sunlight. Regn insisted we stay at Skyland.

'Are you sure? That's where you and Jay always went. Don't you want to have our own place?'

'No. I imagined being here with you so often, Westcott. I requested the room where Rebecca and I always stayed. Hazeltop.'

We slept in the same bed and woke up beside one another. I inhaled before my eyes opened. Regn's presence filled the room. She took me in her arms, held me close. Ran her long fingers along my forehead, kissed me. I desired nothing else in the world. Absolutely nothing.

When she stepped from the privy I waited for her to notice the weathered piece of paper I'd set on the dresser.

'You kept this? Twilight Time,' she read softly. 'I remember that sweater. The picture— it was here, but I don't remember it being taken. Look at my hair then. Where did you—'

'I carried it with me. In my wallet. It's been around the world. You were always with me.

Regn—? I love you. You're the one person I can say that to and not feel foolish. It comes from someplace else.'

Regn held me close as we stood. I looked out the window, feeling the frame of her klein body.

'Oh, Westcott.' Her voice so light. 'I've always loved you. Never, never forget that.'

We'd planned to stay three nights and four days. On the 3ʳᵈ day we took the small trail leading up to Stony Man. Very short, it can be strenuous on a body that requires rest. We stopped frequently. Usually it takes 15 minutes to hike to the overlook. We made it last an hour.

There were other hikers around being spring and the peak of bloom, tourists. Regn and I found a nice rock to sit by. My legs dangled over the edge. Regn's were folded. I leaned against the hard surface, the rock warm through the back of my jacket. Regn leaned into me, my chin on her shoulder.

Let them look, I thought. *Once I came here and wanted to die. Many years ago.*

I watched the horizon. Wondered what Mother was up to. I knew she was thinking the same thing about me. We'd always been connected that way. I didn't want my dying to hurt her, but I knew this was it.

'It hurts so much.'

'What does? Are you all right, West—'

'Yes. I just mean it's so wonderful. This. Just being here. With you. How many times I—'

'I know.' Regn leaned into me, taking my hand, the warmth of her skin, the sun through our hands.

I looked at them. My hands had aged, but they still looked young. Regn's were bonier, but by no means brittle. The skin was not translucent. I looked for the scar on her left hand, by the back of her thumb, from when she was a kid. I couldn't see it, but I knew this detail about her in the same way that her spine silently took in my belt buckle through the knit of her cotton blouse. The brass buckle with the oak tree. Regn never told me, but I knew she loved to look at it.

'Ich liebe dich, Meine Dame.'

'Du bist mein licht.' *You are my light.*

• • •

He hadn't been this happy in almost two decades. There'd been high points and "good" times, but always a shadow in his heart. Today the only shadows were the great cumulus clouds drifting over the valley. He always loved the clouds. Warm blustery days when the wind broke across his forehead and the pillowed giants passed over the grasses. He called clear, still, sky blue days, "blank days." The clouds provided dimension and a sense of company.

When he first met Regn he'd been fresh out of the running gates. It wasn't because it was his first time, but that it had been an affair. There had been no love since that ever came close. Like an athlete who peaks in the height of his youth, Westcott's greatest love affair had already been and continued to be. His heart had aged long before his body. Finally his heart sighed. Only the mountains, the rock he pressed against, heard the valve release. He inhaled, taking Regn inside. He felt those summers long ago alive inside him. And the times his mother had dinner waiting for him when he got home. She'd always accepted him, everything about him, including Regn. The sound of summer with its crickets—the embodiment of youth by his own auditory definition.

'How 'bout some of that homemade banana bread from Big Meadows tonight?'

'That sounds good,' Regn half turned her face. Her voice still as smooth and warm as the sun.

The color of the mountains. Deep, soft, long shadows—it is my greatest dream.

• • •

Back home Regn came up to my room.

I took her in my arms and we moved in a gentle circle, not so much dancing as remembering. Knowing. We weren't parting. We would never part again.

———

I am a most fortunate man. I have no regrets. All the days of my life, I have loved, not the days themselves, but their summation. I have loved someone or something all of my life. It takes the moment of departure to feel there is no yesterday or tomorrow. Only now. I realized this as a young man. This is how I loved. But in the broader sense I could not formulate the sensation of timelessness. Only windows of time existed where, for some odd minutes, I *was* all the years combined. With the imminence of death it becomes clear and lasting. The window widens. No yesterday. No tomorrow. Only now. If you think about it, this is where the story begins.

See you around!

The things I have felt—
The hands that touched me
    become me.
Living is one long continuous goodbye.
This, here, is goodbye.
--W

Dvorak plays
"Humoresque"

© Wheston Grove

"Leaving"

"Within"

EPILOGUE

THE theme song from *Father Knows Best*, starring Jane Wyatt, is entitled 'Waiting.' It plays twice. Once at the beginning of each episode in a slower tempo and then again at the end, a slightly expedited rendition in later seasons. The latter always catches me somehow—I imagine Regn. Taking her in my arms and gliding across an empty dance floor. Everyone I ever knew in this life and those she knew, standing around, honoring our long awaited dance. They smile. But I am not looking at them, nor is Regn. Our peers are not there to judge. They are witnesses of their own volition. Regn and I are looking at each other and we move in a time-honored grace. In hearing the lyrics I return to the place from which I was torn, long ago—another life I loved. Regn is like walking through a front door. In taking her hand, leading her across the floor, as I direct her, she silently brings me home, takes me inside. The song ends much too soon, but somehow it remains endless and the rest can always be believed. It is not an ideal. I knew it once. A different time, a different place. I lived it and knowing what it could be, nothing less ever satisfied. God willing I'll see you all again. As once I was.

Song:

Waiting, for love to find us,
is something worth waiting for.
Someday, my arms will hold you,
my lips will kiss you, forever more.
Yes, waiting can be so lonely,
yet somehow we'll see it through.
Knowing, there's someone waiting
right there just for you.

(turn the page)

HE FELT HIMSELF GO UP LIKE A JETSTREAM. He used to sit in a car and listen to the powerful thrusters, though he might not always see them. But now he was one of them hearing what they always must hear. He heard the earth below and those around searching. He listened from another side, far away, yet still so very close. And then just as the jetstream fades into blindless oblivion he, too, felt himself taken up by the wind. Weightless—he fainted, or so he believed he must have because he awoke.

Why was he walking? He couldn't say nor did he know how long he'd been gone. The avenue was very lengthy, he looked it up and down. He knew without consciously knowing that someone was waiting and he must hurry. It was night and everything deep in the hues of green and blue. It reminded him of another night long ago when he'd walked up the pathway with Birçan to her door. They'd been out dancing. The atmosphere had seemed an ethereal twilight. He'd stepped up close behind her on the front porch, yearning to come in, to come home. The haze of that night showed clearer on this night. The moon was its brightest, he could clearly see the features of the sidewalk, his pale hands, the row of houses. Up ahead a wrought-iron fence—painted white. As he approached he stepped into the blue shadow of the Victorian. No lights were on and the high roof obscured the moon. He knew before opening the gate it would make a noise. A friendly sound. Knew by experience. Having been there many years before. And yet, it felt like yesterday. He closed it behind him, stepped between the boxwoods and went up the partially rotted steps painted burgundy and cream. Lace curtains hung in a window to the right. A bench situated itself on the porch. Wisteria coiled round the support pillars, their pods yet to bloom. The austere soundlessness should have startled a body, but even in the shadows, the deep blue air, he felt the womb of protection. He put his hand to the door handle, it opened and he reentered the passage between.

No one was there, but he strained to see anyway. He knew his way around, just by touch. He moved the sliding doors and cut through the living room into the dining area that gave way to the kitchen's linoleum floor. Aback the kitchen he walked down two steps into the sunroom, which now illuminated itself in a white tide. It was a moon-room. Outside, the paint peeling deck, the perfect square garden, and in the far corner of the yard—to the right—a hardy fig tree that grew outwards rather than upwards. A tall 11-foot wooden fence overgrown with ivy bordered the back wall and on the right a brownish red aluminum fence. He walked the small brick path that cut diagonally across the garden green. In the middle the detached head of a fountain piece. It had become a flower pit—all stone, white gray, a cottage surrounded by a moat of soil that would bloom in the spring if properly tended.

One branch of the tree arced over the outer pathway so that he ducked under it and stepped round the fig leaves. They look like green and plum air balloons, the figs themselves. When squeezed a white sticky substance, very much like glue, buds from the stem. He felt the gray trunk before turning to the ivy. It was a magic book image, one of those pictures you hold close to your face then slowly draw out to see another level, a camouflaged scene. An outline of a door—the ivy slightly yellow along two perpendicular lines—there was something shining through the other side, growing in intensity. He touched the vine. The hingeless door swung open. He hesitated, reluctant to leave this place of memories, memories too vast to recount individually and so a composite profile flashed behind his blue gray eyes.

Standing in the sunlight the door remained open. A small canoe, a hollowed out tree, sat by the river's edge, partially in the water, flowing with the tide. Its other end attached with a rope tossed over an anchored stick. The canoe knew what it wanted. A tree on the river's edge had a gaping hollow alcove from the ground about four feet high and a knob-like structure at its head. He listened to the water flowing—slow without hurry—pure, going exactly where it was meant to course.

A line stretched from the base of the opening down to the river. It was dark in its constant dampness—the cycle of water. And—he looked at it, suddenly becoming very aware of himself. Was he wearing clothes? He did not know. The wet opening intrigued him. Kneeling, he brushed his fingers across the damp earth. Expecting it to be cool, he was surprised at its hearty warmth. He pressed it there for a moment. A woman laughed. He jerked his head and searched to see the direction it had come. She wasn't laughing at him for she didn't know he was there—it was though he was hearing her from afar. It was a happy sound. She was happy. He had made her laugh. He felt himself laughing with her.

His hand felt cold and the laughing turned to an echo. Withdrawing his arm, he turned his palm up to find it was bleeding. There was no cut.

The river guided him without oars, winding and zipping, sometimes gliding or sometimes drifting. A mild waterfall here and then the river came to an abrupt end. The canoe ran aground stopping of its own will.

The young man stepped out. Straining his eyes, in the distance, to his left—a figure. His eyes had always been hard to focus on far away objects, but he saw this one clearly and knew it was a woman. A small but well-postured woman. She wore no shoes. She had clothes but as she approached he discovered he was without. He wanted to hide himself.

She stopped two feet from him. He met her gaze fixedly.

She started to study his length and stopped, detecting the flash of shame in his eyes.

'Don't worry, I brought these for you.' Under her arm a pair of pants, a summer light gray-beige button shirt and a tweed cap. 'You're fine, you were always—'

'No,' he said speaking an answer to something beyond what she'd said.

Looking into his complacent face she began to cry.

'Oh, Westcott,' she said softly and brought him to her, held him.

Feeling her life as he once had, feeling her all the years back, he held her in return, squeezing her small sturdy woman.

Over her shoulder he began to cry silently, tucking his chin into the side of her neck, feeling her warmth of hands on his bare skin.

'How did you know?' he asked, eyes shut. 'You were so sure.'

'Come, put these on.'

She squatted and had him step one foot into each pant leg. Pulling the trousers up, her head came to his groin. He didn't move. He let her without question. She bent forward and kissed lightly the empty nest between his legs, an affirmation of purity. She pulled the zipper and nitched the button. She ran her fingers over his chest, across the graze of his shoulders and down the length of his arms. She slipped the loose shirt around him. Without a word he watched her, felt her, knowing exactly what she was doing. In every move, every stroke, she was reminding him, *I love you.*

- - - - - - -

They walked up a small path. He held her hand in his, the cuff of his shirt rolled up. They stopped. 'Go now and I'll be waiting for you in this field,' she motioned to her side. 'There's someone who's missed you just as I.'

He was reluctant to release her hand. He walked down the road. Beneath a tree, sitting in a chair, was his mother. But how, she's still alive. How can she be here, too? He sprinted, almost a single step in his stride. She took him in her arms. Others started to come from the forest. Others. His grandmother. Instinctively he knew, never having met her.

'It's all right,' she said after a long time. 'I can go now.' He was not used to hearing his mother speak so calmly in letting him go. He knew, at last, she was all right. She was at peace. The way she said it he knew she didn't mean later today, tomorrow, next week. But what was time? And this place apart from it?

- - - - - - -

'Scaaatterbird,' he called from the edge of the tall grass. He saw a hand in the distance, a white flag—a flicker of memory, a handkerchief waving or was it the sun in his eyes?

She lay in the cool of the grass near a giant tree, a canopy of shade.

'She was dreaming—your mother. But *you* are really here. You spoke to her. She could hear you.'

'Are you still al—?'

'No. I am here.'

'When did you—'

'I'm here because you wanted me to be. And *I* want to be. You created this.' Her voice was the color of twilight and dawn, if sound could have a color.

'And what about you?'

'I believed with you.'

'Two visions overlapping, the same vision becoming one.'

They were quiet and sat with each other. He leaned against the tree holding her in front of him, his hands above her left breast, just resting. He stroked her brown-red hair. It became ashen gray like a pigeon's feathers.

'Do you know?' Her voice seemed like the only sound.

'How long—' he felt a wrench in his chest.

'I don't know.'

'Maybe—when we're no longer afraid.'

'Perhaps.'

'We make our own summerland in what we believe,' he said.

'Yes, that's true.'

'Let us.' He shifted the woman he loved to the flat of the earth and undressed her.

He removed his own clothes, appearing as he did when he arrived. He glided down on her, nothing else.

'I think this is how it's done—' he whispered. 'We leave ourselves now—can we hold tight enough to one another. Come together the other side of our—ejaculation?'

She kissed him and he gently rolled to her side. 'Lie on me,' he said. He took her in his arms opening his legs to her. A part of her slipped inside him. Or was it the wind? He cried for the life he'd had. He moved over her again. Wiping the streaks from her eyes. He rested his ear to her breast and listened. All was at peace. Holding her hands, interlocked in his own he said, 'You ready?'

———

My Dear Rebecca,

The items I list here are for you. I hope you will cherish them as I have. Share them with your sister and cousin if you feel they will keep them safe. Your father will find the truth easier to understand while your Aunt Dee might need more time. This is why I leave these possessions to you. I would be heartbroken if Dee threw them away in a fit of anger. My love for my children and grandchildren has never changed. Remember the letter I gave you just before heading off to college? I hope you kept it safe all these years. The time has come for you to open it. Westcott is gone now and if you're reading this so am I. He was an extraordinary man. I loved him and your Grandpa in different ways for very different reasons. Grandpa gave me children, a home, and security. Westcott gave me my soul. For his sake I wish we'd met when I was younger. Perhaps you may know a small part of him in these things he gave to me. I have never been good with words and long letters. Westcott was the writer. I hope and pray you find and know in your life the beautiful love that Westcott and I shared. I am proud of you for being your own person. Maybe it's good to keep the boys at bay for a while. You're independent, strong, and such an attractive young woman. Do something wonderful with your life and have fun. You will.

All my love, always
Oma

Keepsake box with the woman, orange and blue flowers. (The one I kept on the tea cart in our old home).

Small engraved pocket watch. On the back it says, "My beautiful dreamer wake unto me." It no longer works. I always kept it in the tin Westcott gave it to me in—the pretty one with the trees. It probably needs winding or a battery.

Gold acorn.

My silver ring. I loved it very much. Westcott surprised me with it one Christmas.

Sheep pin.

Colorful knitted scarf from Ireland.

Blue raindrop necklace.

My silver dragonfly necklace.

My Volkswagen Christmas Tree ornament. It's missing a small piece, so be careful it's delicate.

And most of all, the copper bracelet you'll find in my jewelry box. I keep it wrapped in the tissue paper so it doesn't tarnish. This is especially for you. When you wear it know I am always part of you and close in mind.

These are the things Westcott gave to me. Now they are yours. Once more they are given in love.

•••

Rebecca had been married eight years now. She reread the sentence to herself, *Maybe it's good to keep the boys at bay for a while. You're independent, strong, and such an attractive young woman. Do something wonderful with your life...* There was no date on the letter. Her Oma was not good at record keeping. It didn't take Rebecca long to discern that anything hand-written or typed for that matter, *and* bearing a date, was from Westcott. He was a natural archivist. With the letter and box of items she found some books and even a small leather journal. The cloth hand-purse with her Oma's name woven in script barely fastened it was so stuffed with letters. *His letters* to Regn. Over the past week she'd periodically been pulling a letter out. As she read, she felt Westcott's love for her Oma as a palpable energy. The papers had long been creased, originally folded by her Oma's long fingers. She wondered when Westcott had given the letters back to her. Reviewing the contents of the box once more, as she had for several days, she picked up the little journal then set it aside, remembering the cassette. It had arrived three days before in a priority mailer with a small recorder, along with other cassettes and some pictures. She'd been expecting the box. Westcott's sister had contacted her. It was the first time they'd ever spoken and it would be the last; no other reason could possibly have brought them together other than Westcott's death. Ellis called to confirm the address was up-to-date, explaining that her brother had left a note with instructions. "The enclosed items are to go to Regn's granddaughter after you have had the chance to sort through them." Ellis had listened to the tape. Now it was in Rebecca's possession. "May Suicide."

What was eerie about the recording was not the devastating soliloquy she'd heard, but its profound commentary on life offered by a man so young. "My name is Westcott Aloysius Rowan. I am 31 years old. This is my voice." It was startling how *old* he had been for his age. Everything he said was true. Though tragic, she couldn't find a single point to argue about. "We all must go...reach a certain age and you've lived your life...now just filling time." The truth was it had frightened the hell out of her. It wasn't morbid. It was honest, so—precise. The madness was all around him, in society, not within him. He couldn't fathom how people just went along in their lives. He felt so deeply. Rebecca had tucked the micro-cassette into the corner of the box three days ago. It haunted her while providing endless sanctuary.

She picked up the pocket journal and opened to where the cloth ribbon had last been placed as a bookmark. She wondered if Westcott had left it there or if her Oma had, wanting her to read this particular passage.

The journal entry began:

Sunday, 6 March 20—
A bit past 11:00 p.m.

Who but I will ever chance to read these pages? My life didn't stop. It never started; it never began. I don't know what to believe anymore and everyone needs something to believe in. I no longer believe in Regn's and my love—(yes, she loves me)—what I mean is, I no longer believe <u>in the power</u> of our love <u>because</u> I lost all belief, "faith" in Regn.

Now what? Move on. To what? I'm not entirely sure what I want. My desires change with mood like the winds. I have a better under-standing of what I do <u>not</u> want—but this leaves a lot of blank spaces, unknown areas.

I'd prefer to embrace the future, but its uncertainty generates pensive anxiety as opposed to excitement. Yes, anything is possible and I believe in my book, but Regn is still a ghost who ties me to the past. I was the love of her life and she, mine. How to let go? Such a large part of my heart remains interred with her.

The date of the entry showed it to be from fifteen years ago. Rebecca reasoned she'd still been too young for her Oma to confide in her. The more she uncovered, the more she wanted to know. As a young girl, she thought she'd known everything there was to know about her Oma. Rebecca had turned to her Oma to tell her about the first boy she kissed. She'd been 14. She'd always felt so grown-up around her Oma, maybe because the latter could be so silly and playful like a child. Rebecca had had so little time to know her Oma as one woman to another. She'd been growing up and by the time she was entering her own, her Oma was moving into the background of her burgeoning life. She picked up an envelope. Inside was a picture of Westcott. He looked to be about her age now, maybe a little younger.

She looked at the date on the back. *Where had the time gone?* Now he was gone. Her Oma was gone. The memory was hers.

'MY NAME IS REBECCA. I've come about the bronze statue.'

The man looks at the young woman, then to the side. 'Oh yes, yes—the statue. You must be the granddaughter.'

The only item of clothing worth noting is a thin bracelet around her right wrist.

A pair of foiled leaves overlap each other, converging. A thin silver wire wraps round the band—a vine, a thread. It is the bracelet Westcott had given Regn on the night they had first made love.

They walk out back to a storage building.

'If you don't mind my saying, your story has generated wonderful business for us lately.'

'Thank you, but it's not *my* story. I guess one always seeks to point out the monetary value of things these days.'

The man glances at her, sensing he's offended the young lady in some way.

'You're referenced in it, aren't you? I mean you met him? I haven't gotten around to reading it. My wife has though.'

Rebecca peers at him, slackening her drawn mouth as if to acknowledge his subtle attempt in apology.

'It's an unconventional read, I'll tell you that. I feel he knew her best and somehow, for me, it's—well, it's as though I'm seeing her for the first time.' She quickly grows silent. She's allowed her thoughts to run freely to a complete stranger. But then she doesn't care. She might have before reading the story but now she realizes what a funny waste it is to hide oneself, to be afraid of each other.

They stand just inside the storage shed. The man begins unwrapping the canvassed tribute. Without prompting Rebecca moves to assist, eager to see.

She steps back, studying the features in the light. Circling and coming round, she examines their expressions.

It's a George Lundeen statue. Westcott had commissioned the bronze sculptor several months prior to his sudden heart attacks. He'd seen his work years before in Virginia and later with Birçan in Loveland, Colorado. His last request was to see the statue placed on Jamestowne Island.

'So, what do you think?' He cannot wait for her to respond of her own will.

'Es ist schön.' Though the man does not recognize the phrase he knows she is pleased by the monument.

'What do *you* think of it?' she replies.

'Well, Miss, not knowing the history behind it, I'm still inclined to say it's a lovely testament.'

Rebecca holds his eyes. *I'm sorry, I misjudged you.* Instead—

'No, I mean what *do you* think of their being laid to rest here—'

He is silent for quite some time.
She waits without waiting.

'It was their right—*is* their right,' he offers more to himself than to her.
Rebecca notices his age for the first time. Though a little heavy in the midriff, he has a full head of hair and his eyes are mottled, slightly tired but kind.

They both stand there studying the figures anchored to a bronze bench, fixed by the metal ore in permanent holding, hand within hand. Age would be difficult to declare on either of them, but it is suggested by the woman's long fingers, the contours of her face—the features have long been in place, sharpening in the finer areas of physiognomy, softening discovered only by touch, in the broader planes—abdomen, breasts. Westcott bears a piercing gaze, melancholic—a skillful feat for any sculptor to distinctly execute. He shows faint traces of sideburns giving way to a dusting of bearded youth. A bracelet rests on Regn's wrist—two leaves overlapping, converging; a tweed cap protrudes from Westcott's brow—no wind may disturb. They look to come alive, stand and walk, side-by-side, amidst the Island's trees.

...
.....
....

THE BEGINNING

Ich Liebe Dich
Seni Seviyorem
I Love You

Giuseppe Tornatore Suite: "Playing Love"
Ennio Morricone interpreted by Yo-Yo Ma

© Wheston Grove

© Wheston Grove

Very few leave an indelible mark. The weight of remembrance is mine—

—Wheston Chancellor Grove

Always

By Wheston Chancellor Grove 2008

About the Author

Wheston Chancellor Grove is a writer and photographer. He loves old train stations and the sound of a distant whistle. He holds an MFA in Creative Writing from Goddard College and has been known to talk to pigeons. He currently lives in Virginia.

www.chancellorscorner.com

ACKNOWLEDGMENTS

WHEN a person dies he or she is gone. For those left behind the fear and alone-ness return full force; life seems cruel, heartless. The machine of society continues unabated, indifferent.

Being resolute in the pursuit of something is not the same as being inflexible. We spend most of our lives trying to find or maintain a foothold, but it is always temporary. In life you only have one person you can turn to, one person you must trust unequivocally. And that is you. Yourself. But.

In trusting yourself you will be misjudged or even accused of being cold, arrogant, impenetrable. It is but a vest of irons, a protective mesh, a façade against Self. Determination allows no room for doubt. Doubt separates the dreamers from the pursuers. Doubt is substitute for fear. Confidence is seeing something through—even though the ending is unsure. And that is life.

You must demand the most of yourself because no one else will. Do nothing halfway, complacency is what the majority succumbs to—one must never be content with settling.

So I say to everyone, the details keep us going, but truly it's all or nothing. The meso-sphere is a breeding ground for discontent. Above all do not become complacent, unless satisfaction is all you seek. But I say do not stop there, the desire, the starvation lets you know you're alive. Preservation is what writers are all about. Excellency is what living is for.

Most of all I must acknowledge five women. And yes I say acknowledge them, not thank them. The women behind the characters of Regn and Birçan. The women whose stories deserved to be told, but which they had not the voice or desire to tell themselves. Seemingly ordinary women who became extraordinary. And my mother, I forgive *you*. I told her time and again she should have been satisfied with having just one child, but no, she insisted on having a second. Me. Against my wishes I was born. To Juliette Binoche, for staying single. Please don't marry, not yet! Lastly, but not last—I said five women—Sara Scott, who *held* me on the cusp of twilight. I gave you the ultimate challenge and imparted the gift of blindness. The room was dim, the timing *imperfect*, and the scent of home beckoning.

I also wish to thank the following: Joan C—for her circumspect proofreading (catching one word or a singular comma—no find was too small). My Editor, you know who you are. It is time! Nurse Susan B. Anthony whose gentleness made it possible for me to hear again. Bill the Shuttle Driver in Vermont. I promised I'd deliver. And to Steve. Yes, just Steve. We shared an hour of life on a flight. You went to Kenyon University and were a psychologist. I hope you read the novella I recommended to you. Marty, the pest guy. One of those rare finds—a gentleman whom I immediately liked and discussed the state of the world with as he gave a puff of the bulb to keep critters at bay (naturally). Captain Ambi, formerly. My friend who showed me how to smoke a tobacco pipe on summer evenings. Also, my "velveteen" pigeon who listened and never said a word during the course of late hours and lonely edits. To the countless others who never stayed…And for everyone who was too busy running in circles. Silence persists. One must make time for what matters most.

Lastly, Magdalena "Leni"—you brought out the best and worst in me. A person cannot begin to know himself without contrast.

MEMORABLE QUOTES FROM WHO HAS KNOWN HEIGHTS: THE MYSTIQUE MEMOIRS OF A MELANCHOLIC MIND

"**E**VERY woman wants her chance at passion, even just once in her life. He wanted the years. He wanted the years without putting in the time."

"Confidence is being sure even when you don't have all the answers. It's a gut feeling. A sensibility that doesn't always have proof going into the situation but most nearly always has evidence on the way out."

"The body is a museum for memories. I am the Smithsonian."

"It was her presence he could not endure without. Her presence which he longed to enjoy with a freedom that would defy the constraints of time."

"Loneliness is an emaciation of the spirit."

"Above all her voice moved him. He had not known that an accent seduced his emotions. But he'd always been drawn to those with an accent. Be it woman or man. It sounded nicer. A lavender husk. More proper, elegant. His attuned ear seemed to be remembering voices from another life, another time. He could never escape the sense that he'd lost a life dear to him and that life was lived in another language."

"She drives him home. It is five in the morning. 'I've never made love all night,' she says. Her right hand rests in his…She drives with her left. They pass the cornbread meadow—a field covered with yellow poppies and black and white cows motionless in the blue mist. Sleeping. A small spread of land in the middle of civilization…it is almost dawn. The streets are peaceful. The world does not hurt at such an hour. There is time."

"One could argue the self-consciousness of youth had me feeling the eyes of everyone in the room, but make no mistake, they were watching intently and some of the men, though I did not yet know the privilege my innocence afforded, envied my position greatly. Regn had always been desired and she knew it. In their eyes I was but a boy, harmless. It would not look proper for them to ask her to dance."

"Regn embodied a time and place I missed. Seeing her, listening to her, was like an old familiar song, long forgotten until it is heard again. When at last our bodies had contact, being held in her arms, or holding her close to my chest…it was the same as coming home. Stepping into the foyer after a long time away. Age was irrelevant. It was an awakening and an unearthing. To love in such a way is not unguarded youth. To love completely is to remember a time and place before; the knowledge of losing it only strengthens it. I wanted to know what entity inhabited this *klein* woman with the languid voice. Who was she at the core, before life changed her?"

"He wanted those overlooked instances—a place at the dinner table—to look up and across at her, fork in midair. To see her enter a room, package in hand. To quietly slip behind her as she stood at the sink and fold his arms around her waist. To argue about nothing and everything, to laugh for the pain of life itself, and to dance gently before going up to bed and falling into endless slumber…He had been a lover to her that day when all he sought to be at that moment, and what she needed most, was a friend. Dancing, holding her in his arms, like a cradled bird, not secure in its abilities to fly independently, he supported her— while the fluttering of her life's fissure anchored him—a tree and a bird."

"The day after the darkest hour is always the most beautiful."

Suggested Reading

Ceely, Jonatha. <u>Mina</u>, Delacorte Press: 2004.

Essex, Karen. <u>Stealing Athena</u>, Doubleday: 2008.

Hall, Radclyffe. "Peter the Swan" <u>The Well of Loneliness</u>, 1928.

Hesse, Hermann. <u>Steppenwolf</u>, 1929.

Horsley, Kate. <u>Confessions of a Pagan Nun</u>, Random House: 2001.

---.<u>The Changeling of Finnistuath</u>, 2003.

Marquez, Gabriel Garcia. <u>Love in the Time of Cholera</u>, Knopf: 1988.

Miller, Andrew. <u>Ingenious Pain</u>, Harcourt Brace & Co.: 1997.

O'Neill, Jamie. <u>At Swim Two Boys</u>, 2001.

Ran, Chen. <u>A Private Life</u>, Columbia University Press (translation: John Howard Gibbon): 2004.

Schlink, Bernhard. <u>The Reader</u>, 1997.

Scholl, Inge. <u>Sophie Scholl und Die Weiße Rose</u>, 1970.

Seton, Anya. <u>Green Darkness</u>, 1972.

Shreve, Anita. <u>Sea Glass</u>, Little, Brown, & Co.: 2004.

Waller, Robert James. <u>The Bridges of Madison County</u>, Warner Books: 1992.

Woolf, Virginia. <u>To the Lighthouse</u>, 1927.

CPSIA information can be obtained
at www.ICGtesting.com
Printed in the USA
BVHW042350240919
559149BV00038BB/212/P